FLOWER GARDENS

PENELOPE HOBHOUSE

FLOWER GARDENS

NEW MILLENNIUM BOOKS

Vancouver

First published in Canada in 2000 by
New Millennium Books
8036 Enterprise Street
Burnaby, BC V5A 1V7
T: 604-415-2444
F: 604-415-3444

British Library Cataloguing-in-Publication Data
A catalogue record for this book is available from
the British Library

The Flower Garden set in Goudy Old Style
by SX Composing, Rayleigh, Essex
Penelope Hobhouse On Gardening designed and type-set
in Caslon 10½ on 13pt by Studio Gossett

Printed and bound in Hong Kong

First Frances Lincoln Edition 1999

9 8 7 6 5 4 3 2 1

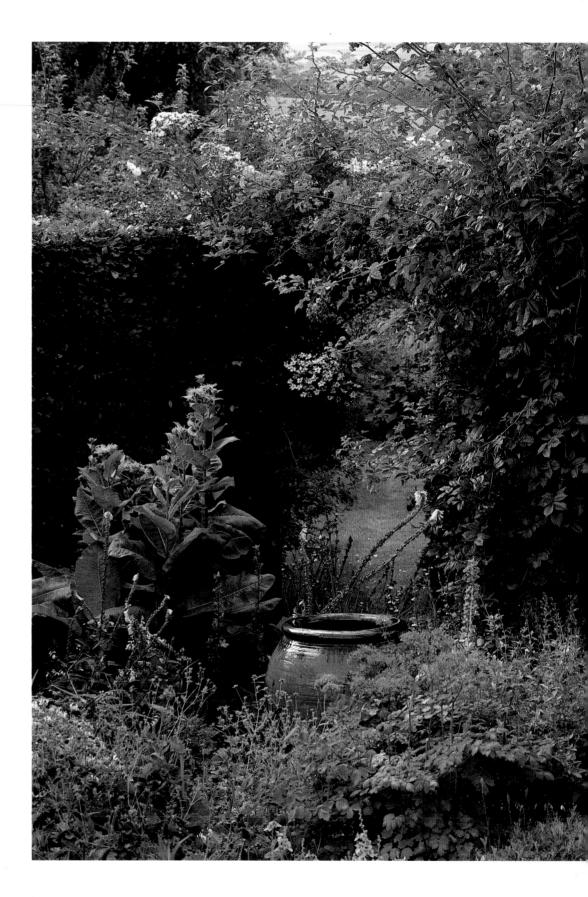

CONTENTS

Introduction 6

INTRODUCTION

When we begin to garden most of us notice individual plants. We fall in love with their beauty and grace before having any clear idea how we might arrange them in a garden. It is the flowers that we find most striking: their colour – often a subtle gradation of tints and shades; the texture of the petals – thick and solid in peonies, fragile and papery in poppies; and their intriguing variety of strange and beautiful shapes. I certainly started like this, wanting to grow certain flowers, rather than beginning with a garden plan and needing to find suitable plants to put in it. I soon extended my 'wants' to include those with wonderful leaves and plant forms as well as interesting blooms.

Even the most irresistible flowering plant, one that I call a 'key' performer, is part of a whole cast; it has to be considered as a component in an overall look as well as for its individual charms. It forms part of the garden. And this is a book about flower gardens rather than simply about flowers as such. In some ways the book's shape follows the broadening perspective I have just described, starting by focusing on flowers in some detail, going on to consider the attributes of a plant as a whole and its potential role in a planting scheme, and then looking at some garden styles where flowers hold the key to the whole effect.

By writing about flowers and how to use them in gardens I feel I am closely involved with the most practical aspects of gardening: not only with the 'hands-on' day-to-day decisions of management, but also with all the design considerations that dictate initial plant and flower choices. My concern in this book is with *flower* gardens as opposed to general principles of garden style and design, although these remain part of a broader philosophy that lies behind all the detail. While considering the more solid virtues of structure, foliage and growing possibilities, I always remember that it is the flowers themselves that in their fleeting and elusive radiance give one the greatest moments of gardening satisfaction.

I feel I am very fortunate to live at Tintinhull, which always seems to me a living, growing example of a true flower garden. It is quite inward-looking, an enclosed oasis, the layout owing little to its setting and more to the trees, walls and hedges that frame it and keep it separate from the surrounding Somerset countryside. Tintinhull's garden is its own world; the flowers have to contribute only to its beauty. It was brilliantly designed and laid out by someone else – we are only guardians for the National Trust – but the garden 'rooms', each with a separate plant or colour theme, provide me with a chance to experiment with all sorts of flowers in different situations. We do have sections in the garden corresponding roughly with the chapter headings in the 'gardens' section of this book. We have different types of border planting – including quite self-conscious colour coordinations – and beds framed by hedges, as well as more natural areas where plants are encouraged to break out of any preconceived role.

Gardening, unlike many other art forms, involves a time scale. Plants change and grow through a season and over the years. By living in a garden and watching plant and flowering performances over a period, one gains some extra sense of what plants can achieve, even allowing for disappointing years of freezing in winter and drought in summer. In fact these trials all give a wider perspective to flower-garden management, and are part of the learning process. I hope this book conveys both the essential joy I find in the beauty of flowers and the pleasures of using flowering plants to make a truly inspirational garden.

Frank Cabot's garden in Canada is eighty miles north of Montreal, near the St Lawrence River. The growing season is short and winters hard, although perennials often lie happily under a protective blanket of snow. The main double borders sloping below the house are planned around an axial grass path which stretches to the tall poplars above. The levels are adjusted by shallow stone risers. Trees and shrubs protect the beds and keep the borders visually separate from the other garden schemes to give more impact. Flower borders are 'made' not only by flowers; attractively coloured and textured leaves are almost as important, providing a frame to set off more fleeting flowers. In July delphiniums, which grow superbly here, back thickly growing clumps of flowering astilbes, cimicifugas and ligularias – all plants chosen for their good foliage as well as for flowering effects.

FLOWERS
IN DETAIL

The attraction of flowers
Plant breeding and selection
Growing healthy flowers

By happy coincidence many of the flowering mechanisms developed by plants to set seed and reproduce also find favour with humans, putting such plants firmly on the list of desirable garden plants. Some wind-pollinated flowers such as catkins and the plumes of grasses possess a subdued beauty. Brightly coloured seeds and berries intended to attract the birds or insects that will ensure their dispersal are also choice plant material for garden display. However, it is with 'flowers proper' that this book is chiefly concerned.

The arrangements developed by flowering plants seeking to attract specific active pollinators, usually from the insect world, offer most excitement for the gardener, with their extraordinary repertoire of alluring colour, pattern and scent. Sometimes form and colour make the flower overwhelmingly conspicuous; at other times the floral parts, while visually subtler, are framed with foliage that gives the plant as a whole some decorative value.

Understanding the botanical technicalities of the flowering process may increase a gardener's awareness and satisfaction in the same way that a familiarity with plant names may sharpen his or her enjoyment. Some knowledge of how these reproductive mechanisms operate may actually be useful – a reminder, perhaps, of the values and disadvantages of double flowers. Other gardeners may deliberately choose flowers for their attractiveness to bees or butterflies. Sometimes such information is simply of interest, deepening our appreciation of a flower's beauty with the knowledge that such-and-such a flower emits its scent in the evening to attract night-flying moths, or that some colour change occurs after fertilization. It may also encourage others to look closely into the hidden centre of a tubular flower to find the patterned pathway that guides the bee to its target.

Here we explore in close-up some aspects of flower form and colour – the 'anatomy' of flowers – before looking in a broader perspective at the garden roles these plants may be called upon to play.

Astrantias have dome-shaped flower-heads composed of tiny florets surrounded by a decorative collar of narrow segmented bracts, giving a charming star-like effect. This arrangement is typical of the Umbelliferae or carrot family; the clusters of small flowers in umbrella-shaped umbels offer an abundance of nectar and convenient landing platforms, making umbellifers popular both with insect pollinators and with the wildlife that preys on insects.

THE ATTRACTION OF FLOWERS

Most of our flowering garden plants are angiosperms, with a decorative flower structure composed of a modified leaf shoot having two functions: to protect the reproductive organs and to assure appropriate pollination.

Flowers pollinated by wind tend to be relatively small and inconspicuous; they produce neither scent nor nectar, and their colouring is incidental rather than being attuned to the vision of some bird or insect. Some are nevertheless valued by gardeners, among them hazel catkins, dierama with slender dangling bells and many ornamental grasses. The more elaborate structures we admire in countless flower species have infinite complexities of colour, form and scent, which evolved over millions of years, closely paralleled by the evolution of living pollinators of various kinds.

These active participators are very often insects, but also include birds, snails and bats. As these creatures travel and visit flowers (usually in search of food), they bring about fertilization by transferring pollen from the flower's male organs to receptive female organs, which then form seed. The male and female organs may be in the same flower, in a separate flower of the same plant, or even (as with most hollies) on separate plants of the same species. In very many instances the flowers whose appearance people find most intriguing have their floral parts organized in such a way as to avoid self-pollination and instead assure cross-fertilization by means of these visiting agents.

There are fascinating evolutionary links between the development of various flower adaptations such as form, colour, nectar and scent and the sensory perception of the different classes of insect pollinator available. The earliest of these were probably wingless insects, succeeded by various forms of beetle. Such insects crawled into primitive flowers to eat the pollen grains, some of which would be distributed over the short distances necessary to assure self-pollination. Certain more evolved flowers developed nectar-secreting glands to attract flies (and later the more intelligent

BELOW LEFT *The Lenten rose* (Helleborus orientalis) *has basin-shaped flowers with distinctive protruding stigmas rising above the golden pollen-covered stamens.*

BELOW *The tightly clustered double flowers of this delphinium cultivar have powerful garden impact. The conspicuous spurs, which in unimproved species provided nectar for pollinators, have become modified into the extra ring of decorative petals.*

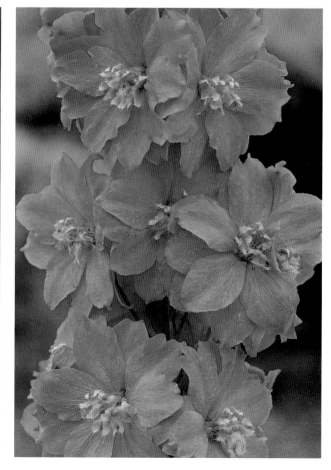

bees, moths and butterflies). These would accidentally brush against the pollen en route to the food store of nectar and so transport pollen to fertilize other flowers or other plants. Flower forms of tubular shape, or with specially adapted nectary structures (such as the conspicuous spurs of aquilegia and delphinium), first developed hand-in-hand with the evolution of insects and birds equipped with an elongated sucking proboscis capable of reaching their nectar.

In order to assure cross-pollination, some species possess special flower shapes, or allow their male and female organs to mature at different moments. The shape of the flower is sometimes designed to attract and admit the intended pollinator while excluding undesirables. Some complicated flowers such as the snapdragon-shapes of antirrhinum and linaria will only 'open' when an insect pollinator of the appropriate size and weight lands on the lower lip. The higher insects such as bees are able to follow sophisticated visual signals marking the path to the nectary, and often have to force their way through the folds of the flower to reach it. In the specialized pollinating mechanism of salvia, the visiting insect gains access to the nectar by knocking against the lower part of the stamen, which causes the top end to swing down and deposit pollen on the creature's back. The individual blooms on a flowerspike of *Lobelia cardinalis* pass through the pollen-producing male phase before the female organs become receptive, and it is possible to compare the older lower flowers, which have reached their female stage, with the upper ones, which function as males on opening.

Scent is another adaptation, aimed to attract from a distance pollinating insects that possess a welldeveloped sense of smell. Flower scents are often extremely pleasing to human tastes, but the smell of rotting meat that lures carrion-flies to pollinate arum flowers demonstrates that this is not invariably so. Some flowers such as night-scented stock, tobacco plants and the Chilean *Cestrum parqui* emit their fragrance only at evening, when colours fade. Others only open as dusk falls. In the case of evening primroses, the flowers open as daylight fails and do not close until dawn. Many attract night-flying moths, which have a keen sense of smell: the evolutionary appearance of honeysuckle in the Eocene era is known to have coincided with the emergence of the long-tongued moths. A particularly specialized relationship in North America is the interdependence between night-

scented yucca and the moth *Pronuba yuccasella*, in which the female moth fertilizes the yucca flower while laying its eggs: moth larvae and flower seeds develop together.

The decorative structure of flowers

The parts of the flower surrounding and protecting the reproductive organs are known as the perianth, and normally consist of a corolla (often divided into petals) and calyx (an outer layer, sometimes divided into sepals). The petals, coloured and often scented, are usually the showiest part of the flower. Sometimes they are separate and arranged to form simple saucer-shaped blooms, such as those of mallow and cranesbill geraniums. At other times they are more elaborately shaped, or fused together into a tube or some more highly specialized shape such as that of pea-flowers. Calyces may be green or brownish, and in some flowers such as clematis and anemone they resemble and actually replace the petals. In flowers such as waterlilies, and in many cacti, the sepals on the other hand

Salvia flowers have the distinctive protruding lips of the Labiatae which offer a platform for visiting pollinators such as hummingbirds or bees with long proboscises. When pollinators touch the lower part of the stamen while seeking nectar at the base of the corolla tube, they release a lever which deposits pollen grains on their backs for distribution to the next flower they visit. The bright blue Salvia patens from Mexico is receptive to any suitable pollinator and, like most American and European salvias, readily produces viable seed in many gardens.

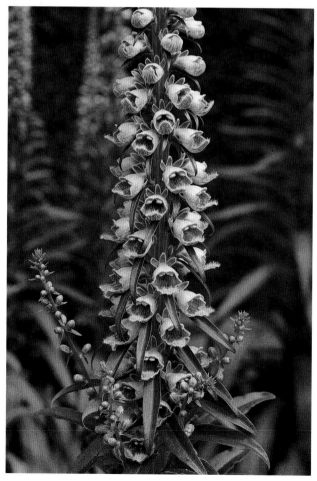

TOP LEFT *The waterlily is one of the earliest known plants to have developed flowers which produced pollen that attracted beetles. Primitive species had a simple arrangement of inner petals merging with stamens and outer petals fusing with sepals. The modern* Nymphaea tuberosa *'Richardsonii' has green-tinged outer sepals.*

TOP RIGHT *In the bog arum or skunk cabbage, as in other aroids, a showy bract or spathe encloses a single spike of tiny male and female flowers which has a heavy scent that attracts pollinating insects. Yellow Lysichiton americanus has a disagreeable odour, while L. camtschatcensis flowers, with white outer bracts, are more pleasingly scented.*

Cape figworts (Phygelius) and foxgloves (Digitalis) are both members of the Scrophulariaceae, with tubular flower-trumpets into which pollinating insects must crawl. In some species the human eye can see 'bee-markings' which guide pollinators to their target. Flowers of the garden cultivar Phygelius aequalis 'Yellow Trumpet' (FAR LEFT) are without distinctive markings, although the parent species and other cultivars with soft red or coral outer colourings have a lemon throat and mahogany lip which attracts insects in their native South Africa. The markings of the species foxglove Digitalis ferruginea (LEFT) are easily distinguished.

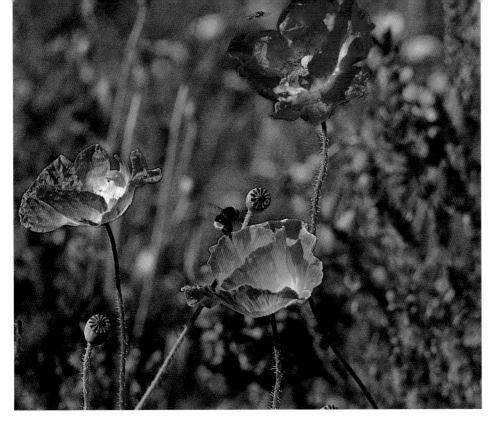

In the single form of the wild field poppy Papaver rhoeas, *the wonderfully translucent papery petals frame a ring of almost equally decorative stamens surrounding a central stigma. The stamens, the male organs, consist of filaments topped with pollen-carrying anthers and attract insects which transfer pollen to the stigma. Later the green seed-capsules split to scatter seed. These poppies hybridize easily and produce different colour forms which can germinate on site in the following spring, although the seeds can remain viable for years in uncultivated soil.*

resemble petals. Occasionally, as in a narcissus, there is no clear distinction between petals and sepals.

The stamens – the male organs consisting of filaments topped with pollen-carrying anthers – are also often decorative features. In winter-flowering shrubs such as hamamelis, wintersweet (*Chimonanthus praecox*) and sarcococcas the flowers are little more than bundles of scented stamens, less susceptible than soft petals to frost and rain damage. Australian trees and shrubs including acacias and callistemons also have flowers in which stamens are most prominent.

Stamens are modified into petals in some plants, resulting in 'double' flowers. These are less likely to produce fertile seed; in the wild they would not reproduce, and in the garden they generally have to be propagated from vegetative cuttings. (For the gardener this is a mixed blessing. A double-flowered Rugosa rose is less likely than a single one to produce the autumn bonus of attractive hips; on the other hand double flowers usually last many more days than single ones, since they are not hurrying to form seed.)

In other flowers it is the female organs that have evolved into a particularly decorative form. In the bearded iris, for example, the true petals are the three 'falls' and the three standards. Each of the three innermost 'petals', however, is actually a female style modified into a flattened petal-like form, with the frilly 'crest' arching outwards to protect its fertile stigmatic surface.

Bracts are a form of modified leaf at the base of a flower stalk or on the stem of a cluster of flowers. When the bracts are bright and decorative they are generally grouped around clusters of very small flowers that have no petals. The pocket handkerchief tree (forms of davidia), all euphorbias (including the exotic-looking poinsettia) and many dogwoods as well as the tropical bougainvilleas have sterile bracts instead of petals. The small flowers are fertile, but the sterile bracts provide an insect- or bird-attracting display. With lace-cap hydrangeas what are loosely identified as decorative flowers are in fact large flattened corymbs of fertile flowers surrounded by a ring of more conspicuous infertile ray florets. In the familiar mop-headed hortensia hydrangeas all the florets are sterile.

The 'flower' of members of the arum family is really a showy bract or spathe, with an interesting role in the pollination mechanism. The actual flowers are enfolded in the swollen base of the spathe, clustered around the central spadix, the lower female ones maturing earlier than the male ones higher up. The spathe's inner surface is lined with minute downward-slanting hairs: these trap flies that have crawled or fallen in, lured by the nectar, for long enough to fertilize the receptive females with pollen brought from a previously visited flower. Gradually the hairs wither and allow the flies to crawl upwards and escape – on their way passing the now-mature male flowers, and so becoming dusted with the pollen, which they may transport to a new flower.

In some species colouring and patterning such as spots or lines, as in horse chestnut, mimulus and eyebright, are designed to provide insects with a route to the nectar. Not all these signals are perceived by the human eye. Bees, wasps, beetles and birds have slightly different vision. Bees, for instance, perceive short wavelengths of light in the ultraviolet range invisible to humans (stamens are often 'lit up' in this way) but cannot distinguish longer-wavelength reds. Birds possess excellent colour awareness, though they lack a sense of smell. Despite their poor sight, beetles can locate large white plants and strong scents.

Having achieved their role in attracting a pollinator, petals normally start to wither, but some, such as those on double flowers, being sterile, are not transformed by fertilization. Those flowers with fragile petals are very transient: rock roses and cistus, day-lilies and giant waterlilies last only for a day, while morning glory flowers shrivel by afternoon. Many flowers that open at specific times perform only for their pollinators: marvel of Peru is called the four o'clock plant for this reason. Most of these plants produce a succession of short-lived flowers, and this quality assures them a place in the garden.

Some of the longer-lasting flowers change appearance dramatically during the flowering period. Buds about to open are often very different in colour from open petals; fading blossoms are tinged with a new range of tones. Some flowers actually change colour once effectively pollinated, usually becoming less rich and vivid as the need to attract passes; leaves also, especially those of crisp grey or silver plants, fade after the flowers have been fertilized.

Colour in flower and leaf

The amazing colour gradations and markings in flower petals are due to the distribution of pigments, most of them soluble in cell sap, and their chemical interaction. Perceived colour is also affected by the molecular structure of the surface texture, which can reflect light differently depending on whether it is smooth and glossy, waxy, matt or velvety. These visual qualities affect our preferences for flowers and the way we plant them, and this more subjective side of flower colour is considered as part of the 'palette' of flowering plants in the following chapter. The chemicals essential to plant growth and development affect the quality of both flower and leaf growth and are indicators of general plant health and of any deficiencies.

Anthocyanins and anthoxanthins are the main flower pigments. Anthocyanins give reddish tints to flowers and leaves, making pelargoniums scarlet, roses red and magenta, and delphiniums mauve, purple and blue. Being water-soluble, these pigments are affected by soil acidity; flowers tend to become redder in acid soil and bluer in alkaline (although *Hydrangea macrophylla* is a noted exception to this rule: a soil with high acidity and high iron content will make its flower bluer). Anthoxanthins produce a range of yellows from ivory to deepest primrose. Sometimes both sets of soluble pigments are present, and colours range through browns, reds and blues. The colour of white petals is sometimes caused by air spaces in the plant tissue, which cause light to be refracted and reflected to make the surface appear white.

Plastid pigments are found in the wall lining of plant cells, and they do not dissolve. The most important plastid is green chlorophyll, which exists principally in leaf and stem cells (and is responsible for their 'greenness'). It also often tinges sepals and flower petals. Chlorophyll is essential for photosynthesis; to achieve this many plants hold their leaves horizontally in order to obtain maximum exposure to light. Thus the leaves of trees present a mosaic pattern when viewed from below, while humbler plants establish a firm upright stance with stiff stalks holding leaves up on a similar horizontal plane. In both cases functional requirements become a decorative asset.

Although much of the time masked by chlorophyll, soluble pigments – which reflect other colours – are also present in leaf cells. In some plants, however, these pigments override the green effects, and leaves

ABOVE LEFT *Some flowers can be pollinated only by night-flying moths. New buds of evening primrose snap open at dusk and the flowers gently close again at dawn. Flowers and stems of* Oenothera speciosa *are pink-flushed, but the pale gleaming upper surfaces of the petals are clearly visible to moths in the darkness.*

Red-toned foliage is not only a feature of autumn, when cold breaks down the chlorophyll in leaves and sugar activates pigments in the sap which turn leaves yellow, red and bronze. In evergreens such as Pieris formosa forrestii *'Jermyns'* (ABOVE CENTRE) *and* Photinia × fraseri *'Birmingham'* (ABOVE RIGHT) *the emergent young leaves are distinctly red-tinged and translucent in spring. Leaf texture is often more significant than colour; the shiny, waxy leaf surface of many evergreens protects against winter dehydration – though the young foliage is vulnerable to late frosts.*

become various shades of bronze, purple, red and pink. In deciduous plants these colours last the whole season, although they generally become darker and less startling towards the end of summer, and purple foliage becomes dark and heavy. In evergreen plants it is the young foliage that displays attractive flushed-tone colours.

In late summer chlorophyll breaks down, producing droplets of carotenoid pigment, which turns the leaf yellow. As nights get colder the sugars build up in the plant tissue (causing the leaves of trees such as cercidiphyllums to exude a strong fragrance of crushed strawberries, and sugar maples to smell strongly of maple syrup). The sugar build-up activates the 'colouring' pigments – the anthocyanins and anthoxanthins – in the sap, and the leaves turn red and golden. In areas of high acidity, such as the east coast of America, autumn colours are startling with fiery and high-toned 'reds'. In more alkaline areas colours are less garish – duller purples and crimsons being commoner than the brighter tones. Similarly in regions with early sharp frosts, leaves produce more vivid autumn colours; a long gradual decline in temperatures, as often experienced in British autumns, allows leaf textures to deteriorate and spoil before the sugars build up.

Variegated or marbled leaves, attractive and useful in gardening schemes, are often a sign of ill-health showing that there are imperfect chloroplasts in the leaf cells. White or yellow edges to a leaf indicate a lack of chloroplasts in the outer layer of leaf cells; leaves with green edges around a central splash or mark of white or gold possess a defective inner layer of cells. Leaves of plants such as hollies, euonymus and elaeagnus with central splashes of pale colour are more likely to revert to plain green, while those edged with white or yellow – including other hollies and elaeagnus as well as many other very decorative hostas and grasses – usually retain this characteristic throughout the summer. In the variegated forms of members of the lily family, including lilies, Solomon's seal, day-lilies, phormiums and hostas, as well as grasses and bamboos, the longitudinal stripes of cream or yellow are formed by the imperfect chloroplasts. Most plants with these markings are technically 'sick' and seldom thrive as well as those with the 'perfect' green foliage; they are always less vigorous and more likely to suffer from drought or disease. In some forms of variegation compensatory feeding may turn the leaves green.

LEFT *Lily flowers are very showy and are colour-coded for insect attraction. Lilium pardalinum from California has attractive upswept spotted 'tepals', which are equal perianth segments rather than true petals, and pronounced stigmas and stamens.*

BELOW *Witch hazels (forms of Hamamelis) have a quite different garden appeal. Flowering in winter, their bundles of spidery stamens resist the rains and frosts that would damage larger, more extravagant petals. Instead of conspicuous patterning designed to lure pollinators equipped with a well-developed visual sense, the flowers of witch hazel are relatively modest-looking, though some species are also sweetly scented.*

PLANT BREEDING AND SELECTION

Surprisingly few of the palette of plants available in nurseries and garden centres are original species. Most have been 'improved' by special breeding programmes in search of more desirable and robust qualities in flower, leaf or form. Sometimes these changes are just to obtain shorter or longer flower-stems, but all are aimed at enhancing the gardening possibilities. This breeding for improvement is a sexual process, not a vegetative one whereby cuttings are taken or grafts made to reproduce a particular plant such as one that has attractive gold and silver foliage. To be certain of obtaining the same 'freak' appearance, it is not possible to use a sexual process.

In breeding, the main objective is to exaggerate features considered useful or decorative and to lose others less obviously desirable. The results of breeding and hybridizing are complicated. In the past breeders would spend years looking for one desirable seedling that demonstrated a noticeable improvement in quality. Today, in theory, the selector or hybridizer chooses two good wild or garden forms (species or cultivars) of a genus and breeds from them, deliberately hoping to produce a strain that inherits the best characteristics of both 'parents'. Of course it may still take time to find the desired combinations, and breeding is aimed not only at producing plants that look good but also at producing those that are disease-resistant, have extra hardiness or some such other more 'hidden' qualities. For final marketing of new hybrids a crucial discovery has been made: that first generation hybrids (called F_1 hybrids on the nurseryman's seed packet) are both uniformly reliable and possess the benefit of hybrid vigour. Such a discovery has transformed the horticultural trade and means that, once a strain is chosen, garden perennials and annuals may be produced by annual cross-breeding from two chosen parents. An additional marketing 'plus' is that the amateur does not find the same uniformity in saved seed but has to buy fresh F_1 hybrid seed each year.

Sometimes scientific breeding alters an harmonious natural balance, and highly bred 'improved' plants, selected for certain exaggerated characteristics such as flowering potential, lack the simple grace of their wild parents. Personally the more I garden, the more I prefer the elegant natural proportions of true species, even though I know that their performance is muted. With

trees and shrubs such reticence would cause no problem, but in the flower garden my choice of perennials and annuals would be more limited and less satisfactory without 'improved' plants. However I do think it would be interesting to lay out a whole scheme using true species alone. I would certainly do this if I had a woodland garden in parts of the United States, where nature's 'produce' can hardly be bettered. But in general we use and are grateful for the thousand and one 'possibilities' provided by the dedicated breeders; from amongst their products we can choose plants exactly suited to any garden scheme. In 'natural'-type gardening, true species often look appropriate; in the formal border we need plants that give precise effects, and those specially bred for longer flowering periods,

ABOVE *Bigeneric hybrids, the product of crosses between two distinct genera, often inherit some desirable qualities from both parents.*
× Heucherella tiarelloides *has the wonderful marbled leaves of* Heuchera brizoides *and the floriferousness of* Tiarella cordifolia, *but with pale pink clouds instead of the foam flower's creamy bells.*

shorter stems and general robustness are a great asset.

The commercial hybridizer and nurseryman exist to satisfy a demand, and the practice of developing and manipulating plants to improve their potential for the ornamental garden is one that goes very much hand-in-hand with garden fashion. Centuries ago in China, chrysanthemums and peonies were hybridized by cross-fertilization, and the Turks improved their native tulips for ornament and use as earnestly as any Dutch nurseryman during the period of Tulipomania in the seventeenth century. The perfectionists who in late seventeenth-century England formed themselves into florists' societies concentrated only on eight specific flowers: anemone, auricula primula, carnation, hyacinth, pinks, polyanthus, ranunculus and tulip. They largely ignored the new flowering plants that were already pouring in from the New World and South Africa. Without understanding the sexuality of flowers (Linnaeus did not publish until the mid-eighteenth century), the florists selected fine or unusual seedlings from a batch, and then propagated them by vegetative means; among them would be some chance natural hybrids. Thomas Fairchild (author of *The City Gardener* published in 1722) crossed a carnation with a sweet William to produce *Dianthus caryophyllus* × *barbatus* – the first scientific hybrid, known as D. 'Fairchild's Mule' – but commercial hybridization had to wait until the mechanics of heredity were more fully understood.

Less than two hundred years ago a chance mating of China roses with Damask roses on the island of Réunion gave rise to repeat-flowering Bourbons,

RIGHT *When the seeds of the annual sweet pea (Lathyrus odoratus) were first brought from Sicily in 1699, the flowers were purplish-red and white, held on graceful upright stems and very sweetly fragrant. By the mid-nineteenth century some self-coloured strains had been developed through natural selection of seedlings. From then on intensive crossing produced ever larger flowers, such as Spencer sweet peas, developed by 1900.*

Unhappily, the more highly bred flowers had almost no scent. Today breeders, while aiming to produce single colours, are redirecting their interest towards older fragrant varieties.

inheriting characteristics from both parents; since then rose breeding has become a fine art. Spencer sweet peas with flat rather than undulating upper petals, Russell lupins with denser spikes than the original Californian *Lupinus douglasii*, Shirley poppies and Excelsior strain foxgloves with better, denser flower-spikes than *Digitalis purpurea* all began as spontaneous seedlings.

Scientific knowledge of plants' sexual reproduction systems, with an appreciation of the genetic material of which chromosomes are made, has now led to geneticists being able to predict and control breeding lines towards certain qualities. Cross-fertilization between families, very rare in nature, is now possible, while hybridizing species between plants in any one genus is almost commonplace. These new skills are exploited to extend flowering seasons, to produce plants with larger flower-heads, and to invent dwarf strains of well-known favourites as well as to extend the range of possible colours. Red delphiniums already exist and in the foreseeable future roses will be blue and tulips black.

Of course, plants and their flowers may also be altered by giving them artificial cultural conditions. In gardening as opposed to the wild, the rigours of nature can be mitigated. Cultivated plants have artificial living quarters where they are watered in times of drought and protected against cold and heat, and where pests and diseases are controlled and weed competition eliminated. It is often noticeable how plants grow bigger and better – sometimes too vigorously – when introduced to these 'softer' conditions. Indeed, native plants grown in 'native' gardens will often become too large or too woody for ordinary garden use, while foreign introductions may well achieve larger flowers and leaves when in a new garden environment than in their own habitats. 'Wild' flowers introduced into a garden may perform much more splendidly than they can do in a competitive native environment; given fertilizers and space, plants respond by growing ever better. A good example is the Burnet rose, which on Scottish shorelines only reaches a few centimetres high but once in good soil will achieve head height.

ABOVE Rosa *'Charles de Mills'*, *with dark crimson cupped double flowers composed of deeply folded velvety petals, inherits its scent and its single flowering period in summer from* R. gallica. *The Gallica rose is one of the ancestors of all our garden hybrid roses, including the Bourbons, although many of its descendants bear little resemblance to the original.*

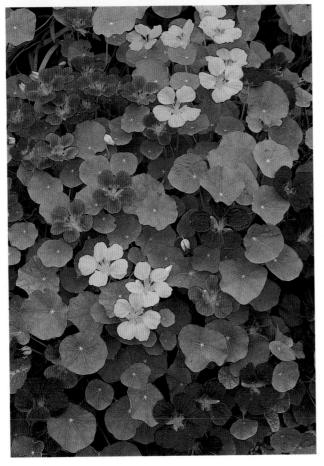

LEFT *In their native Peru annual nasturtiums* (Tropaeoleum majus) *flower in near drought conditions, but when planted in rich, moist garden soil they often produce more foliage than flowers. By cutting back the leaves and withholding water, the gardener can sometimes induce the plant to produce a new crop of flower-buds.*

GROWING HEALTHY FLOWERS

Encouraging plants to flower well is not quite the same as getting them to grow and look healthy. Flowering plants only reach their potential if they are looked after and provided with suitable sites and growing conditions. Their cultural needs have to be correctly balanced. Much of the technical skill of gardening lies in supplying essential elements such as light, water and soil, so that plants may convert carbon dioxide into sugar and starches and absorb certain essential chemicals through their root systems.

But other skills are required to determine the relative proportions of plant foods which are needed at different times of year to obtain good flowers as well as healthy plants. The main elements are nitrogen (N), phosphorus (P) and potassium (K). Magnesium (Mg), calcium (Ca) and sulphur (S) are also essential, and there are another six minor elements (iron, manganese, boron, copper, zinc and molybdenum), besides some trace elements that plants can use. These foods are supplied by putting back plant material taken from the garden – composts of fallen leaves, flower petals, stems and lawn mowings usually spread on the ground as a mulch – or by means of soluble chemicals: the soil must be capable of retaining these nutrient salts until the plants require them (they may be 'leached' away by rain), and each plant should be supplied with each chemical according to its particular needs.

This skilled balancing act between plant food and soil also depends on the nature of the soil itself in each garden, its texture and its fertility. The extent of a garden's alkalinity or acidity, often called sweetness or sourness, is measured by a pH scale. Ericaceous rhododendrons, heathers and camellias and many other plants (often from acid woodlands in America or Japan) will not thrive in alkaline soils. This is because they cannot tolerate lime, since it prevents plants absorbing elements such as iron and manganese which are essential to these calcifuge plants. Peonies and clematis, on the other hand, prefer an alkaline soil. In general the limitation imposed by the existing pH in the garden soil should be accepted, although it is possible to raise a low pH by adding lime. It is difficult, however, to lower the pH with any lasting effects. In the short term, acid-loving shallow-rooted plants may flourish in naturally alkaline soil if top-dressings of peat

Russell lupins, descendants of Lupinus polyphyllus *from California, have been bred for denser flower-spikes and predictable colours for the garden. Plant breeding for visual qualities like these, as well as for greater yield, is increasingly dependent on science rather than on selecting likely seedlings.*

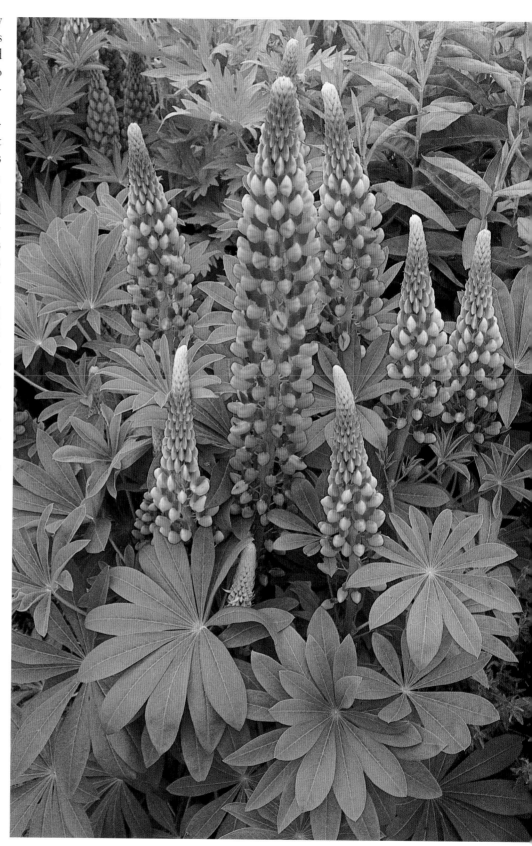

are used regularly and a dressing of flowers of sulphur is given when planting.

Most plants do their best and flower in what might be called their optimum circumstances, producing good blooms seen against a refreshing background of healthy foliage. Most thrive if the soil is regularly mulched with humus-making organic composts, and a balanced complete chemical fertilizer (supplying nitrogen, phosphorus and potassium in one mixture) is used to correct deficiencies and promote growth in spring. But too much rich nitrogen feeding may sometimes be counterproductive, especially for soft-stemmed plants that make extensive growth in one season, encouraging them to put all their energies into leaf and stem production and 'forget' to flower. Their stalks may fail to remain upright, and they may become prone to fungus disease. These plants need a more balanced diet, incorporating the nitrogen essential to all growth but with an increased proportion of phosphorus and potassium. Phosphates (given organically as bonemeal or inorganically as superphosphate) are particularly important for vigorous plants such as annuals and summer-flowering perennials. Potassium (most easily available as sulphate of potash, obtained by grinding up rocks rich in natural potash) helps shrubs to ripen their wood and form next year's flower-buds as well as being quick-acting to improve colour intensity in flowers.

Other plants, especially those that bear grey or 'silver' leaves to protect them against hot sun, thrive in well-drained stony soils approximating to those of their native habitat, and thus do not need rich feeding. Often they only flower as the leaf colour and texture starts to deteriorate. Some plants actually flower best under stress; when threatened with extinction through drought or disease plants hurry to produce the flowers and the seeds which make regeneration possible. In extreme circumstances a cure for woody plants that consistently refuse to flower is to cut around the outer roots in order to put pressure on the plant.

In hot climates, or in unusually hot and dry summers, perennials flower earlier and for much shorter periods. If the soil is well mulched and water-retentive, lack of rain has less ill-effect. In the southern states of America hot days and nights and high humidity reduce the length of flowering time considerably. Farther north in New England or on the west coast of North America the summers are hotter than an average British summer, so the flowering period is also more

limited. On the other hand many sun-loving plants (especially those from South Africa such as phygelius, agapanthus and nerines) flower best and longest during a hot summer or in hot countries. Even in the British Isles there is a marked difference between the sun-lovers' performance in East Anglia and their flowering potential in wetter western coastal districts.

The gardener must therefore be concerned with finding suitable situations and providing the correct soil for individual plants as well as considering appropriate plant associations. It may be worse than useless to put plants that require moisture next to those that need a dry well-drained site, or acid-loving plants close to those requiring alkaline conditions, and so on. The art of gardening lies not only in designing with shapes and colours; in a successful composition plants should look and be happy growing together because they require similar conditions. Some garden design is common sense but is easily overlooked by the flower-gardener who may initially think of colour and leaf association rather than considering these fundamentals. Lavenders do not really thrive in the rich soil demanded by roses; most German-type irises dislike rich soil and do not thrive in well-mulched borders. The gardener must also bear in mind that the foliage of silver and grey plants becomes increasingly green if the

LEFT *The leaves of* Iris foetidissima *are aromatic when bruised – hence its popular name of roast beef plant. Thriving in the shade of deciduous shrubs or trees, this iris has insignificant flowers in summer, but comes into its own in autumn and winter with its decorative orange seed-pods.*

ABOVE RIGHT Pennisetum villosum *is a grass with rather ordinary leaves but worth growing for its lax arching stems carrying long white fluffy flower-heads followed by bronze seeds. Grasses' graceful way of growth, with stems moving gently in a breeze, contrasts well with the more upright habits of tall stiff perennials. Many ornamental grasses look most beautiful in late summer and autumn when other herbaceous plants have lost their glow.*

BELOW RIGHT *Some plants, such as this yellow-flowered* Geum montanum, *are as attractive when carrying seed-heads as they are when in flower. The geum's beautiful wispy seed-heads tinged with pink and buff give the plant an extended season of value in the garden. Many other flowers and grasses are equally decorative at the seeding stage, but some flowers are weakened if left to set seed regularly, and some plants look better for longer if every seed-head is scrupulously removed.*

plants are grown in rich soil, making lax woody growth and being more easily killed in a cold winter.

In order to grow plants successfully, dead-heading and pruning must be undertaken according to the needs of the individual plant – and to its garden role. Flowers are sometimes succeeded by handsome seed-pods or colourful berries that are part of the plant's attraction for gardeners, and so these are treasured for a later-season display: grass-plumes, for instance, may be as beautiful when faded to buff as when they first emerge in summer. In North America autumns are crisp and deterioriation of grassy foliage and many other leaves is delayed to give beautiful effects through the months up to Christmas; in Britain, where damp weather probably follows wetter, cooler summers, the 'fall' display is much more limited.

Dead-heading encourages further flowering as well as improving the colour impact of the remaining blooms on the plant. Many perennials and most annuals and repeat-flowering roses will continue to flower well during the summer season if dead flowers are removed regularly. Gardeners who want to save seed can leave a few flower-heads to mature in relatively inconspicuous places.

Some shrubs (and in particular the repeat-flowering bush roses) also respond to dead-heading, but more generally their summer pruning consists of removing flowering shoots in order to promote the growth of the young wood which will bear next season's flower display. Other woody plants – usually those that bloom late in the season – are pruned back in winter to encourage the growth of new flowering wood.

It is up to the gardener to decide what maintenance is wanted and – with plants that possess the appropriate versatility – to enhance the characteristics that best suit the site. Some plants grown for their foliage may be prevented from flowering in order to preserve the integrity of a colour scheme. Sometimes, as with flowering hedges, later blossom or fruit will be sacrificed to decorative shaping. Shrubs may be either clipped into formal shapes or allowed to grow more naturally. Some climbers, too, do equally well when formally trained as when allowed to grow unrestricted: pillars of standard wisteria, for example, can earn a place in a formal border. The challenge for the gardener is not only in choosing pleasing plants from the wide palette available but also in using horticultural skills to grow them well and as an integral part of the garden style.

THE PALETTE OF FLOWERING PLANTS

Key plants
Companion plants
Massing plants
Plants to use as backdrops
The colour question

Like painters, gardeners seize on the different characteristics of plants to build garden compositions – individual statements or expressions, sometimes within discernible styles or schools, every one unique because of its particular location, and every one changing gradually or dramatically to present a succession of images through time.

Plants, and particularly flowers, are peculiarly unstable building blocks. Flower and leaf colours and forms do not remain static, even for a short period. In a garden picture most flowers have to be considered with their background foliage rather than as isolated colour spots. During a season the behaviour of the plant as a whole has to be taken into account: the transformation effected by flowering may be a radical one, altering the whole colour balance of an area, but the plant's longer-term performance will influence the picture before and after it flowers. Some plants linger, fading gracefully after flowering or assuming new interest in colour or seed, while others rapidly disappear or – perhaps worse – discolour, shrivel and generally become unsightly. Nor do plants retain their size and shape: even the slowest-growing subjects gradually increase in bulk, while some fast-growing annuals and bulbs make measurable growth from day to day.

There is no substitute for knowledge of plants when building successful garden pictures. Every aspect of a plant's appearance contributes something to the effectiveness of the current display. And to achieve the right timing, the cultivation needs of perennials, biennials, annuals, bulbs, shrubs and climbers must all be orchestrated and their behaviour managed.

Plants may be classified by colour or performance, so that each is cast in the role that suits it best. They can be allocated broad categories: key plants, good companion plants, plants for massing, and plants to use as backdrops. Inevitably many plants will not be typecast: they may be capable of many guises – depending on how they are grouped and presented, and on whose ideas are behind the garden design. There is always room for originality.

As finely tuned as paintings, garden pictures use flowers and leaves as the artist's tools, composing them to give delight for an entire season. In this Dutch garden, repeat-flowering catmint, pink clary, erigeron and astilbes are *backed by annual cosmos, heliotrope and cleomes, and perennial* Campanula lactiflora 'Loddon Anna', *purple eupatorium and* Lysimachia clethroides.

KEY PLANTS

The qualities that make a plant stand out from its neighbours or against its background include sheer stature as well as eye-catching colour and striking architectural form. Such accent, or climax, plants sustain a real presence whether they are set in isolation or combined in a graceful group. Inclusion of some of these key plants gives a lift to all garden schemes by punctuating a formal design, emphasizing its structure; they also provide focal points and underpin the seemingly artless compositions of more natural planting styles by giving textual depth and definition to an area of planting.

Unusual plants that attract attention because they are rarities may also be considered as key plants. On a garden tour such specimens will literally stop plantspeople in their tracks. Sometimes scorned by design buffs as collectors' plants, they add spice and provide talking points in a garden (even if they incidentally introduce an element of plant one-upmanship). Many unusual plants are distinguished in less conspicuous and rather more refined ways than the everyday accent plants, so that the plantsman-gardener's task is to allow the light of these subtler stars to shine without being eclipsed by brasher neighbours.

This process of controlled presentation in fact underlies the successful use of all key planting. Using too many accent plants turns a garden picture into a babble of confusion. For a climax to be truly climactic, neighbouring plants must play parts appropriate to the scene. This is demonstrated when foliage acts as a foil to shapely flowering specimens that star in containers used as dramatic focal points. The more extreme the contrast, the more dramatic the climax. A silvery-white thistle spreadeagled against a dark yew hedge represents almost positive/negative white/black contrast; a shining yellow flower-head silhouetted against a murky Venetian smoke bush also exploits extremes of colour contrast. Gentler effects are created when some

In this seaside garden globe-shaped heads of Allium giganteum *on tall stems rise above a sea of massed lavender to make a dramatic keynote in a composition which is given substance by elegant rustling grasses.*

These alliums, flowering in early summer, provide a link between spring bulbs and flowering perennials, but many other species and forms can extend the season to cover summer flowering periods.

other linking ingredients mediate between these extremes – a haze of white gypsophila softens dark foliage, for example.

The effectiveness of a key plant also depends on situation and presentation: a small pot planted with tulips becomes a clear focal point seen against a yew-hedge backdrop. However, when expanded into a bed, the same tulips might in their turn become the background carpet against which yew, clipped into an emphatic topiary shape, could act as climax.

Focus on bulbs

Bulbous plants provide good examples of striking form and flower through the seasons as many of them have the elegant clear-cut lines and definite shape that 'read' well among a group of different textures. In spring, crown imperials with their conspicuous clusters of red, orange or yellow bell-like flowers on statuesque leafy stems stand out against clustered leaves of emerging perennials. The grey-leaved *Fritillaria persica* 'Adiyaman' with dusty blackish-purple dangling bells might be the subtler equivalent for the plantsman.

Taller alliums with multi-flowered spherical heads command attention in early summer. Try growing *Allium christophii*, with its pale amethyst-coloured flowers and grassy leaves that die down gracefully after flowering, or *Nectaroscordum siculum bulgaricum*, which carries drooping greeny-white flower-heads on tall willowy stems. Interplanted among low-growing herbaceous plants – or even among the architectural leaves and elaborate flowers of irises, as at Tintinhull – the shapely allium flower-heads add a texture that lifts what would otherwise be merely pretty.

When in flower, some lilies are key plants through sheer size. Foxtail lilies are both valuable and statuesque: *Eremurus robustus* is the most spectacular in summer borders, with starry lily-like pink flowers on immensely tall stems. The giant lily *Cardiocrinum giganteum* – which takes several years to reach maturity and flower – provides a dramatic centrepiece in a woodland setting.

Lilies proper – *Lilium* species – are incomparably showy for later-season displays. A single-stemmed lily is statuesque, and groups look well as part of border schemes, their crisply outlined flower-heads giving definition to adjacent planting of fuzzier textures. This quality is valuable in more natural situations, too. Groups of golden-rayed imperial lilies are startlingly vivid in woodland gardens in the late season, just as orange-flowered *L. lancifolium* make splendid clumps to contribute midsummer colour in open borders. Lilies are also excellent in containers. We plant Wilson's regal lilies (*Lilium regale*) in stone pots to flank the west door of the house at Tintinhull; as well as their role in emphasizing the entrance, they fill the garden with delicious fragrance and glow white and ghostly at dusk. As pot plants their emphatic role in design is already strong. Moreover it is possible to bring pot-grown plants into play in prime condition, and avoid the business of managing plants in important sites during their off-season phases.

Elements of architecture

Some key plants have handsome foliage and perhaps flower interest that provide good-quality furnishing throughout the year and are thus stars even in the off-season. Two of the shrubby spurges, *Euphorbia characias* and *E.c. wulfenii* (and cultivars of the latter), are among evergreen perennials that remain handsome in all seasons. Gertrude Jekyll grew these in her spring garden to create architectural features above drifts of small bulbs and above the unfolding pleated leaves

Two key plants are part of the bog garden composition in a moist area of Mrs Goossenaert's garden in Holland. The Japanese Iris laevigata *poses in front of a clump of the umbrella plant (Darmera peltata), with large, roughly heart-shaped leaves. Many moisture-loving plants have good decorative foliage which gives them individual eye-catching importance; the darmera also has attractive pink spring flowers which appear before the leaves on long stalks. The stately sun-loving iris, with rich red-purple velvet-textured flowers, revels in humus-rich soil; a 'quality' plant, it could be the main focal point in a garden scheme.*

In a coastal garden in Zeeland, strong clumps of evergreen Salvia officinalis with a bluish-purple flower make statements between the more delicate Knautia macedonica, with yarrow glimpsed in the background. Emphatic planting in repetitive blocks can hold a design together.

of veratrums. The brilliant red-flowered *E. griffithii* 'Fireglow' becomes a colourful focal point in early summer: a single plant will rapidly increase to produce a dense clump of vibrant flower-heads to glow in light shade or under deciduous trees and shrubs.

Hellebores, with elegant foliage and sumptuous white, cream, dusky-mauve and purple-splashed petals, may be grown as single specimens or in groups. Christmas roses (*Helleborus niger*), lenten roses (*H. orientalis*) and other species and hybrids with green and creamy flower-saucers extend the hellebore season

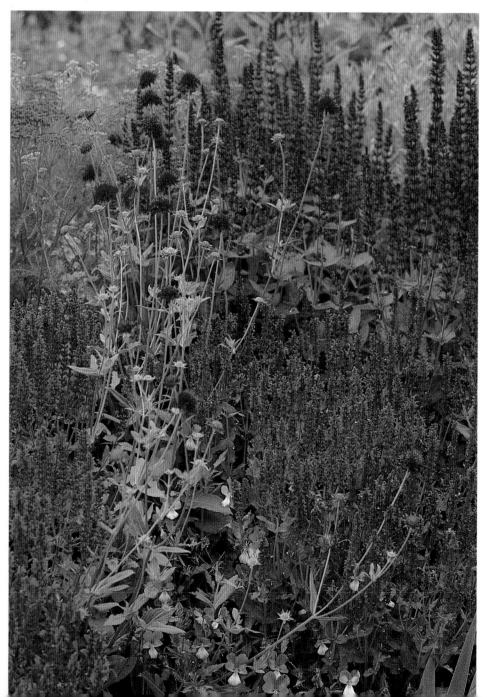

from early to late spring. *H. foetidus* has deeply divided dark evergreen leaves to contrast with neighbouring glossy bergenias and veined hostas; each bell-like pale green flower is edged with maroon, and the plant grows to make a fine individual clump.

There are many different types of Solomon's seal, some with interesting decorative variegated leaves, but none merits more attention than the old-fashioned cottage-garden *Polygonatum* × *hybridum*, with its dangling lily-of-the-valley greeny-white bells held on tall arching stems. Trilliums from America likewise attract the eye in shady borders or light woodland.

Irises with sword-like leaves are also valuable architectural plants, their shapes contrasting with softer textures and more rounded outlines and their flowers, in subtle colours, beautiful for a short season. They are effective on either side of a pathway or in clumps of three or more to give structure to perennial borders. Bearded irises used to be massed in specially designated beds, but such schemes are too extravagant in space and labour to be practical today, so they are teamed with suitable companions that will distract the eye from fading iris leaves.

Bearded irises thrive in well-drained soil and full sun but other garden-worthy irises, such as *I. sibirica* and the common yellow flag (*I. pseudacorus*), need or tolerate moisture around their rhizomes during the growing season, and will even bear some shade. *I. p.* 'Variegata' has eye-catching leaves early in the season although they turn plain green later. Most irises reach their flowering peak in early summer, but the foliage is already decorative much earlier.

Hostas, which produce undulating green, glaucous and golden or creamy variegated leaves, are strong bulky features when set beside delicate flowers such as Himalayan blue poppies. Peltiphyllums, rheums and rodgersias are moisture-loving plants with broad sculptured leaves; and astilbes and meadowsweet have deeply divided or fretted green and bronze-tinted foliage. When massed on a large scale their leaves merge into textured drifts, but these handsome plants retain key status in smaller groupings. All of them also have spectacular flowers: those of hostas are lavender-mauve or white, lily-like and fragrant; peltiphyllums carry pink clustered flowers on tall stalks before the leaves appear in spring; and rheums and rodgersias bear rhubarb-like fluffy panicles. Astilbes and meadowsweet produce flower-plumes in red, pink or white.

Some rules of punctuation

Key plants include some perennials whose architectural quality will, in season, contribute something towards the 'bones' of a garden layout. Sometimes a plant's profile stands out in the crowd so that it can become a valuable pivot of the garden layout, emphasizing a formal design. Repetition of such plants sets up useful rhythms – perhaps the compelling regularity of an avenue, or simply a firm baseline to hold together a more relaxed mixture of border plants.

Kniphofias and yuccas have dramatic punctuating shapes, making them useful features or accent plants for positions in full sun. Kniphofias are more appropriate in small gardens, the clusters of strap-like leaves are a foil for flower-spikes in tones of lemon-yellow through to hotter reds. Some yuccas may be specimens in lawns in larger-scale layouts, or form ideal corner plants framing the end of a border or flanking a gateway. Although less spectacular, I prefer to use those with soft flaccid leaves (such as *Yucca filamentosa* and

Y. recurvifolia) rather than those with dangerous stiff spiked leaf-tips. Yucca foliage alone is striking, but in a hot summer these desert plants produce statuesque flower-spikes of creamy-white bells.

A graceful grass, *Stipa gigantea*, can earn an important place in any scheme: a pair positioned on either side of a path acts as emphasis, perhaps creating a gateway to a new garden area. The large flower-heads, opening purple-tinged and turning to glistening tawny-yellow, look beautiful when seen with the sun's rays glowing through them.

The emerging leaves of silvery artichokes – and the related cardoons (forms of *Cynara*) – also make wonderful corner plants: we use them at Tintinhull to mark the ends of beds, where they contrast in spring with an informal planting of self-seeding small black-flowered violas and sweet rocket, and the pink flowers of *Geranium striatum* 'Glenluce'. Later, the artichokes' tall flower-stems bearing immense thistle-heads become a foil to pink roses, catmint and *Verbena patagonica*. (At

In this very grand garden composition, many of the participants have starring roles. False cypresses, trained into lollipop shapes, with topiary box in the foreground, are framed by a pair of silver-leaved cotton lavender bushes (Santolina pinnata neapolitana). These provide a structured background for good foliage plants and their seasonal flowers. Hostas, violas and opium poppies combine to complete the picture.

Mulleins with large grey (or sometimes green) leaves are statuesque in both foliage and flower. Here in Beth Chatto's garden at White Barn House in Essex a fine group of the biennial Verbascum olympicum *(or of the almost indistinguishable V. bombyciferum), whose branching stems give a candelabra effect, take up an important front-of-border position to make a show for the whole summer.*

Tintinhull this distinguished verbena self-seeds each year to flower by midsummer, its purplish-lilac flowers on tall stems rising like a hazy mist out of the catmint.) The artichokes, incidentally, also look spectacular when massed in a broad bed, to contrast with the green leaves of rosemaries and sages, which like the same sunny position.

Another excellent plant for corners is *Salvia sclarea turkestanica*, with large furry musk-smelling leaves and an architectural spreading habit. Like many of the best salvias, it is biennial. *S. argentea* is architectural in a lower key, usually grown for the wide leaf-rosettes of silvery velvet during its first season. The leaves turn green in the second year, and tall stalks bear typical whitish-green sage-flowers of great charm.

Some perennials are important eye-catchers for their foliage alone, with flowers a fleeting incident. Sun-loving *Melianthus major* bears large silvery-green almost glaucous pinnate leaves. In mild areas brownish-maroon flowers on tall stalks appear in spring, but it is the sculptural quality of the foliage that makes this plant the 'star' of a sunny bed and also spectacular planted in a decorative pot to mark a focal point.

Stars of stature

Some plants become stars through their sheer size. Giant *Ferula communis* does not flower every year, but the towering stems topped with greenish-yellow cow-parsley umbels are worth waiting for, and in the meantime the finely cut midgreen foliage makes handsome furnishing through summer months. Giant kales – with cloudy small white flowers above dark heart-shaped leaves – are climax plants for borders, and especially useful on corners.

Although biennials take two seasons to reach their peak, they can play key roles in a flower garden. Angelica, for example, has large architectural divided leaves during the first season and, in the following year, tall distinguished yellowish-green umbels. I use angelica to give 'body' to kitchen-garden schemes or to fill gaps in first-year border plans. Soaring verbascums, grown as perennials or biennials, have stems to 2.4m/8ft or more above a rosette of green leaves. The yellow flower-spikes, described by Graham Stuart Thomas as 'like a great paint brush in the garden landscape', are borne for almost eight weeks in summer. Metallic-leaved eryngiums, such as the ghostly *Eryngium giganteum*, and silvery *Onopordum acanthium*, may frame pathways or doors. Cottage-garden hollyhocks in warm pinks and reds are deservedly back in favour; today yellow- and black-flowered species add spice to colour schemes. In a warm site the soaring stems of *Campanula pyramidalis* starred with blue or white bell-shaped flowers make an exciting focus in bed or flower pot.

Where there is space to accommodate its invasive roots, allow one of the stately plume poppies (*Macleaya microcarpa*) to tower over neighbouring perennials. It bears striking bronzy-green lobed leaves and panicles of fluffy pinkish flowers in summer. For the really wild garden, the giant hogweed (*Heracleum mantegazzianum*) has huge divided leaves that give a tropical effect in a damp corner; tall stems bear white giant cow-parsley-like flower-umbels. By water or at the edge of a wood these plants look fantastic, but cut stems exude juice that brings up painful blisters. The giant bristly leaves make *Gunnera manicata* an important landscape plant in any waterlogged setting, but floral conical spikes of dull green give it an extra edge.

Small and beautiful

Smaller plants may also be important accents, giving emphasis at ground level; they are quality plants in their own right rather than associates of neighbouring groups. Among these are the spring-flowering pasque flower with its feathery leaves and open petals in tones and tints of mauve and purple with bright yellow centres; later the seed-heads are decorative and airy. Also of distinction are creeping phlox such as *Phlox* 'Chattahoochee' with pink-flushed starry blue flowers, *Viola* 'Irish Molly' with greenish-bronzy-yellow petals, diascias studded all summer with pink flowers above trailing stems, and *Sedum* 'Vera Jameson' with glaucous purple leaves and dusky pink flower-heads. Another good small key plant is *Saxifraga cortusifolia fortunei* 'Wada', which produces wax-like green leaves with startling red undersides and delicate white flowers in late summer.

An edge of quality

Certain perennials add depth of interest to border planting. One of the bluestars (*Amsonia tabernaemontana*), for example, has willowy stems and narrow leaves that are modest yet eye-catching in the early border, and in autumn its foliage and stems turn a tawny-gold. Another good perennial is *Baptisia australis* with its blue-green leaves and blue lupin-like flowers followed by dark seed-pods. Peonies of all types have interesting divided leaves and many are valuable border classics; particularly worth planting are the distinguished herbaceous species such as *Paeonia mlokosewitschii* with its clear lemon-yellow globular flowers and the small *P. cambessedesii* with its exotic red-tinted stalks and leaves. Garden peonies will hybridize to produce some interesting seedlings, probably taking four years to flower.

Gypsophila paniculata 'Bristol Fairy', although often temperamental and short-lived, is worth growing for the cloud of misty white flower-panicles carried in summer, and *Parahebe perfoliata* with its blue-green perfoliate leaves and delicate lavender-blue flowers on arching stems always attracts attention. *Gillenia trifoliata*, a perennial resembling an arching spiraea, carries

Irises and shrubby spurges such as Euphorbia characias wulfenii *are key plants in their own right. Here in full flower at Tintinhull they make a partnership behind* edging mats of Viola riviniana purpurea, Phlox 'Chattahoochee' and grey-leaved Hebe pinguifolia 'Pagei', *this last not yet in flower.*

ABOVE Gaura lindheimeri *tolerates both drought and humidity, and in well-drained soil and full sun produces erect slender stems bearing subdued but charming white flowers that darken to pink as they age. The petals merit close observation.*

ABOVE RIGHT *A bright pink geranium from Madeira with dark stems and fresh green leaves adds distinction to a mass of grey foliage and little companion flowers. Tender in many areas, it self-seeds each season in this Californian garden.*

what William Robinson described as a 'loose panicle of white flowers, distinct and graceful'. These combined with attractive habit and foliage, make it a valued specimen plant. The white-flowering form of *Epilobium angustifolium* is a superlative perennial. Its ethereal flower-spikes enhance a white border and will draw the eye whether the plant is in sun or shade.

Drifts of Himalayan poppies with sculpted hairy leaves and blue or yellow flowers are focal points in woodland glades in early summer. They thrive in west coast gardens in the British Isles and the north-west American states and are matched in splendour by groups of summer-flowering lilies that prefer the same situation in shade. Flowering late in the season and revelling in moist acid loam and half shade, *Kirengeshoma palmata* has dangling yellow bells and distinguished vine-like leaves all season. Toad lilies also like shade and moisture, and their little exotic orchid-like flowers are intriguing at the end of summer.

Other late-summer flowerers need to be baked in full sun. The delicate *Gaura lindheimeri*, with small pinkish-white flowers and willow-like leaves, is modest in size, but a clump is always an eye-catcher in a hot dry border. Most salvia species, of which some are tender sub-shrubs, are valuable towards the end of summer; they revel in hot sun, but do need plenty of moisture. Branching woody plants with dark red or crimson flowers, such as forms of *Salvia microphylla neurepia* and *S. fulgens*, and some species with intense blue flowers, such as *S. guarantica*, deserve important sites.

The tender perennial swamp rose mallow (*Hibiscus moscheutos*) carries wide-open red, pink or white mallow-like flowers of satiny texture, and is one of the most startlingly beautiful late-flowerers in regions with strong summer sun. In a favoured climate the shrub-like French honeysuckle (*Hedysarum coronarium*), also known as sukka sweetvetch, will survive outside; it has glaucous leaves and deep rosy-red pea-like flowers.

Presented in pots

Simply growing plants in a container to some extent signals that they are out of the ordinary, but key plants framed in this way create a lasting impression of beauty and elegance.

Many plants that are perennials in their native habitat are counted as annuals in colder regions. These are best massed, since most put so much energy into their summer flower display that they have little left for developing good leaves or a fine stance. I think of annuals as having specimen potential if they look impressive when grown in pots: *Hibiscus trionum*, with papery cream-coloured petals and a central purplish-brown smudge, is an outstanding example. *Datura meteloides* (now *D. inoxia*) with greyish leaves and wide trumpet-shaped flowers is exotic in an urn; it is a prolific seeder in hot-summer countries (I have seen it spreading in fields in the American Midwest).

Tender woody plants may be grown outside in ornamental pots in the summer and overwintered in a greenhouse – a practice that puts a number of desirable plants within reach of many more gardeners. I use both the marguerite-like *Argyranthemum foeniculaceum*, with its fretwork glaucous leaves and white daisy-flowers, and *Anisodontea capensis*, with its pink flowers, as centrepieces in stone or terracotta jars. These and green- or bronze-leaved cabbage trees (*Cordyline australis* and *C. a. purpurea*) with bunches of sword-like leaves all need full sun. For shade orange-, red- and yellow-flowered mimulus such as *Mimulus aurantiacus* give a late-summer display.

Some of the most interesting plants that do well in containers are woody-based sub-shrubs, which die down each winter in cold or temperate climates and shoot from the base in spring like any hardy herbaceous perennial. Especially good are some of the richly exotic-looking fuchsias, which flower with vigour into the autumn months. I also plant the dahlia-like dark purple-red *Cosmos atrosanguineus* in containers. I find I can get it to flower earlier in summer if I keep specimens in pots over winter, otherwise it performs only from midsummer onwards, occupying valuable flower-bed space during the other months of the year.

In the warmer regions, seedlings of the more tender biennials may survive mild winters outside or be given winter protection: experiment with these rather than following any rule book or zoning formulae. Two geraniums from Madeira, both superlative plants for foliage, form and flower, are monocarpic (dying after flowering and seeding). *Geranium palmatum* is the hardier, and it and G. *maderense* have pink-flushed stems and dark-eyed purplish flowers. They make superb pot plants.

Some of the bulbous plants from hot climates also grow excellently in pots. If thickly mulched in winter, ginger lilies (*Hedychium*) create tropical effects in late borders with their canna-like leaves and heavy fragrance. With generous watering, they may also be grown in pots. Equally exotic in appearance, but hardier, is *Cautleya spicata* 'Robusta', with erect stems and two-ranked leaf-blades; the flower-spikes are dark yellow, each clasped with maroon bracts. Eucomis bulbs (pineapple flowers) come late into leaf when grown in the open, so are easily forgotten; their fleshy basal leaf-rosettes and dense spikes of starry flowers look well in pots, and plants are easy to overwinter.

In her garden at the Old Rectory, Burghfield in Berkshire, Mrs Ralph Merton fills ornamental pots with plants that flow over the edges. Good foliage shapes provide a base for flowers. An American agave with variegated leaves, a clump of hostas, Helichrysum petiolare *'Limelight' and* Euphorbia mellifera *give bulk to* Argyranthemum *'Jamaica Primrose' and deeper yellow* Bidens ferulifolia, *with purple-flowered* Tibouchina semidecandra *lurking in the background.*

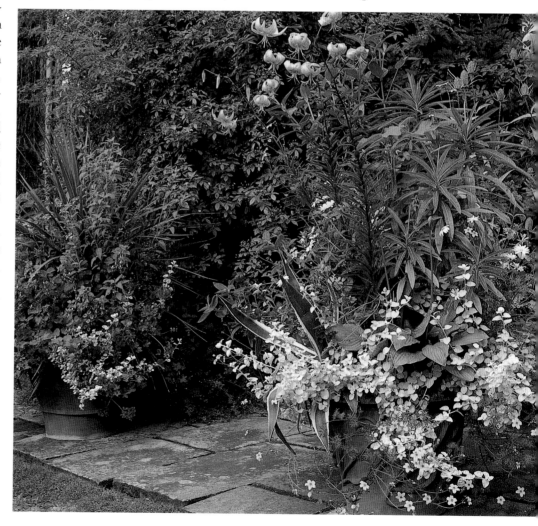

COMPANION PLANTS

These are the essential 'furniture' of garden planting, complementing the framework provided by the architectural key plants and the basic garden structure of walls, grass and so on. Their decorative value is more intimate, less easily registered. Even when grown in a fine group, they do not make a very definite statement on their own; their contribution to the garden scene depends on association. Using them correctly and to best advantage calls for a strong pictorial sense, employed so that neighbouring shapes and colours contribute to the overall garden picture at any given moment.

Most of the hardy herbaceous perennials are companion plants as they are not sufficiently impressive individually to merit key status. When grouped together they are the fundamental components of border schemes. Such plants are important for their flowers and foliage over a long period. While the permutations of perennials seem inexhaustible, especially during summer months, the judicious use of bulbs and specially grown annuals – together with plants that are self-seeders – increases still further the possibility of creating a succession of pleasing associations.

A well-planted garden should have no patches of bare earth. Seeders are especially valuable in the early part of summer before the main perennial groups get into their stride, and drifts of plants grown as annuals are sometimes brought in to complete the colour balance of a section of border planting.

Seeding companions

These come in many guises and include: true biennials flowering and making seed before dying; perennials treated as biennials; and annuals that self-seed and flower next year *in situ* – or are sown by the gardener as local infill. A degree of unpredictability in this kind of companionship creates a relaxed naturalness sympathetic to all but the most manicured layouts. Self-sown plants cropping up in unauthorized spots also rapidly foster an air of mellowness and maturity in newly laid-out garden areas. Allow self-sown seedlings to mature and only weed out those that are indisputably in the wrong place.

Some companion plants make charming informal carpets around and between other more special plants. Low-growing viola species and hybrids seed themselves beneath deciduous shrubs and roses and through paving cracks. They are particularly valuable under delicate-foliaged shrubs such as caryopteris, which come late into leaf. Treat them as biennials and pull them out once flowering is over, unless seedlings are desired for the coming year. Forget-me-nots also flower early; the F_1 hybrids, which look best planted as a mass, come in strong blues. Their seeds produce paler-flowered tints thereafter.

Tall self-seeders may form loose clusters of flowers to weave a colourful infill between permanent plants. In early summer self-seeding aquilegias make graceful clumps at midheight with their muted blue to pinkish-red flowers. Both sweet rocket, in washed-out mauves and whites, and valerian – preferably the white or deeper pink forms – seed in rich border soils and neglected stony ground. Valerian may form natural-looking drifts in gravel or drystone walls. Grey-leaved bright-flowered horned poppies love similarly well-drained garden sites. The Welsh poppy (*Meconopsis*

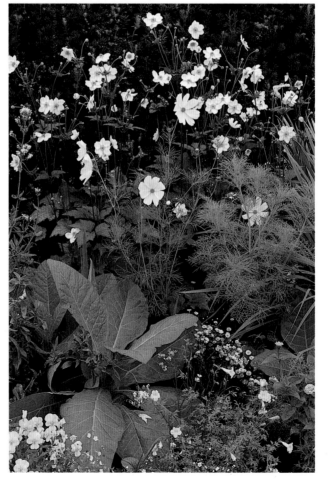

The most effective schemes for beds and borders use combinations of plants that seem to blend together in harmony. In this Dutch garden a white theme is sustained by a companionable group of the perennial Anemone × hybrida *'Honorine Jobert', with distinguished vine-like foliage, and annual* Cosmos bipinnatus, *with more lacy leaves. The leaves of a later-flowering tobacco plant underpin the group, and flowers of violas, zinnias and daisies fill in gaps of bare soil.*

In Phoebe Noble's garden on Vancouver Island, white- and pink-flowered forms of biennial sweet rocket (Hesperis matronalis) and valerian (Centranthus ruber) perform in early summer in front of a large pink Weigela florida – through the branches of which clambers Clematis 'Nelly Moser' with its wide pink and white striped flowers. In this sort of companion planting, promiscuous self-seeders like sweet rocket and valerian are allowed to blend together in happy unison. Any seedlings that stray too far out of line and encroach on a colour scheme where they are less welcome can easily be removed.

cambrica) seeds very freely and will thrive in any soil in sun or shade, adding spots of clear yellow to the background green. The British native woad (Isatis tinctoria), with its brilliant lime-yellow panicles above glaucous leaves, self-seeds in full sun; an interesting alternative for shade is the similarly coloured Smyrnium perfoliatum, which produces less striking flower-umbels but attractive heart-shaped leaves.

Among the self-seeding biennials that are suitable for companion planting are some with more arresting profiles, such as the tall flower-spikes of purple and white foxgloves (Digitalis purpurea and D.p. alba), which look at home in woodland but also thrive in sun. The young green leaves of Miss Willmott's ghost become metallic silver before flowering in their second season, and the burnished flower-heads glisten between low-toned campanulas and brighter-flowered phlox. Mulleins and biennial evening primroses give a pleasingly unplanned air when, with towering flower-

stems, they glow above neighbouring plants – their pale petals opening widest as dusk falls.

Annuals grown from seed sown in spring may be planted in groups among border perennials. The glowing pinks and reds of annual cosmos (Cosmos bipinnatus) make wonderful cut flowers, but are also graceful in a conventional border provided the soil is not too rich. Low-growing grey-leaved gazanias are perennials usually grown as annuals: their wide mainly orange daisy-flowers give colour in the front of borders. Interplanted clumps of violet, pink or white forms of spider flower make pretty dappled patches of blending pastel tones. Alonsoas, however, are straggly growers, whose orange-scarlet twisted flowers do not make distinctive blocks of solid colour; instead they convey a hint of bright tapestry hues to enrich 'hot' border schemes.

The annual delphiniums or larkspurs (Consolida ambigua) are fast-growing upright annuals; giant forms flower at head height, making them almost as valuable in border schemes as true perennial delphiniums – and less trouble. Lower-growing delphiniums are short-lived perennials that flower from seed in the first season, and I prefer them in small drifts complementing taller plants rather than massed in beds.

Tobacco plants, with their sweet scents in evening, are attractive in companionable drifts. Invaluable grouped behind late-summer flowerers is *Nicotiana sylvestris*, which carries soaring spikes of white tubular flowers. Lower-growing *N. langsdorfii* bears sulphur-yellow tubular flowers that fit into any colour scheme.

Fine tuning with tender plants

Some important companion plants are treated as annuals for seasonal garden purposes. These include woody penstemons, felicias and silver-leaved artemisias and helichrysums – sub-shrubs or tender woody plants that often have more presence than annuals but serve a similar purpose, contributing an edge of quality to borders and furnishing containers with interesting colours and textures. Plants may be overwintered or grown from cuttings.

Daisy-flowered felicias, with yellow centres amid blue ray florets, will sprawl like miniature marguerites in the front of sunny flower beds or grow happily in pots, flowering for many weeks if regularly dead-headed. Osteospermums have wide white or pink daisy-flowers and may be grown in the same situations. Penstemons are indispensable border plants with subtly rich colouring; in good soil they flower over a long season. Many are hardy but become rather battered by the end of winter, so it is best to treat them as annuals and take cuttings each autumn. Verbenas are among the most valuable seasonable companion plants. Dark

In Helen Dillon's town garden in Dublin, carefully selected strong colours are combined in the beds near the front door. Spikes of orange-yellow kniphofia and soaring plume poppies (Macleaya cordata) *dominate lower-growing plants, among them yellow lilies, heuchera and penstemon, while the tender Dahlia 'Bishop of Llandaff' gives the colour scheme continuity through the summer. Verbena* patagonica, *with airy flower-heads on a mesh of tall stems, makes a mauve haze in the background.*

green deeply cut leaves make a background for different-coloured clusters of bloom – dark mauve, icy pink and white and many others. Grow them from easily rooted cuttings each year, planted out in drifts at the edge of a bed.

Dahlias, grown from tubers, are valuable for their consistent flowering and are especially useful where colour-scheme continuity is important. Although tall dahlias are stiff, with brittle stalks, few other annuals contribute such height, bulk and floriferousness. (Modern dwarf varieties, on the other hand, seem superfluous, since plenty of other annuals can do their job at the lower level.) All except the graceful airy species *Dahlia merckii* with divided leaves and single pale daisy-flowers need to be planted in blocks that can be easily staked and tied. In return for dead-heading, good rich soil and winter cosseting with a thick mulch to protect them from damage, they flower consistently for many months. A colour enthusiast might well experiment with some of the wide range of flower colours and shapes that exists among the innumerable hybrid strains. Marvels of Peru (*Mirabilis jalapa*) have dahlia-like tubers and may be treated similarly. Fresh blooms of white, yellow or crimson open every afternoon.

Stalwart companions

A handful of good perennials provide long-term under-pinning in border schemes, partnering a series of less enduring plant stars. Leathery-leaved bergenias with creeping rhizomes flower as winter turns to spring. Most are an undistinguished purplish-pink, but *B.* 'Silberlicht' bears white flowers tinged with pink as they age. Mainly evergreen, with the leaves of some forms suffused with purple tones after frost, bergenias give good winter ground cover and may be planted in drifts or even as edging, formally setting off neighbouring flower groups of hellebores, *Brunnera macrophylla*, perennial or biennial honesties and overhead canopies of flowering cherries. Gertrude Jekyll used bergenias in many of her planting schemes. In the Great Plat at Hestercombe, *B. × schmidtii* lines flower beds set in the mown grass where roses, lilies and delphiniums flower later in the season. For early-autumn effects Miss Jekyll allowed *Aster divaricatus* with starry white daisy-flowers on floppy black stems to cascade over bergenias along the edge of a north-facing bed.

Many perennials grown for beautiful flowers contribute foliage interest over a much longer period. The

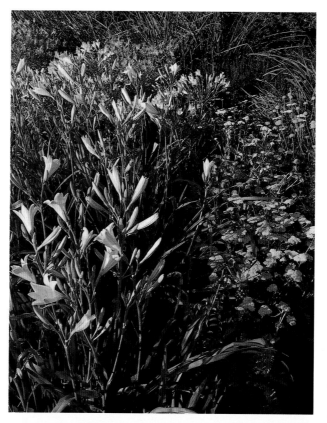

LEFT *In a border at Powis Castle, Peruvian lilies* (Alstroemeria Ligtu Hybrids) *and scented lemon day-lilies* (Hemerocallis lilio-asphodelus) *weave together blending tones of orange, pink and yellow. The grassy foliage of the day-lilies will disguise the fading leaves of the alstroemerias, which begin to look untidy when flowering is over.*

BELOW *In George Radford's garden in Vancouver, large leaves of ligularia make a background foil to the deep red flowers and handsome green foliage of* Paeonia officinalis 'Rubra Plena' *and a more delicate-looking* lactiflora *peony not yet in flower. The fleshy-leaved* Sedum telephium *is in the foreground.*

grass-like leaves of day-lilies make a good foil to neighbouring plants: those of the old favourite *Hemerocallis fulva* 'Flore Pleno' emerge golden-yellow in spring. Such leaf colours look wonderful against sweeps of blue-flowered bulbs or forget-me-nots. Earliest to flower is *H. lilio-asphodelus* (until recently more familiar as *H. flava*) with clear yellow flowers: although each flower lasts only a day, a succession of blooms ensures a long flowering period. Mid- to late-summer species and cultivars produce coarser leaves and lemon-yellow, bronze or orange flowers, which are attractive with neighbouring blues or more startling in 'hot' red and yellow schemes.

Herbaceous peonies flower at the same time as the first roses, to give a border early summer colour and interest, and also look good under the skirts of gracefully arching deciduous shrubs. Both the old-fashioned *Paeonia officinalis*, with its blowzy heads of cottage-garden luxuriance, and the more aristocratic *P. lactiflora* hybrids have valuable foliage that remains decorative – especially if sprayed at intervals against botrytis – through the summer months.

Some of the hardy cranesbill geraniums are more suitable for massing, but the less vigorous associate well with shrub roses and may be planted to make front-of-border drifts in sun and shade. Cutting back after early flowering produces new leafy growth that remains attractive all summer and sometimes colours with the

In a detail of the well-balanced planting scheme in one of the inner compartments of the 'framed' garden near Paris (see pages 152-3), pale Iris 'Rose Queen', hardy Geranium × magnificum (which the camera has made look softer and pinker than it appears to the eye), lime-green Alchemilla mollis and a tall self-seeding Campanula glomerata make a sweep of gentle colour. Choosing plants as suitable companions involves thinking about similar growing needs and good foliage contrasts as well as flowering appearance. Both cranesbill geraniums and alchemillas will produce fresh leaves if cut back as soon as flowering is over.

first frosts. *Geranium renardii* has grey-green leaves and white flowers veined appealingly with streaks of maroon. Revelling in full sun, it contrasts with the more architectural leaves of irises. *G.* × *magnificum* has deeply cut hairy green leaves, which tint red in autumn, and violet-blue flowers. It grows well under the arching branches of the pale yellow *Rosa* 'Frühlingsgold' and around the base of some of the fan-shaped Hybrid Musks such as pale pink *R.* 'Penelope' or subtle apricot-tinged *R.* 'Buff Beauty'. The taller more upright *Geranium psilostemon* also has leaves that colour, but we grow it for its glorious black-centred magenta flowers, which glow next to silvery-leaved artemisias or tower above neighbouring frothy-flowered alchemillas.

Both their light green leaves and their feathery lime-yellow flower-sprays make alchemillas indispensable as low-profile companion plants over a long season. They perform at the same time as pink- or red-flowered heucheras and heucherellas, creating garden pictures when combined with tall glaucous-leaved *Thalictrum flavum glaucum* with fluffy yellow plumes, and groups of blue-flowered delphiniums. Sedums also furnish sunny front-of-border situations with handsome grey-green foliage and have flower-heads composed of a myriad small stars, which are much beloved by butterflies. They look attractive when bronzed by frosts in winter. Above decorative fleshy leaves, the stiff stems of *Sedum* 'Herbstfreude' hold large pink flower-heads which later turn coppery-red.

Essential border perennials

All through a season, borders offer a series of close-up pictures of plant association. They may be based on gentle gradations of colour harmony or more stimulating contrasts, but in order to succeed they are always composed with interesting textures and masses in mind.

A few of the traditional perennials flower early in the season to accompany spring shrubs and bulbs in sun or shade, or flourish beside mounds of delicate young foliage in main borders. Many small, mainly North American woodland plants suitable for naturalizing in peaty soil flower early in the season. Both semi-evergreen *Phlox divaricata* and creeping evergreen *P. stolonifera* flower in spring to grace the front of woodland beds with saucer-shaped blooms on erect stems in association with drifts of trilliums, erythroniums,

uvularias, jeffersonias and, more prosaic, less demanding omphalodes and pulmonarias. Grey-leaved Virginia cowslips like the same conditions for their lavender-blue bells, but forms of *Phlox subulata* and *P. douglasii* are sun-lovers, a substitute for the ubiquitous aubrieta and alyssum to cascade over border edges. Bulbs destined to flower later in the season may thrust through their fading foliage.

Bold clumps of perennial honesty (*Lunaria rediviva*), with hairy leaves and lavender-white flowers will thrive in light shade alongside cream-flowered *Helleborus argutifolius* and evergreen *Euphorbia amygdaloides robbiae* with its green leaf rosettes and pale yellow bracts. We plant clumps of *Lathyrus vernus*, with purple, pink or white pea-flowers, at the back of our main borders; low-growing and flowering in spring, they associate well with fresh young leaves of later-flowering perennials placed farther forward. Mat-forming *Veronica gentianoides* takes a foreground position. Ice-blue flower-spikes rise above glossy basal leaves.

The mat-forming speedwell Veronica gentianoides, *with pale blue flower-spikes above green leaf rosettes, is a very useful plant for the front of the border. It flowers early in summer, so that other plants can be allowed to flop down over its foliage during the rest of the season.*

I grow it grouped to edge a bed in front of yellow-flowered *Paeonia mlokosewitschii* and as a foil to the evergreen bushy spurge *Euphorbia characias wulfenii*. Slightly later flowering, the much brighter Oxford-blue flowers of *Veronica austriaca teucrium* are brilliant when combined with purple-toned leaves and crimson-coloured roses (*Rosa* 'Rosemary Rose' has suitable leaves and flowers) or with shrubs such as the semi-evergreen *Piptanthus nepalensis* with contrasting yellow pea-flowered racemes. *Erysimum* 'Bowles' Mauve' has a drawn-out season, flowering for almost three months after a mild winter. Its pale magenta flowers shine among grey-green leaves; small creeping evergreen spurges such as *Euphorbia myrsinites* and *E. nicaeensis* spill out at its feet.

Portraits of some classic border perennials demonstrate their role as early summer performers. Most Jacob's ladder (forms of *Polemonium*) bear attractive pinnate leaves and flower at the same time as the first roses. The common upright *Polemonium caeruleum* flowers for many weeks, filling in the comparatively flowerless period between German flag irises and traditional summer perennials. At Tintinhull we grow lilac-flowered *P. foliosissimum* as a wide, sprawling clump next to silvery-leaved *Dorycnium hirsutum* (now *Lotus hirsutus*).

Pinnate-leaved galegas are mainstays of borders. Violet-blue pea-flowered *Galega orientalis* is superb but spreads vigorously; it associates well with the yellow of *Thalictrum flavum glaucum* and the scabious-like flower-heads of *Cephalaria gigantea*. The true goat's rue (*Galega officinalis*) flowers at least a month later, producing an ice-cream effect of blue and pink and tying in nicely with tall campanulas and early garden phlox.

Sun-loving alstroemerias are essential border plants, given unobtrusive staking with twigs when the attractive leaves emerge in spring. *Alstroemeria* Ligtu Hybrids have soft-tinted petals, in a range between rosy-pink, bright coral and cool apricot and yellow, which associate with almost any neighbouring flowers. The seed-heads are attractive, but their fading foliage may be an eyesore. Shallow-rooted plants that flower later help disguise unsightly leaves. The hardier orange-flowered *A. aurantiaca* (now *A. aurea*) – a mainstay of Victorian cutting beds and more tolerant of shade – reaches its peak later to coincide with summer perennials.

By midsummer the hardy perennial standbys are in full leaf and many of them are in flower. Achillea, for

example, will be displaying its flat heads composed of tiny daisy-flowers. When combined with its attractive feathery leaves, it makes graceful clumps to associate with other Compositae such as anthemis, or with artemisias and campanulas, or with contrasting foliage of plants such as kniphofias, day-lilies and later-flowering crocosmias. Those achilleas with pale yellow flowers fit into any border scheme; the tall, more vigorous achilleas (such as *Achillea* 'Coronation Gold') carry flat corymbs of glowing yellow that shout for attention; they are best in strong-coloured schemes with neighbouring orange-spiked kniphofias or scarlet lychnis.

If happily sited in full sun and richly fed, astrantias are superb summer neighbours to showy clumps of daisy-flowered anthemis or silver-leaved anaphalis; they are equally effective in a shady corner rising behind the nodding yellow sprays of the low-growing *Chiastophyllum oppositifolium*.

The aromatic artemisias, often with silvery or grey filigree leaves, act as foils to adjacent flower or foliage colour. Some with insignificant flowers form mounds of attractive foliage for flower-bed edges. They need well-drained soil and full sun and are often short-lived; take cuttings each season. Others such as *Artemisia lactiflora*

In early summer Galega orientalis *is dramatic at the end of one of the Tintinhull borders. Somewhat of a 'runner', this goat's rue needs equally vigorous companions or it may overwhelm them in a few seasons. At Tintinhull, to keep planting proportions in balance, it is split up every few years; its contribution to the planting scheme makes this trouble well worthwhile. With completely contrasting habit and foliage effects, silvery-leaved* Artemisia *'Powis Castle' and glossy-leaved* Acanthus mollis latifolius (*not visible in the picture*) *are ideal neighbouring companions.*

have dark green leaves and tall stems bearing tapering cream panicles. Needing a rich moisture-retentive soil, this full-bodied border perennial should be grown in Jekyllian drifts or in bold clumps next to herbaceous plants that need similar conditions, such as yellow-flowered achilleas, cream-plumed aruncus, and later-flowering chelones and purple-leaved lobelias.

Perennial campanulas are essentially companionable sun-lovers with little absolute distinction, yet sturdy clumps with soft blue, palest pink or white bell-flowers blend into border schemes beside plants with stronger foliage or flower impact. Many of the smaller tussocky types are spring or early-summer flowerers, but the taller forms perform from summer onwards. Thread-leaf tickseed (*Coreopsis verticillata*) has bright yellow daisy-flowers; the paler *C. v.* 'Moonbeam' luxuriates in hot summers and flowers into the autumn. Plant in the front of borders, as neighbours to spring-flowering rock roses or summer annuals such as verbenas or ageratums.

Garden phlox are reliable summer and late-summer flowerers. Both *Phlox maculata* forms, with cylindrical clusters of purple, pink or white-flushed pink flowers, and popular *P. paniculata* cultivars (too many to name) make good clumps between other conventional border plants. Although astilbes will thrive in sun (in Europe – not in the hotter states of America), they are perfect shade-lovers for a woodland garden provided the soil is rich and moisture-retentive during the summer months. Plumed flowers in white, pink and red complement the delicate bronze-tinted foliage. They make good companions for drifts of broad-leaved hostas with lily-like scented flowers or for ligularias with green or bronze leaves and vibrant orange daisies. Japanese anemones are also ideal for shady beds or for the back of a border, their pale white or pink-tinted single or double flowers silhouetted against dark hedging late in the season. Their attractive maple-like leaves are an invaluable foil for plants with more insubstantial feathery foliage all through the summer.

At the end of summer the orchid-like flowers of toad lilies attract interest in shady borders; earlier in the season their pleated shining leaves steal the show as they emerge between hellebores and Solomon's seal. The North American Joe Pye weed is imposing. Its garden form *Eupatorium maculatum atropurpureum* is an indispensable late-summer border plant with purple-flushed stems and leaves and wide flat rosy-pink flower-

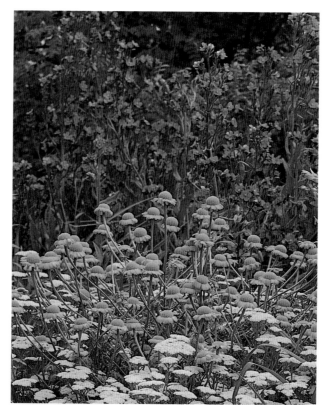

LEFT *In an open bed a clump of a form of blue-flowered* Anchusa azurea *makes a misty backdrop behind the blending yellows of anthemis and achillea. Companion plants must enjoy the same sort of conditions of soil and aspect; all these plants revel in hot sun and need good drainage.*

BELOW *In a garden designed by the Oehme, van Sweden partnership, lavenders and perovskias, both with soft greyish leaves, combine with more strident yellow achilleas to make mounds between tall clumps of swaying grasses. Here the vibrant achilleas, carrying their flat heads on tall stems, brighten the effects with their extreme contrast.*

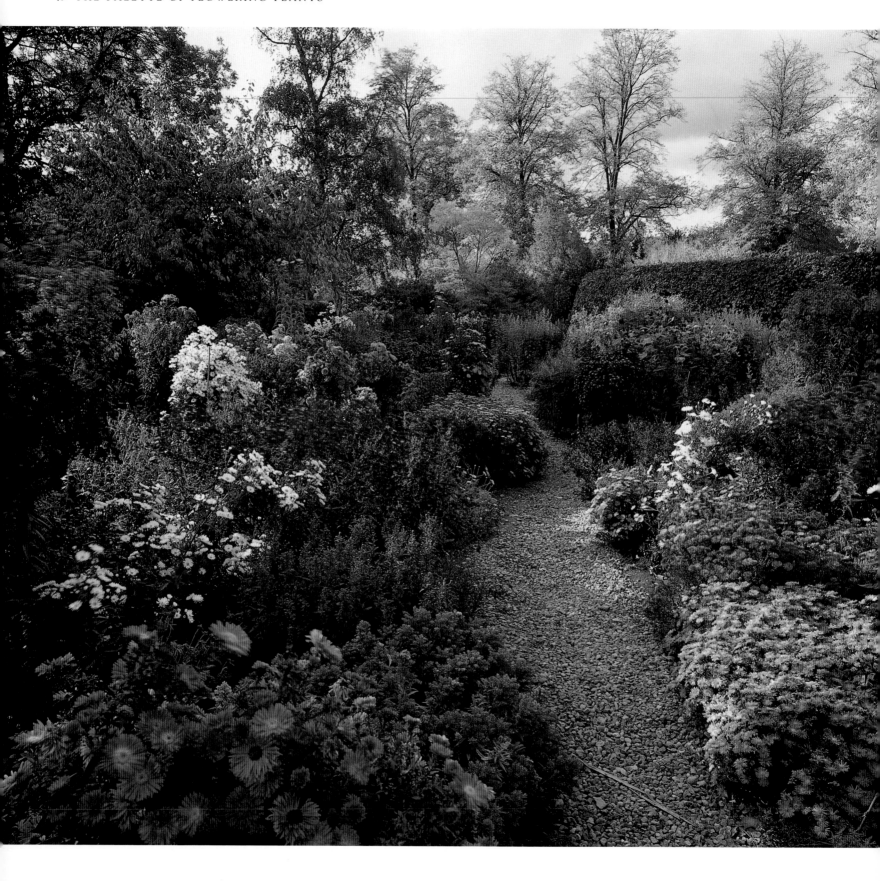

heads; spreading groups are ideal companions to tall spires of blue or white *Veronicastrum virginicum* or turtlehead chelones.

There are many late-flowering asters. These are very desirable and carry the border into winter. *Aster* × *frikartii* seedlings such as A. × *f.* 'Mönch' or A. × *f.* 'Wünder von Stäfa' have delicately rayed blue flowers above grey-green leaves all through late summer and autumn. Other Compositae are included in fine groups of yellow and bronze daisy-flowered helenium, helianthus and heliopsis, all perennials with undistinguished foliage but providing essential colour in the autumn.

Bulbs in companionable drifts

Those tall bulbs whose visible leaves and stems are almost as important as the flowers may look effective growing under tree canopies, around the bases of shrubs and in beds between groups of border plants. Many bulbs come from areas of extreme climates and need growing conditions similar to those in their native habitats. Not all bulbs, therefore, thrive and multiply in drifts in herbaceous and mixed borders.

Nevertheless, many early flowerers – daffodils, tulips, fritillaries, camassias, Byzantine gladiolus, various forms of bulbous and rhizomatous iris, leucojums and alliums (in approximate flowering sequence) – do survive well and contribute drifts of flowers to coincide with spring-flowering shrubs. However, some such as hybrid tulips are best treated as annuals and replanted each year. Tall hybrid daffodils and some of the small narcissus treasures such as *Narcissus cyclamineus* adapt to flower beds. In borders these bulbs need to be sited where perennial foliage may grow up to disguise fading bulb leaves even before flowering time is over. At Tintinhull we grow alliums in the iris bed, Byzantine gladioli to flower through the low-spreading branches of shrubs, *Leucojum aestivum*, which flowers in late spring, as white spears in a densely planted bed of *Rosa gallica officinalis* and stately spring-flowering imperial fritillaries behind summer-flowering perennials.

A tall spire of the regal lily (Lilium regale) soars in front of a bush of flowering Philadelphus 'Belle Etoile'. Most lilies prefer to grow around the base of sheltering shrubs or through some ground-covering plants that give their emergent tips protection from damaging late spring frosts. Deciduous shrubs, with low spreading branches casting only light shade in spring, are particularly suitable neighbours, but low-growing anemones or scillas often provide adequate protection.

At Old Court near Malvern double Michaelmas daisy borders, both beds backed by high hedges, are filled with cultivars of Aster novi-belgii *in a range of white and crimson to dark blue, and mauve A. 'Pink Lace'. Too* *few gardeners use these late flowerers to carry summer into autumn; even fewer can spare space for such a show, reminiscent of Miss Jekyll's wonderful turn-of-the-century daisy borders at Munstead Wood.*

Summer borders may be enhanced by groups of appropriate lilies, *Dierama* species and hardy arum lilies (*Zantedeschia aethiopica*), crocosmias and curtonus (now *Crocosmia paniculata*); as autumn approaches, summer hyacinths (*Galtonia candicans*), crinums and tender *Gladiolus callianthus* precede nerines and amaryllis, which will only thrive in a hot site.

Regal lilies planted in open borders rather than light woodland are susceptible to late frosts, which damage their early shoots and ruin flowering. Provide light but adequate protection by planting them so they grow through branching lithospermums, between biennial honesty plants, behind rhizomatous irises or deep in beds of spreading wood and Italian anemones.

In semi-shade under the canopies of mainly deciduous trees and around the skirts of shrubs, plant bulbs such as erythroniums and trilliums, small corydalis, arisaemas, exotic-looking arums with mottled or 'painted' leaves, and some fritillaries in groups, as they all associate well with other small woodlanders. Other bulbs may spread to naturalize in massed carpets.

MASSING PLANTS

Filoli in California offers supremely clever examples of massed planting (see pages 154-5). Here a breathtaking sea of white arabis provides a soft ground for hyacinths in spring. In the outer frame a blue form of Hyacinthus orientalis *makes a flowery pattern between the clipped box hedging, while a white form makes a more solid impact in the inner rectangle. Formal, geometric layouts look best when planted with precision and groomed so no leaf or flower is out of place.*

Often when intimate plant details are forgotten it is general impressions that remain in the mind to be conjured up for future inspiration. Some of the most memorable garden scenes are composed of massed blocks of flowers or leaves – the simplest kind of planting, dominated by a limited number of varieties rather than a restless combination of dot plants.

A great number of plants are individually beautiful and perform well – perhaps with a long period of summer flowering or with fine foliage that sets off neighbouring flower groups – but they are seldom grown as single specimens. Instead such plants are massed for effect, so they appear as one gently undulating almost horizontal sheet of colour and texture. Mainly low-growing, they are vital ingredients in the pattern-making and bedding-out schemes of formal gardens, such as traditional knot gardens and parterres. In less formal garden areas, massing plants – appropriately chosen to suit soil conditions and aspect – make companion drifts to taller permanently planted perennials and carpet the ground below shrubs, seemingly spreading at will with compositions following the natural contours of the land or the canopies of shade created by overhead trees. On a larger scale appropriate plants may also clothe steep banks where mowing or weeding is difficult – the plants eventually meshing together to form so-called 'ground cover'. In the final analysis a smooth or textured lawn contributing to the layout of the garden and linking areas consists of interwoven grasses, which give a restful and purposeful feeling.

For success with massed planting, whether permanent or temporary, the soil of the whole bed must be well prepared, cleaned and suitably enriched. Permanent plants need conditions approximating to their native habitat: soil that is too rich will encourage lax growth and promote foliage at the expense of flowers. Mediterranean-type plants and those with silver and grey leaves seldom need heavy feeding. On the other hand, the ground for all quick crops should be rich and fertile; annuals growing from seed to flowering in a few months (or even weeks) need every encouragement, especially if they are to flower over long periods. Soil must be regularly forked over and fertilized each time new plants are put in.

Plants for pure colour

The mainstay of jewel-like patterned planting is the improved hybrid, bred for an especially good flower colour, a long-blooming habit or some other such desirable characteristic. The plantsmanly qualities of natural grace and good overall proportion (whose loss is often deplored when flowering potential alone is developed to the highest degree) are not important in situations where plants are to be tightly massed. The gardener chooses 'efficient' plants that quickly blend together to make an impression of dense colour and texture. Seasonal bedding effects call for considerable twice-yearly effort; the plants should need little attention once established in their flowering positions: adequately prepared and enriched soil and regular dead-heading ensure a long flowering performance.

Spring-flowering annuals include velvety-textured pansies and wallflowers with their rich warm colours and airy forget-me-nots. Bulbs such as hybrid tulips are also treated as annuals: they seldom perform well after their first season, and may be lifted after flowering, dried off and used again in successive years in less important sites. Once flowering is over, spring flowerers treated as annuals are removed to make space for the true summer 'bedders', which are set out after the last frost is anticipated. These plants may be used like embroidery silks to create an excitingly wide range of breathtaking colour schemes.

Many summer-flowering annuals are sown *in situ* in spring. Violas germinate and flower in a quick six-week period. Other annuals, insignificant singly but together making pretty patches or sheets of colour, include clarkias, echiums (such as *Echium* 'Blue Bedder'), lavatera, poached-egg flower (*Limnanthes douglasii*) – both decorative and also grown to attract a hover-fly

that feeds on aphids – toadflax, *Malva moschata*, mignonette, Virginia stock (*Malcolmia maritima*) and night-scented stock (*Matthiola bicornis*), blue-flowered nigellas and phacelias. Some of these plants self-seed. The small knotweed *Persicaria capitata* will seed and flower in the front of borders and in rock gardens, while the Kenilworth ivy (*Cymbalaria muralis*) seeds prettily to make a flat cover between bulbs as well as colonizing wall crevices with its scalloped leaves and yellow-eyed blue flowers.

'Improved' hybrids cannot be expected to perpetuate themselves each year in the same bed or border by self-seeding; their seed will not come true. Most hybrid annuals are therefore grown from fresh seed each year and planted out when all danger of frost is over. A greenhouse may be needed to cultivate these tender short-lived plants. Alternatively nurseries and garden centres sell seedlings at the appropriate time, although their range is often limited and only mixed-colour 'bags' may be on offer. If an appealing choice can be found, however, buying annuals is an ideal solution for those with very small gardens. And by happy accident, this style of planting is particularly well suited to the formality of many town plots.

For making stunning carpets of colour or drifts to enhance border schemes in a sunny site, consider any of the following: ageratums with powder-blue flowers, alonsoas, daisy-flowered brachycome, calendulas, gomphrenas, gypsophila with clouds of white

Wonderfully artificial in appearance, sun-loving zinnias are superb when massed in a formal setting. At Filoli the planting is beautifully manicured, each plant always looking in perfect health and bloom and each massed bed having crisply defined outlines. The antithesis of natural-style gardening, Filoli's geometric layout has precise guidelines laid down for planting type and colour. Its success is a matter of choosing just the right cultivar for each area, and it takes a highly developed sense of colour nuances to get the subtle balance required. The garden maintenance alone requires a very high degree of skill.

LEFT *Not all massed planting is of impermanent annuals. Perennials or shrubs, chosen to grow at just the right level, can be equally suitable for achieving an overall cover and will suppress weeds. Here in Mrs Goossenaert's garden in Holland bergenias flower in spring beneath a pink weeping cherry (Prunus pendula 'Pendula Rosea') and are reflected in the pool to give a double image.*

BELOW *In Phoebe Noble's orchard on Vancouver Island the massed planting of the hardy Geranium macrorrhizum in panels beneath fruit trees is wonderfully effective and contrasts well with the mown grass. Once established, this sort of gardening – simple, yet making a positive statement – is not only beautiful, but (apart from mowing) almost labour-free. This is inspirational and deserves to be copied.*

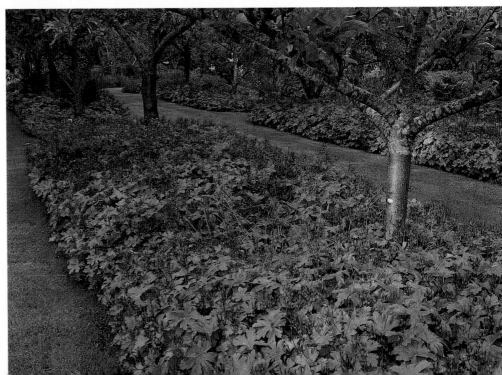

flowers, scarlet linum, lobelias, mesembryanthemums, marvels of Peru, nemesias, pelargoniums (special cultivars are easily grown from F$_1$ seed), petunias, small *Phlox drummondii*, salvias, French and African marigolds, tobacco plants, hibiscus and verbenas. Begonias and impatiens (which grow from seed or cuttings) will even perform well in shade.

Tender plants are also effective substitutes for true annuals. Perpetuated from cuttings (like some of the desirable annual hybrids), they are not so susceptible to late frosts if hardened off appropriately and may be planted out earlier than annuals grown from seed, quickly growing together to cover bare earth. Try soft-stemmed diascias, osteospermums, penstemons and verbenas, with the more woody silver-leaved artemisias, argyranthemums, calceolarias, felicias, helichrysums and salvias. Root them in autumn and overwinter in a frost-free greenhouse.

Permanent carpeting

Permanent planting schemes of low-growing shrubs, perennials or bulbs are labour-saving when compared with seasonal annuals. Some hand-weeding is necessary in the first years but, once established in well-prepared ground, the foliage will mesh together to form a light-excluding carpet that suppresses both annual and perennial weeds. (I prefer not to call this ground cover, which has become associated with rather dreary gardening where beauty and appropriateness are sacrificed to function and low maintenance. Good plants may effectively reduce work without diminishing the quality of performance.)

On a large scale, shrubs such as symphoricarpos, hypericums, pachysandra, viburnums, periwinkles and ivies – grown primarily for foliage effects but often producing worthwhile flowers in season – have wide horizontally spreading branches or suckers to cover the ground. On a more manageable scale, in flower beds and shrubberies, select herbaceous clump-formers such as day-lilies, cranesbill geraniums, tiarellas and tellimas that spread, or ajugas, buglossoides, dicentras, creeping Jennies and lamiums, which have colonizing root systems.

Some sun-lovers have the bonus of good flowers in season as well as beautiful foliage throughout the summer. Substitute these for labour-intensive traditional annuals in quite formal schemes or use as infillers for difficult corners of the flower garden. If the proportions are right these plants are as effective in a small homogeneous group as when massed on the grand scale in dramatic parterres or in woodland scenes. It is not that plants of this type lack individuality: they are often beautiful as single specimens, but are even more effective when massed to grow on a single plane, with flowers and/or leaves all at the same height and

A pair of bronze-leaved smoke bushes stand guard outside the gates to the courtyard at Tintinhull. Both are probably seedlings of one of those with darker purple foliage, such as Cotinus coggygria *'Foliis Purpureis' or* C.c. *'Royal Purple'. Under their skirts the yellow-flowered St John's wort* (Hypericum calycinum) *–* here contained by stonework to stop it spreading – makes an effective foil to its taller neighbours as well as preventing weed growth. In a situation such as this, where immediate effects are important, I prefer simple plant associations rather than a mixture of many kinds of flower and leaf.

At La Garoupe on the French Riviera a wide bed partly shaded by a spine of olive trees is planted with a well-established mass of Chasmanthe aethiopica, a tender bulbous plant with orange-red flowers that is closely related to crocosmia. Massed planting schemes do not have to be formal in intent, although this one follows the line of an avenue. Often using a single plant in quantity rather than a fussy mixture produces the most striking effects. The style of this rather exotic bed can be reproduced in more austere climates using hardy plants such as day-lilies instead of the tender drought-loving chasmanthes.

RIGHT Streamside planting in a garden near the Devon coast is a deliberately informal mix of candelabra primulas and the unusual Portuguese form of St Bruno's lily (Paradisea lusitanica), with grassy leaves and white trumpet-flowers on tall stems. The primulas self-seed in wonderful colour variations and literally cover the soil, forcing out any weeds that germinate. A silver-leaved willow (Salix lanata) also thrives in the moist soil but remains low-growing. To be so effective, this sort of planting must be well maintained; this is not 'wild' gardening, but 'natural' gardening, very much under man's control.

blending into a distant textured carpet – or cushion. Examples of more compact flowering carpeters include ground-hugging acaenas, dwarf campanulas, creeping snow-in-summer curtaining drystone walls and filling in cracks between stonecrops, saxifrages and scented thymes; also Euphorbia cyparissias, Lamium maculatum (with white or pale pink flowers and pretty variegated leaves), Anthemis nobile (used to make chamomile lawns), prostrate veronicas and seeding violas. Glossy-leaved acanthus, alchemillas, the taller euphorbias, cranesbill geraniums (some forms grow well in shade), and grey-leaved California fuchsias (Zauschneria californica) are good on a larger scale.

Some of the plants grown as permanent carpeting are chosen primarily for the colour, shape and texture of their leaves, which are as important through the garden season as any flowers. These plants may be massed in formal patterns or more freely grouped in open borders. Silver- and grey-leaved plants such as shrubby Senecio (now Brachyglottis) 'Sunshine', artemisias, helichrysum and carpeting stachys provide a leafy foil to bright flower colour. Lavenders, rosemaries, santolinas and good foliage forms of Salvia officinalis are all sun-lovers with good-looking and aromatic leaves (and attractive flowers in season). Good foliage perennials for less sunny sites include pig-a-back tolmieas and lamiums with white- and cream-marked leaves (Lamium maculatum 'Beacon Silver' and L.m. 'White Nancy').

Quieter areas of green offer a restful contrast. Ordinary box bushes may be effectively massed together and clipped and trained into flat-topped blocks or undulating waves a metre or even less in height. This makes an interesting alternative to using box as hedging or topiary shapes.

Choose carpeting foliage to suit aspect and soil: only healthy plants successfully cover bare earth in problem areas. Prostrate junipers with green-textured foliage thrive on dry banks, with liriopes and different forms of suckering and invasive mint, including grey-leaved Mentha × rotundifolia 'Bowles' (syn. M. × villosa alopecuroides). In shade, shrubs grown mainly for their leaves include Lonicera pileata, large- and small-leaved ivies, forms of euonymus with green or variegated leaves and acid-loving pachysandras (look for the American Pachysandra procumbens as well as the ubiquitous P. terminalis from Japan). Other shade-tolerant shrubs that also have attractive flowers and/or fruit

are cotoneasters, heathers, hypericums, glossy-leaved sarcococcas (with deliciously scented flowers in winter) and symphoricarpos. All of these are effective spreading through woodland.

Low-growing ajugas with green or coloured leaves and blue spikes, evergreen epimediums, shining-leaved Asarum europaeum, Brunnera macrophylla, sweet woodruff, hellebores, day-lilies, hostas, omphalodes with starry blue flowers, pulmonarias with marbled leaves, forms of comfrey (Symphytum), tiarellas, tellima and yellow-flowered Waldsteinia ternata are all suitable for massing in deep shade. They will grow under shrub branches to cover the soil tightly and make an impenetrable weed-suppressing carpet. Some, such as blue-flowered lithospermums, are determined acid-soil lovers (although the related Buglossoides purpurocaerulea is lime-tolerant); other woodland plants that thrive in shade and moist peaty soil are houttuynias, vancouverias, the even more acid-insistent partridge berry (Mitchella repens), arctostaphylos, maianthemum and gaultheria.

Dog's tooth violets, their attractive spring foliage setting off pink, white or yellow flowers, look their best when colonizing a wood, as at Knightshayes. Pink Erythronium revolutum with brown-tinted foliage frames E. 'White Beauty' (probably a form of E. oregonum), with large cream reflexed flowers and shining marbled leaves. These choice plants prefer an acid soil but are not fussy, and will establish in any shady corner of the garden under the branches of deciduous shrubs such as magnolias, which love the same conditions.

Naturalized drifts

Garden scenes where plants seem to have spread at will evoke something of an idea of paradise. Frank Kingdon Ward thought he had found his own paradise when he first glimpsed the Himalayan blue poppy (*Meconopsis betonicifolia*) in south Tibet in 1926: 'Suddenly I looked up and there, like a blue panel dropped from heaven – a stream of blue poppies dazzling as sapphires in the pale light.' Few of us can grow these Himalayan wonders successfully, but other 'blues' such as buglossoides, Apennine anemones or even the more prosaic forget-me-not make vivid garden carpets. I find inspiration in the sweeps of bluebells in a deciduous wood in spring-time.

Real wild flowers spreading in their native habitat are breathtaking and – appropriately adapted – may inspire garden scenes. Unaided by garden-making techniques, spring rains bring golden eschscholzias and blue-flowered lupins to life to cover Californian hills in broad sweeps of colour. Snakeshead fritillaries are more modest in Oxfordshire meadows. In North American meadows native columbines (*Aquilegia canadensis*) create drifts of nodding red and yellow flowers in late spring. In the British Isles primroses and snowdrops colonize banks to make natural tapestry, also in spring.

Bulbous plants that grow and spread in grass are the ultimate in low maintenance, although the grass-care itself involves a considerable number of man-hours each season. Work out a mowing programme to ensure that grasses do not become too competitive and that bulb leaves are not cut too early. In winter yellow aco-nites carpet a lawn under deciduous trees. Crocus, chionodoxas, muscari, narcissi, scillas and snakeshead fritillaries will all grow happily in mown grass or in a rough orchard. Colchicums, cyclamen and autumn-flowering crocus appear at the end of summer.

Other small bulbs spread to make flowering carpets in beds. Some, such as cyclamen, corydalis, erythro-niums and trilliums also produce decorative foliage. Spring-flowering anemones have a brilliant but fleeting period of flower. Alliums, species tulips and leucojums will all naturalize in beds and give the garden an appearance of age and happy maturity.

I love the idea of massing blue- or cream-flowered camassias to create scenes reminiscent of those glimpsed in their native north-west America. In hot climates blue agapanthus become weeds, seeding and spreading to make panels of colour even under trees.

PLANTS TO USE AS BACKDROPS

Background curtains of climbing plants and wall-trained shrubs provide an extra dimension of beauty behind any planting scheme. Climbers, such as roses and clematis, rising high above a border on walls or trellis, and tall shrubs, in free or pruned shapes, may extend planting and colour themes with their foliage and flowers. Other shrubs or small trees, making a continuous line like a hedge or grouped informally as single architectural keynotes, may provide background interest behind a more free-standing border. Many hedges are grown to provide a mass of mainly one foliage colour to link a whole scheme together, but there are plenty of suitable hedging plants that also contribute flowers.

All these backdrop plants combine with other planting to give individual group effects to complement the planting in front. Vertical plants carry the eye upwards and are especially valuable in small gardens: by introducing a third dimension they make the most use of available space.

The cast of flowering climbers

Some climbing plants are vigorous self-supporters and once established do not need tying in to a frame. Parthenocissus species have adhesive pads that fix the tendrils to any surface. Like ivy, climbing hydrangeas have clinging aerial roots: *Hydrangea anomala petiolaris* is the most common species, and the subtle unshowy beauty of its greenish-white corymbs and fresh green leaves makes a fine background to hellebores, shade-tolerant *Euphorbia amygdaloides robbiae*, pleated hosta leaves and ferns. Schizophragma (*Schizophragma hydrangeoides* and *S. integrifolium*) and the related *Pileostegia viburnoides* also have attractive lace-cap flowers and like shade. The tender evergreen *Trachelospermum jasminoides* with its very fragrant creamy flowers is sun-loving and self-clinging on a warm wall.

The best flowering climbers generally need some supports. Vines have curling tendrils, clematis curling petioles which, with a little guidance, thread themselves through any proffered framework, including the branches of other plants. Climbing roses possess recurved thorns, which hook themselves over wires or branches. Scandent plants such as wisteria and honeysuckle use their stems for twining around supports to produce their flowers in the light.

Wisterias are perhaps the noblest climbers of all, suitable for growing on high sunny walls and pergolas and, in warmer climates, up into tall trees. Their long scented pea-flowered racemes in different tints of violet and mauve or white clothe a flat surface with a scented curtain in late spring. They may also be trained as small standard trees, look elegant when planted as an alley and make focal points in a flower bed in which the drooping flower-heads reach almost to the ground.

Honeysuckles' twining stems decorate trelliswork, pergolas and fences with colourful – and often scented – flowers: different forms flower from spring through summer. Seldom very strong-growing, they are useful in small corners as neighbours to tall perimeter shrubs, and some are shade-tolerant. Delicate summer jasmines also scent the air with fragrance. Blue potato-flowered *Solanum crispum* 'Glasnevin' and the more tender *S. jasminoides* forms may be wall-trained and will scramble over fences or unsightly sheds.

Framing a doorway set in golden Ham stone at The Gables, Mrs Gwen Beaumont's garden in Somerset, the shapely leaves and lacy flower-heads of a climbing hydrangea (Hydrangea anomala petiolaris) make a charming picture with nearby plants. By giving height, climbers add an extra dimension to horizontal planting schemes. Almost every garden needs some sort of frame; this can be achieved by relying on the natural shapes of trees or by letting flowers and leaves weave a background curtain over artificial structures.

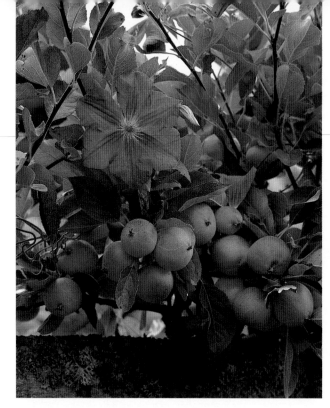

Annual sweet peas (*Lathyrus odoratus*) look wonderful when, like clematis, they are grown on vertical tripods as features in flower beds, in the utilitarian herb garden or even among rows of kitchen vegetables. Plant them four to a tripod in single colours, or allow mixed blues, pinks, mauves and whites to blend in the eye. If regularly picked for the house or dead-headed, sweet peas flower fragrantly for many months.

Clematis and roses

For short periods of flowering some permanent climbers become key features because of the sheer impact of their curtains or garlands of blossom. The most luxuriant flowering climbers will form abstract shapes to carry the planting design upwards – twining through openwork trellis, draping themselves over pergolas or fencing, cascading over roofs, covering the face of stone or brick (perhaps given some framework to help them) or even throwing themselves with romantic abandon high into trees. Less vigorous 'climbers' may fall over balustrading or low walls and sprawl to cover sloping banks. Some climbing plants, however, are best suited when formally trained on supports or walls, where they bring a measured presence to the garden.

Clematis and roses predominate in this category. Different clematis give pleasure for most months of the year – some with a particularly attractive veil of foliage, all with charming flowers (which often become silky

In the best cottage-type gardens orchard trees, vegetables and sweetly scented flowers all grow together within the garden frame. At Chilcombe sweet peas, clambering into twigs in traditional fashion, give height above neat rows of carrots and beetroot. Behind them climbing roses invade old fruit trees to add a touch of wildness.

Fruit trees play host to other climbers as well as roses (LEFT). Clematis 'Perle d'Azur', one of the best late-flowering clematis, entwines the branches of an apple and flowers as fruit develops in late summer.

seed-heads). Many will curtain walls, twine over trelliswork and up tripods, or clamber through neighbouring plants to make glorious displays with small delicate or wide saucer-shaped blooms providing massed colour. Ferny-leaved evergreen *Clematis cirrhosa* curtains a sheltered wall with creamy flowers in earliest spring. *C. armandii*, another evergreen, carries handsome leaves of leathery texture. Like all clematis, it likes its roots in shade but reaches up to flower in more open positions: a perfect solution is to plant it on the sunless side of a wall and allow it to spill over the summit to drape its fragrant blossom on the sunny elevation as a backdrop to sun-loving euphorbias and erysimums, spring-flowering coronillas and mauve- or white-flowered abutilons and the emerging foliage of sturdy perennials.

The *montana* clematis are vigorous and healthy, requiring minimal attention and capable of clothing a large expanse of wall or adorning substantial trees with creamy-, soft or rose-pink flowers. *Alpina* clematis are scramblers, hanging over low walls or balustrades and clambering into the lower stems of climbing roses. Forms of *C. viticella* curtain walls or grow up into small trees; their profusion of small dark purplish-blue flowers looks lovely behind groups of pink phlox or white cimicifugas. At Tintinhull I have allowed them to cascade over metal umbrellas between similarly toned purple-foliaged and contrasting golden-leaved shrubs. *C. flammula*, beloved by Gertrude Jekyll and used to garland all her pergola schemes, bears scented white flowers. Besides the charming clematis species, as summer proceeds a wide range of larger-flowered hybrids come into bloom above the level of most perennials. They are especially useful for growing on frames to give height to a border, to play their part in colour schemes or to create patterns of their own against leafy or man-made surfaces.

Clematis are perfect companion climbers for roses: they will twine up through rose foliage to contribute their flowers at quite another season or be spectacular flowering in unison. Both genera have such a wide range of colours and flower forms that their effects in combination seem unlimited, from almost chintzy floriferousness to delicate embroidered textures.

The choice of backdrop roses is not simply a matter of selecting a colour that works with adjacent planting but also one of mood and style. The more 'perfect' individual rose-buds or 'overblown' open flowers on a

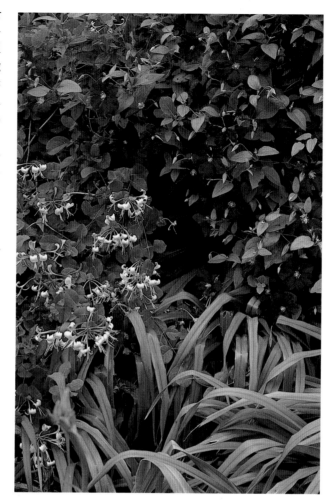

Clematis 'Etoile Violette', with subtle dark violet flowers, performs at the same time as the fragrant climber Lonicera × italica (formerly known as L. × americana), between them totally covering the wall behind and above the leaves of day-lilies. The muted contrast of these complementary colours makes a rich backdrop. Many climbers, accustomed in their native habitats to clambering upwards through natural vegetation, like to grow with their roots in shade and then to flower in the open sun. Here the good effects reflect the fact that the site is naturally satisfactory for all the plants concerned.

larger scale deserve to be admired in close-up. On a pergola or archway, clematis and other twining companions can be allowed to clamber up from below to clothe the roses' bare stems. For a 'curtain' of roses to back a bed or border, clusters of little flower-heads set amid fresh green glossy or rich-looking foliage make a foil to flower colours in the foreground. Paler colours help create a diffused effect, but specific yellows, crimsons or deep reds contribute to a more carefully orchestrated overall colour scheme.

Ramblers are best growing over an open framework; climbing roses are for walls. Ramblers are pruned after flowering to promote flower-bud formation on new shoots that will appear in the succeeding spring; when skilfully executed, this pruning and training gives plants a strong aesthetic impact. A well-pruned climbing rose has its branches stretched in horizontal lines away from a main central stem; the young shoots growing from these laterals produce the most flowers.

For many people Ninfa, the romantic garden in the ruined thirteenth-century village south of Rome, must represent a personal vision of paradise – a Garden of Eden in which man remains a spectator. Roses and other climbers (their identity often a mystery, since extant lists of old nursery orders are imprecise) have been planted to clamber over old walls and into the trees to make floriferous backdrops on a grand, wild scale. The effects of colour, scent and beauty are magical.

OPPOSITE In the walled garden at Mottisfont Abbey a great profusion of old roses fills beds and festoons walls. Backdrop roses are pink 'Blush Rambler' on the rear wall and, to the right, the vigorous Moss rose 'William Lobb', with dark crimson flowers. In the bed (at front left) is a solitary pale bloom of 'Mousseline'; beside it is 'Salet', with few flowers; behind is the taller flower-covered 'Belle Amour', of Alba descent. In the centre deep red Rugosa 'Mrs Anthony Waterer' is visible behind 'Mme Pierre Oger' and 'Bourbon Queen'. On the right is the Gallica rose 'Spong'. Underplanted alpine pinks and self-seeded white foxgloves add to the effect.

Many species and species-type roses, however, such as the early-flowering Banksian rose and *Rosa* 'Mermaid' (of Banksian origins), only need their young shoots tied in after flowering. A favourite climbing rose is 'Gloire de Dijon', which has large buff-apricot to pale orange flowers; these, repeated through the summer, open flat to reveal muddled or quartered centres. A warm wall site permits the monthly rose *R.* × *odorata* 'Pallida' (syn. 'Old Blush China') a succession of charming plant associations. At Tintinhull we intertwine *alpina* clematis, with the semi-double pink flowers of the rose, in a narrow border; sun-loving pink nerines and amaryllis thrive below; Algerian iris with its gentle violet flower-sheaths carried through warmer spells in winter is another perfect companion.

The main flowering flush of some of the stronger-growing climbing roses may be a major part of a distinctive colour plan: deep yellow roses, such as 'Golden Showers', with Hybrid Tea-type flower clusters, complement blue and yellow border schemes. Crimson roses (one of the best is 'Crimson Conquest') blend with a foreground planting of purplish-toned leaves and blue flowers. Deep reds and scarlets of those such as 'Guinée' and 'Danse du Feu' may have a special place in richer, warmer colour schemes. The glowing bright blues of ceanothus are softened by pink climbers: in spring double pink 'Madame Grégoire Staechelin' will accompany *Ceanothus* 'Cascade', while 'Old Blush China' may be teamed with a ceanothus flowering in any summer month.

Some of the more rambling types of roses, both species and cultivars, flower early. Forms of tender scented *Rosa banksiae* and the Cherokee rose (*R. laevigata*), with wide creamy-white fragrant petals, make cascading curtains against a hot wall (with some support) or – in favoured regions such as the American South – grow wild and free into tall trees. Others flower just after the bedding roses and more conventional climbers have completed their first round. With clustered heads of small white yellow-centred flowers, *R.* 'Bobbie James', *R. mulliganii* and *R. filipes* 'Kiftsgate' all look effective grown on tall trellises or allowed to climb into trees, their flowering branches plunging downwards. The vigorous *R.* 'Paulii' has a natural trailing habit and will curtain dull walls and banks with impenetrable prickly stems and a single flush of clove-scented white flowers. (A pink form is less thug-like.)

Other ramblers have a modest demeanour, more

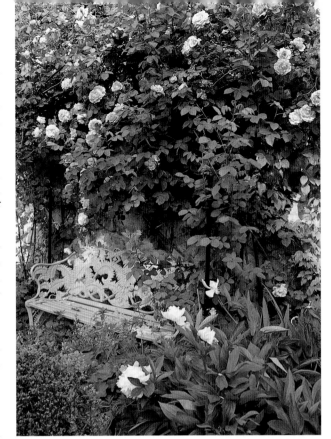

LEFT *The vigorous pink rose 'Constance Spry' and a dark-flowered* viticella *clematis clamber to make a frame behind a cast-iron seat that is almost engulfed by peonies and alchemilla in a garden in southern Holland. Providing height behind borders and beds, plant pictures of this sort give a garden an architectural lift, besides extending the colour range on to a vertical plane.*

suited to the domesticity of pergolas and wall trellises. R. 'New Dawn' is a brilliantly successful pale pink rose with both rambling and climbing remontant habit; its drifts of sweet-scented flowers throughout summer and early autumn provide a perfect gently tinted background in main borders. At Tintinhull it partners philadelphus as well as autumn hydrangeas.

Companion climbers

Less vigorous perennial climbers that die down in winter and some climbing annuals – as well as small-flowered clematis – can be encouraged to twine in and out of shrubs and hedging plants rather than making separate displays.

Flowering through the leaves of hosts. soft-stemmed climbers become key plants that add subtle touches of colour and play a vital part in the whole planting strategy. Red-, orange- and yellow-flowered eccremocarpus and scarlet *Tropaeolum speciosum*, their roots in shade, clamber through yew hedges; canary creeper (*T. peregrinum*) drapes itself over neighbouring bushes at the back of a sunny border and is usually grown as an annual. Passion flowers (*Passiflora*), with exotic blooms, and cup-and-saucer vine (*Cobaea scandens*), with Canterbury-bell-like green flowers set in a saucer-like frill, may be enlisted to reinforce roses and other climbers or to twine through free-standing shrub roses to increase colour impact behind ordinary flower beds, as may annual ipomoeas and the perennial pea (*Lathyrus latifolius*) with pink or glowing white flowers.

Shrubs and climbers performing in the same season are paired for special effects, creating colour incidents of their own with intermingling flowers.

Background foliage climbers

Many of the flowering climbers have tinted as well as more ordinary sombre green leaves, while other climbers are grown specifically for foliage colours that enhance foreground schemes. Some foliage almost upstages planting on the lower plane. Think of an early summer scene where *Actinidia kolomikta* – with tri-coloured leaves splashed with green, pink and white – covers a sunny wall, partnered by a simple border of pink-flowered *Saxifraga moschata* at its feet. In less favoured sites, wall foliage may lift quite low-key plant groups into the realms of garden pictures. The self-clinging deciduous *Parthenocissus henryana* has leaves with white and pinkish markings, which keep their

On the summerhouse at Tintinhull the claret vine has purple-flushed young leaves which mature to a darker purple. By late summer it is entwined with the velvety Clematis × jackmanii of similar colour tone and the brighter orange-flowered Eccremocarpus scaber, *which – although an annual climber – usually self-seeds in profusion. This curtain of leaf and flower makes a background frame to plants arranged annually in ornamental containers. Tall* Lobelia tupa *and silvery* filigree leaves *of* Artemisia arborescens *tower in pots above the trailing South African daisy* Osteospermum ecklonis *and* Sphaeralcea munroana *with pink mallow-flowers.*

glowing colour even in the deepest shade – a quality shared by *Humulus lupulus aureus*, the twining hardy perennial hop with leaves of palest gold. Both provide stunning backdrops of colour in a small basement garden where there is little sunlight; green-leaved lacy ferns and hostas with glaucous-veined leaves are set off by such eye-catching foliage curtains. The evergreen Japanese honeysuckle (*Lonicera japonica* 'Aureoreticulata') – with its golden-variegated leaves turning to golden-bronze in late summer – is another shade-lover that will curtain a dark corner to make an admirable background screen for specific colour effects.

Among shade-tolerant evergreens there are several variegated versions of the larger-leaved ivies: each leaf of *Hedera canariensis* 'Gloire de Marengo' is bordered with grey-green and cream; a Persian ivy (*H. colchica* 'Sulphur Heart', syn. *H.c.* 'Paddy's Pride') has green leaves with a central splash of yellow. Smaller-leaved cultivars of *H. helix* produce a wide range of green foliage shapes and some pretty variegations in gold, cream and silver. At Blickling Hall in Norfolk, ivies are trained inside recessed arches to form a firmly defined colour pattern, an idea worth imitating in more modest surroundings.

Handsome foliage transforms vines into classic curtaining plants. The claret vine (*Vitis vinifera* 'Purpurea') has purple-flushed spring leaves, which mature to dark purple, and those of *V.* 'Brant' are intriguing tones of bronzy-red; both look good behind heliotrope or blue-flowered salvias. Many vines are grown specifically for superb autumnal effects. *V. coignetiae* may drape a wall behind a border in crimson and scarlet in late summer, when grasses and other perennials are assuming bronze and buff leaf tones, or may fling itself up into a tall tree to make a vibrant curtain. Boston ivy and Virginia creeper (forms of *Parthenocissus*) give equally impressive displays. *Ampelopsis brevipedunculata* bears porcelain-blue berries after a hot summer, as spectacular in its way as any floral screen.

More tender climbers such as evergreen *Stauntonia hexaphylla* with violet-tinged white heavily scented flowers in spring deserve a warm corner in full sun. The related *Holboellia coriacea* is very similar. If sharply cut by hard frosts, both often shoot to flower another year. At Tintinhull we grow only the deciduous form of *Schisandra grandiflora*; a twining shrub-like climber, it has pale or dark pink flowers in spring and scarlet berries later if male and female plants are present.

A framework of fruit trees

Fruit trees in espalier, cordon, fan or other formally shaped patterns are architectural in appearance. Planted at regular intervals along a wall or trained along wires as free-standing hedges, their strong outlines become focal points or regular linear features behind beds and borders. They look beautiful all year: in winter bare branches have a clear-cut silhouette; in spring blossom decorates their tiered or slanting boughs, and in late summer the ripening fruit adds a functional air to ornamental planting. Severe annual pruning not only improves appearance but ensures adequate flowering and fruiting, while warm wall sites helpfully protect vulnerable blossom from late frosts and allow wood to ripen.

At Tintinhull espalier pears back pink roses and blue caryopteris. Traditional in old walled gardens, these trained trees are equally valuable in modern small gardens, creating attractive framing divisions without taking up too much space – and at the same time producing fruit crops. Fortunate gardeners find ancient espaliered apples or pears already *in situ* to provide some of the most beautiful and romantic backing to any planting. Happily it is possible to obtain immediate effects in new garden layouts by planting well-grown specimens that have already been trained to two or three branched layers.

At Holkham Hall in Norfolk a fan-trained apple tree espaliered against a high wall plays an architectural role throughout the year and, expertly pruned, serves a functional role as well. In winter the bare branches trace an outline, while in spring and summer blossom and leaf growth are attractive – and the ripening apples are also decorative. Flower gardens, especially borders of perennials which can lack shape and rhythm, benefit from having some more formal focus such as a trained tree as backing. As well as being ornamental and useful, espaliered fruit trees give a garden an atmosphere of maturity.

Trained on walls

Many trees and shrubs will grow sturdier, flower better or develop richer autumn leaf colouring if tied back against a wall and trained into formal shapes. Such plants play an important design role, contributing valuable height to garden compositions. Individual specimens become feature plants at the back of a free-flowing planting scheme; repeated at regular intervals, wall-trained shrubs framed by low-growing plants set up a rhythmic pattern, their clipped formality giving an air of coherence to the overall plan.

In America gardeners are more adventurous than in Europe and extend the range of shrubs trained architecturally beyond the mundane pyracantha. At the Morton Arboretum in Illinois, elegant ginkgos are shaped and tied against a high wall; near Philadelphia grey-leaved Atlas cedars are trained against a house, and elsewhere viburnums, hydrangeas and even *Euonymus alatus*, with scarlet leaves in autumn, have their branches thinned to make rigid flat patterns against a vertical surface, saving space and providing eye-catching features.

When grown against a sheltering wall both ever-green and deciduous shrubs acquire more static shapes than when they are free-standing specimens. Benefiting from the extra protection, abutilons and bay trees develop into regular pyramids; smoke bushes, evergreen *Magnolia grandiflora*, choisyas and osmanthus assume more rounded shapes to resemble wall buttresses and are sometimes clipped to make formal cylindrical or dome-like blocks. I recommend *Itea ilicifolia* with holly-like glossy leaves and greenish-yellow catkin-flowers as a handsome wall shrub for late summer.

Plants from warmer countries also benefit and flower better when given a sheltered wall to grow against. Both pineapple-scented Moroccan broom and the pea-flowered *Piptanthus nepalensis* – semi-evergreen in warm climates but usually deciduous in colder regions – gain from being trained on walls as if they were climbers. Many escallonias are very hardy but *Escallonia* 'Iveyi' with large panicles of white flowers benefits from wall shelter in all but the warmest regions. *Carpenteria californica*, too, performs best when given a sunny wall on which its wood ripens to encourage white flowers the following season. *Fremontodendron californicum* and ceanothus from the west coast of North America make flowering curtains of blossom. The strong hot yellow flower-saucers of the former are effective planted beside solanums with complementary blue flowers or with a foreground planting of silvery foliage with cooling white flowers. Blue-flowered ceanothus in spring is lovely behind spurges with their blue-green leaves and lime-yellow bracts.

Free-standing trees and shrubs

Small trees, large shrubs and shrub roses may be grown as specimens or in assorted groups to provide a free-standing frame to run behind a flower bed. There they make an informal screen, rather than a hedge-like continuous line, and in their own season, covered in flower, they add colour high above eye-level behind foreground planting.

Those that flower in winter or spring become important features where the perennials emerge only in late spring. Evergreen *Viburnum tinus* has white flowers opening from pink buds throughout much of winter and in spring; in summer its attractive green foliage creates a dark background to vibrant flower colours and later in the season it displays metallic-blue fruit clusters. Other tall shrubs flower in early spring on leafless branches. Broad-headed crab apples, thorns and

Many of the shrubby evergreens from California are quite tender if grown in exposed situations, but will perform reliably if given a favourable microclimate. In colder regions most benefit from being grown on a warm sunny wall; bricks give extra heat and ripen the wood in one season to produce flowers in the following summer. Carpenteria californica, first flowered by Gertrude Jekyll at Godalming in 1885, has wide white flowers with central yellow anthers giving the surrounding petals an extra glow. Tied back against a wall it needs a minimum of pruning and makes a fine backdrop to border plants.

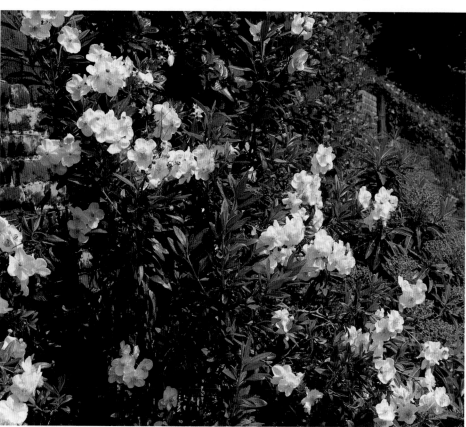

prunus are covered in blossom in spring or early summer and many have decorative fruits and tinted foliage in autumn; their shade provides flower-bed space for hellebores in late winter, woodland-type lilies in summer and autumn-flowering toad lilies. Small hardy cyclamen may carpet the ground under their branches.

In smaller groupings, early-flowering brooms, particularly forms of *Cytisus* × *praecox*, give a fine display in spring borders behind drifts of tulips or blue-flowered camassias. Deciduous magnolias, covered with lily- or star-shaped white or pink flowers on leafless branches, are magnificent in spring and early summer, each one making a backdrop for less magnificent shrubs and providing a summer canopy for shade-lovers. Elsewhere flowering viburnums, spiraeas and deutzias are followed by kolkwitzias wreathed with arching pink blossom. Rounded smoke bushes with green or claret-hued leaves and plume-like airy summer inflorescences frame groups of hardy perennials.

Shrub roses with a natural habit may soar and arch behind smaller shrubs and perennials. Early summer flowerers include *Rosa moyesii* with its rich red flowers followed by flagon-shaped fruits. *R.* 'Complicata'

carries single pink flowers and will scramble into shrubs such as silvery-leaved sea buckthorn (*Hippophaë rhamnoides*). *Rosa soulieana* has waving branches clothed in grey-green leaves and bears creamy-yellow to white small single flowers. Try beautiful *R. nutkana* 'Plena' (formerly known as *R. californica* 'Plena') with its fine foliage, brown prickly stems and gentle pink semi-double flowers. If space is not limited, grow summer-flowering *R.* 'Cerise Bouquet'. Its brilliant cerise-crimson petals are slightly double and 'muddled', borne between almost glaucous dense grey-green foliage on thrusting horizontal stems. This rose is a perfect companion to summer-flowering *Spiraea veitchii*, with its dense white corymbs held on slightly pendulous branches.

Some of the larger-growing cotoneasters are suitable for the back of borders and, in season, are very floriferous, as well as having beautiful late-summer fruits. *Cotoneaster* 'Cornubia' flowers in early summer and has scarlet berries. *C. lacteus* bears milky-white flowers and red fruit while *C.* 'Rothschildianus', a more spreading shrub, has creamy-yellow berries.

The hardiest of the escallonias is the tall *Escallonia rubra macrantha*. Also suitable for hedging, this shrub

In the kitchen garden at Tintinhull flowers surround the vegetables still grown in traditional rows. The layout is given height by occasional pillars of climbers and by some purely ornamental plants such as shrub roses. The pink Rosa 'Wolley-Dod' *(syn.* R. villosa 'Duplex') *with grey leaves is visible lining the perimeter of the garden, while in the foreground* R. 'Geranium', *a hybrid of* R. moyesii, *branches out over white Jacob's ladder* (Polemonium caeruleum album) *and a silvery* Chiliotrichum diffusum *from South America.*

carries rose-crimson flowers and aromatic leaves. It will thrive in sun or shade and is tolerant of all soil types and of salt winds. *E.* 'Donard Brilliance' is a spectacular back-of-border plant, its arching stems wreathed in rose-red flowers in summer. Taller forms of mock orange (*Philadelphus*) may also be grouped at the back of a border; although generally with undistinguished leaves and shape, their highly scented creamy flowers from different species and cultivars contribute for many summer weeks and fit into all colour schemes.

A small tree such as late-flowering *Clerodendrum trichotomum fargesii*, with its fragrant white flowers enclosed in striking maroon calyces, provides a light shady canopy for lily-flowered, elegant-leaved hostas and woodland-type asters. Small-flowered clematis will clamber up through its branches.

Flowering hedges

Hedges may enhance foreground planting, their flower colours being chosen to blend or contrast with schemes and their presence continuing the character of the

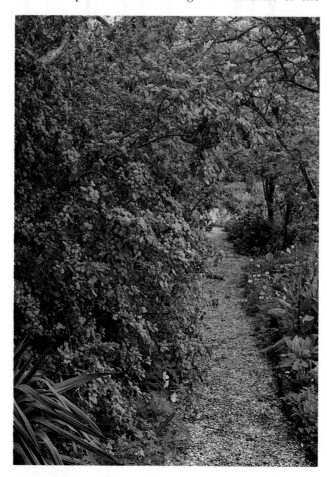

The evergreen shrub Azara serrata *from Chile has distinctive oval toothed leaves and in spring carries clusters of yellow flowers – unfortunately not scented like those of its relative* A. microphylla. *It is nevertheless a handsome plant and gives height edging a path in Somerset.*

surrounding planting on to another level. Such hedges serve the usual purposes of defining spaces and acting as barricades, but do so with perhaps less anonymity than the traditional yew, beech and box grown to provide a uniform background. Since flowering hedges are usually more informal, they can also be less work to maintain, with plants allowed to arch and curve naturalistically rather than being tailored to rigid outlines: flowering shoots, developing from young growth, may be clipped back only after flowering is over (or even later if decorative fruits are also anticipated).

Tall plants providing a background for mixed or perennial borders include berberis with drooping yellow flowers (*Berberis darwinii* has brilliant turquoise berries in midsummer), cotoneasters and evergreen escallonias with sweet-smelling nectar-filled white or pink blooms, and shade-tolerant pyracanthas with white lacy flowers. Lower-growing shrubs may frame beds of rock roses or alpines: hypericums with yellow saucers in summer and autumn, floriferous and long-flowering potentillas, tender hebes suitable for wind-swept sea-coast gardens and, on an even smaller scale, lavenders and rosemary all provide a peak period of flowering as well as leafy-textured hedging.

Rugosa roses with magenta, mauve, pink or white flowers and fresh green crinkly leaves make wonderful informal hedges, either for the outer perimeter or for internal garden divisions. In a wild landscape they make perfect perimeter hedges, blending the domestic garden with the countryside. Their prickly stems effectively deter intruders. Double-flowerers (such as 'Blanche Double de Coubert' and 'Roseraie de l'Haÿ', which both make dense head-high bushes) are more spectacular in flower, but single forms produce most fruit: the single pink 'Fru Dagmar Hastrup' is lower-growing and bushy but delicate in stature, and bears large tomato-like hips.

Hybrid Musks fan from the base to make a free-standing hedge or may be trained on railings or wire. If dead-headed, all flower again. Both apricot-pink 'Penelope' and warm cream-bronze 'Buff Beauty' flower to make backdrops behind the pale-tinted border perennials. Many other roses are also effective as hedges: a low hedge of Rosa Mundi (*R. gallica* 'Versicolor') becomes a sheet of elegant crimson- and white-striped flowers once in a season; the grey-leaved Alba roses with very pale tinted blossoms are less startling, and the foliage stays healthy and glowing all summer.

THE COLOUR QUESTION

Colour is one of the principal contributors to a flower's status as a key, companion, massed or backdrop plant; hence colour's potential role in a garden composition. The first chapter dealt with some more technical aspects of the chemistry of pigments. Here we consider briefly how flower colours are seen and defined before looking at them in context – where they become one small, often almost unidentifiable, factor in the build-up of a complete garden picture.

Colour qualities in flowers

The colours of certain flowers are simple to describe: it is technically feasible to isolate a petal, match it to a colour chart and come up with a name or number that defines a particular clematis or felicia, for example. Some of the massed annuals that combine in a single pool of flower-bed colour may similarly fit into such straightforward colour categorization. Other flower-heads or petals clearly contain a gradation of tones, or even two or more distinct hues, but these resolve when eyes are half-closed or colours are viewed from a distance, so that a resulting predominant 'colour' may be discerned. This is also the case in very intricate flower forms modelled by a great deal of light and shade as well as involving different pigments (think of a full-blown rose, or a wisteria panicle). To handle colours successfully, it is invaluable to be able to 'read' subtleties of tone and to gauge whether the overall effect of a rose, for instance, is a cold, bluish, icing-sugar pink or a warmer-toned more apricot-pink.

Although this sort of impressionistic quality is all-important in gardening, it is only the starting point. The intrinsic colour of a flower is constantly being modified by the changing quality of daylight itself. In fierce sun, bright hues – even the most vivid oranges and scarlets – look faded and slightly yellowed; in temperate countries the fine grey water-laden mist through which everything is seen makes pastel tints appear clearly, while the brightest pure hues seem garish and glaring. At evening it is the pale colours and white flowers that glow as dusk falls, whereas reds and blues fade rapidly into the darkness, even though in early evening light, when the sun's rays are red, the bright 'hot' colours are deepened and mellowed.

Moreover, flowers have to be considered not as isolated colour spots but against their background

foliage, which in all sorts of subtle ways influences their impact – as do other flower and leaf colours in the vicinity. Here gardeners may learn much from the vision and theory of painters, not only about composition, but also about colour harmonies (seen in the close relationship between colours that share some of the same pigment) and contrasts (in colours that are totally dissimilar to one another).

When summarizing some of the more predictable colour phenomena, it is useful to resort to a shorthand. We talk of (say) blue flowers, although we know that 'blue' encompasses a wide variety of tones and shades (think of a typical delphinium spike), and that all sorts of external factors will influence our perception of that blueness. Four distinct areas on the flower palette – white, blue, yellow and red – have a discernible set of effects in garden planting and each is worth looking at briefly.

In Christopher Lloyd's garden at Great Dixter the spring foliage of purple cotinus emerges to make a background foil to orange-toned tulips and biennial forget-me-nots. Bright orange hues are advancing, eye-catching colours, while the deep-toned purples are more sombre and retiring. The blue of the forget-me-nots makes a restful link with blue pigment in the cotinus leaf.

Pure and tinted whites

An unrelieved laundry-white invariably draws the eye and may attract undue attention. The annual *Lavatera trimestris* 'Mont Blanc', *Rosa* 'Frau Karl Druschki', white Japanese anemones and groups of white phlox are all flowers of this perfect whiteness, but fortunately these flowers are seldom seen in isolation; they are almost always accompanied by leaves and other floral or foliage colour, which tends to shadow and soften their extreme whiteness.

In fact, few white flowers are pure white. More often they are faintly tinged with lavender, cream, pale blue or green, or – when set among leaves of strong green – seem suffused with a pinkish tint. The whiteness of others is modified by their shape and texture. Whites such as those of *Rosa* 'Iceberg' and tulip flowers have a solid, three-dimensional mass with glowing white petals moulded by highlights and shadows. Other whites such as poppies and romneya produce papery almost see-through fragile petals around central stamens, while *Clematis recta*, gypsophila and crambes bear small starry flowers held on branched stems to give misty cloud-like diffused colour effects. I much prefer to use the tinted whites: the more glaring laundry-whites are dazzling and seldom restful.

To counteract their potentially eye-catching properties, white flowers are best matched with pastel tints and grey- and silver-leaved foliage, gentle colour values that blend with the whiteness to make gradations of tones, rather than being juxtaposed with dark or bright foliage which emphasizes the strong contrast. For more contrived schemes, the arresting quality of blocks of white flowers may be deliberately exploited to make architectural points, most effectively as repeats along the edge or centre of a border scheme.

White flowers become luminous at dusk and even glow through the night, and so are perfect for beds that may be viewed only at the end of the day. With white-variegated foliage, they will lighten a shady corner.

Neighbouring colours retain their truest appearance when placed beside white flowers, and are optically deepened and enriched, so whites can be used to separate colours that might otherwise clash. Tinted whites do this more gently. The 'white' of the white flowers becomes tinted with the complementary colour of its neighbour. Cream flowers seem perfect companions for all garden flowers. They set off blues, soften harsher yellows, oranges and reds, and are cool and restful.

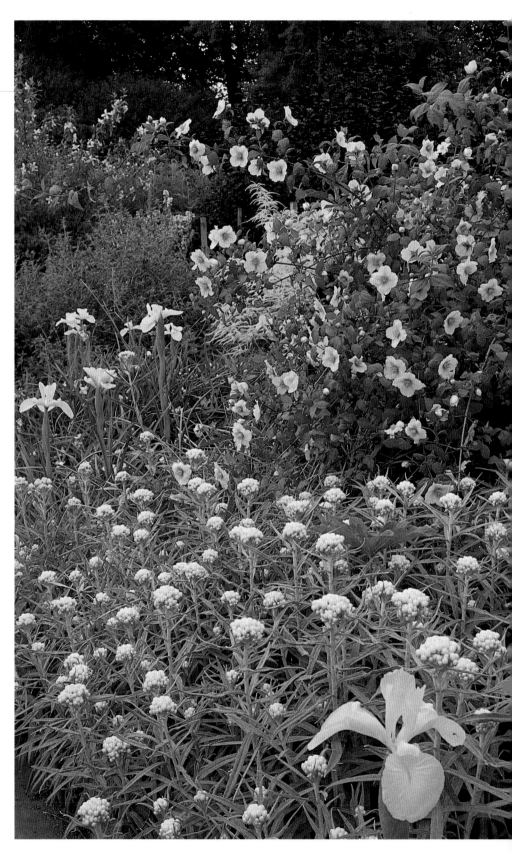

LEFT *Tightly furled button-flowers of silver-leaved* Anaphalis margaritacea *are almost creamy, matching the plumes of* Aruncus dioicus. *The petals of the Dutch iris and the philadelphus are whiter, but yellow touches diffuse their brightness.*

RIGHT *Grey-leaved* Anaphalis cinnamomea *blends behind* Osteospermum ecklonis, *its white daisy-flowers streaked beneath with blue. Silvery* Artemisia canescens *softens the impact of the brightest white flowers.*

BELOW *Clematis 'Mrs Oud' clambers among open flowers of 'Iceberg' rose and reduces their glare.*

BELOW RIGHT *The tulip-shaped flowers of* Magnolia × soulangeana *have purple-pink flushes at the base.*

Blues in the spectrum

Rather as bees do, humans seem to identify blues in different ways. Some flower blues are 'pure', sky-blue, clear and intense; other blues are shadowed with a warmer, redder tone, veering towards violet, mauve or purple. Blue flowers are seldom one-coloured: petals are often darkest in the centre and bluest and palest around the edge. They often include contrasting markings in other colours, such as yellow or orange, which blur the overall blueness and make colour naming difficult. Many colour names for blue – forget-me-not, lilac, lavender and so on – are derived from flowers long familiar to gardeners. However, many of these genera have since been 'improved', and the flowers of these names that we grow today may be quite different from the colour evoked by their name.

Spring carpets of scilla, chionodoxa, muscari, *Anemone apennina* and forget-me-nots, bluebells and brunnera are always rich and satisfying, but not all blues invariably look good together. Himalayan blue poppies lose their glow if planted beside creeping *Gentiana acaulis*, with its short-stemmed trumpets of harsher brilliant blue. In late summer the equally harsh deep blue of ceratostigma is difficult to place: it makes the mauver blue of *Verbena patagonica* look washed out. The blues with a significant proportion of red in their make-up are more difficult to identify, but perhaps easier to use in the garden. These mauve-blues are

the colours of shadow and distance. An avenue of catmint flanking a garden walk will increase the feeling of length, the eye fading away with the flowers into the misty distance. At Tintinhull and elsewhere I use this as a design feature to increase the feeling of space.

Gertrude Jekyll believed that blue gardens do not have to contain only blue flowers, they just have to be beautiful. She recommended adding touches of white, cream or yellow to make the blues more telling. Gardens with blue and yellow flowers are always effective, and may be carried through the seasons without difficulty. Blues brighten oranges and yellows (their opposites on the spectral wheel) and look marvellous with grey foliage. Blues make reds seem redder: even crimson geraniums or roses next to clear blues seem to lose their blue pigment and tend to appear scarlet or vermilion. Strong reds and blues may jar, but softer pale pinks and blues give gentle effects. Low-toned blues, deep violet and mauve are essentials in colour planning, often acting as catalysts between jarring colours.

Leaves of plants such as grasses, hostas, acaena, *Ruta graveolens* 'Jackman's Blue' and tall shrubby euphorbias may be distinctly bluish or glaucous. Quite startling when surrounded by duller green, these look best massed in groups or spreading carpets. They too are often used to enhance and brighten neighbouring pale colours; and in a bolder scheme they look marvellous matched with bright crimson flowers.

RIGHT *Blues do not always go well together, but here the warm tone of potato-flowered* Solanum crispum *'Glasnevin' is perfect above the subtle purplish leaves and sombre flowers of* Salvia officinalis *'Purpurascens'. The silver foliage of* Cynara scolymus *is architectural and acts as a foil to make the blues glow brighter.*

FAR RIGHT ABOVE *Flowers of Jacob's ladder (*Polemonium caeruleum*) are blue, with distinctive yellow stamens and markings. The ferny foliage looks well with the prostrate-growing* Anthemis punctata cupaniana *with its white flowers that enliven the more retiring blues.*

FAR RIGHT BELOW *Blue-flowered catmint makes a gently fading haze, adding space and dimension to a garden rather than a distinctive colour block. In striking contrast, the double white form of feverfew (*Tanacetum parthenium*) grabs attention in the foreground. White valerian behind has a gentler impact, self-seeding freely to soften any semblance of formality implied by whiteness.*

LEFT *Blue-flowered plants make wonderful spreading spring carpets below deciduous shrubs, linking different areas and giving a feeling of space. Here acid-loving blue gromwell (*Lithodora diffusa*) makes a prostrate mat to set off neighbouring flowers and leaves of any colour.*

Yellows and golds

Yellow flowers and golden foliage never seem heavy in a landscape. Whether seen as folded rose petals, feathery alchemillas, angelica umbels, diaphanous evening primroses or flowering shrubs with winter clusters of spider-like stamens, yellow flowers gently draw the eye and seem to give a feeling of airy lightness. Pale and golden leaves may be used to extend space and apparently push the garden perimeters outwards.

In spring, flowering shrubs seem to possess predominantly yellow flowers; under their skirts smaller aconites and crocuses precede primroses and narcissi. The early yellows are often paired with flattering carpets of blue, violet and mauve flowers, which sets a pattern for flowering schemes during the rest of the season. There are fewer yellow-flowering plants in the middle of summer, although roses, cinquefoils, day-lilies and alchemillas provide a wide choice and range of yellows. In traditional yellow and blue summer schemes copied from nature's spring colours, grey foliage of artemisia and lavender provides further subdued contrast. By late summer the yellows have become deeper and more orange in tone, swinging round towards the browns and bronzes of the prolific daisy-flower families, golden rod, tall verbascums and golden-rayed lilies.

Many yellow flowerers produce good foliage so they are often successfully grown on their own or as specimen groups, or are allowed to seed in paths and paving. Whole borders planned with a range of yellow flowers are also attractive and with care will perform all through the summer.

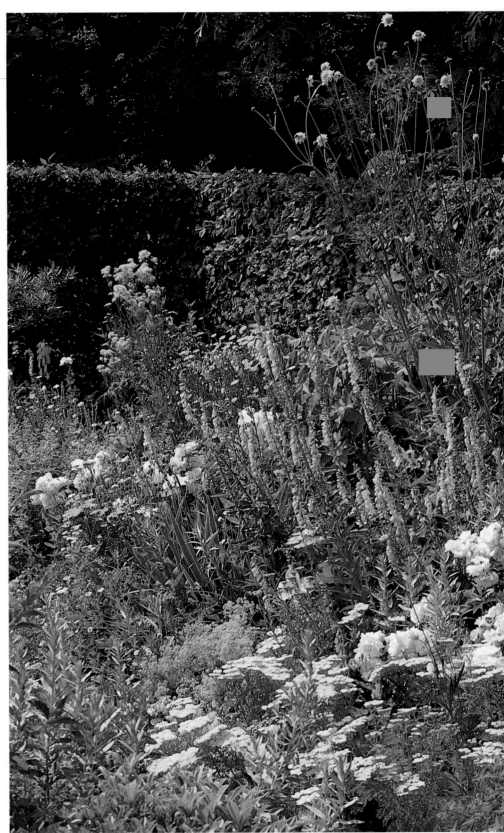

FAR LEFT *Yellows are always light in their effects and seem to glimmer in a garden setting rather than making blocks of solid colour. Here waxy flower clusters of* Lilium *'Connecticut King' look relatively heavy beside diaphanous evening primrose flowers. The dark purple foliage of orach (*Atriplex hortensis *'Rubra') adds a further dimension and a deep note of contrast.*

LEFT *In a border planting with a yellow and white theme, graceful cephalarias rise above pale yellow-flowered thalictrums and creamy-yellow foxgloves (*Digitalis grandiflora*). White roses act as a foil and are repeated to unite the plant groupings. Silvery-leaved* Artemisia ludoviciana *runs like a thread through the foreground planting.*

RIGHT *In this plant group a bright achillea becomes the strong focal point while yellow-toned neighbours like the retiring* Alchemilla mollis *fade beside it. Grey leaves of artemisia and helichrysum blend as background colour to prevent harsh effects.*

RIGHT *Scarlet-reds and harsh yellows – harmonies from the 'hot' side of the spectrum – were often combined in Miss Jekyll's grand border schemes. Telekia speciosa (syn. Buphthalmum speciosum) and Maltese cross (Lychnis chalcedonica) here make a dazzling partnership deliberately designed to jolt the mind and draw the eye from blander colour associations. Most gardens will benefit from some such vibrant colour scheme carefully chosen to enliven the atmosphere.*

BELOW RIGHT *In an ornamental pot Pelargonium 'Lord Bute' and dark-leaved fuchsias, with flowers in toned-down reds, combine above the sultry purple-flushed leaves of a tropical coleus. This sort of planting combination is distinctive without being distractingly flamboyant.*

LEFT *The most eye-catching flowers and foliage in this red border are annuals which produce vivid short-term effects, although bee balm (Monarda 'Cambridge Scarlet') and crocosmias are part of the permanent structure. Scarlet dahlias, verbenas, begonias and Nicotiana 'Crimson Bedder' glow between the seasonal leaves of ricinus, scarlet-stalked ruby chard and beetroot. Berberis × ottawensis 'Superba' and Sedum telephium maximum 'Atropurpureum' have deep purple-toned leaves which pick up the blue pigment of the darker red flowers.*

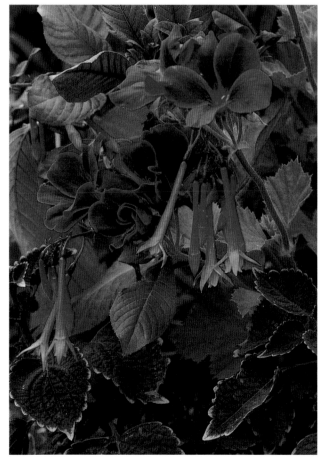

The range of reds

Pure bright reds with dazzling oranges are probably the most controversial of all flower colours. It is impossible for the eye to ignore red features; they stand out and grab the spotlight, and even their own green leaves intensify the redness. By their demand for attention they provoke strong reactions. Most 'good-taste' gardeners dismiss as violent, even vulgar, many of the colours from the 'hot' side of the spectrum. The purest and brightest scarlets and vermilions – reds without any blue pigment to give more mellow crimson shades, and without the traces of yellow that produce more cooling oranges and browns – are certainly vibrant.

This quality of dazzle may also make bright reds desirable. Conventional colour schemes of pale blending pastels and silvery foliage can become dull: bored with sameness, the eyes and mind refocus with the introduction of contrasting bright colour. In a garden these reds – kept from immediate view and deliberately sited around a corner or behind a hedge – jolt the mind and provide surprise focal points. Our red and yellow border at Tintinhull has for some a jarring quality, but I love its contrast with the toned-down greens, greys, and pale flowers of other areas.

Reds are advancing colours, distorting and foreshortening distances, but even this may be turned into an advantage. Small, intimate garden areas become cosier, safer and mysterious if deep reds are set against glowing backgrounds of green hedging.

As with the clear and the reddish-blues, there are to all intents and purposes two sorts of red. Scarlet reds and crimson reds may clash violently or, more maturely, harmonize, with the blue pigment in the crimson toning down and softening the harsher electric scarlets. In the border, reds are best chosen in colour harmonies: oranges and yellows on one side, crimsons and violet-toned flowers stretching away on the other.

Flowers in softer reds – darker shades, or paler pastel pinks – are easier to use and provide less to argue about. These soft colours may pair with blues and, indeed, often share blue pigment in their make-up. Purple-toned leaves provide background colour that harmoniously accentuates the 'blueness'. Pinks, especially when salmon- or apricot-toned, seldom work well with yellows. Mauve, on the other hand, is close enough to blue to make an admirable contrast with most pale and bright yellows.

Colour effects in planting

Gardeners should study colour behaviour in the countryside as well as in the garden, and above all learn how painters and other colour craftsmen have built up colour associations in their work. Looking closely at the blending blue-green weaves of Brussels tapestries, for example, helps us to appreciate how foliage tones set the background for every garden scene (just as in nature, where incidents of bright colour are usually small in proportion to the larger masses of background greens, greys and browns in low tones). Perhaps Impressionist artists have most to teach the gardener. It is their vision, repeated over and over again as a series of glimpses, that adds up to our garden views. Many great garden artists trained as painters: Monet planted his garden at Giverny in order to paint it later, and we can study it translated on to canvas. Gertrude Jekyll, unable to continue her career as a painter owing to deteriorating eyesight, applied her colour lessons

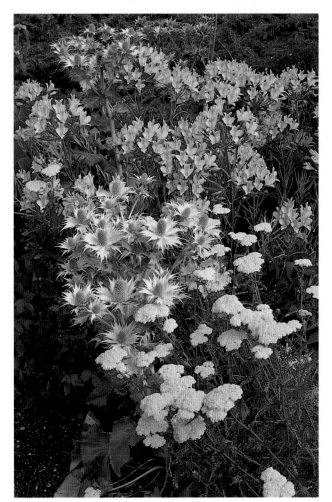

Golden-orange alstroemeria and lemon-yellow achillea are companions to thistle-like Miss Willmott's ghost (Eryngium giganteum) in a border scheme. The almost blue tinge to the silvery leaves and flowers of the eryngium sets off the neighbouring yellows, making them seem brighter and more glowing. Gertrude Jekyll loved to use silvers and greys with pastel colours to make their tints seem stronger, but they are equally effective with the almost strident orange tone of this Peruvian lily.

(many of them derived from Turner) to perfecting garden borders. From Turner she learned the colour values of mist and spray, ice and snow; later she translated his theories of light and used silvery foliage to make neighbouring flowers seem to glow more brightly. She copied the vibrant evening tones of his paintings by using orange and deep violet flowers together.

The principles of colour manipulation remain much the same although the painter works with exact colour mixes, while the gardener labours in a constantly changing world. Both use colours not only in pleasing associations but also to play tricks to convey architectural and linear effects. Dark solid plants such as yew, rhododendron, heavy purple-leaved prunus or beech trees imply weight, while dense twiggy bushes with pale foliage are light and airy. Flower and leaf colours emphasize aerial perspective; painters and gardeners choose cool blues, dull greys and browns and all pale tints to distort space and give the appearance of depth and distance. 'Warm' reds, oranges, shimmering yellows and solid whites foreshorten all dimensions. Thus the length of an avenue or border may be exaggerated, shapes of flower beds apparently altered, and the eye drawn to certain features.

A gardener cannot change colours by mixing pigments as a painter does, but the colours selected will be similarly affected by where they are placed, which colours they are next to, the relative sizes of all the colour groups and the distance from which they are seen. In the three-dimensional garden with planting on different planes, fresh views and colour sequences are unfolding in new and constantly renewed relationships. Whether in a long border glimpsed across a lawn or as plants tightly packed into a container, flower colours behave logically: seen from close to, colours remain in distinct blocks; from farther away they blend and interweave like a Persian carpet.

The colours actually perceived are influenced by all the other elements visible at the same moment, so producing an almost inexhaustible number of possible permutations and combinations. The human eye tends to exaggerate apparent differences, so that colours that seem quite similar (such as two tones of blue) will look very different when placed together; dissimilar colours will, if anything, look even more different when placed side by side. Completely opposite or complementary rainbow colours, the pure undiluted hues such as yellow/violet, orange/blue and red/green – all of which

On the wall at Tintinhull Clematis 'Huldine' makes a curtain of light next to the yellow-green flowers of the shrubby Chilean Cestrum parqui. With petals that are almost translucent and a central boss of greenish stamens, the flowers of 'Huldine' have a quality of whiteness that is easy to use in a garden, flattering neighbours rather than grabbing the spotlight for itself. Tinted whites and pale glimmering yellows are an ideal combination.

as pairs contain no shared pigment – when placed together will each gather intensity and glow more brightly. A 'non'-colour such as grey does not compete with other colours but will make all neighbouring hues appear more vivid and brilliant.

As well as these immediate, so-called simultaneous effects of colour coordination, the colour messages received by the eye will be influenced by a succession of images over short periods of time. The eye after staring for a time at one colour has a tendency to 'see' the image of its complementary or opposite colour. In a garden the eye can be prepared to receive maximum impact from a series of colour schemes. A bright red 'hot' border will appear brighter if it is seen after walking through an area of relatively restful green foliage. Gold and yellow leaf and flower combinations will, similarly, be more effective when viewed after an area containing blue and mauve flowers. Moving from shade into dazzling sunlight creates similar effects.

In her proposals for a series of gardens of 'special colouring' Gertrude Jekyll introduced this principle of viewing colours in succession. Her gardens include a series of areas in which orange, grey, gold, blue or green predominates – each preparing the eye for the next. Surrounded by yew hedges, the orange garden is a lively mixture of yellow- and orange-flowering plants such as coreopsis, heleniums, African and French marigolds, orange lilies and red hot pokers. In the grey garden silvery-leaved cotton lavenders, dianthus and stachys, with grey-foliaged yuccas and catmint, provide the frame to pale pink, mauve and white flowers, all backed with tall tamarisk. The 'gold' section is primarily a foliage garden; hollies, elaeagnus, euonymus, small-leaved box, elders and golden privet (one of Miss Jekyll's favourites) are shrubby masses, and pale yellow snapdragons, coreopsis and helianthus glimmer between them. In the blue garden, where blue flowers are made more telling by creamy aruncus, *Clematis recta*, lilies and yellow thalictrum, the flower borders are again framed with yew. The last garden is one of cool green, different leaf textures and grasses reflecting light to make a tapestry of quiet colour.

For many gardeners some appreciation of colour theory will enrich experiments with living plants and flowers, but can never replace the 'hands-on' approach: at best it provides useful guidelines that may then be adapted to more subtle garden moods, fashions in planting and, ultimately, sheer personal preference.

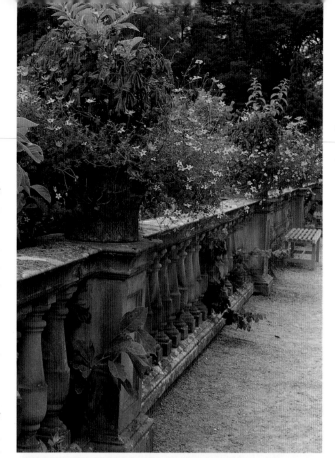

LEFT *In a series of wicker-patterned ornamental pots at Powis Castle, rich red fuchsias are ringed by yellow* Bidens ferulifolia *and blue felicias to make strong statements along a balustrade. In the mid-nineteenth century the pure primary hues of scarlet, blue and yellow were often used together to give the intense effects of bright sunlight. Today planting schemes often seem unnecessarily cautious; brighter combinations of colours can be very effective.*

Border schemes based on bright advancing reds and yellows foreshorten distance and can make spaces seem smaller. The effect is one of intimacy in a garden area (BELOW LEFT) where a grassy path leads between two beds linked by their bright but warm scheme. In the foreground a large-flowered hemerocallis cultivar with vivid orange-bronze petals towers above neighbouring × solidaster and paler yellow lilies, while silver-leaved artemisias weave the patterns together. Yellow and orange flowers and grey leaves sustain the theme in the farther bed, enriched by purple foliage.

Tintinhull's 'hot' border (RIGHT) overflows with red roses, scarlet penstemons and creamy-yellow mulleins and achilleas. The planting may be glimpsed across the lawn, but approaching from one side reveals its effect to be startling rather than overpowering.

At Hidcote (BELOW) scarlet dahlias, red fuchsias and orange-buff hemerocallis blend together, while the dark leaves of Salvia officinalis 'Purpurascens' and Heuchera micrantha 'Palace Purple' in the front and Corylus maxima 'Purpurea' behind serve as catalysts. Grassy miscanthus contributes more airy effects. Facing each other across a central panel of turf, the Red Borders at Hidcote unfold these strong colours in succession as you walk by.

THE NATURAL GARDEN

The essence of natural gardening lies in working with nature rather than against it. Plants are used in ways that they obviously enjoy: they grow with freedom, intertwine with romantic abandon and spread in drifts to match the lie of the land or to complement overhead tree canopies. The natural approach is possible on any scale. True Robinsonian 'wild' gardening, as expounded by William Robinson in the nineteenth century, is most suitable for woodland or for landscapes where trees and hills shape the horizon. The principle of using plants to create such a look of spontaneity, however, may be applied in a pocket-handkerchief flower bed in which hellebores and wood anemones thrive in the shade of a single tree.

This chapter is about growing flowering plants on a modest garden scale, in ways inspired both by the simplicity of nature and by some more intimate wild flower details. In the natural garden, planting schemes appear relaxed and uncomplicated; plants seem to grow as if positioned by accident. Where accent plants are used they subtly enhance the forms and textures of an understated composition rather than punctuate the layout with eye-catching contrasts. Good companionable groups or drifts and natural-looking spreading shapes make abstract patterns, echoing contours and shadows existing in the site.

The myth that wild or natural gardening is virtually labour free should be exploded at the outset. Such gardens may mean less work, but what work there is – from the planning stage onwards – is skilled and sensitive. Natural planting should look as if it requires low maintenance, but this casual appearance is sustained only by selective hand-weeding and considerable annual juggling of plants to retain the relative proportions between the groups. To paint a garden picture informally composed of shapes, flowers and leaves, the natural gardener must have not only a sense of beauty but also a deep knowledge of plant types, their relative growing rates and general needs – skills less vital to the pattern-making formal gardener whose horticultural skills combine with those of the architect.

Mirabel Osler's garden pond in Shropshire has just the right 'natural' touch. The plants look as if they have arrived spontaneously, thriving in the moist soil to spread in drifts that push out into the water's edge. The pond itself has an appropriately informal air, with no hard lines. To keep such a scheme in balance is a demanding task: vigorous plants need firm management.

APPROACHES TO PLANTING

To the real ecologist, gardening with anything other than native species is artificial. In the British Isles adherence to this principle would mean that flower gardens were fairly dull. As a result of the Ice Age, and the islands' subsequent separation from the continent of Europe, the native flora of Britain is not rich in species. Using native plants only would result in charming meadows of delicate wild flowers – suitable for the outer fringes of the garden, perhaps – but the flower garden as a whole would undoubtedly be impoverished.

In many other regions of the world, such as North America, Asia and Australia, which have a wide range of climates and physical conditions, there is a huge diversity of plant material and gardeners have more exciting possibilities for native plant gardens. Most gardeners, however, even if keen on naturalistic results, will want to use foreign plants and good hybrids and cultivars to enhance effects. The gardener's individual skills are employed to give exotic plants growing conditions resembling those found in their native habitats and to grow highly bred garden plants as naturally as possible.

Some naturalistic planting is more psychological than real. An alternative to confining the palette strictly to native flora is to use 'old-fashioned' species in unsophisticated cottage-garden styles of planting. This tradition harks back to a pre-industrial time when gardening was uncomplicated by horticultural sciences and the flood of new plant introductions after about 1600. It may not satisfy the purists, but its rejection of highly bred nurserymen's specimens in favour of unimproved species plants may achieve appropriately simple, natural effects. A few standard fruit trees (if possible old varieties) and some old-fashioned cottage-garden flowers – roses, peonies, columbines, irises, fritillaries – interplanted with rosemary, lavender and lettuces indicate the theme.

Framing wooden steps at the edge of a garden on the Long Island shore, wild flowers flourish in profusion. Here European ox-eye daisies, naturalized as wild flowers in North America, mingle with day-lilies escaped from garden cultivation and a variety of grasses to give the approach a very natural air. Even a native plant purist who declines to use exotics will accept the presence of plants that have been grown around the house for centuries.

Pioneers of natural planting

The earliest and in many ways most influential advocate of the natural garden was William Robinson, who wrote *The Wild Garden* in 1870 at a time when gardening fashions, dictated by the great houses and their influential head gardeners, had established a highly artificial style. Tender bedding-out plants, changed two or three times a year, were being used to implement elaborate colour patterns and massed effects; gardening skills and techniques were intended to demonstrate man's control over nature while showing off the wealth of the garden owners. Hardy plants, both native and introduced, had been relegated to the cutting borders in kitchen gardens; some of the best only survived in smaller rectory and cottage gardens.

Robinson's naturalistic approach seemed revolutionary to his contemporaries, who misunderstood or distorted many of his ideas. He advocated that groups of hardy native and exotic plants (mainly perennials and bulbs) should be encouraged to grow and spread in natural drifts on sloping banks, under the branches of deciduous trees at the edge of woodland, or in moist soil by watersides. After planting, it was hoped, they would multiply naturally and eventually look as if they owed nothing to man's artistic or horticultural interference.

Other pioneering spirits and collaborators such as Gertrude Jekyll took his themes and broadened them for use in the flower garden as well as in the outer areas where garden perimeters fade into countryside. In order to achieve the natural look, the flower garden was treated as if each constituent part provided conditions suitable for certain sorts of plants, and emphasis was put on using plants that were appropriate to each site. There were few obvious climax or architectural plants; instead, blending groups set a theme of happy association and companionship. All this, of course, concealed careful manipulation: the soil and aspect of the site would have been thoroughly considered and, where necessary, adapted and improved in order to give the plants the best chance of success.

Not all naturalistic concepts have come from Britain. Modern gardeners draw on ideals fostered by designers and nurserymen such as Karl Foerster who worked in Germany between the two world wars. Foerster encouraged the use of flowering perennials and grasses in landscapes, and an escape from formality in plant arrangements. Jens Jensen, working in the Mid-

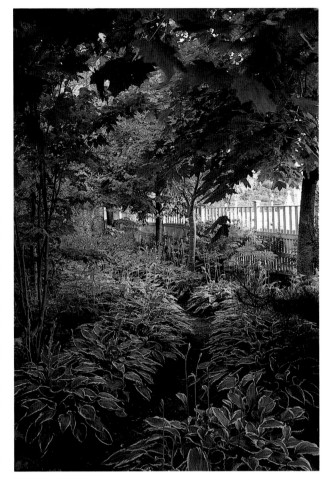

In this New England garden a winding pathway of soft pine-needles leads under the trees and contributes a sense of direction and space. Even plants as sophisticated as hostas, originally from Asia and 'improved' by nurserymen over the last twenty years into a thousand cultivars, assume a natural look when planted in a simple, unpretentious way. William Robinson knew them as funkias and described them as 'noble' plants suitable for massing or edging in shrubberies. Groups of one kind of hosta do not look too exotic and make excellent ground cover.

western states of America, particularly around Chicago, advocated using American native plants in naturalistic designs at a time when most American gardeners – still mainly inspired by traditional European layouts – were choosing imported plants from Europe and sometimes even American natives that had been improved by European nurserymen before returning to be used in gardens in their place of origin.

The new American-style gardens for the 1980s, laid out by Oehme, van Sweden and Associates and planted with prairie grasses and perennials, carry on this tradition today: they are essentially naturalistic in concept. Planting is not confined to American natives, but includes broad sweeps of tufted flowering grasses interlocking with massed rudbeckias, sedums and ceratostigmas, imitating nature at its best. All these pioneers, whether sticking to a 'natives-only' policy or allowing the addition of suitable hardy exotics, choose plants that are suitable to the region and those that are in keeping with the theme of the bed or border.

Nature's inspiration

Like the painter arranging pigments on a canvas, the gardener planning a natural garden must think in terms of creating a balanced composition, using the plants to give height and depth, width and lightness (conveyed by habits of growth and foliage colour), colour and texture, exactly as if he or she were working inside the frame of a picture. Strong accent plants should be arranged in groves or informal groups rather than paired to frame vistas or planted in regular patterns.

A momentary breathtaking glimpse of a foreign countryside embellished with native flowers, exotics to the onlooker, growing wild across the landscape may provide inspiration for garden schemes. The varied climate and scenery, and rich native flora, of North America offer such examples: in the southern states glorious backdrops of wisteria and Spanish moss, along with the Cherokee rose (*Rosa laevigata*) – an escaped introduction – festoon the evergreen live oaks (*Quercus virginiana*); pink-flowered cranesbills (*Geranium maculatum*) flourish by the expressway in the woods of Connecticut; and on Vancouver Island swathes of camassias grow along the shore.

LEFT *Wild garlic* (Allium ursinum) *with dark green leaves and white starry flowers makes an attractive, if pungent, weed-suppressing cover in moist woodlands. Here at Levens Hall it carpets the ground under the branches of the wide beech alley beneath which few plants can thrive.*

ABOVE *Pink-flowered* Allium karataviense *emerges above a mat of sweet woodruff in a charming incident in Catherine Hull's garden on the North Shore near Manchester, Massachusetts. Low-growing spreading plants, if not matting too thickly, make foils for bulbs to push their way through.*

Nature's effects are intended to be improved on by the gardener. Some magical scenes I recall are set in gardens skilfully planned to give truly natural effects, making use of suitable native and introduced flora. I remember with pleasure a field of native meadow anemone (*Anemone canadensis*) in Lincoln Foster's garden in Connecticut – a mass of starry white flowers that made a broad sweep beside a steeply gushing stream. Only a few yards away, on a rocky outcrop, sun-loving European euphorbias (the cypress spurge *Euphorbia cyparissias*) had colonized shallow open soil to seem equally at home. At Mount Cuba, Delaware, small American east coast native flowers spread in broad drifts between mountain laurel and dogwood, while along the stream in the valley Asian primulas had been allowed to establish themselves in natural profusion.

Some of the best small American gardens are those stolen from woodland, where planting follows nature's patterns as closely as possible. By thinning out a few trees to make patterns of light and shade, native acid-loving plants such as maianthemums, arctostaphylos, mitchella, eye-catching arisaemas, bloodroots, heucheras, bluets (*Hedyotis caerulea*), red- and yellow-flowered *Aquilegia canadensis*, sweet rocket (introduced, but now naturalized in New England woods), as well as exotic shade-loving hostas and ferns, spread in natural drifts between dogwood, mountain laurel and native rhododendrons. Biennials (or even annuals) are encouraged to self-seed *in situ* and establish themselves without obvious human interference.

These American examples are matched for me by some in the British Isles. At Glendurgan, Cornwall – a superb natural-style garden – advantage is taken of steep slopes and a mild climate to grow many rare introduced plants: native English cowslips, for example, flower in the rough grass in front of flowering Japanese cherries. Many other great European gardens furnish magnificent scenes of naturalistic planting, closely echoing the magic of recalled scenes of nature. Even if it is not possible to match precisely the particular growing conditions, soils and climates, it may be feasible to introduce similar scenes or incidents into a garden, eliminating obvious signs of control and the appearance of artificiality.

At Sheffield Park, Sussex, giant lilies (*Cardiocrinum giganteum*) are grouped in dappled shade in the woods. White foxgloves glow in the dusk at Knightshayes Court, Devon, and at Winterthur, Delaware, drifts of

pink and white azaleas spread out beneath the tulip trees, and in their turn are underplanted with broad sweeps of native phlox or May-apple and European bluebells. There is nothing simple about any of these gardening triumphs. The giant lilies will only flourish to their full potential if richly fed (Gertrude Jekyll, who used to have manure-filled pits dug for each stand of bulbs, was amused by casual visitors who thought her successes were easy). The white foxgloves at Knightshayes represent years of weeding out mauve-flowered interlopers. The melting colours of the waves of azaleas at Winterthur with their accompanying sweep of colonizing woodlanders have been achieved only after years of patience.

Some gardens may already contain natural features that suggest a theme for naturalistic development, as well as indicating the actual plant types that may be grown – a stream bed, perhaps, beside which to encourage moisture-loving bog plants. The flower

Lenten roses flower en masse at Knightshayes Court. With flower colour varying between cream and blushed purple, Helleborus orientalis *hybrids, often attractively marked, flourish in shady borders. They like rich feeding but need little attention other than tidying of their foliage during the flowering period in early spring. Good colour forms can be selected and grown on from divisions but, left to their own devices, these hellebores will volunteer plenty of good quality seedlings to colonize a suitable site.*

garden may spread into natural woodland, carpeted with drifts of low-growing shade plants and with taller woodland perennials. In some gardens, open banks and meadow valleys provide natural sites for sun-loving colonizers. In others, layers of stratified rock may become the foundation of a natural rock garden for alpine plants that like to put down deep roots in search of moisture (see Natural rock gardens, page 94). Features such as these set the scene, and the planting range may be extended with suitable plants from all parts of the world, so that natives already *in situ* or added discreetly thrive beside drifts of similarly happy exotics.

Themes from elsewhere

For the natural gardener in search of a theme, paintings, carpets, tiles and porcelain may all provide inspiration. The association between art and gardening is a recurrent theme: the romantic landscapes of painters of the school of Claude Lorrain may well have helped to inspire the development of the English landscape movement in the eighteenth century. In its turn, the new landscape ideal, which swept away geometric layouts and plant regimentation to replace them with soft curves and contours, directly influenced the more natural ways of growing plants developed by William Robinson.

The baroque Dutch paintings of the seventeenth and eighteenth centuries – in which snowdrops and anemones, roses and peonies, irises, fritillaries and tulips, lilies and dianthus are displayed together in exuberant if seasonally impossible profusion – may provide a point of departure. When planning a theme for a flower bed, the gardener may emulate the free-style effects of the paintings to follow the seasons. Lavish, informal arrangements overflowing and arching out of elegant vases are worth copying in containers and borders.

The close connection between the Impressionists and their gardens has already been mentioned. Monet created his famous garden at Giverny so that he could paint it and Renoir treasured and preserved the timeless atmosphere of his garden and olive grove at Les Collettes as inspiration for his paintings. Impressionist canvases may act as a direct inspiration to gardeners. Some of the paintings done at the end of the nineteenth century also capture a freedom and exuberance of flower-bed style that deserves study. In the United States, Childe Hassam's portrayals of Celia Thaxter's island garden off the coast of Maine during the 1890s show impressionistic sweeps of flowers growing naturally.

More formal representations of flowers may even stimulate ideas for the natural garden. In the patterns of Persian carpets, stylized flower shapes and colours blend and mingle inside firm geometric structures. The same effect may be achieved within the manicured edges and horizontal lines of backing walls and hedges, the crisp architecture providing a foil to the free-style inner planting. Borders at Hidcote, Sissinghurst and Tintinhull are of this type, described by Vita Sackville-West as 'maximum informality of planting in a formal setting'. Similarly, the flowery meadow glimpsed through the window of an Italian master's painting of the Madonna or the Annunciation may seem horticulturally unrealistic but nevertheless has a charm that merits emulation.

ACHIEVING THE NATURAL LOOK

Whatever your chosen theme, the essence of natural gardening lies in selecting plants that flourish in the soil and climate of the locality and in using them as nature would. This same principle holds good whether your garden is favoured with features lending themselves to naturalistic development, or is a city backyard or suburban rectangle. However urban the site, growing flowers in a natural way involves careful consideration of the soil of the locality so that from the outset the right plants are chosen.

No 'natural' garden, even one in which only natives are grown, will survive without constant reappraisal. Hardy plants growing in conditions they enjoy may quickly get out of control and spoil the balance of the composition. Inevitably some plants grow faster than others; the toughest survive, the weakest go to the wall. To achieve the desired casual look you need to know in depth the habits and requirements of individual plants and their relative rates of growth in successive years.

In theory, introduced plants will do best in any garden site if the conditions approximate to those of their natural habitat. In practice, many good garden plants are no longer 'natural' species, but have been improved to satisfy particular garden conditions. Some requirements are obvious: sun-lovers need an open situation, and shade-lovers prefer woodland conditions – or at

One way of achieving a natural look is to choose garden plants with an ebullient, informal habit so that they cloak man-made structures with flowers and foliage. At Ninfa in Latium, south of Rome, climbers grow in profusion over the old walls of a ruined village. Here pink climbing roses sprawl with luxuriant abandon in the seventeenth-century walled garden. A wonderful assortment of old and new roses thrive in this climate, where the hot sun ripens the wood for next season's performance.

Under the branches of a paperbark maple (Acer griseum) bluebells spread through a woodland area to make a carpet of blue at Le Vasterival, Princess Sturdza's garden near Dieppe. The leaves of lady's mantle will soon disguise the bulbs' fading foliage. In natural gardening it is essential to find plant companions that work together to extend the seasons without a great deal of trouble.

least a predominantly sunless aspect. Identifying more subtle plant needs means knowing more about them.

Those sun-loving plants that are loosely called Mediterranean-type need good drainage and harsh stony ground. If given enriched garden soil, they will make lush growth and quickly outgrow their situations. Until recently native ceanothus or the Matilija poppy (forms of *romneya*) were never seen in a Californian flower garden as they would grow too fast in artificial conditions. However, the modern reliance on simulated 'dry' sites within the garden area means that greater use may now be made of these regional natives.

Some plants, hardly eye-catchers when competing with other species in their native conditions, become quality garden plants when nurtured in a new, slightly alien environment. This is true of a number of the New England Michaelmas daisies. But caution and common sense must be exercised. In natural gardening, acid-loving plants, for example, only look right in a deep loamy soil with a low pH reading. Although horticultural techniques make it possible to change garden soil, plants look better both as individuals and as companions if they are chosen for their suitability for existing conditions. To achieve seemingly uncontrived effects the gardener's improvements should appear minimal.

Trees and taller shrubs have an important role to play in the natural garden. They provide the basic structure of beds and borders, creating areas of shadow and sunlight and acting as scene-setters around which planting schemes may be arranged. The canopies of mature trees give architectural substance that balances the solid mass of the house or other buildings. If starting a new garden from scratch, my advice is to invest in as large a shade tree as can be afforded or, better still, get more than one.

Avoid exotic trees with attention-grabbing foliage or habits, but look for those that are indigenous or have become established in the region over a long period, or fit into a domestic context. Cottage-style gardens are best served by standard fruit trees, prunus (including sophisticated Japanese cherries), crab apples (forms of *Malus*) and thorns (forms of *Crataegus*). Trees and shrubs known and grown in British gardens since the sixteenth century include phillyreas, laurustinus, hollies, spindles, lilacs, laburnum and Cornelian cherries. These are all relatively unobtrusive and lend themselves to the overall pictorial composition of the natural garden.

A question of scale

William Robinson's ideas on the wild garden were conceived at a time when the great estates of England and Scotland still offered the gardener acres of mature woodland that could be developed as large-scale woodland flower gardens. Few gardeners in Europe today have such opportunities – the natural garden at Knightshayes Court is one of the small number of great gardens in an existing wood made in England since 1945.

Most new gardens today are of modest size and are in open situations, usually close to the house. The enthusiastic natural gardener is best able to achieve naturalistic effects by adopting what is often called the cottage-garden style. This should not be confused with

At Crook Hall in Durham, oriental poppies make splashes of vibrant colour in a thickly planted early summer border where plants support each other and spill on to the stone path. This sort of cottage-style gardening depends on seemingly random groupings, but here the repetition of clumps of pink- and blue-flowered cranesbills (Geranium endressii and G. × magnificum) gives the scheme a firm sense of design without loss of informality.

that they appear to have happened naturally. It may not be possible to achieve drifts of bluebells stretching into the distance under deciduous trees, but a woodland theme may be evoked by allowing carpeting plants – including spring bulbs such as wood anemones, cyclamen, scillas and chionodoxa – and perennials – such as hellebores and lady's mantle – to spread under the canopies of trees and shrubs in part of a modern mixed border, or even around the bole of one shade-giving specimen tree.

Beds and borders in the flower garden are usually edged with grass lawns or pathways. Whether curved or straight, they make a firm divide between the planted area and the adjacent areas of turf, gravel or paving. Within even the most formal layout, informal planting can simulate nature's effects. The use of Gertrude Jekyll's free-style planting in drifts transforms regimented border schemes of bright flowers arranged in symmetrical triangles or rectangles into ones where flower colour and leaves intermingle and blend.

At the outer edges of the garden, native and exotic plants may be encouraged to seed and colonize in grass to give dazzling but rather short-lived 'flowery mead' effects. A country garden may be almost imperceptibly linked with its surrounding landscape by the judicious selection of indigenous plants used informally on its perimeter. In an urban situation cultivating a wilder natural style on the garden's edges helps to give a feeling of the country that contrasts with the concrete jungle outside.

the old-style country cottager's utilitarian plot, in which a few flowers were allowed to grow among the vegetables and fruit cultivated for the family's use. The cottage-garden style is an informal manner of planting which focuses on a profusion of flowers, with shade provided by a few ornamental trees and shrubs. Cottage-garden planting brings the naturalistic style into the intimate flower garden. Inside a tight structure of hedges and walls, the actual planting may be exuberant and natural. Flower beds are tightly packed with a mixture of plant types: small trees, shrubs, perennials, annuals and bulbs set in billowing drifts.

Ornamental trees and shrubs not only make informal barriers between areas of the garden but also give some permanent vertical design structure, providing essential pockets of shade for woodland-type flowers. Even if each of these garden pockets is very small, they still provide different aspects where schemes and plant themes may be suitably adapted so

Bulbs for the natural garden

Bulbous plants (those with underground storage organs, whether bulbs, corms, rhizomes or tubers) are best planted in naturalistic groups, spreading themselves between sun and shade as they might in the wild. The most informal effects are achieved by throwing a handful of bulbs on the ground and planting each where it falls rather than in regimented rows or symmetrical groups. These drifts are suitable companions to border shrubs and herbaceous plants.

Given conditions as close as possible to their native habitat, and left to spread by themselves in a relaxed manner, even those bulbs with the most exotic-looking flowers seem at home. Birds and mice may help to distribute their seeds to more distant parts of the garden, as well as in adjacent soil, creating delightfully haphazard effects. In a mature garden, flower beds

Meadow gardening, when successful, is perhaps the most charming of all the 'wilder' garden styles. In Miriam Rothschild's garden in Northamptonshire, white narcissus and tulips flourish in rough grass with wild flowers and even 'weeds'. When naturalized, highly bred tulips will develop smaller flowers each season, making them look less artificial than those with more blowzy flower-heads. This type of gardening works best in poor soil where competitive grasses do not flourish.

carpeted with massed colonies of small spring-flowering bulbs add a naturalistic touch that cannot be achieved in a short span of years; gardening in a natural manner needs time and patience.

Many of these bulbous plants do not need full exposure to sun during the period of summer dormancy, and prefer cooler, slightly shady conditions. Such bulbs include aconites, snowdrops, crocus, cyclamen (there are species that have flowers or attractive leaves throughout the year), scillas, chionodoxas, fritillaries, wood anemones, *Anemone apennina*, species tulips (such as *Tulipa sylvestris*) and small narcissi as well as grape hyacinths. In good border soil bulbs will gradually multiply and flowering may increase if a dressing of bone-meal is given in autumn. They flourish under the branches of deciduous trees and shrubs which, in leaf a few weeks later, shade the soil surface for the rest of the summer. In more open areas of the beds they can be given protective shade from neighbouring herbaceous foliage.

Spring-flowering snowflakes (both *Leucojum vernum* and *L. aestivum*) and dog's-tooth violets from Europe, Asia and America prefer moister soil and will tolerate shade; North American trilliums prefer acid soil and shade. To conserve moisture they should all be given a thick mulch of some organic material as the leaves die

down. Place them carefully so that other plants, such as hart's-tongue ferns or fern-leaved *Corydalis cheilanthifolia*, spread quickly over the bare space as the bulb leaves wither and die down.

Most alliums with grey strap-shaped leaves need more open sites; in their native habitats their bulbs are baked by hot sun in the summer months while they are dormant. Those with mauve spherical flower-heads perform in spring and early summer; their untidy foliage is hidden later by neighbouring perennials. They not only self-sow quite freely but also produce small bulbils attached to the main bulb, which quickly grow large enough to produce flowering plants. The related *Nectaroscordum siculum bulgaricum*, which has pendent bell-shaped greeny-white flowers, flushed purple, quickly seeds in unexpected places and spreads rapidly to make thick flowering clumps, as do two smaller shade-tolerant alliums. *Allium moly*, with spherical yellow heads, flowers in summer; white-flowered *A. tuberosum* waits until near the end of the season to perform in open or shaded sites at the front of borders.

Other useful spreading bulbs include camassias from the western American seaboard, which have starry flowers in early summer; they may be pale blue, rich blue or cream and all prefer an open situation in which they increase naturally. Byzantine gladioli push their way up through the lower leaves of other plants to flower later. The tiny summer-flowering blue-eyed grass (*Sisyrinchium angustifolium*) likes full sun and will seed between paving stones; its taller-growing cousin *S. striatum*, with iris-like leaves, makes drifts of cream at the front of borders. Pacific Coast iris hybrids prefer some shade and do best in an acid soil.

Most of the South African bulbs need hot sun all summer and protected sites in bare unshaded soil; they do not fit into mixed border planting. Exceptions are angel's fishing rods (*Dierama pulcherrimum*) and white-flowered summer hyacinths (*Galtonia candicans*). The former has drooping pink flowers and grass-like leaves; it will seed itself in unexpected corners in sun or part shade. The more fussy galtonias generally need renewing frequently, except in very mild sun-baked gardens. Both of these will flower well next to shrub roses or other plants that do not cast deep shade.

Lilies, often with highly scented flowers, are a large genus, among which are some of the best mid- and late-summer-flowering bulbs. Both shade- and sun-loving lilies grow well in border groups, although the shade-lovers, with muted flower colours, look the more natural. The European turk's-cap martagon lilies, with pinkish to white flowers, are the least fussy and thrive in shade in any soil. Backhouse lily hybrids have martagon genes and are also disease-resistant.

The Canadian *Lilium canadense* bears yellow or dark red flowers and thrives in moist humus-rich acid soil in semi-shade. Although bright orange in flower, the European *L. bulbiferum croceum* and the Asiatic *L. henryi* and *L. lancifolium* are so vigorous that they look relaxed and informal when allowed to spread as large groups between shrubs or vigorous perennials. In the 'hot'-toned borders at Tintinhull, *L. lancifolium* cultivars make effective golden splashes between dark red roses and deep purple foliage plants.

Fruit trees cast little shade and so make excellent host plants to spring-flowering bulbs beneath. At Pitmuies in Scotland drifts of tulips spread through a lush green carpet under flowering apple trees. Red tulips usually suggest a note of formality, but here their random grouping and the accompanying underplanting are all part of a natural approach within the crisply defined frame.

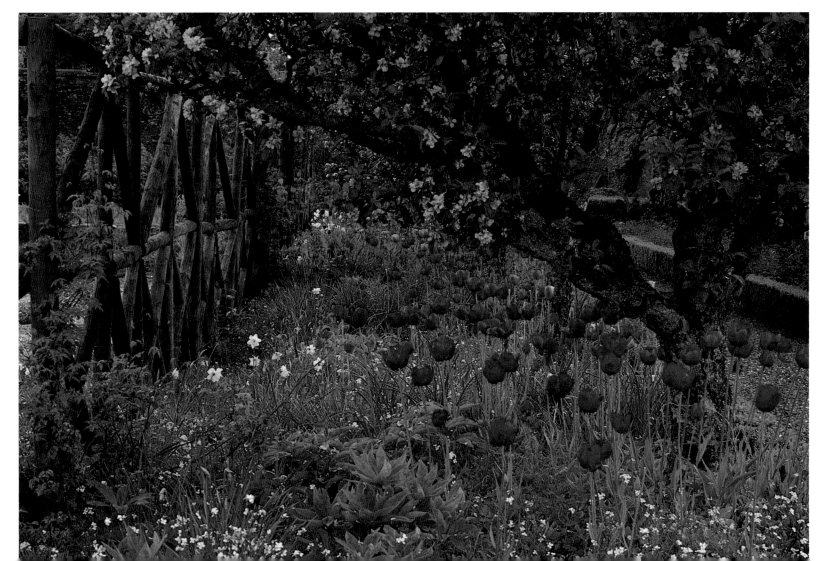

Informal perennials

In natural border schemes, perennials are not regimented into preconceived patterns of foliage and colour; rather, plant groups are allowed to drift into each other and assume different shapes each year; a modicum of disorganization is carefully encouraged. Tall silver-leaved artichokes, verbascums, hollyhocks and foxgloves, instead of being lined up in stands at the back of a bed, spring up at the front to soar above partly hidden lower-growing plants just behind.

Almost any favourite perennial may be encouraged to grow informally, especially if staked unobtrusively early in the season. For quickest results choose those that are romping spreaders and willing self-seeders. However, take care to avoid the most vigorous colonizers in the main flower beds and borders – they are more appropriately grown in wilder outer garden areas where, on an altogether larger scale, they will cover steep banks, grow in woodland glades, or fringe ponds and streams.

Growing flowers naturally means leaving them *in situ* to make their own shapes and patterns over the years; there is therefore greater emphasis on foliage effects and on covering bare earth than on seeking continuous colour displays through the months. In the natural garden the best perennials are those that have attractive foliage before and after flowering, are good neighbours, do not need staking and tying, and seldom require dividing and replanting. Choose pale flowers and those that are recessive in colour – for example, dark blues and violets – so that they will blend together in a scheme. Avoid eye-catching clashes of colour; unless used carefully, orchestrated colour schemes are best left for the formal flower border.

As a general rule, species plants that have shorter flower-heads in relation to stalk length look less contrived than improved varieties with more flower power. Recognizable 'old' garden plants will also look natural: it is modern hybrids and cultivars that strike the jarring note. In general, plants should be chosen to blend with others within the overall scheme, rather than for their individual qualities.

A *white form of* Fritillaria meleagris *rises on slender stems to flower above a sea of speedwell* (Veronica filiformis) *in part of Mrs Goossenaert's garden in Holland. Snakeshead fritillaries seed naturally to multiply in temperate climates even if quite densely underplanted.*

In Jim Reynolds' garden in Ireland all the main flower borders have an informal air with plants closely packed together and almost leaning against one another, making their own lacy patterns. Species and 'old-fashioned' plants often look more appropriate in natural gardens than highly bred flowers, which seem unduly attention-seeking. The subdued palette of pale yellows and creams and whites tinted with mauve sustains the delicacy of these flower pictures. Yellow daisy-flowers contrast with airy white Lysimachia ephemerum *which carries tall flower-spikes above almost glaucous leaves* (RIGHT). *Heart's ease and the biennial Miss Willmott's ghost* (Eryngium giganteum) *take a front position.*

LEFT *Tall flower-heads of* Campanula lactiflora *lean over a foreground mass of* Astrantia major *and* Scrophularia auriculata 'Variegata' *in part of Jim Reynolds' summer border.*

Many of the best and most natural-looking perennials, the most vigorous suckerers, are often un-available from local garden centres as they do not keep in good condition in containers; they should, if pos-sible, be ordered from 'growing' nurseries for spring or autumn delivery. Some of the most suitable species perennials are also willing self-seeders. Seed may be gathered when ripe and sown in the following spring; in most cases plants flower in the next year.

Attractive, natural-looking effects may be achieved in flower beds with some of the more vigorous peren-nials that grow into clumps or thickets in which the contrasting textures of leaves and flowers informally weave themselves together. Alstroemerias, some achilleas, many silvery artemisias, anaphalis, peach-leaved campanulas, *Coreopsis verticillata*, herbaceous clematis, giant *Crambe cordifolia*, galegas (both the old goat's rue *Galega officinalis* and the very desirable *G. orientalis*) and shade-loving Solomon's seal all do this

very well. In all gardens good perennials introduced from foreign countries are often related to less inter-esting indigenous plants: their obvious kinship to native flora helps promote the natural look within flower beds. For example, eupatoriums from the United States, related to European hemp agrimony (*Eupatorium cannabinum*), make sturdy late-flowering clumps in open border sites.

Some low-growing perennials are natural sprawlers; they are often dismissed as so-called ground-cover plants, but the best, with attractive leaves through the season, have good flowering potential. Their spreading habit makes them effective as weed suppressors under shrubs and shrub roses or between sturdy clumps of taller perennials, extending the casual appearance of a planting scheme. Omphalodes, pulmonarias, litho-spermum and rampant buglossoides are all good carpet-ing plants that may be either massed or allowed to weave in and out of other plants in free-style fashion.

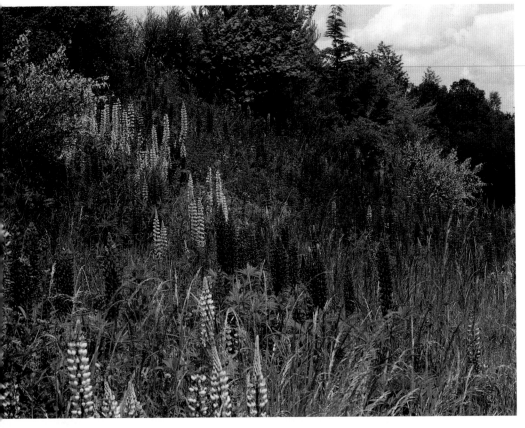

Along a Dorset roadside hybrid lupins with violet-blue, mauve and pink flowers – descendants of the original Lupinus polyphyllus *from western North America – have seeded and naturalized in the grass. The blending tones of these seedlings weave together subtly to give a charming relaxed colour effect that would enhance any garden scheme. Allowing plants to self-seed in a haphazard way often produces effects that are as exciting as carefully planned garden programmes.*

Annuals and biennials

The jungle effects created by the free-style planting of woody plants, hardy perennials and bulbs are further enriched by biennials and annuals that are encouraged to seed themselves in haphazard groups and drifts to colonize any patch of bare soil. The crafty gardener may well direct events by scattering seed (never using a hoe or hand-cultivator) in available spaces.

In spring, biennial honesties (forms of *Lunaria annua* – known as the silver dollar plant in North America) will thrive and spread in the dappled shade of a fruit tree or ornamental cherry. Its mauve flowers make a striking colour contrast to the pale yellow bracts of the almost evergreen perennial spurge, *Euphorbia amygdaloides robbiae*, or the smaller *E. cyparissias*, both of which spread in similar sites. A white-flowered honesty (*Lunaria annua alba*) may flower at the back of beds where shade-loving perennials take over later in the season and if isolated comes true from seed.

Biennial forget-me-nots (forms of *Myosotis sylvatica*) may be allowed to seed freely after flowering each spring and will happily multiply in any shady corner. Plants can be pulled up after flowering is over. Brighter blue flowers and sturdier plants are obtained in named seed packets; they should be sown in early summer and transferred to their flowering sites by autumn.

Biennial foxgloves, for sun and shade, are excellent in an informal garden. The ordinary *Digitalis purpurea* has a dingy pink flower, but white-flowering seedlings, as at Knightshayes Court, may be selected to add grace and interest to a border. The southern European *D. ferruginea*, with coppery-yellow flowers, looks exotic but is not too glamorous for the natural garden. Although a perennial, it is best treated as a biennial.

In open situations statuesque angelicas, evening primroses, tall silvery thistles (forms of onopordum), silybums with green leaves veined with white, and thistle-flowered Miss Willmott's ghost are all worthwhile biennials that mix well with groups of permanent shrubs and perennials; all are species and come true from seed.

The floppy horned poppy (*Glaucium flavum*) with greyish foliage and bright yellow papery flowers will sprawl at the front of a sunny border. Some of the biennial mulleins seed as single specimens between groups of perennials. They provide height, while prolifically seeding violas and verbenas carpet the ground, filling up space at the front of borders.

Periwinkles, often relegated to poor shady sites, flower brilliantly when given more open situations and richer soils. Blue *Brunnera macrophylla*, with forget-me-not flowers in spring, thrives in deep shade; its thick leathery heart-shaped leaves look attractive all summer.

Hardy herbaceous geraniums are prolific flowerers, with colours ranging between mauve, pink and violet, and their mounds of elegant cut leaves fill in gaps between taller perennials or shrubs and fall forward over flower-bed edges for softening effects. Lady's mantle, with gentle light green leaves and feathery lime green flowers, is another spreading perennial that epitomizes the natural look. Grown in drifts at the base of taller plants, it fits into any flower scheme.

If beds are backed by walls, climbing plants – allowed to grow into natural shapes rather than fanned and tied to wires – give a soft curtained backdrop. Draped over walls and climbing up trellis, they also disguise and sometimes completely hide rigid lines of architectural detail or unsightly landscape features. Twining through the branches of neighbouring trees, climbers such as the flame creeper give an air of romantic and wild profusion.

LEFT *Columbines (mostly the ordinary Aquilegia vulgaris with flowers in tones of pink and blue) seed freely in a border in the Walled Garden at Wallington in Northumberland to enhance an early summer scene. Later, as other plants come into flower, the columbines can be dispensed with; as long as a few are allowed to set seed, a selection of new plants will always appear in the following season.*

BELOW *At ground level in Jim Reynolds' Irish garden a patch of pink cranesbills (Geranium × riversleaianum 'Russell Prichard') and little violas – the old-fashioned heart's ease, a prolific seeder – mingle without damaging one another's growth.*

Some annuals, or flowers that may be treated as annuals, are self-perpetuating seeders and look appropriate in natural flower beds. Cultivation of the tall grey-leaved opium poppy (*Papaver somniferum*) is discouraged in the United States and is illegal in public gardens, but I love this plant with its crowded heads of folded white, pink or red petals and encourage it to establish itself as a permanent annual feature; allow the best forms to seed and pull out the least interesting. The catchfly (*Silene armeria*) has oval grey-green leaves and bright rose-pink flower-heads in mid- to late summer and will seed in sunny spots at the front of borders. Venus's navelwort (*Omphalodes linifolia*), with its lance-shaped silvery leaves and whitish flowers in summer, and the tiny ground-hugging knotweed *Persicaria capitata*, with pale pink flower mop-heads, enjoy spilling out on to hot paving or growing between stones.

A display bed of annuals including corn cockles, clary, poppies, marigolds, cornflowers and love-in-a-mist demonstrates the intense effects possible if the flowers have no competition. To achieve this apparently natural profusion, the ground must be cleared each season to prevent coarse grasses and perennial weeds creeping in to weaken flowering potential.

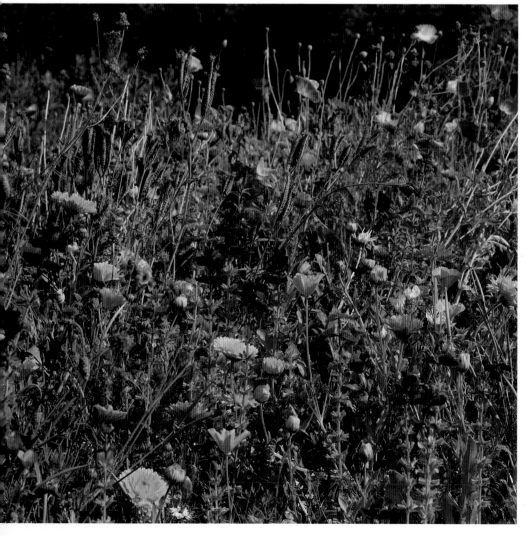

Some tobacco plants such as *Nicotiana sylvestris* seed *in situ* after flowering. Others, such as the very tall and almost woody *N. glauca*, seldom appear spontaneously in the temperate climate of the British Isles; in hotter regions such as California, though, this species seeds freely and has become a roadside weed.

Many annuals are climbers, twining through small trees and shrubs that have flowered earlier in the season and flinging themselves over adjacent plants to give an even more pronounced natural feel. Self-seeding canary creeper (*Tropaeolum peregrinum*) and Chilean glory flowers (*Eccremocarpus scaber*) may well swamp other less vigorous neighbours. Growing up to 3m/10ft in a season, the latter is a perennial in warm climates, and a self-seeding annual in colder regions.

THE MEADOW GARDEN

Meadow gardening is of two kinds: the permanent meadow, of mixed bulbs, annuals, biennials and perennials that are able to survive competition among grasses; and the annual flowering meadow, which is made anew each year in freshly cultivated soil. The permanent meadow, which is never cultivated again once it has been established, may reflect nature at its very simplest, as in the wild flower garden; bluebells and primroses colonize grassy slopes in deciduous woodland, a sea of lesser celandine with fritillaries and leucojums grow in English water meadows in Oxfordshire, and ox-eye daisies flourish on steep banks.

The annual flower meadow, on the other hand, may reach an intensity of dappled colour realized only by alpines in natural meadows when, as the snow recedes from grasslands in spring and early summer, they are in their full flush of bloom. On the California hills native flowers, sheets of annual golden eschscholzias and blue-flowered lupins, bloom after the first spring rains.

But the meadow garden need not be restricted to native regional flora: Flanders poppies, *Agrostemma githago*, *Rudbeckia hirta*, annual phlox and violas create a riot of kaleidoscopic colour. American and British gardeners, with such different native flora, interpret the term meadow gardening in different ways. British native meadows may be a bit dull; a mixture of native and exotic plants will much improve the interest. In North America a gardener can more easily afford to be a native flower freak since he has a greater repertoire of splendid flora on which to draw.

In Suffolk Country Park an annual meadow garden is on a grand scale. Colourful field poppies, cornflowers, corn cockles and daisies mingle against a green background to conjure the image of a rich medieval tapestry or a 'flowery mead'. Although some plants such as the poppies will self-seed, this wealth of colour will not return each year unless the ground is rotovated and resown with a mixture of desirable flower seeds.

Essentially, meadow gardening implies gardening that is done in grass. Much of the success of this sort of gardening depends on creating and maintaining the conditions in which meadow plants will thrive and spread. Meadow gardening does not have to be on a large scale or be part of a larger layout. Meadows may be intimate pockets of planting right against the house or in the front garden. A meadow, sharply delineated by mown grass pathways or other edgings, may seem to take the place of a perennial or mixed border as part of the inner flower garden.

Whether started from scratch or made on a patch of uncut lawn or rough part of the garden, meadows need a foundation crop of various grasses. Mixed with them, hardy flowers, including bulbs, perennials, biennials and annuals are encouraged to naturalize and spread. Their greatest competitors are the vigorous grasses, which gradually tend to push out some of the flowers. Meadows with native or a mixture of native and exotic hardy flowers are easiest to establish in poor soil; Sussex downlands are rich in native flora. In rich soils, grasses, thistles and other hedgerow weeds, including Queen Anne's lace, will usually get the upper hand and most of the flowers will disappear over a period of years. For this reason, ideal as they may seem for the purpose, kitchen gardens, fertilized over decades, are not suitable sites for meadow gardens; nor are old borders and beds, abandoned for economy, or areas of mown lawn where grasses, tightly cut each week in the past, have needed heavy feeding to promote growth.

Meadows may be made by gradually adding bulbs and herbaceous plants to an existing orchard or any rough grass area, the poorer the better; an appropriate mowing timetable using machines with adjustable blades will allow plants to develop leaves and flowering stems and also allow time for seeding. Alternatively, meadows may be established in fresh ground that has been cleaned and rotovated; a grass and flower seed mix, chosen for the soil type and climate, includes perennials, biennials and annuals. Bulbs and established pot-grown plants may be added; planted out individually, they will help to speed up effects but are only feasible for an area of modest size.

Unfortunately, some desirable plants, as well as unwanted weeds, are natural thugs and if left alone will overrun less pushy neighbours, so – however relaxed the garden style – it will be necessary to restrain some plants and encourage others. Grasses, ornamental cow parsley, thistles, nettles, bindweed and brambles, which are colonizers in outer meadows and woods, are popular with many conservationists as part of local ecology (butterflies need nettles to survive). However, in common with undesirable aliens such as ground-elder (which was introduced to Britain to be eaten as salad by the Romans), they love the same conditions as many garden plants, particularly the sites in which bare soil has been improved by cultivation. Such plants need to be controlled.

Both native plants and escaped foreigners can take over when provided with conditions that suit them. In English meadows, strong-growing grasses and even primroses may push out colonies of snakeshead fritillaries, native narcissi, cranesbill geraniums and cowslips as effectively as the farmers' chemical sprays. By watersides, sedges and meadowsweets may be overrun by imported giant heracleums (*Heracleum mantegazzianum*). In North America the European purple loosestrife (*Lythrum salicaria*) is strangling native skunk cabbages (*Lysichiton americanus*) and blocking waterways; in the southern states the kudzu vine (*Pueraria lobata*) is killing native trees and shrubs with its tangled grasp.

The kinds of flowers selected will depend on whether the meadow is in an open sunlit area or in partial shade, as well as on the type of soil. Some meadows are designed to put on a display all through the summer; others for a shorter spring show.

Bulbs such as aconites, snowdrops, crocus, scillas, snakeshead fritillaries, tulips and anemones may be naturalized in grass that is cut quite short during the previous autumn and returned to lawn as soon as possible after the spring flush of flowers; the area may be mown within about six weeks of flowering. Meadows for early and midsummer performance may be brightened with native grassland species – white ox-eye daisies, blue bachelor's buttons, poppies and cranesbill geraniums. In England native orchids, flowering in midsummer, will seed by late summer, allowing the meadow to be cut before having its second fling with colchicums, autumn-flowering crocus and sternbergias in early autumn.

In North America, where there are native flowering plants suitable for every possible meadow environment in different climatic regions, schemes are especially inspirational and wide-ranging. In the north-east a late-season perennial meadow is truly labour saving:

At Great Dixter a starry mass of white-flowered ox-eye daisies and yellow dandelion-like hawkbit grows in the rough grass bordering a mown path. In a sense the area of longer grass is playing the role of a bed in which different flowers perform through spring and early summer. At Dixter seeds have to ripen and fall before the grass is cut in late summer. Meadow gardening is not as simple as it sounds: its success depends on an understanding of all the plants' requirements as well as on choosing a suitable site.

native butterfly weed, eupatoriums, heleniums and heliopsis, purple coneflowers, Michaelmas daisies, golden rods, yarrow and coreopsis glow with waist-high tangled colour among non-invasive grasses; a few naturalized aliens such as day-lilies, teasels and lythrums increase the range. In shadier sites native aquilegias, *Geranium maculatum*, false indigo, claytonias, monardas, dwarf *Iris cristata* and woodland-type Michaelmas daisies grow at different heights.

In the wetter Pacific north-west, where conditions more closely resemble those in the British Isles, established meadows are always threatened by invading perennial grasses and thistles, and acid-loving plants multiply in woodlands and by roadsides. In the Mid-western prairies, where winters are very cold and summers very hot, meadow gardening has assumed a more serious conservation aspect: restored prairie areas (the region's natural habitat now almost wholly destroyed by agriculture) represent a natural plant community in which alien plants may too easily upset nature's balance. Even in controlled garden meadows, plants should be restricted to the innumerable native prairie flowers and grasses as exotics spread too easily.

WATERSIDE GARDENING

Moist places in the flower garden, the edges of streams and ponds, and their calm water surfaces, are all ideal spots for natural flower gardening. For damp spots in the inner flower garden there are spreading clumps of plants that thrive in moisture-retentive soil, such as astilbes, cimicifugas, *Euphorbia griffithii*, filipendulas, hostas, some lobelias, suckering *Lysimachia clethroides*, and ligularias with beautiful heart-shaped leaves and orange flowers. Large-leaved rheums and rodgersias are suitable if the scale is right. As well as their attractive flowers in season, all have interesting foliage through the summer months. The round- or broad-leaved plants can be set alongside those with contrasting spikes such as *Lobelia cardinalis* or the sword-like leaves of irises: yellow flag iris *(I. pseudacorus)* grows in any soil; Japanese *I. ensata* (syn. *I. kaempferi*) and *I. laevigata* need acid soil.

Ponds with natural contours can be edged with groups of plants, the natural effect enhanced by leaving part of the bank clear and encouraging drifts to spread companionably, rather than using single specimens.

The gently sloping banks of ponds and streams, too, provide perfect sites for drifts of hardy flowering plants. Choose spring- and summer-flowering primulas, bog irises, purple loosestrife, rodgersias, *Lysimachia punctata*, peltiphyllums, ostrich plume (*Matteuccia struthiopteris*) and royal ferns (*Osmunda regalis*), marsh marigolds (*Caltha palustris*) and yellow, white or ivory globe flowers (forms of *Trollius*), as well as hostas, astilbes and meadowsweet.

Acorus calamus, with fragrant foliage, bog arums, and various sedges and rushes actually grow in shallow water around the edge. The so-called hardy arum (*Zantedeschia aethiopica*) cannot withstand frozen water around its roots, but will survive low temperatures if the crowns are safely below water level. If winters are not too cold, *Gunnera manicata* from Brazil, with giant bristly, deeply lobed leaves, is a magnificent waterside plant; flowers are conical spikes of dull green followed by orange-brown seed-pods; at the end of the summer season, bend their dying leaves over the crowns to provide frost protection.

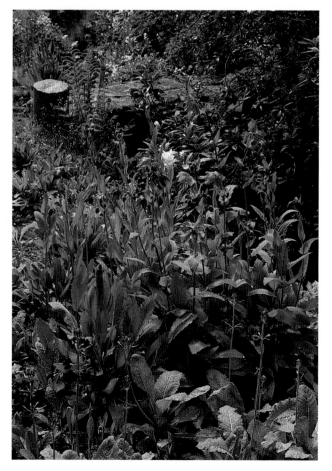

At Kildrummy in Scotland the conditions of acid soil and high atmospheric humidity suit both Himalayan poppies and Asiatic primulas which flourish as they would in their native habitats. Once established, these Robinsonian drifts of plants should be self-perpetuating, but a fine balance is required between providing the moist but not waterlogged soil necessary for meconopsis species and keeping conditions damp enough for the primulas, which do best in more moisture-retentive soils.

Aquatics – plants such as waterlilies that are physiologically adapted to live in soils without oxygen – thrive at various levels in shallow or deeper water. They cannot be grown successfully in swiftly moving streams or where there are changes of current, but lying on the still surface of ponds they further enhance the informal effects of the natural garden and bring nature into formal layouts. In summer their leaves and flowers break up patterns of clear reflecting water, and their spreading horizontal shapes make calm contrast with the fussier silhouettes of neighbouring plants. They only flower satisfactorily in sunlight, but their shining leaves give an exotic tropical air to patches of water in deep shade.

In the Fountain Garden at Tintinhull where the planting is predominantly white the American *Nymphaea odorata* with pointed white petals and greeny-purple sepals flourishes in the shallow water. In the Pool Garden where the water is deeper, *N.* 'Marliacea Rosea', *N.* 'James Brydon' and *N.* 'Escarboucle' bear red and crimson flowers that tone with the hot colours in an adjacent border.

To maximize the naturalistic effects of water features, choose plants that require the same soil type as found in the rest of the garden – unless the pond is in a separate area and can be visually isolated. Plants with quite different requirements and unsuited to an environment often produce a jarring note. Although it is possible to create entirely artificial conditions and to meet plants' different soil and drainage requirements, in practice it is quite difficult to isolate growing areas from the natural environment in any permanent way; water soon leaches through and 'reconverts' the area to its natural conditions.

A water or bog garden will deteriorate more rapidly than almost any other part of the garden. All garden schemes need constant adjustment to make sure that the more vigorous plants do not monopolize space – or that there are no unwanted intruders – but the lush conditions at the water's edge make vigilance particularly important. Even aquatics may spread and take over all the water surface of a pond, leaving no space for sky or trees to be reflected; ideally at least a third of the water surface should be kept clear of spreading leaves. Most of these summer-growing plants are rapid colonizers and have to be divided every few years.

It is not always easy to maintain a clear water surface, especially in a water feature situated in full sun.

LEFT By the water's edge at Heslington Manor in York a candelabra primula (Primula 'Inverewe') grows among grassy-leaved Acorus calamus 'Variegatus'. Behind, waterlilies float on the still surface of the lake. At water margins, as in all natural gardening, there is a constant need to adjust finely tuned planting proportions as some plants increase and spread more quickly than others.

ABOVE In the bog garden at Saling Hall in Essex, pale hosta flowers and tall yellow flower-spikes of Ligularia przewalskii rise from among the elegant tracery of fern foliage and contrasting large-leaved darmeras. All of these plants flourish in good moisture-retentive soil. An ornamental pot provides just the right focus to the lush jungle effects of the planting.

Vast amounts of algae develop quickly and turn clean reflecting water into a green soup. The quick-growing summer-flowerers. – waterlilies, water hyacinths and lotus (*Nelumbo*) – are all oxygenators that play a part in keeping water surfaces clear. Most ponds in full sun will also need further oxygenating plants such as Canadian pondweed (*Elodea canadensis*), that live below water and compete fiercely with the unsightly algae for carbon dioxide.

NATURAL ROCK GARDENS

Windswept alpine slopes in Switzerland and crags and peaks in the Rocky Mountains are the natural homes of countless garden plants. Their special features of soil and climate, however, are not easy to reproduce in an ordinary garden. Many alpine specialists abandon the naturalistic attempt and instead grow their plants in greenhouses where conditions may be totally controlled, or construct raised beds with specially prepared soils in sun and in shade.

The great alpine gardener Reginald Farrer had outcrops of local limestone in his garden at Ingleborough, Yorkshire, where he could satisfy the conditions needed for his precious mountain plants. Many of the grand Edwardian gardens had rockery areas built with limestone slabs brought especially from the Lake District. This is hardly practical or appropriate today.

Although rock gardens are ideal adjuncts to the flower garden, adding new possibilities to the range of plants that may be grown, it is not easy to create a natural-looking rock garden area, or to site it next to other features in the garden. When grown in gardens true alpines, usually snow-covered in winter in their native mountain habitats, need excellent drainage so that their crowns remain dry in winter, as well as deep pockets of soil so that their questing roots can seek moisture during growing periods. They do not require rich feeding. A rock garden, well designed to achieve natural effects, is most often successful if the plant range is limited. Grit-covered sloping screes on an open site with specially prepared drainage, rather than complicated arrangements of rocks, often provide suitable and visually acceptable growing areas. Mediterranean-type plants, with aromatic and silvery leaves and fragrant flowers, after suitable adjustments for soil preferences, will also thrive in these beds, enjoying conditions of heat and drainage similar to their native lands.

Sun and good drainage also suit bulbs from South Africa, shrubs and perennials from California and Chile and some plants from low latitudes in Australia that will survive cold winter temperatures. At Blake House in California, with a view across the bay to the Golden Gates, a sun-facing rocky outcrop has become the home of Mediterranean cistus, Australian melaleucas, New Zealand meterosderos, South African bulbs and native California sun-lovers that naturalize freely and give a wonderful unplanned air to the garden. In drier zones in California, sloping gardens are planted with succulents, which store moisture: agaves, cacti, sedums and sempervivums all thrive, and their glaucous leaves fit naturally into the landscape.

In most natural gardens, however, rock garden areas are best planted simply, with quite ordinary cascading sun-lovers such as mossy phlox, candytuft, cottage-garden pinks, diascias, rosemaries and many silver-leaved plants that will grow between prostrate junipers, ceanothus and brooms. On the shady side of a slope ferns and moss, bloodroots, tiarellas, *Campanula latifolia*, epimediums, roast-beef iris (*Iris foetidissima*), Solomon's seal and grasses such as the tufted luzula will thrive among shrubs such as arbutus that are tolerant of dry soil and shade.

Slopes that provide essential drainage without introducing the harsh lines of retaining walls or raised beds obviously best capture the requisite spirit of relaxed informality, but, even on flat ground, scree-beds may be specially prepared to ensure that water drains away. Plants in ill-prepared beds are far more likely to be killed by water freezing around their crowns than by low temperatures. Many plants from higher altitudes will also survive such conditions if protected from excessive moisture in winter by cloches.

In plantswoman Margaret Charlton's garden north of Vancouver, British Columbia, rough stone walls and terraces maximize the potential of a steep south-facing site and create 'rock garden' conditions that suit a wide range of native and exotic plants. In the foreground are flower-heads of Erysimum 'Bowles' Mauve', Iris sibirica *and* Persicaria affinis 'Dimity'. *Behind, yellow doronicum mingles with the spiky foliage of* Crocosmia 'Lucifer', *and leafy rosettes of* Barbarea vulgaris variegata *set off sedums, alyssum, catmint, phygelius and penstemons.*

A NEW ENGLAND GARDEN

Catherine Hull's rock and woodland garden to the north of Boston is outstanding in its combination of superb plantsmanship with delicacy and taste. The ground falls steeply below the house to provide a naturally varied terrain and in the 1970s the landscape designer Fletcher Steele constructed a pool and pergola, giving the garden a focus around which Mrs Hull has arranged her planting. Natives and exotics grow happily in association in just the way William Robinson recommended in *The Wild Garden*. The rockery – often a tricky subject in garden design – is made with natural stone to look as if it has always existed, and drifts of little woodland plants glimpsed under native trees have the same effect of permanence. All the plants, including many quite fussy alpines, are given conditions in which they thrive.

ABOVE *The foliage of a clump of Solomon's seal, also known as David's harp, provides a distinctive texture in the dappled woodland shade and clothes the stark base of a tree trunk. The plant's graceful lines are particularly attractive in this variegated form, Polygonatum odoratum 'Variegatum', the white leaf-margins clearly visible in the shaded sites in which it flourishes.*

LEFT *In early summer white-flowered dodecatheon, native to North America, thrives in pockets of soil on a rocky outcrop, giving a restrained picture in light shade. To create the best effects Mrs Hull uses simple drifts of one plant type only, rather than 'dotting' plants about more restlessly. Such simple garden schemes disguise great skill and plantsmanship.*

LEFT Mrs Hull uses a low-growing columbine (Aquilegia flabellata pumila) to make a little drift of sophisticated flower colour in the rock garden area. From Japan, this columbine falls into William Robinson's 'exotic' category, but looks perfectly in keeping with the spirit of the site. Planting pockets amid well-placed rocks provide natural-looking frames to set off such small-scale plant treasures.

ABOVE Native American plants such as the little woodland Phlox divaricata spread in drifts in areas where some sunlight penetrates, and biennial Lunaria annua self-seeds to naturalize companionably. Constantly changing light filtering through the tree canopy enhances the natural planting effects. The limited colour range of this flowery mass with its delicate tints and shades sustains the simple mood.

A GARDEN IN HOLLAND

Mrs Goossenaert's garden in the south of Holland is hidden and sheltered from the road by evergreens, so that the areas that open out around the house as you approach along a narrow drive come as a surprise that turns to enchantment as a wealth of plant pictures gradually reveal themselves.

Many good plants establish a strong foundation for gentle naturalistic schemes that seem to flow between one part of the site and another. Each garden view is framed by taller trees and shrubs to make a picture, while at a lower level the planting style is more relaxed and seemingly unplanned. The use of height to break up the space into different areas disguises the extent of the garden, and the resulting air of mystery adds to the feeling of unstudied organization. This sort of gardening –

a mixture of sophisticated planning and a spirit of *laissez-faire* – is the most difficult of all to carry out successfully. It calls for a sure sense of design, well in evidence here, and Mrs Goossenaert also understands the needs of individual plants, juxtaposing those that need sun and good drainage, and accommodating those that enjoy shade. Occasionally more formal elements and intimate or restful areas help to give the garden coherence and provide an important degree of contrast.

Often limited in size by natural topography, Dutch gardens tend to excel in plant association pictures rather than grand effects: when space is restricted, it is essential to be selective, using only the best available plants to create stunning seasonal colour compositions. Mrs Goossenaert deploys this tradition of plantsmanship to equally good effect in her not-so-small garden.

ABOVE *A white-flowered clematis* (Clematis 'Moonlight') *clambers up through a rose into the light to contribute its flowers in season. Intertwined climbers above head height help to make the garden seem relaxed and jungle-like; in reality even these simple effects require considerable manipulation and expert guidance. Plants growing together must enjoy the same conditions, in this case rich feeding and sunlight.*

LEFT *A graceful silver-leaved bush of* Buddleja alternifolia 'Argentea' *is planted in a sea of silver-leaved* Stachys byzantina *to give a wonderful effect, further enhanced in summer when the branches of the buddleja are wreathed with fragrant lilac flowers. It is these touches of brilliance in plant association which distinguish this garden from the run-of-the-mill.*

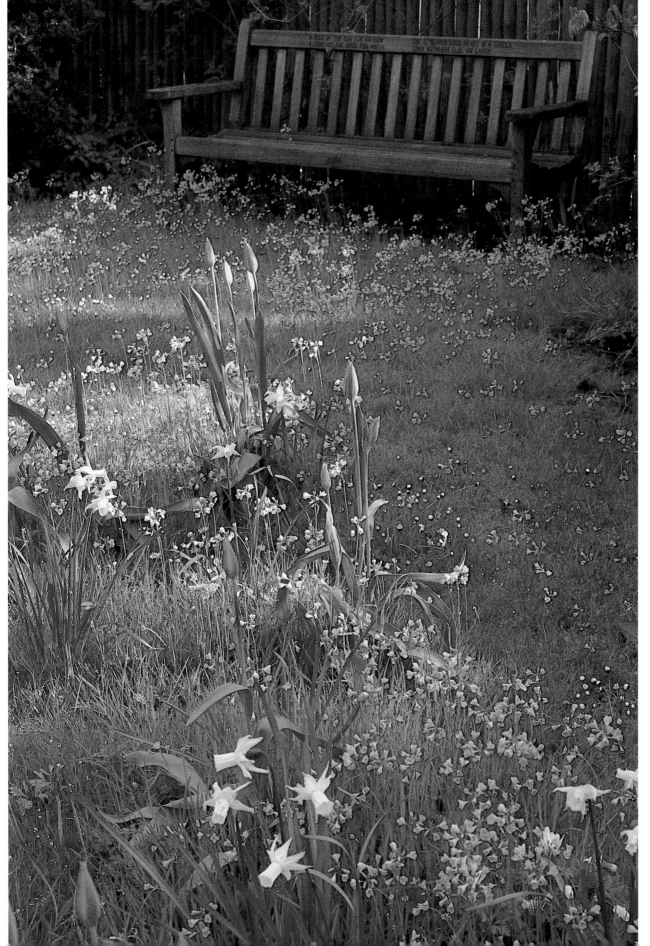

An inviting seat in a spring meadow in the Goossenaert garden. In the grass cuckoo flower or lady's smock (Cardamine pratensis) flowers with the early daffodils, in this case Narcissus 'Dove Wings', and tulips to make a charming scene. This sort of 'wild' gardening is not as easy as it seems; the cuckoo flower should be allowed to set seed and the leaves of the daffodils to wither before the grass is cut. Most of the highly bred tulips will continue to flower when naturalized in grass for many years, their flowers gradually getting smaller and more 'natural'-looking than when grown in specially prepared compost in ornamental pots or beds.

LEFT *In spring the flowers of* Clematis montana rubens *appear when the great* Wisteria sinensis *is also in full bloom. In native habitats climbing and twining plants grow upwards towards the light, clinging to each other to gain support. Both vigorous and hardy (although wisteria flower buds may be damaged by a late frost), wisteria and clematis can be judiciously trimmed after flowering to keep their relative proportions in a garden scheme.*

BELOW LEFT *Dark ivies, leaves of* Hosta sieboldiana *and flowering hydrangea make a restrained autumn picture in which leaf association is as important as the more fleeting flower effects. This garden is full of* such carefully managed scenes, each isolated to give delight and surprise as you make a garden tour.

BELOW *Another part of the garden in late summer where flowers dominate the scene. Stately plume poppies* (Macleaya × kewensis) *and a Rugosa rose with the small-flowered* Clematis viticella *'Purpurea Plena Elegans' growing through it perform above the glaucous leaves of* Hosta sieboldiana. *Using plants with fine foliage in a mixed border gives satisfactory effects all through the season. From spring to autumn the leaves of both plume poppies and hostas act as a foil to all neighbouring flowers.*

LEFT *In a summer border backed by a weeping silver pear (Pyrus salicifolia 'Pendula'), white spikes of* Lysimachia ephemerum *rise behind an exuberant mass of mallow, phlox, campanula and anthemis. Although these effects look easy and relaxed, in practice a border planting like this needs constant grooming to maintain such a balanced picture.*

BELOW *In an intimate corner a more formal note is struck with trimmed box shapes grown in pots to sit on paving. Silver-leaved cotton lavender sets off the more solid greens. The hardy deciduous* Ceanothus × delileanus *'Gloire de Versailles' flowers in late summer.*

A GARDEN IN VERMONT

In essence a 'natural' garden reveals its secrets by degrees; the element of surprise is strong. Unlike a formal garden with a prescribed pattern, or even a border composition viewed across a lawn, the more natural scheme is planned to beckon and entice.

This garden is in the southern Vermont countryside. Although they have split the garden into different 'rooms' each with a distinct scheme, Wayne Winterrowd and Joe Eck have kept planting schemes simple. Trees and shrub shapes dictate the spirit of the garden; they frame the sky overhead and make canopies below which flowers spread in drifts in the summer season. All this is not achieved without a lot of trouble; it is a tribute to the owners' skills that winter protection with evergreen brush makes it possible to grow a wide range of plants beyond their own zone 4 without marring the feeling of spontaneity.

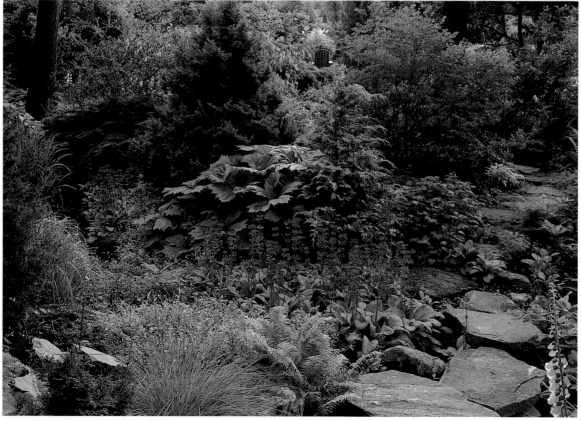

ABOVE *Stepping stones by the stream bed lead to the focal point,* Robinia pseudoacacia 'Frisia' – *described by Wayne Winterrowd as 'the colour of fresh butter all summer'. In the foreground sparkling blue* Meconopsis betonicifolia *contrasts with variegated glyceria leaves and* Primula japonica *'Postford White'.*

LEFT *Moving from shadow into sunlight in the stream garden, pyramidal* Chamaecyparis 'Boulevard' *and bronze-tinted* Rodgersia aesculifolia *provide a background to a drift of pink-flowered candelabra primulas* (Primula japonica) *and blue water forget-me-nots. In this garden statements are made with foliage and the weaving patterns of flowers add their seasonal effects.*

BELOW *Beds surrounding a lawn laid out on three levels with retaining walls built of fieldstone from the site are planted to flower through spring, summer and autumn. The scheme maintains a sense of lightly jumbled informality, with well-nurtured perennials growing in free luxuriance. Peonies, Siberian and bearded iris, hardy border geraniums, day-lilies, phlox, platycodon and asters secure a succession of bloom. On the stone walls scented pinks enjoy the sun and free drainage.*

RIGHT *Self-seeded foxgloves are lit up by sunlight in a clearing. True Robinsonian planting depends on encouraging plants to establish themselves so as to appear natural rather than guided by artifice. For this, plant expertise is as important as an eye for composition. Throughout this garden pines and junipers establish an evergreen framework which gives a strong feeling of unity to disparate planting themes, each of which is appropriate to its situation.*

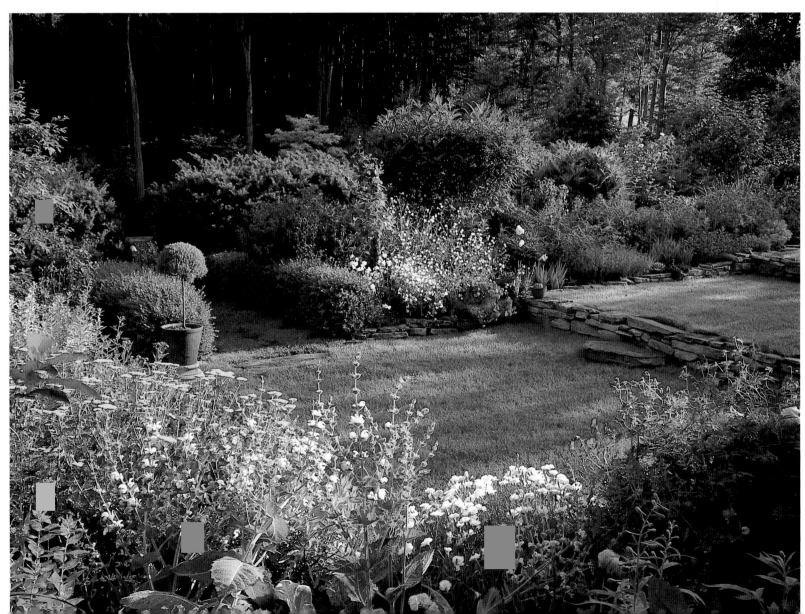

ON THE FRENCH RIVIERA

Some of the most beautiful gardens in the South of France were made between the two World Wars and their terraces and elegant steps reflect the leisured life of those days. Plants here grow only during the winter, as the almost rainless summers are too hot and dry. Silver-leaved plants, with small hairs protecting them from the sun's blast, and those with aromatic foliage containing protective oils flourish best – both native *garrigue* or *maquis* plants and exotics from similar habitats elsewhere in the world.

At Roquebrune Mrs Norah Warre went farther than most of the 'winter gardeners', taking advantage of a favourable microclimate to grow an amazing range of plants from regions with comparable climates, including South African daisies, rare Australians (such as the red-flowered *Templetonia retusa*) and plants from California. Frosts are virtually unknown at Roquebrune; its aspect is protected from icy northern winds, and mature trees now provide further shelter. Lawrence Johnston, who gardened in a colder inland valley at La Serre de la Madone, used to send Mrs Warre newly discovered plants that he could not manage and she grew them successfully in her coastal garden.

Today many of Mrs Warre's rarer plants have gone, but tall Aleppo pines give shade and thriving exotics, naturalized after more than half a century, frame the sea views.

An introduction from Tasmania, Olearia phlogopappa 'Comber's Pink' with mauve daisy-flowers held between silver-green leaves, flourishes beside a pale pink form of Paris marguerite (Argyranthemum 'Mary Wootton'), and spikes of English lavender. Eucalyptus trees, American agave and aloes give a more exotic flavour above sheets of the South African daisy bush (Osteospermum ecklonis), with almost white flowers, blushed blue underneath.

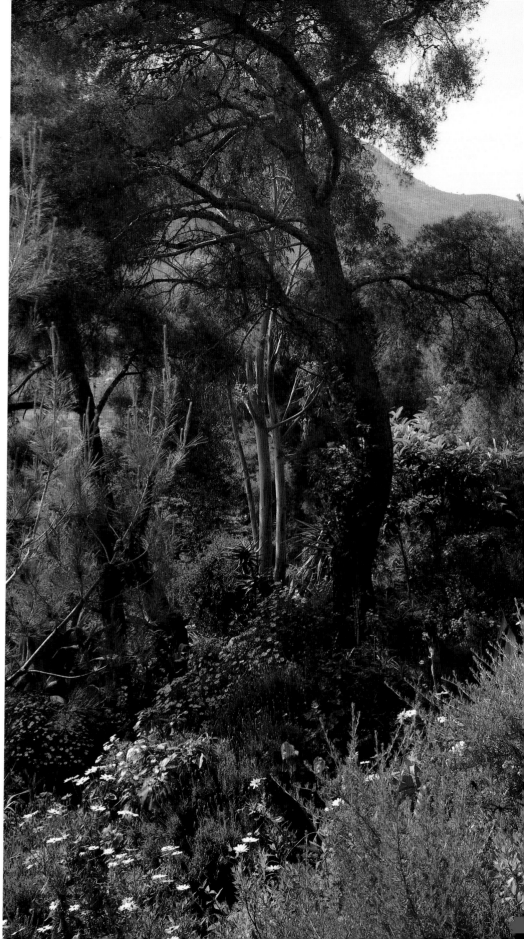

ABOVE *A line of Aleppo pine (Pinus halepensis) along the edge of the terrace gives protection to an orange tree above a drift of German iris. Here exotic plants, revelling in the climate, have become naturalized to give a jungle effect probably far removed from the original owner's intention. Tender roses from Burma and elsewhere in the Far East, such as Rosa gigantea with wide open single white flowers, grow extravagantly to curtain the old terrace walls. The flowering profusion produced by allowing the strongest plants to succeed is possible only in this very favoured microclimate.*

RIGHT *On one of the terraces pines and eucalyptus give some shade from the scorching sun to allow vegetation to cover the old terraces, blurring their more formal lines. Osteospermum ecklonis carpets the ground in a glorious flowering jungle. The garden in maturity, in spite of comparative neglect, still reflects Mrs Warre's plantsman's knowledge; the abundant tender exotics seed and spread today as they would in their native sun-soaked lands.*

THE FLOWER BORDER

Border styles
Schemes and themes

Crathes in Scotland
Stonecrop, New York State
Ashtree Cottage, Wiltshire

The flower border is where plants are brought together not for their individually striking qualities but for the part these plants play as neighbours and companions in an integrated scheme. A border consists of a series of plant groups that link together in a three-dimensional planned picture of jigsaw-like complexity rather than the flat pattern of a knot or parterre. Adjacent flower and leaf colours may be exciting in themselves, but it is for the contribution they make to the whole composition that they are chosen and arranged. Even the most architectural plants, although used to contribute overall design effects, are chosen to enhance the whole scheme and not for any key qualities that draw the eye.

It is the planting style or plant themes rather than the location that define the term border. Originally borders marked the line of lawns, edged paths or ran along the base of walls or hedges. Nowadays the term is used much more loosely; all flower beds in which the planting varies in height and depth and is in different planes are called borders – even an island bed may be a form of border.

BORDER STYLES

Flower borders can be planted with all types of plants. Traditionally they were composed of hardy clump-forming herbaceous perennials with seasonal leaves and flowers at their peak between midsummer and early autumn. Nowadays this sort of scheme is usually supplemented with spring bulbs, early-flowering perennials and drifts of summer annuals for a much more prolonged display. Alternatively a border might be predominantly of shrubs, carefully chosen to flower in succession through the months; the addition of some bulbs and low-growing herbaceous perennials, planted to flower beneath the sweep of deciduous branches, may produce extra seasonal displays.

Borders may also be mixed – that is, planted with a combination of trees and shrubs to give year-round structure and to provide pockets of shade, which are

At Benington Lordship double borders show an eye to design, with repetition of groups of perennials such as clustered spikes of yellow Lysimachia punctata, *magenta* Geranium psilostemon (in the *foreground) and airy greenish lady's mantle making emphatic blocks of colour. Foliage of sword-like iris, arching day-lily and pale-rimmed* Symphytum × uplandicum 'Variegatum' *set off the more brilliant flowers.*

filled in by the seasonal growth of other plants such as upright 'border' perennials in conventional groups as well as shade-tolerant sprawlers and bulbs, biennials and annuals. Many borders in small to medium-sized gardens are of this type.

In practice, the kinds of plants used in each scheme overlap – it is really a matter of personal choice and time available, and there do not have to be too many rules. I prefer to have a few shrubs in a mainly herbaceous border as they give some 'body' and help appearances in winter; they are the permanent feature around which the other plants are replanted and rearranged. All our borders at Tintinhull are of this type. Others find conventional border plant groups, which can all be divided and rearranged as one major spring or autumn task, less demanding.

Whatever plants are used within a border, planting styles can range from the very formal, with repetitive architectural plants and a series of repeated colour patterns flowing through the scheme, to the completely informal or natural style discussed in the previous chapter. Some borders are given a formal outline by crisp box edging; others are backed by horizontal clipped hedges that provide a unifying continuous line of colour to frame the planting in front.

The 'English' herbaceous border

The traditional summer herbaceous border, with its quintessentially 'English' look, developed when beds of hardy perennials, grown as cutting flowers for the great house, were rescued from their Victorian oblivion in the walled kitchen garden and introduced as a focus of attention in the flower garden. The heyday of these great borders was the Edwardian age, when labour was plentiful to groom the plantings. Other garden areas provided interest outside the brief summer weeks when the herbaceous plants were performing.

Herbaceous plants can grow only when ground temperatures are above 5°C/40°F – producing leaves, stems, flowers and seeds in one short season. Hence the temperate climate in England, with no winter or summer extremes, enables a wide range of plants from many variable climates to be grown and borders tend to reach a peak of performance. The flowering periods of many non-native plants are extended by the cool nights and relatively cool days of summer, and seasonal rains maintain growth rates during the hottest part of the year.

ABOVE *In Peter Wooster's Connecticut garden shrubs, grasses, perennials and tender 'fillers-in' texture late summer borders edging trimmed grass paths. Such a personal planting style that disregards the rules dictating plant types can achieve exciting results,* *different plants being used each year to set off the more permanent inhabitants.*

OPPOSITE *In Francis Cabot's garden north of Montreal the growing season is short but strong perennials, often snow-covered in winter, thrive and* *especially enjoy the cool summer nights. Delphiniums, tall Thalictrum flavum glaucum, creamy astilbes and bright yellow ligularias are densely planted so that leaves and flowers interweave.*

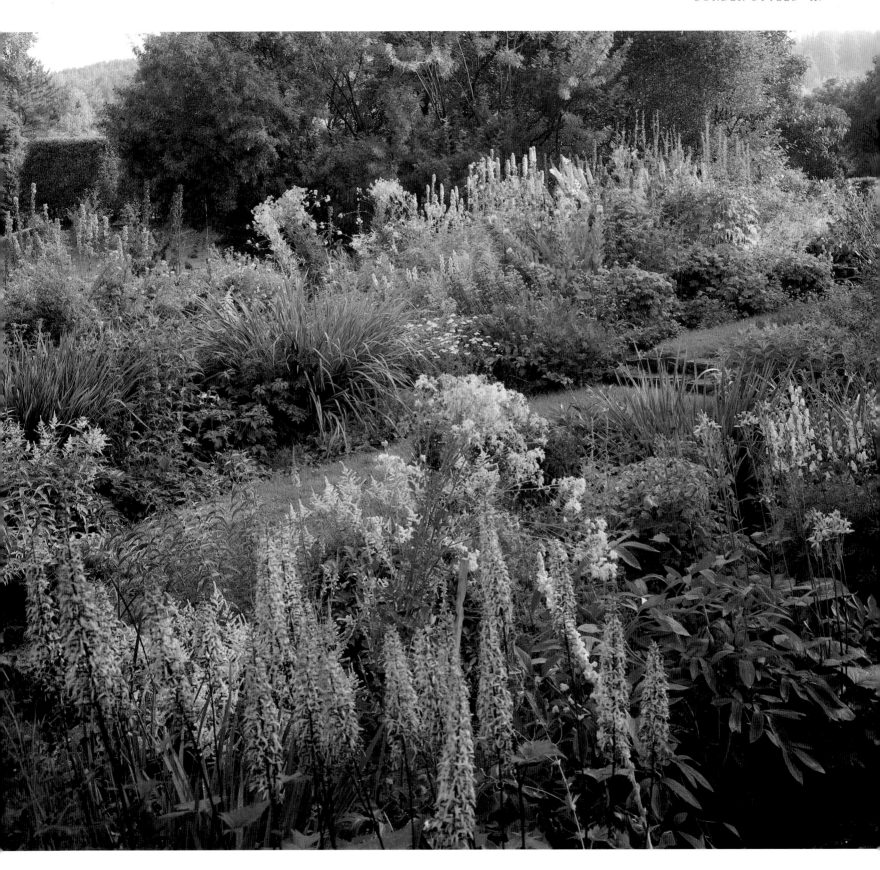

In the garden at Tintinhull we have to get the borders to look good throughout a six-month opening period from April to October. Foliage plants – like sedums and Japanese anemones, which perform from spring to autumn and have beautiful flowers in late summer – become high-priority choices giving the whole scheme an air of luxuriant permanence, and setting off neighbouring clumps of more seasonal flowerers. This border in the Cedar Court is shown at midsummer. It is backed by climbing roses (Rosa 'New Dawn'), scented honeysuckle and intertwining clematis, which flower a little later. In flower are Hybrid Musk roses and clumps of catmint (Nepeta 'Six Hills Giant') – both of which will bloom again in the autumn – and × Heucherella tiarelloides with pink plume-like flowers. A large clump of the white-flowered form of the invasive fireweed or rose-bay willow herb (Epilobium angustifolium album), one of my favourite border perennials, dominates the scheme. The seed of love-in-a-mist (Nigella damascena 'Miss Jekyll') is scattered annually between the rhizomes of bearded irises (now hardly visible) in the narrow frontal border where the globe-shaped Allium christophii also flourishes.

Gardeners all round the world can seek to capture the ethos of the English border style by creating plant associations using perennials that are appropriate to their particular climate and soil. The challenge is greatest in countries with hot summers, especially those where nights are hot. Many herbaceous plants will not tolerate intense heat, especially if it is accompanied by high humidity. For this reason it is more difficult to establish and maintain an English-style border in the south-east of the United States than it is in California. Fortunately, however, many nurseries now give guidelines indicating the tolerance of individual plants to humidity and heat as well as zoning them for frost hardiness. At the other climatic extreme, in cold regions, the main problem is the very short season during which herbaceous plants must make their growth. The fact that the ground may be frozen all winter has compensations, for blankets of snow cover (or thick mulches) protect most border plants from the ill-effects of cold.

Providing winter protection for borderline plants is only one of the tasks of maintaining the herbaceous border. Clump-forming perennials need to be split up and divided every few years or they will cease to flower well. Stems and leaves are cut down each year some time between autumn and the following spring. The soil is mulched and new soft growth is staked and tied in early summer. Gardeners who like their garden to look neat during the winter months will complete the cutting down as soon as leaves fade and stems start to rot; others choose to wait until spring approaches. Those keen on organic methods simply cut down all the stems and leaves, letting them lie where they fall; the new spring shoots push through and in time the dead material rots down to make a mulch.

For the gardener who wants the best possible results in the border at all times, the annual spring or autumn tidy-up is not enough. He or she will spend many hours each week throughout the summer supervising the overall appearance and adjusting the plant relationships within the border. There is always something to do. Fading leaves can be trimmed, dead flower-heads removed, and stalks cut back to encourage other plants to grow over and into the neighbouring flower groups that are already past their peak. Seed is gathered and cuttings taken when appropriate.

In practice the short season of true 'herbaceous' borders is often extended by the welcome addition of bulbs planted in drifts between the perennials. Tulips (small species or the taller hybrids that are treated as annuals), Dutch and English iris, alliums and camassias are at their best in spring and early summer; thereafter their untidy foliage is effectively disguised by the leaves of summer-flowering perennials. Sun-tolerant lilies (and shade-lovers, if planted in the shadow of taller perennial clumps) flower in midsummer, followed by crinums, *Galtonia candicans* and *Gladiolus callianthus* (long known as *Acidanthera bicolor*) in later months. Amaryllis and nerines will only flower well if given a warm site in full sun, ideally at the base of a sheltered wall.

Many annuals are also suitable for growing in companionable clumps and drifts to cover bare soil between groups of perennials. Whereas perennials flower only once in a season (even if over a long period), annuals will bear flowers all summer. In many ways, being temporary and seasonal, they are easier to handle than permanent plants: grown from seed and planted out after the last frosts, they may be fitted in between the existing plants just before flowering time.

In the borders at Jenkyn Place in Hampshire colour planning and the proportions of the plant groupings are superbly and thoughtfully executed. Stone edging frames a beautifully maintained wide border planted with large clumps of traditional hardy perennials. Feathers of creamy Aruncus dioicus *and cloud-like sprays of* Crambe cordifolia *back mounds of* Geranium × magnificum *that flow out over the stone. White and purple forms of* Dictamnus albus *as well as the dark-flowered* Lychnis coronaria *at the front of the border continue the colour theme.*

Borders designed by the late Peter Coats at Buscot Park in Oxfordshire are mixed in content, with small trees, shrubs and perennials contributing to the very successful effect of purple, grey and golden foliage combined with blue-toned and yellow flowers. The blunt-nosed lime-green flowers of Euphorbia characias wulfenii *match the yellows of shrubby* Phlomis fruticosa *in front of dark-leaved* Berberis × ottawensis *'Superba'. 'Blue'-toned* Geranium × magnificum *and catmint spill over the low box hedge.*

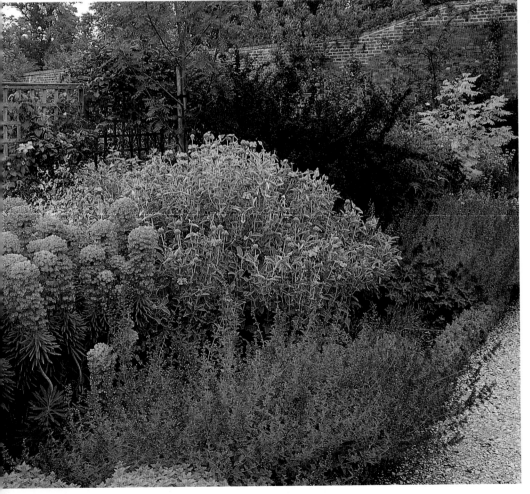

Indeed, annuals can also be effective on their own. Plants chosen especially for their capacity to bloom over a long period without needing their dead-heads removed can be grown from seed and after the initial labour of planting out make a floriferous border that needs relatively little attention. Ageratums, cleomes, godetia, convolvulus, lavatera, nicotiana and salvias can be arranged in groups, the taller towards the back, so that as you walk along the border their colours gradually unfold and blend into each other to create the feel of the traditional herbaceous border in its summer glory.

The shrub border

Composing a flower border using only shrubs calls for a grander time scale as well as a different approach to space. Once planned and established, a shrub border is relatively undemanding to maintain, but there are two important considerations to bear in mind at the outset.

Firstly, these woody plants will take time to reach their full potential. Secondly, since the shrubs will be permanent features, all neighbouring plants chosen must enjoy the same conditions of soil and drainage.

Flower displays are transitory, but shrubs chosen to flower successively will ensure a summer-long performance in the border. Strong architectural plant forms and displays of coloured leaves in season provide year-round interest.

Before planting consider the characteristics of the main plants that set the theme – the natural shape of the shrubs, the foliage colour and texture, seasonal flowering and fruiting performance, and density of growth. (Some woody plants, especially evergreens, are dense and heavy, giving weight to a scheme; others have twiggy growth and pale leaves that bestow an air of lightness.) A balanced border design will include: round-shaped bushes such as evergreen osmanthus and smoke trees; some bushes with branches that fan out from the base, such as Hybrid Musk roses, philadelphus and suckering symphoricarpos; and some that will give definite vertical accents, such as abutilons and variegated buckthorns. Nevertheless, as the border is primarily to be of flowers, it is important to choose good flowering shrubs rather than concentrate too much on foliage textures and shapes. A border scheme should not end up as a Victorian shrubbery.

Consider carefully where to position the shrubs. Plant single specimens so that, on reaching maturity, their branches will just touch those of their neighbours without marring their own graceful outlines. The branches of shrubs planted in groups may interlock, but should not encroach on neighbouring specimens or groups. Creating instant effects by overplanting will give trouble in later years. Planting up a shrub bed is not like planting a forest where alternate trees or lines of trees can be removed at a later date to allow the main specimens (all of similar types) to mature.

Each shrub in a border is an individual with its own growth rate and requirements. When newly established it needs room to breathe and space to put down its roots. Above all, it needs light and adequate moisture. Do not, therefore, surround young shrubs with seasonal annuals or even perennials that have no part in the border's final scheme – tempting though it may be to fill the empty spaces. Unless handled very carefully, such quick-growing infilling plants may all too easily injure the vulnerable young shrubs.

If you have the right sort of acid soil with a low pH and woodland to provide a sheltering canopy, planting low-maintenance azaleas and rhododendrons can be very effective. In this corner of Princess Sturdza's garden in northern France the shrubs – denying light to the soil beneath – are underplanted with shade-tolerant bluebells in a simple scheme. Shallow-rooting shrubs such as these resent attempts to fork over the bed, but appreciate rich top-dressings of organic mulch which help prevent weed germination. These woodland plants look their majestic best grown in appropriate conditions, as they are here, but look ridiculous in smaller borders or open sunlight.

Once established, shrub borders are never dug again unless some of the shrubs have to be removed. A thick organic mulch, applied annually, with the addition of some general fertilizer as growth restarts in spring, will keep the soil fertile and the plants healthy.

All the woody plants in the border need some annual work with pruning shears to ensure a successful performance the next year: dead flowers and flowering shoots must be removed to promote new growth. Shrubs that flower in the spring and early summer generally produce next year's flowering shoots after this year's performance is over and should therefore be pruned immediately. Those that flower towards the end of summer do so on wood produced in the current year and may be pruned back in spring, when frost-damaged shoots are also removed.

RIGHT On a more intimate scale, a shrub border in a town garden depends on shapes and foliage colours more than on flowering seasons. Golden-leaved holly (Ilex × altaclerensis 'Golden King') and Hydrangea macrophylla 'Quadricolor' make effective neighbours in the scheme, but the picture captures a moment when the hydrangea's lace-cap flowers are held on long stems above the variegated leaves and give an extra richness.

The mixed border

A glorious mixture of small trees, shrubs, perennials, biennials, annuals and bulbs arranged as flowering neighbours, the mixed border contains the planting elements of the herbaceous border and the more utilitarian shrub border. However, it is the groups of herbaceous plants that dictate the spirit of the composition, providing firm impressionistic colour patterns, particularly during the summer months. Today the majority of planting schemes are of this type, bringing the natural or cottage-garden style back to the border. No single plant is of major importance for itself: each one is part of the whole scheme.

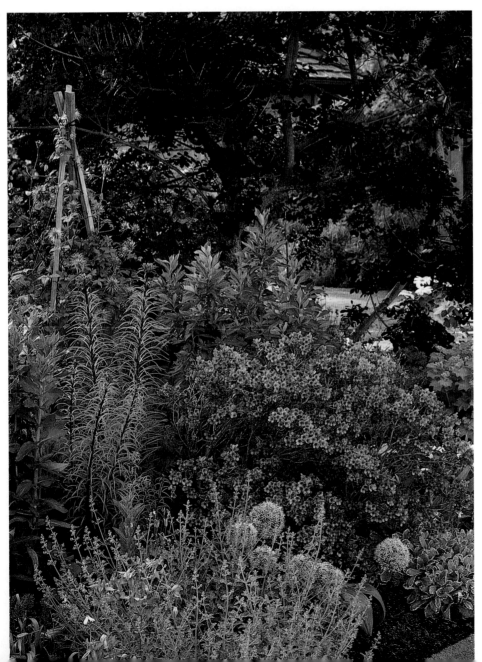

Unlike the shrub or herbaceous border, a lasting blueprint is almost impossible in the mixed border: the relative shapes and proportions change each year and the balance of the composition depends upon the individual's eye rather than on following a rule book. Success also requires a good knowledge of plant needs and behaviour. Over a period of years, if 'soft' material is not divided and replanted, the mixed border can easily turn into something closer to a shrub border, and the impact will gradually be lessened.

Many of the best turn-of-the-century border layouts were of mixed planting. In one of Gertrude Jekyll's borders, for example, woody plants might include a graceful, broad-canopied tree to give overhead protection for spring bulbs and hellebores, while shrubs such as spring-flowering spiraeas and viburnums, autumn hydrangeas and caryopteris, interplanted with drifts of bulbs, extended the season of flowering perennials. Jekyll selected annuals and tender dahlias to enhance permanent planting, sometimes even sinking prepared pots of lilies or similar exotics between more mundane and reliable groups of plants.

The mixed border, with so many different plant elements to consider, is the most complicated border scheme to both plan and maintain. It calls for the skill of the architect in balancing heights and shapes in different planes of planting, as well as the two-dimensional eye of the painter working in one plane. Few gardeners today achieve such amazing results as Gertrude Jekyll and her contemporaries, who had the benefit of skilled assistants in this most labour-intensive form of gardening. Most modern gardeners are better advised to attempt something simpler than the highly orchestrated schemes so dear to the gardeners of the past.

Although perennials set the theme for the mixed border, the small trees and shrubs are put in first. Unlike the shrub border, they should not be planted so that their branches interlock at maturity. They are feature plants, chosen to give an integrated year-round structure to the less sturdy clumps of seasonally growing perennials. If time for gardening is limited, restrict the choice of plants to those that need relatively little attention. Select small trees that cast dappled rather than heavy shade: among those that look good in a border are the very slow growing paperbark maple (*Acer griseum*) and box elder (*A. negundo*, especially its variegated form), dogwoods including *Cornus mas* and

RIGHT *The borders designed by the late Peter Healing at Kemerton are among the most inspiring in England. Although such perfection requires knowledge, skill and lots of hard work as well as a gift for colour arrangement, I think it is worth trying to emulate this achievement. Here a form of Buddleja davidii and a climbing clematis on a tripod frame lower planting of a floriferous Michaelmas daisy, seasonal dahlias, Salvia* farinacea *and verbenas, including the airy V. patagonica.*

OPPOSITE *The border in Susan Riley's garden in Victoria, Vancouver Island, is of mixed planting: shrubs, perennials and bulbs all play major roles in the completion of the scheme. A dark purple-leaved smoke bush (Cotinus coggygria 'Foliis Purpureis') overshadows a pink Rhododendron lepidotum, while lower-growing herbaceous plants and the attractive spherical flowers and handsome leaves of Allium karataviense fill in the foreground. Lilium regale will flower later in the season. This sort of planting is the most visually satisfying: shrub shapes and branches give substance to a scheme while allowing more gently billowing soft-stemmed plants to fill in the detail.*

C. kousa (and of course the American dogwood *C. florida* if it will do well for you – it needs hot summers), laburnums, styrax, halesias, Judas trees, redbud (forms of *Cercis*) and clerodendrums. Among slow-growing shrubs that need little annual cutting back are smoke bush, choisya, the lower-growing Rugosa roses ('Fru Dagmar Hastrup' would be my choice), deutzia and the shrubby potentillas. Mediterranean cistus actually resent being pruned, but are relatively short-lived. In regions with cold climates many shrubs need their unsightly frosted shoots trimmed in spring.

Herbaceous plants should be sturdy enough not to require staking; avoid those that need routine dividing. I avoid labour-intensive delphiniums which need constant attention (rich feeding, staking and protection against slugs) and go for plants such as astrantias, campanulas, eryngiums, eupatoriums, day-lilies, phlox (which do need dividing but never staking), hardy herbaceous geraniums, perennial honesty and catmint.

Choose bulbs and low-growing carpeters that increase naturally without frequent replanting: all the usual scillas, chionodoxas, bluebells and good forms of wood and Apennine anemone for spring; agapanthus, alliums, camassias and lilies for summer display.

To keep the balance of the planting in trim, all borders need some revision in spring or autumn: in the mixed border, where the permanent shrubs create more shade each year, the 'soft' plants will need to be shuffled about more often than in the perennial border, in which there is no competition from woody plants.

In a very broad border with a tall wall or hedge as backdrop, a narrow gravel or paved path towards the back of the planting allows access for maintenance within the main bulk of the border and for any pruning, clipping or training required by backdrop plants. The bed at the foot of a wall can be specially prepared to accommodate the needs of climbing plants and trained shrubs curtaining the man-made surface so that they do not interfere with those of the main scheme. A path also helps to contain the greedy roots of a background hedge as they try to spread into the main planting area and compete for water and nutrients.

LEFT *At Wallington the double borders, viewed from the top of the slope, are a mixture of fading mauves and blues matched with contrasting complementary yellows. Gertrude Jekyll loved this combination. Fortunately there are many suitable hardy plants in these colours to choose from. Here bearded iris, catmint and hound's tongue* (Cynoglossum nervosum) *provide the blues, while clumps of yellow daisy-flowered* Doronicum carpetanum *are eye-catching. The cool colouring gives the illusion of distance, making the borders seem longer than they really are.*

RIGHT *Mauve delphiniums and cranesbills* (Geranium × magnificum), *blue* Nepeta sibirica *'Souvenir d'André Chaudron' and the more startling magenta* Geranium psilostemon, *united by the 'blue' pigment in all the flowers, blend together in one colour harmony in this garden near Heerlen in Holland. All border schemes seem to benefit from some unifying theme such as the repetition of colour blocks or architectural shapes – or, in this case, a unity of tones. The white of the dwarf gypsophila in the foreground picks up the pale silvery variegation in the leaves of the mint* (Mentha suaveolens 'Variegata').

SCHEMES AND THEMES

A border is often glimpsed as a whole from a distance, but is also viewed in detail from close to, and slowly unfolds new incidents of textured colour as it is passed. The series of static plant pictures revealed has not only different nuances from different angles but also shifting permutations as spring, summer, autumn and winter bring changes in appearance and new associations.

A coherent border plan ensures that the whole entity hangs together and works. Most schemes benefit from a unifying theme. This may be provided by the repetitive use of trees, shrubs or perennials chosen for a particular quality of shape or colour. Whether the rhythm is formal or informal, this repeated note turns the whole scheme into an integrated composition.

When making a plan, try to conjure up in three dimensions the colour sequences that unfurl from week to week as different flowers reach their peak then fade. Following the example of Gertrude Jekyll, flower colours may be orchestrated to unfold in different themes based on harmonies or contrasts. As noted earlier, she combined the 'hot' tones of orange, scarlet and crimson in a harmonizing gradation of colours and introduced the cooler colours – blues, greys and pale yellows – in deliberate contrast. At Crathes Castle the main borders, with weaving blues and mauves in earlier summer, become 'warmer' with gold and bronze flower colours as autumn approaches.

Even more important than colour associations is the overall look of the border, the impression of deliberate order. Repeating shapes, colour features and plant groups at least once in any line of vision creates a calming effect; this is particularly valuable in a small garden such as that of Ashtree Cottage, where views of the border are framed by planting that echoes similar themes. Sometimes plants and flower colours are repeated in a studiously regular rhythm to produce formal, mirror-like effects. At other times – like painting a picture – a more free-style composition gives balance and repetition but not exact symmetry, as in Francis Cabot's garden near New York. At Tintinhull we compromise between these two positions. Certain symmetrically placed feature plants hold the border designs together; their choice and disposition depends on a sense of balance. Repeated colour groups aim at stability rather than a mirror-image effect, striving after a naturalistic yet controlled pictorial result.

Successful borders depend not only on making an aesthetically pleasing composition but also on satisfying the plants' growing requirements. Apart from the fact that it will not flourish in the long term, a border scheme will have the wrong 'atmosphere' if adjacent plants do not naturally enjoy similar soil and similar day-to-day feeding and watering.

Mainstays of a classic border, such as phlox, peonies and dahlias need rich feeding. Grey- and silver-leaved plants all require well-drained positions in poor soil in full sun – their silvery appearance is derived from the short hairs that protect the leaves from strong sun rays, enabling the plants to survive long periods of summer drought in their natural habitat. Mediterranean plants such as artemisias, silvery thistles and artichokes will thrive as neighbours.

There are inspiring borders everywhere, magical projects that introduce new plant and colour combinations to lift the heart of the observer. They also

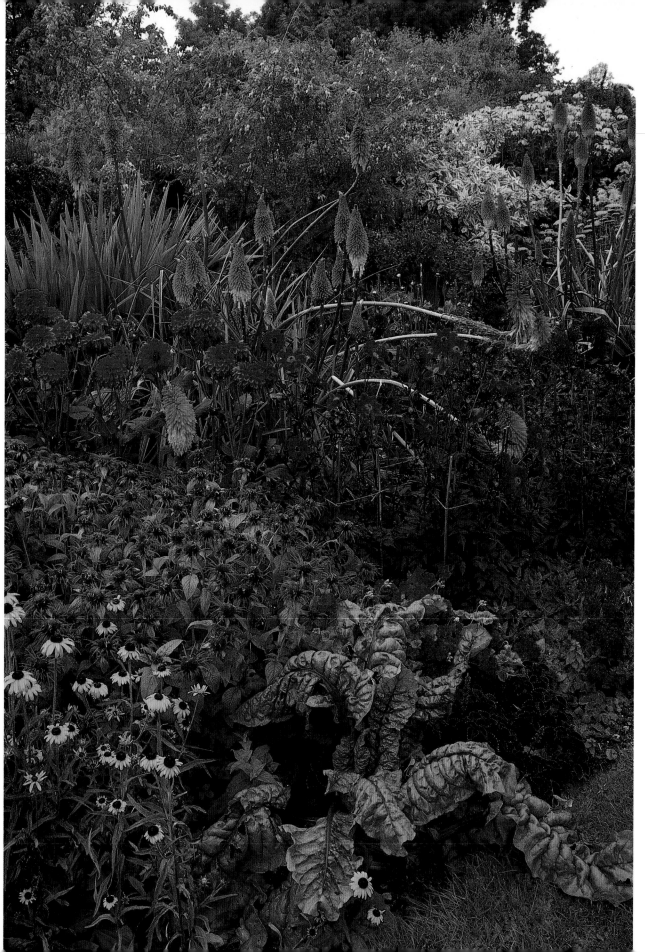

Another border at Kemerton is of 'hot' colours, with flowers of orange, scarlet and yellow matched against red-toned foliage. But the colouring of leaves and flowers gives only part of the picture: textures and shapes of petals and foliage, and even the way they are held, affect the way we see plants as individuals and the roles they can play in planting schemes. In this border red hot pokers, with flower-spikes of tight orange petals grading down to yellow at the base and held on tall stems above rush-like foliage, are a complete contrast to the daisy-flowered semi-double dahlias with their dark bronze-purple leaves and to monardas (Monarda 'Cambridge Scarlet') and rudbeckias in the front of the bed, with wide ray florets around central coloured discs. The red-stemmed crinkled leaves of ruby chard are a striking feature at the edge. I also love the way the graceful arching Rosa moyesii, with its coloured hips, adds an extra dimension at the back of this bed without making too solid a background.

When choosing border companions, the habit and behaviour of each plant has to be considered in detail as well as what you require of the scheme. I prefer the kind of strongly accented heights and depths seen in this Kemerton border to lower, flatter schemes with all the plants growing at one level.

provide models for adaptation. Looking at good borders, especially those in a climatic region similar to the gardener's own, is far more useful than spending hours with graph paper on the detail of the planting.

Planning plant groupings

The artists of the traditional herbaceous border have much to teach gardeners about combining plants to make a beautiful composition on a large scale; many of the visual considerations of deploying flowering plants as neighbours apply even to the more stately pace of shrub borders. But it is with perennials and their bulbous counterparts as supremely unstable building blocks that the glorious effects of herbaceous and mixed borders are achieved.

Apart from possessing soft stems that die down in winter, herbaceous plants have few characteristics in common. Plants such as verbascums and delphiniums soar to head height and more, in contrast to ground-hugging veronicas, creeping mossy phlox and spreading diascias. The flowers are even more varied: peonies and poppies have flat, papery petals that convey strong colour messages. Others – achilleas, eupatoriums and silvery thistles – have tiny airy flowers that form broad, flat flower-heads. The petals of some herbaceous flowers are arranged in a single layer, giving a translucent, ephemeral effect; others are double, providing greater weight and solidity. Astilbe, artemisia and golden rod have feathery flower-heads, while eryngiums and angelicas have spherical umbels.

Although some, such as giant kale or silvery onopordum thistles, are grand enough to stand alone as architectural features, plants are rarely used singly in an herbaceous border; most are planted in groups, as either blocks or triangles. Large municipal borders are often planted in blocks, which makes staking and tying easier but produces a regimented look, destroying all sense of riotous profusion. Triangular shapes are commonly used to plant the garden on paper, but even this method can have an almost too precise military effect. Gertrude Jekyll's preference was for planting in narrow drifts. This means that a number of colours, rather than those only on each side of the group, 'touch' each other, and may be put to great artistic effect.

The size of the groups will depend on the desired effect. If colours are to remain distinct and separate from whatever distance they are viewed, the groups need to be large. If colours are to blend and interweave (except at very close range), the groups should be small. Any groupings, however, must be scaled according to the area of the overall scheme.

The height as well as the potential spread of each group of plants is an important factor in planning the border. Planting with tall groups only at the back and a graduation in heights towards the front can produce a rather unnatural effect. I like to mix the heights in the different planes by creating an arrangement of peaks and valleys which flow through the border. When the tallest plants are at the back to frame foreground planting, smaller plant groups can also grow in their shadow. William Robinson, writing before the end of the nineteenth century, puts the point well:

Do not graduate the plants in height from the front to the back as is generally done, but sometimes let a bold plant come to the edge and . . . let a little carpet of a dwarf plant pass in here and there to the back, so as to give a varied instead of a monotonous surface. Have no patience with bare ground, and cover the border with dwarf plants; do not put them along the front of the border only. Let hepaticas and

The 'border' is defined by a stream in this garden on the Devon coast. Planting a successful scheme is like painting a picture, though plants behave even less predictably than pigments on canvas. Moreover, the palette is limited to those that suit the site; water gardening presents a great challenge as few woody plants are available to give height and substance. Here the composition is dominated by architectural New Zealand flax (Phormium tenax purpureum), with a drift of scarlet candelabra primulas, a scattering of Japanese irises (Iris ensata and I. laevigata) and more primulas in bright painterly colours beneath.

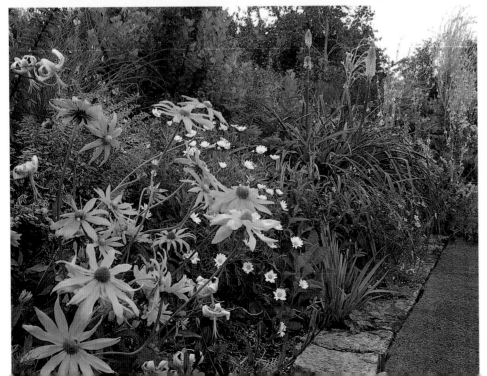

In the pool garden at Tintinhull one border has pale-coloured flowers; the other, across the canal (and also shown on page 71) has red, yellow and cream flowers. Originally designed by Mrs Phyllis Reiss, both today still reflect her vision. They are linked by silvery leaves repeated at intervals along the front of each bed. All the plant groups grow at different rates, so the whole scheme needs constant revision to keep the right proportions of 'spread'. Shrubs and strong-growing perennials tend to grow beyond their allotted space so that there is less and less room for the seasonal planting essential to give the garden the lift it needs, especially towards the end of summer. In general we try to organize a progression of weekly or monthly flowering bursts to peak in different parts of the borders rather than expecting them to be full of colour all through the summer. In quieter moments good foliage plants such as silver eryngiums, miscanthus, sisyrinchiums and variegated symphoricarpos still give interest.

double and other primroses and forget-me-nots, and dwarf phloxes and many similar plants cover the ground among the tall plants . . . at the back as well as the front. Let the little ground plants form broad patches and colonies by themselves occasionally, and let them pass into and under other plants.

As plant groups spread at different rates, parts of a border will need replanning very frequently. Almost as soon as the best possible results have been attained it will be time to do some dividing and reallocating of space. Creating a border is like doing a complicated jigsaw with pieces that are always changing.

Timing the display

Some borders in grand gardens are planned to reach a seasonal peak at a particular time, but in most modest-sized gardens a single border has to look good at all times of the year. This does not mean that the whole bed has to be continually in flower – that would be impossible to achieve. Nor is it easy to try to spread spots of colour through the whole length of a border during the entire season. The best effects are obtained if each part of the border scheme is planned to peak at a particular period, creating a series of progressive seasonal bursts. At these moments flowering plants become stars, like principal actors in a play; at other times, when not in flower, these plants play supporting roles or may even be temporarily off-stage. Managing plants through the gardening season is very much like directing a play through its performance: good timing and synchronization of impact is all-important as both flowers and leaves in turn reach their peak and fade away to make room for new combinations. At any time quieter sections of foliage structure – attractive plant shapes and leaf combinations – make a rich setting for the fleeting scenes played by floral colours.

The importance of herbaceous foliage

The three-month season of peak activity can be extended, and the border's period of beauty lengthened, by choosing flowering plants that have good foliage shape and colour both early and late in the summer. Emphasis is given to contrasts in leaf shape, texture and colour through all the summer months, as well as to the plants' flowering qualities. Sword-like iris leaves, crocosmia, day-lilies, kniphofias and leafy agapanthus contrast with the more rounded shapes of

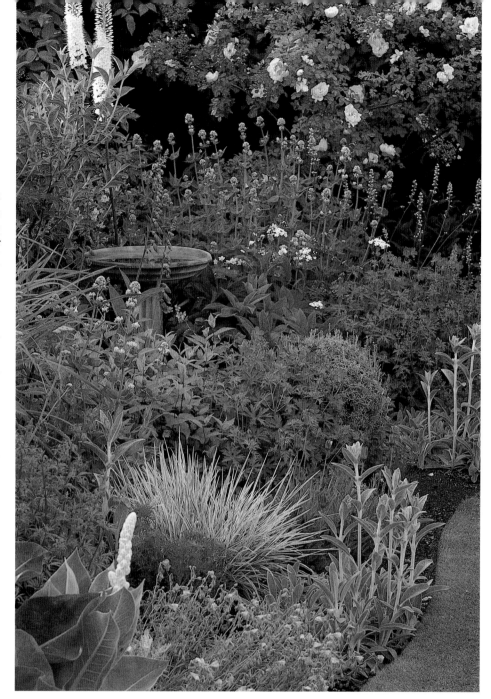

In Susan Riley's garden in Victoria, Vancouver Island, good foliage plants are a high priority for setting off more fleeting seasonal flowers. Silvery Stachys byzantina, verbascum, helianthemum and santolina, the spiky variegated leaves of Phalaris arundinacea picta and a tall grey-leaved buddleja are foundation plants that look good all summer. Behind, soaring spires of Eremurus himalaicus, Rosa 'Nevada' and a drift of white valerian with some blue cranesbills (Geranium 'Johnson's Blue') blend to make a quiet picture with the pink helianthemums and pink-backed floret rays of osteospermum flowers.

alchemilla, hostas, Japanese anemone and elegant *Kirengeshoma palmata*. Smooth, glossy-leaved acanthus are opposed to rough-textured giant kale, tall shimmering grasses rustle next to solid clumps of phlox and Michaelmas daisies.

Plants may be grouped to create harmonies of leaf colour – green, golden, grey, purple and bronze – or may be used in more startling, eye-catching discords. Silvery stachys and artemisias, grey-leaved anaphalis and thalictrums, *Ruta graveolens* 'Jackman's Blue' and spiky glaucous grasses are striking next to the purple-toned leaves of scarlet-flowered lobelias, *Heuchera micrantha* 'Palace Purple' and the spectacular perennial sweet William *Dianthus barbatus* 'Niger'. Leaf colours may extend or contrast with flowering colour themes. Golden and variegated foliage sets off pale and glimmering yellow flowers, glaucous and grey effects make blue flowers dazzling, and purple-leaved shrubs and perennials are a foil to pink, blue and crimson flowers.

The fresh young leaves and shoots of many perennials such as galegas, eryngiums, artemisias and achilleas are beautiful in early summer, and many – including stately grasses – die down gracefully, contributing bronze, buff and yellow tones to the border in late summer and winter. If the stalks and leaves of some perennials, such as alchemilla and cranesbill geraniums, are cut back after flowering, they will produce new mounds of long-lasting foliage; some, such as catmint, will flower again. The leaves of many early-flowering perennials, including euphorbias, hellebores and peonies, are so attractive that they contribute to the border scheme after their flowering season is over, when neighbouring plants are in flower.

Trees and shrubs for structure

A number of shapely evergreen shrubs provide the border with winter structure and, planted at regular intervals to give a definite rhythm, hold the border design together throughout the year. Their shapes and foliage contribute more than their flowers, and they set off the flowers of neighbouring plants. Conifers such as tall junipers, feathery chamaecyparis, Irish yews and, in milder areas, Italian fastigiate cypresses all give this emphasis.

Some shrubs may be pruned into topiary shapes and figures to give a more formal air to a planting scheme. Traditional topiary subjects are evergreen bay, holly, Portugal laurel and yew (both English and Irish – at

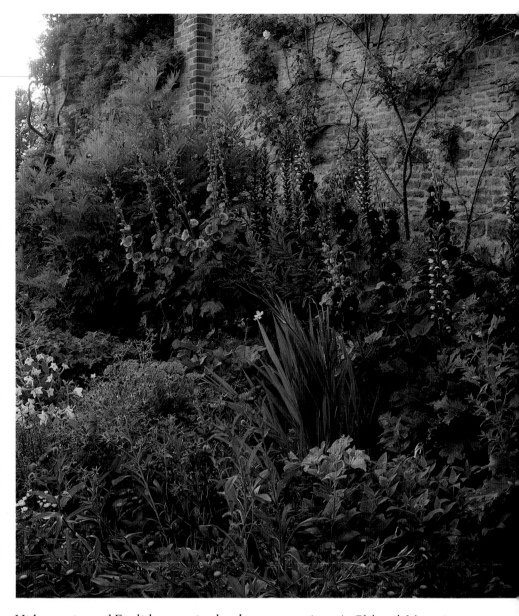

Hidcote trimmed English yews give border structure in the famous Pillar Garden). The neglected phillyrea (especially *Phillyrea angustifolia* and the tree-like *P. latifolia*), pyracantha, *Quercus ilex* and box may also be trimmed into many different outlines. Silver- and grey-leaved shrubs may acquire a formal air by tight clipping – indeed many that grow woody with age benefit from a spring cutting.

Small deciduous trees with green or coloured leaves and a naturally regular outline are also effective design plants. Mop-headed and umbrella-shaped trees are especially useful when space is limited as neighbouring plants can be grown up close to the trunk. Robinias

At Chilworth Manor in Surrey spreading perennials with good foliage, such as glossy-leaved acanthus, provide the best foil to all flower colour; the sword-like green leaves of crocosmia with scarlet flowers are a further contrast. The acanthus bears its own flower-spires of pinkish white next to the gentle tones of assorted hollyhocks.

with pale green foliage (*Robinia pseudoacacia* 'Umbra-culifera') or the golden-leaved form (*R.* 'Frisia') are ideal; the former has a natural globe head and the latter is especially vivid in a dull landscape.

On a smaller scale, silver-leaved willows can be used in the same way. At Tintinhull we grow standard round-headed *Salix helvetica* silhouetted against a yew hedge. Cloud-like smoke trees have a regular shape, but, clothed with branches to the ground, take up more space. Broad-headed thorns (forms of *Crataegus*) and other small ornamental trees such as crab apples and prunus may be included. Those with wide canopies provide pockets of shade for woodland-type plants and

Foliage can really be as important as the more ephemeral and sometimes very fleeting flowers. Here Mrs van Bennekom-Scheffer exploits the different colours, textures and shapes of leaves to the full extent in her garden in Zeeland. Green box, bronze fennel, silver artemisia and stachys and variegated grass give maximum contrast without being overdone. Varying textures including

those of hairy-leaved stachys and smoother wormwoods and grasses reflect light in different ways. The different shapes also give definition, with the dense foliage of the clipped box domes that punctuate the planting making a satisfying foil to the softer and more relaxed outlines of the 'spreaders'.

create pronounced contrasts of light and shadow. Judicious pruning will keep plants within prescribed bounds, although fierce cutting back also stimulates renewed growth.

Shrubs for year-round interest

Many shrubs suitable for the small or inner flower garden blossom in spring; far fewer provide blooms in summer or late summer. In spring, choose from abutilons, chaenomeles, *Choisya ternata* (but be wary of the garish golden-leaved *C. t.* 'Sundance'), corylopsis, cytisus, daphnes, forsythias, magnolias, osmanthus, yellow-flowered *Piptanthus nepalensis*, *Paeonia suffruticosa*, spiraeas and viburnums. For gardens with acid soil, camellias, rhododendrons, pieris and vacciniums may be combined for magnificent, mainly spring, effects, even though they are more suited to woodland scenes.

Summer-flowering border shrubs include both shrub and bush roses, papery-flowered cistus, pink and white deutzias, the dazzling pink-flowered kolkwitzia (*Kolkwitzia amabilis* 'Pink Cloud' is the best), mauve-flowered lavenders, scented philadelphus, potentillas, pyracantha (with berries in autumn), syringa and weigelas. In late summer in most temperate regions (earlier in hot climates) evergreen abelias and arbutus, buddlejas, smoky-blue caryopteris, fuchsias, hydrangeas, hypericums, indigofera, *Itea ilicifolia*, lavateras, perovskias and romneyas all have a high proportion of flower to leaf.

Silver- and grey-leaved shrubs will contrast with more ordinary green foliage in the border, and also provide flowering interest in season. They need full sun and good drainage. Artemisias, helichrysums, lavenders, phlomis, santolinas and shrubby senecios are all worth considering. In regions with a mild climate try leptospermums, hoherias and daisy-flowered olearias. Shrubs with golden, variegated or purple leaves may give stunning results if carefully planned.

There are also shrubs that flower or bear fruit through the winter months. Almost all are scented, and usually their flowers are a tight bundle of fragrant stamens – soft, papery petals would be easily damaged by frost. Mahonias, honeysuckles, shade-loving sarcococcas, many viburnums and witch hazels are good winter performers. Cotoneasters have red or yellow berries that last until Christmas, viburnums carry lustrous, translucent red fruit, while shrub roses bear apple- or flagon-shaped scarlet or orange hips.

Ground-level companions for shrubs

The best companions to shrubs are small bulbs and low-growing herbaceous carpeting plants that will spread beneath the branches and thrive even when lightly shaded during the summer. They will cover the bare earth in the valleys between the shrubs and extend the seasonal colour range of the border. Spring bulbs of the sort that feature in the natural garden are ideal, massed around the base of deciduous shrubs. Those – such as alliums and camassias – that need summer baking during dormancy are not so useful and are best in association with groups of perennials in an open site. Later-flowering drifts of lilies combine well with light-foliaged shrubs, such as corylopsis, caryopteris and perovskia, that allow plenty of sunlight to filter through their branches.

Most lilies can be planted so that they push their spring shoots up through the branches of low-growing and almost prostrate shrubs – in spring their frost-vulnerable tips benefit from the additional protection.

Bunchberry, the charming low-growing dogwood Cornus canadensis – a denizen of acid woodland in the north-eastern American states – is a wonderful carpeter, with attractive leaves and white four-petalled flowers followed by red berries. Its creeping habit makes it a perfect infiller between tall shrubs that require similar conditions. Most of us would give anything in order to be able to grow it. Here in Le Vasterival, Princess Sturdza's garden, it undercarpets rhododendrons and azaleas in the woodland.

Choose shrubs that do not have too dense a habit or too extensive a root system. *Salvia officinalis*, artemisias, cotoneasters, romneyas, and creeping roses and lithospermums are companions for sun-tolerant lilies; in more shady situations they associate with hydrangeas, sarcococcas, stephanandra and symphoricarpos. At Felbrigg Hall, Norfolk, colchicums in late summer make a band of colour in front of a shrub border in which buddlejas, cistus, hebes, hypericums, fuchsias and potentillas have a long period of performance.

Shade-tolerant herbaceous perennials do well when planted under shrubs in a border, although they may need repositioning as young shrubs grow and take up more space. Sun-lovers, however, only do well while areas are still open to the sky. The most suitable low-growing infill perennials are some of the more pushy plants that will drift from patches of open sunlight into the shady areas under the branches. These include acanthus (although preferring to flower in full sun, except in hot climates, it has glossy shade-tolerant leaves), ajugas, *Alchemilla mollis*, *Asarum europaeum*, astrantias, *Brunnera macrophylla*, *Buglossoides purpurocaerulea*, *Chiastophyllum oppositifolium*, dicentras (although the blue-grey leaved forms will lose their leaf colour), shade-tolerant euphorbias, fragrant sweet woodruff (*Galium odoratum*), hardy cranesbill geraniums, hellebores, hemerocallis, hostas, small blue *Iris cristata* or taller clumps of *I. innominata* (both prefer an acid soil), omphalodes, periwinkles, pulmonarias, all forms of Solomon's seal and false Solomon's seal (*Smilacina racemosa*), creeping potentillas, comfreys (forms of *Symphytum*), tellima and the delicate bronze-leaved *Tiarella cordifolia*.

Biennials, especially self-seeders, are as easy to use in the shrub border as they are in the more relaxed natural garden. Those that flourish and multiply in sun and shade include evening primroses, foxgloves, feverfew, honesty, sweet rocket, *Smyrnium perfoliatum* and some of the columbines. The old-fashioned *Aquilegia vulgaris* with clumps of blue- or plum-coloured flowers is very decorative; its various forms are more tolerant of shade than the modern long-spurred hybrids.

Shrubs, perennials and low-growing creepers combine to make the gold and purple border at Tintinhull one of Mrs Reiss's most imaginative schemes. The tall bronze-leaved shrub is Sambucus nigra *'Guincho Purple'; with purple-leaved* Berberis thunbergii atropurpurea *and* B.t. *'Atropurpurea Nana', it contrasts with the golden* Cornus alba *'Spaethii', which is 'stooled' each spring so that its bark will remain red.* Rosa *'Rosemary Rose' has dark bronze-tinted leaves and crimson flowers. Along the front creeping* Persicaria vacciniifolia, *once better known as a polygonum, and bright blue* Veronica teucrium *flower in the semi-shade. Many plants will flower as well in half shade as they do in full sun, often benefiting from the cooler conditions.*

CRATHES IN SCOTLAND

Gertrude Jekyll visited Crathes at the end of August 1895, and later wrote: 'The brilliancy of colour masses in these Scottish gardens is something remarkable. Whether it is attributable to soil or climate one cannot say: possibly the greater length of day, and therefore of daily sunshine, may account for it . . . The flowers of our July gardens, Delphiniums, Achilleas, Coreopsis, Eryngiums, Geums, Lupines, Scarlet Lychnis, Bergamot, early Phloxes, and many others, and the host of spring-sown annuals, are just in beauty.' Whatever the cause, and cooler nights are an additional bonus, the flower borders at Crathes are among the best in the British Isles today. Certainly the hardy perennials thrive to grow taller than in the south, and colours seem more glowing, with flowering extending deep into autumn.

Although the borders were already distinguished, they have changed much since Miss Jekyll's day. They were considerably enlarged by the taking in for ornamental purposes of much of the walled ground still used in the 1890s for fruit and vegetables. The majestic yews are thought to date from 1702, but the main layout within the old walls under the castle owes its inspiration to Sir James and Lady Burnett of Leys. The new mixed and herbaceous borders which they designed from the 1930s are in a series of colour harmonies and themes. The formal Colour Garden below the east walls of the castle was given a spectacular scarlet, crimson and yellow scheme of mixed shrubs and perennials, with dark purple-leaved shrubs such as smoke bush providing weight, all surrounding central features of yew and a small pool. In the lower gardens hedges were introduced to create concealed secret areas all with strong colour or seasonal themes. There are white borders, June borders, main borders where the autumn colour of bronze, orange and gold flowers predominates, as well as a Golden and a Red Garden with a strong emphasis on foliage plants.

LEFT ABOVE *The mainly white borders crossing the lower walled garden, with a clipped Portugal laurel as the central focal point, reach their peak in July. They are mixed in composition, with various forms of scented philadelphus and smaller Hebe albicans as shrubby accents, and with* drifts of bulbs at lower levels. *Strong perennial groups include the tall flower-spikes of* Veronicastrum virginicum album, *feathery-headed* Aruncus dioicus *'Kneiffii', the white-flowered* Tradescantia × andersoniana *'Innocence' and silvery anaphalis.*

LEFT BELOW *Tall Cotswold hybrid verbascums make a foreground point in the main double border leading to the Portugal laurel, and indicate the yellowish-gold tones to come later. Unobtrusive netting stretched over the whole bed in June supports the all-perennial planting.*

ABOVE *The main borders in the central portion of the lower garden create the finest colour effects at Crathes. Early in the season they seem mostly blue and pink. Backed by roses garlanded on chains, the tightly packed perennials here include delphiniums, achilleas, catmint and the* startling magenta cranesbill Geranium psilostemon, *with blue* Veronicastrum virginicum *to the right and leaves of plume poppy in the centre foreground. Later, as bronze and gold daisy-flowers emerge, these borders glow with harmonies from another section of the spectrum.*

LEFT 'Hot' colours fill the Colour Garden in late summer. In the left-hand border purple-leaved Perilla frutescens and the sultry red foliage of Swiss chard 'Vulcan' are lit by red nicotianas, scarlet celosias, deep salmon Agastache 'Firebird', Cuphea ignea and C. miniata 'Firefly' and orange Tithonia rotundifolia. Plants opposite have golden, creamy yellow or variegated leaves: Weigela 'Florida Variegata', the tall grass Miscanthus sinensis 'Strictus' and the shrubby Salvia officinalis 'Icterina' make a background for rioting lady's mantle and spires of Heuchera richardsonii.

RIGHT Shrubs, perennials and annuals harmonize in the beds between the enclosed flower garden and the house. On the left tender Helichrysum petiolare, pink-flowered Salvia involucrata and white argyranthemums are grown each year from cuttings; Ageratum 'Southern Cross', purple-leaved perillas and the azure-blue Salvia patens are raised from seed. Monarda 'Croftway Pink', Rosa 'Bonica', Anthemis 'E.C. Buxton' and silvery stachys survive the winters to make a more permanent frame. On the right helichrysums, Senecio vira-vira and variegated plectranthus provide a leafy background to agastaches, Aster novae-angliae 'Andenken an Alma Pötschke', Argyranthemum 'Mary Wootton', and native Eupatorium purpureum.

STONECROP, N.Y. STATE

The inner flower borders in Francis Cabot's garden are framed by walls, hedges and trellis, all decorated with climbers and trailers or formal espaliers. In this setting hardy herbaceous plants interweave with exotic annuals and tender woody rarities grown from seed or cuttings to peak in late summer. A modern evocation of the Jekyllian masterpieces of the Edwardian age, Stonecrop's success depends upon just three dedicated gardeners with a rare interest in the unusual plants.

Colour schemes inspired by Jekyll but in no slavish imitation exploit rainbow harmonies and contrasts, extending the range to encompass nature's subtler tints and shades and mellowed pigments. There is a complex planted colour wheel. But colour is not the be-all and end-all: the groups of plants, often repeated in each visual glance, establish a firm architectural pattern which matches the strong lines and gives a purpose to the whole conception.

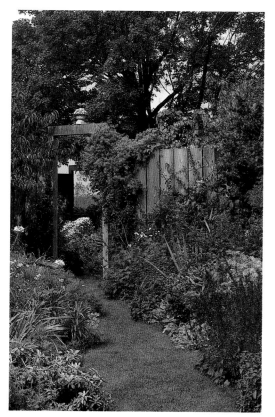

ABOVE *In a broad sweep of border, ornamental kale 'White Peacock', silver-leaved cardoons and artemisias and variegated erysimum provide the cool foliage setting for blue salvias (Salvia farinacea), yellow daisies, white antirrhinums, white cleomes (Cleome 'Helen Campbell') and the tall Boltonia asteroides 'Snowbank', this last a plant seldom grown in England. A Russian vine (Fallopia baldschuanica, syn. Polygonum baldschuanicum) clambering on the trellis at the end of the walk sustains the cooler-toned picture created by the plants in this bed. Nobody can call this kind of planting labour-saving; the task of raising the annuals, tending the perennials and, above all, orchestrating them into subtle colour harmonies each season calls for skill and dedication on the part of the small team of gardeners.*

ASHTREE COTTAGE

Ashtree Cottage lies under a spur of the cold downs just north of Stourhead, in Wiltshire, where winters are long and late frosts are expected. The soil is mainly low pH, allowing Mrs Lauderdale to experiment with many acid-loving plants to add to the shrub roses and traditional border perennials which she grows so well. Given the harsh weather conditions she is very successful, proving once again how loving care and good and wise cultivation can overcome difficulties.

At Ashtree Cottage a narrow rose-clad pergola shelters the almost centrally placed main pathway running from the entrance drive to the house. Thickly filled borders, backed by solid hedges, line the rectangular garden; gently curving edges contain rich tight planting of trees, flowering shrubs, graceful shrub roses, delphiniums and phlox, while lavender, catmint and roses alternate in the light and shade of the narrow beds under the pergola frame. Old apples, a 'new' medlar, white-flowering prunus and a weeping silver-leaved pear give height to the lawn areas and fill the garden with blossom in spring. Unusual trees such as the horizontally branched *Cornus controversa* 'Variegata' show a plantsman's interest.

The planting schemes seem casual but are far from haphazard; repeated themes such as grey and silver foliage and strong clumps of blue delphinium hold the design together. At every viewpoint framed 'pictures' make the garden seem much larger than it is. Behind the house, another garden opens out with views to the high downs.

ABOVE A *detail of the companion planting at Ashtree Cottage: the Gallica hybrid Rosa 'Complicata', underplanted with pinks.*

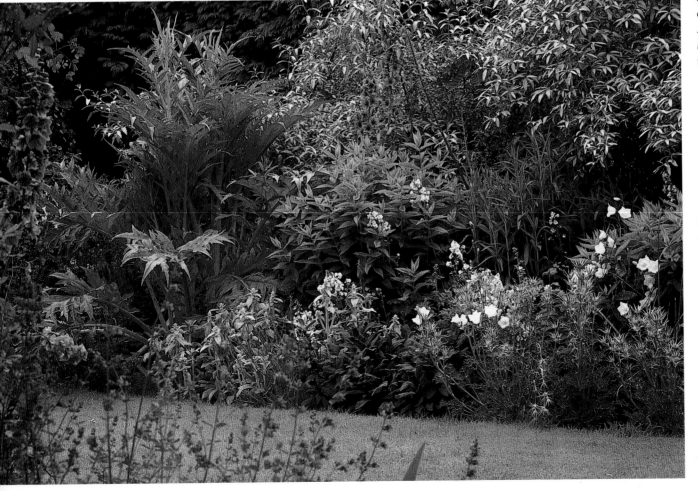

LEFT A *view from the pergola pathway shows a border group against the southern hedge. Purple-leaved sage and silver-leaved perennials and shrubs provide a setting for white-flowered phlox and white Jacob's ladder. The 'silver' group includes a form of Russian olive,* Elaeagnus angustifolia caspica, *with scented yellow flowers in spring, the tall* Cynara cardunculus, *with wide divided leaves, and low-growing* Stachys byzantina *which creeps along in the foreground.*

LEFT *Another view from the pergola is framed by blue delphiniums and blue-flowered* Viola cornuta *which twines among the stems of the long-flowering pink Portland rose 'Comte de Chambord'.*

BELOW *Nearer the house creamy* Sisyrinchium striatum, *with iris-like leaves, grows and seeds beside some Dutch bulbous iris whose pale blue flowers make a strong accent. Beyond, blue and white forms of* Campanula persicifolia *spread through the border.*

THE FRAMED GARDEN

Framing techniques
The living frame
Flowers framed

Chilcombe in Dorset
A garden near Paris
Filoli in California

Frames direct and focus the gaze and present garden scenes as pictures. Gardens designed to exploit framing devices to the full depend on geometry and repetition; plants are manipulated into preconceived schemes and little seems left to chance. This was the fashion that dominated Western gardening until the middle of the eighteenth century; it had a vigorous renaissance in the nineteenth, and is frequently evoked by gardeners of today. In fact there are few gardens where traditionally inspired schemes cannot be adapted or reinterpreted, if only for one small part of the layout: a more formal atmosphere near the house is possible even in a garden where natural effects prevail.

In modern small gardens, with limited and therefore doubly precious planting space, formal styles help create planting opportunities. Garden divisions provide backing for border schemes, and small flower-packed beds – edged with box or framed with brick, stone or gravel – give unity and purpose to a site that might otherwise be meandering lawn. Even the smallest garden can have vistas lengthened by linear or aerial perspective. On a tiny terrace decorative pots of flowering and foliage plants may be put to effective use.

This architectural approach to the garden, of plants framed or framing to create deliberate effects, and the placing of accent plants or massed plants in patterned beds or containers, seems to be the complete opposite to natural gardening. Yet inside this structure, planting styles can be quite wild and free. Any border may be given a frame whether it is planted with strong-growing perennials of different heights or in a more regimented fashion. An arrangement of informal mixed planting in a fine stone or terracotta urn is formalized by its container. Even meadow gardens, with flowers growing in rough grass, may be sharply delineated at the boundaries by mown paths so that they become flower beds set in smoother lawn; in the 'beds' themselves the grass provides a green frame for pointillist colours.

The classically laid out garden at Hazelby House is divided into a series of linked 'rooms', each with framed views into adjacent areas. The geometric garden, with horizontal divisions and vertical hedges, makes the most economical use of space. Here plants frame architectural features – the raised copper bowl, the trellised archway and, on a lower level, the pathway of patterned bricks. At the same time the architecture defines and limits space, and provides satisfying contrasts with the flowing lines and shapes of plants.

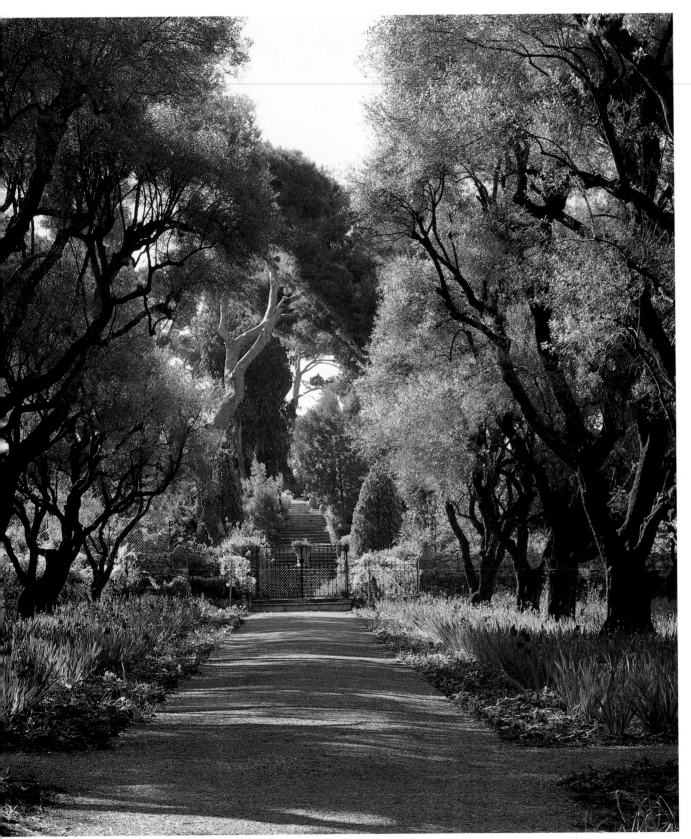

OPPOSITE *Michael Balston makes effective use of symmetry and repetition so that architecture and plants complement one another, hard materials contrasting with the soft billowing shapes of roses and perennials. Overflowing roses line the edges of the main 'frame'. The focal point, the rose-covered archway, reveals a more distant view, at the same time accentuating the graceful outline of the armillary sphere in the foreground. Finally the sphere itself is set off by groups of roses and catmint.*

LEFT *In the Mediterranean sunshine at La Garoupe an avenue of ancient olive trees borders the pathway, giving a sense of distance and framing the steep stairway beyond. The olives shelter tall German irises under the welcome shade of their branches; later in the season the iris flowers are succeeded by clumps of pink cyclamen. Not every garden can be on such a grand scale, but almost all views are best if framed and narrowed to accentuate a distant feature. Avenues can be of trees, shrubs or quite small plants, statues or vases; the size is not important if the eye is correctly directed along a central vista.*

FRAMING TECHNIQUES

The formality inherent in framing involves using symmetry to achieve completeness in each view, with plants regarded as architectural accessories in much the same way as 'hard' garden structures. Deployed in pairs, sets and blocks, key plants with strong outlines – or massed plants marshalled into regular shapes – establish balance, create rhythms and help to manipulate perspective.

A pair of plants such as tall crambes with huge airy umbels of white flowers flanking a seat or ornament emphasizes its role as focal point within the garden area. Plants in a line – continuous as in hedging, or making the separate rhythmic punctuation marks of an avenue – not only delineate the geometry of a layout but will also direct the eye along an axis, emphasizing perspective. Design features found in the great gardens may be adapted for smaller landscapes; the avenue of limes stretching into the horizon to frame a distant temple or hill can be reproduced in miniature with clipped evergreens or by using elegant terracotta urns to line a simple garden path that ends at a welcoming seat or at an accent plant.

When plants reinforce the invitation extended by a path or gateway, they make very compelling framing devices – the frame not playing an enclosing role, but calling attention to something beyond the garden enclosure. A pair of architectural key plants or low box domes surrounded by bulbs and creeping flowers can effectively frame a gate or doorway, or enhance some new flowery delight glimpsed through the opening. Even the most panoramic views are improved when narrowed; by deliberately framing garden vistas and planting schemes, their importance is enhanced. At Newby Hall, Yorkshire, in two rectangular beds flanking a central grass path, branching amelanchiers create a white flowering screen in spring to frame the perennial borders that stretch down the lower slope. In late summer their leaves turn rich crimson and gold.

At Tintinhull converging lines of catmint reinforce the garden axis, framing a distant view into a neighbouring cider orchard. Wings of dark yew, pillars clothed with honeysuckle and graceful arching roses – the grey-leaved Rosa 'Wolley-Dod', *with shell-pink flowers – all play an architectural role in this composition, contributing different patterns of leaf and flower colour through the seasons.*

BELOW LEFT *The garden at Jenkyn Place is divided up into a series of different-shaped 'rooms'. One of the simplest compartments, with four-square symmetry against a backing of clipped yew, has pelargonium-filled pots adding to the formality but giving lightness and colour.*

BELOW RIGHT *At Heslington flowers and leaves contrast with the hard surfaces of stone and brickwork. Beneath a cloud of airy* Crambe cordifolia, *lupins, oriental poppies and pink* Geranium sanguineum striatum *border the geometric pool in which hardy arums and Japanese iris thrive.*

More free-flowing plants become architectural embellishments – climbers, for instance, softening the lines of an archway or pergola like a decorative frieze. Design schemes based on the piquant contrast between a strong garden framework of hard materials such as woodwork and masonry and the exuberant shapes of living plants were a hallmark of the Lutyens–Jekyll partnership, and inspire endless possibilities for modern gardens.

Exploiting contrast

The greatest dramatic effect is achieved when plants are deliberately presented so they exploit contrasts. Instead of 'disappearing' discreetly within a garden as part of a naturalistic scheme, or forming elements of the jigsaw that makes up the integrated border, flowers clearly defined by a frame gain increased impact. Three-dimensional planting becomes two-dimensional in each glance, and, like a painter's canvas in its boundary frame, is separated from the surrounding area so that it stands out and claims attention.

One kind of framed picture is formed by the sculptural shape of an isolated key plant seen in eye-catching silhouette against a plain backdrop. Another occurs when a panel of jewel-like flowers, massed together at the same height, is seen against a smooth expanse of grass or gravel, the simple, definite shape of the bed in itself creating the frame for the decorative contents. Then, of course, there are more three-dimensional frames that create distinct outlines, such as low hedges or walls.

The essence is to provide contrast that will make the most of the feature. Maximum effects are achieved by using more subdued tones and textures as the foil. Inanimate surfaces such as walls, fences and paving are obvious framers, bringing out the vital qualities of the plants that clamber and spill over their rigid forms. But the living frames made by manicured evergreens and smooth lawns can be almost equally hard-edged and abstract when juxtaposed with freer plant shapes. Planting of this kind has always been the very stuff of formal gardens.

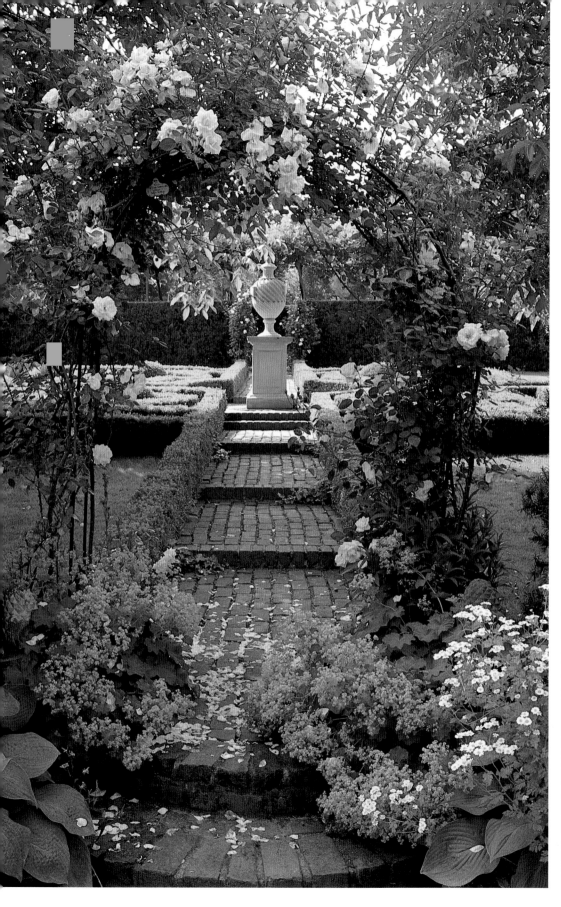

LEFT *Formal box hedges and parterres of scrolled boxwork edge a brick path to frame the focal point of this view in a Dutch garden – an elegant urn on a central plinth. Here the design exploits the contrast between clipped formality in living plants and hard features of garden landscape. The garlanded rose archway frames the entrance.*

BELOW *A statuesque angelica flower-head commands attention as a key plant, without any formal framing devices; a subdued leafy backdrop provides essential contrast to frame the focal point naturally.*

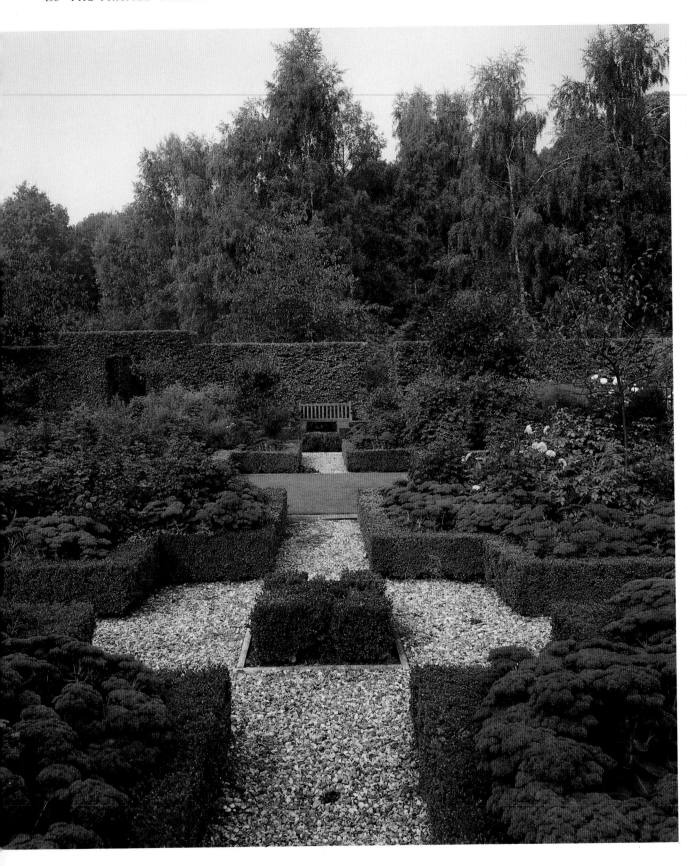

In one of the compartments of this garden near Paris (see pages 152-3), low box hedges framing Sedum 'Herbstfreude', with flat densely clustered pink flower-heads, have been planted symmetrically to give formal definition to the layout. The immaculate gravel and the panel of grass enhance the atmosphere of order, while a tall hedge makes a background to the centrally placed seat. Even the more distant trees play their part in shaping the skyline – something that gardeners can easily overlook at the planning stage. Trees create their own patterns of light and shade and movement; they add an extra dimension to a garden view, having a more human scale and quality than a backdrop of buildings. Here the airy shapes of the birches contrast with the stricter lines of clipped hedging. As well as establishing the garden's style, the trees, hedges and horizontal ground-patterns also create a firm framework in which more free-flowing plant and flower shapes, colours and textures can come and go with the seasons.

THE LIVING FRAME

Flower gardens are framed and accentuated by the permanent planting of trees and shrubs that define space with their shape, outline and mass. On the scale of a whole garden, there is an essential element of contrast: smooth lawns enhance dense trees and shrub canopies that move gently in a breeze, providing movement between shade and sunlight. More solid and static evergreens lend stability and weight.

Trees and hedges set the style of the garden; they also create the design frame inside which flowering associations are assembled to make a satisfactory composition. At Crathes Castle massive L-shaped blocks of yew define space in the centre of the Colour Garden, providing a contrasting focus with mixed borders of red- and orange-coloured flowers in the outer beds. Similar effects are seen at Blickling, Norfolk, where blocks of yew known as the 'Grand Pianos' create a focal point within the great parterre area of more ephemeral flower beds. At Filoli, California, Irish yews with naturally architectural shapes contrast with the flowing lines of flowering plants and provide solid blocks of sombre colour to offset paler tints and fleeting flower performances. In the outer garden, brightly coloured flower beds are framed by a golden-leaved locust tree (*Robinia pseudoacacia* 'Frisia'), cylinder-shaped Irish yews and olive trees, theatrically backed by wild countryside studded with live oaks.

Sombre foliage, used as a living backdrop for colourful foreground planting, is able to achieve dramatic garden contrasts that shout for attention and linger in the memory long after gentler, more reticent schemes have been forgotten. At Packwood House, Warwickshire, the old yews known as 'The Multitude', silhouetted against the sky, make a startling backdrop to colourful flower beds along the brick terrace; elsewhere in the garden low yew hedges grown as buttresses against a high wall frame more intimately the beds of different coloured roses. In the topiary garden at Levens Hall, Cumbria, massed summer-flowering verbenas, contained inside box hedging, set off the giant yew and box shapes behind.

Tall enclosing hedges

In many framed gardens tall hedges break up the broad sweep of lawns into different areas in a manner reminiscent of the style of the seventeenth century. In the garden at Hidcote, Gloucestershire, a series of hedges in different, sometimes mixed, plant materials divide the whole area into a sequence of green rooms deliberately based on Renaissance ideals of symmetry and proportion. These hedges also provide the background frames for luxuriant border planting of hardy plants and roses. The Hidcote style – a combination of formal layout with great informality in planting – has been a major influence on English gardening since it was laid out in the years before the First World War.

Hedging plants that are to make permanent garden compartments or boundaries need to suit the site well enough to grow into more or less regular 'walls' of foliage.

Dark evergreen yew, with its dense tight growth, makes a particularly satisfactory architectural framework for the garden, and enhances the colours and shapes of individual flowers. Its sombre green appears almost black outlined against the sky. Sometimes its intensity and matt effects create almost too much contrast: pure white flowers become dazzlingly bright and garish when outlined against its dark leaves. At Tintinhull we have softened the effects by interweaving grey

Lady Londonderry used Moorish-style arcades instead of solid hedges to separate the Spanish Garden from the 'wilder' woodland areas at Mount Stewart in Northern Ireland. In the 1930s she planted the Monterey cypress, but the National Trust has replaced this with Leyland cypress, which they consider more appropriate and better suited to tight clipping. Planting in the Spanish Garden is a mixture of formality, with sword-like phormiums contrasting with more naturalistic groupings of Kirengeshoma palmata, Hydrangea 'Preziosa' and Hosta sieboldiana elegans which link the scheme with the more relaxed planting style glimpsed through the arches.

and silvery foliage plants between the flowering plants and the yew and searching for white flowers that are gently tinted with pale pink, cream and blue rather than using those of 'laundry' brilliance.

Old yew hedges become interestingly mounded and give any garden an air of antiquity. When yew grows too high and wide it may be rejuvenated by cutting back to the main trunk; this operation is usually done one side at a time to avoid undue shock to the plant. In regions that experience cold winters, such as the north-eastern United States, forms of Japanese yew (*Taxus cuspidata*) are substituted for the common English *Taxus baccata*. A group of hybrids between the two includes *T.* × *media* 'Hicksii' and 'Hatfieldii', which like to grow into pyramidal form and are most suitable for hedging.

Hollies are beautiful slow-growing hedging plants. When still immature, their tips may be severely damaged by frost in a cold spring. Once established, their glowing leaves contrast well with flowers and pale perennial foliage. The spineless *Ilex aquifolium* 'J.C. van Tol' is worth considering; in the north-east United States the Japanese holly *I. crenata* makes a more sober background. Some elegant American hollies such as *I. opaca*, which needs acid soil, do best in areas where summers are hot. The new very attractive *I.* × *meserveae* hybrids produced in Long Island have a distinctive blue bloom to the leaf. Hardy in extremes of cold and heat, they may well be the hedging holly of the future. *I.* × *m.* 'Blue Angel', 'Blue Prince' and 'Blue Princess' all make strong-growing hedges.

In cold climates the most satisfactory conifers for hedging are the various forms of the slow-growing lime-tolerant eastern hemlock (*Tsuga canadensis*) with dense green leaves that are as decorative and useful as yew. In milder regions such as coastal gardens in the British Isles and the more southerly states of the United States, the Chilean yew (*Podocarpus andinus*) forms an excellent framing hedge for planting schemes as well as a thick evergreen screen.

Among deciduous trees, beech and hornbeam hedges are attractive backgrounds to flowers; in spring and summer the foliage is a fresh green, and clipped hedges keep their buff-coloured dead leaves all through the winter. Tapestry hedges of mixed copper and green beech are sometimes chosen to add interest. Field maple (*Acer campestre*) produces fresh young green leaves that turn a brilliant yellow, sometimes flushed

Ann Cox Chambers' garden in Provence, where sunlight is strong and shadows are important for coolness, has a small knot garden in a corner by the house. The pattern outlined in clipped box and punctuated by box domes is infilled with Exacum affine in alternating blocks of mauve and white. The contrast of a soaring Italian cypress, framed by the more bushy shape of a fig tree, provides just the sort of carefully thought out dramatic incident that good gardeners can use to prevent their planting becoming too bland.

RIGHT *At Olivers, near Colchester in Essex, yellow tulips and white pansies in spring are hemmed in by clipped box hedging, and the bed shapes are further framed by stone paving. This strong statement of formality contrasts with the gentle landscape beyond, in which the pool appears as a natural feature, and trees enclose a grassy glade, narrowing the view to a statue.*

BELOW *Mounds of 'Hidcote' lavender used as a hedge spill out over the paving stones to contrast with silvery-leaved Senecio 'Sunshine' behind a seat in the Edinburgh Botanic Garden. Even the simplest architectural object gains from being given a frame of softer plants.*

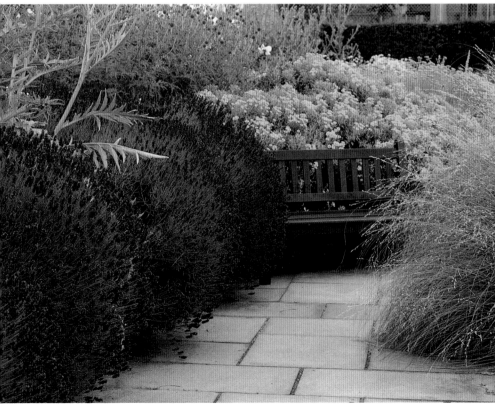

with crimson, in late summer; in Europe it is an ideal perimeter hedge linking garden and countryside.

Roses can make informal hedges to frame inner planting or borders. Suckering Rugosas with fresh apple-green crinkly leaves and scented flowers succeeded by orange or scarlet hips are excellent as background hedging. Ground-cover roses such as *Rosa* 'Max Graf', with its glossy foliage and clear pink yellow-centred flowers, make an informal weed-suppressing frame at a lower level.

Low pattern-making hedging

In the last few years planting low hedging to accentuate formal flower-bed patterns has been found to be more labour-saving than natural planting: modern herbicides control weed growth, and mechanical shears and strimmers have replaced manual tools to make hedge clipping simple and economical. These new beds can be set in stone paving, concrete or reconstituted stone, patterned brickwork, gravel or cobbles, or in a combination of all these different materials. Once laid, they need less maintenance than grass, and plants can tumble over the edges without doing damage.

Tidy horizontal lines of box, lavender, tender rosemary, santolina or thyme, clipped annually, are the most common choice for low hedging, sometimes with fanciful finials or domes to accentuate corners. The scale and type of planting in the beds affects the choice of edging material. Different sorts of box, which may be kept neatly manicured with almost vertical sloping sides and a flat top, are best: few other hedging plants look so good throughout the year. Any box-edged bed appears quite purposeful even when no plants are obviously performing in it; a panel of plain grass is restful framed with cut box.

By far the most common species selected for low hedging is European box: forms of *Buxus sempervirens* or the dwarf Dutch *B.s.* 'Suffruticosa', known since the seventeenth century. If well maintained and clipped every year in early summer, it will keep a narrow outline, making it particularly practical for marking out parterre patterns. In colder climates, substitute forms of Korean box (*B. microphylla*), which have dense bright leaves. European box grows slowly over many years to heights of 3m/10 ft (the 5.5m/18ft hedges at Powis Castle are unique), but most box hedges are restricted to a height of 38–60cm/15–24in, with a spread of about the same extent. Dwarf box grows up to

30cm/12in high, but may be kept much lower; in some parterres it is allowed to grow to only 10–15cm/4–6 in, and coloured gravels are substituted for flowers in the interstices.

European box is known in the United States as American box. There, it tends to grow quickly into mounded shapes; in the hot summers it is difficult to keep its edges crisp and well defined. Broader box hedges, sometimes grown in double rows at different heights (mimicking the sixteenth-century style), may be magnificent, however.

As an alternative, there are a number of hollies that retain a tailored shape. Japanese hollies such as *Ilex crenata* have tiny box-like leaves and may be clipped into dwarf hedges; preferring an acid soil, they may survive cold winters and hot summers. Other American hollies such as inkberry (*I. glabra*), with its dark shining leaves, and yaupon (*I. vomitoria*), with its small box-like leaves, are heat- and drought-resistant. Forms of Dahoon holly (*I. cassine*) thrive where hot summers are accompanied by high atmospheric humidity. In mild areas I have seen *Trachelospermum asiaticum* trained to make a low hedge.

The hardiest hebes also make low compact containing hedges. Grey-leaved *Hebe pinguifolia* 'Pagei' and *H. albicans*, with more glaucous leaves, are salt- and wind-resistant, so they are especially suitable for seaside planting. They need no clipping and bear small dense white flower racemes. Hebe and *Ruta graveolens* 'Jackman's Blue' surround beds of pale pink, yellow and blue flowers in the formal Italian Garden on the lower terrace at Mount Stewart, County Down, in Northern Ireland, where the climate is very mild.

Lavenders, with grey-green linear leaves and flowers ranging from low-toned blues and mauves to pink and white, develop as more informal hedges, each bushy plant growing angular and woody with age. This adds charm in a number of hedging situations, but the lack of definition makes most lavenders unsuitable for formal pattern-making.

Both rosemary and silver- or green-leaved cotton lavender (*Santolina chamaecyparissus, S. neapolitana, S. rosmarinifolia rosmarinifolia* and various cultivars), which has lacy or finely divided foliage, will grow quickly in well-drained soil in a sunny position; they need cutting back each season in spring as they also have a tendency to become woody and are unsightly when bare at the base.

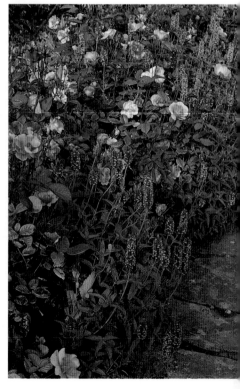

LEFT Ceanothus × delileanus *'Gloire de Versailles'* is set off at Chilcombe by an edging of pink erigerons and companion planting of the biennial musk-scented Salvia sclarea turkestanica. *Low-growing flowers do not detract from the natural shapes of shrubs such as ceanothus.*

BELOW LEFT *At Herterton House in Northumberland, a corner of the physic garden displays a brilliant combination of low-growing plants in a formal way. A central bed of variegated ground elder* (Aegopodium podagraria 'Variegatum') *is framed by bands of armeria and London pride. Plants do not have to be woody to play a formal role: these perennials are clearly defining the garden layout.*

Non-woody edging plants

When considering plants to frame a planting scheme there is no need to be confined to clipped woody species. Low-growing evergreen perennials may be tidied into straight lines or allowed to grow in natural ground-hugging shapes. Wall germander (*Teucrium chamaedrys*), silvery stachys, London pride, *Saxifraga moschata* and alpine strawberries are all good containing plants as are leathery-leaved bergenias with mauve, pink or white flowers and the less coarse *Chiastophyllum oppositifolium* with its yellow tasselled flowers. Set in informal lines, such plants can be controlled or allowed to drift forwards into flower beds and over neighbouring stone or brickwork. As well as providing a foil to the inner flowers, they produce their own bloom in season to extend the sequence of colour.

Gertrude Jekyll loved to plant old-fashioned lamb's ears (*Stachys byzantina*) in gentle drifts round the edge of rose beds, softening the harsh appearance at the base of the branching bushes; nowadays the non-flowering form *S.b.* 'Silver Carpet' is popular. To create similar effects, Miss Jekyll also substituted drifts of lavender for a line of continuous hedging. On the raised terrace at Knightshayes Court, Devon, grey and silver plants edge pink-flowered geraniums and dianthus. Small evergreen thymes with green, grey or variegated aromatic leaves are sun-lovers; they often frame herb-garden beds and may be sheared into shape in spring.

Even perennials that do not retain their winter leaves are suitable edgers. Catmint with its misty blue flowers rising in waving wands above soft grey-green leaves is one of the best. New foliage replaces the old if flower-stems are removed as the flowers fade; flowers will be produced again in late summer. Lady's mantle, with its lime-green flowers arching over light green leaves, is another worthwhile edging plant that may spread under shrubs or fall over the pavement. Some of the herbaceous cranesbill geraniums may also be used as ribbon edging; choose those with attractive leaves all summer as well as seasonal flowers. Less vigorous plants such as mossy phlox, low-growing campanulas and veronicas, sedums and the more tender suckering South African diascias all do well framing small-scale flowering schemes.

ABOVE *A classic knot design outlined in box is filled in with cotton lavender (Santolina chamaecyparissus), a Mediterranean plant grown for centuries in more northerly gardens, and with ageratums, which were introduced from tropical America only in the early nineteenth century. Gardening patterns that date back centuries can be executed with more recently discovered plants provided that the house is not typical of a particular period. Designed by Bruce Kelly, this garden is in Long Island.*

ABOVE RIGHT *At Filoli in California the designs of the different garden areas are scrupulously formal. Here linear beds outlined in box and edged with aubrieta are planted in spring with blocks of flowers. The strict colour effects accentuate the precision of the schemes: polyanthus in mixed colours are segregated from blue varieties by lines of box. Later in summer new colour schemes are implemented and the now bare standard rose bushes come into play.*

FLOWERS FRAMED

Many gardeners like to choose flowering plants appropriate to the style of their house, or to take inspiration from some distinct period theme. In the sunken garden by the old Tudor palace at Hatfield House, Hertfordshire, only seventeenth-century plants form the typical knot patterns, while at Westbury Court, Gloucestershire, flowers known by 1700 grow inside the simple parterre edgings.

In the sixteenth century germander and hyssop, both with midsummer flowers, were standard plants for knot patterns (along with savory, thrift, santolina and thyme) although straggly in habit. From the 1620s box and cotton lavender were also used. As well as the more decorative herbs, typical infilling flowers in these schemes would have been irises, bluebells, crocuses, anemones, columbines, foxgloves, primroses,

At Levens Hall in Cumbria the famous topiary garden is dominated by strange and fantastic shapes in clipped yew and box, their contours set off by low-growing massed annuals. The original garden was designed at the end of the seventeenth century, but many of the topiary pieces, including those of golden-leaved yew, were replaced or renewed more recently. The wonderful spread of Verbena rigida is not historically authentic as the South American verbenas were not introduced until the nineteenth century, although the related vervain was known in the Middle Ages. Antirrhinums, on the other hand, could have been part of the original planting.

cowslips, violas, Jacob's ladder, wallflowers, daisies, peonies, pinks, sweet rocket, fritillaries, native narcissi, lilies and roses – all of which had been grown for centuries. More recently introduced exotics such as crown imperials, tulips and hyacinths from the Middle East and plants such as marvels of Peru and sunflowers from the New World were welcome additions.

By the end of the seventeenth century, despite the fashion for flowerless parterres in the French style, many more plants were becoming available for garden experimentation; a wide range of new bulbs and perennials is listed by contemporary writers. During the next 200 years the stream of new plants became a flood, with colourful petunias, verbenas, salvias, eschscholzias, phacelias and lobelias from all corners of the world providing brighter and brighter hues for bedding-out schemes. In their heyday the Victorian 'bedders' had a greater choice of such plants than is available today.

Historical authenticity of course is not essential in this sort of gardening. The mauve verbenas which set off the topiary shapes at Levens Hall, some of which date from the late seventeenth century, were not introduced until the nineteenth century; in other beds marigolds, which could have been used in the original garden, are grown.

Historical schemes can be inspirational rather than defining a series of rules and may be adapted to suit any size of garden. Jacobean mansions display their appropriately restored seventeenth-century gardens, but the smallest suburban front garden may now be laid out with flower beds edged with box, lavender or santolina, containing any plants or only those known to the gardeners of the period. A Victorian terrace house may have an appropriate Victorian garden with flower beds edged with pebbles and pathways framed by rose-wreathed arches.

At Eastgrove Cottage near Worcester, flowers and foliage, mainly good perennials, are separated by the firm line of a hedge, which provides definition as well as a backing to the two schemes. In the foreground beds penstemons give a good show, while at the back the biennial Salvia sclarea turkestanica, phlox, Miss Willmott's ghost (Eryngium giganteum), achillea and hostas, with the shrubby perovskia, make a setting for the welcoming seat.

Modern flowering schemes are typified by carpets of impatiens, with vigorous modern hybrids flowering prolifically all summer in the sun or shade. But some annuals have more interesting qualities than others. I love the bedding echiums (*Echium vulgare*) with 'mixed' blue, mauve and purple flowers that spread like a soft carpet in the Blue Garden at Crathes Castle, as well as the taller gomphrenas I have seen surviving the heat of summers in Midwest America. I grow the straggling *Salvia sclarea* in a ribbon in our kitchen garden at Tintinhull, and the massed cosmos at Pontrancart in Normandy are positioned so the ferny leaves and airy pink flowers are gently stirred by the wind. Carpeting plants need not be annuals. At Barnsley House, Gloucestershire, a central pathway of flagged stones is framed by panels of green lawn and flanked by old Irish yews; shrubby pink- and white-flowered rock roses (*Helianthemum*), which open their flowers only when the sun shines, make an interweaving patterned carpet with silvery-foliaged neighbours.

Inside low hedges the coloured foliage of shrubs or perennials may be used as foundation planting, massed so that taller flowering bulbs may push up through the foliage in season. Santolinas, variegated or purple-tinged *Salvia officinalis*, and green-and-white variegated lamiums may be hosts to alliums and lilies. Even the variegated form of ground elder may be contained to form a background carpet for bulb flowers. In the White Garden at Sissinghurst, Kent, white tulips push through lamium in a flower bed contained by boxwood.

In a lasting and labour-saving scheme demonstrated in the Fuchsia Garden at Hidcote in Gloucestershire, a simple layout of box-edged beds separated by brick paths frames massed spaces of blue-flowered *Scilla siberica*. Permanently established hardy fuchsias, cut to the ground just before the scillas flower in spring, grow up above the bulbs to flower throughout the summer months.

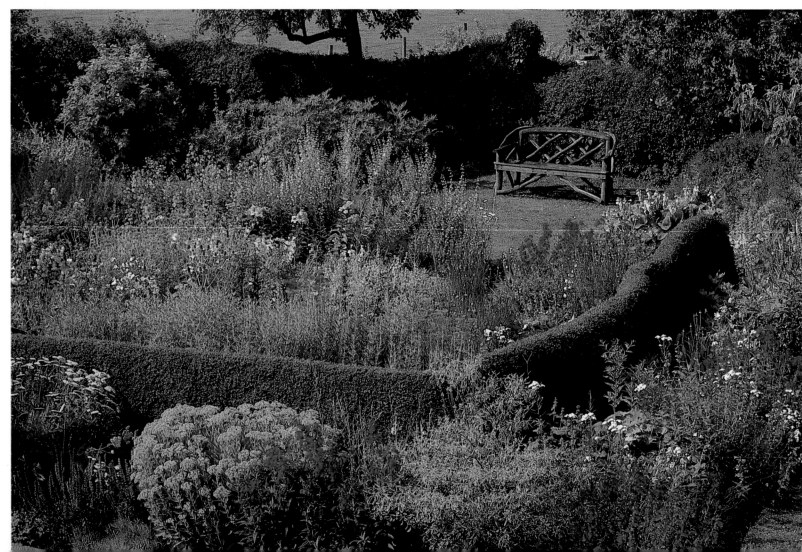

Flowers in containers

The emphasis on manipulation and management, with carefully thought-out arrangements intended to look contrived, is the essence of pictures in the framed garden. Groups of plants in ornamental pots, contained but overflowing, may convey the baroque spirit of a seventeenth-century Dutch flower painting – the plants growing naturally, but with nothing natural or simple about the way they are presented. Just as the Dutch painter had to wait through the summer for each plant to flower in turn in order that their blooms could all be captured realistically on his canvas, so should the gardener plant a container so that it produces a succession of flower and foliage effects for as long as possible. Planting spring bulbs in layers at different depths ensures that they flower at slightly different times. All plants in one container must like the same conditions of soil and aspect, even if they perform in separate seasons. Between each planting the soil is renewed and enriched.

The simplest planting scheme for containers comprises massed annuals, with bulbs, wallflowers, forget-me-nots and pansies for spring followed by summer bedders. Arrangements may be restricted to one plant or one colour. The most traditional container-grown spring bulbs are tulips, which, if a range of types is chosen, may flower for at least six weeks. Favourite summer annuals include pelargoniums, lobelias, petunias and ageratums. All these plants look more appealing if mixed with grey or silvery helichrysums to establish a pattern and enhance the flower colours.

More ambitious schemes for containers introduce woody perennials to act as key or accent plants. Cordylines, phormiums, glaucous-leaved argyranthemums with daisy-flowers (improved versions of Paris daisies), pink-flowered *Anisodontea capensis* and fuchsias are all successful focal points in sunny sites. The soaring chimney bellflower makes a climax plant for the centre of a decorative urn or may be massed for stunning effects in a large container or old cistern. Tender blue-flowered felicias with green or variegated leaves (forms of *Felicia amelloides* or *F. amoena*), silver-leaved *Helichrysum petiolare*, *Senecio vira-vira* and *S. compactus* (now correctly *Brachyglottis compacta* – similar in appearance to *S.* 'Sunshine', but smaller), red- and blue-flowered salvias (which like a lot of water) and small hebes all do well in pots if given adequate moisture and free drainage.

Around the base of these key plants, summer-flowering perennials and annuals ebb and flow as in any planting scheme: diascias (many are tender perennials), red-flowered linums, blue-flowered salvias and verbenas and more run-of-the-mill annuals such as scented tobacco plants, lobelias and petunias, preferably obtained in single colours for a specific scheme. Lilies and hostas, which tolerate shadier sites, thrive in pots containing richer soil.

In winter schemes conifers, hollies (clipped into various topiary shapes) and pyramids or domes of box become central container features. Trailing ivies or lamiums provide colour through the bleaker months, with small bulbs and taller tulips coming up through their low foliage in spring. The edging theme may be extended by training ivy to form a chain or low hedge around the container rim. In a mild winter pansies will flower for three months and forget-me-nots and wallflowers come into bloom for spring display.

Planting an annual scheme in an ornamental container is like arranging a vase of flowers for the house, with living flowers, leaves and the pot itself all contributing to the whole. Here silvery senecio (S. vira-vira) interweaves a scheme of zonal pelargoniums and the dwarfer Pelargonium 'L'Elegante', which will scramble down the sides. Planting is deliberately subdued to fit into the overall garden scheme, with pale-coloured flowers enriched by the silver leaves to give a gentle tapestry effect.

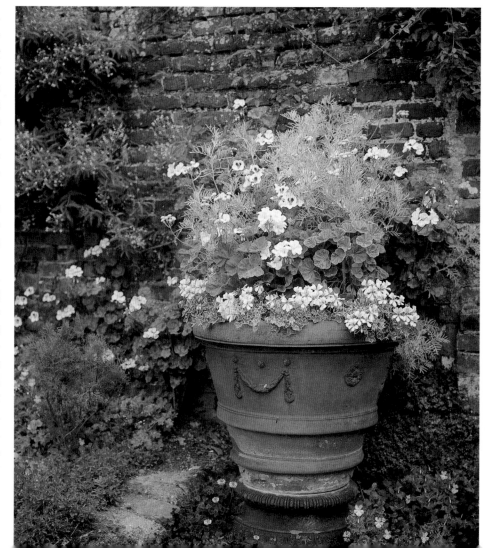

CHILCOMBE IN DORSET

At Chilcombe the walled and hedged garden is laid out in a series of squares and rectangles so that all shrubs and flowers are seen against a background of masonry or foliage. Each separate and secret enclosure could be a garden complete in itself, defined and limited by its perimeter hedge and having its own microclimate in which a wide selection of tender plants flourish. In considering design and the importance of providing a background structure for the flower garden, we must remember that walls and especially wind-filtering hedges are the traditional means of providing shelter. They thus serve a dual purpose, both framing the flowers and improving the aspect. Even when strong gales blow at Chilcombe, plants in these inner garden rooms hardly stir. Furthermore, the garden lies on a steep south-facing slope and benefits from a mild coastal climate; most frosts simply roll away into the valley below.

John Hubbard is a painter whose wife Caryl is also involved in the art world. They use their knowledge of colour to create garden pictures, framing each scene as if it were a two-dimensional painting. They have made the garden together using the basic structure, already divided into a series of rooms, that they found on their arrival. The main garden lies below the house. Here espalier fruit trees, trellis-work arbours for roses and clematis and hedges of mixed beech and yew all make vertical divisions, given broader shape by old spreading fruit trees. On the horizontal level pathways in grass, cobbles or paving define the edges of flower beds and lead the visitor's feet from one secret garden room into another where a different planting theme dominates. None of this means that the garden is either too formal or too diverse and restless. On the contrary, straight lines at head height or ground level are constantly blurred and softened by overflowing plants; a repetition of plant groups in different sections lends stability and effectively links the disparate themes together.

RIGHT *In one of the most intimate garden 'rooms', framed on one side by espalier fruit and on another by a rustic pergola, the planting, mainly of highly scented flowers or plants with aromatic leaves, is distinctly Mediterranean in feel. The air is still and heat is held in by surrounding vegetation and reflected by the cobbled paths. The flowers themselves are in small repetitive groups rather than in broad drifts. Here regal lilies, grey-leaved* Stachys byzantina *and southernwood are backed by* Knautia macedonica, *with small dark purple flowers, and blue-toned salvias.*

RIGHT *The herb garden and salvias in full flower framed by the rose-clad pergola. In the foreground Gillenia trifoliata, used by Indians in North America as a physic, reinforces the 'useful' theme; it flowers beside the marbled-leaved mother of thousands (Saxifraga stolonifera). Climbing and rambling roses with leafy foliage turn the pergola into a shady walk, a strong contrast to the intensity of sunlight and heat in the open garden beyond.*

LEFT *The cobbled paths marking out a cross to divide broad flower beds and plants in pots give the same garden area an almost formal aspect. The Mediterranean atmosphere is enhanced by aromatic herbs. Good King Henry (Chenopodium bonus-henricus), variegated thyme, pot marigold (Calendula officinalis), curry plant (Helichrysum italicum), both purple- and variegated-leaved sage (Salvia officinalis 'Purpurascens' and S.o. 'Icterina'), Jackman's rue (Ruta graveolens 'Jackman's Blue') with glaucous leaves, origanum and lovage (Levisticum officinale) all grow in profusion, scenting the air with old-world fragrance.*

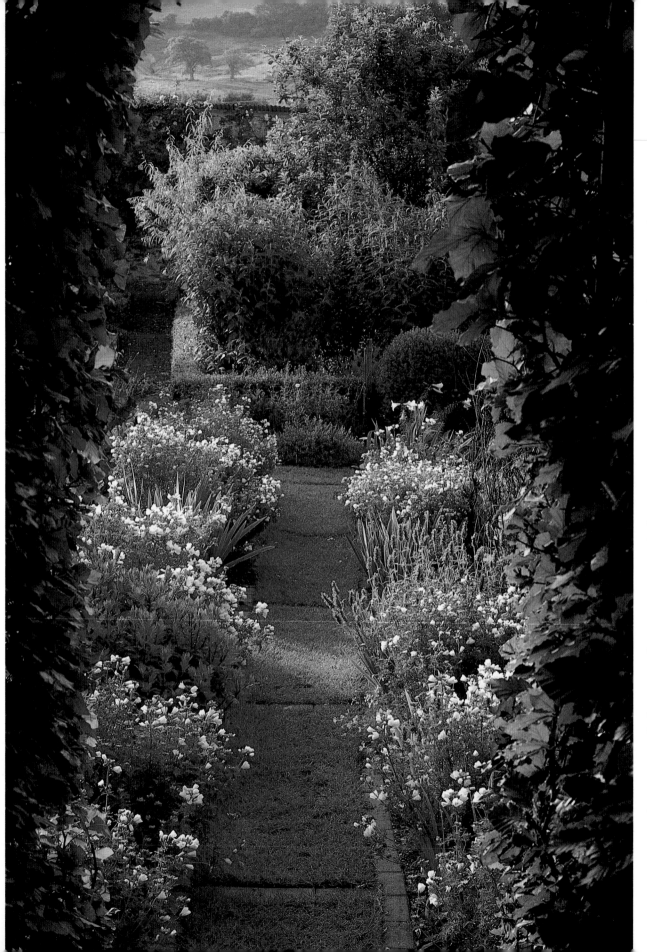

LEFT *Looking from shade into sunlight. A mixed tapestry hedge, clipped to form an archway, frames a broad lawn walk at Chilcombe. This is one of my favourite views, allowing just a hint of open sky beyond. In this tight enclosed garden most of the framed vistas are inward-looking, giving a strong sense of security but potentially claustrophobic in effect. The elegant stone edging and cross pattern is another instance of 'framing'; this time the grass walk is panelled to give definition. The white flowers are self-seeded mallow* (Malva moschata alba).

RIGHT *In the lower garden another hedged enclosure with newly laid paths was for flowers and vegetables. The flowers seem to be taking over: penstemons, silvery-leaved* Lotus hirsutus (*syn.* Dorycnium hirsutum), *daisy-flowered* Felicia amelloides *and* F. amoena, *and cotton lavender – my favourite one,* Santolina pinnata neapolitana *'Sulphurea', with feathery leaves and pale lime-green flowers, which is not grown frequently enough in gardens. On the corner a clump of* Salvia sclarea turkestanica *dominates the scene. Normally biennial, it can be perennial in a climate as mild as that of Chilcombe. With intensely musk-like aromatic leaves and pinkish-grey flower spires, this salvia is a must for every garden.*

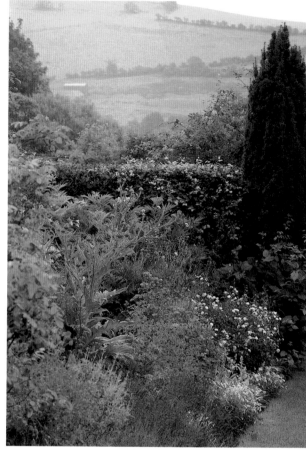

ABOVE *A view of planting on one side of the main borders where the vista terminated by the tapestry hedge is framed by a pair of Irish yews. Shrub roses, tall silvery thistles* (Onopordum nervosum) *and artichokes* (Cynara scolymus), *acanthus with pink spikes, lavender and the double-flowered* Geranium pratense 'Plenum Violaceum' *all grow gloriously together. The almost white leaves of* Stachys byzantina *beside the white violets* (Viola cornuta alba) *make an extra focal point. Backed by the dark yew, the herbaceous* Clematis heracleifolia *is about to open its blue flowers.*

A GARDEN NEAR PARIS

French gardens always seem to have stronger structural elements than those anywhere else in the world. This garden is no exception, yet it belongs to an American, brought up among the woodlands of New England. It has been created in the last twenty years from a waste-land of brambles. The landscape of the owner's background is reflected in a wilder garden area of wooded hillside, but the layout of the main flower gardens at the foot of the slope is formal and geometric. Here planting exuberance and freedom are tamed and reg-ulated by French-style clipped box hedges, which enclose borders and flank lawns.

The series of three gardens is contained within a tapestry hedge of green and copper-leaved beech, hornbeam, cypress and yew. One garden has predominantly blue flowers but is enhanced in true Jekyllian style with neighbours in tones of yellow – bright blue delphiniums set off by pale thalictrums and greenish-yellow lady's mantle. The second is for white flowers: in this clipped spheres of box give formality. The third garden, broken up into inner spaces by low box hedges, has predominantly mauve and pink flowers – roses (especially some of the old ones with magenta colouring), campanulas and autumn-flowering sedums. A description makes the garden sound strict and formal; in fact the lines of the architectural framework are everywhere softened by flowing and soar-ing plant shapes which spill over neat edges with picturesque abandon.

ABOVE *In this luxurious planting of perennials chosen from a palette of blue and yellow tones tall delphiniums, Iris 'Rose Queen', silver-leaved artemisia, hardy cranesbill geraniums and lady's mantle overflow on one side; on the other a similar planting scheme, with foreground Campanula glomerata, links the area together. All flower borders benefit from being given some sort of structural background: island beds are much harder to manage. In this garden the continuous hedge line behind the flowers unifies the planting schemes, while birches beyond the flower garden provide an extra dimension above the hedges to make a dominant frame.*

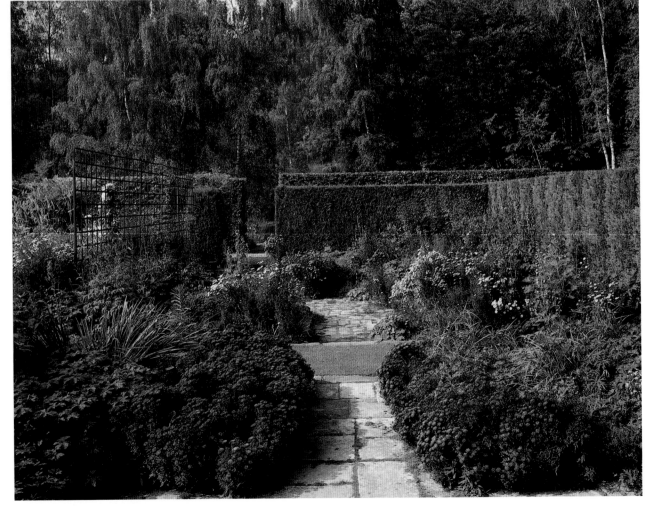

RIGHT *In the flower garden various cross axes help define the spaces as well as indicating views and pathways. Here a main cross way is focused on a tree in the outer garden. Delphinium spikes, framed by trellis and hedges, in their turn frame softer rounded plant shapes, such as hardy geraniums and campanulas, and the sprawlers, such as lady's mantle, which push forward out of the borders. More linear direction is given by the stone edging, which also makes maintenance simpler by allowing flowers to flop without damaging the grass.*

LEFT *Inside the flower garden low-growing asters make lines of colour in late summer; although non-woody, they are used to edge beds in quite a formal manner, framing the inner planting as well as the lawn and paving. They also reflect the horizontal bulk of the tapestry hedge on the perimeter, which gives a vertical definition to the space of the whole area, separating it from the wilder woodland. In small gardens disciplined vertical and horizontal lines contrast with natural plant shapes to provide essential structure. Repetitive planting associations give a distinct feeling of repose.*

FILOLI IN CALIFORNIA

The gardens of Filoli, an hour's drive south of San Francisco, are very formal and impeccably kept, a deliberate contrast to the rugged countryside where beautiful Californian live oaks (*Quercus agrifolia*) provide almost the only vegetation in the burnt ochre-coloured earth. The gardens, now in the charge of the National Trust for Historic Preservation, are nearly 16 acres in extent. Designed by Bruce Porter for William Bowers Bourne II between 1915 and 1919, they are almost Italian in concept, with each area enclosed by hedges. Tall Irish yews (*Taxus baccata* 'Fastigiata') define alleys to resemble the cypress-lined *viales* of Tuscany and grey-leaved olive trees are clipped into cylinder shapes. Espaliered fruit trees accentuate the formal lines.

Each inner garden has a distinct theme. In one, pink flowers and silvery foliage make the pattern of stained glass of a window of

In a tulip bed framed by high box hedges colours are mixed to give an embroidered look. The lily-flowered tulip 'White Triumphator', pink 'Mariette' and golden-yellow 'West Point' are underplanted with a fine stitching of white daisies (Bellis perennis). At first glance effects seem casual, but the bulbs are very carefully planted to make a uniform pattern. At Filoli all planting schemes are as exact and each bed is repeated with mirror-image planting to complete the symmetry of the layout. In this part of the garden one of the beds frames a circular pool and a standard wisteria, while another surrounds a sundial.

Chartres cathedral; in another a maze is laid out in boxwood; another is Dutch in conception; yet another is an Elizabethan knot. Colour schemes used in the annual beds are as originally planned. Fine collections of trees and superb roses, magnolias, azaleas, rhododendrons and camellias are all grown with consummate skill. To some the geometry and precision is overpowering, but I find it completely satisfying, and a fine reminder of how background framing and symmetry of effects can make an incomparable setting for flowers. Filoli may represent an extreme in manicured perfection, but it sets a fine standard which other gardens could mould and alter to a more relaxed approach and a smaller scale. Inside each scheme trees give an extra dimension: honey locusts, Japanese maples, dawn redwoods, standard wisterias as well as more tender shrubs such as New Zealand tea trees (forms of *Leptospermum*) and *Luma apiculata* with peeling brown bark.

In the annual borders beyond the knot gardens scarlet zinnias (Z. 'Dreamland'), blue- and white-flowered salvias (including the blue Salvia farinacea 'Victoria') and clary (Salvia viridis 'Claryssa') with a distant view of white cosmos, have a more relaxed air. They appear as pleasantly jumbled drifts and blocks of rich colour and reduce the tension in the garden. The scale and ebullient style of these annuals contrasts with the more obviously controlled areas of planting, but the containing frame is none the less present.

In the Elizabethan knot garden, dwarf berberis and germander (Teucrium chamaedrys) are clipped tightly into low hedges to mark out a formal pattern beside beds of lavender cultivars which, as they grow older, make broader sweeps of mauve and blue flower colour. Everywhere at Filoli, inside each enclosure containing different plant themes or colour schemes, linear hedges define the planting within the beds. As lavender bushes mature and develop a pleasantly gnarled woody appearance, they give the whole garden a feeling of age without detracting from their structural role as low hedging plants.

PLANTS FOR THE FLOWER GARDEN

An A to Z guide

Choosing plants for the flower garden is like assembling a cast of actors to rehearse a play. Before making a definite choice of flower – or actor – you need to understand their qualities and limitations, to predict what sort of encouragement they may require to perform well – and even to judge whether they are suited to your particular garden setting.

In the following pages I have chosen those plants that I most enjoy experimenting with – there are hundreds more that I like to use. Each seems to have some specially valuable attribute, either as a single specimen or used in a group, which makes it 'essential' to the gardener – or, at least, to my ideal garden. I am often asked how we choose the plants for the flower garden here in Tintinhull. I cannot give a definitive answer. The descriptions that follow demonstrate how many different qualities we are looking for and perhaps will be helpful in pinning down that elusive *je ne sais quoi* which makes one determine on a particular plant.

For each plant we have included as many useful attributes as possible. Flower and foliage, height and spread, times of flowering and colour variations are all considered. Also included are hardiness zones and a chart (on page 215) which indicates temperatures below which certain plants cannot live. More practically I think, there is a 'usefulness' zoning indicator (in square brackets) which will tell gardeners whether the plant will grow well in their region, especially if given a favourable microclimatic situation. Although none of us wants a plant that will only just survive, most of us like to take a few risks across the margins of safety, and sometimes plants prove surprisingly accommodating.

Some shrubs and small trees are included, particularly those which seem to belong comfortably in the flower garden. I have not described hedging plants in detail here. Some, such as box, yew and holly, are mentioned in the previous chapter as part of the living background to flowers, but a full discussion belongs in a book about general garden styles.

In John Sales' garden in Gloucestershire, border planting is traditional, with a rich tapestry of flower and foliage colour flanking a central pathway. The shapes and textures of grassy and spiky leaves contrast with jagged hellebore foliage and soft lady's mantle. Choosing plants to make an effective scheme is like doing a jigsaw, but you have to hold all the shapes, sizes and tones in your mind's eye as you think the border through its seasonal performance.

ABELIA

(Caprifoliaceae)
A. × grandiflora is a graceful arching semi-ever-green shrub of garden origin with glossy purplish leaves. Pink tubular flowers, slightly scented, are borne for a long period in late summer. Sun; protect from cold wind.
MEDIUM SHRUB H: 1.5–1.8m/5–6ft
s: 90–120cm/36–48in z: 6[6–10]

ABUTILON

(Malvaceae)
A. vitifolium (Chile) is a pyramidal semi-evergreen shrub with soft vine-like grey-green leaves; bell- or saucer-shaped flowers of pale mauve or lilac in early summer. Fast growing; best planted against a sheltering wall. Cut back hard after flowering. *A. × suntense*, its hybrid with *A. ochsenii*, bears smaller deep violet flowers slightly earlier.
MEDIUM SHRUB H: 2.4m/8ft or more s: 1.5m/5ft or more z: 9[9–10]

ACAENA

(Rosaceae) New Zealand burr New Zealand
Evergreen perennials making dense low ground cover of attractive pinnate leaves, grey-green in *A. buchananii* and intense blue-green in *A. adscendens* 'Glauca'. Full sun and well-drained soil. Good for paths and paving, especially for disguising ugly pavement joints.

H: 2.5–5cm/1–2in s: 25–50cm/10–20in z: 6[6–9]

ACANTHUS

(Acanthaceae) bear's breeches
southern Europe
Semi-evergreen or herbaceous perennials with sculptural deeply cut foliage. Well-drained soil; in cold regions mulch in winter.
A. mollis (Latifolius group; from Portugal) has large glossy green arching leaves and handsome 45cm/18in spikes of pink/white foxglove-like flowers in summer. Hardier than the species.
H: 90–120cm/36–48in s: 90cm/36in z: 8[6–10] or colder if mulched

ACHILLEA

(Compositae) yarrow Europe, western Asia
Herbaceous perennials whose flower-heads are dense corymbs of crowded daisies. Sun and well-drained soil; tolerates drought.
A. 'Coronation Gold' has ferny green leaves and vivid yellow flowers in summer. Needs staking.
H: 90cm/36in s: 30cm/12in z: 3[3–10]
A. grandifolia with grey-green dissected leaves, has dull white flowers in early summer. Needs staking.
H: 75cm/30in s: 30cm/12in z: 3[3–10]
A. ptarmica 'Boule de Neige' (syn. *A.p.* 'The Pearl'), with bright white double flowers in summer, is clump-forming and invasive.
H: 45cm/18in s: 60cm/24in z: 3[3–10]

A. × taygetea has lemon-yellow flowers in summer above finely dissected grey leaves. Needs good drainage.
H: 45cm/18in s: 15cm/6in z: 3[3–10]

ACONITUM

(Ranunculaceae) Europe, Asia
A. napellus (common monkshood, helmet flower) is a deciduous perennial. *A.* 'Bressingham Spire', another perennial, has indigo-blue flower-spikes above deeply cut dark green leaves in late summer. *A.* 'Ivorine' is a perennial with hooded creamy-white flowers in early summer. Sun or part shade and moist rich soil.
H: 90cm/36in s: 30cm/12in z: 6[6–9]

AGAPANTHUS

(Liliaceae/Alliaceae) blue African lily
S. Africa
Sun-loving deciduous perennials with strap-shaped leaves and rounded umbels of mainly blue flowers in late summer. Fertile moist but well-drained soil.
A. campanulatus albus (bell agapanthus) has flat-tish heads of white flowers that blend to a creamy-green effect. Best tightly massed. Mulch in winter.
H: 75–100cm/30–40in s: 35–45cm/14–18in z: 8[8–10]
A. Headbourne Hybrids bear rounded umbels

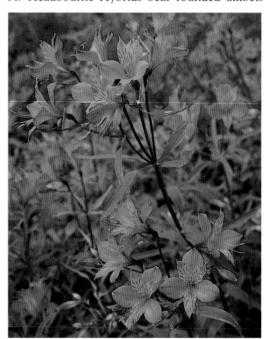

ABOVE *Alstroemeria aurea*
LEFT *Abutilon × suntense*

ranging from dark blue through violet and pale blue to white: choose plants when in flower. Reliably hardy, but mulch in very cold regions.
H: 60–120cm/24–48in   s: 35–45cm/14–18in
z: 8[8-10]

AJUGA
(Labiatae)   bugle, bugleweed   Europe
A. reptans forms are vigorous spreading evergreen perennials making carpeting ground cover on ordinary moist soil in part shade. Ovate leaves may be green, purple-bronze, cream-variegated or tricolour – bronze, pink and green. Blue flower-spikes enrich the colour scheme in summer.
H: 10cm/4in   s: 15cm/6in   z: 3[3–10]

ALCEA
(Malvaceae)   hollyhock
A. rosea (China) provides a colourful backdrop to a late summer border, but the beautiful mallow-flowers on immensely tall spikes are worth appreciating close to. Single and double forms are available, as well as single or mixed coloured flowers in reds, pinks, yellows and white. A.r. 'Nigra' has maroon flowers that are so dark they are almost black. Grow as a perennial or biennial in sun and rich, well-drained soil.
H: 1.5–3m/5–10ft   s: 90cm/36in   z: 2[2–10]

ALCHEMILLA
(Rosaceae)   lady's mantle   eastern Europe to Asia Minor
A. mollis is a deciduous perennial making a mound of light green umbrella-shaped leaves: serrated leaf edges sparkle with droplets of rain or dew. Carries clouds of soft lime-green flowers in summer. Seeds freely in full sun or part shade, and may be invasive.
H: 30cm/12in   s: 35cm/14in   z: 3[3–8]

ALLIUM
(Liliaceae/Alliaceae)
Different allium species flower all through the summer months, mostly with flower-heads in shades of pinkish-mauve, though others are yellow or white. These bulbous perennials are useful for interplanting in herbaceous beds – the flower-spikes and onion-leaves providing contrast of form and texture. All need good drainage and most prefer sun.
A. cernuum (N. America) has drooping heads of lilac-pink in summer. Colonizes rapidly but is still small enough to grow under shrub roses.
H: 45cm/18in   s: 15cm/6in   z: 5[3–8]

A. christophii (Turkestan) has huge but delicate spherical heads composed of a web of pale amethyst-coloured stars; they rise on stout stems above untidy leaves to make statuesque accents between groups of perennials in early summer.
H: 60cm/24in   s: 45cm/18in   z: 5[5–10]
A. schubertii (eastern regions of Mediterranean, central Asia) is a version of A. christophii with irregular-shaped flower-heads of lilac-pink in spring. Although the bulb is hardy, the leaves and flower stem are frost tender.
H: 60cm/24in   s: 45cm/18in   z: 5[5–10]
A. tuberosum (Far East) has flat heads of dark-eyed white flowers in summer. Grow in sun or shade at the front of a border.
H: 45cm/18in   s: 23cm/9in   z: 5[4–10]

ALONSOA
(Scrophulariaceae)   mask flower   Peru
Half-hardy perennials often grown as annuals in sunny site on rich well-drained soil.
A. warscewiczii makes a compact bush, with deep green leaves and reddish stems. Has bright orange-scarlet spurred flowers in late summer.
H: 30–60cm/12–24in   s: 35cm/14in   z: 9[9–10]

ALOYSIA
(Verbenaceae)
A. triphylla (syn. Lippia citriodora; lemon verbena from Chile) has lemon-scented leaves and panicles of tiny pale mauve flowers in late summer. This tender deciduous shrub, for a container or sheltered wall in temperate climates, may be trained into a formal shape.
MEDIUM SHRUB H: 1.5m/5ft   s: 1.2m/4ft
z: 9[8–10]

ALSTROEMERIA
(Liliaceae/Alstroemeriaceae)   Peruvian lily   Chile
Tuberous-rooted herbaceous perennials with strap-shaped leaves making spring ground cover. Clusters of attractively marked lily-flowers appear in summer. Stake unobtrusively with twigs. Slow to establish (most are best grown from seed), but eventually invasive; mulch for frost protection until settled. Sun or part shade.
A. aurantiaca (now correctly A. aurea) has flowers in varying yellows and oranges. Hardy, vigorous and relatively easy to transplant after flowering.
H: 90cm/36in   s: 30cm/12in   z: 7[7–10]
A. Ligtu Hybrids are grey-leaved, with flowers in blush pinks, brighter coral tones and soft yellows.
H: 60cm/24in   s: 30cm/12in   z: 7[7–10]

AMSONIA
(Apocynaceae)   blue dogbane, bluestar   N. America
A. tabernaemontana is a deciduous perennial with erect willowy stems clad in long narrow leaves.

Amsonia tabernaemontana

Both stems and leaves turn golden in late summer. Terminal clusters of starry pale blue flowers are borne in summer. Sun and moist fertile soil.
H & S: 60–90cm/24–36in z: 3[3–9]

ANAPHALIS
(Compositae)   pearl or pearly everlasting
A. *margaritacea* (N. America, eastern Asia) is a deciduous perennial with downy grey leaves and large heads of pearly-white everlasting flowers with yellow eyes in late summer. Sun or part shade and well-drained soil.
H & S: 30–45cm/12–18in z: 3[3–9]

ANEMONE
(Ranunculaceae)   windflower
The spring-flowering European species are compact deciduous perennials with tuberous roots. Summer-flowering Japanese anemones are larger, fibrous-rooted border plants.
A. *apennina* (Europe) has carpeting ferny leaves and blue daisy-flowers in spring. Rich soil and part shade; loves to naturalize through borders under deciduous shrubs.
H & S: 10–15cm/4–6in z: 6[6–10]
Japanese anemones are low-maintenance plants with clumps of palmate dark green leaves, for sun

or part shade and fertile, well-drained but moisture-retentive soil. Slow to establish and eventually invasive, but worth having for the leaves and the display of late-summer flowers. Most garden plants are hybrids: A. × *hybrida* 'Honorine Jobert' has long-lasting pure white flowers with conspicuous yellow stamens. A. × *h.* 'Prince Henry' ('Prinz Heinrich') has deep rose double flowers.
H: 60–90cm/24–36in s: 45–60/18–24in
z: 6[6–10]
A. *nemorosa* (European wood anemone) has simple flowers – usually creamy-white – in spring, though some forms are pink or blue. Naturalizes in part shade under shrubs in soil rich in leaf-mould.
H & S: 15–20cm/6–8in z: 3[3–9]

ANGELICA
(Umbelliferae)   archangel, wild parsnip
Europe, Asia
A. *archangelica* is a dramatic biennial or perennial with deeply dissected fresh green leaves. Large greenish-yellow flower umbels top 1.8–2.4m/6–8ft stems in summer. Sun or part shade and rich soil.
H: 60–150cm/24–60in s: 90cm/36in
z: 4[4–9]

ANISODONTEA
(Malvaceae)
A. *capensis* (S. Africa) is a tender evergreen shrub with attractive green leaves and pink flowers from spring through to autumn, perfect for growing as a centrepiece in an ornamental pot. Root cuttings in late summer and keep frost free.
SMALL SHRUB H & S: 90cm/36in z: 10[9–10]

ANTHEMIS
(Compositae)   Europe
A. *tinctoria* 'E. C. Buxton' is a variety of ox-eye chamomile or golden marguerite with cool lemon-yellow daisy-flowers in summer above attractive deeply cut mid-green leaves. Cut back this deciduous perennial after flowering. Sun and well-drained soil.
H: 75cm/30in s: 45cm/18in z: 3[3–10]

ANTHERICUM
(Liliaceae/Anthericaceae)   southern Europe
A. *liliago* (St Bernard's lily) is an herbaceous perennial with slender spikes of delicate trumpet-shaped white flowers in early summer above clumps of grass-like leaves. Cut back after flowering unless seed-heads are wanted. Sun or part shade and good soil, preferably acid.
H: 45–60cm/18–24in s: 30–38cm/12–15in
z: 8[8–10]

AQUILEGIA
(Ranunculaceae)   columbine
Herbaceous perennials for moist, well-drained soil in sun or part shade. Divided foliage resembles large-scale maidenhair fern; in early summer funnel-shaped flowers have spurred petals.
A. *canadensis* (N. America) has dainty red-spurred lemon-yellow flowers and light green leaves. Grow in naturalized drifts.
H: 45–60cm/18–24in s: 30cm/12in z: 3[3–10]
A. *vulgaris* 'Nora Barlow' is an old variety of the European granny's bonnet – with spurless pink/red/green/blue double flowers and glaucous leaves. Seeds true.
H: 90cm/36in s: 45cm/18in z: 3[3–10]

ARBUTUS
(Ericaceae)   strawberry tree   southern Europe,
Asia Minor
A. *unedo* (Killarney strawberry tree) is evergreen with glossy dark green leaves. Dangling panicles of white pitcher-shaped flowers in late summer intermingle with strawberry-like fruit. Can be a lawn specimen or part of a border scheme. Sun or

Asphodeline liburnica

Anemone apennina

Aquilegia vulgaris 'Nora Barlow'

part shade; protect from cold winds. Ericaceous, but lime-tolerant.
SMALL TREE/LARGE SHRUB H: 5–6m/15–20ft
s: 3–4m/10–12ft   z: 8[8–10]

ARGYRANTHEMUM
(Compositae)
These tender chrysanthemums, which are easy to overwinter from cuttings taken in late summer, grow into attractive shrubby plants that flower prolifically. Ideal as focal points in large pots on a wall or terrace in full sun.
A. foeniculaceum (formerly *Chrysanthemum foeniculaceum*; marguerite, Paris daisy from the Canary Islands) is an evergreen perennial with deeply divided silvery-grey almost glaucous foliage and white daisy-flowers in summer. A. 'Jamaica Primrose' bears lovely pale yellow single flowers, complemented by deeply cut green leaves.
H & S: 60–90cm/24–36in   z: 9[9–10]

ARTEMISIA
(Compositae)
Shrubs and perennials grown for grey and silver leaves that make an attractive foil for other plantings. Survive low temperatures in full sun and well-drained soil.
A. absinthium 'Lambrook Silver', a cultivar of the European absinthe or common wormwood, is a semi-evergreen sub-shrub with woody stems bearing silver-grey dissected leaves. Pale yellow flowers appear in summer.
H & S: 90cm/36in   z: 4[4–10]

A. ludoviciana (white sage from N. America) is an herbaceous perennial with silvery-white felty leaves and silvery-grey flowers in summer. Suckers freely and may be invasive.
H: 120cm/48in   s: 60cm/24in   z: 5[5–10]
A. pontica (south-eastern and central Europe) is a suckering perennial that has smoky-grey feathery foliage and makes good ground cover or pathway edging in sun.
H: 45–75cm/18–30in   s: 45cm/18in   z: 5[5–10]
A. 'Powis Castle' is an evergreen sub-shrub, making a sturdy pewter-toned cushion of fine-cut leaves.
H: 60cm/24in   s: 45cm/18in   z: 8[8–10]
A. schmidtiana 'Silver Mound' is a perennial that makes low mounds of silvery grass-like silky foliage.
H: 10cm/4in   s: 25cm/10in   z: 4[4–10]

ARUM
(Araceae)   south-eastern Europe
A. italicum pictum (correctly *A.i. marmoratum*) has leaves that unfurl in autumn and grow to full lushness in spring – glossy arrow-shapes veined in creamy-white. Spikes of red berries take the place of leaves in late summer. Seeds true. This tuberous perennial makes attractive ground cover in sun or part shade.
H: 38cm/15in   s: 30cm/12in   z: 6[6–10]

ARUNCUS
(Rosaceae)   goatsbeard   northern hemisphere
A. dioicus is a deciduous perennial that makes an attractive clump of elegant fern-like foliage.

Creamy-white plumes of astilbe-like flowers rise 2.1m/7ft tall in summer. An essential border companion plant for making bold groups. Sun or part shade and rich moist soil.
H: 120cm/48in   s: 90cm/36in   z: 3[3–9]

ASARUM
(Aristolochiaceae)   wild ginger
A. europaeum (Europe) is an evergreen rhizomatous perennial that makes creeping ground cover in moist shade or part shade. Handsome dark green glossy leaves, shaped like a rounded heart, hide inconspicuous greenish-brown flowers in spring. Attractive to slugs.
H: 12–15cm/5–6in   s: 20–30cm/8–12in
z: 4[4–8]

ASPHODELINE
(Liliaceae/Asphodelaceae)   Jacob's rod
Mediterranean
A. lutea (king's spear, yellow asphodel) makes architectural perennial clumps of stiff stems clad in semi-evergreen grey-green grassy leaves. Tall racemes of shiny yellow starry flowers in early summer are followed by attractive seed-heads. *A. liburnica* is a shorter form. Rhizomatous rootstock increases slowly. Sun or part shade and well-drained soil.
H: 90–120cm/36–48in   s: 30cm/12in   z: 6[6–10]

ASTER
(Compositae)   N. America
Herbaceous perennials grown for daisy-like flowers. Sun or part shade and rich but well-drained soil.
A. divaricatus (white wood aster) has sprawling wiry black stems that bear a profusion of little white starry flower-heads in late summer to autumn. Tolerates dry shade.
H & S: 45–60cm/18–24in   z: 3[3–9]
A. × frikartii is one of the best later-flowering plants, with freely borne yellow-centred lavender-blue flowers from late summer onwards. *A. × f.* 'Mönch' is the best.
H: 60–90cm/24–36in   s: 38–45cm/15–18in
z: 5[5–10]
A. lateriflorus 'Horizontalis' has compact twiggy stems that bear small dark green leaves with distinctive horizontal habit. Is crowned with a hedge-like mass of tiny palest silvery-lilac flowers with browny-pink centres in autumn.
H: 60–90cm/24–36in   s: 30cm/12in   z: 3[3–10]
A. novae-angliae 'Andenken an Alma Pötschke' (Michaelmas daisy, New England aster) bears

heads of long-lasting rich cherry-red flowers in late summer to autumn. Tolerates moister soils.
H: 90–150cm/36–60in s: 45–60cm/18–24in
z: 4[4–9]

ASTILBE
(Saxifragaceae) eastern Asia
Deciduous perennials with handsome ferny foliage and long-lasting plumes of flowers. Moist or even boggy soil. Sun (in Europe) or part shade in the hotter zones of N. America.
A. rivularis has elegant leaves, very deeply divided and luxuriant. Tall plumed panicles of long-lasting creamy-green flowers, which appear in summer, are attractive even when fading to buff.
A. × arendsii hybrids in white, pinks and reds all have attractive sometimes bronze leaves: choose flower tones to suit individual schemes.
H: 1.8m/6ft s: 1.2m/4ft z: 4[4–9]

ASTRANTIA
(Umbelliferae) masterwort
Deciduous perennials with attractive palmate leaves and dainty flowers in summer, each one a miniature posy of florets in a circle of pointed bracts. Moist rich soil in sun or part shade.
A. major (Europe) has flowers that look greeny-white. A. m. 'Sunningdale Variegated' has young leaves extensively splashed with cream – one of the best variegated perennials. Needs shade to retain this colouring.
H: 60–90cm/24–36in s: 38cm/15in z: 4[4–9]
A. maxima (Europe, eastern Caucasus) has three-lobed leaves and shell-pink flower-heads, surrounded by a deeper pink frill of bracts.
H: 45–75cm/18–30in s: 30–45cm/12–18in
z: 4[4–9]

BALLOTA
(Labiatae) Crete
B. pseudodictamnus has pale woolly-textured rounded leaves. Cut back this evergreen sub-shrub in spring to keep a compact shape and to encourage new growth of silvery-green foliage. Full sun in front of border and good drainage.
H: 30–60cm/12–24in s: 45–60cm/18–24in
z: 8[8–10]

BAPTISIA
(Leguminosae) false indigo
eastern N. America
B. australis is a handsome border perennial with blue-green trifoliate leaves and spikes of indigo-blue pea-flowers in early summer. Dark grey almost black seed-pods are attractive later. Allow to establish in rich moist acid or neutral soil in sun. Tolerates heat and humidity.
H: 60–120cm/24–48in s: 60cm/24in z: 3[3–9]

BERGENIA
(Saxifragaceae)
Large rounded leathery green leaves spread slowly to make substantial evergreen perennial ground cover, good for anchoring front-of-border planting. Full sun or shade; happy in most conditions. Some hybrids carry particularly attractive leaves or flowers: B. purpurascens has purple-flushed leaves in winter. B. × schmidtii has 30cm/12in sprays of clear pink flowers in early spring. B. 'Silberlicht' ('Silver Light') produces pure white flowers slightly later; these become pinkish as they mature.
H: 30cm/12in s: 45–60cm/18–24in z: 4[4–10]

BOLTONIA
(Compositae) N. America
B. asteroides is a perennial that bears masses of pale lilac Michaelmas-daisy flowers above grey foliage in late summer to autumn, making pretty back-of-border infill to complement hydrangeas and other perennials. Easy to grow in sun or part shade and any fertile soil; tolerates heat and humidity.
H: 1.2–2.1m/4–7ft s: 1.2m/4ft z: 3[3–10]

BRUNNERA
(Boraginaceae) western Caucasus
B. macrophylla (Siberian bugloss) makes effective late-spring perennial ground cover, with intensely blue forget-me-not flowers in early summer glowing among heart-shaped hairy dark foliage. As leaves gradually darken and coarsen, allow neighbouring plants to eclipse them with summer flowers. Sun or shade and moist soil; does not tolerate humid heat. B. m. 'Hadspen Cream' is an elegant variegated form that needs protection from drying winds and sun.
H: 45cm/18in s: 60cm/2ft z: 3[3–10]

BUDDLEJA
(Loganiaceae)
Buddlejas like full sun and good loamy soil. Lime-tolerant.
B. alternifolia (China) can grow as a spreading deciduous shrub or be trained as an elegant small tree. Lanceolate leaves are a dark grey-green. Rounded clusters of very fragrant pale lilac flowers appear in summer on the previous year's growth.

Astrantia major

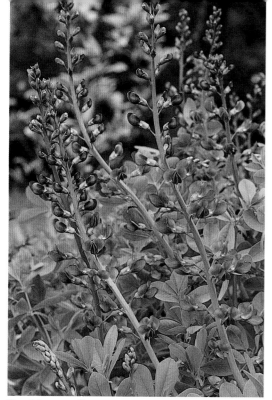

Baptisia australis

B.a. 'Argentea' is a less vigorous silver-leaved form for a small garden.
LARGE SHRUB H & S: 4–6m/12–20ft z: 6[6–9]
B. crispa (syn. *B. paniculata*; from northern India) is a beautiful semi-evergreen shrub for a warm wall in sun. Deeply toothed white-felted leaves make a shimmering dusty-silvery-grey mass, the perfect background for terminal clusters of fragrant lilac-pink flowers with orange throats, which appear in summer on the current year's growth.
MEDIUM SHRUB H: 1.8–3m/6–10ft
s: 1.2–2.4m/4–8ft. z: 9[8–10]
B. davidii (butterfly bush from China) is a decid-uous shrub with terminal trusses of fragrant lilac-purple flowers in late summer on new season's growth. Garden forms offer a colour range from warm red-purple through violet to blue. *B.* 'Lochinch', its hybrid with *B. fallowiana*, has violet-blue flowers and grey woolly leaves with paler undersides. Its misty colouring and graceful habit suit mixed pastel-toned plantings.
MEDIUM SHRUB H & S: 2.7m/9ft z: 6[6–10]

BUGLOSSOIDES
(Boraginaceae)
B. purpurocaerulea is an attractive and useful perennial carpeter, with purplish-blue flowers in late spring to early summer. Vigorous and lime- and shade-tolerant.
H: 40cm/16in s: 90cm/36in z: 4[4–10]

BUPLEURUM
(Umbelliferae) thoroughwax central and southern Europe to Asia
B. fruticosum (shrubby hare's ear), an evergreen shrub of attractive bushy habit, is quick-growing. Subtle colourings of shiny blue-green young foliage and, from midsummer onwards, greenish-yellow flower- and seed-umbels are an effective foil for neighbouring planting. Full sun or part shade. Provide wind shelter and frost drainage.
MEDIUM SHRUB H: 1.8m/6ft s: 3m/10ft
z: 8[8–10]

CALENDULA
(Compositae) marigold
C. officinalis (pot marigold from southern Europe) has large, cheerful daisy-flowers in yellows and oranges; named varieties may offer double flowers, more compact habit and pinkish or pastel tones. Undemanding annuals with a long summer flowering period, thriving in sun and poor soils. Often self-seeds.
H: 30–60cm/12–24in s: 23–45cm/9–18in
ANNUAL

CALLICARPA
(Verbenaceae)
C. bodinieri (China) is a deciduous shrub grown principally for its clusters of deep lilac-coloured fruit carried among rose-tinted autumn foliage. Both male and female shrubs are necessary for fruiting. Insignificant lilac-coloured flowers appear in midsummer. Sunny sheltered position and good garden soil.
MEDIUM SHRUB H & S: 1.5–1.8m/5–6ft z: 5[5–9]

CALTHA
(Ranunculaceae) marsh marigold
Europe, N. America
C. palustris bears numerous rich yellow 25mm/1in flowers in spring above mounded perennial clumps of shiny rounded green leaves. Thrives in damp soil near water, but will flourish in drier shaded sites provided the soil is rich and moist.
H: 30–60cm/12–24in s: 45cm/18in z: 3[3–10]

CAMPANULA
(Campanulaceae)
Border campanulas are easy to grow in good well-drained soil in sun or shade. Flowers in summer. Perennial species make useful colonizers, but tall flower-spikes often need staking.
C. lactiflora (Caucasus) is a perennial with open branching stems clothed in lanceolate leaves, and panicles of bell-shaped flowers in attractive 'washed-out' shades of blue.
H: 90–150cm/36–60in s: 38–45cm/15–18in
z: 6[6–10]
C. latifolia 'Brantwood' is a cultivar of the peren-nial giant bellflower (Europe, Asia). Produces long tubular flowers, in rich violet-purple, above a handsome rosette of rounded leaves.
H: 120–150cm/48–60in s: 38–45cm/15–18in
z: 3[3–10]
C. medium (Canterbury bell from southern Europe) carries large showy bell-shaped flowers in blues, whites and pastels over a long period.
H: 38–90cm/15–36in s: 30cm/12in z: 8[8–10]
or grow as ANNUAL/BIENNIAL
C. persicifolia (peach-leaved or willow bellflower from Europe, northern Africa, Asia) is a peren-nial with blue or white saucer-shaped flowers that stud tall stems clothed with narrow leaves.
H: 30–90cm/12–36in s: 30–45cm/12–18in
z: 3[3–10]
C. pyramidalis (chimney bellflower, steeple bells; from southern Europe) is a short-lived perennial, often grown as a biennial. Tall spires clad in cool blue or white bell-shaped flowers make an arrest-ing pillar of colour above a pyramid of heart-shaped basal leaves.
H: 120–180cm/48–72in s: 45–60cm/18–24in
z: 8[8–10]
C. takesimana (Korea) is a superlative perennial that should be better known. Tubular bell-shaped white flowers, borne on stems arching upwards from a rosette of large leaves, are lilac-mottled outside, maroon-spotted inside.
H: 60cm/24in s: 45cm/18in z: 5[5–10]

CAMPSIS
(Bignoniaceae) trumpet creeper, trumpet vine
Deciduous climbing shrubs that make a dense curtain of attractive pinnate foliage and produce huge drooping clusters of 75mm/3in orange-scarlet tubular flowers in late summer. Full sun, well-drained rich soil and a sheltered site.
C. grandiflora from Asia has wider flowers and is more tender than *C. radicans* from N. America, which is hardy to zone 5.
CLIMBER H: 9–12m/28–40ft z: 7[7–10]

CARDIOCRINUM
(Liliaceae) giant lily
C. giganteum (Himalaya, Tibet) is a dramatic cli-max plant for the light shade of a shrubbery or woodland glade. In summer a spectacular spire of 15cm/6in greenish-white trumpet-flowers emerges

Centranthus ruber

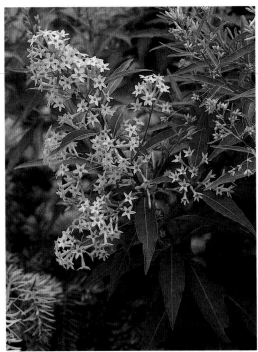

Cestrum parqui

from a deep whorl of glossy heart-shaped leaves. Bulb dies after flowering, but produces offsets that take 3–5 years to mature. A good flowering group is slow to establish but well worth the nurturing and waiting. Moisture-retentive but well-drained soil enriched with plenty of humus is vital.
H: 1.8–3m/6–10ft s: 0.9–1.2m/3–4ft z: 6[6–9]

CAREX
(Cyperaceae) sedge
Grass-like perennials with arching leaves that thrive in sun where soil is cool and moist.
C. *elata* 'Aurea' (Bowles's golden sedge) has leaves striped in green and yellow, turning to gold in summer and then buff.
H: 60cm/24in s: 45cm/18in z: 5[5–9]
C. *oshimensis* 'Evergold' (syn. C. *morrowii* 'Evergold') makes shaggy rounded clumps of foliage that remain effective all year, the leaves brightly variegated in green and yellow.
H: 20–30cm/8–12in s: 15–20cm/6–8in
z: 8[8–10]

CARYOPTERIS
(Verbenaceae) eastern Asia
C. × *clandonensis* is a small deciduous shrub with narrow grey-green aromatic leaves that make a smoky background to clusters of lavender-blue tubular flowers that appear in late summer: several

darker blue forms exist. Sun and well-drained soil.
SMALL SHRUB H & S: 60–120cm/24–48in
z: 7[6–10] (may be cut to ground below zone 7)

CEANOTHUS
(Rhamnaceae) Californian lilac N. America
Evergreen species are tender, wall-loving shrubs, needing favourable sites, though many hybrids are hardier. Deciduous ceanothus are even hardier. Plant in good garden soil.
C. *arboreus* 'Trewithen Blue' grows fast to become a tree-like evergreen shrub in warm gardens, spectacular in late spring and early summer with long panicles of deep blue scented flowers. Its relatively large soft leaves make its hardiness unreliable.
LARGE SHRUB H: 5m/15ft s: 6–8m/20–25ft
z: 9[9–10]
C. 'Burkwoodii', also evergreen, has shiny green leaves with grey undersides and bright blue flowers from midsummer through to autumn.
MEDIUM SHRUB H: 1.8–3m/6–10ft
s: 1.8–2.4m/6–8ft z: 8[8–10]
C. 'Cascade' has arching branches making an elegant weeping evergreen shrub. Small intensely blue flowers appear in early summer.
LARGE SHRUB H & S: 3m/10ft z: 9[8–10]
C. × *delileanus* hybrids are deciduous and hardy enough for open borders, contributing useful flower colour at the end of the season. Prune hard

in spring. C. 'Gloire de Versailles' has a strong open habit and long panicles of pale blue flowers that fit beautifully into misty schemes.
MEDIUM SHRUB H & S: 1.8–2.4m/6–8ft z: 6[6–10]

CELASTRUS
(Celastraceae) climbing staff vine, bittersweet
C. *orbiculatus* (north-eastern Asia) is a strong-growing deciduous climber that will twine over walls, fences, tree stumps etc. Inconspicuous summer flowers are of less interest than the pea-sized bright orange-scarlet fruits, freely borne in autumn against a background of yellowing foliage.
CLIMBER H: to 10m/30ft z: 5[5–10]

CENTRANTHUS
(Valerianaceae) valerian
C. *ruber* (Jupiter's beard, red valerian, fox's brush; from Europe and other Mediterranean regions) is a short-lived perennial with panicles of tiny rosy-red flowers (white in the form C.*r. albus*) from summer onwards above fleshy grey-green leaves. Discard leggy plants after flowering. Tolerates poor, well-drained soils, and is happy to seed and naturalize in walls and paving.
H: 45–90cm/18–36in s: 30–45cm/12–18in
z: 4[4–10]

CERASTIUM
(Caryophyllaceae)
C. *tomentosum* (snow-in-summer from southern Europe) is an evergreen perennial that makes a silvery foliage mat covered in early summer by starry saucer-shaped white flowers. Quickly spreads to soften paving and masonry. Sun and well-drained soil.
H: 15cm/6in s: 60cm/24in z: 3[3–10]

CESTRUM
(Solanaceae) S. America
C. *parqui* is a half-hardy narrow-leaved deciduous willowy shrub bearing plumes of small greeny-yellow tubular flowers – musk-scented at night – in late summer. Sunny, sheltered site and good loamy soil. Prone to frost damage, but if cut back hard sends out new flowering shoots.
MEDIUM SHRUB H & S: 1.2–1.5m/4–5ft z: 8[7–10]

CHELONE
(Scrophulariaceae) turtlehead N. America
C. *obliqua* forms perennial clumps of stiff leafy stems and flowers in late summer to autumn, with deep rosy-purple spikes of curious snapdragon-shape flowers to augment a border scheme. Sun or

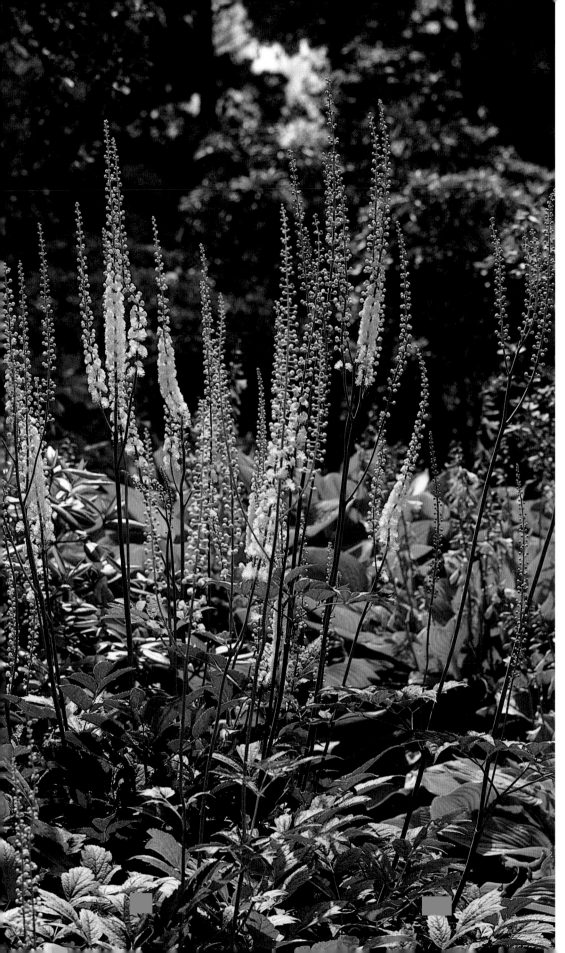

part shade and deep light soil or near water.
H: 60–90cm/24–36in   S: 45–60cm/18–24in
Z: 3[3–9]

CHIASTOPHYLLUM
(Crassulaceae)   Caucasus
C. *oppositifolium* resembles a miniature bergenia, its small succulent dark green leaves making it a useful edging or carpeting evergreen perennial in sun or part shade. Small golden-yellow flowers appear in sprays on 20cm/8in reddish stalks in late summer. Spreads quickly by stem-rooting, and tolerates poor conditions.
H: 10cm/4in   S: 30cm/12in   Z: 6[6–10]

CHIONANTHUS
(Oleaceae)   fringe tree
C. *virginicus* (N. America) is a large deciduous tree-like shrub with fragrant white flowers consisting of strap-like petals. Flowers in midsummer.
LARGE SHRUB H: 7m/22ft   S: 3m/10ft   Z: 5[5–9]

CHIONODOXA
(Liliaceae/Hyacinthaceae)   glory of the snow
Turkey
C. *forbesii* (syn. C. *luciliae*) has short racemes of intensely blue white-eyed flowers that appear with blunt strap-shaped leaves in early spring. In autumn plant groups of bulbs in well-drained soil in short grass or borders, in sun or part shade.
H: 15cm/6in   Z: 4[4–10]

CHOISYA
(Rutaceae)   Mexican orange   Mexico
C. *ternata* is a handsome evergreen shrub with aromatic glossy leaves and sweet-scented orange-blossom flowers in spring. May be massed in part shade or planted more architecturally in formal areas. Shelter by a wall in a cold site, and protect from full sun in hotter areas. Well-drained soil. Look for the new compact form if space is limited.
MEDIUM SHRUB H: 1.5–1.8m/5–6ft
S: 1.8–2.4m/6–8ft   Z: 8[8–10]

CIMICIFUGA
(Ranunculaceae)   bugbane
Graceful perennials for the back of a border or informal planting among shrubs. Tall wands of bottlebrush-flowers appear above clumps of elegant ferny leaves. Prefer cool moist places; intolerant of high humidity.

Cimicifuga racemosa

C. racemosa (black cohosh, black snakeroot; from eastern N. America) has fragrant feathery white flowers on 2.4m/8ft branching stems in summer.
H: 1.2–1.5m/4–5ft   s: 0.6m/2ft   z: 3[3–10]
C. ramosa (China) produces 30cm/12in spires of white flowers from late summer into autumn. *C.r.* 'Atropurpurea' is a purple-leaved form.
H: 1.5–2.1m/5–7ft   s: 0.9–1.2m/3–4ft   z: 3[3–9]

CIRSIUM
(Compositae)   thistle   central Europe
C. rivulare atropurpureum is a deciduous perennial grown for the sculptural shape of its bristly pinnate leaves as well as for the deep wine-red pincushion-flowers that appear in summer. Sun and damp soil.
H: 60–120cm/24–48in   s: 60cm/24in
z: 4[4–10]

RIGHT *Clematis viticella* 'Purpurea Plena Elegans'
BELOW *Clematis recta*

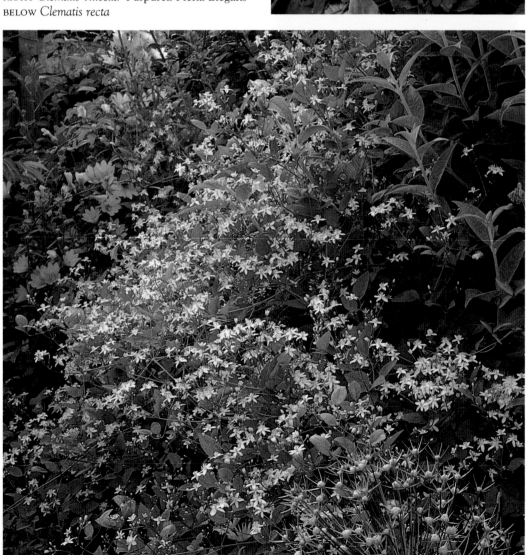

CISTUS
(Cistaceae)   rock rose, sun rose
Mediterranean
Sun-loving evergreen shrubs massed with white or pale pink flowers like single roses in early summer. Flowers last only a day, but are borne in long succession. Not reliably hardy; suitable for dry rocky banks or sheltered corners. Prefer poor well-drained soils.
C. × cyprius, *C. ladanifer*'s hybrid with *C. laurifolius*, has sticky olive-green leaves and papery white flowers, 75mm/3in wide, with a crimson blotch. Vigorous and one of the hardiest cistus.
MEDIUM SHRUB H: 1.8–2.4m/6–8ft
s: 2.1–2.7m/7–9ft   z: 8[8–10]
C. ladanifer (gum cistus) is a stiff upright bush with dull green leaves. The 60mm/2½in flowers have a chocolate blotch at each petal base and yellow centres.
MEDIUM SHRUB H: 1.8m/6ft   s: 1.2m/4ft
z: 8[8–10]
C. 'Silver Pink' is an attractive compact hardy shrub. Clusters of clear pink yellow-centred flowers are freely carried above leathery dark green leaves with grey undersides.
SMALL SHRUB H & s: 60–90cm/24–36in
z: 8[8–10]

CLEMATIS
(Ranunculaceae)
The climbing species and hybrids are indispensable for curtaining walls, garlanding pergolas, decorating plain evergreens and leafy shrubs, and disguising stumps. Full sun, roots in shade. All like well-drained fertile soil with some lime. Choose from wide range available, selecting flowers in the colouring, scale and season that suit your situation.
C. alpina (southern and central Europe) and *C. macropetala* (Siberia, northern China) are both scrambling spring-flowering deciduous species, typically blue and not too vigorous.
CLIMBER H: 1.8–4m/6–12ft   z: 2–6[2–9]
C. armandii (China) is a vigorous evergreen, with long leathery dark green leaves and creamy-white clustered flowers in spring. Feed generously. Not reliably hardy.
CLIMBER H: to 10m/30ft   z: 8[8–10]
C. cirrhosa (Balearic Islands) has ferny evergreen leaves. Drooping creamy flowers with purple-spotted insides appear in spring. Not reliably hardy.
CLIMBER H: 3m/10ft   z: 8[8–10]
C. flammula (fragrant virgin's bower from southern Europe) has bushy deciduous growth. Panicles

of small pure white fragrant flowers appear in late summer. Grow through trellis or low spring-flowering shrubs of open habit.
CLIMBER H: 3m/10ft z: 7[7–10]
C. heracleifolia 'Wyevale' is a perennial that forms a leafy shrub-like mound, with clusters of deep blue hyacinth-flowers in late summer.
H: 60–90cm/24–36in z: 3[3–9]
C. 'Huldine' has almost translucent white petals, palest mauve outside and with greenish stamens. Cut back this deciduous climber hard in winter to encourage summer flowering on young wood.
CLIMBER H: 4m/12ft z: 5[5–10]
C. × *jackmanii* is a large-flowered deciduous clematis hybrid (*C. viticella* is one parent) producing violet-purple flowers for many weeks from midsummer. Prune in late winter and train into shape during spring. A wonderful companion for bronze foliage and deep red flowers.
CLIMBER H: 4m/12ft z: 5[5–10]
C. montana (central and western China, Himalayas) is rampant, a beautiful deciduous backdrop in a big enough garden. The species has white flowers in early summer; many varieties have pink or lilac tints and are slightly less vigorous. Prune after flowering if necessary to control spread.
CLIMBER H: to 12m/40ft s: 5–6m/15–20ft
z: 5[5–10]
C. recta (ground clematis from southern Europe) is a perennial with a tendency to sprawl. Makes superb clumps with 180cm/6ft stems carrying starry white flowers to produce a cloud effect in early summer. A companion to early-flowering thalictrums and crambes.
H: 60–150cm/24–60cm. z: 3[3–10]
C. viticella types are moderately vigorous deciduous climbers, with nodding bell-shaped flowers in shades of blue and purple in summer. *C. v.* 'Purpurea Plena Elegans' is rose-purple, a densely packed rosette of sepals. *C.* 'Abundance' has soft purple flowers. Grow on walls and through neighbouring shrubs, and prune hard in early spring.
CLIMBER H: 2.7–4m/9–12ft z: 5[5–10]

CLEOME
(Capparidaceae) spider flower
tropical America
C. hassleriana (syn. *C. spinosa* of gardens) is a late-summer flowering annual with clusters of pink and white or violet flowers that appear at the tips of hairy stalks. Plant seed in late spring. Group in sunny beds and borders for a pretty weaving mass of pastel colour.
H: 90cm/36in s: 45cm/18in ANNUAL

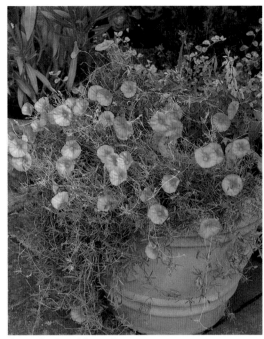
Convolvulus althaeoides

CLERODENDRUM
(Verbenaceae) Far East
C. trichotomum makes a strong-growing deciduous shrub, best as a lawn specimen in a sunny sheltered site, where suckers may be controlled. Very fragrant white star-shaped flowers with persistent maroon calyces appear in late summer, followed by turquoise berries. Those of *C. t. fargesii* are a lighter blue.
SMALL TREE H & S: 3–5m/10–15ft z: 6[6–10]

COLCHICUM
(Liliaceae/Colchicaceae) autumn crocus
C. speciosum (Turkey, Caucasus) has large crocus-like flowers 15cm/6in high in shades of pinkish mauve; *C. s.* 'Album' is white. Plant in drifts in sun or shade for an autumn carpet in grass or at the edge of a shrubbery, where there is space for the dense spring foliage. Allow corms to naturalize and increase.
H: 30–40cm/12–16in s: 23–30cm/9–12in
z: 4[4–10]

CONVALLARIA
(Liliaceae/Convallariaceae) lily-of-the-valley
Europe, Asia, N. America
C. majalis 'Fortin's Giant' is a perennial that is larger and later-flowering than the species: dainty waxy white flowers in late spring are bell-shaped and very sweetly scented. The mid-green leaf-

spikes make good summer ground cover in shade and humus-rich soil. Creeping rhizomes colonize quickly once established, becoming invasive in favourable conditions.
H: 20cm/8in s: 30cm/12in z: 3[3–9]

CONVOLVULUS
(Convolvulaceae)
All like light well-drained soil and full sun, and need frost protection in exposed sites.
C. althaeoides (southern Europe) is a deciduous semi-climber with silvery grey-green dissected foliage and trailing stems. Funnel-shaped shell-pink flowers in summer open wide in sun. Grow in a container or over a wall where the root-run is contained but the plant can sprawl in charming abandon.
H: 15cm/6in s: 45–60cm/18–24in z: 8[7–10]
C. cneorum (evergreen silverbush from southern Europe) is an evergreen shrub. Its small narrow leaves have a silky silvery sheen. White funnel-flowers open from pinkish buds in early summer.
SMALL SHRUB H: 45cm/18in s: 60cm/24in
z: 8[8–10]
C. sabatius (syn. *C. mauritanicus*; ground morning glory from northern Africa) also forms a sprawling perennial mat of grey-green ovate leaves. In early summer twisted flower-buds open to wide funnel-flowers of deep lavender blue. Cut back hard to encourage spring growth.
H: 15cm/6in s: 60cm/24in z: 9[8–10]

CORDYLINE
(Liliaceae/Agavaceae) evergreen cabbage palm
New Zealand
Evergreen trees and shrubs grown for handsome palm-like foliage. Cordylines are tender or half-hardy; in cold districts, grow as pot plants about 90cm/36in tall for architectural emphasis and shelter in winter.
C. australis (cabbage tree) has branches bearing dense clusters of sword-like leaves atop an erect stem. Produces huge drooping panicles of fragrant creamy flowers in summer in a favourable site.
SMALL TREE H: 8m/25ft s: 1.8–3m/6–10ft
z: 9[9–10]

COREOPSIS
(Compositae) tickseed N. America
C. verticillata (thread-leaf tickseed or coreopsis) is an erect bushy perennial with very fine hair-like foliage and loose corymbs of rather brassy yellow daisy-flowers in late summer. *C. v.* 'Moonbeam', which has paler flowers to associate in a cooler

Cosmos atrosanguineus

scheme, flowers for longer, enduring intense summer heat. Dead-head to prolong flowering. Sun and well-drained soil. Slow to establish.
H: 45–60cm/18–24in S: 30–45cm/12–18in
Z: 3[3–10]

CORNUS
(Cornaceae) dogwood
The dogwoods described are graceful middle-storey deciduous trees or shrubs with flower interest in spring and attractive autumn leaves.
C. alternifolia 'Argentea' (N. America) is a handsome small tree with tiered branches of delicate silver and green foliage. Flat corymbs of small flowers appear in late spring.
SMALL TREE H: 4m/12ft S: 3m/10ft Z: 4[4–9]
C. controversa 'Variegata' (China, Japan) also has horizontal branches in wedding-cake tiers, and the alternate leaves are cream-edged. Like *C. alternifolia* 'Argentea', on a larger scale, it is elegantly architectural even when leafless in winter.
MEDIUM TREE H & S: 8m/25ft Z: 6[6–10]
C. florida (flowering dogwood from eastern USA) is an elegant spreading shrub or small tree. Four petal-like white bracts surround tiny green flowers in late spring. Susceptible to late frosts.
LARGE SHRUB/SMALL TREE H: 3–5m/10–15ft
S: 6m/20ft Z: 5[5–9]
C. kousa chinensis (China) is a small upright tree with spreading branches and inconspicuous flowers set in showy white bracts in early summer. Lime-tolerant. Plant in woodland with some shade from fierce summer sun.
LARGE SHRUB/SMALL TREE H: 3m/10ft
S: 2.4–3m/8–10ft Z: 5[5-9]

C. nuttallii (Nuttall's West Coast dogwood from western N. America) has conspicuous white bracts in late spring, which take on a pink tinge in sun. Leaves colour in autumn. Acid soil essential.
LARGE SHRUB H: 5–6m/15–20ft
S: 2.4–3m/8–10ft Z: 8[8–10]

CORONILLA
(Leguminosae)
C. glauca (southern Europe) has delicate grey-green evergreen leaves. Its delightful pale yellow pea-flowers, borne intermittently all winter, are at their best in spring. Grow as a wall shrub or as a sprawling bush in full sun to accompany violet-flowered abutilons.
MEDIUM SHRUB H & S: 2.1m/7ft Z: 9[9–10]

CORYDALIS
(Papaveraceae)
C. cheilanthifolia (China) makes neat evergreen perennial clumps of fresh green ferny leaves and bears little spikes of yellow miniature snapdragon-flowers all summer. Self-seeds and spreads in a cool site. Good for interplanting with bulbs.
H & S: 25–30cm/10–12in Z: 5[5–10]

CORYLOPSIS
(Hamamelidaceae)
C. pauciflora (Japan) is a pretty deciduous shrub of open habit for a shady mixed border or a woodland glade. Drooping pale yellow cup-shaped cowslip-scented flowers are carried in spring, just before the leaves open. Grow above blue-flowered scillas or anemones.
MEDIUM SHRUB H & S: 1.8m/6ft Z: 6[6–9]

COSMOS
(Compositae) Mexico
C. atrosanguineus (black cosmos) is an unusual dahlia-related perennial with long-lasting chocolate-scented velvety-maroon flowers in late summer. The slightly tender tubers may be lifted in winter or protected with a thick mulch. Sun and deep moisture-retentive soil. Striking grown in a container.
H: 75cm/30in S: 30cm/12in Z: 9[7–10]

COTINUS
(Anacardiaceae) smoke tree
C. coggygria (smoke bush, Venetian sumach; from Europe to Caucasus) is a deciduous shrub with bronzy-green ovate leaves that give good autumn colour. Panicles of tiny purple flowers in summer create a smoky hazy texture amid the foliage. Named forms have purple leaves.
MEDIUM SHRUB H & S: 2.4m/8ft Z: 5[5–10]
C. obovatus (syn. *C. americanus*; chittam wood from south-eastern USA) is more upright deciduous shrub with purplish-pink leaves that shade in summer to glaucous-green and colour brilliantly in autumn.
LARGE SHRUB H: 3m/10ft S: 1.8–2.4m/6–8ft
Z: 6[6–9]

COTONEASTER
(Rosaceae)
Low-growing cotoneasters are architectural shrubs and make shapely ground covers. Taller ones offer good back-of-border furnishing or screening.
C. conspicuus (Tibet) is semi-evergreen, its branches clothed with pink buds opening to white flowers in summer. Soft red berries are carried in autumn. Its arching mound-like habit is attractive on a dry bank.
MEDIUM SHRUB H: 1.8–2.1m/6–7ft
S: 1.5–1.8m/5–6ft Z: 6[6–9]
C. 'Cornubia' is semi-evergreen, with long dark green leaves and creamy flowers in early summer. Large red fruits are prolific and long-lasting.
LARGE SHRUB/SMALL TREE H & S: 6m/20ft
Z: 7[7–9]
C. horizontalis (herringbone cotoneaster from China) has stiffly spreading fan-like branches that provide a useful base to anchor upright forms. Foliage colour and dark red berries glow in autumn. Use this deciduous shrub to spread over neighbouring pavements or against walls.
SMALL SHRUB H: 0.6m/2ft S: 1.8–2.1m/6–7ft
Z: 6[6–9]

C. *lacteus* (China) is evergreen, with large oval leaves, grey beneath. Milky-white flowers in summer are followed by late-ripening red fruits. Good for hedging.
LARGE SHRUB H: 3–5m/10–15ft
S: 2.4–4m/8–12ft Z: 7[7–9]
C. 'Rothschildianus' is evergreen, with a more spreading habit and light green leaves. Fruit is creamy-yellow.
MEDIUM SHRUB H: 1.8–3m/6–10ft
S: 3–5m/10–15ft Z: 7[7–9]

CRAMBE
(Cruciferae) kale
C. *cordifolia* (colewort, giant kale; from the Caucasus) is a dramatic perennial with large rough heart-shaped leaves and tall stems bearing a cloud of tiny white flowers in early summer. Stalks need firm staking. Trim off any damaged leaves as they appear during summer. A statuesque back-of-border or cornerstone plant for sun and deep well-drained soil.
H: 1.8m/6ft S: 1.2m/4ft Z: 6[6–9]

CRATAEGUS
(Rosaceae) thorn
C. × *lavallei* is a dense-headed deciduous tree with long glossy leaves. Clusters of white single flowers appear in early summer, and orange-red fruits in autumn. Drought- and wind-resistant.
SMALL TREE H: 5–6m/15–20ft S: 3–5m/10–15ft
Z: 5[5–9]

CRINUM
(Liliaceae/Amaryllidaceae) S. Africa
C. × *powellii* is free-flowering and relatively hardy. Bright green strap-shaped leaves emerge from the enormous bulb in spring, followed by stout stems bearing umbels of fragrant pink or white trumpet-shaped flowers in late summer. Sun and rich deep soil; in cold districts protect by a heat-reflecting wall and with a winter mulch.
H: 45cm/18in S: 30–45cm/12–18in
Z: 9[7–10 when mulched]

CROCOSMIA
(Iridaceae) montbretia S. Africa
Sheaves of sword-like leaves from corms provide useful textural contrast in borders, with elegant branching spikes of tubular flowers contributing eye-catching colour in summer; the related montbretia colonizes and may be invasive. Sunny well-drained site. Named hybrids are hardier and make important contributions to border colour schemes:
C. 'Lucifer' is robust but elegant, with brilliant flame-red flowers in midsummer.
H: 120cm/48in S: 23cm/9in Z: 7[5–10 when mulched]
C. 'Solfaterre' has bronze-tinged leaves and pale apricot-yellow flowers, together creating an understated smoky tone.
H: 60cm/24in S: 15cm/6in
Z: 8[7–10 when mulched]

Cyclamen repandum

CROCUS
(Iridaceae) Levant, southern Europe
C. *sativus* (saffron crocus) is a cormous perennial with large rich purple dark-veined flowers opening to reveal red stigma and orange anthers. Flowers appear with the leaves in late summer to autumn. Plant in drifts in sun and rich soil; needs a warm site to thrive.
H: 10cm/4in Z: 4[4–10]
C. *tommasinianus* (Yugoslavia) flowers in spring, in a range of shades from lavender-blue to deep reddish-purple, and there is a white form. This sturdy hardy corm happily colonizes in short grass.
H: 75mm/3in Z: 4[4–10]

CYCLAMEN
(Primulaceae) Mediterranean
Hardy species of cyclamen make attractive carpets of subtly patterned foliage and pinkish-toned flowers in partly shaded sites. Well-drained soil, rich in humus.
C. *hederifolium* (sowbread) is a tuberous perennial with marbled ivy-like leaves in winter and early spring. These disappear and are succeeded by flowers in shades of mauve to pale pink and white in late summer and autumn.
H: 10cm/4in S: 10–15cm/4–6in Z: 5[5–10]
C. *repandum* is a tuberous perennial with arrow-shaped leaves. Scented flowers with twisted petals in pale pinks, whites and deep carmine appear in spring. Sheltered site.
H: 15cm/6in S: 15–20cm/6–8in Z: 8[8–10]

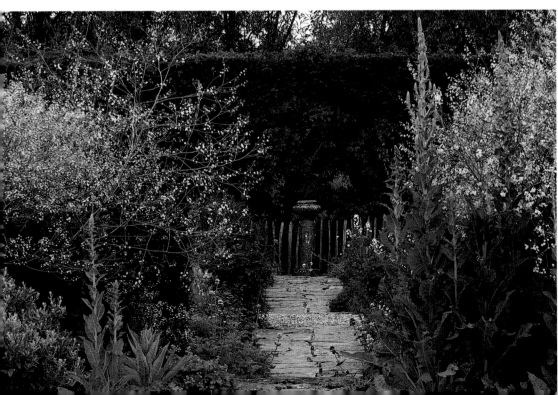

Crambe cordifolia

CYNARA

(Compositae)   Europe

C. cardunculus (cardoon) is a striking architectural perennial. Its bold clumps of deeply divided silvery-grey leaves are effective punctuating a design as well as massed in large-scale textural groups. Stout branching stems bear large violet thistle-flowers in summer. Sun, with some shade in hot climates, and well-drained fertile soil; winter mulch in cold areas.

H: 1.8m/6ft s: 0.9m/3ft z: 8[6–10 when mulched]

CYTISUS

(Leguminosae)   broom

C. battandieri (Moroccan broom, Pineapple broom) is a slightly tender semi-evergreen shrub with silvery trifoliate leaves and racemes of pineapple-scented pea-flowers in summer. Protect near a sunny wall. May be pruned and tied back.
LARGE SHRUB H: 5m/15ft s: 2.4–4m/8–12ft z: 8[8–10]

C. × praecox 'Warminster' (Warminster broom) is a hardier deciduous shrub. The sprays of flat stem-like leaves are insignificant until covered with a profusion of creamy-coloured flowers in early summer. Full sun and well-drained soil.
MEDIUM SHRUB H & S: 1.5–1.8m/5–6ft z: 7[7–9]

DAHLIA

(Compositae)   Mexico

Dahlia hybrids offer a wide spectrum of long-lasting colour for late summer. Many of the more extravagant forms are best massed (and carefully staked) in grandiose bedding schemes; the following have enough character to make eloquent contributions to mixed plantings. Most tubers are tender but if thickly mulched will survive low temperatures.

D. 'Bishop of Llandaff' has elegant pinnate foliage of a metallic bronze-purple colour, which sets off the bright scarlet of the peony-flowers and adds its richness to border schemes of glowing or sombre reds.
H: 120cm/48in s: 60cm/24in z: 9[8–10 when mulched]

D. merckii (bedding dahlia from Mexico) is a slender elegant hardy species bearing simple single pink to lavender flowers. Planted in a block, it seldom requires staking.
H: 1.8m/6ft s: 0.9m/3ft z: 9[8–10 when mulched]

Dahlia merckii

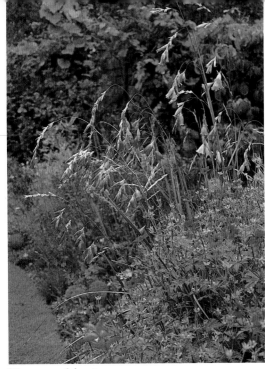

Dierama pulcherrimum

DAPHNE

(Thymelaeaceae)

D. × burkwoodii 'Somerset' is semi-evergreen and one of the faster-growing daphnes, with very fragrant pink flowers in early summer. Sun or part shade and well-drained site.
SMALL SHRUB H & S: 90–120cm/36–48in z: 6[6–9]

D. odora 'Aureomarginata' (China, Japan) with a spreading habit has variegated glossy evergreen leaves and fragrant pink flowers in spring. Is more vigorous and hardier than its green-leaved type.
MEDIUM SHRUB H & S: 1.5–1.8m/5–6ft z: 8[8–10]

DARMERA

(Saxifragaceae)

D. peltata (formerly *Peltiphyllum peltatum*; umbrella plant from California and Oregon) has round heads of starry pinkish-white flowers carried on tall stems in spring, before the shield-shaped leaves emerge to make a dense low perennial mound of handsome rounded foliage. Good for autumn colour. Sun or shade, but likes moist soil: plant in a bog-garden or at the waterside with primulas and other moisture-loving perennials.
H: 60–120cm/24–48in s: 60–90cm/24–36in z: 6[6–9]

DATURA

(Solanaceae)

D. inoxia (formerly *D. meteloides*; from Texas) is an exotic shrubby perennial with hairy greyish leaves and fragrant creamy-white trumpet-flowers 15cm/6in long borne in summer. Likes hot sun. Usually grown as an annual border plant in rich soil; also good in containers.
H: 90cm/36in s: 75cm/30in   ANNUAL

DELPHINIUM

(Ranunculaceae)

Tall spires of large-flowered hybrids are a classic ingredient in traditional herbaceous borders. Sun and richly fed well-drained soil.

D. × belladonna hybrids are compact perennials producing graceful loose flower-spikes from mid-summer. The branching stems may not need staking. Flowers are white, and blue from palest to navy. *D.b.* 'Lamartine' is a deep violet-blue.
H: 90–135cm/36–54in s: 60cm/24in z: 3[3–10]

D. elatum hybrids are perennials producing stately erect spikes crowded in summer with flowers in every gradation of blue, plus white, pinkish-lavenders, mauves and violets, some with contrasting eyes. Choose from named colour forms. Stake stems individually in early summer.
H: 0.9–2.4m/3–8ft s: 0.6–0.9m/2–3ft z: 3[3–10]

DEUTZIA

(Hydrangeaceae)

D. × rosea is a compact deciduous shrub with gracefully arching branches bearing clusters of wide bell-shaped pink flowers in summer. Sun

and well-drained soil, with plenty of moisture-retentive compost to encourage flowering.
SMALL SHRUB H & S: 90cm/36in z: 6[6–9]

DIANTHUS
(Caryophyllaceae) pink
Pinks make sprawling tufts of grey-green spiky grass-like leaves that are often evergreen. Fragrant flowers in shades of pinks and white, single or double, and often marked or zoned in a deeper tone, appear in summer; modern hybrids often flower again in late summer. Full sun or part shade and gritty well-drained soil.
H: 25–38cm/10–15in s: 30cm/12in z: 4[4–10]
D. barbatus (sweet William from eastern Europe, Asia) is a cottage-garden perennial often grown as a biennial. Crowded flattened flower-heads range in colour from white through pinks to carmine and crimson-purple, and are often zoned in two tones. Is often sold as a mixture of colours; a mass in a bed or border front makes a mosaic pattern of harmonizing colours. Single colours are sometimes available. *D.b.* 'Niger' has dusky purple-tinged foliage and dark red almost black flowers. Sun and rich moist well-drained alkaline soil. Sow seed outdoors for summer transplanting to next year's site.
H & S: 30–60cm/12–24in z: 4[4–10]

DIASCIA
(Scrophulariaceae) twinspur S. Africa
D. vigilis (syn. *D. elegans*) makes a loose perennial mound of erect and sprawling leaf-clad stems, tipped throughout the summer months with racemes of pale pink-lipped flowers. Makes an attractive bedding or container plant for temperate regions: overwinter cuttings. Sun or part shade and rich well-drained but moisture-retentive soil. *D.* 'Ruby Field' is a relatively hardy hybrid with deep coral-pink flowers.
H: 30–45cm/12–18in s: 45cm/18in
z: 8–9[8–10]

DICENTRA
(Fumariaceae) bleeding heart
D. formosa (N. America) has pretty lacy grey-green leaves. Drooping heart-shaped flowers borne in early summer are pinky-mauve. Low clumps of foliage make good perennial ground cover in the part shade of shrub roses of the same classic 'rose' tones. *D.f.* 'Stuart Boothman' produces a subtle combination of pink flowers and smoky-grey foliage.
H & S: 30–45cm/12–18in z: 3[3–10]

DICTAMNUS
(Rutaceae) burning bush, gas plant
southern Europe, Asia
D. albus (dittany, fraxinella) is a handsome long-lived perennial with aromatic leaves. White flowers with long stamens emit volatile oil and are carried in erect spikes for a short period in early summer. They are followed by attractive star-shaped seed-pods. Sun or part shade. *D.a. purpureus* has mauve flowers with darker veining.
H: 60–90cm/24–36in s: 75cm/30in z: 3[3–10]

DIERAMA
(Iridaceae) angel's fishing rod, wandflower
S. Africa
D. pulcherrimum has a corm that forms tufts of grass-like evergreen leaves that anchor long arching 'wands' of flowers in summer – silvery calyces opening to hanging bell-flowers of pale to deep rose-pink. Looks lovely reflected in water. Well-drained soil, preferably in sun, though part shade is tolerated. Self-seeds in unexpected corners.
H: 180cm/72in s: 30–60cm/12–24in z: 9[8–10]

DIGITALIS
(Scrophulariaceae) foxglove
Tall spikes of thimble-shaped flowers in early summer make charming vertical emphasis in informal plantings. Part shade or sun, but not too hot, and ordinary humus-rich soil.

Dictamnus albus and *D.a. purpureus*

Eryngium giganteum

D. ferruginea (rusty foxglove from southern Europe, central Asia) is a perennial best treated as a biennial. Has tall stems of fine small coppery-yellow flower-trumpets with rust-coloured veining.
H: 90–120cm/36–48in s: 30–45cm/12–18in z: 4[4–10]

D. grandiflora (yellow foxglove from Europe, Caucasus, Siberia) is a stockier clump-forming evergreen perennial with large creamy-yellow flowers and slightly shiny leaves.
H: 60–90cm/24–36in s: 30cm/12in z: 4[4–10]

D. lutea (small yellow foxglove from south-western Europe, north-western Africa) is a graceful perennial with slender tapering spires of slim pale yellow tubular flowers. Self-seeds freely.
H: 60–90cm/24–36in s: 30cm/12in z: 4[4–10]

D. purpurea alba (western Europe) is the lovely white form of the common biennial or perennial foxglove. Allow to naturalize in woodland and 'wild' areas. Weed out seedlings with reddish leaf-stems, which produce pink flowers.
H: 90–150cm/36–60in s: 45–60cm/18–24in z: 3[3–10]

DODECATHEON
(Primulaceae) American cowslip, shooting star N. America
D. meadia is a perennial with a rosette of long smooth leaves, reddish at the base, that die away after flowering. In early summer stout 60cm/24in stems bear loose umbels of nodding cyclamen-like flowers with reflexed petals, in shades from palest pinky-white to purplish-rose. Shade or part shade and damp humus-rich soil.
H: 30–45cm/12–18in s: 30cm/12in z: 4[4–9]

ECCREMOCARPUS
(Bignoniaceae) Chilean glory flower Chile
E. scaber is a perennial climber that seeds freely and may be grown as an annual against a warm wall or curtaining shrubs in colder areas. Has attractive pinnate leaves and racemes of tubular orange-scarlet flowers from midsummer onwards. Crimson-red, yellow and orange forms are available and usually come true from seed. The fire colours are lovely in 'hot' schemes, brightening dark green neighbouring foliage like lamps.
CLIMBER H: 2.4–3m/8–10ft z: 9[9–10] or grow as ANNUAL

ECHINOPS
(Compositae) globe thistle
Imposing perennials with divided thistle-like leaves and spherical flower-heads on wiry stems in late summer. Sun and ordinary garden soil.
E. 'Nivalis' is a splendid, elegant foliage plant, with grey spiky leaves and greyish-white drumstick flowers.
H: 180cm/72in s: 60cm/24in z: 3[3–10]
E. ritro (eastern Europe, western Asia) is compact, with jagged green leaves, grey beneath, and grey stems bearing deep steel-blue globular flower-heads.
H: 60–120cm/24–48in s: 60cm/24in z: 3[3–10]

EPILOBIUM
(Onagraceae) fireweed
E. angustifolium album (northern hemisphere), a white form of the very invasive rose-bay, French or great willow herb, is sufficiently well-behaved to allow in the garden, where it makes a superlative perennial in sun or shade. Tall spires of ethereal white flowers, giving a ghostly effect, top stems clothed in narrow green leaves in summer. Seed capsules open to reveal glistening seeds resembling feathery hairs.
H: 90–150cm/36–60in s: 60cm/24in z: 3[3–9]

EPIMEDIUM
(Berberidaceae) barrenwort, bishop's hat
Once established, these perennials spread to make attractive weed-suppressing ground cover in sun or shade. Prefer a cool position and tolerate root competition under shrubs. Roughly heart-shaped veined leaves colour to pink and bronze in winter, and in some species almost hide the sprays of small flowers in spring.
E. grandiflorum 'Rose Queen' has loose spikes of deep pink white-spurred flowers held above the leaves.
H: 23–30cm/9–12in s: 30cm/12in z: 5[5–9]
E. pinnatum colchicum (Caucasus, Iran) is almost evergreen and has bright yellow short-spurred flowers.
H: 23–30cm/9–12in s: 30cm/12in z: 5[5–9]

ERANTHIS
(Ranunculaceae)
E. hyemalis (winter aconite from Europe) is a perennial with a ruff of bright green leaf-like bracts around the single buttercup-flower in midwinter, massed flowers forming a glowing carpet of golden-green under deciduous shrubs and trees. Clumps of its deeply cut leaves may be mown with the grass in spring.
H & S: 75–100mm/3–4in z: 5[5–9]

EREMURUS
(Liliaceae/Asphodelaceae) foxtail lily
E. robustus (giant desert candle from Turkestan) has immensely tall flower-spikes of peachy-pink, soaring from a perennial clump of lax strap-shaped leaves in summer. Grow in sun and rich well-drained soil at the back of a border where bushy neighbours can spread to fill the vacuum left when the leaves die away untidily after flowering.
H: 1.8–2.7m/6–9ft s: 0.9m/3ft z: 6[6–9]
E. Shelford Hybrids are more compact perennials,

with grass-like foliage and, in summer, flowers from palest pink and yellow to rich coppery-orange.
H: 180cm/72in s: 75cm/30in z: 6[6–9]

ERIGERON
(Compositae) fleabane
E. karvinskianus (bonytip fleabane, Mexican daisy; from central America) is a sprawling slightly shrubby perennial with wiry stems bearing a mass of white daisy-flowers later tinged with pink. In a warm climate it flowers from spring to autumn, colonizing well-drained spots such as drystone walls and paving.
H: 15–45cm/6–18in s: 60cm/24in z: 9[9–10]

ERYNGIUM
(Umbelliferae)
Handsome plants with steel-blue, silvery or marbled white leaves.
E. giganteum (Miss Willmott's ghost from Cauca-

Digitalis ferruginea

sus, Iran) is a biennial: grow in sun to encourage the leaves to fade from green in spring to shimmering almost translucent grey, a beautiful foil for the pale blue-grey thistle-heads at midsummer. Well-drained soil. Freely self-seeds.
H: 90–120cm/36–48in s: 60cm/24in z: 5[5–10]
E. × zabelii 'Violetta' is of more compact stature and perennial. Large flower-heads and ruffs of delicate bracts borne in summer are violet-blue.
H: 60–75cm/24–30in s: 45cm/18in z: 5[5–10]

ERYSIMUM
(Cruciferae)
E. 'Bowles' Mauve' (also listed as E. linifolium 'E. A. Bowles' and Cheiranthus 'Bowles' Mauve') is a short-lived woody perennial. Clear pale magenta spikes of wallflower-like blooms are borne above bushy mounds of grey-green leaves for many weeks in early summer. Take cuttings each spring and plant out in late summer. Sun; dislikes high humidity.
H: 60cm/24in s: 45cm/18in z: 8[8–10]

ERYTHRONIUM
(Liliaceae) dog's-tooth violet, dog tooth violet
Thriving in rich woodland soil, clumps of these small hardy tuberous perennials grouped around shrubs and trees are among the most desirable early-summer flowerers. E. grandiflorum and E. 'Pagoda' are both slow spreaders.
E. grandiflorum has plain green leaves and bright yellow flowers.
H: 30–45cm/12–18in s: 15cm/6in z: 4[4–9]
E. 'Pagoda' has luminous yellow flowers with reflexed turk's-cap petals above marbled leaves.
H: 30–45cm/12–18in s: 15cm/6in z: 4[4–9]

ESCALLONIA
(Escalloniaceae) S. America
These glossy-leaved evergreen shrubs that flower in summer make attractive hedges, specimens and wall plants for sheltered sunny gardens in temperate zones. Choose one of appropriate size, habit and flower colour for your garden layout.
E. 'Apple Blossom' is one of the more compact, with pinky-white flowers. Its regular form makes it a useful anchor plant in borders.
MEDIUM SHRUB H & S: 1.5m/5ft z: 8[8–10]
E. 'Donard Seedling' has a weeping habit that makes an attractive cascading hedge, the dark green leaves softened with pinkish-white flowers in summer.
MEDIUM SHRUB H: 1.8–2.4m/6–8ft
s: 1.5–1.8m/5–6ft z: 8[8–10]

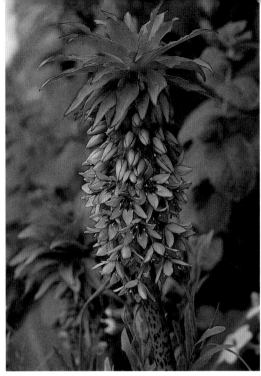

Eucomis bicolor

E. 'Iveyi' has a regular pyramidal shape that makes a solid buttress-like mass against a sunny wall. Erect panicles of white flowers cover the shrub in late summer.
LARGE SHRUB H: 3m/10ft s: 1.8–2.4m/6–8ft
z: 8[8–10]

ESCHSCHOLZIA
(Papaveraceae)
E. californica (California poppy) is usually grown as an annual, though in warm regions it is a short-lived perennial. Orange poppy-flowers appear above ferny blue-green foliage in long succession from early summer if dead-heads are removed regularly. Cultivar flowers range from cream through yellows and oranges to pinks and reds. Plant a whole bed in a bright mix, sowing seed in situ in poor soil in a sunny site.
H: 20–45cm/8–18in s: 30cm/12in z: 9[9–10]
or grow as ANNUAL

EUCOMIS
(Liliaceae/Hyacinthaceae) pineapple flower
S. Africa
Large bulbs produce rosettes of lax fleshy leaves in spring and eye-catching flower-spikes in late summer. Each pineapple-cluster of starry flowers is topped by a tuft of leaf-like bracts. Grow in a sunny sheltered spot or in a container, and protect with thick mulch or in a greenhouse during winter dormancy.
E. bicolor has pale green flowers, edged with

purple, and brownish-maroon spotting on the stem.

H: 45cm/18in   s: 30cm/12in   z: 9[8–10]

E. comosa is elegant and more colourful, with a slight pinkish-lilac tinge to flowers, which have conspicuous dark centres.

H: 75cm/30in   s: 30cm/12in   z: 9[8–10]

EUCRYPHIA

(Eucryphiaceae)   Australasia, S. America

These shrubs have glossy leaves and creamy-white cup-shaped flowers that open to reveal central yellow stamens. Most are acid-loving.

E. × *intermedia* 'Rostrevor' is a quick-growing evergreen with an erect habit. Flowers in late summer. Grow behind kirengeshomas and toad lilies. Relatively lime-tolerant.

LARGE SHRUB H: 3m/10ft   s: 1.8–2.4m/6–8ft
z: 9[9–10]

EUPATORIUM

(Compositae)   boneset, hemp agrimony

E. coelestinum (southern USA, W. Indies) is a hardy perennial form of the annual ageratum with bright blue clustered flowers from late summer. Thrives in hot sun.

H: 30–90cm/12–36in   s: 30–45cm/12–18in
z: 6[6–10]

E. ligustrinum (Mexico) is an evergreen shrub that grows upwards against a warm wall or forms a rounded free-standing bush. Shiny elliptical slightly serrated leaves are attractive all year. In late summer clouds of small pinky-white flowers create a gypsophila effect.

MEDIUM SHRUB H & s: 1.2–2.4m/4–8ft   z: 9[9–10]

E. maculatum atropurpureum (Joe Pye weed from N. America) is a clump-forming deciduous perennial. Whorls of pointed purple-veined leaves on purple stems provide a fine feature through summer months for the back of a border. Late-season large flat flower-heads are deep rosy-purple. Sun or part shade and rich moist soil.

H: 1.2–1.8m/4–6ft   s: 0.9–1.2m/3–4ft   z: 3[3–10]

EUPHORBIA

(Euphorbiaceae)   spurge

Representatives of this richly varied genus with attractive foliage and conspicuous petal-like bracts play important roles in different areas of the flower garden.

E. amygdaloides robbiae (Mrs Robb's bonnet from

Asia Minor) is a suckering perennial spreader, useful for making evergreen ground cover in poor soil or woodland. Produces dark green rosettes of leathery foliage. Thrives and spreads in shade, but the long-lasting pale yellow bracts in spring perform best in full sun. Purple-leaved forms are stunning in lightly shaded beds between erythroniums and trilliums.

H: 30–60cm/12–24in   s: 30–45cm/12–18in
z: 8[8–10]

E. charasias and *E.c. wulfenii* (Mediterranean regions) are similar, forming rounded clumps of erect stems clothed in linear glaucous blue-green leaves. Evergreen foliage is architectural and remains handsome all year, and the flower-spikes curve over attractively in the months before flowering, in early summer. *E. charasias* has black-eyed bracts; those of *E.c. wulfenii* and its numerous cultivars are pure greenish-yellow with a yellow centre. Dead-head when flower-heads become unsightly, but avoid skin contact with the milky sap. Sun or part shade and well-drained site.

SMALL SHRUB H: 90–150cm/36–60in
s: 90cm/36in   z: 8[8–10]

E. cyparissias (cypress spurge from Europe) has delicate light green deciduous foliage that resembles a mass of miniature conifer seedlings and bright lime-yellow flowers in early summer. Spreads by underground runners to make weed-suppressing perennial ground cover in sun or part shade. Though invasive, it is not a strangler and so can underplant shrub roses.

H: 30cm/12in   s: 30–45cm/12–18in   z: 3[3–9]

E. griffithii 'Fireglow' has vibrant tomato-red bracts in early summer. The red and orange tones of its good-looking foliage enrich 'hot' colour schemes all season. More tolerant than *E. cyparissias* of shade and of moisture, it spreads to form perennial clumps but is not unduly invasive. *E.g.* 'Dixter' is more compact, with slightly less vivid bracts.

H: 90cm/36in   s: 60cm/24in   z: 5[5–9]

E. myrsinites (southern Europe, Asia Minor) is a fleshy-leaved evergreen perennial with trailing stems clothed in ice-grey leaves bearing lime-yellow bracts in spring. Needing sun and good drainage, it is best allowed to sprawl in a rockery or over the low wall of a raised bed.

H: 15cm/6in   s: 30–38cm/12–15in   z: 5[5–10]

EURYOPS

(Compositae)   Africa

E. acraeus (formerly *E. evansii*) is an evergreen shrub with erect stiff stems clothed in linear leaves of an intense silvery-grey. Take cuttings in late summer. A good furnishing plant for the front of a sunny well-drained border.

SMALL SHRUB H: 45–60cm/18–30in
s: 45cm/18in   z: 9[9–10]

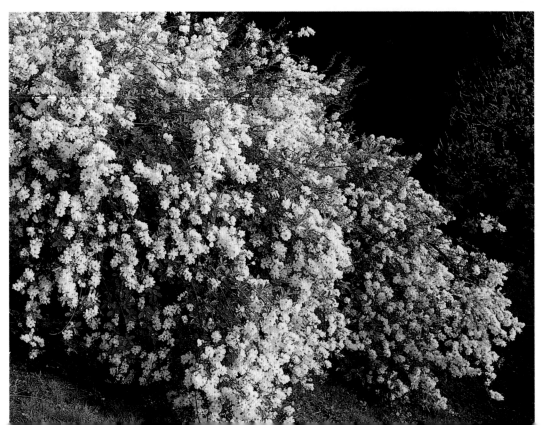

Exochorda × *macrantha* 'The Bride'

EXOCHORDA

(Rosaceae) pearlbush Asia

E. × macrantha 'The Bride' is a compact deciduous shrub, suitable as a lawn specimen or to grow in mixed border schemes. Its graceful arching branches are wreathed with masses of delicate white flowers in early summer. Sun or part shade.

SMALL SHRUB H: 0.9–1.5m/3–5ft
s: 1.2–1.8m/4–6ft z: 5[5–9]

FELICIA

(Compositae)   blue daisy, blue marguerite
S. Africa

F. amelloides is a half-hardy semi-woody perennial of upright habit with pale blue daisy flowers in summer. Dead-head to ensure continuous flowering. Can be grown in a container as well as a sunny border.

H: 45cm/18in s: 30cm/12in z: 9[9–10] or grow as ANNUAL

FERULA

(Umbelliferae)   giant fennel   southern Europe

F. communis is an herbaceous perennial making a mound of finely dissected leaves, a soft glinting green texture that is an excellent foil for more defined flower and leaf shapes near by. When well-established, large stout stems bearing wide heads of greenish-yellow cow-parsley flowers soar to 2.4m/8ft in summer. Sun and deep well-drained soil.

H: 60cm/24in s: 90cm/36in z: 6[6–10]

FESTUCA

(Gramineae) fescue

F. glauca (blue fescue from central and south-western Europe) is a tufted perennial grass with fine grey-blue leaves and compact habit. Straw-coloured flowers in summer and dead leaves mute the somewhat luminous blueness. Good for edging and front-of-border groups. Sun and well-drained soil.

H: 30cm/12in s: 45cm/18in z: 4[4–8]

FILIPENDULA

(Rosaceae) meadowsweet Japan

F. purpurea forms handsome clumps of divided foliage from which rise flattish heads of tiny deep pink flowers towards the end of summer. Best in part shade, but tolerates sun provided the soil is deep and moist. A good back-of-border or water-side perennial.

H: 90–120cm/36–48in s: 60cm/24in
z: 6[6–9]

FOENICULUM

(Umbelliferae) fennel Europe

F. vulgare purpureum (bronze or copper fennel) is a form of the edible herb with a mahogany tinge to the young feathery thread-like leaves; these become a softer bronze later in the season. In a border the smoky effect of the foliage relieves a mass of more solid 'leafy' foliage. Flat umbels of tiny yellowish flowers of this short-lived perennial appear atop tall stems in late summer: remove them if you want to prevent a rash of seedlings. Sun and poor or ordinary well-drained soil.

H: 0.9–1.8m/3–6ft s: 0.6m/2ft z: 4[4–10]

FRANCOA

(Saxifragaceae)   Chile

F. sonchifolia (bridal wreath) makes a perennial clump of hairy deeply lobed leaves; graceful wands of small deep pink flowers appear to make a long-lasting 'wreath' in summer. Seed-heads remain attractive for many weeks. Good evergreen ground cover in warm climates; in colder areas it may be container-grown, wintered under glass.

H: 60–90cm/24–36in s: 45–60cm/18–24in
z: 8[8–10]

FRITILLARIA

(Liliaceae) fritillary

F. imperialis (crown imperial from Persia) is a majestic plant known in gardens since the late sixteenth century. A ruff of bright green glossy leaves surrounds the stout stem. In spring the stem top bears a hanging cluster of large bell-shaped flowers beneath a tuft of leaf-like bracts: choose clear yellow, burnt orange or red flowers to complement neighbouring colours. Bulbs increase slowly in fertile well-drained soil, preferably where they can bake in summer sun. Good for a spring border.

H: 90–120cm/36–48in s: 30cm/12in z: 5[5–10]

F. meleagris (snakeshead from northern Europe) bears bell-shaped flowers dangling singly or in pairs from a grass-like stalk in spring. Flowers have chequered markings – white faintly mottled with green, or pale and deep tones of purplish-pink. A native of damp meadows, this bulbous perennial is lovely naturalized in grass, but also thrives in dry borders.

H: 30cm/12in s: 10–15cm/4–6in z: 5[5–9]

F. persica 'Adiyaman' from the Middle East is similar to the crown imperial in habit and needs. Its racemes of more slender dangling conical flowers are in shades of remarkably murky blackish-purple.

H: 100cm/40in s: 30cm/12in z: 6[6–9]

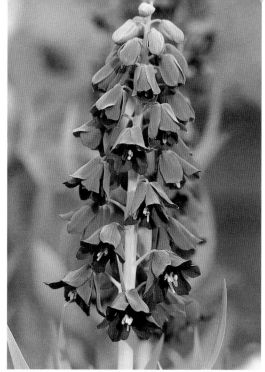

Fritillaria persica

FUCHSIA

(Onagraceae)

Fuchsias hardy to your region make useful border plants: from innumerable hybrids and cultivars choose fuchsias to suit climate and colour schemes or grow selected favourites as annuals and in pots, taking cuttings each autumn.

F. magellanica molinae (syn. *F.m.* 'Alba') is a deciduous shrub that has pale pink flowers in summer and autumn.

LARGE SHRUB H: 3–4m/10–12ft s: 1.8m/6ft
z: 7[7–10]

F. 'Thalia' is a good variety for bedding in a 'red' scheme: its deciduous dark green leaves are shadowed beneath with red, and the clusters of graceful long trumpet-flowers in summer are a soft orange-scarlet.

SMALL SHRUB H: 90cm/36in s: 60cm/24in
z: 9[9–10]

GALANTHUS

(Liliaceae/Amaryllidaceae)   snowdrop

G. elwesii (giant snowdrop from Asia Minor) flowers slightly later than *G. nivalis*.

H: 10–30cm/4–12in s: 5–7.5cm/2–3in

G. nivalis (common snowdrop from Europe) is an indispensable early-spring carpeting bulb. Its pendent white flowers and grey-green leaves relish the light and air beneath leafless deciduous shrubs, and equally appreciate shade in summer.

H: 7.5–20cm/3–8in s: 7.5–15cm/3–6in
z: 2[2–9]

Galega × hartlandii

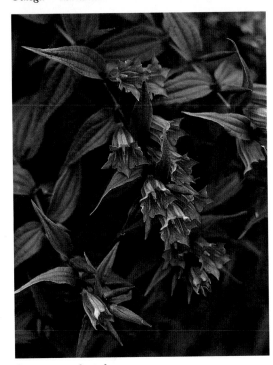

Gentiana asclepiadea

GALEGA

(Leguminosae) goat's rue

G. *officinalis* (southern Europe, Asia Minor) is an old cottage-garden perennial with tall bushy clumps of light green pinnate leaves. Pea-flowers in summer are white or a pale washed-out blue, but there are good garden forms such as G. × *hartlandii* which have warmer tones of lilac, lavender or pinky-mauve. Good 'fillers' for borders in sun or part shade.

H: 90–150cm/36–60in s: 75–90cm/30–36in
z: 4[4–9]

G. *orientalis* (Caucasus) is similar except the erect flower-spikes are violet-tinted blue and carried for many weeks in late spring. A rampant but valuable spreader.

H: 90–120cm/36–48in s: 60cm/24in
z: 5[5–9]

GALIUM

(Rubiaceae)

G. *odoratum* (sweet woodruff from Europe, Siberia) may be invasive but its whorls of narrow green leaves make attractive perennial ground cover in shady sites. Clusters of white starry flowers appear in early summer.

H: 15–25cm/6–10in s: 30cm/12in z: 3[3–9]

GALTONIA

(Liliaceae/Hyacinthaceae) summer hyacinth
S. Africa

G. *candicans*, a useful late-flowering summer bulb, has erect stems bearing elegant loose spires of bell-shaped scented white flowers, shaded or marked with green, above long lax greyish leaves. Interplant in borders among earlier performers. Sun and rich well-drained soil. Unless drainage is excellent, treat as an annual, lifting bulb in autumn for frost-free overwintering.

H: 120cm/48in s: 30cm/12in z: 8[7–10]

GAURA

(Onagraceae) south-eastern USA

G. *lindheimeri* is a perennial that forms an open bush of willow-like foliage. Wiry stems bear tall spikes delicately set with small pinkish-white flowers from summer to autumn. Not vigorous enough for border competition, but worth finding a special place for: a clump is an eye-catcher in late summer. Sun and well-drained soil.

H: 90–120cm/36–48in s: 60–90cm/24–36in
z: 6[6–10]

GAZANIA

(Compositae) S. Africa

Gazanias form compact grey-leaved clumps of daisy-flowers – mainly orange and centrally zoned with brown. Named hybrids come in a wide range of yellows, browns, pinks and warm reds, often with vivid zoning. Flowering from summer onwards, they are useful as colour-grouped bedding in the front of a border. Perennials usually grown as annuals from overwintered cuttings.

H: 15–30cm/6–12in s: 30cm/12in z: 9[9–10]
or grow as ANNUAL

GENISTA

(Leguminoseae) broom

G. *aetnensis* (Mount Etna broom from Sardinia, Sicily) is an almost leafless shrub with a cloud of golden-yellow flowers carried in midsummer on arching rush-like branches that give a graceful appearance all season. Grow next to more 'solid' bush-like shrubs and underplant with lower-growing flowerers. Sun and ordinary or poor well-drained soil.

LARGE SHRUB H: 5–6m/15–20ft
s: 5–5.5m/15–18ft z: 8[8–10]

GENTIANA

(Gentianaceae) gentian

G. *acaulis* (trumpet gentian from Europe) is a prostrate-growing evergreen perennial, with brilliant blue trumpet-flowers in early summer above mats of glossy leaves. Flower performance may be unpredictable. Sunny open site and moist humus-rich soil.

H: 7.5cm/3in s: to 45cm/18in z: 5[5–9]

G. *asclepiadea* (willow gentian from Europe) is a graceful perennial for a shady border. Arching leafy stems bear clusters of flowers in various shades of blue in late summer. Deep moist humus-rich soil, preferably (but not necessarily) acid. A valuable specimen plant for sun or shade, when not jostled by competitive neighbours.

H: 90cm/36in s: 60cm/24in z: 5[5–9]

G. *sino-ornata* (western China, Tibet) is an autumn-flowering and acid-loving prostrate evergreen perennial. Glowing blue flowers above leafy mats are streaked with deep blue and green.

H: 15cm/6in s: 30–38cm/12–15in z: 5[5–9]

GERANIUM

(Geraniaceae) cranesbill

Most of the hardy cranesbills have a fine early flowering period. Cut back stems and leaves as flowers fade to produce new leafy growth attractive for the rest of the season. Some cranesbills are best in ground-covering masses; others are more distinguished and merit places in a border.

G. 'Ann Folkard' is a perennial with yellow-green leaves like those of its parent, G. *psilostemon*. Large purplish-magenta flowers, in summer, are black-veined and black-centred.

H & S: 45cm/18in z: 5[5–10]

G. *clarkei* 'Kashmir Purple' has large saucer-shaped flowers, with thin red veining on purple petals, in summer. Deeply dissected foliage of this perennial is upright and branching. Sun.

H & S: 45cm/18in z: 4[4–10]

G. 'Johnson's Blue' makes a sprawling mass of elegant delicately lobed leaves; violet-blue flowers appear over a long period from early summer.

H: 30–60cm/12–24in s: 60cm/24in z: 5[5–10]

G. × *magnificum* has dark-veined violet-blue flowers in early summer above an upright perennial clump of handsome lobed mid-green leaves that tint to red in autumn. A good front-of-border companion to pale yellows and pinks.

H: 45–60cm/18–24in s: 60cm/24in z: 3[3–10]

G. *maderense* (Madeira) is a striking semi-evergreen perennial with large ferny leaves and, in early summer, purplish-pink flowers dark-veined at centre and with petal edges white-veined. Seeds prolifically: overwinter seedlings under glass in cold areas. Sunny sheltered site.

H: 90–120cm/36–48in s: 60–90cm/24–36in z: 10

G. *nodosum* (Europe) is one of the more compact perennial species that revels in shade: give it a corner to itself where it will self-seed and colonize vigorously. Flowers – which appear throughout the summer – are pinkish-lilac and the leaves are shiny and attractive.

H & S: 45cm/18in z: 5[5–9]

G. *palmatum* (Canary Islands) has divided anemone-like leaves and purplish-red flowers in late summer. The foliage, tinged with pink or red, of this semi-evergreen perennial is good underplanted with *Viola riviana purpurea* (formerly known as *V. labradorica purpurea*). Seeds prolifically: overwinter seedlings under glass in cold areas. Sunny, sheltered site.

H: 45cm/18in s: 60cm/24in z: 8[8–10]

G. *psilostemon* (Armenia) has striking magenta flowers with black eyes and veins in summer, beautifully echoing the tones of purple-bronze foliage such as that of *Rosa glauca* and wonderful with dark pink shrub roses. Its lax perennial clump of elegant leaves may need some support. Leaves colour well in late summer.

H: 75–120cm/30–48in s: 90–120cm/36–48in z: 5[5–10]

G. *renardii* (Caucasus) forms neat perennial clumps of velvet grey-green leaves and has starry white flowers veined with maroon in early summer. Open situation.

H & S: 30cm/12in z: 4[4–10]

Geranium clarkei 'Kashmir Purple'

Geranium maderense

Geranium renardii

GILLENIA

(Rosaceae)   bowman's root, Indian physic
eastern N. America
G. trifoliata is a tough wiry but graceful perennial with reddish stems and trifoliate leaves, resembling an arching spiraea. Loose clusters of dainty starry white or pink-tinged flowers in summer are succeeded by attractive red calyces. Slight preference for acid soil, and part shade in hot areas.
H: 60–120cm/24–48in   s: 60cm/24in
z: 4[4–9]

GLADIOLUS

(Iridaceae)
G. callianthus (formerly *Acidanthera bicolor*; from eastern Africa) is a graceful species with grassy leaves and fragrant dark-blotched white flowers that appear in late summer. Grow as a hybrid gladioli, lifting corm in autumn and planting out in a sunny position in late spring.
H: 90cm/36in   s: 30cm/12in   z: 9[8–10]
G. communis byzantinus (Byzantine gladiolus from Europe) is an early-flowering species with typical sword-like gladiolus leaves and vivid reddish-purple flowers in early summer. Seeds and colonizes readily in light soils: keep this cormous perennial in an emphatic clump, to harmonize with *Geranium psilostemon*, Rugosa rose *R*. 'Roseraie de l'Haÿ' or a purple cotinus. Sun or part shade.
H: 90cm/36in   z: 7[7–10]

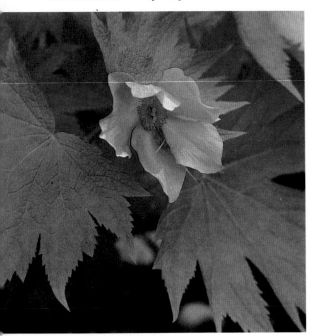

Glaucidium palmatum

GLAUCIDIUM

(Paeoniaceae)   Japan
G. palmatum is a handsome-leaved perennial woodlander bearing large delicate poppy-flowers of pale lavender (or white, in the form *G.p. leucanthum*) in late spring. Retentive humus-rich acid soil; protect from sun and wind.
H: 60–120cm/24–48in   s: 60cm/24in   z: 6[6–9]

GLAUCIUM

(Papaveraceae)   horned poppy, sea poppy
Europe, other regions of Mediterranean
G. flavum is a sprawling unruly perennial bearing bright yellow cup-shaped papery flowers in late summer above very attractive pale grey-green lobed leaves. It can be perennial given sun and poor well-drained soil; otherwise grow as an annual or biennial and allow to self-seed.
H: 25–60cm/10–24in   s: 45cm/18in   z: 5[5–10]
or grow as ANNUAL/BIENNIAL

GOMPHRENA

(Amaranthaceae)
G. globosa (globe amaranth from India) is a bushy half-hardy annual with clover-like 'everlasting' flower-heads, in white, yellow, orange or pinkish-purples, which appear in late summer. Good for bedding or growing in a pot. Hot sun and well-drained soil.
H: 30cm/12in   s: 15–25cm/6–10in   ANNUAL

GUNNERA

(Gunneraceae)
G. manicata (Brazil), with its giant umbrella-like leaves, adds a dramatic element to a large garden. Furrowed and puckered kidney-shaped leaves, up to 3m/10ft across, are brown-tinged and, in summer, almost hide exotic club-shaped flower-buds. This herbaceous perennial prefers marshy ground, providing scale and substance to waterside drifts of pink and red primulas and astilbes. Feed well; protect crown from frost.
H: 1.8–3m/6–10ft   s: 2.4–3m/8–10ft
z: 7[7–10]

GYPSOPHILA

(Caryophyllaceae)   baby's breath
G. paniculata (eastern Europe, Siberia) is a perennial making a long-lasting froth of tiny white flowers in summer. Perfect for infilling gaps between pastel- or strong-coloured neighbours, and for concealing withering stalks and heads of earlier-flowering perennials. Avoid disturbing deep fleshy roots of established plants. Grow from cuttings, which root quickly as shoots appear in late spring. Sun and well-drained deep and preferably limy soil. Pinkish and double forms are also grown. *G.p.* 'Bristol Fairy' with double white flowers is often temperamental, but well worth trying.
H & s: 90–120cm/36–48in   z: 3[3–10]

HALIMIUM

(Cistaceae)   Mediterranean
H. lasianthum is a half-hardy cistus-like evergreen shrub with grey-green leaves and, in late spring and early summer, rock-rose flowers whose golden-yellow petals have mahogany basal blotches. Sun and well-drained soil: a rock garden or raised bed suits perfectly.
SMALL SHRUB H: 45–90cm/18–36in
s: 60–120cm/24–48in   z: 9[9–10]

HEBE

(Scrophulariaceae)   shrubby speedwell,
shrubby veronica   New Zealand
Hebes are invaluable furnishing shrubs for foliage texture and flower colour. Hardiness varies according to species, but all like sun, well-drained soil and plenty of moisture – none tolerates a cold climate.
H. albicans is a dense compact evergreen shrub with rounded glaucous leaves and short white flower-spikes in spring. Good for low ground cover and front of a border.
SMALL SHRUB H & s: 60cm/24in   z: 8[8–10]
H. buchananii is a dwarf evergreen that makes a spreading cushion of little rounded leaves, sprinkled with white flowers in summer.
DWARF SHRUB H: 5cm/2in   s: 15cm/6in
z: 7[7–10]
H. hulkeana is untypical: its attractive evergreen leaves are glossy green, toothed and ovate. Delicate lavender flowers in large loose panicles are borne in early summer. In cold regions grow in a pot.
SMALL SHRUB H: 90–120cm/36–48in
s: 60–120cm/24–48in   z: 9[9–10]
H. 'Midsummer Beauty' is evergreen and has purplish-tinged leaves and long lavender racemes throughout summer.
MEDIUM SHRUB H: 1.8m/6ft   s: 1.5m/5ft
z: 8[8–10]
H. pinguifolia 'Pagei' is a prostrate evergreen shrub with small blue-grey leaves and short white flower-spikes in early summer. Good for ground cover under roses and open shrubs.
SMALL SHRUB H: 15–25cm/6–10in   s: 90cm/36in
z: 6[6–10]

Hebe hulkeana

Hebe albicans

H. rakaiensis is one of the hardier evergreen hebes with dense pale green foliage and white flower racemes in summer.
SMALL SHRUB H: 50cm/20in S: 70cm/28in
Z: 6[6–10]

HEDERA
(Araliaceae) ivy
Best in part shade and moisture-retentive soil, ivies are indispensable both as an evergreen backdrop and as ground cover. Scale, shape and colour of leaves all contribute to a wide range of overall textures.
H. canariensis 'Gloire de Marengo' has wide triangular leaves on long pink leaf-stalks. Cream margins, wider at the base, surround dark and grey-green central markings.
CLIMBER H: 5–6m/15–20ft Z: 8[8–10]
H. colchica (Persian ivy) has heart-shaped leaves, the largest of the genus. It climbs rapidly but does not make dense cover. *H.c.* 'Sulphur Heart' leaves have central splashes of yellow.
CLIMBER H: 6–10m/20–30ft Z: 8[8–10]
H. helix (common ivy from Europe) has a wide range of useful named varieties. *H.h.* 'Angularis Aurea' has leaves shaded in gold while *H.h.* 'Digitata' (finger-leaved ivy) has leaves divided into five narrow lobes, making a dark lacy curtain of foliage. *H.h. hibernica* has distinctive large leaves.
CLIMBER H or s: 4m/12ft Z: 5[5–9]

HEDYCHIUM
(Zingiberaceae) ginger lily, gingerwort
India
Hedychiums are spectacular evergreen perennials in warm situations; in temperate zones, given a sunny sheltered position, they survive some frost, the canna-like leaves dying down in winter. Plant fleshy rhizomes shallowly in organically rich moist soil. Good in pots if generously watered. Cut down spent flower-spikes and mulch well after flowering.
H. gardnerianum (kahili ginger) produces a spike of clear yellow orchid-like heavily scented flowers, with prominent red stamens, in late summer and early autumn. Broad glaucous leaves add to this tropical effect in late borders.
H: 1.5–1.8m/5–6ft s: 0.9m/3ft
Z: 9[9–10]

HEDYSARUM
(Leguminosae)
H. coronarium (French honeysuckle, sukka sweetvetch from Europe) is a vigorous shrubby biennial or short-lived perennial with lax stems, pale green-grey pinnate leaves and spikes of small fragrant subtle red pea-flowers borne in summer. Suits both pale-flowered and brighter colour schemes. Sun and well-drained soil.
H: 75–120cm/30–48in s: 45–60cm/18–24in
Z: 5[5–9] or grow as ANNUAL

HELENIUM
(Compositae) sneezeweed
eastern N. America
These clump-forming perennials are good for late-summer borders. Hybrids of *H. autumnale* have daisy-like flowers, each with a prominent central boss, in a wide range of yellows and coppery-reds. Sun and moisture-retentive soil.
H. 'Moerheim Beauty' is compact and has rich bronze-red flowers from late summer to autumn.
H: 90cm/36in s: 30–45cm/12–18in
Z: 3[3–10]

HELIANTHEMUM
(Cistaceae) rock rose, sun rose
Spreading evergreen foliage of small dull green leaves provides good front-of-border furnishing all year. Short-lived papery flowers open with the sun in summer. Very well-drained and slightly alkaline soil. Choose named varieties for leaf and flower colour. Two attractive grey-leaved cultivars are *H.* 'Wisley Pink', with soft pink flowers, and *H.* 'Wisley Primrose', a delicate yellow, both of which are a foil to pale border schemes.
DWARF SHRUB H: 15–25cm/6–10in s: 60cm/24in
Z: 5[5–10]

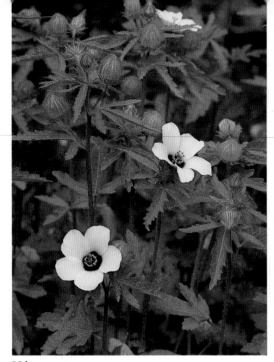

Hibiscus trionum

HELIANTHUS

(Compositae) sunflower USA
Although coarse rather than elegant, sunflowers still make an important contribution to a late colour scheme.

H. annuus (annual sunflower) grows very tall, with coarse heart-shaped leaves and huge cart-wheel heads of sunny yellow daisy-flowers with brown or purplish centres. Grow in a group at the back of a sunny border to make a challenging splash of colour in late summer.
H: 90–300cm/36–120in s: 30–45cm/12–18in
ANNUAL

H. decapetalus and its forms are clump-forming perennials for the back of a sunny border. *H.* 'Capenoch Star', in summer, produces flowers of a pale cool yellow that combines more easily in colour schemes than many of the brighter-toned hybrids.
H: 1.2–1.5m/4–5ft s: 0.6m/2ft
z: 5[5–10]

HELICHRYSUM

(Compositae)
H. petiolare (S. Africa) is a sprawling evergreen sub-shrub. Heart-shaped pale green leaves covered with short white pile clothe horizontally branching stems and form an attractive silver-grey foliage companion to neighbouring plants, and an indispensable furnishing background for key plants in containers. Sprays of pale creamy flowers may appear in summer. Sun and well-drained soil: tolerates drought rather than humidity.

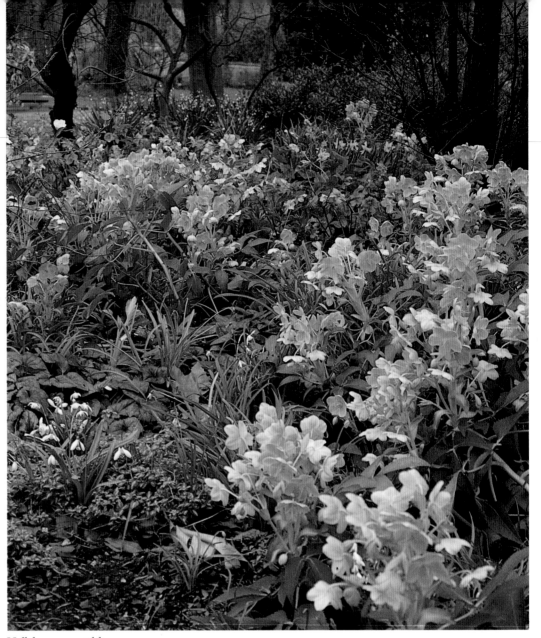

Helleborus argutifolius

H: 30–60cm/12–24in s: 45–75cm/18–30in
z: 9[9–10] or grow as ANNUAL

H. rosmarinifolium (syn. *Ozothamnus rosmarini-folius*; snow-in-summer from Tasmania) is an up-right evergreen shrub similar to rosemary in appearance, with white woolly stems and leathery leaves. Little white flowers open from an attrac-tive corymb of reddish buds in early summer.
MEDIUM SHRUB H: 1.8–2.7m/6–9ft
s: 0.6–1.5m/2–5ft z: 9[9–10]

HELICTOTRICHON

(Gramineae) south-western Europe
H. sempervirens is an ornamental perennial grass making a dense arching clump of narrow steel-blue leaves that contribute colour and texture in a grey/white garden. Feathery buff flower-heads 120cm/48in tall appear in summer. Sun and well-drained soil. Not invasive. Tidy away dead growth in spring.
H: 60cm/24in s: 30cm/12in z: 4[4–9]

HELIOTROPIUM

(Boraginaceae) cherry pie, heliotrope Peru
H. arborescens becomes an evergreen shrub in warm climates. Handsome corrugated foliage is deep green, often bronze-tinged. Tightly clus-tered heads of fragrant flowers, from late spring through till winter, are violet-purple or white. May be trained to form an attractive standard.

Sun and fertile well-drained soil.
SMALL SHRUB H: 45–120cm/18–48in s: 30–
75cm/12–30in z: 9[9–10] or grow as ANNUAL

HELLEBORUS
(Ranunculaceae) hellebore
H. argutifolius (Corsican hellebore) makes shrub-like perennial mounds of remarkable grey-green trifoliate leaves, with prickly edges and conspicuous veins, which are virtually evergreen. Pendent clusters of creamy-green flowers appear in spring and last for weeks. Protect from strong wind; in hot areas, shade from scorching sun.
H & s: 60–75cm/24–30in z: 7[7–10]
H. orientalis (Lenten rose from Asia Minor) is an evergreen perennial that hybridizes freely to produce charming saucer-shaped flowers in a range of subtle colours from white through blush-pink to maroon and dusky purple, often flushed with green and speckled with purple inside. Flowers appear in late winter or early spring amid glossy deeply divided leaves. Part or full shade, cool conditions and deep rich soil.
H & s: 45–60cm/18–24in z: 3[3–10]

HEMEROCALLIS
(Liliaceae) day-lily
Light to mid-green grassy leaves spread to make almost evergreen perennial ground cover: foliage often dies down for only a short period in winter. Lily-like flower-trumpets are fragrant and short-lived, but produced in long succession. Modern summer-flowering hybrids (there are many wonderful American forms) come in a good colour range from clear yellow to orange, apricot, buff and bronze. Sun or part shade, and any soil that is not too dry.
H. citrina (citron day-lily from China, Japan) has lemon-yellow flowers in late summer.
H: 105–120cm/42–48in s: 60–90cm/24–36in
z: 3[3–10]
H. fulva 'Kwanzo Variegata' has leaves striped with cream, which make a focal point in spring. Flowers are similar to those of *H.f.* 'Flore Pleno', an old cottage-garden favourite with fragrant tawny orange-toned double flowers in summer; its pale golden foliage in spring is a wonderful foil to sweeps of blue flowers.
H: 120cm/48in s: 90cm/36in z: 3[3–10]
H. lilio-asphodelus (syn. *H. flava*; lemon day-lily from south-eastern Europe to Japan), is a pale yellow species with recurving petals, which flowers in late spring and early summer.
H: 60–90cm/24–36in s: 45cm/18in z: 4[4–10]

Hoheria glabrata

HESPERIS
(Cruciferae) southern Europe, western Asia
H. matronalis (damask violet, dame's violet, sweet rocket) is a cottage-garden perennial to mass in informal borders. Evening-scented white, pink and mauve cruciform flowers are borne in loose clusters above narrow dark green leaves in early summer. Dead-head to encourage further flowering. Freely self-seeding. Grow as a biennial, since older plants deteriorate to woodiness. Sun.
H: 60–120cm/24–48in s: 45–60cm/18–24in
z: 3[3–9]

HEUCHERA
(Saxifragaceae) alumroot, coral flower
N. America
H. × brizoides hybrids form perennial mounds of rounded scalloped hairy leaves, mottled grey and green, which are evergreen except in very cold areas. Woody roots spread to make good ground cover in well-drained soil – in full sun for best flowering performance and in part shade for foliage only. Slender panicles of flowers held well above the foliage on wiry stems appear in early summer. Choose a named form to harmonize with neighbouring flower and foliage colour. *H. × b.* 'Coral Cloud' has coral-pink flowers.
H: 45–60cm/18–24in s: 30–45cm/12–18in
z: 3[3–10]
H. micrantha 'Palace Purple' is a perennial grown for its handsome bronze foliage with rich deep red undersides.
H & s: 60cm/24in z: 4[4–10]

× HEUCHERELLA
(Saxifragaceae)
× H. tiarelloides is an evergreen perennial hybrid between heuchera and tiarella with tiny pink flowers in early summer and soft green leaves without the typical heuchera marbling. Grows in similar conditions to heuchera and is an excellent border plant.
H: 45cm/18in s: 30–45cm/12–18in
z: 3[3–10]

HIBISCUS
(Malvaceae) rose mallow
H. moscheutos (swamp rose mallow from USA) is a handsome perennial species with toothed slightly lobed ovate leaves. The satiny wide-open mallow-flowers may be 15–20cm/6–8in across and are white, pink or crimson, borne in summer. Sun and moist rich soil. Easily raised from seed.
H: 0.9–1.5m/3–5ft s: 0.9m/2ft z: 4[4–9]
H. trionum (flower-of-an-hour from Africa) is an annual with dark green serrated leaves. Large cream mallow-flowers with purplish-brown centres appear in late summer, typically opening only in the morning. Sow seed each spring.
H: 75cm/30in s: 30cm/12in ANNUAL

HOHERIA
(Malvaceae) New Zealand
Hoherias are upright-growing deciduous and evergreen shrubs flowering well in full sun. Evergreen forms are tender, but *H.* 'Glory of Amlwch' (*H. glabrata × H. sexstylosa*) is semi-evergreen with

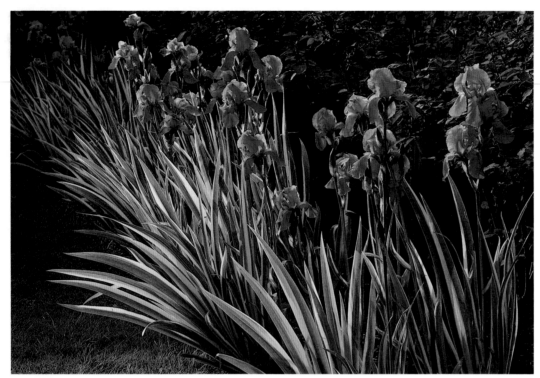

Iris pallida 'Variegata'

large white mallow-like flowers in summer. Both *H. glabrata* and *H. lyallii* are good hardier species.
LARGE SHRUB H: 7m/22ft s: 5m/15ft
z: 9[9–10]

HOSTA

(Liliaceae/Funkiaceae)   plantain lily
eastern Asia
Grown primarily for their leaf colour and texture, these herbaceous perennials also contribute flower colour during summer months. Almost every good garden hosta has leaf variegation with markings in gold, cream or white.
H. fortunei 'Aureomarginata' has its broad sage-green leaves outlined with a band of creamy-yellow. Pale lilac flowers are carried aloft in loose spires in summer. Vigorous and good for ground cover.
H: 75cm/30in s: 60cm/24in z: 3[3–9]
H. 'Royal Standard' has rich green heart-shaped leaves, veined and puckered. Fragrant lily-like white flowers tinted with lilac appear in summer. Robust; tolerates all but the hottest sun as well as part shade.
H: 60–90cm/24–36in s: 60cm/24in
z: 6[6–10]
H. sieboldiana elegans is a form with the finest of the dramatic large seersucker leaves of this splen-did species, in a deep blue-grey. Dense heads of pale lilac-lavender flowers appear in summer just above the foliage.
H: 75cm/30in s: 60cm/24in z: 3[3–9]
H. ventricosa has lush evenly veined foliage of a shining dark green. Bell-shaped late-summer flowers are richly toned violet.
H: 60–90cm/24–36in s: 60cm/24in
z: 3[3–9]

HUMULUS

(Cannabidaceae)   hop   America, Asia, Europe
H. lupulus is a vigorous perennial climber with attractive palmate leaves and scented green seed-heads. *H.l. aureus* its golden-leaved form, is less vigorous and less free-flowering, but twines upwards in deepest shade to make vertical accents of soft luminous foliage against which yellows and dark blues look their best. Flowers in autumn. Tolerates a dark basement garden in the city or any back yard.
CLIMBER H: to 3m/10ft z: 5[5–9]

HYDRANGEA

(Hydrangeaceae)
Deciduous woodland plants preferring part shade and moisture-retentive rich loam, but often happy in containers and town gardens.

H. anomala petiolaris (Japanese climbing hydrangea) is a deciduous climber that makes ground cover on banks and clambers up walls and stumps by means of self-clinging rootlets. In early summer large flat corymbs of greenish-white flowers are ringed with sterile white florets.
CLIMBER H: to 18m/60ft z: 5[5–9]
H. arborescens (eastern N. America) is a lax shrub with greeny-white sterile florets forming a glob-ular head from midsummer to early autumn. The species is more graceful than some of the popular cultivars.
MEDIUM SHRUB H & S: 1.2–1.8m/4–6ft z: 5[5–9]
H. aspera villosa (China, Himalayas) is one of the best hydrangeas for sun, provided the roots are cool and moist. Leaves, stems and flower stalks are clothed in soft hairs; pinkish-mauve flowers in late summer are large and flat. Late frosts can damage flowering shoots.
MEDIUM SHRUB H & S: to 2.4m/8ft z: 7[7–10]
H. paniculata 'Grandiflora' has large showy creamy-white terminal panicles of sterile florets in late summer, which become pinkish with age.
LARGE SHRUB H & S: 4–5m/12–15ft z: 4[4–9]
H. quercifolia (south-eastern USA) has oak-leaf foliage that colours magnificently in autumn. Flowers freely with white panicles of mixed fertile and sterile flowers in summer. Best against a wall, sheltered from wind and shaded from hot sun.
MEDIUM SHRUB H: 1.8m/6ft s: 1.2–1.8m/4–6ft
z: 6[6–9]

HYPERICUM

(Guttiferae)   St John's wort
Shrubby hypericums spread rapidly by under-ground runners to make ground cover that is mainly evergreen and studded with shining golden-yellow flowers in summer months.
H. olympicum (south-eastern Europe and Asia Minor) is deciduous, with grey-green ovate leaves. *H.o.* 'Citrinum' bears clusters of attractive lemon-yellow flowers. Well-drained soil and full sun.
DWARF SHRUB H: 23–30cm/9–12in s: indefinite
z: 6[6–9]

IBERIS

(Cruciferae)   candytuft   Mediterranean
I. sempervirens is a low spreading evergreen peren-nial with dark green leaves covered by a mass of white or pinkish-white flowers from spring to early summer. Trim after flowering to keep a compact shape. Sun and well-drained slightly alkaline soil.
H: 30cm/12in s: 90cm/36in z: 5[5–10]

IMPATIENS

(Balsaminaceae)   touch-me-not

Most impatiens garden cultivars are grown as bright summer-flowering annuals to decorate shady beds and borders.

I. balfourii (western Himalayas) makes a leafy mass topped with delicate purplish-pink flower racemes. Self-seeds and may become invasive. Shade or part shade and rich moist porous soils.
H: 60–90cm/24–36in s: 30cm/12in z: 10 or grow as ANNUAL

INDIGOFERA

(Leguminosae)

I. heterantha (Himalayas) is a sun-loving deciduous shrub with fresh green pinnate leaves and rosy-purple pea-flowers, which are borne from midsummer through to autumn. Not reliably hardy: give wall protection in marginal areas. Cut back severely in spring to remove any frost damage and encourage flowering.
MEDIUM SHRUB H: 1.5–1.8m/5–6ft
s: 1.2–1.5m/4–5ft z: 8[8–10]

IRIS

(Iridaceae)

Irises provide essential contrast of foliage form in garden planting – whether the emphatic verticals of sword-like spikes or the curving lines of grassy leaves – and the wide range of flower-colour is an ephemeral bonus in season.

I. orientalis (butterfly iris from Asia Minor) makes a stout clump of stiff sword-like leaves and spreads rapidly in good rich moist soil, swamping weeds. Early summer flowers are white with a broad yellow stripe in recurving fall petals. Plant good summer foliage to hide dying stems of this beardless rhizomatous perennial.
H: 120cm/48in s: 38cm/15in z: 4[4–9]

Pacific Coast hybrids (mostly derived from *I. douglasiana* and *I. innominata*) are beardless rhizomatous perennials with coarse grass-like evergreen leaves and early-summer flowers of blue-purple, lavender, yellow, orange and various whites intricately marked with veining. Well-drained humus-rich soil, preferably lime-free; they tolerate part shade.
H: 23–45cm/9–18in s: 30cm/12in z: 7[7–9]

I. pallida pallida (syn. *I.p. dalmatica*; orris from Europe) is a bearded rhizomatous perennial with greyish-glaucous almost evergreen leaves harmonizing with pale lavender-blue flowers in late spring and early summer. Grow in a sunny dry spot where rhizomes can bake all summer. Variegated

forms with yellow- or white-striped foliage increase more slowly and flower less freely.
H: 90–120cm/36–48in s: 60cm/24in
z: 3[3–10]

I. pseudacorus (water flag, yellow flag; from western Europe, northern Africa) likes a damp place and acid soil, but will accommodate itself to a border where it will grow less tall. This beardless rhizomatous perennial produces deciduous blue-green sword-like leaves and heads of up to five yellow flowers in early summer. The form with variegated leaves is decorative in early summer.
H: 90–120cm/36–48in s: 30cm/12in
z: 4[4–9]

I. sibirica (Europe, northern Asia) is a beardless rhizomatous perennial making a compact tall sheaf of grassy foliage. Flowers in many shades of blue on branching stems in early summer. Sun. Tolerates moist and drier fertile soils.
H: 75–120cm/30–48in s: 45–90cm/18–36in
z: 4[4–10]

I. unguicularis (Algerian iris, winter iris) loves poor soil at the base of a sunny wall. Slightly scented violet flowers are borne in winter on low stems, often partly hidden among long grassy leaves. Avoid disturbing this evergreen beardless perennial, but cut down foliage in spring to allow rhizomes to bake.
H: 30–45cm/12–18in s: 30cm/12in
z: 8[8–10]

ISATIS

(Cruciferae)

I. tinctoria (woad from southern Europe, western Asia) is a biennial with a rosette of long dark green leaves and in early summer a mass of tiny lime-yellow gypsophila-like flowers that turn into dangling shiny dark seed-pods. Readily self-seeds. Sun and rich well-drained soil.
H & s: 90cm/36in z: 4[4–9]

ITEA

(Iteaceae)   central China

I. ilicifolia is an evergreen shrub with lax holly-like leaves and long fragrant racemes of greenish-yellow flowers in mid- to late summer: the catkins have long-lasting colour and fragrance. Sun, and a sheltering wall in areas of marginal hardiness.
LARGE SHRUB H: 3m/10ft s: 1.8m/6ft
z: 9[8–10]

JASMINUM

(Oleaceae)   jasmine Asia

J. officinale (common white jasmine) is a vigorous

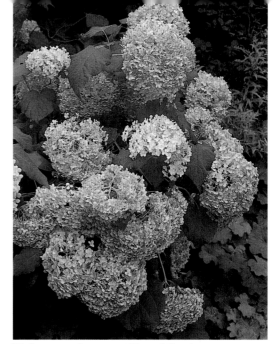

Hydrangea arborescens 'Grandiflora'

deciduous climber, twining upwards to weave an intricate mesh of mid-green pinnate leaves and clustered white tubular flowers that scent the garden in summer. Does well in sun and ordinary soil, but if well fed will make luxuriant foliage growth to clothe arbours and screen dull fences.
CLIMBER H: 10m/30ft z: 8[7–10]

KIRENGESHOMA

(Hydrangeaceae)   Japan

K. palmata is a perennial of great dignity, with beautiful pale green vine-like leaves set on dark ebony stems. In late summer elegant foliage is complemented by dangling shuttlecock flowers of pale butter-yellow held above leaves. Superb in a foliage border where soil is rich moist and slightly acid.
H: 90–120cm/36–48in s: 60–90cm/24–36in
z: 5[5–9]

KNIPHOFIA

(Liliaceae/Asphodelaceae)   red hot poker, torch lily Africa

Conspicuous tall flower-spikes rise above lax grassy leaves, providing sharp contrast of form in the border as well as eye-catching fire-colours or gentler lemon-yellows. Feature or accent plants for sun and well-drained – but not dry – soil.

K. caulescens is a perennial with strange elephant-like self-rooting stems and good bluish-green evergreen foliage. Thick flower-stems with 'pokers' of coral-red buds open to pale lemony-white in autumn. Cultivars may provide specific colour for early, mid- and late summer schemes. *K.* 'Maid

Lavatera 'Barnsley'

of Orleans' is a dwarf hybrid with pale cool creamy-yellow flowers in summer.
H: 90–120cm/36–48in s: 60cm/24in
z: 7[7–10]

KOLKWITZIA
(Caprifoliaceae) beauty bush western China
K. amabilis 'Pink Cloud' is one of the best deciduous shrubs to flower in early summer. Drooping branches of soft hairy leaves are draped with soft palest pink bell-shaped flowers opening from dark pink buds. Gentle colouring works well with other hues as well as with deeper pinks and strong reds. Attractive bark in winter. Sun and well-drained soil.

LARGE SHRUB H: 1.8–4m/6–12ft s: 1.2–3m/4–10ft
z: 5[5–9]

LAMIUM
(Labiatae) dead nettle Europe, Asia
L. maculatum with white-splashed leaves makes attractive – but often over-enthusiastic – semi-evergreen perennial ground cover in shade or part shade. Flowers in mid-spring. Pale pink- or white-flowered varieties are much less invasive than the type with its dull mauvy-pink flowers. *L.m. roseum* has pink flowers. *L.m.* 'Beacon Silver' with rosy-pink flowers has more shining silvered leaves; it thrives in part shade, but is not as hardy as other cultivars. *L.m.* 'White Nancy' is low-growing with white flowers and silver leaves; it thrives in shade.
H: 20–40cm/8–16in s: 30cm/12in z: 3[3–10]

LANTANA
(Verbenaceae)
L. camara (W. Indies) is a tender evergreen shrub with handsomely veined ovate leaves and domed clusters of little tubular flowers ranging from white through yellow tones to brick-red. Varying colours within a flower-head give a rich glowing effect. Often grown as a bedding plant or in a pot to flower all summer.
SMALL SHRUB H: 45–120cm/18–48in
s: 30–90cm/12–36in z: 10 or grow as ANNUAL

LATHYRUS
(Leguminosae) everlasting or sweet pea
These peas, most of them climbers, all thrive in sun and rich well-drained soil.
L. latifolius albus (everlasting pea from Europe), white form of the mauvy-pink perennial pea, creates a spectacular mass, sprawling down over a bank or trained over earlier-flowering perennials and shrubs to add late-summer interest. Grow from seed or delve deeply to find roots to divide. Cut back in winter to remove dead stems, taking care not to damage host plants. Sun.
CLIMBER H: 3m/10ft z: 5[5–10]
L. nervosus (Lord Anson's blue pea from S. America) is a rare but fine perennial with delicate sprays of fragrant periwinkle-blue flowers in summer and grey-green leaves.
CLIMBER H: 1.5m/5ft z: 9–10 or grow as
ANNUAL
L. odoratus (annual sweet pea from Italy) can be grown up tripods or frames to create pillars of colour in borders. Cut the scented flowers or dead-head them to prolong flowering from summer into early autumn. Choose cultivars from white ones through to pinks, mauves, violet-blues and rich maroons.
CLIMBER H: to 3m/10ft ANNUAL
L. rotundifolius (Persian everlasting pea from eastern Europe, Asia Minor) is an herbaceous perennial with rounded leaves of deep green. Clusters of warm pink-toned flowers are borne in summer.
CLIMBER H: 1.8m/6ft z: 5[5–10]
L. vernus (spring vetchling from Europe) is a non-climbing perennial that makes an attractive clump of pinnate pointed leaves when combined with little purple vetch-like flowers in late spring. There are good colour forms.
H: 38cm/15in s: 30cm/12in z: 4[4–9]

LAVANDULA

(Labiatae) lavender southern Europe

Misty grey-green linear leaves of lavender make short-lived low hedges or rounded cushions of foliage to contrast with more solid leaf-forms of neighbouring plants. Scented flower-spikes attract bees, whose humming contributes to the mellow atmosphere of a summer garden. Sun and well-drained soil.

L. angustifolia is evergreen and bears flower-spikes, of the eponymous pale 'lavender' colour in late summer, held above silver-grey leaves. Some cultivars are hardier than the type.
SMALL SHRUB H & S: 90–120cm/36–48in
Z: 6[6–10]

L.a. 'Hidcote' is a denser, more compact shape, with deep purple-blue spikes.
SMALL SHRUB H: 30–60cm/12–24in
S: 45–60cm/18–24in Z: 6[6–10]

L. stoechas (French lavender) is an evergreen shrub with stems clad in grey-green aromatic leaves. Terminal heads of dark purple flowers, each topped with a tuft of fluttering bracts, appear in summer.
SMALL SHRUB H & S: 30–60cm/12–24in
Z: 9[9–10]

LAVATERA

(Malvaceae) tree mallow Europe

L. 'Barnsley' is a fast-growing semi-evergreen shrub with downy sage-green leaves. Bears veined pinky-white mallow-flowers, each with a deep pink eye, throughout summer. Prune hard in spring. Sun and good drainage.
MEDIUM SHRUB H & S: 1.5–2.4m/5–8ft
Z: 8[8–10]

L. 'Rosea' is a semi-evergreen shrub bearing a profusion of large wide-open rich pink flowers in late summer, complemented by soft grey-green lobed foliage. Grows quickly to furnish a new border, and provides useful late-season colour.
MEDIUM SHRUB H & S: 1.5–2.4m/5–8ft
Z: 8[8–10]

LEPTOSPERMUM

(Myrtaceae) Australia, New Zealand

Slightly tender evergreen shrubs of pyramidal shape for warm walls and favoured sites in temperate zones. Plenty of sun, good drainage and acid or neutral soil.

L. grandiflorum has silvery foliage and wide white flowers in late spring and early summer.
LARGE SHRUB H: 3m/10ft (taller in warm climates) S: 2.1m/7ft Z: 9[9–10]

L. lanigerum also has silver leaves, but its flowers, borne from late spring, are smaller.
LARGE SHRUB H: 3m/10ft S: 2.1m/7ft
Z: 9[9–10]

LEUCOJUM

(Liliaceae/Amaryllidaceae) snowflake Europe

L. aestivum (summer snowflake) is a bulb that thrives in a damp water-meadow and naturalizes in grass, throwing up long stems of pendent white bell-flowers with green markings in late spring. Sun or part shade.
H: 60cm/24in S: 15cm/6in Z: 4[4–9]

L. vernum is smaller and flowers earlier, almost before leaves appear.
H: 15–20cm/6–8in S: 7.5–10cm/3–4in
Z: 4[4–9]

LILIUM

(Liliaceae) lily

The more splendidly formal of these bulbous perennials are best seen alone or with non-competing companion plants, making a focal point in a container or against a foliage background. Others contribute texture and colour to mixed plantings.

L. auratum (golden-rayed imperial lily from Japan) has brilliant creamy-white petals with golden bands and wine-red spotting. Plant bulb in rich acid soil in shade, but allow late-summer flowers to emerge in sun. Grow behind earlier-flowering hellebores or small evergreen shrubs.
H: 90–180cm/36–72in S: 23cm/9in
Z: 5[5–9]

Backhouse hybrids (*L. martagon* × *hansonii*) have turk's-cap flowers in summer in shades of white, cream, yellow, buff, orange and wine-red, above whorls of mid-green leaves. Vigorous and free flowering in semi-woodland or an ordinary site in part shade: Lime-tolerant.
H: 120–150cm/48–60in S: 25–30cm/10–12in
Z: 4[4–9]

L. candidum (Madonna lily from Asia Minor)

Kolkwitzia amabilis

Lathyrus vernus

Lilium candidum

needs a warm sunny position in neutral or alkaline soil in a container or in front of a heat-reflecting wall. Several fragrant pure white open trumpet-flowers are borne in summer.
H: 120–150cm/48–60in s: 23cm/9in z: 4[4–9]

L. lancifolium (syn. L. tigrinum; tiger lily from Far East) is good for a late-summer border in sun. Orange turk's-cap flowers are spotted and flecked with black and purple. Prefers acid soil.
H: 90–180cm/36–72in s: 23cm/9in z: 3[3–9]

L. regale (regal lily from China) has loose clusters of funnel-shaped creamy-white blooms with yellow centres, shaded with purple on outside, in summer. Easy to grow in a pot or clump in an herbaceous border where perennials protect emergent shoots from late frosts. Sun or part shade, e.g. light woodland. Acid or alkaline soil, enriched with loam, leaf-mould and compost.
H: 90–180cm/36–72in s: 30cm/12in z: 4[4–9]

LINUM
(Linaceae) flax

L. grandiflorum (Algeria) is an annual flax with saucer-shaped red flowers in summer; L. g. 'Rubrum' is brighter crimson-red. Grow in a pot or make drifts in a flower bed.
H: 30–50cm/12–20in s: 15cm/6in ANNUAL

LIRIOPE
(Liliaceae/Convallariaceae) lilyturf

L. muscari (big blue lilyturf from eastern Asia) makes compact evergreen perennial clumps of grassy dark green foliage; excellent for edging or ground cover in sun or shade. Whorls of deep purple flowers are a bonus in late summer.
H: 30cm/12in s: 45cm/18in z: 6[6–10]

LOBELIA
(Campanulaceae)

L. cardinalis (cardinal flower from USA) is a perennial with a basal rosette of green or bronze leaves above which spikes of lipped scarlet flowers make a splendid display in late summer. Hybrids (often with L. fulgens) offer subtly different leaf and flower colour tones: L. 'Queen Victoria' has deep red flowers and beetroot-coloured foliage; L. 'Dark Crusader' has flowers of even deeper red, with coppery-green foliage; L. 'Cherry Ripe' is a brighter cerise-scarlet. Sun and rich damp soil. Give winter protection in cold areas.
H: 90cm/36in s: 30cm/12in z: 4[4–9]

L. tupa (Chile) is an attractive tender sub-shrubby perennial with dark erect stems bearing long downy pale green leaves. Curious red-brown flowers are borne in tapering racemes in summer. Sun and good moist soil; shelter from wind.
H: 1.5–2.1m/5–7ft s: 0.9m/3ft z: 9[9–10]

LONICERA
(Caprifoliaceae) honeysuckle

Climbing and twining honeysuckles make attractive leafy backdrops or vertical accents; choose from the range of flower colour and season to suit adjacent planting and the sun/shade aspect of the site.

L. × brownii (scarlet trumpet honeysuckle) is semi-evergreen, with long glaucous downy leaves and whorls of orange-scarlet flowers in spring and again in late summer. Its exotic colouring looks good as a background to other tender sun-loving plants, and it is not too vigorous for such mixed planting. L. × b. 'Dropmore Scarlet' is a good form.
CLIMBER H: 3–5m/10–15ft z: 3[3–9]

L. etrusca (Mediterranean regions) is semi-evergreen and bears fragrant large cream to yellow showy flowers in midsummer. Sun.
CLIMBER H: 4m/12ft s: 1.8m/6ft z: 8[8–10]

L. × heckrottii is deciduous and has long fragrant flowers, pinkish-purple opening to yellow, throughout summer.
CLIMBER H: 4m/12ft s: 1.8m/6ft z: 6[6–9]

L. japonica 'Halliana' is semi-evergreen (deciduous in zones 5-6) and vigorous, bearing scented flowers, white fading to yellow, in sun or shade all summer.
CLIMBER H: 4m/12ft z: 5[5–9]

L. × tellmanniana, a hybrid of the following species, is tender with bronze-yellow flowers, reddish in bud, in summer. Produces handsome bronze deciduous foliage, but no fragrance. Thrives in shade.
CLIMBER H: 5m/15ft z: 8[8–10]

L. tragophylla (Chinese woodbine) is deciduous shade-tolerant and vigorous; its flowers in summer are a beautiful pure yellow, but unscented.
CLIMBER H: 6m/20ft z: 6[6–9]

LOTUS
(Leguminosae)

L. hirsutus (syn. Dorycnium hirsutum; from southern Europe) is a spreading evergreen sub-shrub with downy grey-green leaves, making a soft mound of grey to spill over walls or on to paths. Pink and white clover-like flowers are borne in summer, and attractive reddish-brown seed-pods are carried all winter. Prune back half the branches each spring to encourage new shoots with fresh young foliage. Sun and poor well-drained soil.
H: 30–60cm/12–24in s: 60cm/24in z: 8[8–10]

Matteuccia struthiopteris

Linum grandiflorum 'Rubrum'

LUNARIA

(Cruciferae) honesty Europe

L. annua (silver dollar plant) is a biennial, self-seeding to make useful background colour in spring and early summer. Flowers are mauve to purplish-crimson and look less garish when in shade; white-flowered and variegated-leaved forms come true when grown separately. Has attractive papery seed-heads. *L. rediviva* is its perennial cousin, with fragrant lavender-white flowers; good for shade.

H: 60–90cm/24–36in S: 60cm/24in Z: 6[6–10]

LUPINUS

(Leguminosae) lupin

L. arboreus (tree lupin from California) is a quick-growing sprawling semi-evergreen shrub with attractive digitate lupin leaves and little spikes of scented pea-flowers in cool yellow or tones of purple and blue, borne in summer. Sun and well-drained soil.

SMALL SHRUB H: 120cm/48in S: 90cm/36in
Z: 8[8–10]

LUZULA

(Juncaceae)

L. sylvatica (great woodrush from south-western Europe) is an evergreen rhizomatous perennial making handsome tufts of grassy leaves in damp shade. Loose clusters of brownish flowers appear in early summer. Spreads slowly to make rough ground cover, ideal for woodland edges; small groups provide contrast of form.

H: 45cm/18in S: 30cm/12in Z: 5[5–9]

LYSICHITON

(Araceae)

Both species of this genus of deciduous, perennial bog plants thrive in moist soil near water. In spring striking arum-like spathes emerge, followed by massive smooth ovate leaves.

L. americanus (yellow skunk cabbage, bog arum; from Canada, northern USA) has clear yellow green-tipped spathes. Seeds freely once established.

H & S: 60–120cm/24–48in Z: 7[7–9]

L. camtschatcensis (white skunk cabbage from Siberia, Japan) has pure white spathes.

H & S: 45–90cm/18–36in Z: 7[7–9]

LYSIMACHIA

(Primulaceae) loosestrife

L. clethroides (gooseneck loosestrife, shepherd's crook; from China, Japan) has starry grey-white flowers carried in gently arching spikes in late summer. May sucker and be invasive in damp soils, but fortunately this herbaceous perennial thrives in drier sites.

H: 90cm/36in S: 60cm/24in Z: 3[3–10]

L. ephemerum (south-western Europe) makes a lovely perennial clump within a grey/white garden. Glaucous-grey leaves in spring later turn green. Tall slender spikes of delicate greyish-white flowers appear in summer. Sun (but not too hot) or shade and preferably moist soil.

H: 90cm/36in S: 30cm/12in Z: 6[6–9]

LYTHRUM

(Lythraceae) loosestrife

Lythrums grow in any reasonable soil and freely provide spires of late-summer flower colour in shade. Good garden forms are derived from two perennial species.

L. salicaria (purple loosestrife from northern temperate zones) has grey-green willow-like leaves and tall magenta flower-spikes. *L. s.* 'Feuerkerze' is an intense rosy-red.

H: 60–90cm/24–36in S: 45–60cm/18–24in
Z: 3[3–10]

L. virgatum (wand loosestrife from eastern Europe) is similar, but more delicate. Flowers are in warm pink tones.

H: 60–90cm/24–36in S: 45–60cm/18–24in
Z: 3[3–10]

MACLEAYA

(Papaveraceae) plume poppy Far East

M. microcarpa is a strikingly architectural back-of-border perennial, with large deeply lobed leaves, bronzy-green above and felted greyish beneath. *M. m.* 'Kelway's Coral Plume' has tall fluffy plume-like panicles of tiny pink-tinted flowers in summer. Sun and well-drained deep loamy soil. May be invasive.

H: 1.5–2.4m/5–8ft S: 0.9–1.2m/3–4ft
Z: 4[4–10]

MALVA

(Malvaceae) mallow

M. moschata (musk mallow from Europe) is a perennial, but not long-lived. In summer spikes of open funnel-shaped rose-pink flowers (or white in *M. m. alba*) cover bushy foliage of soft green leaves, deeply lobed and cut. Full sun and ordinary garden soil; tolerates poor dry soil. Allow to seed *in situ*.

H: 60–75cm/24–30in S: 60cm/24in
Z: 3[3–10]

Malva moschata alba

MATTEUCCIA

(Aspleniaceae)

M. struthiopteris (ostrich plume fern, shuttlecock fern; from the northern hemisphere) is a moisture-loving rhizomatous perennial; suitable for a bog-garden or waterside site. Its 'shuttlecock' of bright spring greenery makes a perfect backdrop for primulas or blue poppies. Part shade, but tolerates sun; avoid drying winds.

H: 90–150cm/36–60in S: 60–90cm/24–36in
Z: 2[2–9]

MATTHIOLA

(Cruciferae) stock

M. bicornis (night-scented stock from Greece) is an annual grown for its vespertine scent. Trivial lilac flowers, opening at night in summer, are scattered over untidy bushes of grey-green leaves. Plant in drifts between more striking neighbours.

H: 38cm/15in S: 23cm/9in ANNUAL

M. incana (southern Europe) is the parent of many of the richly scented garden hybrids with dense

Meconopsis × sheldonii

Monarda 'Cambridge Scarlet'

flower spikes, including the Brompton and Ten-week Stocks. The species is a short-lived perennial with narrow felty grey-green leaves and spikes of mauve flowers in summer.
H: 30–60cm/12–24in   s: 30cm/12in
z: 8[8–10]

MECONOPSIS
(Papaveraceae)   poppy
M. *betonicifolia* (Himalayan blue poppy from Asia) is an herbaceous perennial bearing pale blue papery-textured flowers 55–75mm/2¼–3in across, which open in summer on slender stems above grey-green leaves. The larger deeper blue flowers of M. *grandis* appear slightly earlier. M. × *sheldonii* is a desirable hybrid of the two preceding species, with large nodding pure blue flowers. All these Asian poppies need relatively mild winters and like rich deep lime-free soil in a sheltered site with humidity and part shade – a woodland glade is ideal.
H: 90–120cm/36–48in   s: 45cm/18in
z: 7[7–9]
M. *cambrica* (Welsh poppy from western Europe) is a perennial best treated as annual, since tap roots are difficult to eradicate. Clear yellow flowers are borne all summer above fresh green ferny leaves. Flourishes in any soil and position, seeding freely.
H: 30–60cm/12–24in   s: 30cm/12in
z: 6[6–9] or grow as ANNUAL

MELIANTHUS
(Melianthaceae)
M. *major* (India, S. Africa) is a beautiful exotic-looking foliage evergreen sub-shrub, with large deeply serrated grey-green pinnate leaves. In warm areas brownish-maroon flowers appear in spring, but the plant is often grown only for its striking architectural foliage. Leaves cut down by frost shoot again in spring. Full sun and well-drained soil.
H: 1.5–3m/5–10ft   s: 1.2m/4ft   z: 9[8–10]

MERTENSIA
(Boraginaceae)
M. *pulmonarioides* (syn. M. *virginica*; Virginia cowslip from eastern USA) has blue-grey foliage and leafy stems bearing drooping clusters of fragrant lavender-blue bell-like flowers in late spring to early summer. Disappears in midsummer: grow ferns to take its place. A perennial woodlander for acid loam in shade or part shade.
H: 30–60cm/12–24in   s: 45cm/18in   z: 3[3–10]

MIMULUS

(Scrophulariaceae) monkey flower
M. aurantiacus (monkey musk from western N.
America) is an evergreen shrubby perennial of
sprawling habit, with sticky mid-green leaves on
brittle stems. Pale translucent yellow-orange
50mm/2in trumpet-flowers appear all summer.
Give cuttings winter protection in cold areas. Prefers dry sunny position, but tolerates shade.
H & S: 30cm/12in z: 9[9–10]

MIRABILIS

(Nyctaginaceae)
M. jalapa (four o'clock plant, marvel of Peru; from
tropical America) flowers prolifically in summer.
Fragrant 30mm/1¼in trumpet-flowers, ranging
from crimson through pink to white and yellow,
open mid-afternoon and fade next morning. Dahlia-like tubers may be lifted for overwintering indoors in cold areas, or raise plants annually from
seed. Sun and moderately rich soil.
H: 60–90cm/24–36in s: 60cm/24in
z: 10[9–10]

MISCANTHUS

(Gramineae) Far East
M. sinensis is a giant ornamental perennial grass
with blue-green white-ribbed leaves. Is clump-
forming but not invasive, making an excellent
windbreaking backdrop. Sun and rich moist soil;
tolerates sandy soils given sufficient rainfall.
H: to 1.8m/6ft s: 0.9m/3ft z: 5[5–10]
M.s. 'Gracillimus' is more compact. Its narrow
sage-green leaves fade in winter to straw-colour.
H: 30–75cm/12–30in s: 45–60cm/18–24in
z: 5[5–10]

MONARDA

(Labiatae) bergamot
M. didyma (bee balm, Oswego tea; from N.
America) is a tall summer-flowering border perennial for sun or part shade and enriched moist soil;
may be invasive. 'Cambridge Scarlet' bears rich
scarlet flowers with deep crimson calyces in dense
whorled heads up to 75mm/3in across.
H: 75–90cm/30–36in s: 45cm/18in
z: 4[4–10]

MYOSOTIS

(Boraginaceae) forget-me-not Europe
M. alpestris has clusters of fragrant azure flowers
with yellow centres in early summer. Allow this
short-lived perennial to naturalize, but replace
every few years with new plants grown from seed

Mirabilis jalapa

sown the previous summer. Part shade and well-
drained soil with organic matter, or a rock garden.
H: 7.5–20cm/3–8in s: 15cm/6in z: 5[5–9]
M. sylvatica is a similar but larger plant: named
forms of this biennial have deeper blue flowers, in
early summer. Self-seeds readily in a shady border.
H & S: 30cm/12in z: 5[5–9]

NANDINA

(Nandinaceae) sacred bamboo China
N. domestica is an elegant evergreen shrub that
grows like a bamboo with unbranched stems. Very
large delicate pinnate leaves are usually tinged
with pink. Large terminal panicles of small white
flowers in summer ripen to scarlet or white fruits.
Rich moist well-drained soil; shelter in cold areas.
MEDIUM SHRUB H: 1.2–1.8m/4–6ft
s: 0.6–0.9m/2–3ft z: 8[8–10]

NARCISSUS

(Liliaceae/Amaryllidaceae) daffodil
Most narcissi will happily naturalize in grassy
glades or under deciduous trees. To make bright
focal points early in the year plant these bulbous
perennials in containers.

N. cyclamineus (Iberian Peninsula) has solitary
flowers of rich yellow with cyclamen-like swept-
back petals and long trumpets in late winter and
early spring. A dainty species for fine grass or a
peaty pocket in a rock garden or even a border.
Enjoys dampish soil. Cyclamineus hybrids are
taller and more resilient.
H: 15–20cm/6–8in z: 5[5–10]
N. pseudonarcissus (Lent lily, wild daffodil; from
Europe) has pale almost white petals with lemon-
yellow trumpets in spring. Native to damp
meadows.
H: 20–35cm/8–14in z: 3[3–10]
N. tazetta (Mediterranean regions, Asia Minor,
Far East) is for a frost-free area, preferably where
its bulb can be sun-baked in summer, or for forcing for a pot display. Clustered heads of small fragrant cream and papery-white flowers appear from
late autumn to mid-spring.
H: 30–45cm/12–18in z: 9[9–10]
N. 'Tresamble' has the swept-back petals and pendent flower-heads of the Triandrus group. Clusters of two or three creamy-white flowers, each
with an open cup, appear in early spring.
H: 20–35cm/8–14in z: 3[3–10]

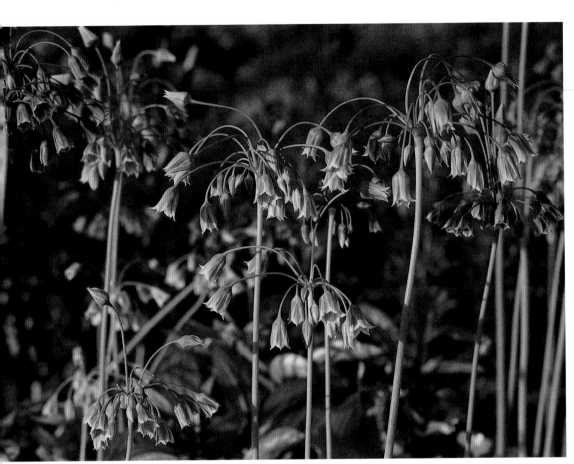

Nectaroscordum siculum bulgaricum

NECTAROSCORDUM
(Liliaceae/Alliaceae)

N. siculum bulgaricum (sometimes known as *Allium bulgaricum*; from southern Europe) has leaves and bulb with the characteristic onion smell of allium when bruised. Leaves are long mid-green and keeled. In early summer umbels of pendent bell-shaped greeny-white flowers, marked with dull purple, are carried on tall wiry stems. Seeds in unexpected places. Useful shape and texture for mixed borders. Vigorous enough to naturalize in grass or to form colonies between shrubs.
H: 60–120cm/24–48in s: 25cm/10in z: 5[5–9]

NEPETA
(Labiatae) catmint

Catmints are hardy perennials that like well-drained soil and sun.

N. × faassenii has soft grey-green leaves and a profusion of arching spikes of lavender-coloured flowers in early summer. Cut back after flowering to encourage a crop of late-summer flowers. Useful for edging, making a billowing low hedge, or for ground cover.
H: 30–60cm/12–24in s: 45cm/18in z: 3[3–10]

N. nervosa (Kashmir) makes a good-looking rounded bush of long narrow green leaves with pronounced veining. Bears bright blue flowers all through late summer.
H: 30–60cm/12–24in s: 30cm/12in z: 4[4–9]

N. 'Souvenir d'André Chaudron' (syn. *N.* 'Blue Beauty') has almost bronze leaves and long-lasting pale blue flowers in summer. Useful for a border.
H: 45cm/18in s: 25cm/10in z: 5[5–10]

NERINE
(Liliaceae/Amaryllidaceae) S. Africa

N. bowdenii provides valuable colour at the end of summer. Umbels of fine lily-like pink flowers are borne on strong bare stems just before the strap-shaped leaves re-emerge after dying down in early summer. Hardy, but bulb appreciates a sunny site with warmth reflected by a wall in marginal districts. Well-drained soil.
H: 45–60cm/18–24in s: 15–20cm/6–8in z: 8[8–10]

NICOTIANA
(Solanaceae) tobacco plant

N. alata (flowering tobacco, jasmine tobacco; from S. America) is a perennial often grown as an annual. Tubular flowers, ranging from white (often tinted yellow or green) to red and purple, offer scent as well as colour throughout summer. Sticky green leaves are good weed-smotherers. Sun and well-drained rich soil.
H: 60–90cm/24–36in s: 30cm/12in z: 9[9–10] or grow as ANNUAL

N. glauca (southern Bolivia, northern Argentina) is a sprawling tender semi-evergreen shrub with lax branches bearing smooth grey-green leaves. Only its tubular flowers in summer and early autumn betray the family resemblance. Worth coaxing as a desirable foliage perennial or annual; may be invasive in warm areas.
LARGE SHRUB H: 3m/10ft z: 9[9–10] or grow as ANNUAL

N. langsdorfii (Brazil, Chile) is a perennial grown as an annual. Strange pendent sulphur-yellow flowers appear in early summer.
H: 75cm/30in s: 30cm/12in z: 9[9–10] or grow as ANNUAL

N. sylvestris (Argentina) is a majestic perennial, but grow as annual in cold areas. Pendent clusters of almost lily-like long white flower-tubes are borne above large leaves in late summer. Good grouped at the back of a border. Sun or light shade. Self-seeds *in situ*.
H: 150cm/60in s: 30cm/12in z: 9[9–10] or grow as ANNUAL

NIGELLA
(Ranunculaceae) love-in-a-mist

N. damascena 'Miss Jekyll' has clear blue corn-flower-heads in a halo of thread-like bracts amid delicate grassy foliage. Sow seed *in situ* in spring for summer flowering. Self-seeds readily to make a flowery carpet in summer – between iris rhizomes, for example, its flower-heads disguise unsightly iris leaves.
H: 45–60cm/18–24in s: 25cm/10in ANNUAL

NYMPHAEA
(Nymphaeaceae) waterlily

Waterlily hybrids, chosen for their colour, may charmingly continue a flower theme into formal or informal ponds. Available water depth, plant hardiness, size and vigour are all factors to consider when selecting these perennial water plants, as well as flower colour and form. The hardy *N.* 'James Brydon', for example, has 10cm/4in flowers of rose-crimson, which tone with its maroon-splashed leaves and might echo a planting of deep-coloured astilbes and bronze rodgersias at the water's edge or, in more formal schemes, might complement near-by borders of hot strong colours. Free-flowering and compact; suitable for water depths to 45cm/18in.

OENOTHERA
(Onagracaeae)   evening primrose
O. biennis (biennial evening primrose from N. America) is a biennial that has rosettes of long green leaves from which arise erect stems bearing clusters of pale yellow flowers from midsummer onwards. Delicate colour of newly opened flowers gleams at twilight and perfectly complements blues and murky purples. Readily self-seeds in weed-like numbers. Sun and well-drained soil.
H: 50–100cm/20–40in   s: 30cm/12in
O. speciosa (showy primrose from southern USA) is a compact but invasive perennial. Bowl-shaped flowers in delicate faded pinks and whites appear in summer during the daytime.
H: 15–60cm/6–24in   s: 60cm/24in   z: 5[5–10]

OMPHALODES
(Boraginaceae)   navelwort
O. cappadocica (Turkey) forms perennial clumps of long-stalked green leaves. Sprays of azure-blue flowers, reminiscent of a distinguished forget-me-not, are produced in spring. Grow in drifts at the edge of a woodland or under shrubs. Part shade and peaty soil.
H & S: 15–23cm/6–9in   z: 6[6–10]
O. linifolia (Greek forget-me-not, Venus's navelwort; from Greece) is a biennial best grown as an annual. Charming almost bluish-white flowers are produced in summer above pale silvery leaves. Sow seed in early spring; overwintered plants can damp off and young plants are vulnerable to slugs. Can be grown in a container in sun for a froth of blossom.
H & S: 30cm/12in   z: 6[6–9] or grow as ANNUAL
O. verna (blue-eyed Mary from Europe) is a semi-evergreen perennial using rooting runners to spread more quickly into a carpet of heart-shaped foliage decorated with sprays of small blue flowers in spring. Evergreen in frost-free areas.
H: 15–20cm/6–8in   s: 30cm/12in   z: 5[5–9]

ONOPORDUM
(Compositae)
O. acanthium (cotton thistle, Scotch thistle; from UK) is a statuesque biennial foliage plant, beauti-

ful at the back of a border, with purple flowers at midsummer. Ethereal silvery-grey leaves and branching stems look ghostly at twilight and are a mainstay in 'white' gardens – but spines armouring the entire plant are painful to hands of weeders and to soft leaves of neighbouring plants. Allow to self-seed and remove young plants in the wrong place, or dead-head. In cold areas grow seed in individual pots and overwinter. Sun or part shade and rich soil.
H: 180cm/72in   s: 75cm/30in   z: 6[6–10]

OSMANTHUS
(Oleaceae)
Hardy evergreen shrubs for any situation, making dense bushy shapes of dark and glossy green, with fragrant flowers in spring.
O. decorus (Asia) has hard smooth oblong leaves forming a dense graceful domed shape, ideal for introducing a touch of formality. Slow-growing. Sun or part shade.
LARGE SHRUB H: 3m/10ft   s: 1.8m/6ft   z: 8[8–10]
O. delavayi (China) has handsome dark green toothed leaves. Showy white flowers in axillary clusters, rather like those of a jasmine, smother this shrub in late spring. Clip into shape after flowering: may be used for hedging. Prefers an open site in sun.
MEDIUM SHRUB H & S: 1.8–2.4m/6–8ft   z: 8[8–10]

OSMUNDA
(Osmundaceae)
O. regalis (royal fern; world-wide except Australasia) is a handsome deciduous perennial with pinnate leaves, resembling those of *Dryopteris filix-mas* (male fern), that unfurl from copper-toned crosiers in spring. Moist humus-rich soil.
H & S: 90–120cm/36–48in   z: 3[3–9]

OSTEOSPERMUM
(Compositae)
O. ecklonis (S. Africa) is a slightly tender sprawling evergreen sub-shrub with a profusion of blue-centred white daisy-flowers all summer. Sun and fairly fertile well-drained soil. Drought-tolerant.
H: 60–90cm/24–36in   s: 30–60cm/12–24in
z: 9[9–10]

PACHYSANDRA
(Buxaceae)
P. procumbens (N. America) is a semi-evergreen perennial – less vigorous than *P. terminalis* – which is lovely in a woodland setting. Spikes of white or purplish flowers are borne in spring.

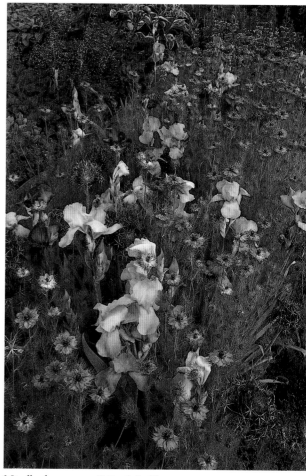

Nigella damascena 'Miss Jekyll'

P. terminalis (Japanese spurge) is a creeping shrubby evergreen perennial that can be massed to make ground cover under deciduous and evergreen trees and shrubs. Clusters of diamond-shaped smooth leaves with toothed edges make a handsome contrast to both grass and rougher foliage. Spikes of inconspicuous whitish flowers appear in spring. Acid-loving, but shallow roots tolerate lime provided they have plenty of leaf-mould.
H: 30cm/12in   s: 45cm/18in   z: 5[5–9]

PAEONIA
(Paeoniaceae)   peony
This decorative genus includes a wide range of shrubby and herbaceous plants with gorgeous showy flowers framed by architectural divided foliage. Leaves make good ground cover and often colour well in spring and autumn. Rich well-drained soil. Disturb roots as little as possible.
P. cambessedesii (Balearic Islands) is a slightly

Papaver somniferum

tender perennial that needs a special site in sun where thrusting neighbours will not overwhelm it. Late-spring flowers are deep rose-pink with darker centres, and the foliage is particularly handsome, exotically tinted with deep red stalks and undersides.

H & S: 45cm/18in z: 9[9–10]

P. lactiflora (Mongolia, Siberia) garden hybrids are numerous, with attractive mid- to deep green foliage and large flowers in all shades of pinks and whites from early summer. Varieties of these perennials include singles, doubles, semi-doubles and so on, but the single forms, often with conspicuous yellow stamens, are the most elegant. A valuable border plant.

H: 45–105cm/18–42in s: 60–90cm/24–36in
z: 2[2–10]

P. mlokosewitschii (Caucasus) is a perennial and earliest to flower. Fat cherry-buds herald spring and open to clear lemon-yellow globular flowers with golden anthers clustered among blue-green leaves. By midsummer pods open to reveal shining black seeds nestling in a crimson lining.

H & S: 60cm/24in z: 5[5–10]

P. officinalis (common peony from southern Europe and Asia) is a tuberous perennial with flowers in late spring. Single and double forms are available, in whites, pinks and reds. Fresh green foliage lasts well all summer. Good under and with shrub roses.

H: 75cm/30in s: 90cm/36in z: 2[2–10]

P. suffruticosa (moutan from China, Tibet) is a deciduous shrub with single white flowers, blotched with crimson to maroon at the petal base, in a framework of pale green leaves. There are many wonderful cultivars with pink or yellow flowers, usually grafted.

MEDIUM SHRUB H & S: 1.5–1.8m/5–6ft z: 5[5–9]

P. wittmanniana (Caucasus) is a handsome perennial with rather coarser leaves. In late spring produces pale single flowers, from white to yellow, with crimson filaments in centre.

H: 90cm/36in s: 60cm/24in z: 5[5–10]

PAPAVER

(Papaveraceae) poppy

P. orientale (oriental poppy from Armenia) is a perennial with flamboyant tissue-paper flowers in white, pink, scarlet and vermilion amid pale bristly deeply cut leaves. Makes an exciting early-summer climax in a border. After flowering the plants sprawl untidily and are best veiled by later-flowering neighbours. Sun and deep well-drained soil.

H: 60–120cm/24–48in s: 60–90cm/24–36in
z: 3[3–9]

P. rhoeas (field poppy from Europe) with papery scarlet petals on delicate stalks colours wildflower meadows in summer. Garden varieties, the Shirley poppies, make useful annual front-of-border fillers in drifts of pinks, whites and reds.

H: 60cm/24in s: 20cm/8in ANNUAL

P. somniferum (opium poppy from Greece and the Orient) is an annual with smooth pale grey-green leaves. Peony-flowered varieties have double flowers in white, pink, red and purple in summer. Endures very high temperatures.

H: 75cm/30in s: 30cm/12in ANNUAL

PARAHEBE

(Scrophulariaceae)

P. catarractae is a neat little evergreen sub-shrub. A mound of mid-green leaves is covered by a mass of pale whitish-mauve speedwell-flowers in summer. Sun and well-drained soil.

H: 15–20cm/6–8in s: 30–45cm/12–18in
z: 9[9–10]

P. perfoliata (often listed as *Veronica perfoliata*; digger's speedwell from Australia) is an unusual distinctive evergreen sub-shrub with waxy-grey oval leaves clasping and encircling long arching stems. Elegant racemes of lavender-blue flowers in late summer will trail gracefully over the edge of a low sunny wall.

H: 60cm/24in s: 45cm/18in z: 8[8–10]

PARTHENOCISSUS

(Vitaceae)

These self-clinging deciduous creepers clothe walls to make rich foliage backdrops to borders, and are particularly dramatic with vivid autumn colouring.

P. henryana (Chinese Virginia creeper) has attractive palmate leaves of velvety dark green variegated with white and pink along midribs and veins. Variegation persists after the dark green leaves have turned to fiery red in autumn. Shade.

CLIMBER H: 8–10m/25–30ft z: 8[8–10]

P. quinquefolia (Virginia creeper from N. America) has serrated five-leaflet leaves that turn a brilliant crimson in autumn.

CLIMBER H: 20m/70ft z: 3[3–9]

P. tricuspidata 'Veitchii' (Boston ivy from China, Japan) has variable leaves, often with three leaflets or three lobes.
CLIMBER H: 15m/50ft z: 4[4–9]

PELARGONIUM
(Geraniaceae) geranium
Pelargoniums are invaluable for their colour: dense rounded flower-heads bloom all summer if dead-heads are removed. Grow named forms from seed or choose colours carefully to fit in with orchestrated schemes of summer bedding.
P. 'The Boar' has pretty salmon-pink flowers and dark foliage. Perennial, but grow as annual from seed or as cutting.
H & S: 90cm/36in z: 10 or grow as ANNUAL

PENNISETUM
(Gramineae)
P. alopecuroides (Argentina, eastern Asia, eastern Australia) is a perennial grass with narrow grey-green leaves forming a dense clump. Bottle-brush flower-spikes appear in autumn. Sun; protect from frost.
H: 90cm/36in s: 45–60cm/18–24in z: 5[5–10]

PENSTEMON
(Scrophulariaceae)
northern and central America
Penstemons make a valuable contribution to summer and autumn borders with freely produced loose spikes of tubular flowers in lovely rich colours. Border varieties are often only half-hardy but root easily from cuttings to be grown as annual bedding (left *in situ* they become unsightly in winter and succumb to cold spring wind). Keep dead-headed. Sun and well-drained fertile soil.
P. 'Garnet' (correctly *P.* 'Andenken an Friedrich Hahn') is a semi-evergreen perennial with flowers of deep purple-red from midsummer to autumn. Flowers tone particularly well when planted under pink shrub roses.
H: 75cm/30in s: 60cm/24in z: 8[8–10]
P. heterophyllus is a semi-evergreen alpine variety with narrow grey-green leaves and spikes of blue flowers in summer.
SMALL SHRUB H & S: 45cm/18in z: 5[5–10]
P. 'Schoenholzeri' has scarlet flowers that glow beside other 'hot' colours from midsummer to autumn. Vigorous bushy semi-evergreen perennial.
H: 90cm/36in s: 60cm/24in z: 8[8–10]

PERILLA
(Labiatae)
P. frutescens (China) is an annual needing hot sun to ripen the seed. Has handsome red-purple leaves, ovate and pointed and attractively textured with veining. Spikes of white flowers appear in late summer.
H: 60cm/24in s: 30cm/12in ANNUAL

PEROVSKIA
(Labiatae)
P. atriplicifolia (Russian sage from Afghanistan to Tibet) is a graceful deciduous sub-shrub with grey-blue leaves and open panicles of violet-blue tubular flowers throughout late summer: the effect of the whole plant in a border amounts to more than the sum of its parts. Named forms have bluer flowers. Is generally cut to the ground each winter and shoots again from the base. Suckers may be invasive. Sun and good drainage.
H: 90–150cm/36–60in s: 45–60cm/18–24in z: 6[6–10]

PERSICARIA
(Polygonaceae) knotweed
P. campanulata (formerly *Polygonum campanulatum*; from the Himalayas) has attractively veined and brown-marked leaves that appear in early spring. Wide branching flower-heads of tiny shell-pink bells last for many weeks from midsummer to early autumn. Colonizes moist or cool soil to make perennial ground cover in part shade or non-scorching sun, but its easily controlled shallow roots make it less alarmingly invasive than other knotweeds.
H & S: 90cm/36in z: 6[6–9]
P. capitata (formerly *Polygonum capitatum*; from the Himalayas) makes charming low ground cover for mild areas, with dark green brown-marked foliage and a long succession of little rounded pink flower-heads throughout summer. Perennial in its native habitat; in cold zones overwinter indoors and grow as an annual, or allow to self-seed.
H: 10–15cm/4–6in s: 30–45cm/12–18in
z: 9[9–10] or grow as ANNUAL

PHILADELPHUS
(Philadelphaceae) mock orange
A range of species and hybrids of deciduous shrubs varying in size and flowering time provide scented white flowers for many weeks in shrub borders and woodland.
P. 'Belle Etoile' is a compact shrub with single white flowers opening wide to display maroon-blotched petal bases in summer.
MEDIUM SHRUB H & S: 2.4m/8ft z: 5[5–9]

Perovskia atriplicifolia 'Blue Spire'

Philadelphus coronarius

Philadelphus 'Innocence'

P. coronarius (southern Europe) has richly scented creamy-white flowers in early summer, and is not fussy about soil or site. Its golden-leaved and variegated forms need part shade.
MEDIUM SHRUB H & S: 1.8–3m/6–10ft z: 5[5–9]
P. 'Innocence' bears single pure white flowers in summer. Leaves have distinctive cream and white variegation.
MEDIUM SHRUB H: 2.4m/8ft s: 1.8m–2.4m/6–8ft
z: 5[5–9]
P. 'Virginal' has wide-opening double white flowers in summer on upright branches.
MEDIUM SHRUB H: 2.4–3m/8–10ft
s: 1.8–2.4m/6–8ft z: 5[5–9]

PHILLYREA
(Oleaceae)   southern Europe, northern Africa, Middle East
Phillyreas are slow-growing evergreens with a dense mass of glistening foliage to clip into formal shapes as emphatic foils for exuberant flowering companions.
P. angustifolia rosmarinifolia makes a compact dome-shaped bush, with narrow plain dark green leaves.
SMALL SHRUB H & S: 60cm/24in z: 8[8–10]
P. latifolia is an elegant tree similar to an olive, its small leaves revealing pale undersides and fluttering attractively in a breeze.
SMALL TREE H & S: to 5m/15ft z: 8[8–10]

PHLOMIS
(Labiatae)
P. fruticosa (Jerusalem sage from the Mediterranean) is a sprawling bushy evergreen shrub with hairy grey-green foliage and whorls of bright yellow flowers carried in leaf axils in summer.
SMALL SHRUB H: 90–120cm/36–48in
s: 60–90cm/24–36in z: 8[8–10]
P. italica (Balearic Islands) is, in summer, a beautiful combination of silver-grey felted leaves and palest dusty-pink flowers. Prune hard, if necessary to ground level, in early summer to make a shapely upright evergreen bush. Slightly tender until well-established. Sunny sheltered site and well-drained soil.
SMALL SHRUB H: 30–45cm/12–18in s: 30cm/12in
z: 8[8–10]

PHLOX
(Polemoniaceae)
The *Phlox* genus provides flower colour for almost every season and section of the garden.
P. 'Chattahoochee', a trailing woodland-type short-lived perennial, is a valuable early-flowering front-of-border plant. In summer and autumn purple-eyed flowers of a rich soft blue fade to pale lavender-blue in a lovely blended mixture. Leaves are dark, hairy and rather pointed. Part shade and cool soil.
H: 25cm/10in s: 30cm/12in z: 4[4–9]
P. divaricata (wild blue phlox from north-eastern USA) – a probable parent of *P.* 'Chattahoochee' – forms an open perennial mat of semi-evergreen foliage. Bears loose clusters of light blue or lavender flowers in spring. Needs woodland conditions of part shade and moist humus-rich soil.
H & S: 30cm/12in z: 4[4–9]
P. douglasii (western N. America) is an evergreen perennial forming a dense sub-shrubby mat of mid-green leaves. Garden forms have flowers in tones of pink, mauve and white in early summer. Good for front of a sunny border.
H: 7.5cm/3in s: 45cm/18in z: 5[5–8]
P. drummondii (Texas) is a half-hardy annual, flowering from midsummer onwards with dense flower-heads in shades of reds, pinks, lavender and white. There are garden varieties of more compact habit with various flower shapes and colours.
H: 38cm/15in s: 23cm/9in ANNUAL
P. maculata (wild sweet William, meadow phlox; from eastern USA), a perennial, freely produces tall cylindrical spikes of fragrant mauvish flowers from late summer on. Feed richly and divide periodically for best results. Useful late-flowering plant for an open border or part shade. Feed richly and divide periodically for best results. Rich moisture-retentive well-drained soil. *P.m.* 'Alpha' has dark-eyed flowers of soft lilac-pink. *P.m.* 'Omega' is white with a slight lilac tinge and a violet eye.
H: 60–120cm/24–48in s: 45–60cm/18–24in
z: 3[3–9]
P. paniculata (border phlox, garden phlox; from north-eastern USA) is a perennial with, in summer, many good named varieties in a wide spectrum ranging from violet-blues to reds, sometimes with a darker eye. If possible choose from a flowering plant rather than a catalogue description to ensure the right tone for a scheme. Heavy pyramidal flower panicles may need staking. Feed richly and divide periodically for best results. Good for open border. Part shade and rich moisture-retentive well-drained soil.
H: 45–150cm/18–60in s: 45–60cm/18–24in
z: 3[3–9]

Phygelius × *rectus* 'African Queen'

P. stolonifera (creeping phlox from south-eastern USA) makes a low evergreen mat of oval leaves with loose clusters of rose-purple flowers in late spring; named forms come in pink, white and blue. Makes good perennial ground cover in part shade. Tolerates sun that is not too intense.
H: 15–20cm/6–8in s: 30cm/12in z: 3[3–9]
P. subulata (moss phlox from eastern USA) makes a dense perennial mass of thin evergreen leaves with pink or mauve flowers in late spring. Named forms include good tones of pink, red and lavender. Good for front of a sunny border.
H: 7.5cm/3in s: 45cm/18in z: 3[3–8]

PHORMIUM
(Agavaceae/Phormiaceae)
P. tenax (New Zealand flax) is an evergreen perennial with tough sword-like leaves rising from the ground in a huge fan, making a striking architectural focal point and a valuable contrast with most other foliage shapes and textures. Panicles of dark brownish-red flowers tower above the leaves in summer. Sun and moist but well-drained fertile soil. Withstands salt, drought and city atmosphere. Provide winter protection in cold areas. *P. t. purpureum* has grey-green leaves with a purplish sheen. There are many tender cultivars and hybrids with variegated and purple leaf tones.
H: 1.8–3m/6–10ft s: 1.2m/4ft z: 8[8–10]

PHYGELIUS
(Scrophulariaceae) S. Africa
These sub-shrubby plants are evergreen in warm areas, but may be grown as herbaceous perennials in colder gardens in sunny sheltered well-drained sites.
P. aequalis is a spreading sub-shrub with salmon-buff flowers from midsummer to autumn. *P. a.* 'Yellow Trumpet', a compact form, has spikes of palest yellow slender tubular flowers.
H: 75cm/30in s: 50cm/20in z: 8[8–10]
P. × rectus are hybrids between *P. aequalis* and *P. capensis* (Cape fuchsia). *P. × r.* 'African Queen' has light red flowers with yellow throats from midsummer to autumn. *P. × r.* 'Winchester Fanfare' bears pendulous flowers of dusky red lined with yellow from midsummer to early autumn.
H: 75cm/30in s: 50cm/20in z: 8[8–10]

PILEOSTEGIA
(Hydrangeaceae)
P. viburnoides (China) is a good self-clinging evergreen climber with dull green leaves and creamy flowers in terminal panicles in late summer and autumn. Ideal for lighting a dark corner or shady wall. Slow-growing, it takes time to establish.
CLIMBER H & S: 6m/20ft z: 9[9–10]

PIPTANTHUS
(Leguminosae)
P. nepalensis (evergreen laburnum from the Himalayas) is a short-lived semi-evergreen shrub. Racemes of bright yellow pea-flowers in late spring are set amid silver-haired young leaves, which later turn into elegant long leaflets, dark green above and greyish below. Sun; plant by warm wall and shelter from cold wind.
LARGE SHRUB H & S: 2.4–4m/8–12ft z: 8[8–10]

PLUMBAGO
(Plumbaginaceae)
P. auriculata (syn. *P. capensis*; from S. Africa) is an evergreen climber with lovely panicles of ice-blue primrose-like flowers for many months in summer, amid soft green elliptical leaves. Tie its lax stems to a wall or allow to sprawl over neighbouring plants. Cut back after flowering and water sparingly in winter. Overwinter in a frost-free greenhouse and in spring put out in its pot, or plant out, to transform a sunny corner with its flowers.
CLIMBER H: 5m/15ft s: 3m/10ft z: 9[9–10]

PODOPHYLLUM
(Podophyllaceae)
P. hexandrum (syn. *P. emodi*; from India) is a rhizomatous perennial colonizing slowly in a moist shady border. Deeply lobed leaves emerge folded downwards like a furled umbrella and open to show coppery-brown markings. Saucer-shaped pink or white flowers in early summer are followed by egg-shaped red fruits, which are edible, though the plant is poisonous.
H: 30cm/12in s: 45cm/18in z: 5[5–9]

POLEMONIUM
(Polemoniaceae) Jacob's ladder
Polemoniums are pretty border perennials for sun or part shade and ordinary garden soil. Cut back spent flower stems to freshen up ferny foliage.
P. caeruleum (Asia, Europe) makes a basal clump of bright green pinnate leaves and produces loose clusters of bell-shaped lavender-blue flowers with orange stamens in early summer.
H: 60–90cm/24–36in s: 30–60cm/12–24in
z: 3[3–9]
P. foliosissimum (western N. America) has erect stems carrying dark green pinnate leaves and ter-

Podophyllum hexandrum

minating in dense clusters of cup-shaped flowers of rich lilac-blue, produced in long succession throughout summer.
H: 75–90cm/30–36in s: 60cm/24in
z: 4[4–9]

POLYGONATUM
(Liliaceae/Convallariaceae)
P. × hybridum (David's harp, Solomon's harp) is an elegant shade-loving spreading perennial for a border. Long arching stems bear horizontally held elliptical leaves all along their length, and green-tinged white bells hang downwards in clusters during early summer. Pale green leaves emerge to camouflage anemone and fritillary flowers as they fade in late spring, and their simple lines become the perfect foil for shapely ferns and acanthus and for massed darker small-leaved foliage.
H: 90–120cm/36–48in s: 60cm/24in
z: 4[4–10]

POLYSTICHUM
(Aspleniaceae)
P. setiferum (soft shield fern from Europe) has dainty elegant fronds and thrives in most conditions. This evergreen or semi-evergreen perennial tolerates drought, but is most luxuriant in a cool shady site.
H: 60–120cm/24–48in s: 90–150cm/36–60in
z: 5[5–9]

POTENTILLA

(Rosaceae)   cinquefoil

These useful hardy deciduous shrubs have a long flowering period. Their brown stems and seedheads are attractive all winter.

P. fruticosa 'Abbotswood' has abundant white flowers against a mass of greyish leaves throughout summer and autumn.

SMALL SHRUB H: 90cm/36in   s: 120cm/48in
z: 2[2–9]

P. f. arbuscula (Himalayas, northern China) has sage-green leaves and brown shaggy stems in winter. Clusters of large rich yellow flowers are borne from early summer to autumn.

SMALL SHRUB H: 60cm/24in   s: 150cm/60in
z: 2[2–9]

P. f. 'Elizabeth' is dome-shaped and has rich canary-flowers, freely produced late spring to early autumn. Good for hedging or in groups.

SMALL SHRUB H: 90cm/36in   s: 120cm/48in
z: 2[2–9]

P. f. 'Vilmoriniana' has intense silver leaves primrose-flowers from late spring to early autumn, and a more upright habit than *P. f.* 'Elizabeth'

SMALL SHRUB H: 120cm/48in   s: 90cm/36in
z: 2[2–9]

PRIMULA

(Primulaceae)   primrose

Asian species prefer part shade in cool humus-rich soil – moist or well-mulched, but not waterlogged in winter. Given a suitable site, their contribution of flower colour and form is stunning.

P. florindae (giant cowslip, Tibetan primrose; from western China, Tibet) is a handsome vigorous perennial for a moist site, with long-lasting summer flowers. Several tall stems bearing fragrant drooping sulphur-yellow flowers powdered with white rise from a clump of large rounded leaves.

H: 60–90cm/24–36in   s: 60cm/24in
z: 6[6–9]

P. pulverulenta (western China) is a candelabra-type perennial, with wrinkled green leaves and tiered flowers carried on stems covered in floury meal in early summer. Garden cultivars have tones from almost crimson with a darker red or purple eye to softer pink tints. Plant in drifts at a pond's edge, with bronze rodgersia foliage or gunnera leaves as a background.

H: 60–90cm/24–36in   s: 45cm/18in
z: 6[6–9]

P. sikkimensis (Himalayan cowslip) is a slighter version of *P. florindae*, with narrower leaves and pale yellow flowers in summer. This perennial is less easily grown.

H: 45cm/18in   s: 23–30cm/9–12in
z: 6[6–9]

P. vulgaris (common primrose from Europe) is a perennial that should be encouraged to colonize shrubberies and woodland areas, the simple pale yellow flowers evoking the arrival of spring.

H: 15cm/6in   s: 23cm/9in   z: 5[5–9]

PRUNUS

(Rosaceae)   flowering cherry

P. maackii (Manchurian cherry from China) is deciduous and has outstanding golden-brown bark that flakes as it ages. Shows up best in a group planting, glowing against a plain background, a carpet of yellow aconites reflecting its brightness.

MEDIUM TREE H: 12m/40ft   s: 6m/20ft   z: 2[2–9]

P. 'Ukon' (Japanese cherry) is deciduous and has long-lasting green-tinged creamy double flowers in midspring set amid bronze young leaves, a beautiful combination against a dark backdrop.

SMALL TREE H: 5–6m/15–20ft   s: 5.5–8m/18–25ft
z: 6[6–9]

PULMONARIA

(Boraginaceae)   lungwort

Pulmonarias make useful perennial ground cover in moist shady sites, but two species with shapely leaves offer more textural interest than most.

P. angustifolia (blue cowslip from central Europe) has elliptical leaves of plain dark green. These emerge in spring with the flowers – sprays of pink buds unfurling to blue cowslip-flowers.

H: 23–30cm/9–12in   s: 30–45cm/12–18in
z: 3[3–9]

LEFT *Primula florindae*   ABOVE Candelabra primulas

P. longifolia (western Europe) has long narrow pointed leaves spotted with white, and the dense clusters of blue spring flowers last into summer, later than most of the genus.
H: 30cm/12in s: 45cm/18in z: 5[5–9]

PULSATILLA
(Ranunculaceae)
P. vulgaris (pasque flower from Europe) has purple flowers that appear in spring before the delicate finely cut foliage has fully emerged. Silky hairs give this perennial a silvery sheen. Full sun and well-drained dryish chalky soil.
H & s: 23–30cm/9–12in z: 3[3–9]

PYRUS
(Rosaceae) pear
P. calleryana 'Chanticleer' (Bradford pear), a cultivar of the Chinese wild pear, is deciduous and has a graceful pyramidal habit. Carries a mass of white blossom in spring and good rich leaf colouring in autumn.
MEDIUM TREE H: 15m/50ft s: 6m/20ft
z: 5[5–9]
P. salicifolia 'Pendula' (weeping silver pear) has gracefully drooping dark stems and willow-like silver leaves. Its colour shimmers against a dark backdrop, but also contributes well to beds of mixed planting. Prune lower branches to keep a graceful shape to this deciduous tree.
SMALL TREE H: 8m/25ft s: 6m/20ft
z: 6[6–9]

RANUNCULUS
(Ranunculaceae) buttercup
R. aconitifolius (Europe) makes strong leafy perennial clumps of dark green buttercup-foliage. Wiry branching stems bear loose clusters of dainty white flowers in early summer. Beautiful white button-flowers of double-flowered *R. a.* 'Flore Pleno' (fair maids of France) make elegant contrast with the dark foliage. Sun or part shade and moist soil.
H & s: 90cm/36in z: 4[4–9]

REHMANNIA
(Gesneriaceae) China
R. elata (syn. *R. angulata*) is a long-blooming self-seeding perennial with strange hooded foxglove-like flowers of rose purple with spotted inner markings in early and midsummer. Useful in a border. Sun or shade and well-drained soil.
H: 60–90cm/24–36in s: 30–60cm/12–24in
z: 8[8–10]

RESEDA
(Resedaceae) mignonette
R. odorata (northern Africa) is a hardy cottage-garden annual with honey-scented fluffy flower-spikes, greenish-yellow in the species but red-tinged in some named varieties. Plant in groups as a subtly toned front-of-border filler.
H: 30–60cm/12–24in s: 15–23cm/6–9in
ANNUAL

RHEUM
(Polygonaceae) ornamental rhubarb   China
R. palmatum is one of the best foliage perennials for waterside with deeply toothed broad rough leaves, green tinged with purple in the type, while *R. p.* 'Atrosanguineum' (syn. *R. p.* 'Atropurpureum') has vivid red young foliage that turns deep wine-purple as it matures. Tall plumes of white, pink or red astilbe-like flowers are borne in summer. Sun or part shade and deep moist soil.
H & s: 1.8m/6ft z: 5[5–9]

RICINUS
(Euphorbiaceae) castor oil plant
R. communis (tropical Africa) is a tender evergreen tree-like shrub of upright habit grown for its handsome palmate leaves. Grow as an annual from seed sown the previous summer, and over-wintered free from frost, to make attractive textural contrast in border plantings. Red- or bronze-leaved forms are valuable too.
SMALL SHRUB H: 150cm/60in s: 90cm/36in
ANNUAL

RODGERSIA
(Saxifragaceae)
Deciduous perennials that flourish in moist soil, rodgersias spread quickly to make weedproof mats of handsome greeny-bronze leaves that contrast beautifully with light green or feathery foliage. Pink or cream plumes of flowers are a bonus in midsummer.
R. aesculifolia (China) has large crinkled bronze chestnut-leaves that set off clustered plumes of creamy-white flowers, and also harmonize with neighbouring pink-toned flowers.
H: 90–150cm/36–60in s: 60–75cm/24–30in
z: 4[4–9]
R. pinnata 'Superba' is a striking cultivar with very deep green bronze-flushed pinnate leaves and brilliant pink astilbe-like flowers.
H: 90–120cm/36–48in s: 60–75cm/24–30in
z: 4[4–9]
R. tabularis (now correctly *Astilboides tabularis*;

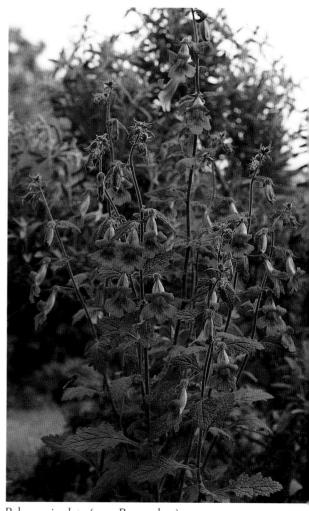

Rehmannia elata (syn. *R. angulata*)

from China, Korea) has smoother umbrella-shaped light green leaves like a small gunnera. Produces tall panicles of creamy-white flowers.
H & s: 90cm/36in z: 4[4–9]

ROMNEYA
(Papaveraceae) California poppy, tree poppy
California
R. coulteri is an herbaceous perennial with deeply lobed glaucous leaves. Huge papery-white poppy-flowers, yellow-centred and fragrant, appear in late summer and autumn. *R. c.* 'White Cloud' has even more splendid flowers. Slow to establish, but potentially invasive: grows into a substantial shrub in warm climates, where it flowers earlier. In colder zones is cut to the ground by frost. Well-drained deep soil, and sun and shelter in cold areas.
H & s: 1.2–1.8m/4–6ft z: 8[8–10]

Rosa 'Albertine'

Rosa 'Penelope'

ROSA

(Rosaceae)   rose

This summary concentrates on roses that combine gracefully in general plant compositions rather than those chosen for perfection of individual bloom, which usually demand privileged treatment in the garden. The list could be expanded infinitely: here are some examples.

Roses for mixed borders

Many roses merit 'key' status in borders, though some rank as companion plants.

Hybrid musks are valuable shrubs with a branching fan-like habit – good for combining with lower-growing herbaceous perennials – and huge trusses of flowers in midsummer, with a second flush in late summer if dead-headed. Colours vary from pure white to some bright pinks (*R.* 'Penelope' is a gentle pink) and the warm cream-bronze of *R.* 'Buff Beauty'.

Modern shrubs – many of which are the result of crosses between Hybrid Teas and various species roses – offer a wide range of shrubs, some displaying the elegant and thrifty habit characteristic of a species parent. A wide choice of flower colour is available, with main flowering in summer and some intermittent blooms later. Plants are robust and relatively disease- and trouble-free. Favourites are the gigantic *R.* 'Cerise Bouquet' and pale yellow *R.* 'Frühlingsgold'.

Bush roses are grown less for habit than for flower impact. This grouping includes highly developed Hybrid Teas, with shapely flowers best massed in formal settings in areas of the garden that can be bypassed in winter when the pruned bushes are unsightly. More suitable for border schemes are Floribundas, with informal clustered blooms, and their parent Polyanthas – compact bushes with small flowers in closely packed bunches.

Roses for informal planting

In less formal garden areas many of the species roses and their near hybrids contribute attractive foliage and subtly beautiful flowers in season. *R. pimpinellifolia* (Scotch or Burnet rose) forms a suckering thicket of fern-like leaves and has forms with pink or white double or single flowers in early summer followed by black hips. Flourishes in poor soil and shady beds. Where its root-run is contained, makes a charming hedge for the more formal flower garden.

Alba roses flower once, in early summer, and have soft grey leaves, an attractive shape and pretty pale pink or white double or semi-double fragrant clustered flowers. *R.* 'Alba Maxima' and *R.* 'Great Maiden's Blush' are favourites.

Rugosa forms have apple-green deeply veined wrinkled leaves and very thorny pale wood. Scented flowers from white to pink and deep wine-crimson are freely borne all summer, followed by globe-shaped red hips. Make attractive and impenetrable hedging. Rugosa roses are hardy, trouble-free and tolerant of salt-laden winds, and many Rugosa hybrids have inherited these useful qualities. *R.* 'Fru Dagmar Hastrup' has single pink flowers and good fruit, and does not grow too large.

Roses as backdrops

On a larger scale, roses curtain vertical surfaces or cascade over banks to add a third dimension of flowers to garden layouts. Perhaps the loveliest backdrops are created by species and cultivars with small or clustered flower-heads combining in massed colour effects.

Rambling and twining roses need the framework of a trellis or pergola for support. Many Ramblers have *wichuraiana* breeding: *R.* 'Albertine' has reddish-copper buds opening to strawberries-and-cream pink; *R.* 'Albéric Barbier' bears cream flowers and glossy green leaves. The more vigorous such as *R.* 'Bobbie James' may be allowed to clamber into trees. *R.* 'Paulii' has single white flowers and prickly branches that will flow down a wall or clothe a slope. Trailing *R.* × *jacksonii* 'Max Graf' produces gold-centred rose-pink flowers.

Climbing roses are for walls, and may be pruned spring into architectural shapes. Stronger-growing climbers usually have a main flush of flowers in early summer and then repeat on and off throughout the rest of the summer: choose deep reds or rich yellows to enhance specific colour schemes, or paler tones for a less eye-catching backdrop. A modest old-fashioned climber is *R.* × *odorata* 'Pallida' (syn. 'Old Blush China'), the rose with delicious semi-double pink flowers that appear in almost every month of the year.

ROSMARINUS

(Labiatae)   rosemary

R. officinalis (southern Europe, Asia Minor) is an evergreen shrub with greyish-green linear leaves and pale mauvish-blue flowers in spring. Deserves a place in every garden, sprawling informally or clipped into a low hedge. Improved forms offer brighter blue flowers and a choice of upright or more compact habit, but are often less hardy.
MEDIUM SHRUB H: 1.8–2.1m/6–7ft
s: 1.5–1.8m/5–6ft z: 8[8–10]

RUDBECKIA

(Compositae)   coneflower   N. America

R. laciniata (cutleaf coneflower) makes a robust perennial clump of deeply cut leaves to provide late-summer colour at the back of a large-scale border. The species has large yellow flowers with drooping ray florets and greenish cones. *R.l.* 'Golden Glow' is a double form with brassy yellow flowers. May be invasive.

H: 1.8–2.1m/6–7ft s: 0.6m/2ft z: 3[3–10]

SALVIA
(Labiatae) sage

Sages tend to have handsome textured leaves and spikes of tubular flowers ranging from subtle to showy. Hardy culinary sage is a useful foliage plant, while many of the more tender New World species are worth nurturing for their ornamental flowers in striking colours. Needs sun and good drainage.

S. argentea (eastern regions of Mediterranean) is grown principally for its rosette of large silver-white hairy leaves with crinkled and toothed edges. This biennial virtually becomes a perennial if the flower-buds are removed, in summer. (I personally like the low-key whitish-green flower-spires.)

H: 90cm/36in s: 60cm/24in z: 5[5–10]

S. farinacea 'Victoria', a cultivar of the tender mealy sage, is a perennial usually grown as an annual. Long-lasting flower-spikes of intense violet-blue appear in late summer on branching felted stems with grey-green foliage.

H: 45cm/18in s: 30cm/12in z: 9[9–10] or grow as ANNUAL

S. fulgens (cardinal sage from Mexico) has velvety flower-spikes of vivid scarlet, in late summer, above this evergreen sub-shrub.

H: 60–90cm/24–36in s: 45cm/18in z: 9[9–10]

S. guaranitica (S. America) is a semi-evergreen sub-shrub with rough dark green leaves. Intense royal-blue sage-flowers appear in late summer and autumn. Mulch well. Not reliably hardy: cuttings may be rooted in autumn.

H: 150cm/60in s: 60–90cm/24–36in z: 9[9–10] or grow as ANNUAL

S. leucantha (Mexico) is a tender evergreen sub-shrub with arching grey-white stems and textured leaves. In late summer and autumn slender sprays of little lavender-white flowers are produced in conspicuous felted violet-toned calyces.

H & s: 60–90cm/24–36in z: 9[9–10]

S. microphylla neurepia (Mexico) is a tender evergreen shrub with fresh green leaves and a succession of little brilliant scarlet flowers from early summer to autumn.

SMALL SHRUB H: 120cm/48in s: 90cm/36in z: 9[9–10]

S. officinalis (sage from southern Europe) and its various forms make useful matt-textured foliage plants – low-growing bushy evergreen shrubs, with variegated or purplish leaves to tone with different colour schemes. Small spikes of violet-blue tubular flowers appear in summer.

SMALL SHRUB H: 60cm/24in s: 45cm/18in z: 7[7–10]

S. patens (Mexico) is a compact leafy tuberous perennial that bears loose spikes of bright blue hooded flowers on branching stems in late summer and autumn. Is evergreen in a warm climate, becoming woody with age; sow seed each spring in colder areas.

H: 45–75cm/18–30in s: 30–45cm/12–18in z: 9[9–10] or grow as ANNUAL

S. sclarea turkestanica (Turkestan) is a biennial or short-lived perennial with wrinkled leaves and sturdy stems carrying sage-flowers with conspicuous lavender-purple bracts in summer.

H: 90cm/36in s: 45cm/18in z: 8[8–10]

S. uliginosa (bog sage from S. America) is a perennial carrying loose spires of bright azure-blue flowers on tall arching stems in late summer. Not reliably hardy: protect from frosts, or root cuttings in autumn for overwintering. Relatively moist soil and warm site.

Rosa × *odorata* 'Pallida' (syn. 'Old Blush China')

H: 150cm/60in s: 45–60cm/18–24in z: 8[8–10] or grow as ANNUAL

S. viridis (syn. *S. horminum*; clary from southern Europe) has showy coloured bracts in different muted shades of purple-blue, soft rose-reds, pinks and white that tone together well and last from mid- to late summer.

H: 45cm/18in s: 23cm/9in ANNUAL

SANGUINARIA
(Papaveraceae) bloodroot

S. canadensis 'Multiplex' (syn. *S.c.* 'Plena') is a rhizomatous perennial and double form of the wildflower of Canadian woodlands. Flower-heads of tightly packed creamy-white petals are freely carried in spring from folds of leaves. These later open out flat to display handsome grey-green lobes and provide ground cover until they die down in summer. Part shade and well-drained rich loamy acid soil.

H: 15–23cm/6–9in s: 30cm/12in z: 3[3–9]

SANTOLINA
(Compositae) cotton lavender southern Europe

Santolinas are useful small evergreen shrubs,

Salvia viridis 'Rose Bouquet'

Selinum tenuifolium

hardy where full sun can ripen the wood and where roots are not waterlogged in winter. Vigorous spring pruning keeps the shape neat and prevents woodiness. Good for edging, low hedges and ground cover.

S. chamaecyparissus makes a dense rounded bush, greenish in spring but silvery later. Small yellow button-flowers in summer may be trimmed off where they vie with cool pastel schemes of mauves and pinks.
SMALL SHRUB H & S: 45–60cm/18–24in
z: 7[7–10]
S. rosmarinifolia rosmarinifolia (syn. *S. virens*) has narrow pale green leaves and attractive sulphur-yellow summer flowers. *S.r.* 'Primrose Gem' has paler yellow flowers.
SMALL SHRUB H: 60cm/24in s: 90–120cm/36–48in z: 7[7–10]

SARCOCOCCA

(Buxaceae) Christmas box, sweet box Asia
These little glossy-leaved evergreen shrubs have tiny intensely fragrant flowers in midwinter, followed by coloured berries. Are handsome when grouped to make ground cover in shade of taller golden-leaved shrubs.
S. hookeriana digyna and the slightly smaller *S. humilis* (which suckers) have black fruits.
SMALL SHRUB H & S: 38cm/15in z: 7[7–9]

SAXIFRAGA

(Saxifragaceae) saxifrage
Although many species are alpines and thrive in well-drained rocky sites, most adapt happily to ordinary border conditions.
S. cortusifolia fortunei 'Wada' is a semi-evergreen or herbaceous perennial with rosettes of glistening leathery rounded leaves, green above and carmine below. Sprays of starry white yellow-centred flowers appear on red stems in autumn. Good for a cool sheltered corner.
H & S: 30cm/12in z: 7[7–9]
S. moschata (Pyrenees to Caucasus) is an evergreen perennial forming a moss-like cushion of deeply divided bright green leaves. Forms have pink or yellow saucer-shaped flowers in summer.
H: 7.5–15cm/3–6in s: 30–45cm/12–18in
z: 5[5–9]

S. stolonifera (mother-of-thousands, strawberry begonia; from eastern Asia) has rounded or kidney-shaped leaves marked with silvery veining and with reddish undersides. Airy racemes of little white flowers appear in summer. This evergreen perennial colonizes by long overground runners ending in little plantlets. Tolerates shade and damp or dry soils.
H: 23–30cm/9–12in s: 30cm/12in z: 7[7–10]
S. × urbium (London pride) is an evergreen perennial. Makes a weed-smothering mat of fleshy apple-green leafy rosettes above which a haze of pink flowers is borne on wiry stalks in early summer.
H & s: 30cm/12in z: 5[5–9]

SCILLA

(Liliaceae/Hyacinthaceae) squill
Spring-flowering hardy bulbs that are at home in any well-worked soil.
S. bifolia (southern Europe and Asia Minor) has loose racemes of mauve-blue to blue flowers in early spring; there are also pink and white forms. Naturalizes in grass. Tolerates shade.
H: 5–10cm/2–4in s: 10cm/4in z: 5[5–10]
S. peruviana (Cuban lily from western regions of Mediterranean) has dense blue flower-heads rising above substantial clusters of strap-shaped leaves in early summer. Plant in a warm spot.
H: 23–30cm/9–12in s: 20cm/8in z: 8[8–10].
S. siberica (Siberian squill from central and southern Russia) has three or four stems each with a few brilliant blue bell-shaped flowers in early spring.
H: 5–10cm/2–6in s: 10cm/4in z: 4[4–9]

SEDUM

(Crassulaceae) stonecrop
These herbaceous sedums make strong plants for open sunny borders, their fleshy glaucous leaves and flat heads of crowded starry flowers in late summer associating well with neighbours in sun and well-drained soil.
S. 'Herbstfreude' ('Autumn Joy') is a perennial with long-lasting large domed heads of rich pink that turn salmon-copper and rusty-red.
H & s: 60cm/2ft z: 4[4–10]
S. spectabile (ice plant from eastern Asia) is an herbaceous perennial with pale green fleshy leaves that emerge in spring and grow slowly into a clump. Flowers at the end of summer, heavy flower-heads of cool dusty-pink often sprawling outwards. *S.s.* 'Brilliant' has flowers of stronger pink. Useful for the front of a border.
H & s: 30–45cm/12–18in z: 4[4–10]

S. telephium 'Munstead Dark Red' is a perennial and has flat flowers, of sombre dusky-red, held on compact stems with darker green leaves.
H & S: 45–60cm/18–24in   Z: 4[4–10]

SELINUM
(Umbelliferae)
S. tenuifolium (Himalayas) is a graceful cow-parsley-like perennial with finely cut ferny leaves and flat umbels of black-anthered white flowers in summer. Part shade; dislikes intense heat.
H: 90–150cm/36–60in   S: 60cm/24in
Z: 4[4–8]

SENECIO
(Compositae)
S. 'Sunshine' (now correctly *Brachyglottis* 'Sunshine') is an evergreen shrub with grey felted leaves. Spring pruning and summer shaping encourages fresh leafy growth in place of bright yellow daisy flowers, which mar the plant's predominantly silver colour and compact habit. Flowers in early to midsummer. Good as a specimen, to frame corners of traditional borders, or massed in a group.
SMALL SHRUB H & S: 120cm/48in   Z: 8[8–10]

SILENE
(Caryophyllaceae)   campion
S. uniflora 'Flore Pleno' forms a low perennial mat of grey-green leaves covered with white carnation-like flowers from mid- to late summer. Sun and well-drained soil.
H: 15cm/6in   S: 30cm/12in   Z: 4[4–9]

SILYBUM
(Compositae)
S. marianum (milk thistle from Mediterranean regions) makes a rosette of dark glossy leaves, spined and lobed, with veins marked in white to give a marbled variegation. Branched stems of purple thistle-flowers appear in late summer and often self-seed in a sunny site. Overwinter seedlings in pots in cold climates.
H: 60–120cm/24–48in   S: 60cm/24in
ANNUAL/BIENNIAL

SISYRINCHIUM
(Iridaceae)
S. striatum (Andes) is a semi-evergreen perennial with grey iris-like leaves. Slender spikes of pale creamy-white star-shaped flowers appear in summer. Seeds prolifically once established. Sun and

well-drained humus-rich soil. *S.s.* 'Aunt May' has leaves boldly striped with creamy-yellow, is more tender and needs protection from intense sun.
H: 45–60cm/18–24in   S: 23–30cm/9–12in
Z: 7[7–10]

SMILACINA
(Liliaceae/Convallariaceae)
S. racemosa (false Solomon's seal, false spikenard; from N. America) is a deciduous perennial woodlander. Arching stems bear pairs of pale veined leaves like those of Solomon's seal, with lemon-scented fluffy cream flower-plumes in spring. Part shade and deep rich soil.
H: 45–90cm/18–36in   S: 30–45cm/12–18in
Z: 3[3–9]

SMYRNIUM
(Umbelliferae)
S. perfoliatum (southern Europe to Caucasus) has heart-shaped leaves clasping the stems and small heads of cow-parsley flowers in early summer. This short-lived perennial or biennial seeds freely once established. Allow to naturalize on the garden's edge in shrubberies or light woodland.
H & S: 45–60cm/18–24in   Z: 5[5–9]

Smilacina racemosa

Smyrnium perfoliatum

SPARTINA

(Gramineae)   prairie cord grass
S. pectinata 'Aureomarginata' has graceful narrow arching leaves striped with yellow. Pendulous green flower-spikes are draped with purple stamens in season. Dry soil, to curb invasiveness of this rhizomatous perennial.
H: 1.8m/6ft   s: 0.9m/3ft   z: 5[5–9]

SPHAERALCEA

(Malvaceae)   globe mallow
S. munroana (western N. America) has trailing stems bearing hairy lobed and cut leaves. Produces little mallow-like flowers in tones from red to apricot and pink all summer. Sun-loving and drought-tolerant deciduous sub-shrubs for poor well-drained soil.
H: 30–90cm/12–36in   s: 30–45cm/12–18in
z: 8[8–10]

SPIRAEA

(Rosaceae)
Deciduous shrubs to mass in informal planting or for use as border plants between perennials. There are forms with spring, summer and late-summer flowers.

LEFT *Stipa gigantea*

S. 'Arguta' (bridal wreath, foam of May) carries white flowers all along its stems in spring.
MEDIUM SHRUB H & s: 1.8–2.4m/6–8ft   z: 4[4–9]
S. thunbergii (China, Japan) has small narrow pale green leaves that turn yellow in autumn. White flower-clusters appear before leaves in spring.
MEDIUM SHRUB H: 1.5–1.8m/5–6ft
s: 1.8–2.4m/6–8ft   z: 4[4–9]
S. veitchii (China) has long downy arching branches covered with dense flat corymbs of tiny white flowers in midsummer – a good foil to an arching shrub rose. Rich moist soil.
LARGE SHRUB H & s: 3m/10ft   z: 6[6–9]

STACHYS

(Labiatae)
S. byzantina (lamb's ears from the Caucasus to Iran) is an evergreen perennial making attractive low clumps of felted silvery leaves. Woolly flower-spikes of mauvish-pink, borne by the type in summer, mar the smooth carpet effect and need trimming – unless seedlings are welcome. Opting for the sterile cultivar *S.b.* 'Silver Carpet' avoids these complications. Sun and well-drained soil.
H: 30–45cm/12–18in   s: 30cm/12in   z: 4[4–10]
S. grandiflora (syn. *S. macrantha*; from the Caucasus) has distinctive green triangular leaves and deep purple lipped tubular flowers carried in

SOLANUM

(Solanaceae)   S. America
Semi-evergreen climbers for a sunny position.
S. crispum (Chilean potato tree) has slightly scented purple-blue potato-flowers with yellow centres from midsummer. *S.c.* 'Glasnevin' is a brighter blue and has a longer flowering season. Has a bushy scrambling habit: allow to clamber over stumps and sturdy shrubs or train on a wall.
CLIMBER H: 5–6m/15–20ft   z: 8[8–10]
S. jasminoides 'Album' is more tender, but where it is suited bears an abundance of clustered bluish-white yellow-centred potato-flowers in summer and autumn. Allow to twine upwards or to tumble down a sunny bank.
CLIMBER H: 3–5m/10–15ft   z: 9[9–10]

× SOLIDASTER

(Compositae)
× *S. luteus* has open heads of light canary-yellow daisy-flowers on wiry leafy stems in summer. Useful as a low-key border perennial.
H: 60–75cm/24–30in   s: 45–60cm/18–24in
z: 4[4–10]

Symphytum × *uplandicum* 'Variegatum'

Symphytum caucasicum

whorls in early summer. Grow this perennial beside bare-stemmed shrub roses, perhaps selecting the pink or violet forms for harmonizing tones. Sun or part shade.
H: 30–60cm/12–24in   s: 30–45cm/12–18in
z: 3[3–10]

STAUNTONIA
(Lardizabalaceae)
S. hexaphylla (north-eastern Asia) is a twining evergreen that bears exotically scented violet-tinged white flowers in spring. Grow over host trees and shrubs in a sunny sheltered spot.
CLIMBER H: 10m/30ft   s: 3m/10ft   z: 8[8–10]

STEPHANANDRA
(Rosaceae)
S. tanakae (Japan) is a graceful deciduous shrub with arching red-brown stems and lobed leaves of a fresh green that show up well in shade or against dark evergreens. Autumn tints are muted orange tones. White star-shaped flowers are borne in summer.
MEDIUM SHRUB H & s: 1.5–2.1m/5–7ft
z: 6[6–9]

STIPA
(Gramineae)   feather grass
S. gigantea (Spain) makes a dense perennial clump of grey-green almost evergreen foliage. In summer produces tall plumes of oat-like flower-heads, opening purple-tinged and becoming a shimmering tawny-yellow. Sun.
H: 90–180cm/36–72in   s: 60–90cm/24–36in
z: 6[6–10]

SYMPHYTUM
(Boraginaceae)   comfrey
S. caucasicum (Caucasus) makes good coarse perennial ground cover in shade, but is invasive. Rough-textured greyish leaves turn green in summer. Loose sprays of forget-me-not blue tubular flowers glow in spring.
H & s: 60cm/24in   z: 3[3–9]
S. × uplandicum 'Variegatum' is a handsome slow-growing perennial specimen plant with typical hairy borage-leaves, pale green margined with creamy-white. Pink-budded flowers open to pale violet-blue in late spring and early summer. Part shade and deep moisture-retentive soil.
H: 90cm/36in   s: 60cm/24in   z: 4[4–9]

SYRINGA
(Oleaceae)   lilac
All the following small-leaved lilacs are useful in borders next to perennials or herbaceous plants.
S. meyeri 'Palibin' (Korean lilac) is deciduous and has lilac-pink flowers in early summer. Perfect for a small garden.
SMALL SHRUB H & s: 1.2m/4ft   z: 5[5–9]
S. microphylla 'Superba' bears a flush of pretty scented rosy-pink flowers in early summer, and continues to flower intermittently until autumn. Leaves are small and deciduous.
SMALL SHRUB H & s: 1.2m/4ft   z: 4[4–9]
S. × persica (Persian lilac from Iran to China) is deciduous and has a graceful habit. Abundant pale pink scented flowers appear in late spring.
S. × persica 'Alba' is a white form.
MEDIUM SHRUB H: 1.8–2.4m/6–8ft   s: 1.8m/6ft
z: 5[5–9]

TAGETES
(Compositae)   marigold
T. erecta (African marigold from Mexico) is grown for its glowing late-summer colour at the front of a border. Single or double flowers above deeply cut and scented glossy green leaves may be yellow, gold or orange: choose hybrids in the tone you prefer.
H: 60–90cm/24–36in   s: 30–45cm/12–18in
ANNUAL

TANACETUM
(Compositae)
T. haradjanii (Anatolia) is a superb evergreen sub-shrubby perennial carpeter, its little fern-like silvery leaves creeping to form a dense mat. Full sun and well-drained gritty soil.
H: 15cm/6in   s: 30–38cm/12–15in
z: 8[8–10]

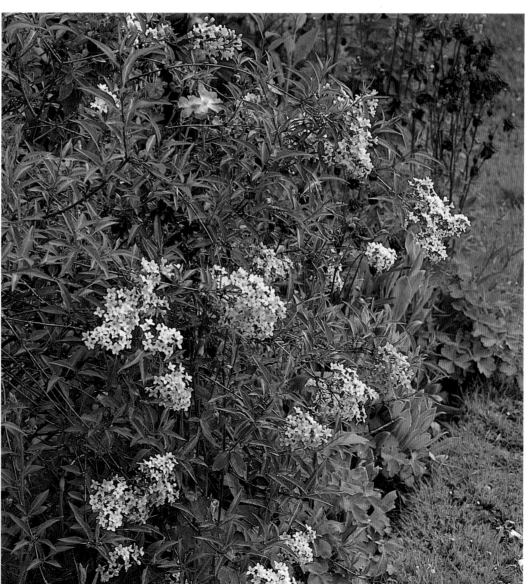

Syringa × persica

TEUCRIUM
(Labiatae)   germander

T. chamaedrys (wall germander from Europe) is a shrubby perennial with neat dark green leaves and spikes of pale pink-lipped inconspicuous flowers in summer. Good for ground cover and hedging.
H: 25–30cm/10–12in   s: 30–45cm/12–18in
z: 5[5–10]

T. fruticans (tree germander from southern Europe) has small simple aromatic leaves, green above and hairy below, giving this evergreen shrub an overall impression of silver-grey. Pale lavender flowers in summer continue into winter in a warm site. Grow in a mixed border or in dry soil against a wall.
SMALL SHRUB H: 120–150cm/48–60in
s: 90–120cm/36–48in   z: 9[9–10]

THALICTRUM
(Ranunculaceae)   meadow rue

Thalictrums are graceful perennials with elegant ferny leaves that make delicate masses of foliage to contrast with more sculptural neighbours in both formal borders and cottage-garden mixtures.

T. aquilegiifolium (Europe, northern Asia) has glaucous green leaves resembling those of aquilegia. Tall open panicles of fluffy flowers in early summer are usually mauve; *T. a.* 'Thundercloud' is deep purple. *T. a. album* is a most attractive white form with grey-green leaves.

H: 60–90cm/24–36in   s: 30–45cm/12–18in
z: 5[5–10]

T. delavayi (western China) has daintier foliage, and the sprays of tiny pinkish-mauve flowers which appear in summer, are more open, with conspicuous yellow staments. *T. d.* 'Hewitt's Double' has long-lasting double mauve flowers without the touch of yellow.
H: 120–150cm/48–60in   s: 45–60cm/18–24in
z: 5[5–10]

T. flavum glaucum (syn. *T. speciosissimum*; yellow meadow rue from Europe) has beautiful glaucous divided leaves and tall stems with fluffy yellow flowers in summer. From spring to autumn leaves associate well with other grey-green foliage. Stake firmly but unobtrusively.
H: 90–150cm/36–60in   s: 45–60cm/18–24in
z: 6[6–10]

T. rochebrunnianum (Japan) creates an effect similar to that of *T. delavayi*. Its mass of elegant glaucous foliage is crowned by large loose panicles of pale purple flowers with light yellow stamens in summer.
H: 120–180cm/48–72in   s: 45–60cm/18–24in
z: 5[5–10]

THYMUS
(Labiatae)   thyme

Thymes boast an attractive combination of grey-green leaves and tiny pinky-mauve flowers in summer. Plant creeping thymes where the foliage may be brushed or bruised to release the bonus of scent: in border edges and paving cracks, or carpeting lawns and seats. Sun and good drainage.

T. × citriodorus is an evergreen with forms offering coloured or variegated leaves as well as a lemon scent.
DWARF SHRUB H: 5–20cm/2–8in   s: 30cm/12in
z: 4[4–10]

TIARELLA
(Saxifragaceae)

T. cordifolia (foam flower from N. America) makes attractive weed-suppressing perennial ground cover in shade between shrubs. The low evergreen mat of rich green lobed foliage is bronze-tinted in winter; creamy-white feathery spikes of flowers shimmer above the leaves in early summer.
H: 15–30cm/6–12in   s: 30–45cm/12–18in
z: 3[3–9]

TOLMIEA
(Saxifragaceae)

T. menziesii (pig-a-back plant from western USA) is a perennial that is sometimes semi-evergreen. Produces an attractive mound of hairy maple-like mid-green leaves and spires of greenish or copper-tinted small flowers in early summer. Little plantlets form on old leaves and root easily to make new

ABOVE *Tiarella cordifolia*

RIGHT *Tricyrtis formosana*

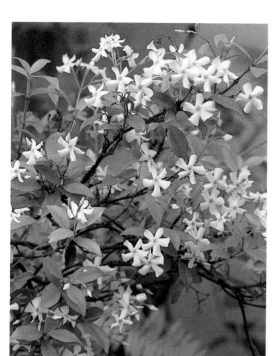

Trachelospermum asiaticum

plants. Good for ground cover in shade or moderate sun. *T.m.* 'Taff's Gold; irregularly variegated with creamy-yellow, resembles dappled sunlight.
H: 15–30cm/6–12in   s: 30–38cm/12–15in
z: 8[8–10]

TRACHELOSPERMUM
(Apocynaceae)
These evergreen twining climbers have dark green glossy leaves that turn red and yellow in winter. Fragrant creamy-white jasmine-like flowers appear in summer. Tender: good for warm microclimates (or conservatory walls) in temperate zones.
T. asiaticum (Japan, Korea) is the hardier species with neat small leaves and a compact habit that will clothe a wall densely with foliage.
CLIMBER H: 5m/15ft   z: 8[8–10]
T. jasminoides (China) is vigorous, with longer glowing leaves and a more sprawling habit that may need some training into shape.
CLIMBER H: 6m/20ft   z: 9[9–10]

TRICYRTIS
(Liliaceae/Convallariaceae)   toad lily
Toad lilies have exotic flowers, like little upturned lilies, in late summer. Plant these perennials where the flower detail may be examined and enjoyed. Part shade and moist soil.

T. formosana (Taiwan) carries sprays of purple-speckled mauve flowers, with yellow throats, on branching stems clothed in glossy dark green leaves.
H: 60–90cm/24–36in   s: 45cm/18in   z: 5[5–9]
T. hirta (Japan) has upright unbranched stems and hairy leaves. Flowers are whitish, spotted with lilac, and greenish-white in the form *T.h. alba*.
H: 30–90cm/12–36in   s: 60cm/24in   z: 5[5–9]

TRILLIUM
(Liliaceae/Trilliaceae)   wake robin, wood lily
Woodland perennials that flower in spring, trilliums have leaves, sepals and petals in sets of three. Shade and acid rather moist loam. Good for borders.
T. grandiflorum (snow trillium, white wake robin; from eastern USA) has shining leaves with pronounced veins making a dome-shaped plant. Funnel-shaped pure white flowers have slightly reflexed petals.
H: 30–45cm/12–18in   s: 30cm/12in
z: 3[3–9]
T. sessile (toadshade from central USA) produces leaves marbled in grey-brown and deep green. Dark maroon stemless flowers are held upright.
H: 20–30cm/8–12in   s: 23–30cm/9–12in
z: 5[5–9]

TROLLIUS
(Ranunculaceae)   globe flower
Trollius make attractive clumps of dark green deeply cleft leaves all season, with shapely flowers in late spring and early summer. These herbaceous perennials prefer waterside sites, but also thrive in borders where soil is moisture-retentive.
T. × cultorum garden hybrids have big globe-shaped flowers resembling double buttercups. Colours include a range of yellows and oranges. *T.* 'Alabaster' is a delicate ivory-cream; *T.* 'Canary Bird' has clear pale yellow flowers.
H: 60–90cm/24–36in   s: 30–45cm/12–18in
z: 4[4–9]

TROPAEOLUM
(Tropaeolaceae)
T. peregrinum (canary creeper from Peru) is a vigorous short-lived deciduous perennial climber usually grown as an annual. Has light green lobed leaves and bright clear yellow flowers, with green spurs and fringed petals, in summer and autumn.
CLIMBER H: 4m/12ft   s: 0.9m/3ft   ANNUAL
T. speciosum (flame creeper, flame nasturtium, Scotch flame flower; from Chile) is a deciduous

perennial whose six-lobed leaves are as decorative as green flowers against a dark-leaved host. Small brilliant scarlet nasturtium-flowers are borne continuously in late summer. Cool acid soil.
CLIMBER H: 3–5m/10–15ft   s: 0.6–0.9m/2–3ft
z: 8[7–9] or grow as ANNUAL
T. tuberosum (Bolivia, Peru) is a more tender deciduous perennial climber, suitable for a sunny wall in temperate zones. The mass of slightly glaucous lobed leaves is lit up in late summer by spurred tubular flowers in tones of red and yellow, borne on red stems. *T.t.* 'Ken Aslet' is earlier flowering.
CLIMBER H: 3m/10ft   s: 0.9m/3ft   z: 9[8–10] or grow as ANNUAL

TULIPA
(Liliaceae)   tulip
A progression of different tulips provides flowers from mid-spring well into early summer. With their elegant sculptural flower-heads, the hybrids and cultivars of these bulbous perennials are for deploying in deliberately orchestrated colour schemes. Simpler forms of species tulips are for more informal groupings.

Tropaeolum tuberosum

Tulipa acuminata (syn. *T.* 'Cornuta')

Species

T. acuminata (syn. *T.* 'Cornuta'; horned tulip; actually an old cultivar), in late spring, bears red or yellow flowers whose slender petals each end in a twisting point.
H: 45–60cm/18–24in   s: 10–12cm/4–5in
z: 3[3–9]

T. clusiana (lady tulip from Iran to Kashmir) has narrow erect grey-green leaves. Slender white flowers flushed with crimson on the outside petals, creating a striped effect, appear in late spring.
H: 23–30cm/9–12in   s: 7.5cm/3in   z: 3[3–10]

T. kaufmanniana (waterlily tulip from Turkestan) bears short stems and slender creamy flowers that open wide into a star-shape in early spring. Petals are flushed red at the base and on the outside. Kaufmanniana hybrids are stockier plants, often with two-coloured flowers and attractively marked leaves.
H: 12–25cm/5–10in   s: 15cm/6in   z: 3[3–10]

T. sylvestris (Europe, western Asia, northern Africa) produces slender grey-green leaves and delicately fragrant pale yellow flowers in late spring. Plant in part shade under deciduous trees and shrubs.
H: 38cm/15in   s: 10cm/4in   z: 3[3–10]

Hybrids and garden cultivars

T. 'Golden Apeldoorn' (Darwin) has rich golden-yellow flowers with black bases in late spring.
H: 60cm/24in   s: 15cm/6in   z: 3[3–10]

T. praestans 'Fusilier' carries four to six brilliant orange-scarlet flowers on each stem in spring. Good on a rockery to complement dwarf azaleas.
H: 25cm/10in   s: 12cm/5in   z: 3[3–10]

T. 'Purissima' (Fosteriana) has large outer petals of milky-white to cream; grey-green leaves are attractive before flowers emerge in spring.
H: 50cm/20in   s: 15cm/6in   z: 3[3–10]

T. 'Queen of Night' (Single Late) produces large flowers of deep velvety-maroon in late spring.
H: 70cm/28in   s: 15–20cm/6–8in   z: 3[3–10]

T. 'White Triumphator' (Lily-flowered) is tall-stemmed, with beautiful creamy-white reflexing petals. Flowers over a long period in late spring and early summer.
H: 65cm/26in   s: 15cm/6in   z: 4[4–9]

VANCOUVERIA
(Berberidaceae)

V. hexandra (Vancouver fern from western USA) spreads in woodland conditions – even dry shade – to form perennial ground cover of dainty fresh green foliage, the lobed leaflets resembling little ivy leaves. Wiry stems hold loose panicles of little white flowers above the leaves in late spring or early summer.
H: 15–45cm/6–18in   s: 100cm/40in   z: 5[5–9]

VERATRUM
(Liliaceae/Melanthiaceae)   false hellebore

These perennials grow best in rich soil in part shade, or at least out of scorching sun.

V. nigrum (black false hellebore from Europe, Asia) is a remarkable foliage plant. Large leaves, folded and pleated like a fan, push through the soil in early spring to make arching mounds of fresh green (which slugs unfortunately find irresistible). Established plants produce imposing flower-stems, bearing brownish-maroon plumes composed of tiny stars, in late summer.
H: 90–150cm/36–60in   s: 60cm/24in   z: 3[3–9]

V. viride (Indian poke from N. America) has stems clothed in leaves. Dense panicles of starry light yellow-green flowers are borne in summer – a beautiful foil to the pleated foliage.
H: 1.2–2.1m/4–7ft   s: 0.6m/2ft   z: 3[3–9]

VERBASCUM
(Scrophulariaceae)   mullein

Verbascums have large basal leaves of leathery green or felted grey from which soar stout stems bearing flower-spikes in summer. Their architectural quality makes valuable accent plants in well-drained and sunny mixed borders.

V. chaixii (southern and central Europe) forms a handsome perennial clump of ground-covering grey leaves and slender spires tightly massed with small yellow flowers with purplish eyes.
H: 75–90cm/30–36in   s: 45cm/18in
z: 5[5–10]

V. olympicum (Turkey) is a biennial giant mullein with huge rosettes of felted silvery leaves and a woolly candelabra-stem bearing clustered yellow flowers. Sow seeds *in situ*, or select self-sown seedlings to flower the following year.
H: 1.8–2.4m/6–8ft   s: 0.9m/3ft   z: 6[6–10]

V. 'Vernale' is virtually a larger version of *V. chaixii* with branching flower-spikes of bright yellow flowers.
H: 1.8–2.4m/6–8ft   s: 0.9m/3ft   z: 6[6–10]

VERBENA
(Verbenaceae)

V. patagonica (syn. *V. bonariensis*; S. America) is an outstanding perennial grown as an annual in cool climates. Produces strange square stems and umbrella-like clusters of tiny lilac-purple scented flowers rising above neighbouring plants in mid-summer. Allow to seed between lower-growing silver- or grey-leaved plants such as lavender to make an airy network of scent and toning colour at midheight.
H: 90–150cm/36–60in   s: 60cm/24in
z: 9[8–10] or grow as ANNUAL

V. rigida (vervain from southern Brazil to Argentina) is often grown as an annual, but is perennial in mild areas. Leafy branching upright stems are topped by glowing violet-purple flower-heads in summer.
H: 30–60cm/12–24in   s: 30cm/12in
z: 9[8–10] or grow as ANNUAL

Garden hybrids

Half-hardy or tender perennial bedding verbenas are often grown as annuals from seed and may be propagated by cuttings for overwintering. Make cushions of attractive dark green deeply cut leaves, transformed in late summer into a mass of often vividly coloured flower-heads, many with a white eye. Good old cultivars propagated from cuttings, include: *V.* 'Hidcote Purple' (deep rich purple); *V.* 'Loveliness' (pink); *V.* 'Silver Anne' (soft pink and scented). *V.* 'Sissinghurst' is shrubby and un-scented but a vivid eye-catching pink.
H & s: 50cm/20in   ANNUAL

VERONICA

(Scrophulariaceae)   speedwell

Veronicas are easily grown perennials in sun.

V. austriaca teucrium (southern Europe, northern Asia) forms a loose mound of erect or sprawling stems and toothed oval leaves for the front of a border. Soft spikes of intensely blue flowers are borne in summer.
H & S: 30–45cm/12–18in Z: 5[5–10]

V. gentianoides (gentian speedwell from Caucasus) is a front-of-border species forming a mat of glossy-leaved rosettes that produce spires of ice-blue flowers in early summer.
H: 30–60cm/12–24in S: 45cm/18in Z: 5[5–9]

V. virginica (correctly *Veronicastrum virginicum*; blackroot, bowman's root; from eastern N. America) is an elegant ethereal plant that contrasts well with neighbouring bushy shapes and domes. Erect stems bear horizontal whorls of slender mid-green leaves and terminate in delicate flower-spikes of palest blue, lilac-pink or white in late summer.
H: 120–180cm/48–72in S: 45–60cm/18–24in
Z: 4[4–10]

VIBURNUM

(Caprifoliaceae)

This large genus has a vast number of excellent species and hybrids, offering interesting flowers, foliage, fruit and form in varying permutations.

V. × bodnantense is a deciduous shrub bearing clusters of sweetly scented pink tubular flowers on leafless branches from late autumn through most of winter. Young growth is bronze-flushed; autumn leaf colour is good too.
LARGE SHRUB H & S: 2.7–4m/9–12ft Z: 7[7–10]

V. × burkwoodii (China) is one of the best hybrids, producing scented pink-tinted white flowers for many weeks from late spring. Undersides of the dark green leaves are grey-brown and felted. A good evergreen wall shrub in warmer zones: deciduous in zone 5. Hardy and unfussy about soil.
MEDIUM SHRUB H: 2.4m/8ft S: 2.7–4m/9–12ft
Z: 5[5–9]

V. × carlcephalum is deciduous, with good autumn colour; large rounded heads of fragrant creamy-white flowers open from pink buds in late spring.
MEDIUM SHRUB H: 2.4m/8ft S: 1.8–2.1m/6–7ft
Z: 5[5–9]

Verbena patagonica and *Anemone × hybrida*, *Nicotiana sylvestris*, *Lablab purpureus* (syn. *Dolichos lablab*) and *Macleaya*

Viburnum sargentii 'Onondaga'

V. opulus 'Xanthocarpum' is deciduous and a garden form of the European guelder rose with clear golden-yellow fruits. Is good in early winter against glowing autumnal foliage.
LARGE SHRUB H & S: 4–5m/12–15ft
Z: 3[3–8]

V. plicatum 'Mariesii' is deciduous and strongly architectural, with horizontally tabulated branches laden in early summer with white flowers as if with snow. Good for autumn colour.
MEDIUM SHRUB H: 2.4–3m/8–10ft
S: 3–5m/10–15ft Z: 5[5–8]

V. sargentii 'Onondaga' is deciduous and has bronze-tinged young leaves that also colour well in autumn. 'Lacecap' panicles of white flowers opening from pink buds in early summer later turn into deep red berries.
MEDIUM SHRUB H & S: 1.5–2.1m/5–7ft
Z: 3[3–9]

V. tinus 'Eve Price' forms a compact rounded evergreen bush with the dark healthy-looking leaves typical of laurustinus. Deep pink buds open to flat corymbs of pinkish-white flowers from late autumn to early spring, followed by blue-black fruits. Tolerates shade. Good for hedging.
SMALL SHRUB H & S: 90–120cm/36–48in
Z: 8[8–10]

VINCA
(Apocynaceae) periwinkle
Vincas spread to make evergreen ground cover of handsome glossy dark green simple leaves, with flowers as a colour bonus. Although tolerant of shade and neglect, these perennials look and flower better if given an open site, rich feeding and an annual dead-heading and trim.

V. difformis (western regions of Mediterranean) carries beautiful pale blue flowers all through winter.
H: 30cm/12in S: 60cm/24in Z: 9[9–10]

V. minor (lesser periwinkle from Europe) has rich blue, plum or white flowers, often double; those of *V.m. atropurpurea* are very deep purple, and of *V.m.* 'Azurea Flore Pleno' double and a clear blue. Flowers appear in spring and early summer, often continuing until the frosts.
H: 15cm/6in S: 60cm/24in Z: 4[4–10]

VIOLA
(Violaceae) heart's ease violet, pansy
V. cornuta (horned violet, tufted pansy; from the Pyrenees) makes a spreading straggling perennial carpet of fresh green leaves topped with tall stems bearing lilac-blue flowers (white in *V.c. alba*) in summer. Dead-head or shear to encourage further flowering. Cool moist soil.

Viola riviniana purpurea (formerly *V. labradorica purpurea*)

Viola cornuta

Wisteria sinensis

H: 15–30cm/6–12in s: 30–38/12–15in
z: 6[6–10]
V. obliqua (syn. *V. cucullata*; from eastern N. America) is a rhizomatous perennial. Dainty violet-flowers in shades of lavender, with darker tracery on lower petals, appear in late spring and early summer.
H: 25–30cm/10–12in s: 30cm/12in z: 4[4–8]
V. riviniana purpurea (formerly known as *V. labradorica purpurea*) is a rhizomatous perennial with dark purple leaves and bright violet-blue flowers in early summer; leaves turn dark green by the end of summer. Grow next to grey foliage, beneath roses, or in formal bedding patterns: informality creeps in as plants self-seed readily.
H: 15cm/6in s: 30–38cm/12–15in z: 3[3–9]
Garden forms
Two old 'viola' or tufted pansy cultivars that flower from spring to autumn, and are evergreen perennials, are V. 'Irish Molly', with curiously attractive greenish-bronzy-yellow flowers, and V. 'Jackanapes', with rusty red-brown upper petals, bright yellow lower ones. Propagate from cuttings. V. 'Bowles' Black', another classic, seeds freely between plants in a blue border, making

deep shadow-tones. This short-lived perennial flowers from spring to autumn.
H: 10–15cm/4–6in s: 23cm/9in z: 6[6–8]

VITIS
(Vitaceae) vine
Clinging vines can be trained to make shady curtains and canopies of leaves or can be allowed to ramp through suitably robust host trees and shrubs.
V. 'Brant' is deciduous and has leaves that turn a mysterious tone of deep bronzy-red in autumn, while the veins remain green. Bears red-purple grapes.
CLIMBER H: 6m/20ft z: 6[6–10]
V. coignetiae (Japanese crimson glory vine) is a bold vigorous deciduous climber. Large broad heart-shaped leaves are smooth on top but felted with reddish hairs beneath. Autumn colour is dramatic, as the common name suggests.
CLIMBER H: to 27m/90ft z: 5[5–10]
V. vinifera 'Purpurea' (claret vine, teinturier grape) is a cultivar of the common grapevine and deciduous. Purple-red leaves all summer darken to a deeper shade in autumn.
CLIMBER H: 6m/20ft z: 6[6–10]

WISTERIA
(Leguminosae)
Nothing can be more beautiful than the early-summer festoons of long pendulous racemes of pea-flowers, in lilac, pale mauve or white, of these deciduous twiners, draping pergolas or arbours or growing into old trees.
W. floribunda 'Multijuga' (syn. *W.f.* 'Macrobotrys') is a form of Japanese wisteria with 90cm/36in long fragrant racemes, lilac tinged with violet-purple, and light green pinnate leaves.
CLIMBER H: to 9m/27ft z: 5[5–10]
W. sinensis (China) is more vigorous, with scented 30cm/12in long racemes of mauve or deep lilac borne on leafless branches. *W.* 'Black Dragon' is a hybrid with dark purple double flowers.
CLIMBER H: to 18m/60ft z: 5[5–10]

YUCCA
(Agavaceae)
Yuccas are statuesque and long-lived evergreens, useful all year for emphasis and for contrast with leafier neighbours. Magnificent flower-spikes add drama in late summer. Desert plants, they thrive in sun and poor sandy soil with minimal moisture.

Y. filamentosa (Adam's needle from south-eastern USA) is an evergreen shrub with fairly stiff glaucous green leaves edged with dangling filaments. *Y.f.* 'Variegata' has leaves striped and margined with cream, but may be less hardy. Carries erect panicles of creamy-white fragrant bell-flowers.
SMALL SHRUB H: 60–75cm/24–30in
s: 90–120cm/36–48in z: 4[4–10]
Y. recurvifolia (south-eastern USA) has narrow arching evergreen leaves in huge elegant rosettes on a slow-growing trunk. Elegant flower-spikes of creamy-white.
SMALL SHRUB H & S: 90–180cm/3–6ft
z: 6[6–10]

ZANTEDESCHIA
(Araceae)
Z. aethiopica (arum lily, calla lily; from S. Africa) is a tuberous perennial usually grown in the hardy form *Z.a.* 'Crowborough', which tolerates drier border conditions (the species likes moisture, even waterlogging). Flowers in late spring; flaring pure white spathes surround a scented yellow spadix. Is also a handsome foliage plant, with broad spear-shaped glossy dark green leaves. Rich moist soil; protect from frost until established.
H: 90–120cm/36–48in s: 30–60cm/12–24in
z: 9[8–10]

ZAUSCHNERIA
(Onagraceae) California fuchsia
Z. californica latifolia (syn. *Epilobium canum latifolium*) is a sub-shrubby perennial making a mound of pale grey hairy leaves above which slender erect stems bear scarlet trumpet-flowers in late summer. Mass plants in a sunny site. Needs good drainage: useful for a rockery or raised bed.
H: 30–90cm/12–36in s: 45cm/18in
z: 8[8–10]

ZINNIA
(Compositae)
Z. elegans garden cultivars, grown as half-hardy annuals, look best in bright sunlight but are often too startling to mass as front-of-border infills: showy flowers, in summer and early autumn, are often bi-coloured and sold as gaudy mixtures. Some are available in separate colours; others in harmonizing blends. Plants grow quickly from seed, and colours may be chosen for specific schemes when first flowers appear; or mixtures may be sown and undesirables rogued out.
H: 15–75cm/6–30in s: 20–60cm/8–24in
ANNUAL

INDEX

Page numbers in **bold** refer to the illustrations

Zone chart

Approximate range of average annual minimum temperatures

1	below −45°C/−50°F
2	−45°C/−50°F to −40°C/−40°F
3	−40°C/−40°F to −34°C/−30°F
4	−34°C/−30°F to −29°C/−20°F
5	−29°C/−20°F to −23°C/−10°F
6	−23°C/−10°F to −18°C/0°F
7	−18°C/0°F to −12°C/10°F
8	−12°C/10°F to −7°C/20°F
9	−7°C/20°F to −1°C/30°F
10	−1°C/30°F to 4°C/40°F
11	above 4°C/40°F

The hardiness zone ratings given for each plant – indicated in the text by the letter Z and the relevant number – suggest the approximate minimum temperature a plant will tolerate in winter. However, this can only be a rough guide. The hardiness of a plant depends on a great many factors, including the depth of its roots, its water content at the onset of frost, the duration of cold weather, the force of the wind, and the length and heat of the preceding summer.

ACKNOWLEDGMENTS

Author's Acknowledgments

I owe so much to Frances Lincoln and her team. I doubt if other authors are as fortunate. Frances herself is always involved from the very beginning, and so are Erica Hunningher, her editorial director, and Penny David, who has been my right hand in editing all my books. They are there to provide a total infrastructure, ready to criticize and cajole as well as to give inspiring advice at every moment of writing. Caroline Hillier and Louise Tucker have made the book beautiful using the pictures Anne Fraser, with untiring efforts to get the best and most appropriate for every page, has discovered. The photographers seem to become more and more skilful each year, capturing images of plants and gardens that are both inspirational and informative. Tony Lord has given invaluable help with the horticultural content, including identifying plants and their correct names. It would have been impossible to complete the book without all these links in the chain of production.

I would also like to thank the National Trust for allowing me and my husband John Malins to be guardians of Tintinhull. I could not have written about flower gardens without the inspiration which Tintinhull gives me and the lessons I learn from working here. But I could never have written this book at all without my husband John to help me. I am most grateful to him for all his patience.

Publishers' Acknowledgments

The publishers would like to thank the following people and organizations who kindly allowed us to photograph their gardens:
Richard Bisgrove; Beth Chatto; Helen Dillon; John and Mary Hawgood; John and Caryl Hubbard; Frank Lawley; The National Trust (Wallington); The National Trust for Scotland (Malleny House); Jim Reynolds.

The publishers are also grateful to the following individuals for their help in the production of this book:
Jo Chisholm, Serena Dilnot, Susan Kennedy and Sarah Mitchell for their editorial contribution; John Laing and Claudine Meissner for design work.

Horticultural Consultant   Tony Lord
Editor   Penny David
Art Editor   Louise Tucker
Picture Editor   Anne Fraser
Production   Adela Cory

Editorial Director   Erica Hunningher
Associate Art Directors   Tim Foster, Caroline Hillier
Production Director   Nicky Bowden

Photographic Acknowledgments

R=right   L=left   B=bottom   T=top   M=middle

Nic Barlow 52, 79
Deni Bown 168, 195
Boys Syndication/Jacqui Hurst 56
Geoff Dann 45 © FLL
John Fielding 159, 160, 166B, 170R, 172, 177R, 180R, 202T, 208T
Garden Picture Library: Stephen Robson 55; Marijke Heuff 173B, 187; David Russell 180L, 197
Giancarlo Gardin 94L, 104, 105
John Glover 194T
Nancy-Mary Goodall 69, 167T
Mick Hales 7, 54, 109, 110, 135B, 139, 140
Jerry Harpur 24 (designers: Oehme, van Sweden and Associates), 39B (designers: Oehme, van Sweden and Associates), 61L (designer: Arabella Lennox-Boyd), 73, 74 and 75 (designer: Edwina Von Gal), 91, 102, 103, 108, 128, 129, 133, 135T, 141T, 144L, 145, 146, 157, 207 (Peter Wooster)
Marijke Heuff 23 (Beeuwkes), 25, 26 (van Bennekom-Scheffer), 27 (Adriaanse), 32 (Greve), 37 (Great Dixter), 44T, 53T (Greve), 61BR (Goossenaert), 63L and 63BR (van Bennecom-Scheffer), 64L (Ton ter Linden), 64R and 65 (Greve), 67T (Ton ter Linden), 68 (Beth Chatto), 70B (Ton ter Linden), 83, 84L, 92, 94R, 98, 99, 100, 101, 117 (Greve), 123, 125, 137L (Greve), 142BR, 201R (Beth Chatto), 204R (Goossenaert)
Saxon Holt 30R, 33, 35B, 42, 43, 44B, 76R, 95, 96, 114, 121, 144R, 154, 155, 164L
Jacqui Hurst all © FLL: 34, 38, 49, 71T, 77 (reproduced by permission of The National Trust and the Knightshayes Garden Trust), 84R, 85, 87R
Michèle Lamontagne 147
Andrew Lawson 1, 2 (Powis), 10, 11, 12TL, TR and BL, 14, 15, 17, 18, 19, 20, 21T, 29, 30L, 31, 35T © FLL (Powis), 39T © FLL, 41, 47 (Marwood), 48, 58 © FLL (The Gables), 60 © FLL (Crathes), 62, 63TR, 66 (Kemerton), 67B (Kemerton), 112, 115, 118, 119 (Marwood), 120, 126 © FLL, 127 © FLL, 130, 131, 137R, 141B, 143 © FLL, 148, 149, 150, 151L, 158R, 161R, 163, 164R, 166T, 169B, 170L, 171, 173T, 174, 175, 176T, 179R, 181, 182, 183, 184, 185R, 188B, 189, 190, 191, 192, 193, 194B, 196L, 198, 199L, 201L, 202BL, 203, 204L, 205T, 206, 208BL and BR, 209
Georges Lévêque 36, 46, 80, 113T, 124, 134, 138, 152, 153
Tony Lord 51, 59, 61TR, 70T, 71B, 76L, 93B, 136R, 176B, 177L, 178, 188T
Marianne Majerus 13 © FLL, 53B, 88 © FLL, 93T, 113B © FLL, 122, 196R
S & O Mathews 111, 162, 165, 186L
Clive Nichols 57, 136L
Elizabeth Rodgers 97
Smith Collection 16, 158L, 161L, 169T, 177M, 179L, 185L and M, 186R, 199R, 200, 202BR
Rosemary Weller 9, 12BR
Elizabeth Whiting and Associates/Jerry Harpur 82 (Miriam Rothschild), 86, 89, 107
Peter Woloszynski 40
Steve Wooster all © FLL: 4, 21B (Beth Chatto), 28 (Beth Chatto), 50, 81, 87L, 116, 142T and BL, 151R, 205B (Beth Chatto)

Penelope Hobhouse
On Gardening

Penelope Hobhouse
On Gardening

Photographs ANDREW LAWSON

Watercolours JEAN STURGIS

In gratitude to the National Trust
for allowing me to live and learn at Tintinhull

CONTENTS

MY SORT OF GARDENING

Fortunately, gardening is a continuous learning process. Every day spent gardening, every visit to a garden, every book read, and every plant planted, for oneself or as part of a scheme for others, add to experience. These different bits of knowledge shape the way one plans, plants and dreams.

In making and looking after gardens – thinking out design schemes and using plants – there can never come a point when all the possibilities have been tried. Each site has its own individual advantages and problems, each plant will react a little differently depending on the conditions it is given and where it is put. Often features inherent in the site point in a firm direction. An open situation in a hot climate calls out for the welcoming shade given by old trees and by Italian-style pergola walks and arbours. Established trees and natural water demand gentle styling rather than a shift to formality; superb landscape surroundings need framing, not screening, while planting for privacy becomes more and more a priority not only in inner city gardens but also in much of the countryside. All planting success will depend on local and seasonal weather variations, the prevailing wind, frost pockets and rain shadows, all of which can play havoc with the best-laid plans.

Above all, gardens change as they develop. Plants grow and mature at different rates and their grouping and relationship to each other need constant revision. Plants grow out of their site or have a limited life span and need replacing. Even Capability Brown's groves of beech, shaped for appreciation two hundred years after his time, eventually reach a peak which is automatically followed by decline. Most of us plan for a few years ahead only, and few designers or amateur gardeners, except in the most formal of themes, can hope to

In the borders lining the cross path of the Kitchen Garden, Verbena bonariensis *flowers among roses and self-seeded* Malva moschata. *All the beds at Tintinhull are a mixture of shrubs, perennials, bulbs and annuals. This sort of planting was central to the garden philosophy of Phyllis Reiss, which I have inherited.*

allow for all eventualities. The more modest the scale the more frequently changes are made; in fact, a detailed planting plan is almost always altered by eye at planting time. A garden plan is not like an architectural blueprint, it can and must be revised as the garden is planted and begins literally to grow. It is not only the planning, planting and anticipation that make gardening enthralling, there is also the pleasure of changing and adjusting as the expected or unexpected happens. Watching a garden grow and having to adapt it each year makes gardening endlessly interesting. Next year can always be different and better.

Thomas Church, the great American designer who worked mainly in California, pointed out, in *Gardens are for People*, the difference between those basic principles of garden design which can be applied to any site, and the development of individual style, which remains a matter of taste. The former can be learned and put into practice. But the style which emerges, the combination of layout and planting detail, remains personal. Design ideas are quite different from principles, and it is the combination of the ideas with the principles that defines a style. The success of the style depends on its appropriateness to a site and on a fair degree of practical plant knowledge, both in choosing plants and in knowing how to grow them well. Each visit to a garden, great or small, adds to gardening maturity, and so does each gardening day or week.

More practically, Thomas Church defines the fundamental principles of design as unity – house and garden must flow together, linked by the repetition of hard or soft features; function – there should be a clear working relationship between house, garden and utility areas; simplicity – by which he basically means not having too many disparate ideas; scale – getting right the relationships between house and trees, hard surfaces and plants. This last is more difficult to define, but the best way to develop a feeling for satisfying proportions is by looking at good design wherever it is to be found, whether in houses and gardens or drawings and pictures.

To these prerequisites can be added the importance of attention to light and shade, closely related to scale and grouping: an open

7

glade in a dark wood, a pool reflecting the sky above, light filtering through foliage and, as Sylvia Crowe says (in her *Garden Design*) 'the sudden blaze of sunlight appearing at the end of a chasm of evergreen' in an Italian garden. The colour and texture of plants act as further controls in garden design, influencing space and distance almost as much as perspective does. Flower colour is ephemeral, but the greens, greys, bronzes and purples of foliage add weight or lightness, close in a view or allow it to travel into the distance.

After many years of working as a gardener and designer I do now feel that I have developed a style which influences all my gardening efforts. It is tempting to call it the 'Tintinhull' style, because I learned it, in large part, from Tintinhull, the Somerset garden where I have lived and worked for the past fourteen years.

The garden at Tintinhull, which now belongs to the National Trust, was established, mostly during the 1930s and 1940s, by Phyllis Reiss, one of the great gardeners of the twentieth century. At Tintinhull I have been the decorator rather than the designer, using Mrs Reiss's inspired 'bones' – trees, walls and hedges and the framework of garden divisions – as the background to all planting.

Working in Phyllis Reiss's garden I have absorbed her sense of scale and structure and learned the importance of repetition in planting to prevent the restlessness produced by too much variety. I have had the chance to experiment further with her colour schemes and to develop some of my own idiosyncrasies in colour harmony. It has been at Tintinhull, above all, that I have really come to appreciate the idea of 'gardens within a garden'. For Tintinhull is a garden divided into a series of linked 'rooms', very much in the style of Hidcote and Sissinghurst, but on a more modest scale. The layout is essentially formal, constructed on a grid pattern, with lawns, paths and hedges all meeting at right angles. A main axis, a pathway of cut stone flags, runs from east to west along the south side of the garden. All the lateral compartments are hedged with English yew or surrounded by walls, while border areas are connected by a series of deep 'valves', pathways which lead through formal breaks in the flower beds. Borders and beds run parallel to the walls and hedges, which mark the boundaries and create the vertical barriers between the different sections and provide a backdrop for flowering plants. Tall trees – evergreen oaks, a cedar of Lebanon and a colonnade of old yews – balance with the mass of the house and provide pockets of alternating shade and sunlight. (Soon I shall be leaving Tintinhull, and perhaps my clearest memory, when I do not live there any more, will be of the outline of tree shapes against the sky.) As at Hidcote and Sissinghurst, the detailed planting inside this structure is informal, with coloured flowers and leaves weaving patterns for different schemes.

The combination of geometric 'bones', which give definition and structure to a garden, and free natural-style planting leads to a degree of informality. Sometimes the framework is so disguised by

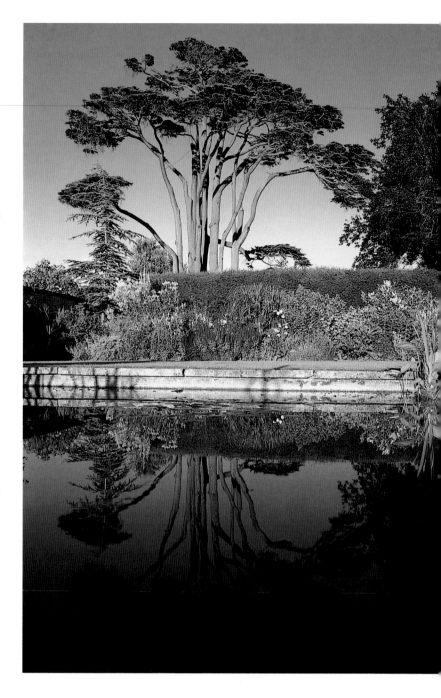

Above: *The garden at Tintinhull is dominated by the old cedar of Lebanon. Here, its many trunks and tiered branches, distinctly outlined against the summer sky, are mirrored in the reflecting water of the pool.*

On pages 10–11: *The long view back towards the façade of Tintinhull House, through the symmetrically arranged foliage plants flanking the axis path that links the 'rooms' on the south side of the garden.*

N

West beds

North borders

Foliage beds

White garden

FOUNTAIN GARDEN

borders

KITCHEN GARDEN

South

South wall border

Gallica rose beds

Dry ridge

Azalea beds

Eastern pathway

Oaks

North-west bed

Hot borders

Summerhouse

POOL GARDEN

South border

MIDDLE GARDEN

North-east bed

beds

Pale borders

Purple and gold border

Yew

Magnolias

South border

EAGLE COURT

North border

CEDAR COURT

Cedar tree

Yew

Cedar

Magnolia

Magnolia

TINTINHULL HOUSE

border

5m / 15 ft   5m / 15 ft

East border

ENTRANCE COURTYARD

the cottagey planting style that it is no longer immediately obvious. Some people think of Tintinhull as a formal garden because of the strict layout, others believe that it is informal because of the luxuriant, almost jungle-like, planting. Vita Sackville-West described Hidcote as a formal garden with a maximum of informality in the planting and Tintinhull is an offshoot of Hidcote. Mrs Reiss lived near there before coming to Tintinhull.

Since I have lived at Tintinhull and come to appreciate the strict geometry of each compartment and how each room is linked to the next to make the whole an integrated design, the 'gardens within a garden' theme underlies all my thinking, on whatever scale I work. This is true whether a design is formal or informal – the idea of separate garden compartments does not have to be implemented in geometric shapes. Although remaining a traditionalist at heart, I have found that, even in the most informal gardens, I can create rooms which reflect different moods, making use of the whole ambience of the site, which, in the end, is what matters.

I have taken Tintinhull as a role model for some other gardens. A garden I designed in Michigan is very much in the Tintinhull spirit, although none of the features actually copies any at Tintinhull: in the Michigan garden, planting is designed to keep the eye on the level of a colonnade of 'Bradford' pears and on the avenues of crab apples which frame the centre, rather than on the distractions of neighbouring houses. In a much smaller garden at the back of a house in Campden Hill Square in London we divided the typical city space, which sloped upwards, into three horizontal 'rooms' – a flat courtyard, a terrace and an open circular lawn – all with distinct yet linked planting schemes. In a herb garden I designed for the New York Botanical Garden a formal central knot pattern is surrounded by borders very much in the Tintinhull tradition of mixed planting, with symmetry and balance being as important as plant varieties. In my new garden at Bettiscombe in Dorset, the basic layout, which is not unlike that of Tintinhull in style, though much smaller, simpler and less labour-intensive, is now nearly complete. The elements that compose the framework are in place. It awaits further planting.

Gardening at Tintinhull, working inside a strong framework, is much easier than gardening in a wilder situation, in woodland, by streams or in a naturalistic cottage garden. Structure is just as important in the more natural garden but it must be subtler and less obtrusive, more like painting than architecture. In place of geometry the more impressionistic composition depends on free-growing plant groups to provide visual structure and give background, height and balance. On whatever scale, from trees and shrubs down to low-growing groundcover, the character of the plants becomes more important; it is their sculptural quality and how they relate and contrast with each other that provide the background to the garden and actually construct the design. Building up layers of planting to

make a coherent picture requires both an artist's talents and an expert's knowledge of plants and their individual needs and habits. My greatest design challenge has been a garden in Fort Worth, Texas, where steep slopes and contoured lawns made geometry impossible and I had to achieve an organized natural look using many plants with which I was at first quite unfamiliar. In Fort Worth the soil is highly alkaline and in any twenty-four-hour period temperatures can swing rapidly between extremes of cold and heat, so plants have a tough time. Getting the right plants to withstand the stressful climate was of vital importance, and I needed a lot of local horticultural advice before I could begin to compose pictures, even in my mind's eye.

So, Tintinhull has been a great inspiration. I have also had the good fortune to see a lot of other gardens, in the British Isles, in Europe and in the United States. My most important formative period was probably the 1970s when, before moving to Tintinhull in 1979, I visited many of the great Italian Renaissance gardens. I believe every gardener should have this experience, or if this is impossible should determine to study pictures and read about the philosophy behind the gardens. It was in Italy that I began to understand the use of three-dimensional as well as two-dimensional space and how it was employed to relate and balance with the mass of the house. These old gardens are basically laid out in a series of separate but closely linked rooms, with the central pathways and features aligned on villa doorways and windows and other architectural elements. On hillsides, terraces adjust levels and provide views to the countryside. Massive trees – evergreen oaks, pines and cedars, many of them two or three hundred years old – guard and shelter the villas, shaping the skyline and providing areas of shade to alternate with bright sunlight. Cypresses grown as specimens or as hedges, with both vertical and horizontal lines, provide sharp contrast with more rounded tree shapes. You do not need to know any history to understand the simple beauty of these gardens. Their patterns have influenced all our gardening lives.

In America many of the most intriguing gardens have been made to set off or flow with new buildings. The best of these have a haunting beauty quite different from the traditional Renaissance symmetries. One garden, the Bagley Wright garden north of Seattle, which I saw a few years ago, is constantly in my mind. A low concrete-and-glass house, designed by Arthur Erikson, lies in a forest clearing with a dramatic western view over and above Puget Sound, set off by a geometric reflecting pool where water flows imperceptibly over the boundary edge as if into the chasm below. On the eastern side, a meadow, contoured by Cornelia Hahn Oberlander, stretches back like a vast lake of light behind the house, a total contrast to the dark forest beyond. White daisies grow in the grass.

It is interesting, however, that the most successful formal garden of the twentieth century is also to be found in the United States, at

Filoli in California. Filoli is another garden designed as a series of rooms, and it is a perfect example of symmetry and careful grooming. Planting as well as design is formal and repetitive. Like the classic Italian gardens to which its layout is related, it is a perfect place to train your perceptions. The principles on which these formal gardens are based can also be applied to more naturalistically styled gardens where there is no obvious geometry. Once your eye is attuned to balance you can dispense with rigid symmetry.

Of course, I have also been influenced by books. For me both Thomas Church's *Gardens are for People* (1955) and Russell Page's *The Education of a Gardener* (1962) are a constant source of inspiration. I remember always how Russell Page, in his first chapter, stresses the

This garden on the Isle of Oronsay was designed to fit into the local landscape and to offer protection against battering salt-laden winds. A grid of hedges and hurdles safeguards the plants.

importance of interpreting the landscape in which a garden is set before attempting any gardening detail. For example, in a cliffside garden I was asked to design in Maine, the formal themes I usually prefer would have been inappropriate, so all planning and planting was done to extend the natural feeling, with groups of hardy evergreen spruce providing shelter from salt winds as well as framing vistas to the ocean.

I also frequently re-read Sylvia Crowe's *Garden Design* (1958), in which she vividly describes Phyllis Reiss's layout and planting at Tintinhull, comparing the enclosed garden rooms to an Islamic garden, which represents, for the devout Muslim, a terrestrial paradise, a foretaste of heaven to come. In 1990 I made something very like an enclosed Islamic garden in Austin, Texas.

So, gradually over the years, I have come to feel more certain not only of my own style preferences but also of my attitudes and philosophies. I like enclosures, framed views not vast panoramas, trees which shape the visible skyline and balance with a house, horizontal lines – especially hedges, edges of lawns and pools and pathways – which meet at right angles and reflect a general symmetry. I love soft planting and plant shapes, billowing curves softening the hard lines of paths or hedges, but I do not like pointless meandering curves, often introduced in a rectangular city garden plot to disguise the straight boundary lines. In a natural landscape curves work in association with the lie of the land, and relate to overhead tree canopies or follow the natural direction of a stream. (And in Thomas Church's famous El Novillero garden at Sonoma, California, the abstract shape of the swimming pool reflects patterns in the valley landscape below.)

Sometimes my gardening philosophy clarifies what I do not like rather than what I do. Far more jarring, to me, than any garish colour combination is the sight of plants with entirely different cultural requirements growing alongside one another. Appropriate planting is vital to the success of a garden: it is essential to choose plants which will not only do well in any particular spot but will also associate happily with any indigenous neighbouring plants. As an extension of this, I prefer on the whole to grow species plants. I find that new plant hybrids or cultivars, especially when bred for longer and thicker flower spikes, for particular colour effects, shorter stems (no staking), or extended flowering periods, tend to lose some of their subtle qualities. The peculiar grace of a plant often comes from its own natural colour and from the proportions between flowers, leaves and stem. None the less, especially as I continue to design in different climatic regions, I appreciate the plants specially bred to cope with difficult conditions. And, of course, there are many old favourites among hybrids and cultivars which, as vast improvements on the original type plant, one uses all the time.

Beth Chatto's first Gold Medal winning garden at the 1977 Chelsea Flower Show was a lesson to all gardeners. Silver and grey plants of Mediterranean type grew together on a well-drained bank, while moisture-loving plants were gathered around the margin of a pool. Yet in spite of her example there are still gardens at shows where acid-loving plants are displayed next to those which tolerate only lime, sun-lovers next to the shade-tolerant, drought-tolerant next to bog plants, almost, it seems, deliberately to confuse the uninitiated, who may believe that gardening is like that.

Opposite: *In this modern garden in Michigan, vertical alleys of crab apples and lines of 'Bradford' pears create areas of light and shadow as well as dividing up the garden into 'rooms'. The horizontal lines of paths and pool edge meet at sharp right angles and handsome pots are symmetrically placed to flank the pool.*

Below: *Lady's mantle, creeping campanulas and a crimson Gallica rose soften the hard lines of the steps between the Pool Garden and the Kitchen area at Tintinhull.*

Each plant should be envisioned as an individual mature specimen but also needs to be perceived in its subordinate position as a contributor to the whole garden picture. I find it useful to keep lists of plants with special qualities to which I can refer when I want particular effects. Deciduous shrubs such as berberis, corylopsis, deutzias, dogwoods, hazels, philadelphus and viburnums work well in a mixed border, sheltering low-growing spring bulbs with their canopies and allowing space for good clumps of perennials for the summer garden, as well as giving attractive winter structure. Evergreens such as box, winter-flowering mahonias, choisya and osmanthus are the sort of shrubs which unite a border scheme throughout the year. In a natural landscape small trees or large shrubs such as magnolias, dogwoods and, if the soil is sufficiently acid, stewartia, styrax and tupelos (*Nyssa sylvatica*) provide a variation in strong shapes. Accents or focal points can be provided by dogwoods with tiers of tabulated branches (either *Cornus controversa* 'Variegata' or *C. alternifolia* 'Argentea') and viburnums such as *Viburnum plicatum* 'Mariesii', with a dense spreading habit. Perennials with sculptural leaves provide scale and definition at a lower level and are not wholly dependent on flowering for their appeal: crambes, euphorbias, thalictrums, macleayas, eryngiums, Japanese anemones and hostas are among the most common foliage plants which give borders a long season of interest. Others, in contrast, have more spiky effects: irises, phormiums, sisyrinchiums and yuccas which in their turn set off low-growing bergenias or mounds of silvery artemisias.

All the planting at Tintinhull is mixed: trees, shrubs, perennials, biennials, annuals and bulbs cover the earth in each section, and unity of design is achieved by distinct colour schemes and themes rather than by massed formal planting. These schemes are as suitable for a natural-style garden as for Tintinhull's right-angled beds and borders. Except for occasional 'framed' beds for seasonal bulbs and annuals (as in my Michigan garden), or in cutting gardens, I almost always mix woody and soft-stemmed plants. At Tintinhull, usually, colour groups are repeated in each line of vision; here this helps to introduce an air of formality, but I find this kind of linking equally useful in the more undulating beds and contoured shapes of a wild garden.

All the planting at Tintinhull is very close, with no bare earth to be seen; annuals and bulbs are fitted in between the more permanent plants. Any bare space is thickly mulched. Plants, usually in quite large groups (of at least five), cover the soil and weave together in as natural a way as I can control. Not only does the close planting look almost jungle-like, but, by preventing weed germination, it reduces maintenance. In a more naturalistic garden the planting style is only an extension of this: larger drifts spread in abstract patterns in less obviously structured surroundings. Even a 'wild' site needs a design frame, a series of balances and matching shapes.

After design and planting have been considered, there remains a third element essential to success: the general health of the garden. Maintaining soil and plants in good condition is an ongoing process, but the foundations for vitality are laid in the earliest stages. Planting in unprepared soil or soil with perennial weeds, for example, is wasteful and unproductive. In the worst situation it may be necessary to give two seasons to providing adequate drainage, then digging, cleaning and mulching to ensure the best start for plants. It is not always easy to persuade clients new to gardening that so much preparation is vital. I am personally applying this lesson to my own new garden at Bettiscombe, in which the basic soil is almost unworkable clay. Mistakes of planning can be corrected later, but if planting is done too soon it will be difficult subsequently to dig and incorporate compost and grit to lighten the soil, and it can be impossible to get rid of perennial weeds. Many old gardens have tired soil in which the plants cannot take up nutrients, as essential humus-making organic mulches have not been regularly added. When I came to Tintinhull, the soil, although workable, had for some years had only artificial fertilizers and routine digging in of well-rotted compost was needed to restore it to health. Fortunately, we were able to incorporate quantities of compost as we renewed the planting in each area.

After many years of designing and working in gardens, I now feel that I can walk into a garden and make a quick analysis of its successes and failures from a design point of view. More practically, I can usually judge the garden's state of health. Such appraisal becomes much easier as judgment matures, but it is always difficult to make an objective assessment of one's own garden. Even the greatest gardens have some features that work well and others that work less well; sometimes gardens become restless or overdesigned, with just too many different features. While a formal layout is always easily interpreted, occasionally a more natural garden has a true atmospheric grandeur and yet resists rigid design analysis, the garden concept seemingly having developed without being made to a rigid plan.

Whether the effect sought is formal or naturalistic, a garden is not meant to resemble nature; all gardening is artificial. Just as a painter or a sculptor arranges shapes and colours, so the gardener assembles plants. The art of gardening lies in creating a composition that is truly satisfying.

In all the beds at Tintinhull the planting is mixed, with a spring emphasis on bulbs which thrive between deciduous shrubs. Aconites, snowdrops, scillas and invasive bluebells, with a few groups of dark tulips, successively carpet the soil in the purple and gold border of the Cedar Court, providing interest from the New Year until taller plants, shrubs and flowering perennials start to perform in May.

A wisteria, trained carefully against the Ham stone wall of the old stable block at Tintinhull, in full flower in May. Occasionally the buds are damaged by late frost, but most years the wall is draped with long purple racemes that make a magnificent display in the austere setting of the Courtyard.

A restrained approach
Planting up pots
Ceanothus and a few favourite evergreen shrubs

THE COURTYARD

I FAVOUR THE IDEA that the approach to a garden should be relatively austere: architectural, not flowery, giving little or no hint of what is to come in the garden beyond. Gertrude Jekyll wrote about this, suggesting that, as well as being quiet in its planting, the approach to a garden should, ideally, be on the shady side of the house. The full glory of the main garden, on the sunny side, should first be seen from inside the house itself, so that a relationship is established between the building, its occupants and the garden. Suggestions of the excitement to come may be fleetingly conveyed in advance; at Tintinhull a wooden door in the courtyard wall, left open always except in severe storms, allows a welcoming, comforting glimpse of the Cedar Court to the north of the house as one turns into the yard. Even a closed door offers an invitation to further exploration.

An arrival area (and especially an arrival courtyard), presents a special opportunity for restraint in planting. The decoration should be minimal: trees and shrubs trained into architectural shapes, free-standing or as clipped buttresses against walls. If there are flowers there should be relatively few different sorts. A wisteria can make a purple curtain in spring (as at Tintinhull), Virginia creeper clinging by tendrils to walls might provide a lush green surface in summer, with a spectacular display of orange and red in autumn. If a wall is in shade a climbing hydrangea, *Hydrangea anomala* ssp. *petiolaris*, or the related *Schizophragma hydrangeoides*, both with attractive lacecap greenish flowers, can smother masonry with a pattern of twisted stems, green-leaved in summer. If space allows, topiary evergreens or annuals might be regimented in pots or arranged in a disciplined patterned parterre surrounded by low hedges of box.

Of course, these are just ideas and must be adapted for any particular site. If the arrival area is on the gardening side of a house, the thinking needs to be rather different. Helen Dillon's front garden in Dublin, for example – a magical place, hardly separated from a tree-lined street – is full of delightful planting.

However, as a principle, the muted approach is well worth considering. Many urban and suburban front gardens where unity and simplicity should be the norm have too many features in them: a pond, a rockery, a weeping specimen tree, mounds of earth which mimic the contours of a landscape garden in miniature, different plants which give a spotty effect. A well laid out parterre with box-edged beds, planted with tulips in spring followed by summer and winter annuals, with more permanent massed lavenders or cotton

lavenders if in sun, or sarcococca in shade, would be much less fussy. The geometry of the parterre might be in some way linked with the architecture of the house.

In most regions of the United States the planting of the front garden, visible to passers-by and to the owner, is solved quite differently. There, without boundary fences between neighbours, flowing lawns planted with specimen trees link adjacent properties to give coherence to a whole street or neighbourhood. The only individual planting in the front may be under the house walls, where evergreens anchor the building to the soil and often grow tall to create desired privacy, leaving the opportunity for personal gardening styles to develop in the fenced backyards hidden behind. I find this democratic attitude to sharing the front landscape very attractive.

At Tintinhull an almost square courtyard, originally a traditional stable yard, reached through gates on the roadside, is now used as the approach for all visitors. (During the previous centuries a door in the lane gave access to the Eagle Court garden and main entrance hall.) This courtyard, surrounded by walls, is paved with old stone blocks, each about the width of a narrow brick (8cm/3in) but longer (30cm/12in rather than 23cm/9in). They have probably been in position for more than a hundred years, and were originally planned for horses, not motor cars. Larger stone flags cover an area next to the seventeenth-century mullioned façade of the house and make for smoother walking.

For hard surfaces tarmac and cement and man-made paving slabs, although durable and requiring no weedkilling, are the least attractive of materials. Stone flags, slate or cobbles are all much more interesting and desirable, and they can sometimes be obtained from reclamation sites at quite reasonable prices.

For more simple effects, local gravel – a surface often found in traditional kitchen gardens – can be edged with boards. I have used gravel at Bettiscombe for the arrival court, my utility area and paths in the walled garden. The honey-coloured surface looks both

The view into the garden at Tintinhull from the Courtyard. This narrow glimpse, framed by spreading cotoneasters and the branches of the magnolia beyond, gives just a hint of the profusion of planting to be discovered. The pots inside the doorway are planted for spring with lily-flowered 'Burgundy' tulips.

The little blue Anemone blanda *has proliferated under the mahonia in the Courtyard. Small spring bulbs – snowdrops, muscari, scillas, chionodoxas and different anemones – have spread through all the flower beds at Tintinhull.*

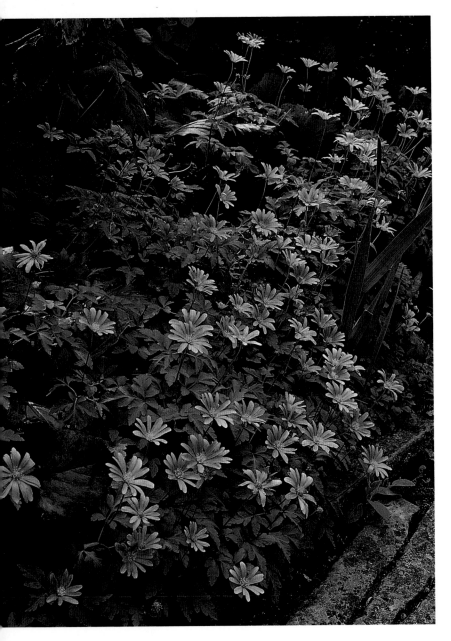

attractive and workmanlike. If there is space for a lawn, line it with narrow boards, stone or brick: this will reduce the hours spent edging the grass.

At Tintinhull the south-facing wall of the house, on the lane, has a sun-loving winter-flowering clematis (*Clematis cirrhosa* var. *balearica*). With deeply cut delicate evergreen leaves and nodding bell-shaped creamy-green flowers for many months – especially in a mild winter – followed by silky seed tassels, it always earns its position. The variety *C.c.* 'Freckles' has more open flowers spotted with maroon. A yellow Banksian rose (*Rosa banksiae* 'Lutea') flowers in spring and has to be pruned immediately after flowering to allow new growth to form and ripen sufficiently for flowering the following season. An old native silver birch grows unusually tall to tower over the courtyard. A vast wisteria (*Wisteria sinensis*) is trained on the wall of the stables opposite the gates. Pruned lightly at midsummer and again, more severely, in winter, it flowers without leaves in early spring. Pots of tulips followed by summer-flowering annuals flank the front and kitchen doors. Ideally that should probably be all, but another bed next to the road and a trellis to hide the oil storage tank give extra plant interest. A tall aspen poplar, *Populus tremuloides*, hides an electricity transformer, with mahonias (the Oregon grape, *Mahonia aquifolium*) and Japanese anemones spreading through the bed beneath it. A thickly set *Phillyrea latifolia* and the rare similar but smaller-leaved *Maytenus boaria* from Chile, both evergreens, give definition in winter. The scented white multiflora rambling rose 'Bobbie James', its large individual flowers with overlapping petals held in clusters, flowers at midsummer to smother the trellis.

A narrow pathway that forms part of the entrance area of this garden in Michigan is edged with a harmonious assembly of golden plants – a yellow hollyhock, golden-foliaged hostas, Lilium auratum *and* Berberis thunbergii *'Aurea'.*

Planting up Pots

P LANTS GROWN in containers for decorating terraces, courtyards and porches give any garden a feeling of luxury and extend its season. Evergreens followed by bulbs, pansies or forget-me-nots last through winter and spring and in summer plants – of a single sort or a mixture – can be massed to resemble an indoor scheme of cut flowers.

Placed singly in key positions, the pots themselves, full or empty, provide focal points: a pair can frame a doorway; in formal rhythms they emphasize and enhance a design. I seldom use small containers, preferring large, elegant pots

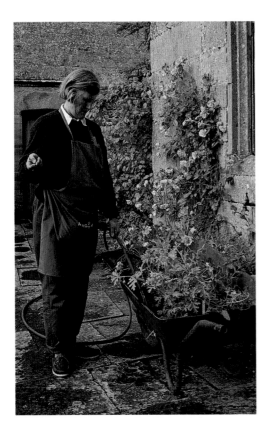

even in a restricted space. A small enclosed garden will benefit from an out-of-scale ornament. The most beautiful containers, in wood, stone, lead or pretty handmade terracotta (preferably frostproof), are expensive, but I try to avoid the flat, textureless surface of plastic or fibreglass. In certain situations tin, painted or weathered silvery grey, is as satisfying as grander materials. Beside the kitchen door in the Courtyard at Tintinhull I have three upturned rhubarb forcers which I fill with tulips for spring, followed by summer-flowering annuals. The illustration (*above*) shows an arrangement of *Argyranthemum* 'Pink Australian', *Salvia buchananii*, osteospermum and *Helichrysum petiolare*.

Soil preparation is important. At Tintinhull we make our own compost, and we find that a good mixture for general use is one-third each by volume of plain garden soil, peat (or a peat alternative) and coarse sand. We add water-retentive granules and

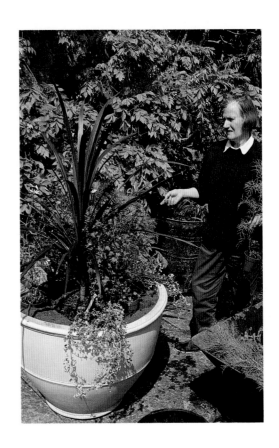

a slow-release fertilizer. But of course it is easier to use a ready-made compost, which can be bought to suit the requirements of particular plants.

Planting is a simple matter, but it is essential to make sure the plants are adequately watered before being transferred to their permanent home. I generally fill a wheelbarrow with water and soak the plants in it until all air-bubbles disappear (*opposite, bottom left*). This summer I planted the big pots on either side of the stable doors with an arrangement of blue verbenas, dark pink pelargoniums, paler argyranthemums, dark-flowered osteospermums, *Cosmos bipinnatus*

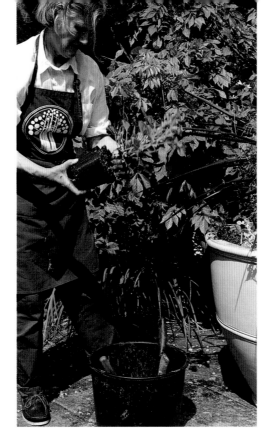

'Sea Shells', helichrysums and the pink-flowered *Anisodontea scabrosa*, surrounding purple-leaved cordylines. With containers as large (and as stable) as this I sometimes economize by putting polystyrene in the bottom to fill up some of the space; then I add compost to within about 10cm/4in of the rim. When doing a mixed colour scheme, I put in any large plants, such as the cordylines, then position the smaller plants, still in their pots, around them (*opposite, bottom right*). Once I am satisfied with the arrangement I take them out of the pots (*left*) and plant them. I always plant very tightly, starting in the centre and working outwards, leaving as little bare soil as possible. To finish off I add extra compost, bringing the level up to 5cm/2in below the rim (*below left*), then spray the whole arrangement with water to clean off any soil remaining on the leaves (*below*). Don't forget your pots once you have planted them – regular feeding and watering is essential throughout the growing season. We give annuals and quick-growing perennials a balanced liquid feed every two weeks.

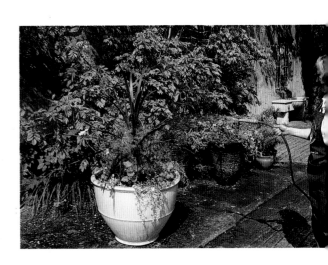

Ceanothus and a few Favourite Evergreen Shrubs

Ceanothus arboreus 'Trewithen Blue'

A T TINTINHULL evergreen ceanothus, growing as buttresses against brick or stone walls, are a mainstay not only for their brilliant blue flowers carried in sequence between spring and early autumn but also for their strong vertical and structural quality. When I started to garden seriously it was with a passion for evergreen shrubs, which provide such solace in winter when other shrubs – albeit many with beautiful bark or twigs – are bare. Although I have since been distracted, especially while at Tintinhull, by the delights of flowers and colour, I still study the habit and quality of evergreens and enjoy their infinite variation in leaf shades, texture and shape, as well as their contribution towards the essential 'bones' of a garden. Together with trees shaping the skyline and the horizontal and vertical lines of hedges and grass, these shrubs are the most important plant ingredients in any garden.

Walled gardens are particularly suitable for the Californian ceanothus and, of course, for many of the other exciting evergreens from California, as well as those from the Mediterranean and the southern hemisphere. Walls, especially brick, reflect heat and encourage wood to ripen and harden: this not only means that the plant is more resistant to cold weather, but also makes flowering the following season more likely.

My experience of ceanothus began with the spring-flowering *Ceanothus arboreus* 'Trewithen Blue', which I first saw at Trewithen garden in Cornwall, many years ago. Large soft rich green leaves clothe strong tree-like stems and the flower heads are a clear blue. It grows happily facing west on a wall of the Courtyard at Tintinhull.

Forms of *C. impressus*, with small hard leaves on densely branched stems which can be trained espalier-like on a wall, flower in late spring. 'Puget Blue' has magnificent dark blue flowers emerging from almost purple buds. Another spring flowerer is *C.* 'Cascade', taller with an almost pendulous habit, weeping forward when tied back against the wall. With narrow leaves it has clear blue flowers. It has inherited characteristics from the hardy *C. thyrsiflorus* with paler flowers, which performs a little later, in midsummer, and has some white-flowered forms, besides the prostrate *C.t.* var. *repens*, ideal for draping over a low wall or being encouraged to spread out over paving. *C.* 'Burkwoodii' flowers twice, in summer and again in autumn, while *C.* 'Autumnal Blue' carries pale blue flowers from late summer onwards.

I especially like evergreens with unshowy – but often fragrant – flowers, and leaves with subtle shapes and textures. There are various osmanthus, such as *Osmanthus heterophyllus* and its coloured-leaf forms, usually translucent in young growth, as well as the dense *O. armatus*, with jagged-toothed edges to the leaves and scented white flowers in autumn, and the larger dense olive-green *O. yunnanensis*, with tiny ivory-white scented flowers in late winter. *O. decorus* (*Phillyrea decora*) has a solid look; a handsome spreading dark green shrub, it is suitable for trimming into topiary domes and a splendid alternative to box. The Alexandrian laurel, *Danaë racemosa*, is another good edging plant; a small shrub that will endure deep shade, it was popular in the gardens of the Italian Renaissance. Its flowers are insignificant, but in autumn it carries bright red berries above its glossy, curiously flattened leaves.

The Mediterranean phillyreas are also among my favourites. *Phillyrea latifolia* is a small tree or large bush with glittering and fluttering green leaves, rather like a small evergreen oak in general appearance. Known as the farmyard tree, it is an ideal complement to stone or brick. A specimen can be allowed to make a dense bush or trained on a single trunk to make a broad-headed tree. The small narrow-leaved *P. angustifolia* is also desirable; its long thin leaves are almost glaucous when young. Much grown in the seventeenth century for topiary, it can be trimmed almost as tightly as the dwarf 'Suffruticosa' box (although it is not so hardy).

The invaluable evergreen viburnums are discussed on pages 120–21. The evergreen hollies also really deserve a chapter to themselves: in this confined space I can only mention a few of the most special. The hardy American inkberry, *Ilex glabra*, with small shining green leaves on a compact bush and small black berries, should be seen more often. Requiring an acid soil, it is resistant to salt winds and is an ideal shrub for seaside as well as for inland gardens. On quite a different scale, the Chinese *I. fargesii* and the Japanese *I. latifolia* are tree-like shrubs with the largest leaves of all hollies, those of *I. latifolia* having serrated edges.

I. pernyii is easily recognizable by its triangular spined leaves.

For a seaside garden or one in a mild climate, daisy-flowered olearias, mainly from New Zealand, are desirable evergreen shrubs. They remain much neglected because they are temperamental, disliking fierce sun – they die of sunstroke – but needing light. They have a superb range of leaf types, from the holly-like *Olearia × macrodonta* to soft grey-green *O. phlogopappa* varieties from Tasmania. If the climate is not on your side, try **growing** them in containers. *O. traversii* has rich grey-green leaves densely covered below in white felt. It is quick and vigorous and used as hedges in the Scilly Isles. One of the

Azara microphylla

Olearia phlogopappa

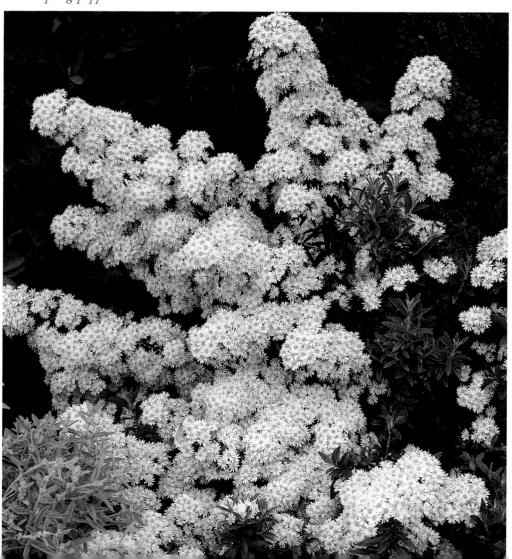

hardiest is *O.* 'Waikariensis'. Silver-leaved with showy white daisies, it has survived many years at Tintinhull.

Some of my favourite evergreens are definitely for warm areas. The true myrtles (*Myrtus communis*) from southern Europe, as well as those from the southern hemisphere (including *Lophomyrtus* and *Eugenia*), are among the best tender evergreens. *M. communis* hardly needs describing, but *M. luma* from Chile, with flaking cinnamon-coloured bark, is distinctive. All adapt well, at least for several years, to being grown in containers. The bay rum, *Umbellularia californica*, with a strong pyramidal habit and leaves that are intensely aromatic when crushed, is highly desirable for a sheltered spot. And no garden that has a suitable climate should be without the lacy-leaved *Azara microphylla* from Chile, with yellow vanilla-scented acacia-like flower puffs in early spring. Also from Chile, *Drimys winteri*, growing naturally into a pyramidal shape but happy to be trained back against a wall, has translucent leaves and creamy-white scented flowers in early summer.

The box domes at Tintinhull stretch as an avenue through the Eagle Court and the Middle Garden. Flanking the main pathway of diamond-shaped flagstones, and clipped annually to retain their shape, the domes link the garden compartments.

Formal symmetry in a walled garden
Structural planting
Flowers through the seasons
Box and yew topiary
A passion for hellebores
Euphorbias in the garden

THE EAGLE COURT

WITH ITS BOX topiary and mixed planting schemes, the Eagle Court is the most formal of the gardens at Tintinhull. Occupying the area below the main west-facing façade of the house, it has a symmetry that balances the architecture. The horizontal expanse of terrace, grass forecourt and perimeter borders almost matches the vertical house wall in extent. It is an outside room, a three-dimensional space. The effect is accentuated by the two yews beyond the north wall, matching a tall crab apple and flowering cherry in the south border. Curtaining climbers and wall shrubs decorate the walls and add to the atmosphere of green seclusion.

In this garden there is an almost exact correspondence between architectural features and plants used as the equivalent of architecture. The symmetry of the walls is reinforced by the eight topiary box bushes down the centre and the horizontal shapes made by the green panels of grass. Although the perimeter borders appear to be planted informally, in fact there is repetition of blocks of shapes and colours, very much in Phyllis Reiss's style and conveying a strong design message. This sort of planning sets a rhythm for all the beds in the garden, through which formality, cloaked and almost disappearing in free riots of colour, binds each scheme together. For me, in designing for others and now in creating beds of my own at Bettiscombe, repetition without exact symmetry seems to provide an essential key.

Although the Eagle Court is a self-contained area – as are all the Tintinhull compartments – an axial path of York stone slabs, flanked, here and in the Middle Garden, by the avenue of box domes, leads from the front door steps westward right to the end of the garden, terminating in the Fountain Garden's arbour of clipped bay. The pathway was laid down during the First World War, and the box domes (*Buxus sempervirens*) were added in the 1920s.

The west side of the house dates from about 1720. As a classical addition to the farmhouse built a hundred years earlier, it almost doubled its size, as well as enhancing its elegance. For two centuries the Eagle Court was used as an entrance from the main approach lane. Visitors reached the front door from a side gate in the south wall. All the brick walls which mark the boundaries of the courtyard were built during the eighteenth century and may be contemporary with the façade. Stone eagles set back on gate piers frame the narrow entrance to the Middle Garden. Although the south-facing wall would have been especially suitable for espalier fruits, it is probable that little gardening was done here until Mrs Reiss's day. After 1933 she turned it into a flower garden.

Mauve and lavender abutilons, blue ceanothus, euphorbias and early clematis dominate the Eagle Court in spring. In the foreground is Abutilon × suntense, *probably the most beautiful of the garden abutilons hardy in our part of England.*

Structural Planting

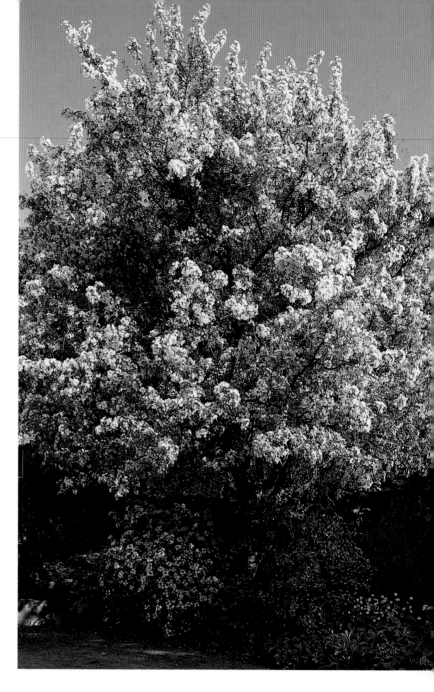

Altffough since coming to Tintinhull we have had to renew much of the detailed planting in this area, the main structural plants – including the topiary box, the crab apple, the cherry and a large mahonia (*Mahonia japonica*) that flowers in January – are Mrs Reiss's original plants. One of her most successful combinations has been the partnership between a pair of shrubs, Mexican orange (*Choisya ternata*) and *Corylopsis pauciflora*, planted in both the north-east and the south-east corners. Both shrubs are tolerant of sun or shade so the pairs developed at almost equal rates in different conditions. Recently we replaced those in full sun, which had grown ungainly in the last years. The partnership in the north-facing bed (in the comparatively shady south-east corner by the door into the lane) still survives, probably now at least forty years *in situ*. The choisya is trimmed annually after flowering, to prevent its branches encroaching over beds filled with hellebores.

The less hardy evergreen abutilons, ceanothus, shrubby euphorbias and lavenders in full sun in the south-facing border all have relatively short lives. Besides being susceptible to severe frosts they are always vulnerable to wind turbulence, an unwelcome characteristic caused by the wall and funnelling through the narrow west entry, the path of the prevailing wind. In a typical mild wet autumn these quick-growing evergreens put on a lot of new lax growth which can be cut back by succeeding winter frosts, weakening the plants at least for a season. Needing little feeding, they might do better if starved in a more Mediterranean-type soil than we give them. Mrs Reiss did not grow euphorbias in the garden; these are our additions. They play an important role in these sunny beds, with blue-green linear foliage in winter and acid-yellow flower spikes over months in early spring, ideal to complement the bright blue of flowering ceanothus. She certainly knew them, for Margery Fish, her neighbour at East Lambrook Manor, was a euphorbia enthusiast, stocking many different species and varieties in her nursery. Perhaps she worried about the poisonous properties of the milky juice found in the stalks. If the climate is suitable I always use shrubby euphorbias in spring schemes, and add other less woody ones where possible. I like to combine the lemon-yellow of their flowering bracts with mauve flowers such as ordinary honesty or Byzantine gladiolus or with the lavender flowers of glaucidiums.

A further contribution we have made to this part of the garden is the twisting *Stauntonia hexaphylla* on the wall. Reputedly tender, this evergreen climber from Asia, with deliciously fragrant flowers

Mrs Reiss planted this tea crab, Malus hupehensis, *in the 1940s. Flowering gloriously in May, it also acts as a host to schisandra and clematis, while under its canopy flourish choisya,* Itea ilicifolia, *hellebores, perennial* Lunaria rediviva, Anemone *'Prinz Heinrich' and bergenias.*

in spring, rarely shows signs of frost or wind-chill damage. I first saw it at East Lambrook, growing over the Old Malt House. Another elegant evergreen, the *Itea ilicifolia*, is about twenty years old. It was here when we came and may have been planted as a replacement for one planted by Mrs Reiss.

These evergreens are accompanied by perennials which also keep their winter foliage. Throughout the year there are the contrasting leaf textures and different greens provided by hellebores, hart's-tongue ferns and leathery-leaved bergenias in the shady beds, and, planted in blocks beneath the stone eagles, evergreen epimedium (*Epimedium pinnatum* ssp. *colchicum*) with delicate yellow flowers at the end of March. All demand frequent manicuring, especially in spring, when frosted shoots, dead leaves and flower heads need trimming. If it were my garden I would replace the labour-intensive bergenias with masses of suckering sarcococca (*Sarcococca humilis* and *S. confusa*), to provide scent in the New Year and glossy foliage throughout all the seasons.

In full sun clumps of sword-like iris and silvery artemisias lighten the more sombre darker shades throughout the summer months. For closer viewing there are Japanese anemones with maple-like leaves, glossy rosettes of late-flowering toad lilies (*Tricyrtis formosana*) that shine in the shade between clumps of hellebores and, on the sunny side, the fern-like foliage of Jacob's ladder, the ordinary *Polemonium caeruleum*. There are ferns (*Polystichum setiferum* and its form, *P.s.* Acutilobum Group), happily accommodated in cracks between stone, brick or paving, and two different corydalis, the weedy grey

fluffy *Corydalis lutea* and the desirable *C. cheilanthifolia*, everywhere.

The character of the whole scheme in the Eagle Court is dependent on its most formal architectural features: the central domes of box, with leaf colours and patterns that continually change as young shoots emerge and fade between darker leaves, and the patterns made by the green panels of grass which, mown and edged next to lichen-textured stone, dignify the horizontal space. Phyllis Reiss's layout of paving, paths and grass, combined with the verticals of trees, topiary and walls, creates a completely satisfying whole. Sometimes it is possible to believe that the more flowery seasonal events are unnecessary.

By late summer the holly-leaved Asian Itea ilicifolia, *happy in the north-facing border with the wind-protection offered by the crab, is a fountain of yellow-green catkin-like racemes composed of tiny scented flower heads. Nearby, the oak-leaved hydrangea,* Hydrangea quercifolia, *which performs best if tied back against a wall, provides autumnal leaf tints, as well as trusses of white summer flower heads. The woodland aster,* Aster divaricatus, *has myriad white stars for a six-week period in late summer.*

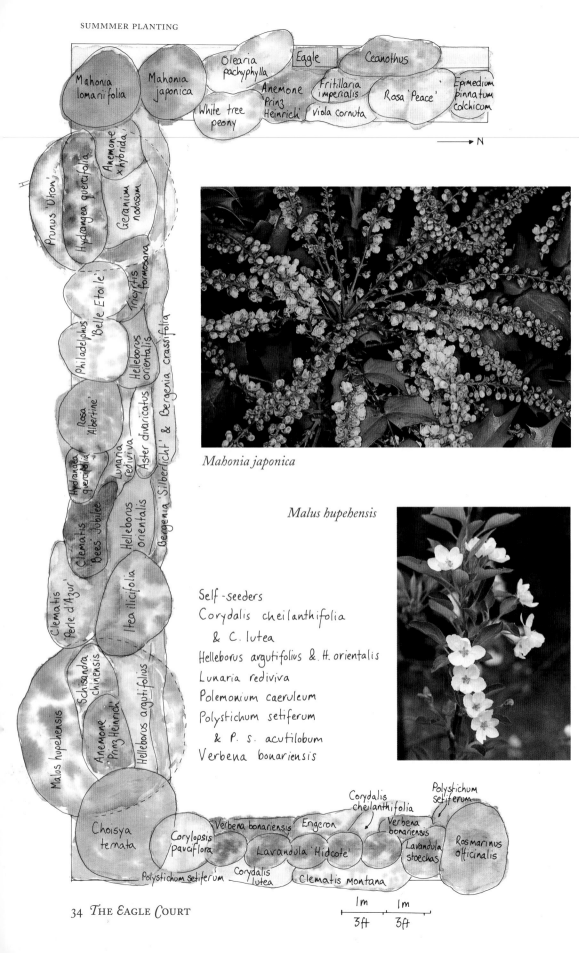

The garden plan labels (top bed, left to right):

- Mahonia lomarii folia
- Mahonia japonica
- White tree peony
- Olearia pachyphylla
- Anemone 'Prinz Heinrich'
- Eagle
- Ceanothus
- Fritillaria imperialis
- Viola cornuta
- Rosa 'Peace'
- Epimedium pinnatum colchicum

→ N

Left bed (top to bottom):

- Prunus 'Ukon'
- Hydrangea quercifolia
- Anemone x hybrida
- Geranium nodosum
- Tricyrtis formosana
- Philadelphus 'Belle Etoile'
- Helleborus orientalis
- Bergenia crassifolia
- Rosa 'Albertine'
- Aster divaricatus
- Hydrangea quercifolia
- Lunaria rediviva
- Bergenia 'Silberlicht' & Bergenia crassifolia
- Clematis 'Bees Jubilee'
- Helleborus orientalis
- Clematis 'Perle d'Azur'
- Itea ilicifolia
- Schisandra chinensis
- Anemone 'Prinz Heinrich'
- Helleborus argutifolius
- Malus hupehensis
- Choisya ternata

Bottom bed (left to right):

- Corylopsis pauciflora
- Verbena bonariensis
- Erigeron
- Corydalis cheilanthifolia
- Verbena bonariensis
- Polystichum setiferum
- Lavandula 'Hidcote'
- Lavandula stoechas
- Rosmarinus officinalis
- Polystichum setiferum
- Corydalis lutea
- Clematis montana

Self-seeders
Corydalis cheilanthifolia
    & C. lutea
Helleborus argutifolius & H. orientalis
Lunaria rediviva
Polemonium caeruleum
Polystichum setiferum
    & P. s. acutilobum
Verbena bonariensis

Rosa 'Peace'

Mahonia japonica

Malus hupehensis

Verbena bonariensis

Lavandula 'Hidcote'

1m   1m
─── ───
3ft   3ft

Clematis 'Prince Charles'

Cestrum parqui

The border plan (illustrated plant map):

Solanum crispum 'Glasnevin'
Chaenomeles speciosa 'Moerloosei'
Clematis alpina 'Frances Rivis'
Eagle
Anemone 'Prinz Heinrich'
Rosa 'Peace'
Anemone 'Prinz Heinrich'
Aquilegia
Nerine bowdenii
Abutilon × suntense
Purple Iris
Epimedium pinnatum colchicum
Rosa 'Peace'
Agapanthus africanus
Penstemon venustus
Nerine bowdenii
Tree peony
Euphorbia characias wulfenii
Skimmia hexaphylla
Nerine bowdenii
Salvia patens
Yellow Tulips
Abutilon × suntense
Agapanthus africanus
Lilium regale
Iris sibirica
Salvia sclarea turkestanica
Yellow Iris
Iris sibirica
Clematis montana
Salvia cacaliifolia
Nicotiana langsdorffii
Artemisia 'Powis Castle'
English lavender
Ceanothus 'Cascade'
Agapanthus africanus
Teucrium fruticans
Abutilon vitifolium
Nicotiana langsdorffii
Clematis 'Prince Charles'
Salvia cacaliifolia
Euphorbia characias wulfenii
Artemisia 'Powis Castle'
Cestrum parqui
Lavandula angustifolia
Iris sibirica
Lilium regale
Polemonium caeruleum
Abutilon × suntense
Yellow Iris
Clematis 'Bill Mackenzie'
Ceanothus 'Puget Blue'
Agapanthus africanus
Salvia sclarea turkestanica
Perovskia atriplicifolia
Rosa 'Helen Knight'
Coronilla glauca
Yellow hollyhocks
Coreopsis 'Moonbeam'
Yellow Tulips
Lilium regale
Nicotiana glauca
Salvia patens
Choisya ternata
Ceratostigma plumbaginoides
Clematis montana
Rosmarinus officinalis
Corydalis cheilanthifolia
Polystichum setiferum acutilobum
Corydalis lutea
Lavandula 'Hidcote'
Clematis montana
Verbena bonariensis
Polystichum setiferum
Corylopsis pauciflora

Ceanothus 'Puget Blue'

Polemonium caeruleum

Agapanthus africanus

Coronilla valentina ssp. *glauca*

Nicotiana glauca

Flowers through the Seasons

Groups of biennial Salvia sclarea var. turkestanica *in the Eagle Court have their stems tied together for support. This unconventional method of staking also works for tall crambes and verbascums.*

In the north-facing shady bed next to the lane, spring flowering opens with the cream or dusky purple flowers of massed Lenten hellebores (*Helleborus orientalis* of gardens) and the creamish-green flower cups and toothed leaves of the Corsican hellebore (*H. argutifolius*), below the still leafless crab apple and cherry. The hellebores start to flower early, the first blooms opening in bleak February periods, just as *Mahonia japonica* sheds its yellow racemes after weeks of scenting this part of the garden. They are at their most floriferous in mid-March.

By April the edging elephant's ears, *Bergenia* 'Silberlicht', produces almost white flowers. Overhead the best of all cherries, *Prunus* 'Ukon', with yellowish-green double flowers in April, is succeeded by the tea crab apple, *Malus hupehensis*, with scented white flowers opening from soft pink buds. Clematis (*Clematis* 'Bees' Jubilee' is an early flowerer, with *C.* 'Perle d'Azur' towards the end of summer) clamber through its canopy and twine in the

Species and cultivars of shrubby philadelphus scent the garden in midsummer. Philadelphus *'Belle Etoile', here in full blossom, grows in the half-shaded north-facing border above hellebores, perennial honesty and late-flowering asters.*

rambling June-flowering rose 'Albertine' and over the wall. There are many other possible flowering combinations between roses and clematis, and their habits and flowering periods make them especially suitable companions in gardens of any size. We added an unusual climber, *Schisandra chinensis*: it has pinkish-white flowers in early spring but, lacking a mate, does not produce fruit. All these scrambling plants perform much better and look tidier if helped by gentle teasing and tying-in. It is not enough to cut them back according to a rule book. Lower down, the perennial honesty, *Lunaria rediviva*, is one of the earliest perennials to flower, taking over from the Lenten and Corsican hellebores. It is a prolific seeder.

The larger wall shrubs are mostly spring-flowering. The white flowers of *Choisya ternata* appear in April, at around the same time as the flowers of *Clematis montana* and the primrose-yellow bells of *Corylopsis pauciflora*.

June-flowering *Philadelphus* 'Belle Etoile', with wide creamy flower petals, maroon-flushed at the base, is one of the best of the mock oranges. It grows happily in shade beside the oak-leaved *Hydrangea quercifolia*, the leaves of which colour sombrely in autumn. There is no space available in this bed for July flowers but by the end of August white-flowered starry wood asters (*Aster divaricatus*), with wiry black stems, flop over the edging of bergenias. We took this scheme straight from an illustration in one of Gertrude Jekyll's books (*Colour Schemes for the Flower Garden*).

In the south-facing border opposite, mauve-flowered *Abutilon* × *suntense* and *A. vitifolium* grow as pyramids between blue ceanothus (*Ceanothus* 'Puget Blue' and *C.* 'Cascade'), which are layered and tied back to give a flatter contrasting effect. When young these ceanothus are given winter protection with curtains of nylon net. They flower in spring, at the same time as the abutilons.

Beneath the shrubs, groups of yellow tulips – originally the scented 'Mrs Moon' but more recently, as these bulbs became

After flowering begins, the green twine is wrapped around the individual woody stems and zigzagged across to make an almost invisible cat's cradle.

difficult to obtain, the more vibrant-hued 'West Point' – are interplanted with clumps of June-flowering iris – an unidentified German type with lemon-coloured flowers – and hardy agapanthus, their blue flowers covering any possible August gap. Siberian iris with strong upright stems and leaves make architectural groups which when in flower extend the blue theme.

Although all this works quite well, the planting schemes in this border easily get out of hand and become a tangle of climbers and shrubs which spread out to weaken the growth and flowering performance of bulbs and low-growing perennials. The planting needs constant readjustment. Over the years, instead of tackling it as a whole, we have retained existing plants and added some for quick effects without allowing adequate space, bolstering up the scheme with late-flowering annuals in the prescribed blues and yellows. Probably the real problem lies in trying to imitate someone else's scheme without having exact plans or plant lists.

If it were my decision I would probably redesign the border adhering to the idea of blue and yellow but sharpening the colour effects with silvery leaves. I might well adjust the planting to include only shrubs and climbers for spring effects – ceanothus, abutilon, coronilla, corylopsis and choisya (for foliage as well as for its scented white flowers), with cream and yellow lilies and annuals, grown from seed and from cuttings from tender plants, contributing much of the summer colour. I would omit all perennials. This sounds labour-intensive, but it is the sort of gardening I enjoy and can do well. The blues and yellows would cover a broad spectrum from blueish-mauve to violet and from cream to purest primrose-yellow. Bulbs would allow me to bolster early-summer effects with masses of globular-headed mauve alliums to flower after the yellow tulips, followed in succession by blue brodiaeas, golden lilies (*Lilium* Golden Splendor) and regale lilies (both *L. regale* and *L.r.* Album Group), and separated by the strong clumps of existing agapanthus. The aspect

Biennial Salvia sclarea *var.* turkestanica *flourishes near* Lilium regale *Album Group in the south-facing border. Ideally this salvia, when it has finished flowering, could be replaced by pots of late-flowering bulbs – perhaps acidanthera (*Gladiolus callianthus*) or Galtonia candicans, the summer hyacinth.*

suits sun-loving blue-flowering salvias (*Salvia patens, S. cacaliifolia* and *S. guaranitica*), among the best and brightest summer blues. Annuals would include yellow and lime-green tobacco plants (*Nicotiana langsdorffii* and *N.* 'Lime Green'). To set all these off I would have the silvery *Artemisia arborescens* 'Faith Raven', its filigree leaf shapes shimmering near the back with *Senecio viravira*, and plant *Artemisia* 'Powis Castle' or *Lotus hirsutus* along the front.

For a border I designed near a swimming pool in the gardens at Royaumont in the Ile-de-France, I was asked to use mainly blue and grey plants. I included very little green foliage but concentrated on giving bulk and depth with grey-leaved shrubs. With more space at my disposal, I was also able to plant a background hedge of silvery sea buckthorn (*Hippophaë rhamnoides*).

To return to the Eagle Court at Tintinhull: in the corner between the north and west walls, the fast-growing *Solanum crispum* 'Glasnevin' is rampant and produces its blue flowers through most of the summer months. By mid-June the bush rose 'Peace', one of Mrs Reiss's favourites, is in bloom in the west border. It will flower again in September.

A planting of a few summers ago, in the south-facing border of the Eagle Court. The grey leaves of English lavender and glaucous euphorbia leaves provide a foil for yellow and blue flowers. The lavender flowers coincide with blue agapanthus to complement Argyranthemum *'Jamaica Primrose'.*

In snug beds at the base of the house wall, Algerian iris, *Iris unguicularis,* flowers in warm spells in winter, between clumps of *Corydalis lutea* and ceratostigma; small starry ipheons spread in the cracks between the stone flags. Climbing roses (the apricot 'Climbing Lady Hillingdon' and dark red scented 'Guinée'), intertwined with clematis (*Clematis viticella, C.v.* 'Purpurea Plena Elegans' and *C. campaniflora*) and *Schizophragma integrifolium* are all trained on the lower part of the façade.

Near the house, on the narrow terrace separated from the lawn and outer borders by a low wall, large Italian-style pots (made with reconstituted Ham stone but mellow and lichen-covered with age) are planted simply with regale lilies to flower towards the end of June. Other containers here are for seasonal displays; arrangements are changed at intervals through the summer and depend on back-up greenhouse work. On the steep steps leading down from the front door, in shade until early afternoon, there are pots of *Francoa sonchifolia,* the dark-flowered chocolate-scented *Cosmos atrosanguineus* and *Galactites* (thistles with elegant veined or variegated leaves). Twin pots against the wall contain hybrid bomareas trained to twine on bamboo canes. Kept in the greenhouse to get maximum heat until almost in flower, the green *Zinnia* 'Envy' is brought out for July and August. Below the wall a stiff ribbon edge of lavender (*Lavandula* 'Hidcote') is softened by self-seeding *Verbena bonariensis,* with flat mauve heads carried on tall square-shaped stems in August and September. Sprawling bushes of rosemary and seedlings of French lavender (*Lavandula stoechas*) frame the terrace and pathway.

Although in the Eagle Court, especially in April and May, the characteristic colours of spring prevail – particularly blues and yellows – none is pure and bright in hue. They are pale or darker hues which fade gently away into mauve and cream shades and tints. Except for some orange crown imperials (*Fritillaria imperialis*), supplied in error for the pale yellow form some twelve years ago, there are no colours from the warmer segment of the spectrum. Instead strong accents are provided by plant shapes and good foliage, which extend through all the seasons. Greens and greys and the shapes and densities they convey are most important in this garden. Pure undiluted primary colours seldom look effective placed together and I prefer to separate cool colours from the warmer hues. This is a part of my general garden philosophy which was acquired, I think, both by reading Gertrude Jekyll's books and from looking after Mrs Reiss's garden.

The blue and silver border at Royaumont contains many of the same colour elements as the Eagle Court. Blue caryopteris and salvias are united by silvery artemisias. Hydrangea arborescens *produces pale globular heads in late summer, above a carpet of hosta leaves.*

Box and Yew Topiary

THE CLASSIC mushroom-like domes of clipped box (*Buxus sempervirens*) at Tintinhull are a very simple sort of topiary – so simple and severe that to topiary fans intent on complicated fanciful shapes they probably seem quite dull. They are intended, however, not as decorative adjuncts but rather as a deliberate part of the garden design. Clipped and groomed immaculately, and as architectural as the old brick walls and gateways, they frame the pathway and control perspective.

Inspired at Bettiscombe by Tintinhull themes, I have used English yew to create similar rhythmic effects. Two avenues of eight yews each – one inside the walled garden, the other outside – are being trained as pyramids. Although now only 2m/7ft tall, they will develop to 4.5m/15ft in height with at least a 1.8m/6ft square base. Together with the existing walls and grass, they are the most important elements in the design of the garden, linking front and back into an integrated space.

Topiary, defined today as the art of shaping trees and shrubs by clipping and training, has a long history. The word derives from the Greek *topia* meaning landscapes, refined in the Latin *topiaria opera*, used by Pliny the Elder to indicate any kind of ornamental gardening; Pliny attributed the invention of tree-clipping to Matius at the end of the first century BC. References to the clipping and shaping of cypress, ivy and box in both Cicero's and Pliny the Younger's letters – the latter had his gardener's name outlined in box – indicate a strong interest in sculptural forms and definition in early gardening. Although little is recorded of any topiary practices in medieval Europe, there was a dramatic revival of interest from the fifteenth century on. In the famous Rucellai garden in Florence, created in the second half of the fifteenth century, evergreen shrubs were trained on withy (willow) frames into 'spheres, porticoes, temples, vases, urns, apes, donkeys, oxen, a bear, giants, men, women'. In the accounts for Hampton Court there exist bills for the withy materials on which plants – evergreen and deciduous – were trained. These date to the middle of the sixteenth century, and the resulting topiary is described by a visiting German in 1599.

In his essay 'Of Gardens' (1625) the eminent English philosopher and essayist Francis Bacon stated his preference for simple shapes such as 'little low hedges round like welts, with some pretty pyramids ... and in some places fair columns' – this in a century which saw almost every known small tree or shrub being ruthlessly tortured into elaborate, often frivolous, topiary shapes. At this period the 'ordering' of trees and shrubs into alleys and shapes was far more important – at least in the French and Dutch schools of gardening – than growing flowers. The inspiration for much modern topiary derives from shapes created in the seventeenth century.

For the edging to the beds in the Herb Garden at the New York Botanical Garden in the Bronx, I chose a hardy Japanese box cultivar, Buxus microphylla 'Winter Gem', which survives both harsh winter temperatures and hot summers. Clipped at intervals throughout the summer – in the heat of New York it grows fast – the knot retains its neat geometric shape.

Left: *We find that the simplest way to trim the box domes is to start by cutting a wide strip from the bottom to the top, to act as a marker. Tarpaulin sheets laid around the bush catch the clippings.*

Right: *Once the marking strip has been cut, it is fairly easy to trim neatly all around the bush. We only remove the young growth, usually about 5cm/2in, made since the previous year's annual trim. Clipping should be tightest around any gaps, as this will stimulate new growth.*

Like Francis Bacon, I prefer simple strung-out lines rather than whimsical features – perhaps because subconsciously I associate the more fanciful peacocks or rabbits with an alarming amount of fiddly work. I find the traditional evergreens such as box, yew, phillyrea and holly the best suited to topiary. I like topiary used as architecture and positively dislike shapes which have no relationship with house or garden. I admire topiary collections, as at Levens in Cumbria or Ladew in Maryland, and love the topiary kings and queens at Haseley Court in Oxfordshire.

Aspiring topiarists should remember the time element. The simplest sort of clipping, such as that of the Tintinhull domes, takes many years to develop to its required architectural form and scale. The domes, now 1.5m/5ft high and the same across at the bottom, have been there since the 1920s. They were almost certainly obtained already shaped and probably 60–75cm/2–2½ft in height; small bushes would have looked ridiculously out of scale with the house, brick walls and stone eagles. Nurseries for ready-made topiaries have probably existed whenever topiary has been fashionable. The famous topiary shapes in yew and box that once ornamented the garden at Compton Wynyates in Warwickshire were installed in 1895, a product of the late-Victorian cult of period revivalism, planted to convey an 'antique' atmosphere and link the Tudor house with its past. We know that the pieces were obtained ready-made, mainly from the nursery of the aptly named Herbert J. Cutbush of Highgate and from Joseph Cheal of Crawley, who also provided plants at Hever Castle for the labyrinth and golden chessmen in that contemporary garden.

Of course it is easiest, if expensive, to buy plants ready-trained from a specialist. But much of the pleasure of the effect lies in its creation: ideally, plants to be made into new topiary shapes should be obtained some years earlier and trained in a nursery situation. Rounded shapes are much easier to cut and control than those with right angles and square edges. Pyramids and battlements cut in a hedge need a fine degree of precision in cutting. The lines should be marked with strings first. For arches, spheres and niches and for the fanciful shapes – peacocks, hens, animals, chessmen – it is advisable to have frames on which the plants are trained. Light iron or willow are both suitable but, of course, the iron will last longer. In some cases the frame itself will be attractive during the formative years. For the most complicated shapes more than one plant will be necessary. Judiciously chosen young shoots are trained and tied to the frame; others are clipped back. Strong outward-growing shoots must be tied in at an early stage or may have to be removed altogether. The more the plant is cut the more natural 'breaks' will occur, with more than one young shoot taking the place of each one that is cut. Old-fashioned shears or good pruners and a small saw are better tools for topiary than machine-driven hedge-cutters, as many of the shoots must be cut off individually.

Once formed, topiary is not a lot of work but immaculate grooming is essential. Clipping of established shapes is of course much easier than clipping to make new ones. At Tintinhull the annual clipping, usually completed in June, is done by eye; over the years, however, not all eyes have judged accurately and some domes are more pudding-shaped than others. Perhaps, to ensure uniformity, we should make a standard portable frame in laths or willow which would fit exactly over each dome the whole operation takes two days. In spring, as growth begins, the bushes are given an artificial fertilizer – an all-rounder with lots of nitrogen – and a top-dressing of compost. Apart from this no other attention is required – except, perhaps, after snowfalls, when it is important to knock the heavy snow off with some sort of light switch, or even with your hands.

One of the pleasures of topiary lies in the reflection of light from differently angled surfaces in sun and shadow. Then, in spring fresh green growth contrasts with the older darker green leaves; contrasts experienced again a few weeks after the annual cut. This is especially true of box and yew, which are pre-eminent for more detailed topiary, although forms of holly and phillyrea, recommended in 1629 by John Parkinson, can look particularly appropriate in a garden in a seventeenth-century style.

The trimming of the first dome has been completed and the bush looks very fresh and tidy. Within a week of clipping the leaves turn brown, but after another few weeks the bushes are beautiful again, with a rush of pale new foliage.

during clipping. We cut back all of the year's growth to keep the domes the same size, but if you need to reduce size or to correct any asymmetry you can be much more ruthless. If you want to encourage an increase in size you should clip twice during the summer, removing half the new growth each time. In climates with hotter summers, such as most areas of the United States, ordinary *Buxus sempervirens* puts on so much mounded growth that it is almost impossible to keep it as trim as we manage in the British Isles. In the famous boxwood gardens of Virginia mature box bushes are allowed to develop their own sprawling shapes.

After they have been cut our bushes are fed with a dried organic fertilizer, scattered by hand to make sure it reaches the base of each plant. There are sixteen box plants and

A Passion for Hellebores

HELLEBORES COULD become a grand passion. Their flowers – in most forms actually sepals – come in a wide range of muted colours: creamy-blushed purples, plum, pink, primrose-yellows, greens and mysterious blue-black, many with delicate spotting on the inside. Individually beautiful, their flowering in midwinter and spring makes them particularly precious and welcome. And they are not only flowerers. Their green foliage, deeply divided like the fingers of a hand and in some cases evergreen, is almost as desirable as the flowers and makes them attractive in the garden throughout the year.

Hellebores are generally good companion plants and, liking shade (although tolerant of sun), can be placed in corners where many other plants would not thrive – under the outer rims of the canopies of deciduous trees and shrubs, for example. Any ordinary well-drained fertile soil will do for most hellebores. All benefit from dressing with rich compost, and a dark mulch added just before flowering helps to set off the blooms as well as conditioning the soil and improving fertility. They do need periodic grooming: dead or blemished leaves should be removed in early spring, to show off the flowers at their best, and again in summer; the stems of the taller varieties, such as *Helleborus argutifolius* and *H. foetidus*, can be unobtrusively staked.

Most of us, unless already hellebore specialists, will start by growing those that are easiest and grow quickest; these include the Lenten hellebores (*H. orientalis* of gardens), the Corsican *H. argutifolius*, and the stinking hellebore, *H. foetidus*.

Everyone finds space for some of the Lenten hellebores, a range of hybrids based

Helleborus orientalis

Helleborus orientalis Ballard's Strain

On pages 46-7, left to right:
Helleborus orientalis
Helleborus foetidus
Helleborus argutifolius

Helleborus orientalis

Helleborus torquatus 'Pluto'

Helleborus × sternii

Helleborus lividus

on *H. orientalis* and often called simply Orientalis hybrids (botanically they are *H. × hybridus*). They are among the toughest of the group, well able to stand extremes of heat and cold. Their flowers are sculptured saucers in tints and shades between blush-white and plum, often spotted inside with crimson and maroon and subtly flushed with green. They seed freely, the seed germinating around the crown and some-times under the leaves of a mature clump.

The Lenten hellebores look good with appropriate spring companions such as snowdrops, erythroniums, epimediums and wood anemones, which all enjoy the same conditions. For summer effects shade-tolerant lilies such as the Turk's cap lily (*Lilium martagon*) and toad lilies (*Tricyrtis formosana*) can be planted between the hellebore clumps.

I could not be without the Corsican species *Helleborus argutifolius* – as handsome as a shrub and growing to over 1m/3ft in height and spread, with bold spiny grey-green leaves and clusters of green-cupped flowers. Grow it with similar Mediterranean hillside plants: shrubby euphorbias, rosemary, lavenders, brooms and cistus. Its more tender relative

H. lividus can be a wonderful pot plant, but needs winter protection. The hybrid of these two species, *H. × sternii*, has a distinctive pink blush to the back of its leaves.

H. foetidus – native all over Europe with the best forms coming from the south – has narrow finely fingered leaves and cylindri-cally shaped small pale green flowers, each with a reddish band at the tip. Forms of it grow to 1.2m/4ft. It has a wilder appearance than other hellebores and will thrive and flower in any rough corner, but repays extra attention and sprucing up for a more visible flower bed.

I have never been charmed by the Christmas rose, *H. niger*, or any of its forms or hybrids. I do not want large white flowers, much preferring the grace and subtle interest of the green hellebores. I would like to have again some of the green-flowered subspecies of *H. multifidus*. Many years ago I treasured *H.m.* ssp. *bocconei* from central Italy. I recommend a collection of 'greens' in which I would include this, along with *H. viridis* – a British native – and forms of the sought-after *H. torquatus* from Serbia, with sepals dusky purple outside and green-coloured inside.

Euphorbias in the Garden

WITH THEIR handsome foliage and elegant habit, euphorbias or spurges are among the most diverse and useful of garden plants. The grandest are feature plants in their own right, while lower-growing species and hybrids play a humbler role, enhancing the effect of more striking neighbours. Some are shrubby plants, others perennial clump-formers or stoloniferous spreaders. Most prefer full sun and good drainage, thriving in Mediterranean conditions, but others, especially the wood spurge, *Euphorbia amygdaloides*, and its variants, enjoy dappled shade. All are tap-rooted and, grown from seed or cuttings, should be transplanted in their early stages before the roots become pot-bound – a common cause of failure.

Among the most handsome of the sun-lovers is the shrubby *E. characias*. This bold evergreen with narrow greyish leaves makes a graceful shape 1.2 m/4 ft high and across. It

Above: *Euphorbia characias* ssp. *wulfenii* 'John Tomlinson'

Right: *Euphorbia griffithii* 'Fireglow'

Below: *Euphorbia mellifera*

bears fine yellow flowers (or rather, strictly speaking, bracts) with deep brownish-purple centres for two months each spring. A short-lived species, it is a natural infiller, seeding between paving stones and in dry walls. The best forms are cultivars of *E.c. wulfenii*, such as 'Lambrook Gold' (originally found by Margery Fish in her garden at East Lambrook) and 'John Tomlinson'. The biennial stems produce clustered leaves in one year and flower spikes the next; the latter need cutting back as the flower head fades. Propagate these cultivars from cuttings of the young growth in spring or summer.

If you have a sheltered garden the tender *E. mellifera* from the Canary Islands deserves a place in full sun. Growing to 1.8m/6ft to make a rounded bush, it has beautiful velvet-textured veined green foliage and honey-scented pinkish-brown flower heads.

In contrast the evergreen species *E. myrsinites* from southern Europe and Asia Minor only grows to 20cm/8in; it has trailing stems with pointed glaucous fleshy leaves and, in early spring, bright lime-green terminal inflorescences, which assume a pinkish tint as they fade. This euphorbia likes very well-drained soil: grow it over a low wall or in a tub, perhaps beside blue-flowered *Scilla bifolia*, a plant of the same native habitat. Even more attractive is the taller *E. rigida* (*E. biglandulosa*), with spiralling leaves clasping the stems and bright yellow flowers.

From the eastern Himalaya comes *E. griffithii*: its cultivars *E.g.* 'Fireglow' and 'Dixter' have brick-red and orange flowers respectively, carried over greenish-orange foliage. Enjoying any good soil in sun or part shade, the spreading roots quickly establish to make substantial groups. Another Asiatic spurge, *E. sikkimensis*, does best in moist soil. Its translucent red leaves with white veins are startling as they rise through the soil in spring; much later in the season flower heads on spaced willowy stems are flat and greenish-yellow. We grow it pushing through a blue pulmonaria.

Forms of the spring-flowering woodland spurge *E. amygdaloides* are more muted in appearance. They are companion plants rather than striking on their own. *E.a.* var. *robbiae*, an almost evergreen colonizer with broad darkest green rosettes and yellowish-green spring flowers, is an admirable groundcover plant to lighten a dark corner.

The small feathery *E. cyparissias*, although disappearing in winter, is another groundcover plant; however, it does not like to be shaded by overhead plants. It runs freely but if controlled is most appealing, making a carpet of lacy lime-green stems in early summer. Its woodland cousins *E. dulcis* and *E. stricta* are almost weeds but very desirable for their rich autumn colouring. Allowed to weave and seed around shrubs and perennials they make a fine cover for awkward areas of bare soil.

Right: *It is important to wear gloves, and to work with care, when deadheading the large woody euphorbias (varieties of* Euphorbia characias *and* E.c. *ssp.* wulfenii *cultivars), as the lactose glue which oozes out from a cut stem can produce a skin rash or damage the eyes. Leaving a few flowers – those which show least – to set seed, I cut off most of the long-stemmed flower heads as near to the base of the plant as I can reach.*

In the Middle Garden, running from sunlight into the shadow of the evergreen oaks and between the two outer borders with their casual planting, the central pathway and box domes play a major role in holding the design together. A view from the attic windows reveals the pattern of symmetrically arranged golden foliage plants in the Fountain Garden beyond.

A woodland garden
Drought-tolerant planting
Seasonal performance
Encouraging self-seeders
Anemones for spring and autumn
Elegant hydrangeas

The Middle Garden

MUCH LESS CAREFULLY arranged than the Eagle Court, the Middle Garden has a more natural 'woodland' style, with less obvious architectural planting and a less immediately identifiable colour scheme. But although planting seems haphazard, with single small specimen trees and shrubs of different heights, there is still essential balance and symmetry. The design is held together by some strong features, such as the repetition of the pattern of clipped domes of box flanking the axial stone pathway that continues to the western end of the garden. The taller bushy planting is linked on the horizontal level with massed groundcover. Except for the central pathway, all the horizontal patterns formed by grass and groundcover plants curve rather than making right-angled bends. Curving flower beds enfold a central lawn, the lawn panels becoming a well of light in the midst of thick planting. On the north side, a narrow grass pathway, framed by upright junipers, reveals the rectangular canal in the Pool Garden and allows access. The vista in reverse, from the Pool Garden summerhouse down the canal into the Middle Garden, is centred on a replica of an eighteenth-century urn, set on a plinth against the south wall.

The planting is dominated by two tall evergreen oaks (*Quercus ilex*) on the south-west corner. While creating a wide pocket of dense dry shade (their roots extend well beyond their overhead canopies), these leafy trees effectively screen noise and movement from the neighbouring village lane and, of course, frame the sky. Smaller trees combined with large shrubs accentuate the perimeter planting along the outer wall and make a division between the Middle Garden and the Fountain Garden to the west and the colourful Pool Garden on the north. Smaller shrubs, graceful mauve- and pink-flowered shrub roses and other woody plants, carry the garden through all the seasons, a plant theme allowing a certain amount of licence in replacement and improvement.

At first glance there may seem to be no distinctive scheme or guidelines; there are no strongly shaped plant blocks and the effects

A reproduction of the eighteenth-century Kent's Urn is framed by the flowers and leaves of the woodland plants along the south border in the Middle Garden. By late summer pink Japanese anemones, well established between hydrangeas, provide the main flowering interest in beds which in spring are carpeted with woodland anemones and erythroniums. Heathers supply winter colour.

achieved are pictorial rather than architectural: a composition of light and shade, openness and density, with touches of balancing colour, shades and hues dominated by pinks and mauves. Partly because there are fewer fixed rules, but also because each plant becomes part of the overall scheme rather than having much individual importance, we have found this area the easiest to restore to the character intended by Mrs Reiss. If we add new plants they are immediately integrated rather than remaining obvious additions. The point about this garden is that the framework, although firmly present, is unobtrusive. It is disguised by naturalness in planting. I find it sets a theme for a relaxed sort of planting which often proves more suitable for implementation in a client's garden than more formal hedged schemes or geometric patterns.

Natural planting, done by eye and whenever possible implemented on site rather than from a blueprint, is far more difficult than laying out formal patterns to a rule book. Much of my design work is superimposed on an existing garden layout; occasionally it has to be integrated into awkward sloping terrain with existing trees. Few clients want a garden even as formal as Tintinhull. American garden owners, especially, want a style that fits into their native, often thickly wooded, landscape. In a garden I designed in Austin, Texas, giant live oaks (*Quercus virginiana* – the American south's equivalent to the holm oak, *Quercus ilex*) are dominant features. Curving drives, pathways and beds are all related to the oak canopies which frame the sky and, with their roots, control the ground area which can reasonably be planted. Lawn walks alternately widen and narrow to make pools of light between the groves of dark oak; shrubs, undercarpeted with smaller plants, integrate a naturalistic pattern, very much in the same style as the Middle Garden at Tintinhull, though on a much larger scale.

Mrs Reiss also had clear-cut practical objectives, the most important of which was to ensure that this part of the garden would be screened from the adjacent Pool Garden by thick perimeter planting. She chose to do this with mixed shrubby planting, rather than by emphasizing the edges with a line of trees or hedging plants. Until 1947 the Pool Garden was a tennis court and this planting may have been left over from those days. A rigid row of screening trees or large shrubs would have drawn attention to a court and accentuated its straight netting. Mrs Reiss knew that thick planting of high and low shrubs mixed together would make a much more effective visual barrier.

Erythronium revolutum

Urn

Clematis armandii

Hydrangea aspera Villosa

Hydrangea aspera sargentiana

Hedera helix 'Conglomerata'

Galium odoratum

Spiraea japonica 'Anthony Waterer'

Hydrangea paniculata 'Praecox'

Prunus 'Ukon'

Polygonatum × hybridum

Hydrangea arborescens

Anemone × hybrida

Berberis vulgaris 'Atropurpurea'

Erythronium dens-canis,
Erythronium 'White Beauty',
Erythronium revolutum and
ferns in drifts

Anemone nemorosa,
A. apennina
A. ranunculoides
and A. × hybrida -
in drifts

Clematis 'Niobe'

Ferns

Erythroniums

Clematis × jouiniana

Hemerocallis fulva 'Flore Pleno'

Self-seeders
Anemone apennina
Cyclamen repandum
Daphne mezereum & D.m alba
Digitalis lutea & D. purpurea
Geranium maderense
Helleborus orientalis
Hesperis matronalis
Lunaria annua
Oenothera biennis
Scilla siberica

N

Clematis × jouiniana

Erythronium dens-canis

Geranium palmatum

Erythronium 'White Beauty'

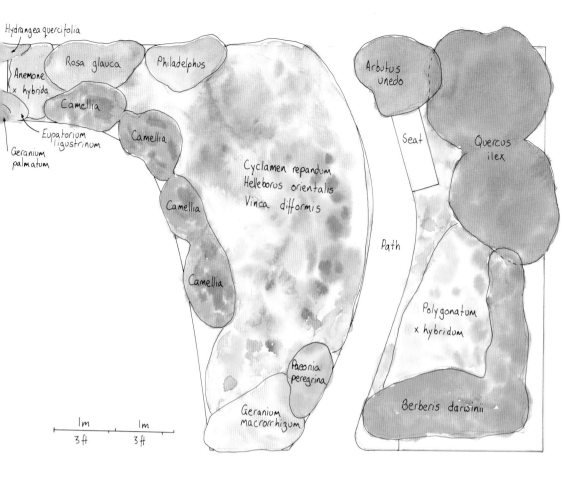

Hydrangea quercifolia

Rosa glauca

Philadelphus

Anemone
× hybrida

Camellia

Eupatorium
ligustrinum

Camellia

Geranium
palmatum

Camellia

Cyclamen repandum
Helleborus orientalis
Vinca difformis

Camellia

Arbutus
unedo

Seat

Quercus
ilex

Path

Polygonatum
× hybridum

Camellia

Paeonia
peregrina

Geranium
macrorrhizum

Berberis darwinii

1m   1m
───   ───
3 ft   3 ft

Arbutus unedo

Scilla siberica

Vinca difformis

Paeonia peregrina

Polygonatum × hybridum

Bupleurum fruticosum

Buglossoides purpurocaerulea

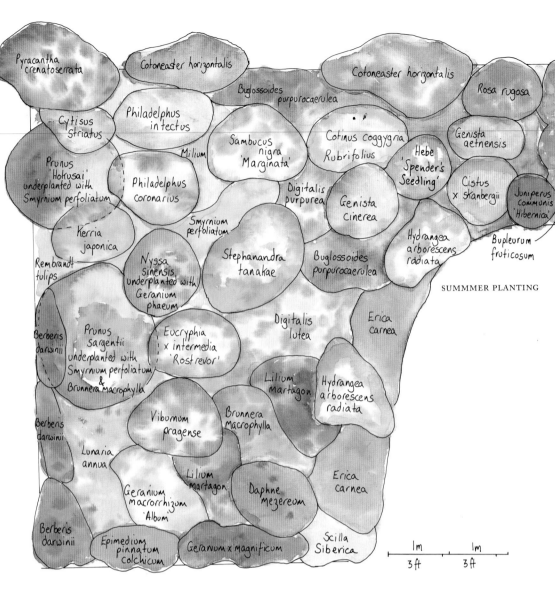

Pyracantha crenatoserrata

Cotoneaster horizontalis

Cotoneaster horizontalis

Buglossoides purpurocaerulea

Rosa rugosa

Cytisus striatus

Philadelphus intectus

Milium

Sambucus nigra 'Marginata'

Cotinus coggygria Rubrifolius

Hebe 'Spender's Seedling'

Genista aetnensis

Prunus 'Hokusai' underplanted with Smyrnium perfoliatum

Philadelphus coronarius

Digitalis purpurea

Genista cinerea

Cistus x skanbergii

Juniperus communis 'Hibernica'

Smyrnium perfoliatum

Kerria japonica

Nyssa sinensis underplanted with Geranium phaeum

Stephanandra tanakae

Buglossoides purpurocaerulea

Hydrangea arborescens radiata

Bupleurum fruticosum

Rembrandt tulips

SUMMMER PLANTING

Berberis darwinii

Prunus Sargentii underplanted with Smyrnium perfoliatum & Brunnera macrophylla

Eucryphia x intermedia 'Rostrevor'

Digitalis lutea

Erica carnea

Berberis darwinii

Lilium martagon

Hydrangea arborescens radiata

Viburnum pragense

Brunnera Macrophylla

Lunaria annua

Lilium martagon

Erica carnea

Berberis darwinii

Geranium macrorrhizum 'Album'

Daphne mezereum

Epimedium pinnatum colchicum

Geranium x magnificum

Scilla Siberica

1m / 3ft   1m / 3ft

Lilium martagon

Daphne mezereum

Geranium × magnificum

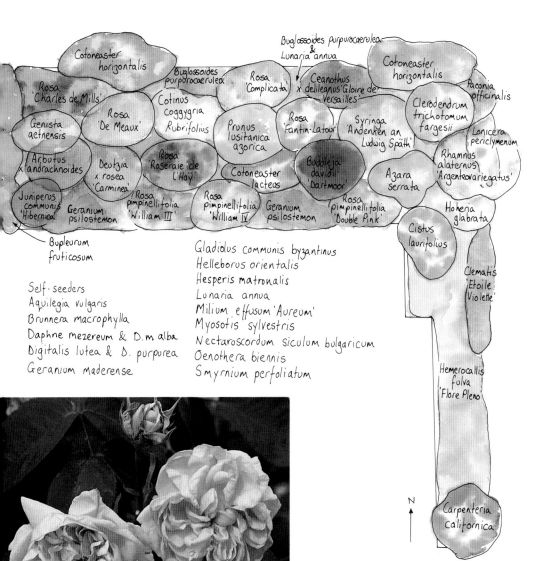

Cotoneaster horizontalis

Rosa 'Charles de Mills'

Buglossoides purpurocaerulea

Rosa 'Complicata'

Buglossoides purpurocaerulea & Lunaria annua

Ceanothus x delileanus 'Gloire de Versailles'

Cotoneaster horizontalis

Genista aetnensis

Rosa 'De Meaux'

Cotinus coggygria Rubrifolius

Rosa 'Fantin-Latour'

Prunus lusitanica azorica

Syringa 'Andenken an Ludwig Späth'

Clerodendrum trichotomum fargesii

Paeonia officinalis

Arbutus x andrachnoides

Deutzia x rosea 'Carminea'

Rosa 'Roseraie de l'Haÿ'

Cotoneaster lacteus

Buddleja davidii 'Dartmoor'

Azara serrata

Rhamnus alaternus 'Argenteovariegatus'

Lonicera periclymenum

Juniperus communis 'Hibernica'

Geranium psilostemon

Rosa pimpinellifolia 'William III'

Rosa pimpinellifolia 'William IV'

Geranium psilostemon

Rosa pimpinellifolia 'Double Pink'

Hoheria glabrata

Bupleurum fruticosum

Cistus laurifolius

Clematis 'Etoile Violette'

Self·seeders
Aquilegia vulgaris
Brunnera macrophylla
Daphne mezereum & D. m alba
Digitalis lutea & D. purpurea
Geranium maderense

Gladiolus communis byzantinus
Helleborus orientalis
Hesperis matronalis
Lunaria annua
Milium effusum 'Aureum'
Myosotis sylvestris
Nectaroscordum siculum bulgaricum
Oenothera biennis
Smyrnium perfoliatum

Hemerocallis fulva 'Flore Pleno'

N

Carpenteria californica

Azara serrata

Hoheria glabrata

Clematis 'Etoile Violette'

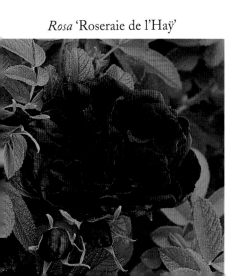

Rosa 'Fantin-Latour'

Rosa 'Roseraie de l'Haÿ'

Gladiolus communis ssp. *byzantinus* with *Geranium psilostemon*

Drought-tolerant Planting

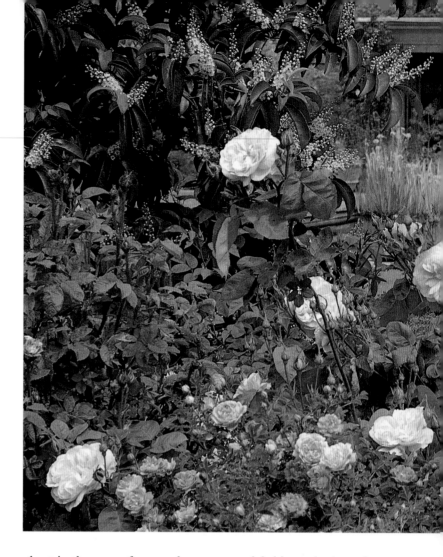

A gap in the screen of roses and evergreen and deciduous shrubs on the north side of the Middle Garden allows a glimpse through to the Pool Garden's central canal and the summerhouse.

Although at Tintinhull each compartment is linked by paths, carefully planned vistas and a repetition of planting, any individual section, when you are in it, remains almost totally hidden from adjacent areas. In 1980, our first summer at Tintinhull, it was four years after the severe drought of 1976. We found that many of the larger shrubs in the wide beds of the Middle Garden, those separating it from the Pool Garden to the north, had never fully recovered from the stress occasioned by lack of water and were gradually deteriorating. They no longer operated as a dense screen but left more open views and in many cases needed replacing. Our first task was, so far as possible, to save the old plants (this was achieved, to some extent, by hard pruning and feeding). We also wanted to introduce new shrubs – mainly bulky and evergreen with broad, rounded shapes rather than staccato verticals – to help provide a permanent and effective screen. With a projected pattern of hot summers to come, the intention was that these shrubs should be as drought-tolerant as possible, as well as being able to withstand freak cold winters.

We replaced much of the original planting and also added shrubs of our own choice. Among these, in the north-east bed in full sun, are Mediterranean-type evergreens, including a form of Portugal laurel from the Azores (*Prunus lusitanica* ssp. *azorica*) with golden-green foliage and the magnificent *Arbutus × andrachnoides* (a hybrid of the Greek *A. andrachne* and *A. unedo*), with peeling cinnamon-red bark. In a corner of this bed, sheltered from wind chill and turbulence, a tender evergreen, *Azara serrata* from Chile, with clusters of yellow stamen-like flowers in July, grows beside a replacement *Hoheria glabrata* from New Zealand, with cherry-like white blossom crowding the branches in the same month. Both will flower well in a year following a hot summer. Down the middle of the bed, part of a spine of taller shrubs, are an upright evergreen cotoneaster, the vigorous *Cotoneaster lacteus* we first admired as a tall hedge at Glasnevin in Dublin, with long-lasting clusters of red fruits, and the bushy *Rhamnus alaternus* 'Argenteovariegatus', its leaves marbled grey and cream. Bushes of the glaucous-leaved Mediterranean *Bupleurum fruticosum* now flank the pathway vista to the Pool Garden. This shrub needs an annual spring trim. It is a tedious task, to be done slowly with secateurs, but well worth the effort: the carefully sculpted rounded shapes look glorious in summer when the bushes produce their umbels of yellow flowers, turning to buff-gold as the seed ripens.

Some large shrub roses, such as *Rosa* 'Complicata', *R.* 'Fantin-Latour' and the Rugosa 'Roseraie de l'Haÿ' grow between the shrubs, along with the Gallica 'Charles de Mills' and Centifolia 'De Meaux'. The smaller suckering Scotch burnet roses (varieties of *R. pimpinellifolia*) which do so well at Tintinhull – 'Double Pink', white 'William IV' and magenta-flowered 'William III' – thrive along the southern edge of the bed. A pretty pink deutzia (*Deutzia × rosea* 'Carminea'), quite modest in size when we came in 1980 but possibly planted by Mrs Reiss, has grown to make a 2m/7ft spread. *Buddleja davidii* 'Dartmoor', with purple-crimson flowers, strikes a dark note.

In the north-west bed there had been less drought damage and new shrubs grew quickly to complement old plantings which have survived and are still healthy after forty years or so. Among the latter the more tender *O. armatus,* one of E.H. Wilson's introductions, with thick leaves edged with spiny teeth, very like a large holly, which flowers as summer ends. Although these osmanthus all come from the Far East, none of them looks at all exotic. These would be a start, together with *Phillyrea latifolia,* one of the finest small trees from the Mediterranean basin, with flickering finely toothed leaves, translucent when young, and a broad canopy. I have seen it in groves in its native habitat and it is spectacular at Hatfield House in Hertfordshire, where it grows along the courtyard balustrading. There are also exotic hollies, again from the Far East, among them *Ilex fargesii* and *I. latifolia.*

Along the northern edge of the Middle Garden are Mrs Reiss's fans of herringbone cotoneaster (*Cotoneaster horizontalis*), pruned to cascade and spread over the path beneath, with glorious autumn foliage and berries, one of her most successful ideas. Some people might scorn the use of such an ordinary plant in an important situation but it seems just right to me; I like to use it in my designs, draped against balustrading or a low wall. *C. microphyllus,* with smaller habit and leaves, can be used in a similar way.

The use of groundcover plants in this area is classical: both evergreen and deciduous shrubs make a layer of planting under the limbs of the small trees, while low-growing plants – shrubs and perennials – cover the ground and keep it moist in summer and suppress weed germination. Bulbs come mainly in spring, and other taller summer-flowering perennials and biennials find just enough bare earth to survive and flower beside denser carpeting plants.

Under the north-facing wall along the lane spring bulbs provide the predominant groundcover. Scillas and anemones, cyclamen and erythroniums are succeeded by scented woodruff (*Galium odoratum*). In the middle beds there are more perennials, especially blue-flowered *Buglossoides purpurocaerulea,* intermixed with other blues such as self-seeding forget-me-nots and *Brunnera macrophylla.* In the shadiest part in the north-west bed there are crane's-bill geraniums and, encouraged by us, self-seeding *Smyrnium perfoliatum* with lime-yellow bracts in spring. All of these knit together to make an effective barrier against weed germination.

The old favourite daylily *Hemerocallis fulva* 'Flore Pleno' is massed under the west-facing 'Eagle' walls, its young golden foliage emerging in late winter. *Cyclamen repandum,* Solomon's seal (*Polygonatum × hybridum*), Lenten hellebores and the white-starred winter-flowering periwinkle *Vinca difformis,* now mixed with a self-made blue form, spread happily in the dry soil under the deep shade of the evergreen oaks, where little else would flourish.

Throughout the whole of the Middle Garden, wherever there is space among the drifts of groundcovers, scented mauve and white mezereums (*Daphne mezereum* and *D.m.* f. *alba*) and sweet rocket are encouraged to seed casually, alongside many biennials such as evening primrose, honesty, foxgloves and *Geranium maderense.*

are broad-headed spring-flowering cherries, backed by a tough *Pyracantha crenatoserrata* that produces clouds of white in early summer, a tall variegated elder (*Sambucus nigra* 'Marginata') and a neighbouring philadelphus (*Philadelphus intectus*) which grows to 4m/13ft. The most successful additions have been a tough evergreen viburnum from Prague (*Viburnum* 'Pragense'), lime-tolerant *Eucryphia × intermedia* 'Rostrevor', brown-stemmed *Stephanandra tanakae* and a scattering of shrub roses.

If space permitted or if I were making a similar new bed I would probably use some more of my favourite evergreen shrubs for their foliage and general appearance. These were among my greatest interests when I was gardening at Hadspen House (also in Somerset), in the 1970s. I particularly enjoy the different Asiatic holly-like osmanthus, especially *Osmanthus heterophyllus* (including the variegated varieties), small-leaved *O. delavayi* (for its deliciously scented spring flowers) and dome-shaped dark-leaved *O. decorus.* All of these are hardy. I used to grow two Chinese species at Hadspen: *O. yunnanensis,* a fast-growing small tree or large shrub with olive-green leaves and tiny fragrant white flowers in late winter, and

Seasonal Performance

In a mild spell in January the white periwinkle starts to perform under the tall evergreen oaks. During the next two months seedling hellebores followed by the sweetly fragrant carmine-flowered *Cyclamen repandum* emerge through the periwinkle foliage, both plants continually colonizing any neighbouring pockets of bare earth under shrubs. Mrs Reiss had camellias here but these, suffering from neglect, were removed, to be replaced with unnamed red camellias taken as cuttings from a friend's garden in Italy. The original planting scheme, before the roots of the oaks had spread so far, also included some small rhododendrons, but these have succumbed to drought. The soil at Tintinhull is almost neutral, but conditions do not really suit ericaceous plants, and even the camellias require frequent doses of sequestrene.

By March spears of Solomon's seal appear nearer the boles of the trees. The evergreen *Berberis darwinii* from South America, planted as a hedge between the Middle Garden and the Fountain Garden, also flowers early, its yellow blooms replaced in midsummer with glowing turquoise fruits. The cherries, as planned by Phyllis Reiss, flower in an organized succession. Round-headed Sargent's cherry, *Prunus sargentii*, also renowned for the splendid autumn foliage effects rare in cherries, opens the season with single pink flowers; *P.* 'Hokusai' has large semi-double flowers a little later, and a more spreading habit. Beside the wall *P.* 'Ukon' is taller, with yellowish-green flowers. This tree and the specimen in Eagle Court have been badly damaged by birds who attack dormant buds in winter, leaving long straggly limbs without flower or leaf, and they should soon be replaced. Evergreen *Clematis armandii* clambers over the wall and into neighbouring shrubs, scenting the spring garden with its fragrant white flowers; it needs cutting back after flowering, a task easily neglected in the busiest time of early summer.

Under the wall native wood anemones (*Anemone nemorosa*) are massed to produce a spring carpet of white and green, while the ground-hugging yellow-flowered *A. ranunculoides* yearly increases its spread and escaped seedlings – distributed by birds – of blue-flowered *A. apennina* appear everywhere. *Cyclamen repandum* seeds freely here among clumps of Solomon's seal and crowns of creeping scented woodruff. This 'natural' planting is given more formality with blocks of erythroniums, their shining leaves making focal points even before the flowers open their nodding heads in late spring. We grow white *Erythronium* 'White Beauty' and the yellow form of the species, *E. revolutum* from Californian woodlands, as

well as *E. dens-canis,* the native European dog's-tooth violet, known as the trout or fawn lily in the United States, and much loved for its glaucous spotted leaves and violet-pink swept-back flower petals. Corms need time to establish and should be left undisturbed. As flowering ends the leaves begin to die down and by midsummer they are cleared away to leave an empty space in the garden scheme. I have found that ferns, which emerge relatively late in spring, can be grown successively between the erythronium corms without inhibiting their vigour.

In the north-west bed a kerria – the single-flowered *Kerria japonica* – and a tall *Genista cinerea* flower early. Both survive well in this dry area, as does the interesting *Smyrnium perfoliatum* from central Asia. Beneath are three shade-tolerant groundhuggers, all members of the Boraginaceae family. *Brunnera macrophylla*, with forget-me-not-like flowers, rapidly increases by annual self-seeding. *Buglossoides purpurocaerulea* has arching tip-rooting stems, capable of colonizing any area very rapidly. These two combine with ordinary biennial forget-me-nots to make swirling blue patterns under the yellow-flowered shrubs and the smyrniums with their acid-yellow bracts. The smyrniums and forget-me-nots are pulled out as soon as the seed is ripe and dispersed. The long questing fronds of the buglossoides (perhaps still more easily recognized by its old name of lithospermum) need cutting back by mid- to late summer or they will almost strangle some of the plants. In a small garden – or even here – the less vigorous form of brunnera, *Brunnera macrophylla* 'Hadspen Cream', with leaves delicately splashed with white, could be an alternative, or the more elegant and slightly earlier-flowering *Pulmonaria angustifolia*, or a bugle, *Ajuga reptans*.

In early summer, in the north-east bed, the tall old lilac (*Syringa vulgaris* 'Andenken an Ludwig Späth') chosen by Mrs Reiss has dark violet flowers and twiggy burnet roses have pink, white and magenta clustered flowers. By full summer mauve and pale pink shrub roses with scented white-flowered philadelphus and the one floriferous pink deutzia dominate the main beds. Crane's-bill geraniums make good companions, their mainly pale colouring matching the gentle hues of the roses. They have a long flowering season and stretch back in drifts under the shade of the earlier-flowering cherries and towards the big evergreen oaks. The most striking is the tall *Geranium psilostemon*, with magenta petals and a black eye, sited in full sun. All of these hardy geraniums have to be cut back to the ground after flowering; they will then produce fresh new foliage to

Above left: *The scented flowers of* Cyclamen repandum *are pinkish-carmine. Reputedly tender, it thrives at Tintinhull.*

Above right: *The native wood anemone* (Anemone nemorosa) *flowers with* Cyclamen repandum *in the shaded south border.*

improve the beds' late-summer appearance, and occasionally some more flowers as well.

Throughout this area colour schemes are seasonal, almost monthly 'episodes' rather than all-over themes; spring yellows precede dark purples and pinks, then come swathes of blue ground carpeting, then pinks and mysterious purples from old roses, followed by the dark-flowered *Buddleja davidii* 'Dartmoor' and pink- and white-flowered hydrangeas. I really prefer this sort of colour planning to the more self-conscious arrangements in other Tintinhull beds. I enjoy the monthly variations.

Some of the roses flower again, if briefly, but during the rest of the summer and autumn most of the flower and leaf interest of the central beds is located on the northern side, facing the Pool Garden. This show accompanies the main peak of the Pool Garden borders,

which is in July and August, and is more strictly colour orientated. In the north-west bed the golden Mount Etna broom (*Genista aetnensis*) is startling near a purple-bronze-leaved smoke bush (*Cotinus coggygria* Rubrifolius Group); pale evening primroses (*Oenothera biennis*) glow at dusk to link the colour scheme with the red and yellow border in the Pool Garden. The blue-flowered deciduous *Ceanothus × delileanus* 'Gloire de Versailles' correspondingly links the north-east bed with the pale-coloured Pool border. A new *Clerodendrum trichotomum* var. *fargesii* has fragrant white flowers enclosed in maroon-purple calyces. Later the flowers become turquoise-blue berries, still surrounded by the colourful calyces, resplendent for the autumn scene.

Along the outer wall bed, hydrangeas are grouped together in the light shade to give a solid impact as they flower in late summer above the ferns, Solomon's seal and ground-hugging scented woodruff. They include *Hydrangea aspera* Villosa Group, *H. arborescens*, *H. paniculata* 'Praecox', *H. quercifolia* and the velvet-leaved *H. aspera* ssp. *sargentiana*. The most drought-tolerant and most effective in flower is *H.a.* Villosa Group, but its new growth and flower buds are especially vulnerable to late spring frosts. At Tintinhull a young plant needs protecting in its first seasons.

Encouraging Self-seeders

Aquilegia vulgaris with *Rosa* 'Rosemary Rose'

Gladiolus communis ssp. *byzantinus*

I FIND THAT a practical approach to managing mixed borders, in which every iota of soil should be covered by plants, is to encourage proliferation of self-sown seedlings. They will extend the theme adopted for any one area, fill every empty space and, allowed to flower in season where they germinate, give the attractive and seemingly unplanned natural look that I am always seeking.

At Tintinhull we use this self-seeding method throughout the garden, in the formal colour borders as well as in the more natural-style beds in the Middle Garden. We do, however, limit the numbers of different plants in each area, believing that it is more effective to have an abundance of any one kind rather than just a few examples of a great variety. In most areas we have distinctive, easily recognizable colour schemes, so the seeders are chosen to augment and enrich these schemes.

This method of gardening fits perfectly into my garden philosophy. It sounds labour-saving and up to a point it is, but I have not adopted it to save time or work; it is done for effect. It does require a certain amount of skill and effort, particularly in weeding, for, to the uninitiated, many of these young seedlings look just like weeds. Maintenance depends on an observant eye and a controlling hand, or the garden will look a mess by midsummer and deteriorate even more in the following months.

Instead of being trimmed back in an orderly manner after flowering, as part of normal garden routine, at least a proportion of the desirable seeders must be allowed to set and disperse seed as flowering finishes. It is sufficient to keep just a few specimens of each plant for this purpose; you can also, of course, gather and scatter the seed. If space permits, the well-organized gardener can even grow examples of self-seeders in a nursery area, allowing them to set seed there, then gathering it and scattering it where required.

I like to have strong woody plants in all borders: these establish a skeleton structure. They are placed with great care, their architectural role and contribution to the whole scheme without question. Around them are arranged the more permanent perennials. In the main borders at Tintinhull shrubs and perennials occupy 90 per cent of the space. In the Middle Garden and other more natural-looking areas there are more shrubs but perennials have less emphasis. Instead, self-seeding biennials and annuals play a major role. As the shrubs become established, probably in the second year after planning a scheme, other plants – mainly biennials and annuals but also some perennials – are encouraged to seed, to fill in the background around the shrub shapes. Unlike quick-growing bedding annuals, designed for massed effects in full sun, most of these plants do not need a richly prepared soil, but will look after themselves and flourish in poor conditions. They germinate wherever there is light and space. They colonize unlikely corners and spread in dappled shade. Though their beauty is often fleeting, they give an established air to a garden.

In all areas I use both tall plants and those which have more of a groundcover weed-suppressing role. In light shade smyrniums, foxgloves, evening primroses and lythrums give the required height; in sun verbascums, opium poppies, silver thistles, Miss Willmott's ghost and

Forget-me-nots in the Kitchen Garden

Nigella damascena 'Miss Jekyll'

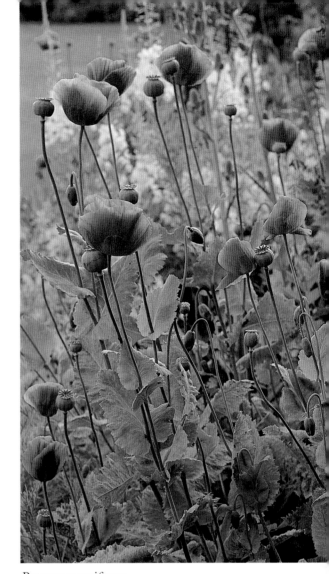

Papaver somniferum

Viola 'Bowles' Black'

silybums are encouraged to seed and then selectively weeded out to achieve the look I want. In the Middle Garden we leave all the grannies' bonnets (*Aquilegia vulgaris*) in their different blues, while both here and in the Kitchen Garden ordinary forget-me-nots make a sea of blue in spring wherever space allows. Also in the Middle Garden are mauve-flowered Byzantine gladiolus and *Nectaroscordum siculum* ssp. *bulgaricum*, with nodding pinkish-green flowers; both are prolific seeders and seeds are probably moved around by mice or ants. In the Cedar Court we have encouraged the brightest blue love-in-a-mist, *Nigella damascena* 'Miss Jekyll', to seed itself between the rhizomes of the German flag irises. It makes a froth of intense colour above finely cut green leaves when the iris flowering is over. In the Kitchen Garden biennial sweet rocket (*Hesperis matronalis*) scatters its seeds behind clumps of summer roses. Among other prolific self-seeders at Tintinhull are violas (we have *Viola* 'Bowles' Black' in the Kitchen Garden); flaxes, including the annual scarlet *Linum grandiflorum* that we grow for pots around the pool; and poppies – the opium poppy, *Papaver somniferum*, the Welsh poppy, *Meconopsis cambrica* (which needs to be strictly controlled) and two horned poppies, *Glaucium corniculatum*, with scarlet flowers, and *G. flavum*, with clear yellow petals. Our rather special self-seeders include the unusual apricot-coloured *Collomia grandiflora*, which we have in the pale borders.

There are also always new plants to be tried. By taking advantage of self-seeders an established bed can readily be given a fresh look, a new lease of life, without changing the main feature plants.

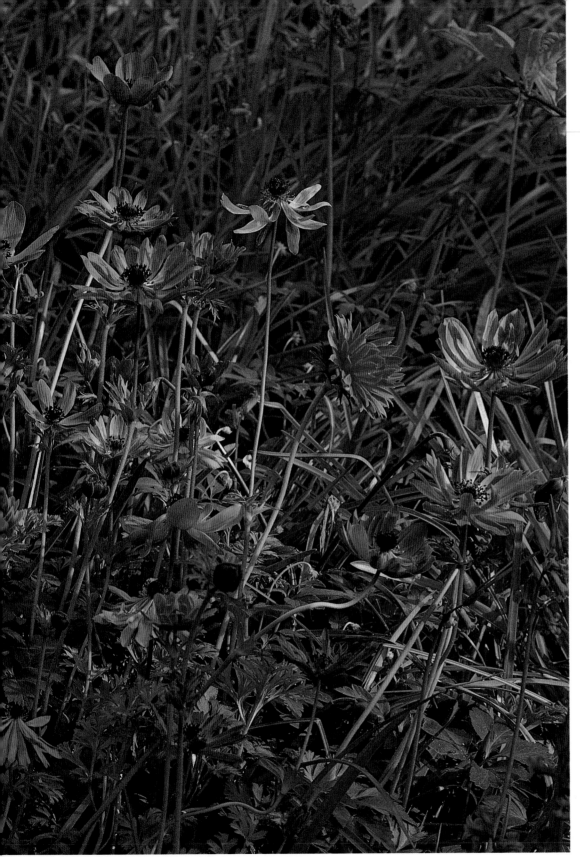

Anemone coronaria St Brigid Group

Anemones for Spring and Autumn

GARDEN ANEMONES fall into quite distinct categories, with very different garden effects. The genus is divided between those which have tubers or rhizomes and flower in spring, and those with a fibrous rootstock, which flower in late summer and can be part of main border schemes. The spring flowerers require a well-drained humus-rich soil and tolerate dry conditions during summer dormancy. The tall autumn flowerers need adequate moisture during their growing season through the summer.

Most familiar are the different species of spring anemone and the wind flowers or poppy anemones (*Anemone coronaria* hybrids). The spring anemones are shade-tolerant small naturalizers, mainly from Europe and the Middle East. Given a few years to establish, they will spread in drifts of colour under deciduous trees and shrubs and between snowdrops, hellebores, dog's-tooth violets and other shade-loving woodlanders such as creeping phlox from North America and the evergreen spurge, *Euphorbia amygdaloides* var. *robbiae*. The British native white wood anemone, *A. nemorosa*, is a great colonizer. It has many beautiful forms, among them *A.n.* 'Vestal', a double white, and *A.n.* 'Allenii', with pale lavender blooms. *A. ranunculoides* is similar, but lower-growing and with small yellow flowers. *A. apennina*, from Italy, south-eastern Europe and the eastern end of the Mediterranean, remains my favourite. A little taller than the earlier-flowering *A. blanda*, but otherwise very similar, it has deeply dissected fern-like leaves and erect stems carrying wide blue or white – occasionally pink – flowers, which turn towards the sun. At Tintinhull, with beds cultivated intensively for more than half a century, both the blue Apennine anemone and the white-flowered wood anemone have naturalized freely, the seeds of *A. apennina* distributed by birds to all parts of the garden, while *A. nemorosa* and its yellow cousin, *A. ranunculoides*, appear to increase only by their creeping rhizomes. Seed is set and the leaves die down soon after flowering. Here, with so many, we can afford to ignore them during the rest of the year, but in a new garden their positions should be clearly marked.

The *A. coronaria* hybrids, the type itself traditionally introduced to England in sacred soil by Crusaders from the Holy Land, are sun-lovers and mainly seen as the popular double-flowered St Brigid and single De Caen florists' flowers. More tender, the bulbs can be protected, or planted at any time in spring to give a display a few months later. The related hybrid *A. × fulgens* is the most brilliant of all scarlet flowers, the black centres outlined in yellow. The pasque flower (*Pulsatilla vulgaris*), with ferny foliage, a close anemone cousin, is another sun-lover.

The autumn-flowering anemones, often given the all-embracing title of Japanese anemones but actually including many from China, are usually forms of *Anemone × hybrida*, *A. vitifolia*, or the earlier species *A. hupehensis* from China (which will tolerate more summer heat and drought). Introduced after 1844, they can all be invasive but are strangely difficult to get established or even to move as mature plants. With broad maple- or vine-like rough leaves, which make them attractive throughout the growing season, these perennials contribute washes of white or pink to border effects through the last weeks of summer and are the flowering backdrop to many autumn borders. There are many good garden forms, all with wide segmented flowers and golden centres. *A. hupehensis* 'Hadspen Abundance' has rich pink almost double flowers, *A. h.* var.

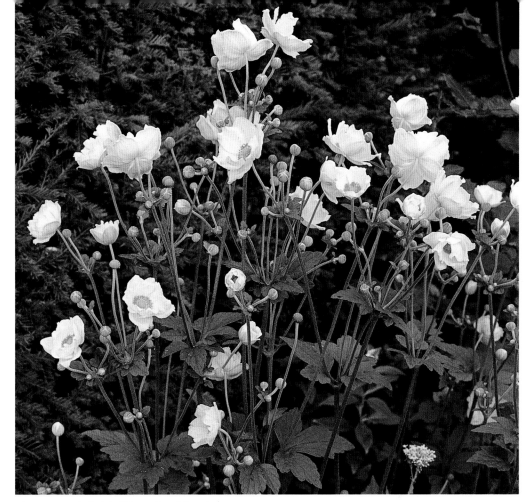

Anemone × hybrida 'Honorine Jobert'

japonica 'Prinz Heinrich' is clear pink, *A. × hybrida* 'Queen Charlotte' single and paler. The star is *A. × h.* 'Honorine Jobert', a ghostly white with tall stems rising above dark foliage. Although tolerant of light shade, most of these anemones, even if originally placed at the back of a border, will gradually push forward towards a sunnier site; they are best allowed to thrive where they will. They should be given a thick mulch during the winter months and if they have to be moved must not be allowed to dry out before replanting. Unlike many other late performers, they need no staking.

On page 66, above: *Anemone blanda*
On page 66, below: *Anemone coronaria*
On page 67: *Anemone nemorosa* 'Allenii'

Anemone apennina

Elegant Hydrangeas

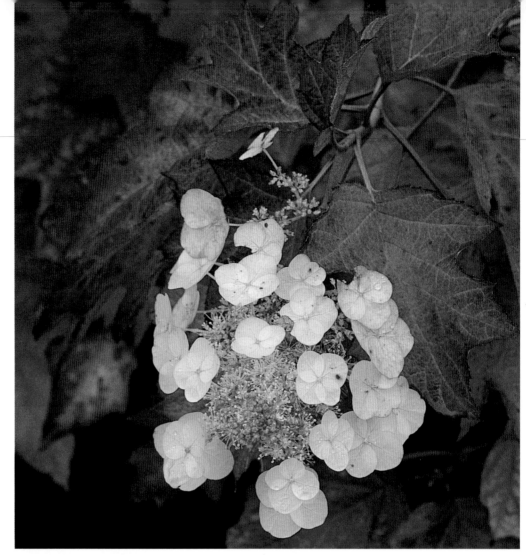

Hydrangea quercifolia

Hydrangeas are woodland plants and they look 'right' when grown in dappled shade in naturalistic gardens. As a total contrast, they have an architectural role. A pair can frame a gateway or define a vista, or a single specimen can be treated as a focal point. They also make marvellous container plants, especially for town gardens. Invaluable for their late-summer flowers, they continue to look good all winter, the flower heads generally deepening in colour with maturity and remaining decorative throughout the cold months until pruning time in spring. As an added bonus, most hydrangea flowers are well suited to drying for indoor arrangements.

With hydrangeas, success depends on wise pruning. Most flower on the previous year's growth. In early spring the stems that flowered last year are cut right to the ground, but as a general rule young shoots should not be touched (although if a bush has become very thick it may be best to remove some of the weakest of the new stems). After pruning the plant should be fed generously with an organic fertilizer to stimulate basal growth for next year's flowers. A few, including *Hydrangea paniculata* and *H. arborescens*, which flower at the tip of the current year's growth, can be treated more ruthlessly. With these, cut back the previous season's wood in late spring.

Although hydrangeas thrive more naturally in an acid loam, so long as they are well cared for and well fed most will tolerate akalinity or even chalk. However, I have to say that I covet the incredibly vivid wash of blue produced by mop-headed hortensia hydrangeas growing in rich acidic loam. Flowers achieve the deepest blue tones in a soil of pH 4.5 to 5.5. In limy soil the colour of the sterile florets becomes a muddy blueish-pink. If, like me, you garden on neutral or alkaline soil it is well worth considering growing the blue forms in containers with a specially prepared mix of acidic soil, or soil that has been treated with a blueing compound of aluminium sulphate.

The macrophyllas and serratas are the most domesticated of the hydrangeas. They are all clump-forming, producing new shoots from the base each season. Others suitable for smaller gardens are *H.* 'Ayesha' (of macrophylla origins) and *H. involucrata* 'Hortensis'. The larger hydrangeas, forms of *H. paniculata* (including 'Grandiflora' and 'Praecox' and the lovely new cultivar 'Kyushu'), and summer-flowering grandees such as the velvet-leaved *H. aspera* ssp. *sargentiana* and *H. heteromalla* Bretschneideri Group look their best in a woodland situation.

At Tintinhull we do well with *H. arborescens*, a medium-sized shrub with slender pointed leaves which bears its round mops of greenish-white sterile flowers from mid- to late summer. *H. aspera* Villosa Group also is nearly always a success, although a late spring frost can badly damage new growth. The colour of its large inflorescences is pink at Tintinhull but in more acid soil it is lilac-blue.

The tender Chinese *H. aspera* ssp. *sargentiana* is a noble shrub valuable for its foliage effects, as is the hardy American *H. quercifolia*, the oak-leaved hydrangea, with leaves which colour crimson in autumn. *H. aspera* ssp. *sargentiana* is augmented by large blueish (even in our soil) inflorescences in summer, while the oak-leaved hydrangea has sterile conical pinkish flowers, produced on last year's wood, so it will not flower in a cold climate. It can be trained as a wall shrub, and usually flowers and colours up well when it has the extra protection offered by a wall.

We grow all of these hydrangeas in the north-facing border in the Middle Garden, our nearest approach to a woodland situation, where wood and Apennine anemones, self-seeded *Cyclamen repandum* and clumps of erythroniums fill in the groundwork in spring. When in flower the hydrangeas are accompanied by drifts of pink Japanese anemones.

There are also climbing hydrangeas. Among the most popular, and deservedly so, is the self-clinging *H. anomala* ssp. *petiolaris*, which will climb to 20m/70ft along and up a shady wall, or can be encouraged to trail over a bank. With greenish-white lacecap flower corymbs, it is a slow starter but vigorous enough later. The tender evergreen *H. seemannii* has leathery leaves and creamy-white flower panicles. The related *Pileostegia viburnoides* and *Schizophragma hydrangeoides* – both members of the Hydrangeaceae – are also desirable for north-facing or shady walls. These two are self-clingers but can be guided when young. They both need some spring protection in their early years but are completely hardy as they mature.

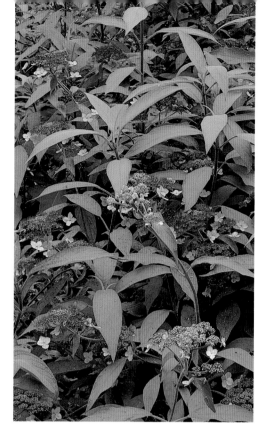

Hydrangea aspera Villosa Group

Hydrangea anomala ssp. *petiolaris*

Hydrangea macrophylla 'Générale Vicomtesse de Vibraye'

Schizophragma hydrangeoides 'Roseum'

The view back to the house from the white seat at the end of the Fountain Garden. Tall yew hedges, spiky iris, white roses, the double avenue of box and the larger trees frame the façade. The layers of planting on different planes are integrated in a way that is typical of Tintinhull.

Gardens within gardens
A golden scheme
A white garden
A foliage garden
Caring for grey and silver plants
The distinguished dogwood family
Different daisies

THE
FOUNTAIN
GARDEN

I LOVE THE IDEA of a one-colour garden. Blue gardens, yellow gardens, pink and purple gardens are all attainable as extensions of other existing schemes. Only white gardens and hot-coloured gardens need to be set aside, hidden and framed by screens of hedges to come as a complete visual and emotional surprise. The white garden has a special charm at the end of the day, with whites and pastels glowing in the evening light, while reds and dark violets fade to nothing as dusk falls. Heavily scented white and cream flowers, or flowers with petals of the palest tints, set among greys, silvers and greens ... it seems an entrancing dream.

At Tintinhull an enclosed white area forms the central feature of the Fountain Garden, the garden 'room' at the end of the axial walk. While each of the other 'rooms' at Tintinhull has a single theme, the Fountain Garden is subdivided by free-standing yew hedges (about 2m/7ft high) into a geometric complex of very small gardens, each with a separate plant or colour theme, arranged more or less as a square around the central white garden. In front of and behind the hedges are symmetrically laid out paths and beds, with different plant emphases depending on aspect. Some beds are in deep shade, others receive sun for most or part of the day. The whole area, at the

farthest western point of the garden, is also enclosed on two sides by the south and west perimeter walls, at the base of which is space for more flower beds.

The view from the Middle Garden takes your eye through two beds with a golden colour scheme, across the white garden with its central pool, and through openings in the yew, to terminate at an arbour of bay laurel sheltering an inviting white seat under the west wall. The bay laurel, clipped in an archway above the seat, is repeated as large, dense blocks (two cubes 3m/10ft × 1.2m/4ft × 1.2m/4ft) against the wall on either side. The seat looks east towards the main classical façade of the house, a view narrowed by foreground wings of yew, a pair of giant dogwoods with variegated leaves and, in season, statuesque silver Scotch thistles. In the distance the domes of box line the path below the tall eagles and frame the front door and steps.

The seat also allows a resting place in an intimate garden area, an area hidden from view until entered, and entirely devoted to the foliage effects of trees such as the dogwoods and lower-growing shrubs and perennials. A shady border around the back of the yew, under the south wall, also has a distinctive planting scheme. But it is the overall arrangement, and its relationship to the main axial path and the adjacent Kitchen Garden, which is of fundamental importance to the design. As in the rest of the garden, Mrs Reiss carefully planned vistas, entrances and exits to provide moments of surprise and satisfaction. She probably did it not with an elaborate scaled drawing but with bamboo canes and string – much the most satisfactory method if you can be on the spot.

From the central pool another view between the yew hedges opens to the north and carries the eye up the middle path of the Kitchen Garden to a typical Somerset cider orchard reached by a gate at the farthest end, a distance of some 45m/150ft. This is the only outside vista at Tintinhull. Even so the orchard is really an extension of the ornamental garden, rather than true countryside. Sheep are occasionally allowed in to graze beneath the trees. They give a delightful rural effect.

Two tall crab apples, *Malus* 'John Downie', flank the exit to the Kitchen Garden. This is perhaps the best-fruiting variety of all the crabs, with symmetrical heads bearing white blossom in spring and golden fruit in late summer. In spring daffodils line the central pathway of the vista through the Kitchen Garden and by June giant catmint overflows the edges. Opposite this entrance the garden ends at the perimeter wall on the south, where another pair of crabs, *Malus tschonoskii*, frames a shrub, the oak-leaved *Hydrangea quercifolia*. With white flower trusses, tinged slightly pink, and superb autumn foliage in a range of yellow, purple and scarlet, the hydrangea thoroughly earns its keep in this important position. Besides contributing to the formal planting scheme, the crabs are intended to screen activities across the public road.

Opposite: *In the two foliage beds at the west end of the garden, the two dominant giant dogwoods* (Cornus controversa *'Variegata'*) *rise above the rounded shapes of phlomis and brachyglottis and the leaves of the lower-growing hostas. White annual honesty* (Lunaria annua alba) *has seeded to give a spring display that complements the blue forget-me-nots.*

Above: *Looking north, beyond the silvery standard willows, the yew wings and the 'John Downie' crab apples, and through the hedges of catmint which stretch towards the cider orchard at the far end of the Kitchen Garden.*

A Golden Scheme

Yew hedge

1m 3 ft | 1m 3 ft

Lilium Golden Splendor
Tanacetum parthenium 'Aureum'
Anemone apennina & Anemone 'Honorine Jobert'
Lysimachia nummularia 'Aurea'
Lamium maculatum 'Aureum'
Tanacetum parthenium 'Aureum'
Philadelphus coronarius 'Aureus'
Philadelphus coronarius 'Aureus'
Philadelphus coronarius 'Variegatus'
Physocarpus opulifolius 'Luteus'
Philadelphus coronarius 'Aureus'
Philadelphus coronarius 'Aureus'
Lonicera japonica 'Aureoreticulata' (clipped)
Hosta ventricosa
Lilium martagon, Scilla siberica & Meconopsis cambrica
Hosta sieboldiana 'Frances Williams'

THE FIRST SECTION of the Fountain Garden, immediately next to the Middle Garden, is reached by descending shallow central steps, an extension of the axial stone pathway, under the overhanging branches of the evergreen oaks. The levels on either side are adjusted by low stone walls, fringed with the hedge of *Berberis darwinii*, which helps to give a feeling of separateness. Still known as the azalea beds, this completely shaded area is divided into two

In the azalea beds golden-leaved Philadelphus coronarius *'Aureus' and a lingering* Rhododendron luteum *are undercarpeted with a medley of feverfew (*Tanacetum parthenium *'Aureum'), anemones, autumn-flowering colchicums, spring cyclamen (*Cyclamen repandum*) and self-seeded white honesty. By midsummer the leaves of most of the golden-foliaged plants become a more solemn green.*

Self seeders
Anemone apennina
Meconopsis cambrica
Scilla siberica
Tanacetum
   parthenium 'Aureum'

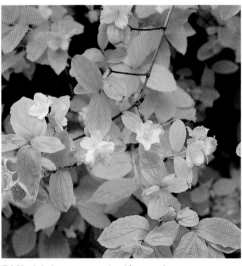

Philadelphus coronarius 'Aureus'

Meconopsis cambrica

Yew hedge

Lysimachia nummularia 'Aurea'

Anemone 'Honorine Jobert'

Lilium Golden Splendor

Scilla siberica,
Colchicum speciosum

Lamium maculatum 'Aureum'

Colchicum speciosum & Lilium Martagon

Rhododendron luteum, with Anemone apemina & Tanacetum parthenium 'Aureum'

Rosa glauca

Philadelphus coronarius 'Aureus'

Lonicera japonica 'Aureoreticulata' (clipped)

Colchicum speciosum

Lilium Martagon

Hosta ventricosa

Hosta ventricosa

Hosta ventricosa

squares, with tall yew hedges providing a background to yellow and white scented flowers and plants with golden leaves. Originally the two beds were planted by Phyllis Reiss with the fragrant *Rhododendron luteum*, the well-known yellow species (then still known as *Azalea pontica*), underplanted with blue *Scilla siberica*. Today, although a few azaleas remain, the soil is too dry for them to thrive – the roots of the oaks penetrate deeply into these beds, soaking up all moisture – so we have extended and partly replaced the original theme with golden-leaved forms of various plants, both shrubby and herbaceous, all of which enjoy shade. In spring the beds are mulched heavily with organic compost to keep in as much moisture as possible. The scillas, increasing annually, are backed up by drifts of slightly later-flowering Apennine anemones, the blues complementing the glowing golden leaves of prolific self-seeding feverfew (*Tanacetum parthenium* 'Aureum'), which appear early in spring. Taller shrubs include sweet mock orange, *Philadelphus coronarius* 'Aureus', with scented white flowers in midsummer; and the evergreen honeysuckle, *Lonicera japonica* 'Aureoreticulata', with golden-green speckled leaves, is clipped into dome-like features along the path edge. The yellow-flowered Welsh poppy, *Meconopsis cambrica* (another seeder), golden-leaved creeping jenny (*Lysimachia nummularia* 'Aurea') and the gold-variegated form of *Lamium maculatum* prolong the yellow and gold motif. Yellow-flushed *Lilium* Golden Splendor and martagon lilies spearing between glaucous-leaved hostas complete the scheme.

This may all sound a bit much, but cut off from other areas of the garden this golden 'picture' is seen in isolation and could be a prototype for any gold garden. In a plan for a larger space with more sun (implemented at Pyrford Court in Surrey) Miss Jekyll recommended additional plants in the same theme. She included plants with golden and gold-variegated leaves; among the former were a golden plane tree (*Platanus* × *acerifolia* 'Suttneri'), elders (both *Sambucus nigra* 'Aurea' and *S. racemosa* 'Plumosa Aurea'), privet (*Ligustrum ovalifolium* 'Aureum'), *Cassinia fulvida* and golden-leaved box. To these we could temptingly add fresh-foliaged *Physocarpus opulifolius* 'Luteus', with leaves which retain their golden tinge through the summer months, and the golden perennial hop (*Humulus lupulus* 'Aureus'). Among variegated golds she used good backbone plants such as hollies, elaeagnus and euonymus.

Elsewhere in her writing Miss Jekyll recommended having a blue garden next to a golden one, to be followed in its turn by a garden with grey leaves, explaining how the juxtaposition of the colours would enhance the effect of each scheme. Gold and yellow complement blues, so when they are placed side by side each of them appears more vivid. Grey makes all associated colours glow more boldly.

However, at Tintinhull I think I would prefer the preparation for the white garden to be a quiet area of more solemn green.

Lonicera japonica 'Aureoreticulata'

Lilium Golden Splendor

Scilla siberica

A White Garden

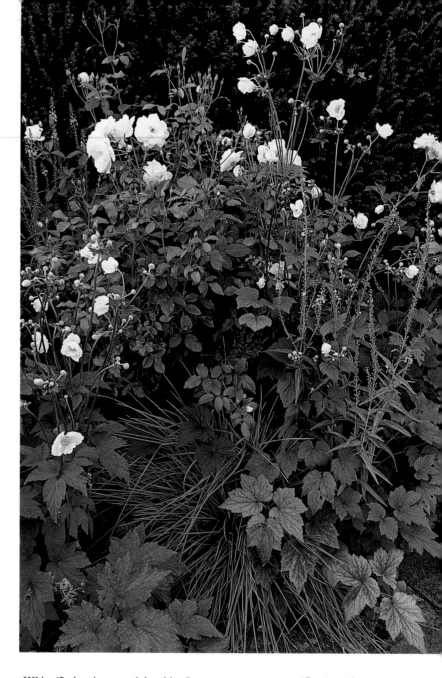

White 'Iceberg' roses with white Japanese anemones and Lysimachia ephemerum *perform late beside the spikes of glaucous grass,* Helictotrichon sempervirens. *'Iceberg' has its first flush of flowering in early summer, but flowers again later if carefully deadheaded.*

R INGED BY YEW HEDGES and invisible until the last approach – except in late summer, when a froth of white Japanese anemones crowds the edges of beds to break the vista – the white garden consists of four equal triangular beds and a central pavement framing a circular pool. The planting is quite formal, with repetitive, rather than mirror-image, groups of silver- and grey-leaved plants with white or pale flowers. In this part of the garden none of the beds gets full sun and the yew hedges cast bands of shade. Standard globe-shaped willows – the small silver-leaved *Salix helvetica* – are placed in the corners where the hedges meet. Pruned into shape each winter, they act as architectural features and, after ten years' growth, rise above the horizontal level of the clipped hedges. They will soon need to be replaced. These silvery-leaved willows, along with leptospermums and artemisias, and the variegated ivies (*Hedera helix* 'Glacier') used as edging, separate the dark green of the yews from the flowers, toning down extreme contrasts and considerably reducing the glare of the white effects. We have introduced these silvers gradually in the last ten years.

Over the time we have been tending the beds we have tried to return to a planting scheme more like Mrs Reiss's original intention. As we have frequently been told by visitors that Mrs Reiss had always used pale-tinted flowers and had never envisaged the garden as specifically a 'white' one, we have felt free to experiment. The garden is still basically white, but most of the bulbs, shrubs, roses, perennials and annuals have off-white or creamy flowers rather than the more startling pure white. For example, when we came in 1979 'Iceberg' roses dominated the planting, to make a great show in summer. We have removed some of these and instead planted the more gentle-toned cream rose 'Margaret Merril', with its slight wafting fragrance. Other plants have been chosen to extend the season into the latter part of the summer. However, we may have made a mistake in that, instead of completely reorganizing all the four beds, we have restored and 'improved' them piecemeal, adding plants each year. The garden might look better if, at some appropriate moment, we had made a new plan and redone the planting as a whole scheme.

In this part of the garden the flowering season opens with the ivory flowers of tulip 'Purissima'. There are several groups, along with scattered clumps of white honesty (*Lunaria annua alba*), followed by a white-flowered Brompton stock (*Matthiola incana*), the latter replaced annually from cuttings or seed sown in the open

in June. The seeds from the previous year's biennial honesty germinate by March, so must not be buried in a thick carpet of mulch.

Other early-summer flowers include cream *Primula* 'Lady Greer' in a relatively damp shady corner, and in sun a white variety of grey-leaved *Lychnis coronaria* the latter unreliable as a perennial but encouraged to replace itself by annual seeding *in situ*. In the three more open beds there are massed plantings of white campanulas. The glossy foliage of a creamy water lily, *Nymphaea odorata*, almost fills the pool, and pots of *Senecio smithii* sit on a ledge submerged by water. These moisture-loving plants from Chile and the Falkland Islands, with grey-green puckered leaves, have 30cm/12in stems carrying white yellow-centred daisies.

Important features are two beds set in the paving. In these a white-flowered form of agapanthus (*Agapanthus campanulatus* var. *albidus*), with greenish buds and decorative seedheads, making thick clumps after forty years of being undisturbed, flowers reliably every August. A few Venus' fishing rods (*Dierama pulcherrimum*), also known as wand flowers, have seeded among the agapanthus, where they get adequate drainage and full sun to flower in July. Covering a range from deep pink to blush, their flowers offer a welcome touch of colour among the near-whites. They are also volunteer seeders, but care must be taken not to weed out the tiny tufted grass-like seedlings, happily germinating in cracks in paving during spring.

We found *Lysimachia ephemerum* in the two sunniest beds. With glaucous leaves all summer and delicate white flowers on tall stems in autumn, it is one of the best perennials. In a shady corner we have added one of my other favourite perennials, the invasive creeping *L. clethroides*, with arching white flower spikes. These, with the white anemones (*Anemone* × *hybrida* 'Honorine Jobert') and the delicate *Allium tuberosum*, with chive-like leaves, carry the garden into autumn. White colchicums (*Colchicum speciosum* 'Album') flower in September. In spring we usually add some summer hyacinth bulbs (*Galtonia candicans*), as few seem to survive the winters. I also intend to plant another late-flowering bulb, the charming *Gladiolus callianthus* 'Murieliae' (more familiar as *Acidanthera murieliae*), with sweetly scented flowers and grassy leaves.

For me as for many others, the ideal white garden is the one at Sissinghurst. Here is a garden where the quality and texture of the leaves is as noticeable as the flowers. Moreover, especially when viewed from the tower above, the Sissinghurst white garden clearly demonstrates the importance of design. As well as the geometric box-edged beds arranged around the central rose-covered bower, there are blocks of silver and green foliage plants set out to give quite a formal effect.

At Tintinhull the yew hedges make a fine background, but ideally I would like to edge the beds with box. It is always a good move to hide the unsightly bases of roses and late-summer perennials – in a small area every fading leaf or defect of growth is very visible. I would also grow blocks of flowers rather than naturalistic clumps. I might grow no roses but get my effects from flowers such as arum lilies (*Zantedeschia aethiopica*), summer hyacinths (*Galtonia candicans*) and, in the sunniest corner, a huge mound of spreading

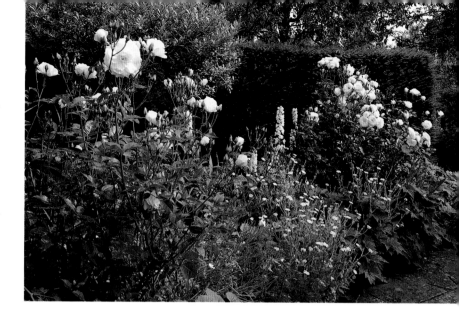

In a corner of the white garden a silvery willow and white 'Iceberg' roses glow against the dark yew hedge. White delphiniums and white Lychnis coronaria *are followed by white Japanese anemones; silver-foliaged plants soften the effect.*

romneya with grey foliage and papery poached-egg flowers. Blocks of *Lotus hirsutus*, blue-leaved rue (*Ruta graveolens* 'Jackman's Blue'), silvery stachys and white lavender (the large *Lavandula angustifolia* 'Alba', which is heavily scented) could alternate with white galega, regale liles, white dictamnus, a white-flowered form of *Salvia officinalis* (admired at Mottisfont), all of which have attractive leaves and habit even when not flowering. In my garden at Bettiscombe I am planning to include a white area with very few white flowers – in general I want few perennials and hope to get effects with shrubs, bulbs and annuals. On my hottest brick wall a white wisteria for spring will accompany a white Banksian rose; there will be a white *Solanum jasminoides* 'Album' for later in the summer. The last two are slightly tender, but the garden is sheltered and it is only five miles from the English Channel. Grey-leaved olive trees and olearias with white flowers will be undercarpeted with glossy green *Acanthus mollis latifolius* with pale pink flower spikes in summer. As Miss Jekyll wrote in *Colour Schemes for the Flower Garden*, 'It is a curious thing that people will sometimes spoil some garden project for the sake of a word. For instance, a blue garden … may be hungering for a group of white lilies … but it is not allowed to have it because it is called the blue garden and there must be no flowers in it but blue flowers. I can see no sense in this … Surely the business of the blue garden is to be beautiful as well as to be blue. My own idea is that it should be beautiful first, and then just as blue as may be consistent with its best possible beauty.'

Lunaria annua alba

Agapanthus campanulatus var. albidus

Rosa 'Margaret Merril'

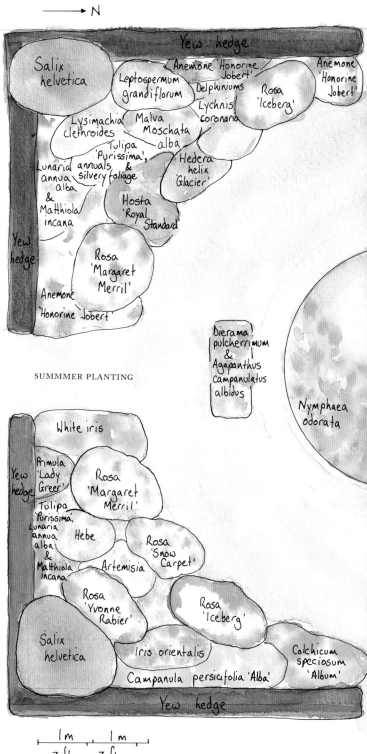

SUMMMER PLANTING

Dierama pulcherrimum

Colchicum speciosum 'Album'

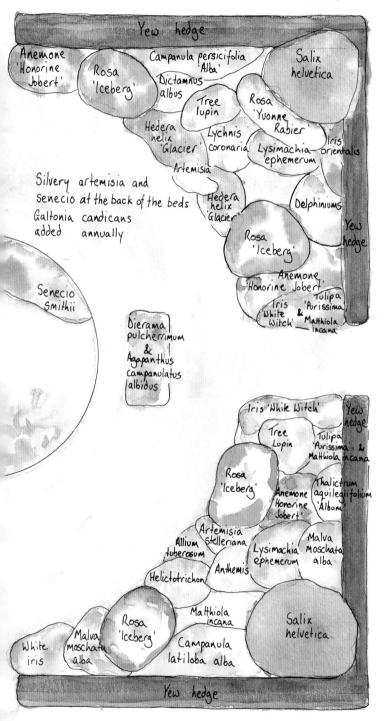

Yew hedge

Anemone 'Honorine Jobert'

Rosa 'Iceberg'

Campanula persicifolia 'Alba'

Dictamnus albus

Salix helvetica

Tree lupin

Rosa 'Yvonne Rabier'

Hedera helix 'Glacier'

Lychnis coronaria

Iris orientalis

Lysimachia ephemerum

Artemisia

Silvery artemisia and senecio at the back of the beds
Galtonia candicans added annually

Hedera helix 'Glacier'

Delphiniums

Rosa 'Iceberg'

Yew hedge

Anemone 'Honorine Jobert'

Senecio smithii

Tulipa 'Purissima' & Matthiola incana

Iris 'White Witch'

Dierama pulcherrimum & Agapanthus campanulatus albidus

Iris 'White Witch'

Yew hedge

Tree lupin

Tulipa 'Purissima' & Matthiola incana

Rosa 'Iceberg'

Anemone 'Honorine Jobert'

Thalictrum aquilegiifolium 'Album'

Artemisia stelleriana

Allium tuberosum

Lysimachia ephemerum

Malva moschata alba

Anthemis

Helictotrichon

Rosa 'Iceberg'

Matthiola incana

Salix helvetica

White iris

Malva moschata alba

Campanula latiloba alba

Yew hedge

Galtonia candicans

Nymphaea odorata

Matthiola incana

A Foliage Garden

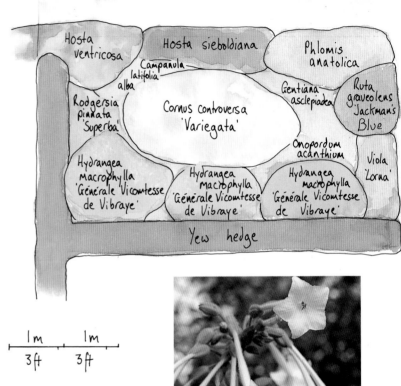

THE THIRD compartment in the Fountain Garden is reserved almost entirely for foliage plants. It has little to do with Mrs Reiss but was planted with inspiration by Paul Miles, during his time as a National Trust Gardens' adviser, now fifteen or more years ago. No one seems to know what was there before his time.

After some bad winters many of the Miles plants have died off, but the theme of his planting remains. The area is dominated by the fine pair of giant dogwoods (*Cornus controversa* 'Variegata') with tabulated layered branches, showing off the cream-edged leaves carried on red-tinged stems. The dogwoods have grown to 3.5m/12ft, rising high above the yew hedges. Beneath the trees are glaucous and variegated hostas, rodgersias, biennial Scotch thistles (*Onopordum acanthium*) and Jackman's rue. Three mop-headed hortensia hydrangeas, *Hydrangea macrophylla* 'Générale Vicomtesse de Vibraye', have clear blue flowers carried early in the season. White *Anemone* × *hybrida* 'Honorine Jobert' and blue-flowered willow gentians (*Gentiana asclepiadea*) perform late.

A large *Phlomis anatolica* occupies one corner by the white seat and *Brachyglottis* 'Sunshine' the other. Behind the seat a self-clinging vine, *Parthenocissus henryana*, its dark leaves netted with strange silvery veins, and turning scarlet in autumn, covers the brick wall. The general effects depend on leaf colours and textures but there are always plenty of flowers.

On one side of the back wall beyond the bay arbour the flowering season is opened in early spring by the hardy *Viburnum* × *burkwoodii*, with its scented globular heads of pink-tinted buds unfolding to white. On the other side *Clematis rehderiana*, carrying primrose-yellow cowslip-scented bells from September until the frosts, climbs over a frame alongside the wall.

Nicotiana sylvestris

Self-seeders
Aquilegia vulgaris
Gladiolus byzantinus
Lunaria annua
Myosotis

SPRING PLANTING

N

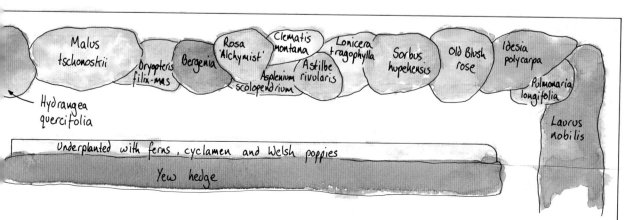

Plan labels (top diagram):

N →

Laurus nobilis | Clematis rehderiana | Clematis 'Miss Bateman' | Akebia quinata | Photinia | Laurus nobilis

Parthenocissus henryana

Hosta ventricosa | Lychnis coronaria alba

Brachyglottis 'Sunshine'

Cornus controversa 'Variegata'

Gentiana asclepiadea 'Alba'

Ajuga reptans

Viola 'Lorna' | Onopordum acanthium | Anemone 'Honorine Jobert'

Yew hedge

In the narrow bed (hardly 45cm/18in wide) under the south wall, there is, besides the crab apples mentioned earlier, a pair of *Sorbus hupehensis*. *Podophyllum hexandrum* and *Saxifraga fortunei* 'Wada' both revel in the shade but need a thick mulch of homemade compost to keep surrounding soil moist. A clump of giant *Astilbe rivularis* proves how effective a large-scale plant can be in a small space. Here it creates a wonderful jungle-like atmosphere, and the invasive roots are contained by paving. Most of these plants have been added since 1979.

Farther along the wall the soil is drier where the roots of the evergreen oaks have spread from the Middle Garden, but the glossy-leaved *Buxus balearica* from the Mediterranean islands and the smaller *B. harlandii*, a dome-shaped bush with bright green leaves, probably originating from China, thrive here in conditions which obviously suit them. They look at home with the oaks.

Lonicera tragophylla

Parthenocissus henryana

Plan labels (bottom diagram):

Malus tschonoskii | Dryopteris filix-mas | Bergenia | Rosa 'Alchymist' | Clematis montana | Asplenium scolopendrium | Astilbe rivularis | Lonicera tragophylla | Sorbus hupehensis | Old Blush rose | Idesia polycarpa | Pulmonaria longifolia | Laurus nobilis

Hydrangea quercifolia

Underplanted with ferns, cyclamen and Welsh poppies

Yew hedge

Hydrangea quercifolia

Caring for Grey and Silver Plants

GREY AND SILVER foliage plants are a perfect foil to both green and purple-tinged leaves and to all flower colours. While contributing a gentle atmosphere overall, their neutral tones make neighbouring flower or leaf colours seem more vibrant. Arranged in repetitive groups they integrate schemes as firmly as topiary pieces.

At Tintinhull silver and grey plants are used throughout the white beds in the Fountain Garden, and in the Pool Garden plantings of silvery artemisias unite the hot and the pale borders. In the swimming pool border at Royaumont (*opposite above*), where lacy perovskias and artemisias intermingle with clumps of caryopteris, salvias and agapanthus, the silver foliage plants heighten the effects of the flowers.

TAKING CUTTINGS

Silver plants are often slightly tender and may not survive a hard winter, so I take cuttings of semi-mature shoots towards the end of summer.

With *Artemisia arborescens* 'Faith Raven', as with most of the silvery plants, I take heeled shoots (*left*). Some artemisias, such as *A. stelleriana*, often have side shoots which can be pulled from the base of the plant (*top left*). These may well have an embryo root system. All cuttings should be placed at once in an airtight polythene bag (*above left*) and transferred to pots as soon as possible – within a few hours at the most.

Back in the potting shed, I prepare 8cm/3in pots of mixed peat (or a peat alternative) and grit (or perlite). I trim the heeled shoots, or, if they are more than 15cm/6in long, cut across a node where the side shoots join the main stem (*top right*). Then I pinch off the leaves from the lower half of the stem (*above right*), dip the end of the stem in water and press the bare tip into a hormone rooting powder. The cuttings are then placed in the pots, about six to each pot – I use a dibber to make the planting holes (*opposite, below left*). With *A. stelleriana* stems I just pinch off the lower leaves and pop the shoots in the pots (*opposite, below centre*). The soil around the cuttings should be carefully firmed (*opposite, below right*).

I then put the pots in a mist propagator, arranging them on the heated compost surface at the very edge of the mist bench, so that they get just enough spray but not too much. In these conditions cuttings of *A. arborescens* 'Faith Raven', *A.* 'Powis Castle', *A. stelleriana* and most other 'silvers', including the glaucous *Argyranthemum foeniculaceum*, will root in a few weeks. More woody plants such as *Teucrium fruticans* and woolly-leaved willows take longer. Using a mist propagator there is a danger that cuttings may get too moist and rot. It is less

risky to root them in an airtight tray or in a pot covered with polythene on a window sill, where condensation will provide all the moisture needed. Cuttings taken from more mature wood can be left to root in a frost-free greenhouse over the winter months. However, at Tintinhull we are always pressed for time and space, and I find that the speed of rooting in the propagator makes up for the extra care needed. As a precaution, we usually keep a stock plant in a pot in the greenhouse during the winter, and take additional cuttings from this in spring, as the days lengthen and new shoots become available.

Artemisia stelleriana is more likely to rot than the taller, lacier artemisias such as *A.* 'Powis Castle' and *A. arborescens* 'Faith Raven' but it is also hardier. Once plants are cuttings and the compost slip out together, and I gently separate the cuttings – here, of *A.* 'Powis Castle' (*opposite, below left to right*). Holding one in a prepared pot, I add compost around the roots (*left*), fill the pot almost to the top and firm the soil gently around the plant. Then I tease out the remaining plants and pot them on in the same way (*below*). I shall pot on again when the pot seems full of the artemisia's spreading root system, but with a firmer hand, as the potting soil mixture should by now be adhering to the roots in a ball. If it is not, and the ball disintegrates, potting on has been attempted too early.

PLANTING OUT

Before beginning to plant I usually soak the pots and water the ground thoroughly. When planting 'silvers' I do not add fertilizers – these plants like poor situations. I dig a good-sized hole for each plant, tip it

rooted they can be kept in a closed frame over winter, so long as the frame is opened to allow air circulation on fine days.

POTTING ON

After plants have established a root system (you will notice small fibrous roots just emerging from the base), they should be potted on into individual pots. If you use too large a pot there is a risk of overwatering, so choose a pot of an appropriate size and be prepared to pot on again at least once, and sometimes two or three times, before plants can be put out in the open.

I add grit to a proprietary potting compost and put some of the mixture in the bottom of the required number of pots (*opposite above*). Then I give the base of the old pot a sharp tap, so that the rooted

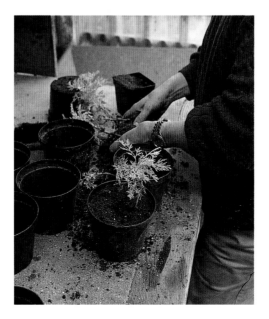

carefully out of its pot and plant it, firming it in well. *A. stelleriana*, which I am planting here (*above*), is one of the few silver-leaved plants which will tolerate dry shade, so it is ideal for growing near the base of a yew hedge or behind taller plants. I use it mainly in the Fountain Garden, where it goes in the shadier corners, leaving the taller *A. arborescens* and *A. a.* 'Faith Raven' to go where there is more light.

The Distinguished Dogwood Family

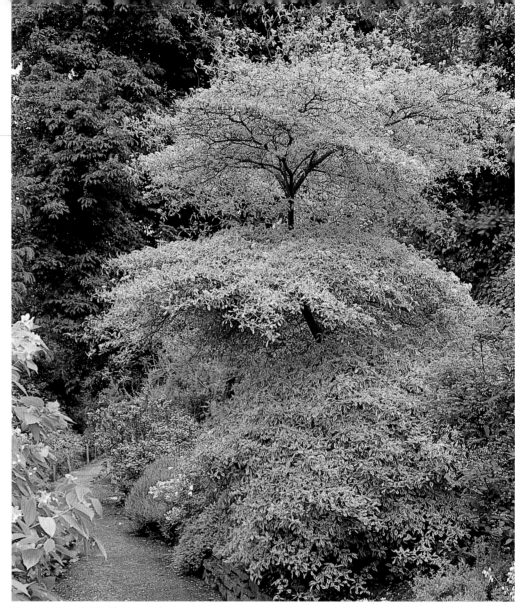

Dogwoods, or cornels, from Europe, Asia and America, range in size from trees (the Pacific dogwood, *Cornus nuttallii*, and the majestic Asiatic giant dogwood, *C. controversa*) to the sub-shrub *C. canadensis* from North American woods. In between there are many shrubby dogwoods. We grow some of these for their startling red, yellow or green polished young stems, spectacular when bare in winter. Other – often stately – shrubs are grown for their habit or their flowering bracts, foliage or fruit.

C. controversa, with tabulated branches, is beautiful in its green form, and the more commonly grown *C.c.* 'Variegata', its leaves marked with creamy yellow turning to white, is even more striking. The handsome pair of *C.c.* 'Variegata' in the Fountain Garden makes a dramatic feature. Both these and the more delicate American *C. alternifolia* 'Argentea' (above the steps at the garden entrance) have a distinctive habit, growing like tiered wedding cakes. They are at their most impressive against a dark background.

The dogwoods with coloured stems make interesting additions to almost any garden scheme. *C. alba*, from Siberia and China, has forms with several different bark colours. The Westonbirt dogwood, *C.a.* 'Sibirica', has the most brilliant colour of all the red-stemmed varieties, but 'Elegantissima', with deep red young stems, offers the additional interest of cream-variegated leaves through the summer months, and 'Spaethii', with bright red stems, has leaves margined and marked with gold ('Spaethii' is in the purple and gold border in the Cedar Court). The sober plum-red twigs of the European native

Cornus alternifolia 'Argentea'

hedgerow dogwood, *C. sanguinea*, being less exotic-looking, are suitable for a natural pond area, as are the deeper, almost violet-plum twigs of *C. stolonifera* (*C. sericea*) from North America. A form of *C. stolonifera*, *C.s.* 'Flaviramea', has greenish-yellow bark. Another American, *C. racemosa*, has white fruits in autumn as well as rose-coloured stems in winter. Most of these dogwoods grown for the colour of their young stems should be cut right back almost to ground level at least every other spring. If you prune *C. racemosa* more selectively, leaving a

Cornus alba 'Elegantissima'

Cornus kousa var. *chinensis*

Cornus kousa var. *chinensis*

proportion of the older wood, you will get the fruits too.

Other dogwoods have decorative flowers or coloured bracts. The European Cornelian cherry, *C. mas*, is a woodland plant. It has tiny yellow starry flowers carried before the leaves unfurl in early spring. Fruits follow but are generally hidden by the leaves, which colour well in autumn. In a warm, sheltered garden, the tender evergreen *C. capitata* may eventually become a small tree; it has creamy-sulphur flower bracts followed by fleshy strawberry-like fruits. A hardier alternative is the superb *C. kousa* or its more lime-tolerant variety *C.k.* var. *chinensis*, both with creamy bracts turning slightly pink and with notable autumn colour. At Tintinhull Mrs Reiss angled the view of the *C.k.* var. *chinensis* in the Cedar Court so that it could be seen from the Courtyard on arrival. It grows fast, and there are several variants, including the semi-evergreen 'Norman Hadden', probably a hybrid between *C. kousa* and *C. capitata*. Sadly, the American dogwood *C. florida* prefers hotter summers and more acid soil than we can provide at Tintinhull and seldom performs to its true potential in Britain, even in the mildest regions. The Pacific dogwood, *C. nuttallii* from the Pacific west coast, a magnificent tree in its native habitat, is even firmer in its preference for acid soil. The little stoloniferous bunchberry, *C. canadensis*, is a woodlander for acid soils, where it will spread into drifts, starred with white flowers, among other typical plants from north-east America, all of which I love but in my neutral to alkaline soil can never grow.

Different Daisies

THE DAISY-FLOWERED Compositae family includes among its members many wonderful garden plants. The daisies grown as annuals are invaluable in beds and containers, loving sun, withstanding drought and having long flowering periods. Some of them will grow to 2.5m/8ft in a season. For a children's garden I designed in America – a temporary affair – our theme came from one of Monet's paintings, with tall dramatic 'avenues' of sunflowers (*Helianthus annuus*) creating secret shady tunnels.

But not all Compositae have wide daisy flowers with distinctive ray florets; some members of the group are grown mainly for their leaves, with little button rayless flowers so clustered in dense heads as to be almost unrecognizable as true daisies. Among these are some of the helichrysums. The drought-tolerant *Helichrysum petiolare* has soft silver leaves on twisting stems which spread out over the edge of containers, while allowing more colourful plants to twine in between. Other shrubby helichrysums with interesting foliage (*H. italicum*, the curry plant, for instance) look marvellous massed in sunny beds or grown in pots. Many of the silver-leaved artemisias can be treated in the same way.

The biennial Scotch thistle, *Onopordum acanthium*, with silvery-grey fiercely armed foliage and stem, is an architectural plant growing as high as 2.5m/8ft in its second season, so it is ideal to mark a gateway or make a focal point. In the Fountain Garden two of them flank a path, framed against a dark wall of yew. Flowering stems break from near the ground in candelabra fashion, and tiny clustered flower buds open to deep purple shaving brushes. I also love another statuesque biennial, the milk thistle, *Silybum marianum*, with green leaves veined in white. The seeds from both these plants will germinate the following spring to flower a year later.

Many of the tender decorative chrysanthemums have been given a new genus, *Argyranthemum*. Perhaps the most beautiful of these is the almost shrubby glaucous thread-leaved *A. foeniculaceum* of gardens, a variant of the marguerite, with sprays of small white daisy flowers all summer (so long as dying flowers are regularly removed). There are now several *Argyranthemum* cultivars and hybrids with more silvery leaves and flowers in various

Silybum marianum

Osteospermum jucundum

Brachyscome iberidifolia

colours. I especially like 'Mary Wootton', with pale pink flowers, and yellow 'Jamaica Primrose', with wide flowers that appear almost luminous. These plants will grow into sizeable shrubs during a summer season and are well able to cope with the robust cut-and-thrust life of a border, jostled by adjacent plants. Cuttings will root readily in the autumn and should be kept in a frost-free greenhouse or cold frame through the winter. It is easy to train them into standards: just tie the main shoot to a cane and remove any side shoots.

The sub-shrubby perennial osteo-spermums from South Africa need hot sun, good drainage and protection from wind. Given those prerequisites they will survive temperatures down to -5° to -10°C (23° to 14°F) but it is advisable to take cuttings as an insurance. They will make dense mats in a season. Pink-flowered *Osteospermum jucundum* is reasonably hardy at Tintinhull. The more tender *O. ecklonii* has wide white daisies, the ray florets backed in dusky blue, with centres of dark blue. Gazanias, also from South Africa, like similar conditions but are less shrubby in habit.

Blue marguerites from South Africa, species and cultivars of *Felicia*, both *F. amelloides* and its various forms, and the Swan river daisy, *Brachyscome iberidifolia* from Australia, with blue or white flowers, thrive in hot situations and look good in pots. I have always grown felicias from cuttings and brachyscomes from seed.

Zinnias, though now separated from the Compositae into Asteraceae, are still daisies. We usually grow the green-flowered 'Envy', a cultivar of *Zinnia elegans*. Lacking hot sun, we keep it in the greenhouse until it is nearly in flower and grow a group together

in a handsome pot by the front door rather than placing it in a mixed planting. I would like to try the unzinnia-looking *Z. angusti-folia*, each of its stems surmounted by orange daisies, but do not know if it would enjoy our summers. I have seen it in Texas growing with forms of the ferny-leaved *Tagetes tenuifolia*, known as signet marigold.

Zinnia angustifolia 'Orange Star'

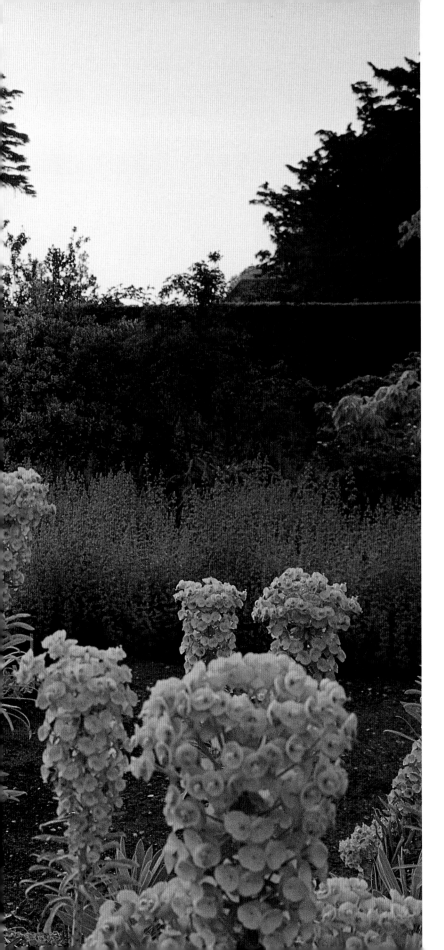

Euphorbias and catmint edge paths in the Kitchen Garden, almost obscuring plantings of more utilitarian vegetables. The view looking east shows the old cedar of Lebanon at the far edge of the Cedar Court. Honeysuckles grown as verticals on metal frames give height – as do shrubs such as hollies and viburnums – while the yew hedge, separating the Kitchen Garden from the Pool Garden, makes a splendid backdrop to the mixed planting.

THE KITCHEN GARDEN

THE KITCHEN GARDEN at Tintinhull remains essentially a working garden, where traditional fruit and vegetables are grown. But, as in the kitchen gardens of the past, seasonal flowers from fruit trees and in borders have a strong influence on its general character.

Twiners grow on wires and tripods to give vertical effects among the low serried rows of more pedestrian vegetables. Sweet peas for cutting and French runner beans with scarlet flowers in summer are in traditional rows, and the more unusual blue hyacinth bean (*Lablab purpureus*, also known as *Dolichos lablab*), with purplish leaves and dark blueish-purple flowers, is exotic on willow frames. The 'cottage' style, with functional paths providing access to beds and with flowers and useful crops almost intermingled, has a charm of its own. It provides a link not only with the grand walled gardens of the past but also with the real cottage gardens of agricultural workers, where vegetables and soft fruit would be grown of necessity, with flowers as decorative additions along path edges.

The Tintinhull Kitchen Garden is attractive enough on its own to provide a model for the main garden area of any modest-sized house. While most of my clients like to have some space for fruit and vegetables, few allow me to mix ornamental plants between or around the rows – although I can usually persuade them to have central pathways lined with catmint, lavender or woody sages, and to use rosemary and mints in an ornamental way. In the west end of a windswept walled garden I designed on Oronsay, off the west coast of Scotland, crops grow in rows beside the greenhouse. At Wormsley in Oxfordshire the scale is quite different, and grand greenhouses and vegetable and soft fruit beds occupy almost a quarter section of the 2-acre walled garden layout. Another vast assemblage of beds contains flowers for cutting. At Herriard Park in Hampshire, where I helped design a new garden, we planned a herb garden, a garden for vegetables and a greenhouse to look as attractive as the flower garden beside the house. In none of these gardens do the kitchen areas intermix with the more flowery beds. However, at Ston Easton, a country house hotel near Bath, rows of flowers (perennials and annuals) for cutting for the house intermingle with herbs and other vegetables for the kitchen. Hotel guests may enjoy a stroll between rows of peas and beans. At Bettiscombe I intend to make my kitchen garden a separate design feature: ultimately I will grow my favourite vegetables – courgettes, lettuce, small French beans and perhaps early potatoes – in raised beds in an enclosed garden concealed by hornbeam hedges.

The old kitchen garden at Tintinhull measures approximately 64 × 27m/210 × 90ft. Of this, during the last fourteen years, we have stolen from cropping plants a 1.5m/5ft border around the edge. And though the centre beds are used primarily for vegetables we also treat them as a nursery for the whole garden, sowing the seed of annuals and biennials in rows among the lettuce, beans and cabbage.

Above: *On the Isle of Oronsay in Scotland an old walled kitchen garden, dating to the fourteenth century and attached to the Priory, has been turned into mixed ornamental, vegetable and fruit gardens. Although frosts are unlikely, fierce salt winds can devastate the plants, so I installed a network of willow hurdles and privet hedges (backed, until they are established, by windproof netting) to give wind-protection.*

Opposite: *Looking east, past the stone vase at the western edge of the garden and through the yew arch into the Pool Garden. In early spring daffodils, tulips, primroses and forget-me-nots bring seasonal colour to the rose border.*

When we first came we used the outer border for single plants on trial: the planting here too had a nursery atmosphere rather than a feeling of permanency. Over the years, however, the worthwhile plants have been retained and divided to make clumps of their own; shrub roses have grown large, and groundcover seeders and spreaders have established themselves as part of the random and cottagey scene. Many of the new plants have a semi-domestic connotation or are useful herbs, which makes them specially suitable for growing adjacent to vegetables. There are shrub roses with apple-like hips, the gilded rosemary – a form of *Rosmarinus officinalis* with striped leaves, grown in the sixteenth century – southernwood, lavenders, lovage, *Salvia officinalis*, angelicas (both the stately *Angelica archangelica* for preserving and the less common *A. gigas*, with

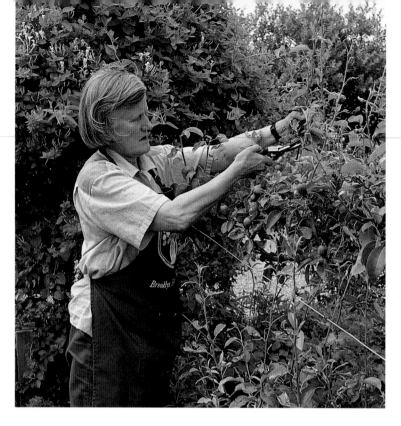

The espalier pears have new shoots pruned back in midsummer. They are pruned more severely in the winter while they are dormant. When young, the main lateral and top shoots are encouraged to make the desired pattern of espalier. In maturity, any excess spurs are removed and lateral shoots are tied down to ensure that they stay horizontal.

Sweet peas need frequent cutting if you want them to flower for a long period; a shoot that is allowed to form seed will not continue to flower. Our sweet peas, grown in rich soil on a traditional framework of bamboos, are constantly being cut for the house.

bronze stems, from Asia). In spring, biennial dyer's woad, *Isatis tinctoria*, with grey-green foliage, produces loose racemes of acid-yellow flowers. The invasive double-flowered bouncing bet (*Saponaria officinalis* 'Rosea Plena'), still used for washing valuable old tapestries and crewel work, flowers in August, its roots contained – just – in a far corner.

This garden, on a lower level than all the other areas, is in a cruciform pattern, with gravel paths dividing the vegetable beds into four separate areas. The central axis path is edged with daffodils and catmint and a stone-paved cross path has on either side pink roses backed by rows of espaliered pear trees. Japanese honeysuckle (*Lonicera japonica* 'Halliana') twines on eight ironwork trellis posts to mark the corners of the rose beds. We doubled up the catmint, *Nepeta* 'Six Hills Giant', to form a continuous line along the centre – previously it was widely spaced – and now it makes a truly impressive show. The avenue of misty mauve flowers leads the eye into the orchard beyond the northern boundary and back towards

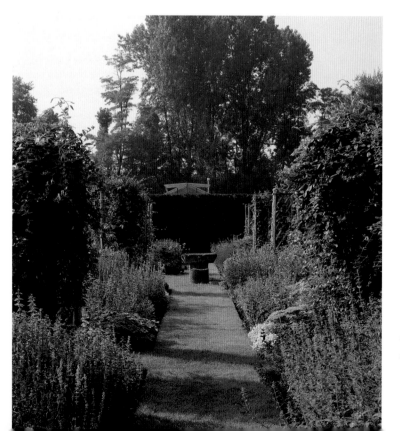

At Royaumont in the Ile de France, fruit trees have been trained as espaliers and honeysuckles grown on wooden trellis pillars, a theme I adopted from the Kitchen Garden at Tintinhull. The beds were planned for cutting flowers but annual blue and clary salvias and autumn-flowering sedums have proved too attractive to pick.

Towards the end of the summer the red dahlias lined out in the Kitchen Garden bloom brilliantly beside the catmint, in flower for the second time, and herbs. On the willow frames the blue hyacinth bean (Lablab purpureus, *also known as* Dolichos lablab) *is just coming into flower. Nearby, a sowing of forget-me-nots for spring flowering has germinated.*

the Fountain Garden, extending the feeling of distance. The catmint is so strong and vigorous that, using a sharp spade, we were able to cut off the requisite number of extra groups from the existing planting. Delicate aromatic grey-green leaves make low hummocks attractive for eight months of the year. Lax arching stems carry lavender-coloured flowering shoots 1m/3ft high and wide in early June. These are cut back after the flowers fade – probably at the end of the month or even later, depending on the weather – encouraging new foliage growth, followed by a second but less spectacular flowering in late summer.

The old espaliered pears were replaced in 1982: we grow 'Pitmaston Duchess', 'Doyenné du Comice' and 'Williams' Bon Chrétien'. Mrs Reiss had the pink rose 'Else Poulsen', but we have replaced most of these with 'Mevrouw Nathalie Nypels'. Very similar to 'Else Poulsen', with like habit and shining young bronze leaves, although somewhat paler flowers, 'Mevrouw Nathalie Nypels' flowers even more prolifically, and is much less susceptible to disease. We have kept two 'Else Poulsen' at the central corners to remind us of Mrs Reiss's original preference. Below the roses and spilling out on to the paving we grow the small catmint *Nepeta nervosa*, with catkin-like flowers in pale blue. If the dying flower heads are regularly removed it will flower all summer. Bushes of *Caryopteris* × *clandonensis* 'Heavenly Blue' grow between the roses and by the end of summer scatterings of tall *Verbena bonariensis* spear up between roses and caryopteris to make a mauve haze. At the four outer corners of these borders giant silver-leaved cardoons, *Cynara cardunculus*, give architectural focus, while biennial sweet rocket (*Hesperis matronalis*), blue- and pink-flowered columbines and small violas such as *Viola riviniana* and *V.* 'Bowles' Black' seed freely in any of the gaps.

At the south end of the Kitchen Garden the view into the Fountain Garden is framed by ornamental trees: pyramidal pear trees (*Pyrus calleryana* 'Chanticleer') and *Malus* 'John Downie'. At the east end, steps from the pink rose walk lead up through an archway in the yew hedges into the Pool Garden. The view back from the Pool Garden down the steps is one of the most important in the garden, terminated by a stone vase on the west side.

A bird's-eye view of the garden would reveal quite distinct seasonal colours. In spring yellow narcissi line the central axes, by midsummer a mist of blue catmint and pink shrub roses is dominant. Later, shrubs and perennials, often with pink or white flowers, give interest. Many of the ornamentals, added round the edge since Mrs Reiss's day, are evergreen and keep up winter appearances.

The central vegetable beds with cabbages, Brussels sprouts, leeks and spinach (or Swiss chard) do not always look manicured, but as adjacent areas are cleaned and dug (in any available moment) they convey a satisfactory feeling of use and care.

A clump of Allium tuberosum *flowers in late summer between the bushes of rose 'Mevrouw Nathalie Nypels' and verbena. 'Nathalie Nypels' flowers all season if regularly deadheaded.*

In late summer self-seeded musk mallow (Malva moschata) *flowers between the pink roses 'Mevrouw Nathalie Nypels', while* Verbena bonariensis, *bearing flat mauve flowers on tall strong stems, pushes*

through. Bushes of blue caryopteris are ranked along the back of the beds where the scented honeysuckle Lonicera japonica *'Halliana' flowers on metal frames.*

1m 1m
3ft 3ft

Self-seeders
Alchemilla mollis
Anemone blanda
Aquilegia vulgaris
Brunnera macrophylla
Dicentra formosa
Fritillaria meleagris
Helleborus orientalis
Leucojum aestivum
Polystichum setiferum

SPRING PLANTING

Yew hedge

Viburnum carlesii

Rosa gallica officinalis
Scilla siberica
Leucojum aestivum 'Gravetye Giant'

Malus 'John Downie'

Hydrang[ea]

Bergenia stracheyi

Senecio doria

Anemone nemorosa 'Robinsoniana'

Lonicera seedling

Paeonia Veitchii

Pulsatilla vulgaris

Daphne Collina

Erythroniu[m]

Hemerocallis fulva 'Kwanzo Variegata'

Euphorbia griffithii 'Dixter'

Pulmonaria

Papaver orientale

Teucrium scorodonia

Polystichum setiferum

Pulmonaria

Saxifraga

Anemone nemorosa 'Robinsoniana'

Hemerocallis fulva 'Kwanzo Variegata'

Papaver orientale 'Black and White'

Pulmonaria officinalis 'Sissinghurst White'

Pulmonaria rubra

Yew hedge

Hydrangea

Malus 'John Downie'

Rosa gallica officinalis
Scilla siberica
Leucojum aestivum 'Gravetye Giant'

Hydrangea

Viburnum carlesii

Photinia serrulata

N

Clematis recta

Halimium ocymoides

Hosta × tardiana

Brunnera macrophylla 'Hadspen Cream'

Daphne pontica

Brunnera macrophylla

Cerastium tomentosum

Tulipa orphanidea

Geranium sanguineum striatum

Euphorbia griffithii 'Fireglow'

Daphne × burkwoodii 'Somerset'

Geranium Clarkei 'Kashmir Purple'

Actaea rubra

Lathyrus vernus 'Alboroseus'

Helleborus orientalis

Lychnis coronaria

Erythronium 'Pagoda'

Laurus nobilis

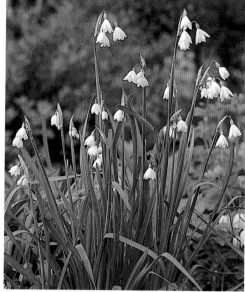

Leucojum aestivum 'Gravetye Giant'

Cerastium tomentosum

Lathyrus vernus 'Alboroseus'

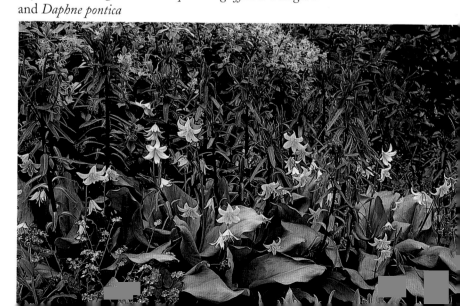

Erythronium 'Pagoda' with *Euphorbia griffithii* 'Fireglow'
and *Daphne pontica*

Daphne × burkwoodii 'Somerset'

Lonicera japonica 'Halliana'

Stipa gigantea

Vinca difformis

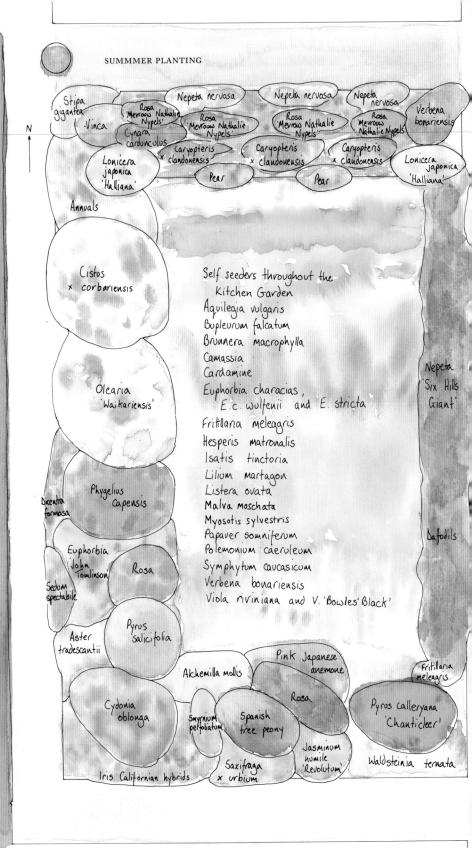

N

Stipa gigantea

Nepeta nervosa   Nepeta nervosa   Nepeta nervosa

Vinca   Rosa 'Mevrouw Nathalie Nypels'   Rosa 'Mevrouw Nathalie Nypels'   Rosa 'Mevrouw Nathalie Nypels'   Rosa 'Mevrouw Nathalie Nypels'   Verbena bonariensis

Cynara cardunculus   Caryopteris × clandonensis   Caryopteris × clandonensis   Caryopteris × clandonensis

Lonicera japonica 'Halliana'   Pear   Pear   Lonicera japonica 'Halliana'

Annuals

Cistos × corbariensis

Olearia 'Waikariensis'

Dicentra formosa   Phygelius capensis

Euphorbia 'John Tomlinson'   Rosa

Sedum spectabile

Pyrus salicifolia

Aster tradescantii

Alchemilla mollis   Pink Japanese anemone

Cydonia oblonga   Smyrnium perfoliatum   Spanish tree peony   Rosa   Pyrus calleryana 'Chanticleer'

Jasminum humile 'Revolutum'   Waldsteinia ternata

Iris Californian hybrids   Saxifraga × urbium   Fritillaria meleagris

Nepeta 'Six Hills Giant'

Daffodils

Self seeders throughout the Kitchen Garden
Aquilegia vulgaris
Bupleurum falcatum
Brunnera macrophylla
Camassia
Cardamine
Euphorbia characias,
   E.c. wulfenii and E. stricta
Fritillaria meleagris
Hesperis matronalis
Isatis tinctoria
Lilium martagon
Listera ovata
Malva moschata
Myosotis sylvestris
Papaver somniferum
Polemonium caeruleum
Symphytum caucasicum
Verbena bonariensis
Viola riviniana and V. 'Bowles' Black'

Euphorbia characias ssp. *wulfenii*
'John Tomlinson'

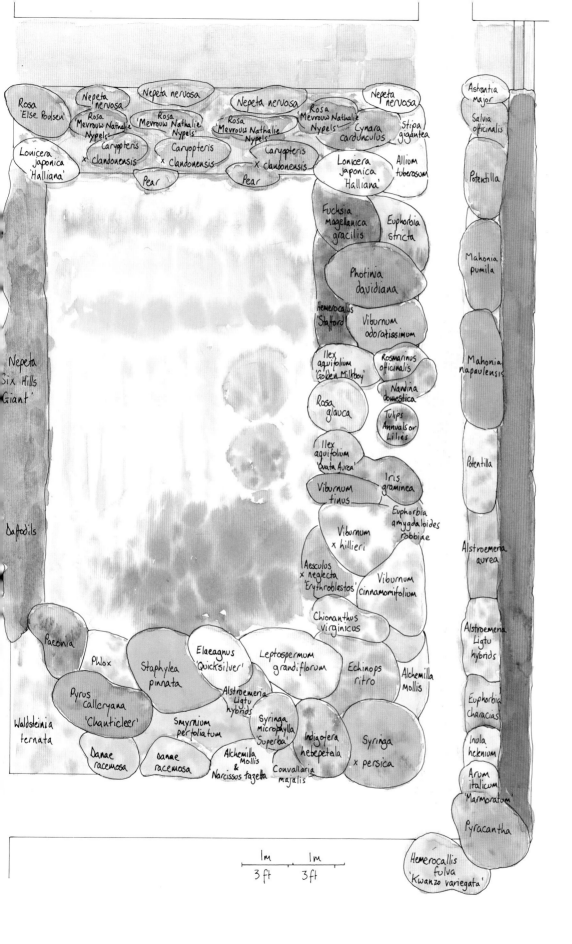

Rosa 'Else Poulsen'

Rosa 'Mevrouw Nathalie Nypels'

Nepeta nervosa

Nepeta nervosa

Nepeta nervosa

Nepeta nervosa

Rosa 'Else Poulsen'

Rosa 'Mevrouw Nathalie Nypels'

Rosa 'Mevrouw Nathalie Nypels'

Rosa 'Mevrouw Nathalie Nypels'

Cynara cardunculus

Stipa gigantea

Caryopteris × clandonensis

Caryopteris × clandonensis

Caryopteris × clandonensis

Lonicera japonica 'Halliana'

Allium tuberosum

Lonicera japonica 'Halliana'

Pear

Pear

Fuchsia magellanica gracilis

Euphorbia stricta

Photinia davidiana

Hemerocallis 'Stafford'

Viburnum odoratissimum

Ilex aquifolium 'Golden Milkboy'

Rosmarinus officinalis

Nepeta 'Six Hills Giant'

Nandina domestica

Rosa glauca

Tulips Annuals or Lilies

Ilex aquifolium 'Ovata Aurea'

Iris graminea

Daffodils

Viburnum tinus

Euphorbia amygdaloides robbiae

Viburnum × hillieri

Aesculus × neglecta 'Erythroblastos'

Viburnum cinnamomifolium

Chionanthus virginicus

Paeonia

Phlox

Staphylea pinnata

Elaeagnus 'Quicksilver'

Leptospermum grandiflorum

Echinops ritro

Alchemilla Mollis

Pyrus Calleryana 'Chanticleer'

Alstroemeria Ligtu hybrids

Smyrnium perfoliatum

Syringa microphylla 'Superba'

Indigofera hebepetala

Syringa × persica

Waldsteinia ternata

Danae racemosa

Danae racemosa

Alchemilla Mollis & Narcissus tazetta

Convallaria majalis

Astrantia major

Salvia officinalis

Potentilla

Mahonia pumila

Mahonia napaulensis

Potentilla

Alstroemeria aurea

Alstroemeria Ligtu hybrids

Euphorbia Characias

Inula hekenium

Arum italicum 'Marmoratum'

Pyracantha

Hemerocallis fulva 'Kwanzo variegata'

1m
3 ft
1m
3 ft

Rosa 'Else Poulsen'

Caryopteris × *clandonensis*

Aesculus × *neglecta* 'Erythroblastos'

Smyrnium perfoliatum

Crinum × powellii

Symphytum caucasicum

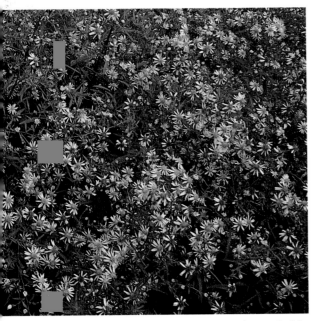

Aster ericoides

Gaura lindheimeri

Angelica archangelica

Ilex aquifolium
Rosa 'Wolley-Dod'
Symphytum caucasicum
Rosa 'Wolley-Dod'
Paeonia suffruticosa 'Duchess of York'
Rosa 'Wolley-Dod'
Phlomis
Crinum × powellii
Scilla peruviana
Crinum × powellii
Scilla peruviana
Crinum × powellii

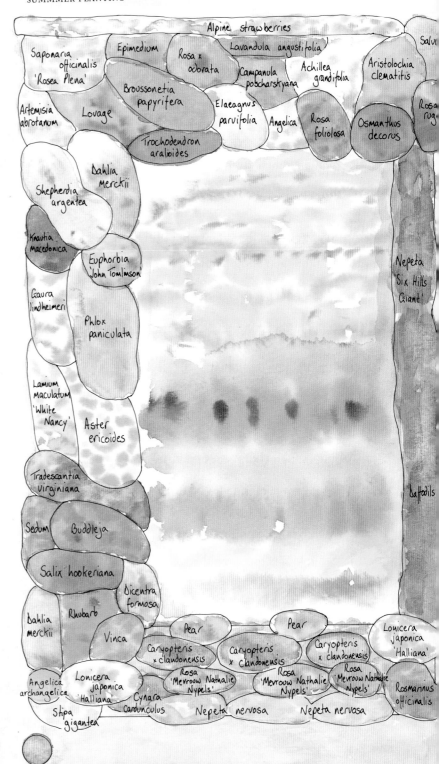

SUMMMER PLANTING

N

Alpine strawberries

Saponaria officinalis 'Rosea Plena'
Epimedium
Rosa × odorata
Lavandula angustifolia
Salvi
Campanula poscharskyana
Achillea grandifolia
Aristolochia clematitis
Artemisia abrotanum
Lovage
Broussonetia papyrifera
Elaeagnus parvifolia
Angelica
Rosa foliolosa
Osmanthus decorus
Rosa rug
Trochodendron araloides
Shepherdia argentea
Dahlia Merckii
Knautia Macedonica
Euphorbia 'John Tomlinson'
Gaura lindheimeri
Phlox paniculata
Nepeta 'Six Hills Giant'
Lamium maculatum 'White Nancy'
Aster ericoides
Tradescantia Virginiana
Sedum
Buddleja
Salix hookeriana
Dicentra formosa
Dahlia merckii
Rhubarb
Pear
Pear
Lonicera japonica 'Halliana'
Vinca
Caryopteris × clandonensis
Caryopteris × clandonensis
Caryopteris × clandonensis
Angelica archangelica
Lonicera japonica 'Halliana'
Cynara Cardunculus
Rosa 'Mevrouw Nathalie Nypels'
Rosa 'Mevrouw Nathalie Nypels'
Rosa 'Mevrouw Nathalie Nypels'
Rosmarinus officinalis
Stipa gigantea
Nepeta nervosa
Nepeta nervosa
Daffodils

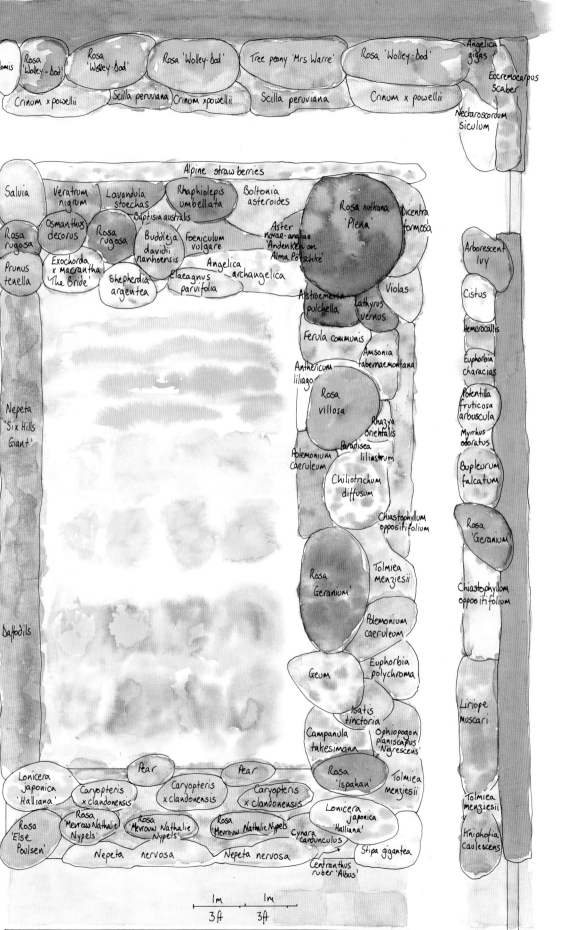

Phlomis
Rosa 'Wolley-Dod'
Rosa 'Wolley-Dod'
Rosa 'Wolley-Dod'
Tree peony 'Mrs Warre'
Rosa 'Wolley-Dod'
Angelica gigas
Eccremocarpus scaber
Crinum × powellii
Scilla peruviana
Crinum × powellii
Scilla peruviana
Crinum × powellii
Nectaroscordum siculum

Alpine strawberries

Salvia
Veratrum nigrum
Lavandula stoechas
Rhaphiolepis umbellata
Boltonia asteroides
Rosa nutkana 'Plena'
Dicentra formosa
Osmanthus decorus
Baptisia australis
Rosa rugosa
Buddleja davidii nanhoensis
Foeniculum vulgare
Aster novae-angliae 'Andenken on Alma Pötschke'
Rosa rugosa
Exochorda × macrantha 'The Bride'
Shepherdia argentea
Elaeagnus parvifolia
Angelica archangelica
Prunus tenella
Violas
Alstroemeria pulchella
Lathyrus vernus
Ferula communis
Amsonia tabernaemontana
Anthericum liliago
Rosa villosa
Rhazya orientalis
Paradisea liliastrum
Polemonium caeruleum
Chiliotrichum diffusum
Chiastophyllum oppositifolium
Nepeta 'Six Hills Giant'
Rosa 'Geranium'
Tolmiea menziesii
Polemonium caeruleum
Euphorbia polychroma
Geum
Daffodils
Isatis tinctoria
Campanula takesimana
Ophiopogon planiscapus 'Nigrescens'
Rosa 'Ispahan'
Tolmiea menziesii
Pear
Pear
Lonicera japonica 'Halliana'
Caryopteris × clandonensis
Caryopteris × clandonensis
Caryopteris × clandonensis
Lonicera japonica 'Halliana'
Rosa 'Else Poulsen'
Rosa 'Mevrouw Nathalie Nypels'
Rosa 'Mevrouw Nathalie Nypels'
Rosa 'Mevrouw Nathalie Nypels'
Cynara cardunculus
Nepeta nervosa
Nepeta nervosa
Centranthus ruber 'Albas'
Stipa gigantea

Arborescent Ivy
Cistus
Hemerocallis
Euphorbia characias
Potentilla fruticosa arbuscula
Myrrhus odoratus
Bupleurum falcatum
Rosa 'Geranium'
Chiastophyllum oppositifolium
Liriope muscari
Tolmiea menziesii
Kniphofia caulescens

1m 1m
3ft 3ft

Paeonia suffruticosa 'Mrs Warre'

Crinum × powellii 'Album'

Scilla peruviana

Ophiopogon planiscapus 'Nigrescens'

Rhaphiolepis umbellata

THE GALLICA ROSE BEDS AND THE DRY RIDGE

ON THE SOUTH side of the Kitchen Garden, beneath the yew hedge that separates it from the Fountain Garden, two rectangular beds are planted with a carpet of *Rosa gallica* var. *officinalis*, the apothecary's rose. This is another of Mrs Reiss's inspired ideas, well worth copying in other gardens.

The apothecary's rose, also known as the red rose of Lancaster, has richly scented semi-double rosy-crimson flowers, with prominent yellow anthers. A sport of the deep pink *Rosa gallica*, a rose grown in Europe from the earliest recorded times, it has been known in cultivation since the fourteenth century. Produced after the main flush of midsummer roses, the flowers last about three weeks provided they are not damaged by rain. After flowering is over things are less satisfactory. The flower heads should be removed, for aesthetic reasons; if this task is neglected, the rose looks a mess.

There is a standard *Viburnum carlesii* positioned at the far end of each bed. Blue scillas make a carpet beneath the roses in early spring and by April *Leucojum aestivum*, the summer snowflake, is flowering as freely as it would in a damp meadow, each 60cm/2ft stem holding its flower head above the developing roses. Its white bell-shaped flowers resemble snowdrops but have out-turned green tips and hang in a loose cluster. The form we grow is the best, *L.a.* 'Gravetye Giant', which had its origin in William Robinson's garden at Gravetye Manor in Sussex. It seeds itself in neighbouring beds.

An old lonicera hedge once grew on the other side of the Gallica rose beds. We removed it, to leave a ridge supported by a low wall. This is the only raised bed in the garden and, well drained and partly shaded, provides ideal conditions for small plants we treasure.

This was always considered a temporary scheme, so it had no planting plan and suitable plants were added on impulse; at first around the base of the hedge and later to fill the available space. At the eastern end, where there is some shade and moisture, a clump of the variegated form of the old daylily *Hemerocallis fulva* 'Kwanzo Variegata' makes a focal point at the end of the long eastern path. It is a coarse plant but in early spring its leaves are valuable. *Bergenia stracheyi* from the Himalaya, a miniature elephant's ears with rounded leaves, makes neat rosettes on the edge of the bed. A temperamental plant, it has white flowers, decorated by green calyces in spring. Near it is a clump of *Euphorbia griffithii* 'Dixter'. Similar to the popular *E.g.* 'Fireglow', with vivid brick-red bracts and colourful leaves, which thrives at the far end of the ridge, it is more muted, with a reddish tinge to the foliage. Next comes a

Above: *The apothecary's rose looks wonderful when in flower, massed in the bed in front of the yew hedge. Using one plant in quantity is an effective way of making a section of the garden appear much larger than it really is. On the dry ridge opposite,* Halimium ocymoides *flowers beside* Geranium sanguineum var. striatum.

Opposite: *On the ridge at the south end of the Kitchen Garden planting is very tight. In spring hellebores seed among the brunnera under the skirts of a large* Daphne pontica, *and* Euphorbia griffithii *'Fireglow' spreads among erythroniums. Summer snowflakes flower in the back bed.*

rough-leaved perennial, *Senecio doria*, with bright yellow daisies in summer – less desirable but easier to grow than purple-flowered *S. pulcher*, which we lost. *Paeonia veitchii* from China is small and slow to establish. It is seldom more than 30cm/12in high, with suckering stems bearing finely cut leaves and pink flowers with cream anthers in late spring. If there were space I would like to have many more species peonies. The ferny leaves of the native pasque flower, *Pulsatilla vulgaris*, found on chalk downs, emerge early to protect the soft silky buds and purple flowers with golden stamens. Later the copper-brown seedheads are as attractive. There are erythroniums and white- and pink-flowered forms of *Pulmonaria saccharata*. Snow-in-summer (*Cerastium tomentosum*) carpets a corner of the steps. *Tulipa orphanidea* Whittallii Group was a gift; it is quite modest, with slender flowers of dull red with a green mark on the outside of the segments. Nearby is an exuberant purple-flowered *Geranium clarkei* 'Kashmir Purple', which flowers prolifically in late spring, and there are small-leaved hostas (such as

the glaucous *Hosta* × *tardiana*) and a variegated form of blue-flowered brunnera (*Brunnera macrophylla* 'Hadspen Cream'). By April the delicate cut foliage of baneberry, *Actaea rubra*, from north-east America, is spearing through the soil. In July, after bearing fluffy white flowers, the actaea has clusters of poisonous pea-sized green berries which quickly turn a glowing red. (A white-berried form is even more desirable.) There is *Daphne* × *burkwoodii* 'Somerset', with pinkish highly scented flowers in sun, and in shade a vast bush of the evergreen yellow-flowered *Daphne pontica*, its flowers fragrant in the evening. Other plants and seedlings include leucojums, alchemillas, and snakeshead fritillaries (*Fritillaria meleagris*) volunteered from nearby beds. Drought-loving deciduous ferns grow in the shadiest parts of the low walls. The effects are random and cottagey, almost a relief from the more ordered colour schemes and plant themes found in most of the garden. However, this sort of 'natural' planting needs constant care, or fast-growing thugs will overwhelm less vigorous plants.

THE SOUTH BORDERS

A T THE SOUTH END of the garden, under one of the shapely pears, clumps of my favourite Alexandrian laurel, *Danaë racemosa*, with waving fronds of glossy leaves and dark red berries, are beginning to bush out, 1m/3ft high and wide, above lower groundcover. This shade-lover from the Mediterranean region, so often seen in Italian gardens, thrives in hot dry summers. We introduced *Smyrnium perfoliatum*, with acid-yellow bracts, to this part of the garden and it has begun to spread in the light shade under the pears, on one side next to spreading alstroemeria – the Ligtu hybrid pink form – in a patch of sunlight, and on the other next to clumps of multicoloured *Iris* Californian hybrids planted under a quince (*Cydonia oblonga*). The leaves of smyrniums in the first two seasons much resemble ground elder. It does not flower until three years after being sown. Now, after five years, it is flowering annually, and it threatens to overwhelm the lower *Waldsteinia ternata*, which is meant to make a neat square on the two 'pear' corners. Other volunteers have already spoiled the intended symmetry. Seedling martagon lilies, snakeshead fritillaries, wild cardamine or cuckoo spit (a favourite but easily weeded out), tway-blades (*Listera ovata*) and common aquilegias all find the waldsteinia area a perfect breeding ground. I wonder if Phyllis Reiss allowed these intruders? She probably did, and welcomed them. Any plant lists and plans are apt to become sacrosanct once committed to paper and seldom represent the original designer's maturing wishes.

At the edge of these beds, to add height and mark the division between ornamentals and kitchen garden proper, we have added the relatively new (to commerce) *Elaeagnus* 'Quicksilver' (once thought to be a variety of the Russian olive, *E. angustifolia*, but with the suckering habit of the lower-growing *E. commutata*). With its silvery leaves and wonderfully scented yellow flowers, it is spectacular in late spring. It is a better flowerer than *E. angustifolia* but it has a fault, for by late summer it is dropping its leaves and looks as if it is dying. For this reason I hesitate to place it in the gardens of clients and remain faithful to the true Russian olive. Nearby, the upright *Staphylea pinnata* bears drooping white panicles in late spring, followed by baggy green capsules through the summer. This shrub, from south Europe and western Asia, has been grown in Britain since the sixteenth century. On the other side of the path, a tree peony, from seed brought from Spain, has grown tall. Its pink flowers present a foil to the silver elaeagnus leaves. All of this is underplanted with *Alchemilla mollis* and Japanese anemones.

Rose 'Geranium' has scarlet flowers in early summer. These are followed by orange flagon-shaped pendulous fruits which remain decorative for many months. Growing tall and wide at the top, this rose does not make dense shade, so many small plants can be grown next to it. They help to disguise the ugly woody base which develops over a period of years.

THE EASTERN PATHWAY

THE EASTERN pathway, running beside a narrow bed under the yew hedge which separates the kitchen area from the Pool Garden, has acquired a character of its own, more or less separating it from the rest of the kitchen area. Evergreen and deciduous shrubs and low perennials flop over each side of the path.

This was the first area in which we planted more experimentally. An alcove with a copper pot, in which are planted tulips followed by summer-flowering annuals (or, more recently, lilies), is framed by two large hollies, *Ilex aquifolium* 'Golden Milkboy' and *I.a.* 'Ovata Aurea', grown to make architectural pyramids, both with startling golden patterns or splashings on their leaves. In the former the gold is in the centre of the leaf, while the latter has green leaves margined with yellow. Taller evergreen shrubs screen this path from the vegetables. *Photinia davidiana* (formerly *Stransvaesia davidiana*) is trained as a standard; *Viburnum* × *hillieri*, tender glossy-leaved *V. odoratissimum* and the sacred Chinese bamboo, *Nandina domestica*, are all mature specimens. The deciduous Persian lilac, *Syringa* × *persica*, has scented mauve flowers in late spring, and the fringe tree, *Chionanthus virginicus*, bears drooping white panicles in early summer. The shrubs along this side of the 'secret' pathway, and the yew hedge on the other, are underplanted with spreading plants. *Arum italicum* 'Marmoratum', with marbled cream and green leaves in winter, shrub-like, glaucous-leaved *Euphorbia characias* and the soft-stemmed *E. amygdaloides* var. *robbiae* are evergreen, as are grassy-leaved *Liriope muscari* and *Chiastophyllum oppositifolium* – a small creeping plant with yellow flower tassels in summer, ideal for edging in half-shade. Also under the shrubs (although it would probably prefer a more open situation), *Iris graminea*, the grassy-leaved plum tart, flowers early. Its apple-scented flowers, nestling in the long leaves, have purple styles and violet falls. On the sunny side, under the yew hedge, the spreading *Alstroemeria aurea* competes with neighbouring Ligtu hybrids in shades of pink.

A pair of grasses, *Stipa gigantea*, with purplish-golden flower heads, arch almost to meet on either side of the entrance to the rose/pear walk, at the bottom of the steps from the Pool Garden. With wands reaching to 2m/7ft, this is my favourite perennial grass, best viewed against a western sky in the evening. Beyond the more open end of the eastern pathway, shrub roses are a feature. One of the most beautiful of the old roses, Damask rose 'Ispahan', with fragrant light pink semi-double flowers, grows on the inner side of the path, as does *Rosa* 'Geranium', with scarlet waxy flowers.

The old copper container, in light shade, is perfect for summer felicias and Salvia cacaliifolia, *both of which flower for many months. At Bettiscombe I am going to grow the spreading blue grass,* Elymus arenarius, *in the same pot, but in full sun.*

Growing nearby is *R. villosa* (*R. pomifera*), with grey leaves, wide single pink flowers and the largest apple-like hips. The tall large *R. nutkana* 'Plena', better known as *R. californica* 'Plena', with graceful arching branches, grows on a corner; it has grey-green leaves and double pink flowers. Between these large roses grow St Bernard's lilies, *Anthericum liliago* and St Bruno's lilies, *Paradisea liliastrum*. These are very similar, both flowering in early summer with white tubular flowers on spikes, but St Bernard's lilies are taller and more substantial. Both *Rhazya orientalis* from Asia and the closely related North American *Amsonia tabernaemontana*, also in this border, have small starry flowers in misty blue, and untidy grassy leaves. The giant fennel, *Ferula communis*, from the shores of the Mediterranean, has a tracery of delicately divided leaves in spring, from which, occasionally, 2m/7ft stems bear great umbelliferous yellow cow-parsley heads in summer. Tap-rooted, it must be grown from seed and transplanted to its permanent site when young.

The North Borders

At the northern boundary of the Kitchen Garden, in front of the holly hedge, tall bushes of grey-leaved *Rosa* 'Wolley-Dod' (*R. villosa* 'Duplex') have pink flowers in profusion followed by large apple-like fruits. Now 3m/10ft tall, they tower above a line of pink- and white-flowered forms of *Crinum × powellii*. The crinums, beautiful in flower in late summer, are difficult to manage. The leaves come through the ground early and their tips are always scorched by frost, with blemishes remaining all through the season. I have tried throwing over light coverings of some protective material when late frosts are threatened but still have not solved this problem. Grey-leaved comfrey, *Symphytum caucasicum*, contributes pale blue flowers on tall stems which rise behind the crinums in early summer. It is an excellent plant for sun or half-shade, easily grown from seed and distributing itself naturally if allowed to do so.

Lavenders, shrubby sages and alpine strawberries thrive and spread under the light shade of *Elaeagnus parvifolia* and the male form of the rare Chinese paper mulberry, *Broussonetia papyrifera*, which bears long catkins in spring. (In China and Japan the exfoliating bark of large plants was used for making paper and the bark fibre for making cloth.)

Nearby is *R. foliolosa*, a pink North American rose that grows only 1m/3ft high and wide; with no thorns and suckering freely it is suitable, if grown on its own roots, for hedging or massing and – like *R. nitida* and the swamp rose, *R. palustris*, neither grown at Tintinhull – it is a good choice for moist areas. Also in sun at this end of the garden, *Exochorda × macrantha* 'The Bride' flowers early with the daffodils, opening the shrub season with its double white flowers. In the same area false indigo, *Baptisia australis*, with blue pea flowers and grey leaves, flowers in midsummer, black seed pods hanging on until well in the autumn. Close by is one of the last flowers to bloom, daisy-flowered *Boltonia asteroides*, a first cousin to the Michaelmas daisy tribe. It has silvery leaves and yellow-centred white flowers. It grows near the cerise-scarlet *Aster novae-angliae* 'Andenken an Alma Pötschke', the brightest of all Michaelmas daisies.

THE WEST BEDS

ON THE WESTERN fringe of the garden two large *Euphorbia characias* ssp. *wulfenii* 'John Tomlinson' make a magnificent splash, their 30cm/12in flower heads a strong acid-yellow. In my opinion this is a better form than Margery Fish's euphorbia 'Lambrook Gold', its bracts more pointed and its habit more graceful. These giant euphorbias have a short life span and cuttings are taken every spring. Cistus, olearias, late-flowering asters and annuals flourish along this western boundary. We often store summer-flowering perennials here in rows during the winter months; each year a few are kept back as emergency stopgaps for the main borders. A spreading clump of scarlet Cape figwort, *Phygelius capensis*, first came here in this way, and has been allowed to stay.

Below: Angelica archangelica *and silvery cardoons make a handsome setting for the stone vase at the end of the rose walk. Edible plants, with superbly decorative foliage, they link the ornamental appearance of the Kitchen Garden with its more mundane aspect.*

Above: *Orderly rows of potatoes and carrots are edged on one side by catmint and on the other by mixed planting that includes white-flowered* Cistus × corbariensis *and forget-me-nots. The dark-leaved plant is sweet william,* Dianthus barbatus Nigrescens Group, *the foliage of which turns purple after a cold winter. It has been lined out for use in the hot borders in the Pool Garden.*

Left: *The view into the old cider orchard on the north side of the garden is framed by rose 'Wolley-Dod', crinums, Rugosa roses and phlomis species. This vista is the only glimpse of the outside world from the Tintinhull garden.*

Sowing Seed in Open Ground

Forget-me-nots for early spring are planted throughout the garden. They are allowed to seed, germinate and flower in the following season wherever they choose to establish themselves. But the intensity of blue decreases each season, so every few years, in June, we sow a batch of a named myosotis from one of the reliable seed catalogues.

So long as the ground is well prepared, sowing the seed of annuals or biennials is very easy. Our problem is always finding a suitable space for a row in the already packed Kitchen Garden. Stretch a string between two pegs, make a shallow trench with the back of a rake and carefully scatter the fine seed along the row (*above, right and far right*). Rake a little soil over the top but do not firm it in (*right*). Then water the soil, using a watering can with a fine rose

(*below right*). The row should be labelled with the name of the plant and the date of planting – I usually put the label in before I even begin the sowing, as it is so easy to forget to do it afterwards.

By September the young plants have usually made quite a lot of growth (*below left*), and they should be moved to the situations in which they will flower the following spring, so that roots get well established before cold weather sets in. This moving always presents us with another difficulty, as the current year's annuals are still in fine condition and it is difficult to make space without discarding plants which are contributing to the summer display. One solution is to pot up plants individually and keep them in cold frames for the winter, ready to plant out in early spring. In fact it is always advisable to keep some potted plants in reserve in case the winter is severe.

Gardening is never a matter of a cut-and-dried list of tasks – when you are doing one thing you will always see something else that needs attention. When I was watering my forget-me-nots I noticed that the blue hyacinth bean, *Lablab purpureus* (*Dolichos lablab*), was looking a bit dry, so I took the rose off the watering can and gave it a good soaking.

Taking Rose Cuttings

W HILE NURSERYMEN usually feel constrained to graft roses on to a chosen stock rose, in your own garden, free from the necessity to guarantee uniformity of strength and vigour, you can increase your rose supply by rooting cuttings. Not all cultivated roses are sufficiently vigorous to do well on their own roots – highly bred Hybrid Teas, for example, really need to be grafted – but I would certainly recommend taking cuttings of species and other strong-growing roses. Apart from the intrinsic satisfaction, there is also a practical advantage: most roses grown on their own roots will not produce suckers, which can easily develop when a plant is grafted on to a stock rose; and removing suckers is one of the most tedious of garden tasks.

All twenty-four plants of the Polyantha rose 'Mevrouw Nathalie Nypels' in the double border of the Kitchen Garden are from two original plants obtained in 1980. I take cuttings of semi-mature wood around the middle of the summer (*above right*). Using sharp secateurs I cut off non-flowering shoots 20–25cm/8–10in long, making sure they have a heel of the old wood attached (*above, far right*), and pop them quickly into a plastic bag to prevent them drying out. In the potting shed I snip off some of the upper leaves (*right*), remove the lower leaves and trim off the heel with a razor blade or a very sharp knife. Alternatively, I cut up pieces of longer stems, making the base cut just below one node (where the leaves join the stem) and the upper cut just above another. I then plunge the whole shoot in a fungicide to prevent disease, and dip the rooting end into a hormone rooting powder to stimulate root growth.

About six semi-mature cuttings should fit around the edge of an 8cm/3in pot filled with a mixture of peat (or peat alternative), loam and vermiculite (*below right*). It is possible to root in pure vermiculite, but I use loam as it provides some nutrition for the young cuttings if I am too busy to pot on as soon as they have rooted. I keep the cuttings in a mist propagator with underheating, positioning them where they will be kept moist, but not drowned. New young shoots on the cuttings indicate that a viable root system has been established. In the moist warmth of the propagator cuttings taken at midsummer usually develop roots by early autumn, and at that point I pot them up individually. They are then transferred to a cold frame for the winter. They can be planted out the following spring, to perform in their first year.

Alternatively, hardwood cuttings can be taken in autumn. They are treated in the same way as semi-mature cuttings, except that they are planted out about 20cm/8in apart in an open trench with some coarse sand at the bottom to encourage rooting. Or they may be kept covered in a closed airtight frame. They will be rooted by the spring, but should be left undisturbed until the following autumn when they can be potted up.

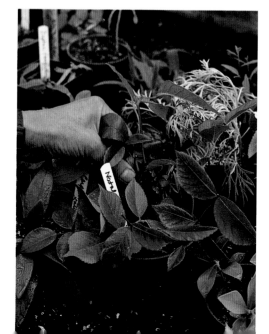

Using Shrub Roses

S HRUB ROSES ARE infinitely useful in the garden. Both the 'old' roses – including species and varieties, most often garden crosses already centuries old – and the more modern hybrids have distinctive characteristics which make them striking as garden features. At the same time, with their lax but graceful habit, they fit effectively into mixed planting schemes, happily associating with other shrubs – such as viburnums, deutzias and philadelphus – and with soft-stemmed herbaceous plants.

Shrub roses are year-round plants, their shapes and stems, and sometimes beautiful fruits, gracing the garden even in winter. In spring the arching branches protect spring-flowering bulbs. Summer foliage effects are very variable: leaves can be mat (most of the Gallicas) or glossy green, glaucous purple-flushed grey (*R. glauca*) or silvery grey (*R.* × *alba* and *R. villosa* types) to fresh crinkled apple-green (most of the Rugosas); occasionally they are fragrant (*R. eglanteria*). The old species and garden hybrids have a limited flowering period, with a main flush in early or midsummer. Their flowers, often deliciously fragrant, are mainly in a range from dark crimson through mauve to palest pink or white. However, since the 1900s selective breeding has produced many modern shrub roses with an extended flowering period and in a wider colour range. David Austin's 'English' roses combine shrubby characteristics with a degree of perpetual flowering.

Some shrub roses are vast and spreading, suitable for the larger garden and appropriate for curtaining old trees; these include the species *R. mulliganii*, the famed *R. filipes* 'Kiftsgate', the desirable 'Bobbie James' and 'Rambling Rector' and,

Rosa filipes 'Kiftsgate'

Rosa 'The Garland'

Rosa 'Rambling Rector'

Miss Jekyll's favourite, 'The Garland'. Then there are the healthy suckering roses, which need not be underplanted. Among these are the spring-flowering Scotch burnet roses, varieties and hybrids of *R. pimpinellifolia*, and the American species *RR. virginiana*, *palustris* and *nitida*, which are useful end-of-season performers. Among the bushy Rugosas there are roses of all sizes for mixed companion planting. With apple-green crinkly leaves and carmine, pink or white flowers followed by large red or orange hips, they can be used as garden features, for hedging and, as they are impervious to salt winds, for seaside planting. Some of the Rugosa hybrids, such as the trailing 'Max Graf', are glossy-leaved groundhuggers. Other prostrate roses are the dense and prickly species *R. × paulii* and its pink hybrid 'Paulii Rosea'. 'Raubritter', with dense globular pink flower heads, will clothe banks and suppress weeds.

Personally, even when I am gardening in a small space, I prefer to have a few large shrub roses rather than the more compact and – to me – less graceful varieties. Any garden can find room for the grey-leaved *R. glauca*, which creates little shade and fits in with all mixed planting. Among old roses, Gallicas are the smallest: their gloriously

'Complicata'

ped and scented flowers make up for ir lack of distinction in habit. Another of favourites is 'Irène Watts' which grows to 60cm/2ft across. It has peachy-pink ers opening from pointed buds.

grew some shrub roses in my first house garden when I was a complete inner, choosing those I had liked in other gardens. At Hadspen I extended the range, mixing them with other shrubs. I remember planting the pink-flowered modern shrub *R.* 'Complicata' to grow through quick-growing sea buckthorn, *Hippophaë rhamnoides*, later adding blue-flowered *Clematis* 'Perle d'Azur' to clamber between the grey leaves of the upper branches of the buckthorn for late-summer effects, and underplanting the scheme with *Geranium* × *oxonianum* 'Wargrave Pink'. Elsewhere I experimented with roses interesting for their foliage, bark or translucent thorns. *R. omeiensis*, now *R. sericea* ssp. *omeiensis*, from the Himalaya, has fern-like foliage and stout branches armed with bright translucent red thorns. *R.s.* ssp. *omeiensis* f. *pteracantha* has brown stems clad with wedge-shaped thorns. The smaller *R. primula* has brown thorny stems and fern-like leaves. *R. roxburghii*, the burr or chestnut rose, which thrives in the southern states of America, is distinct, with tawny-brown slightly angular stems and flaky bark. The flowers are shell-pink.

At Tintinhull we have massed beds of the old apothecary's rose, *R. gallica* var. *officinalis*, at the south end of the Kitchen Garden, and the grey-leaved *R.* 'Wolley-Dod' (*R. villosa* 'Duplex'), grows as a towering hedge at the north end. We have the true *R. villosa* (*R. pomifera*) at the edge of the eastern pathway, with *R. nutkana*

'Plena', *R.* 'Geranium' and the Damask rose 'Ispahan' nearby. We also grow both old and modern shrub roses as companion plants scattered throughout all the borders in the garden. With few exceptions we stick to scented roses with a traditional colour range.

Unless you are a collector, the shrub roses in your garden must be easy to manage, healthy and vigorous. Rose replant disease is a recurring problem in many gardens, including Tintinhull. When we first came we had to sterilize or replace the soil wherever there had been roses or members of the Rosaceae family (see page 207). If your garden is similarly affected you may need to do the same, or, alternatively, not grow roses in that part of the garden for at least five years.

Shrub roses, old and new, like rich feeding with organic mulches. Generally, little pruning is needed, but if necessary whole branches can be cut back after

flowering and in winter the oldest wood can be cut to ground level, opening out the centre of the bush. Any frost-tipped shoots should be removed in early spring. You can avoid the chore of removing suckers by growing the roses on their own roots (see page 111). These roses should never be sheared off at a uniform height to make a frill of new growth. It is their graceful habit, as much as their flowering beauty, which makes them such an asset in the garden.

Rosa 'Ispahan'

Hardy Geraniums

When I began to garden, my first 'scheme' was a small collection of shrub roses underplanted with crane's-bill geraniums. The twining stems, thick foliage and gentle flowing habits of geraniums seemed to make them especially suitable for growing around the base of bare rugged rose stems. The flower colours, also, in misty blues, dark velvet-purple and brighter pinks and magentas, often enlivened by deeper veining, seemed to tone successfully with all the shrub roses I had. From that day, I have valued their many qualities.

There are hardy geraniums to suit most

Geranium maderense

Geranium pratense 'Plenum Violaceum'

situations. They are invaluable for infilling between more disciplined upright plants, happily weaving their way to cover the soil. None seem fussy about the soil type but most show some preference between sun or shade and dry or moist situations. Some, including *Geranium cinereum*, *G. macror-rhizum*, *G. phaeum*, *G. platypetalum*, *G. clarkei* 'Kashmir White' and 'Kashmir Purple', *G. pratense* 'Plenum Violaceum', *G. renardii* and *G. sylvaticum*, make wide hummocks. A few, such as *G. psilostemon*, with black-centred magenta flowers and

autumn-tinted foliage, grow more upright. A third category is tender and includes two stars, the self-seeding *G. maderense* and *G. palmatum*. Both are handsome foliage plants with clusters of pink-mauve flowers. The taller *G. palmatum* is most ornamental and is good for containers; *G. maderense* seeds prolifically at Tintinhull, surviving in sheltered corners through all but the hardest winters.

The geraniums most commonly grown are violet-blue *G. × magnificum*, *G. × oxonianum* and its hybrids and cultivars (the

Geranium phaeum 'Album'

On pages 118-19, left to right:
Geranium phaeum
Geranium clarkei 'Kashmir White'
Geranium pratense 'Mrs Kendall Clark'

very vigorous *G. × o.* 'Claridge Druce', with grey-green leaves and magenta-pink flowers, and *G. × o.* 'Wargrave Pink', with brighter pink petals than the type) and forms of the much lower-growing smaller magenta *G. sanguineum*. Of these I like best 'Glenluce', with clear pink flowers, which I use as a carpet under pink roses.

My favourites – for the veined beauty of their flowers and their natural habit – are varieties of *G. pratense*, the meadow crane's-bill. As their name suggests, they prefer open, field-like conditions. *G. pratense* itself is tall and graceful, increasing around the garden by self-sown seed. Good varieties include *G.p.* 'Striatum', with veined petals, and *G.p.* 'Mrs Kendall Clark', with pearly-grey flowers. The double forms with rosette-like flowers are most compact for border grouping; both lavender-blue *G.p.* 'Plenum Caeruleum' and the richer violet-blue *G.p.* 'Plenum Violaceum' make long-flowering companions for strong perennials. Two varieties of *G. clarkei*, 'Kashmir Purple' and 'Kashmir White', have many of the *pratense* characteristics, but, spreading by rhizomes, are lower-growing.

I particularly admire those geraniums which really prefer shade; so much the better if they will also tolerate dry conditions. The European *G. nodosum* grows to 45cm/18in, with glossy leaves and small lilac flowers; it self-seeds under evergreens, its flowers paling if in full sun. Equally tolerant of shade is *G. phaeum*, the mourning widow, with small dark maroon, almost black, flowers; its white variety is even more desirable.

A Wealth of Viburnums

Viburnum × carlcephalum

Evergreen and deciduous viburnums are among the best and most versatile of shrubs, with beautiful white or pink-flushed flowers, good black, red or turquoise fruits (provided there is the necessary cross-pollination) and, in many cases, striking autumn foliage. There are winter-, spring- and autumn-flowering viburnums, and there are many cultivars suitable for the smaller garden.

Growing in sun or semi-shade, viburnums like moist conditions. They enjoy a rich loamy soil but are not at all fussy about whether it is acid or alkaline. Pruning consists of removing old or dead wood in spring, at the same time carefully cutting back any of the evergreen varieties which take up more than their allotted space. They can be propagated from late-summer cuttings of semi-ripe wood. All deciduous viburnums allow small bulbs and little woodlanders to grow under their skirts, while the bushier evergreens can be trained against walls to save space.

Deciduous viburnums

In autumn and early winter, and continuously in mild spells through the succeeding few months, the remarkably frost-resistant rose-tinted flowers of the deciduous *Viburnum farreri* waft their scent through the garden. The hybrid *V. × bodnantense* 'Dawn' also flowers from late autumn to early spring, its rich rose-red buds opening on the leafless stem to white flushed with pink. *V. carlesii*, its many garden cultivars and its hybrid *V. × carlcephalum* all flower in early spring. All are pink-budded, fragrant, medium-sized and compact, and can be trained to make round-headed standards.

V. sargentii 'Onondaga', with maple-like leaves, bronze when young and again in autumn, flowers early. It is a compact bush for the smaller garden. When space is not a problem, forms of the guelder rose, *V. opulus*, are highly desirable. The sterile cultivar with creamy snowball flowers *V.o.* 'Roseum' (*V.o.* 'Sterile') is wonderful in late spring, and the yellow-fruited *V.o.* 'Xanthocarpum' is decorative later.

Perhaps the loveliest form of the prized Japanese snowball, *V. plicatum*, is *V.p.* 'Mariesii', with tabulated branches bearing white lacecap flowers. The foliage colours well for the late summer. It is an architectural shrub to be paired for corners or used singly as a focal point. A smaller version, *V.p.* 'Nanum Semperflorens' (*V.p.* 'Watanabe'), grows slowly into an almost conical shape. *V.p.* 'Grandiflorum' has large white sterile flower heads.

Both *V. dilatatum* and the lofty *V. betulifolium* would be worth growing for their clusters of redcurrant-like fruit alone, but these are large shrubs, more suitable for woodland. To ensure cross-pollination, several, from different sources, should be grown in a group. An American hybrid of *V. dilatatum*, *V.* 'Oneida', grows to 3m/10ft only, and has creamy-white flower trusses and dark glossy leaves.

Evergreens

Forms of the evergreen laurustinus, *Viburnum tinus*, are robust winter-flowering shrubs. They have a dense bushy habit and are clothed to the ground with glossy green leaves, which makes them suitable for hedging. Their pink-budded flat white flowers are followed by metallic blue fruit.

Viburnum × bodnantense 'Dawn'

Viburnum plicatum 'Mariesii'

Viburnum × burkwoodii

Viburnum tinus 'Eve Price'

I prefer the more compact cultivar 'Eve Price', with attractive flattened heads of carmine buds and pink-tinged flowers.

V. × burkwoodii is one of my favourite viburnums. With leaves shining above but brownish-felted beneath, it produces scented pink-budded flowers from midwinter until late spring. For very cold areas, *V.* 'Pragense', bred in Prague and adapted to a continental climate, is an alternative; neither leaves nor buds are ever damaged by frost. *V. rhytidophyllum* is another useful plant which will thrive in a cold garden; it will also tolerate chalk. *V. henryi* is not often seen, but it is a handsome open shrub with narrow glossy green leaves and fragrant white flower panicles in early summer. *V. × hillieri* 'Winton' is semi-evergreen and bears masses of creamy-white flower panicles in midsummer. Also summer-flowering, and very attractive, are *V. cinnamomifolium*, with interesting reddish stalks to the leaves, and *V. cylindricum*, which has leaves with a waxy metallic sheen.

On a spring day at dawn in the Pool Garden, trees from behind the walls are reflected in the central pool. Beside the summerhouse the acid-yellow of the large euphorbias contrasts with the differing blues of ceanothus and spiky *Iris pallida* ssp. *pallida*. The flag iris, *Iris pseudacorus*, in the water, can spread at an alarming rate, but its leaves and flowers unify the scheme.

THE POOL GARDEN

ALTHOUGH THE Pool Garden is hidden away in the centre of the garden complex, direct axes and cross views to other garden sections unite it with the design as a whole. Screened from other areas by tall yew hedges on either side, it has a classical rectangular layout. The plan is simple, and the volume of space created by symmetrically arranged lawns and water, by vertical walls of yew and by the sky overhead, harks back to the enclosed Muslim garden and the Italian Renaissance garden which derived from it.

Until 1947 the whole Pool Garden space, enclosed on the east and west by yew hedges and on the north by a wall, was a tennis court. Mrs Reiss raised £500 by the sale of an old cider orchard across the road and used the money to lay out the canal with its flanking grass panels and the main borders and to build the summerhouse. She dedicated this new garden area to the memory of her nephew, a pilot killed in the last year of the 1939–45 war.

In fact the area is not an exact rectangle but its irregularities, including a definite slant to the south, are disguised by clever planting. Mrs Reiss gave the pool and summerhouse central positions and made the flower beds flanking the summerhouse asymmetrical. This adjustment, although of minimal necessity here, is worth remembering, for the principle can be applied to any awkwardly shaped site. If the dominant features of the garden space are centred and aligned, the eye will overlook irregularities, perhaps in awkward perimeter lines, and will automatically home in on the geometry. It is surprising how many seemingly formal gardens are made in shapes that are not symmetrical and do not have straight edges. In some, particularly the linear gardens made by the French in the seventeenth century, the laws of perspective controlled distance and size, and plants were deliberately set closer together or further apart to create definite effects. The same rules of vision can be applied to planting and, in conjunction with the principles of colour theory, they can be used to deceive the eye and make a satisfactorily balanced picture.

The summerhouse in the Pool Garden, with its view down the formal pool to the urn in the Middle Garden, is the natural centre of the whole garden at Tintinhull. All routes around the garden lead to it. Seats are placed invitingly in the shady interior, and decorative pots, filled with exotic or fragrant plants, are arranged to give

Left: *The Pool Garden at midday, looking south, with the Middle Garden's tall spreading holm oaks reflected in the pool. All still-water schemes should be managed so that at least two-thirds of the water surface is kept clear of aquatics. In the end borders, part of the Middle Garden scheme, the variegated elder and the pyracantha are in full flower.*

Right: *On the corner of the summerhouse, the dark purple flowers of* Clematis *'Jackmanii Superba' entangle with bronze-leaved* Vitis vinifera *'Purpurea'. Regale lilies, blue salvias and white argyranthemums grow in the pots just in front of the building.*

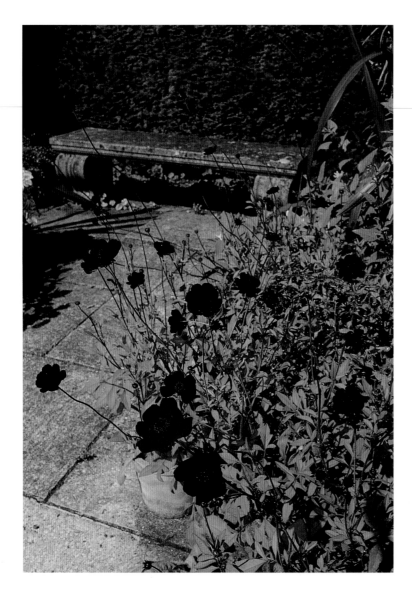

pleasure. From here the distinctive colour schemes of the two contrasting main borders in the Pool Garden can be viewed and appraised simultaneously.

The Pool Garden's rigid architectural layout is interlaced with loose organic planting. Small trees, shrubs and soft-stemmed plants growing in naturalistic profusion overlap the stiff lines of walls, hedges and front border edges. Hedge-clipping, mowing and edge-trimming are done by rule, but the management of the free-style planting is more demanding. It requires a good knowledge of the plants' behaviour and needs, as well as a trained eye for proportion and colour. This is what might be called 'skilled' rather than 'high' maintenance. It is the sort of gardening challenge that I enjoy and often suggest to clients.

Each of the two main borders has a break in the centre. In one a seat is framed by plain yew; the other reveals the archway over the steps which descend to the Kitchen Garden and the rose walk. Both colour schemes are typically Tintinhull in style but, as in any mixed border, the shapes of plants and the colours and textures of leaves play an important supporting role. The border scheme on the west side of the garden has strong and bright colours, a 'hot' mixture; the eastern borders are planted with groups of predominantly pale-coloured 'cool' flowerers. Both schemes are planned to reach a peak from mid- to late summer, but both include a few spring-flowering shrubs – *Cytisus* × *praecox* and a smoke bush in the hot borders, deutzias and *Viburnum plicatum* 'Mariesii' in the pale borders, philadelphus in both.

Although the Pool Garden is self-consciously designed for colour patterns and repetitions, a more naturalistic spirit is introduced, as in all the other Tintinhull 'rooms', by encouraging a certain amount of spontaneous seeding. In the hot borders soaring verbascums establish in both the back and the front of the beds, while in the paler composition grey-leaved opium poppies seed in drifts between established clumps of perennials.

The main colour impact begins in June, when the defined colour schemes become recognizable. Throughout the summer, plants in containers – at the corners of the pool, in and outside the summerhouse, on steps and in the alcove of yew at the south end of the hot borders – bulk up the adjacent border colour schemes. Green leaves in different textures and sizes and more self-consciously placed grey and silver foliage plants, laced through both schemes, link and integrate the borders, bringing out the paler hues and exaggerating the more vivid. Although planted as naturally as possible, with tightly packed colour drifts interweaving to blur sharp-edged divisions, these beds are the most 'dressed' in the garden. At summer's peak the pale west-facing borders are most spectacular in the early morning mists; the scheme opposite is mellowed and rich in evening light, as shadows lengthen and the sun drops below the high hedge.

Above: *Chocolate-scented* Cosmos atrosanguineus *grows in terracotta pots by the stone bench in the south-west corner of the Pool Garden, beside an annual cuphea. This cosmos is quite hardy if protectively mulched during the winter months, but as it comes through the soil very late I prefer to keep it safe in pots.*

Opposite: *A corner of the Pool Garden, looking especially romantic in the early morning light. Tumbling lady's mantle (*Alchemilla mollis*) covers the ground beneath large-leaved* Crambe cordifolia*, while a vertical yellow-flowered verbascum and a self-seeded* Eryngium giganteum *contribute their contrasting flower and leaf textures. Scarlet 'Frensham' roses in the background give a hint of the hot colours which are the main theme of this border.*

The Hot Borders

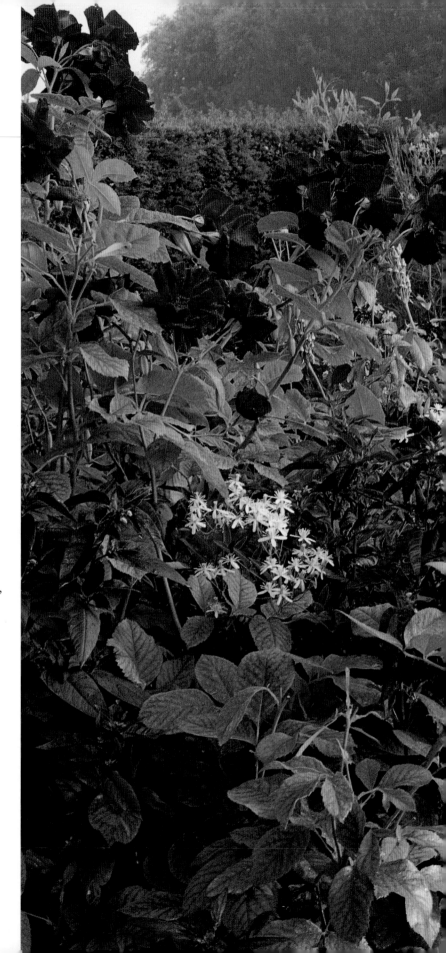

The western borders are primarily intended to convey strong colour sensations. As you turn to face them, hot colours blast the retina and compel a second or two of refocusing, especially after the eye has become accustomed to the softly tinted colours of the pale beds. Scarlet, vermilion and crimson reds, with yellows and oranges, all from one segment of the colour wheel, assail the perception; even the pockets of gentle silvery foliage, mainly senecios (now *Brachyglottis* 'Sunshine') and *Artemisia* 'Powis Castle', although allowing some relief, by contrast make the strong neighbouring hues even more arresting.

When we came to Tintinhull in the winter of 1979–80 these borders had been half-emptied in preparation for soil sterilization, mainly against replant diseases. In spring we removed the rest of the plants, storing many through the summer for replanting in the following autumn and spring. The plans for the replanting scheme, which we implemented, were drawn up by Jim Marshall, the National Trust Gardens' Adviser who had taken over responsibility for Tintinhull in the previous year. Mrs Reiss left no planting plans or even plant lists for these borders, and Jim's drawings were mainly based on what we had found still in the beds and on photographs showing red 'Frensham' roses, blue delphiniums and bright yellow achilleas. The roses were planted in four repetitive clumps (two clumps of three in each bed). Jim also put in green-leaved smoke bushes (one in each border – one has since died) and two groups of shrubby variegated snowberries. He used *Potentilla* 'Gibson's Scarlet' and tall orange tiger lilies, both of which have been a huge success. Red dahlias were to be added each year.

Like all detailed plans which include a mixture of shrubs and perennials, these blueprints were only a start. Each season since then, usually in spring, we move groups about to get relationships

I particularly enjoy the view looking along the red and yellow border. By our later years at Tintinhull the midsummer colouring was less hot than it had been earlier, when we had more orange and red flowers. Last summer, when this photograph was taken, the brilliant red of the 'Frensham' roses mingled with the pale blooms of Clematis recta, Nectaroscordum siculum ssp. bulgaricum, Lilium regale, Aruncus dioicus *'Kneiffii' and* Verbascum *'Vernale', the dark purple foliage of* Lysimachia ciliata *'Purpurea' and the yellow-edged leaves of* Symphoricarpos orbiculatus *'Foliis Variegatis'.*

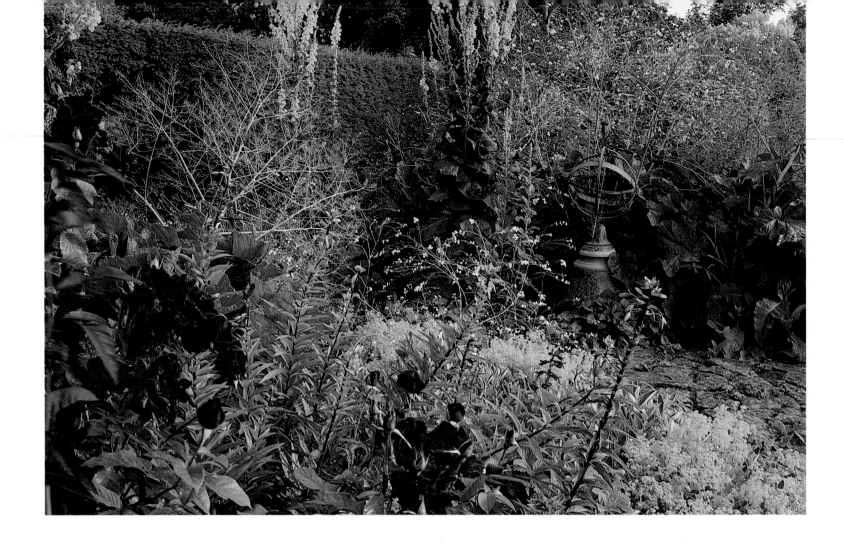

Tall verbascums and crambes, Alchemilla mollis *and 'Frensham' roses thrive around the armillary sphere in the central division of the hot borders. The background frame of the dark green yew hedge and the classical ornament give definition to the luxuriant cottage-style planting.*

right and try new combinations. At first we used only plants recommended to us by the Trust but gradually we became more adventurous, trying suitable new plants and giving up those which failed to get the effects we wanted and believed Mrs Reiss had striven for. The Trust had already replaced *Artemisia absinthium* 'Lambrook Silver' with the bushy *A.* 'Powis Castle', not in existence during Mrs Reiss's time. In breaking with tradition by using a 'new' plant they set a precedent for our experimentation over the next years. (Recently in the United States I met an even more interesting form, *A. absinthium* 'Huntington Gardens', with more distinguished habit, but I have not yet been able to find it in Britain.) We planted delphiniums behind the red roses, as she had done, but Jim must have chosen the wrong shade of blue. For three years we cut off their flower heads as they came into bloom, finding their contrast with the roses too acute. A more purple blue, with some red in it, might have been more successful.

To the 1981 plans we have added scarlet *Crocosmia* 'Lucifer' and some of the bronze-leaved lobelias such as *Lobelia* 'Dark Crusader' (we dig this up in autumn, in spring divide it in containers, and

replant it in early May). More recently we have put in the perennial purple-leaved *Lysimachia ciliata* 'Purpurea'; with its small yellow flowers nestling between the coloured leaves, and a spreading habit, it is perfect for the scheme. At first, as recommended by the Trust, we used red penstemons, grown annually from cuttings and overwintered in cold frames, to bulk up the front of the beds. *Penstemon hartwegii* and *P.* 'Garnet', both dark red, as well as the more vivid 'Scarlet Fire', fitted exactly into the colour harmonies. However, in one hard winter we lost all our cuttings and the following summer we used scarlet tobacco flowers instead, planting four strong clumps of *Nicotiana* 'Scarlet Bedder' along the front of the beds. The next year we substituted tender woody red salvias, which I prefer; but for this scheme it is important to choose those with clear or dark red flowers, avoiding the more cherry hues. *Salvia fulgens*, *S. coccinea* and *S. elegans* all work well (they are useful in the middle of the border as well as along the front edge). More recently we have used red and yellow figwort (*Phygelius*) from South Africa to get our foreground effects. I first admired groups of red- and yellow-flowered forms at the Cambridge Botanic Garden and, as we seemed to be getting hotter and drier summers, decided to attempt a similar combination. *Phygelius × rectus* 'African Queen' and *P. aequalis* 'Yellow Trumpet' now make suckering groups.

The 'Frensham' roses remain a mainstay of the whole border, particularly spectacular in June, but blooming in bursts throughout the rest of the summer. There are few late-flowering red shrubs or perennials to take over when 'Frensham' leaves off, so annuals and tender shrubby plants such as the salvias (overwintered as rooted cuttings) are important to keep the scheme going. We often use dahlias such as 'Bishop of Llandaff' and 'Bloodstone' which fill in during the latter half of the season. We have few yellows and oranges in the early months of summer but many Compositae contribute later. Daisy-flowered achilleas, rudbeckias and bigeneric × *Solidaster hybridus* are essentials, but we avoid the more bronze-flowered heleniums. Creams are also easy to find and we use more of these than in Mrs Reiss's time, softening some of her brightest colour associations. A tall bushy broom, *Cytisus × praecox*, flowers early, quickly followed by cream-flowered camassias which tend to seed throughout, as also does *Nectaroscordum siculum* ssp. *bulgaricum*. Corner plants of architectural *Crambe cordifolia* have wide umbels of small white flowers rising above massive heart-shaped green leaves, to make a statement by the end of May. A large group of cream-coloured *Clematis recta* opens beside tall glaucous-leaved thalictrum (*Thalictrum flavum* ssp. *glaucum*). *Achillea filipendulina* 'Gold Plate' has flat heads of harsh yellow; if I were to follow my own preference, I would replace this with one of the paler cultivars. Red-hot pokers – an unnamed variety we found here – and tall mulleins (*Verbascum* 'Vernale'), allowed to seed through the two beds, make vertical accents. *Crocosmia* 'Lucifer' is a shaft of scarlet in late summer. If there is any space we add groups of *Nicotiana langsdorffii* and *Argyranthemum* 'Jamaica Primrose', which fit equally appropriately into the opposite cool scheme. We have also encouraged orange- and red-flowered forms of *Eccremocarpus scaber* and the yellow canary creeper (*Tropaeolum peregrinum*) to seed freely and twine among shrubs and perennials to further extend the colour scheme.

Over the years we have experimented with colour sequences, finding it best to repeat each vivid hue at least once within the range of vision, but also striving to blend in the same progression colours which are adjacent to each other on the colour wheel. Drifts of pale cream and primrose next to brighter buttercup, then oranges, then scarlets and so on to deeper reds and crimson.

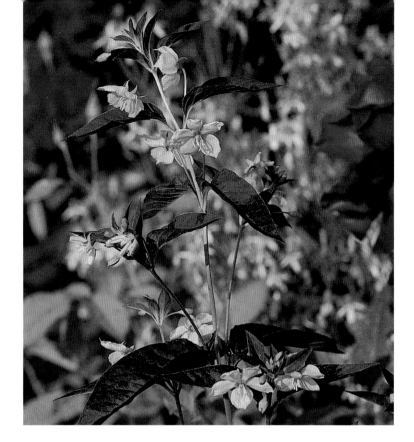

Above: *Like most loosestrifes,* Lysimachia ciliata *'Purpurea' is a rapid colonizer. This cultivar is splendid beneath the 'Frensham' roses, its purple leaves and pale yellow flowers their perfect complement.*

Below: *The tall* Reseda luteola *has pale yellow spikes which seem just right as an addition to the stronger oranges, yellows and reds. It grows to 1.5–1.8m/5–6ft but needs no staking. We hope that it will self-seed with the years and fill in any bare patches of soil.*

Lobelia
'Dark Crusader'

Crocosmia masoniorum

Lilium henryi

Crocosmia 'Lucifer'

Sisyrinchium striatum

Cotinus coggygria

Heuchera micrantha
'Palace Purple'

Self seeders
Achemilla mollis
Camassia
Eccremocarpus scaber
Eryngium giganteum
Euphorbia stricta
Nectaroscordum siculum
   spp. bulgaricum
Oenothera biennis
Sisyrinchium striatum
Tropaeolum peregrinum
Verbascum 'Vernale'

SUMMMER PLANTING

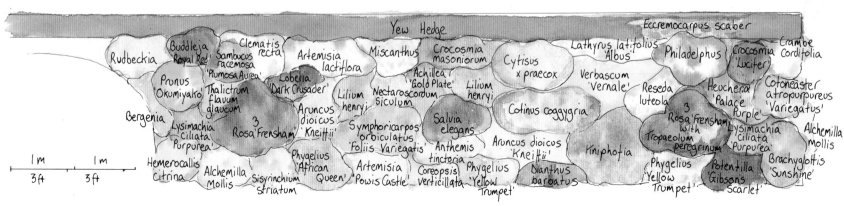

Yew Hedge — Eccremocarpus scaber

Rudbeckia · Buddleja Royal Red · Clematis recta · Sambucus racemosa 'Plumosa Aurea' · Artemisia lactiflora · Miscanthus · Crocosmia masoniorum · Cytisus x praecox · Lathyrus latifolius 'Albus' · Philadelphus · Crocosmia 'Lucifer' · Crambe Cordifolia

Prunus Okumiyako · Thalictrum flavum glaucum · Lobelia 'Dark Crusader' · Achillea 'Gold Plate' · Lilium henryi · Nectaroscordum siculum · Lilium henryi · Cotinus coggygria · Verbascum 'Vernale' · Reseda luteola · Heuchera 'Palace Purple' · Cotoneaster atropurpureus 'Variegatus'

Bergenia · Lysimachia ciliata 'Purpurea' · 3 Rosa 'Frensham' · Aruncus dioicus 'Kneiffii' · Symphoricarpos orbiculatus 'Foliis Variegatis' · Salvia elegans · Aruncus dioicus 'Kneiffii' · Kniphofia · 3 Rosa 'Frensham' with Tropaeolum peregrinum · Lysimachia ciliata 'Purpurea' · Alchemilla mollis

Hemerocallis citrina · Alchemilla Mollis · Sisyrinchium striatum · Phygelius 'African Queen' · Artemisia 'Powis Castle' · Anthemis tinctoria · Coreopsis verticillata · Phygelius 'Yellow Trumpet' · Dianthus barbatus · Phygelius 'Yellow Trumpet' · Potentilla 'Gibson's Scarlet' · Brachyglottis 'Sunshine'

1 m / 3 ft   1 m / 3 ft

Alchemilla mollis and
Brachyglottis 'Sunshine'

Salvia fulgens

Nectaroscordum siculum ssp. *bulgaricum*

*Nicotiana
langsdorffii*

Rosa 'Frensham'

× *Solidaster hybridus*

Phygelius × *rectus*
'African Queen'

THE PALE BORDERS

THERE IS A MUCH greater choice of plants suitable for the beds with cooler colours, and here, rather than colour harmonies based on a narrow segment of the spectrum as in the west border, we have more definite associations and repetitions, with colours taken from a wider range. Indeed, there are so many perennials to choose from that selection and repetition is the key; without this the whole scheme would collapse into bland chaos. Interestingly, over the years, as we have fiddled with the planting in this area, we have gradually eliminated all yellows except for thalictrum and cephalaria, both of which flower in early summer before the main purpose of the border scheme becomes apparent, and *Argyranthemum* 'Jamaica Primrose' for late-summer performance; all of these have very pale flower colour. Blues, mauves, pinks and some creamy whites are now the predominant colours, with tones of blue used more frequently than any other. This reflects my own preferences for harmonies.

Without strong, eye-catching hues, the success of the overall design depends on unity of purpose. Each colour group, usually but not always of the same plant, is repeated either twice in the length of the two sections which comprise the border or twice in one of the sections. In early summer clumps of brilliant blue *Galega orientalis* flower at opposite ends of the two beds, while ordinary bicoloured goat's rue, *G. officinalis*, flowering a few weeks later, has a more central position. White-flowered epilobium (*Epilobium angustifolium album*) appears both near the centre and closer to the southern end. A pair of white Rugosa roses, *Rosa* 'Blanche Double de Coubert', underplanted with glossy-leaved *Acanthus mollis latifolius* and *Polemonium* 'Lambrook Mauve', frames the seat between the beds. Clumps of pink and mauve phlox are distributed in less formal fashion throughout both sections. White and cream flowerers are the white mugwort (*Artemisia lactiflora*), blackroot (*Veronicastrum virginicum album*) and a bugbane, the snakeroot (*Cimicifuga racemosa*), all with interesting foliage which contributes from early in the season. Groups of violet-blue *Salvia nemorosa* 'Lubecca' give a darker tone.

Although the scheme is by no means a formal pattern, many similar plant drifts and clumps touch and weave together to give an impression of unity. There are clumps of pale blue aster (*Aster × frikartii* 'Mönch') and low-growing pink diascias – a South African plant revelling in hot sun – almost symmetrically placed along the front edge. These, together with silver-leaved artemisias and the

Above: *The uncommon apricot-flowered* Collomia grandiflora *groups itself in early summer in front of* Erysimum *'Bowles' Mauve'. This collomia, acquired by accident, is a self-seeder and an invaluable addition to the pale borders.*

Right: *In my last summer at Tintinhull all the perennials and annuals were newly planted in the pale borders. Bright carmine* Silene armeria, *opium poppies, silvery* Artemisia *'Powis Castle', white epilobiums and felicias give quick seasonal effects in a new planting scheme.*

dark yew hedge, hold the design together through the long season. Perhaps all this sounds rather too carefully arranged, but informal notes are sounded with annual opium poppies, peony-flowered in pink and mauve, encouraged to seed in drifts between flower groups. Another annual seeder, the little known *Collomia grandiflora* from western North America, with distinct apricot flowers, also seeds *in situ* at one end, while *Silene armeria* with bright pink flowers and glaucous leaves spreads at the other. Each year the tiny knotweed, *Polygonum capitatum*, germinates between the cracks along the stone edging in front of the beds. Encouraging these annual effects with self-seeders is a very personal way of gardening.

These eastern borders were completely emptied in the autumn of 1981. They were replanted, after the soil had been sterilized, in the spring of 1982. In 1992–3 they were again redone. Because of this disturbance – all the perennials were stored in the Kitchen Garden

Left: Deutzia setchuenensis, *the last of the deutzias to flower at Tintinhull, produces its innumerable white star-like blossoms in July and August. This deutzia is reputedly not entirely hardy, but the Tintinhull plant never seems to be affected by severe winters.*

Below left: *The pinkish-blues of goat's rue,* Galega officinalis, *fit perfectly into the pale border theme. The earlier-flowering G. orientalis, which has dark blue flower spikes and is more of a spreader, also plays an important role in these borders.*

Opposite: *The fireweed,* Epilobium angustifolium album, *with white flowers opening from green-tinged calyces, is one of my favourite perennials. Later in the year the epilobium's seedheads, the seeds enclosed in 'cottonwool', are almost as attractive as the flowers, and last for many weeks. Although this plant does spread – by creeping rootstock – seed seldom germinates, so it is not too difficult to control.*

from early autumn until spring – during 1993 we had to use more annuals and tender plants than usual to bulk up the newly replanted groups of perennials. *Gaura lindheimeri* (a perennial but treated as an annual here), blue-flowered salvias and felicias and mauve *Penstemon venustus* all contributed to the picture.

The appearance of the whole plant or each group of plants throughout the growing season is almost as important as the flower power which is, at best, only fleeting; and in both the east and the west borders plants are chosen for their foliage as well as their flowers. In the hot borders *Crambe cordifolia*, the giant sea kale with umbels of tiny white flowers, is grown for its architectural habit and huge heart-shaped leaves. It is matched by the smaller but equally valuable glossy-leaved *Acanthus mollis latifolius* in the pale borders. Eryngiums have an almost metallic sheen to the leaves. Some vigorous growers, such as the giant crambe, need constant manicuring, with dying leaves removed almost on a daily basis.

Although the hot borders are described as mainly red and yellow, cream flowers and grey foliage are important ingredients, and these are repeated in the cool beds opposite. In the early years we opened our season in April with swathes of dark tulips, 'Queen of Night' in the west beds and pink 'Queen of Bartigons' in those to the east, to give a hint of the themes planned for summer. More recently we have abandoned any early bulbs but allow the mixed greens and textures of emerging perennials, framed by a few early-flowering shrubs, to give us a quieter pleasure.

The Pale Borders 137

Yew hedge

Thalictrum flavum glaucum
Deutzia gracilis
Eupatorium maculatum 'Atropurpureum'
Miscanthus sinensis
Artemisia lactiflora
Cimicifuga racemosa
Delphiniums
Acanthus Mollis latifolius
Rosa 'Blanche Double de Coubert'
Veronica gentianoides
Lilium regale
Dahlia 'Gerrie Hoek'
Lepechinia Salviae
Deutzia gracilis
Nicotiana langsdorfii
Dahlia 'Gerrie Hoek'
Verbena hastata
Eryngium giganteum
Galega orientalis
Epilobium angustifolium album
Verbena hastata
Gaura lindheimeri
Phlox
Gaura lindheimeri
Phlox
Ballota pseudodictamnus
Galega officinalis
Phlox
Salvia nemorosa 'Lubecca'
Galega officinalis
Euphorbia characias
Phlox
Argyranthemum 'Jamaica Primrose'
Morina longifolia
Penstemon venustus
Salvia patens
Artemisia 'Powis Castle'
Felicia amelloides
Aster × frikartii 'Mönch'
Artemisia 'Powis Castle'
Diascia vigilis

1m   1m
3ft   3ft

Self·seeders
Collomia grandiflora
Eryngium giganteum
Lathyrus vernus
Papaver somniferum
Polygonum capitatum
Silene armeria
Viola 'Bowles' Black'
Viola riviniana Purpurea Group
Viola sororia 'Freckles'
Verbascum 'Vernale'

Lilium regale

Verbena hastata

Cimicifuga racemosa

Eryngium giganteum

Argyranthemum 'Jamaica Primrose'

Felicia amelloides

Phlox paniculata 'Franz Schubert'

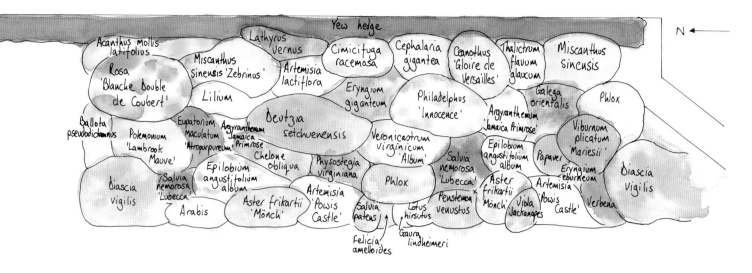

Yew hedge

Acanthus mollis latifolius
Lathyrus Vernus
Cimicifuga racemosa
Cephalaria gigantea
Ceanothus 'Gloire de Versailles'
Thalictrum flavum glaucum
Miscanthus sinensis

Rosa 'Blanche Double de Coubert'
Miscanthus Sinensis 'Zebrinus'
Artemisia lactiflora
Eryngium giganteum
Philadelphus 'Innocence'
Galega orientalis
Phlox

Lilium
Deutzia setchuenensis
Argyranthemum 'Jamaica Primrose'
Viburnum plicatum 'Mariesii'

Ballota pseudodictamnus
Eupatorium maculatum 'Atropurpureum'
Argyranthemum 'Jamaica Primrose'
Veronicastrum virginicum 'Album'
Epilobium angustifolium album
Papaver

Polemonium 'Lambrook Mauve'
Chelone obliqua
Physostegia virginiana
Salvia nemorosa 'Lubecca'
Eryngium eburneum

Diascia vigilis
Epilobium angustifolium album
Phlox
Aster frikartii 'Mönch'
Diascia vigilis

Salvia nemorosa 'Lubecca'
Artemisia 'Powis Castle'
Penstemon venustus
Artemisia 'Powis Castle'
Verbena

Arabis
Aster frikartii 'Mönch'
Salvia patens
Lotus hirsutus
Viola Jackanapes

Felicia amelloides
Gaura lindheimeri

Rosa 'Blanche Double de Coubert'

Physostegia virginiana

Epilobium angustifolium album

Diascia vigilis

Viola 'Jackanapes'

Salvia patens

Penstemon venustus

The Summerhouse Beds

THE UNEQUALLY SIZED summerhouse beds that frame the sitting area are backed by stone walls. Climbing pink and red roses, twining clematis, celastrus (*Celastrus orbiculatus* from Asia) and a perennial sweet pea (*Lathyrus rotundifolius*) make a woven background to plants chosen to take the scheme through all the months of the year. Evergreen *Osmanthus heterophyllus*, with glossy holly-like leaves, and the broad shape of the St Lucie cherry (*Prunus mahaleb*) on one side balance with shining *Piptanthus nepalensis* and a vast *Ceanothus* 'Cascade' on the other. A wide bush of *Phlomis fruticosa* gives protection to emerging clematis shoots. In one or other of the borders, sometimes in both, we grow my favourite Bowles' wallflower (*Erysimum* 'Bowles' Mauve'). If the winter has been kind it will flower for many months in spring, its bushy habit, grey-green leaves and clear mauve-pink flowers a perpetual joy. We always keep some specimens as a reserve in case of a hard winter. Rooted the previous summer, they are safe in our cold frames. Spring-flowering *Daphne × burkwoodii* 'Somerset', with delicate pink buds and fragrance, is almost evergreen, as is the blue-flowered flag iris (*Iris pallida* ssp. *pallida*) – a real blue and not a purple blue – which flowers in May. Clumps of *Salvia officinalis* and the tender

In the western summerhouse border in spring, the tender Euphorbia mellifera *flowers near* Erysimum *'Bowles' Mauve', and scented* Daphne × burkwoodii *'Somerset'. Behind, against the yew hedge, the St Lucie cherry,* Prunus mahaleb, *is also in bloom.*

Euphorbia mellifera (which may well succumb to hard frosts) are grown for their year-round foliage.

In the west summerhouse bed, the wider of the two, a superb spring performance is given by the St Lucie cherry, with myriad small white flowers in early spring, more subdued than the showy Japanese cousins. It spreads its branches above the prized yellow species *Paeonia mlokosewitschii*, with wide yellow papery flowers (followed by scarlet fruit) held on tall stems above glaucous leaves. The tall silver-leaved Moroccan broom, *Cytisus battandieri*, has primrose-coloured tassels smelling deliciously of pineapples. Nearby is another pale yellow flowerer, *Asphodeline lutea*, with grassy foliage. *Parahebe perfoliata*, with pale blue veronica flowers above grey leaves, is almost evergreen, but benefits from being cut to the ground in spring. It is a determined sun-lover, as also are the small rose 'White Pet', with clusters of pink buds opening to white all through the summer (if regularly deadheaded), *Philadelphus* 'Manteau d'Hermine', a small-leaved mock orange, and *Calamintha nepetoides*, with catmint-like aromatic flowers and foliage. Into any empty spaces we fit lower ground-hugging plants such as *Codonopsis clematidea*, *Sedum* 'Ruby Glow', with glaucous leaves, and *Viola*

riviniana Purpurea Group. A sub-shrub, *Cestrum parqui*, has yellow flowers in July and August, smelling musk-like in the evening.

The scrambling *Convolvulus althaeoides* twines its silvery leaves through the roses, producing its pink flowers in later summer, at the same time as *Clematis* 'Huldine' with greenish-white sepals curtains the back wall. In the last few years *Rehmannia elata* from China, with hooded, foxglove-like, mauve flowers, a plant still relatively new in gardens, has looked exotic in front of the climbers. Though it may not survive a cold winter there is no need to worry, for germinated seedlings will appear at the base of the parent in the following spring. As a precaution we usually grow extra plants from seed. *Penstemon venustus*, very similar to 'Sour Grapes', with

The Moroccan broom, Cytisus battandieri, *with silvery foliage and pineapple-scented flowers in late spring, benefits from the protection and reflection of a warm south-facing wall. In the summerhouse west bed the pale cone-shaped yellow flowers contrast admirably with blue iris and penstemons.*

Above: *The double pink rose 'Climbing Shot Silk' is luxuriant against the wall behind the summerhouse east bed in spring. A salmon-coloured perennial sweet pea,* Lathyrus rotundifolius, *twines through its lower branches and unsightly base to give an extended season of flower. Below are blue irises and Jerusalem sage.*

Right: *The iris-like* Sisyrinchium striatum *flowers in the front of the summerhouse border. The pale yellows and creams of the sisyrinchium seem to have the effect of calming harsher tones, while its slender leaves, although on a small scale, lend architectural coherence to this part of the border.*

mauveish-blue flowers which seem to fit into almost any colour scheme, ensures a sequence of flowers through the summer months (it is also a stalwart performer in the pale border theme). Grown from cuttings each year but often surviving *in situ*, it will flower again in summer if deadheaded after its first flush.

The other, narrower, bed on the east side of the summerhouse has very similar planting. In spring the effects are dramatic, with large clumps of *Euphorbia characias* ssp. *wulfenii* 'Lambrook Gold', its swaying stems of heavy-headed acid-yellow bracts showy in front of one of the most graceful and hardy of the evergreen ceanothus, *Ceanothus* 'Cascade'. On the wall, 'Climbing Shot Silk' is the second rose to flower at Tintinhull each year (the yellow Banksian rose on the south wall of the house is usually first). With double shining petals in pale pink, 'Shot Silk' is trained back hard against the wall;

later, *Lathyrus rotundifolius*, a salmon-pink perennial sweet pea, twines around its stems. Small-flowered *Clematis viticella* 'Purpurea Plena Elegans', with overlapping double flowers, smothers the wall in August and September. In a corner the purple-leaved grape vine, *Vitis vinifera* 'Purpurea', pruned to a few buds each spring, will drape itself over the front pediment of the summerhouse, its leaf colours matching the dark flowers of cherry pie, the fragrant heliotrope, growing in pots below for summer display. *Origanum laevigatum* 'Hopleys', with similar flower hue, is under the wall.

Along the front edge of this narrow border, clumps of rose 'White Pet' flower all summer long to match those in the west bed. From mid-June onwards a larger shrub rose, bronze-leaved *Rosa* × *odorata* 'Mutabilis', has single flowers of pink fading to yellow, next to *Cistus* × *skanbergii* with clear bright pink papery flowers.

Clematis 'Huldine' · Celastrus orbiculatus · Cestrum parqui · Rosa 'Crimson Glory' · Lonicera sempervirens
Osmanthus heterophyllus · Prunus mahaleb · Penstemon venustus · Cytisus battandieri · Bupleurum fruticosum · Phlomis fruticosa · Daphne x burkwoodii 'Somerset'
Yew hedge · Philadelphus 'Manteau d'Hermine' · Ruta graveolens 'Jackman's Blue' · Paeonia mlokosewitschii · Penstemon venustus · Iris pallida pallida · Carpenteria californica
Brunnera macrophylla · Iris pallida pallida · Parahebe perfoliata · Lamium maculatum album · Asphodeline lutea · Codonopsis clematidea · Viola riviniana · Euphorbia mellifera · Convolvulus althaeoides · Lamium maculatum 'Roseum'
Rosa 'White Pet' · Euphorbia mellifera · Rosa 'White Pet' · Viola riviniana · Rosa 'White Pet' · Rosa 'Allen Chandler'
Rehmannia elata · Phlomis anatolica · Sedum 'Ruby Glow' · Calamintha nepetoides · Rehmannia elata · Verbena

Self-seeders
Rehmannia elata
Sisyrinchium striatum

Clematis 'Huldine'   *Paeonia mlokosewitschii*

Iris pallida ssp. *pallida*

Cytisus battandieri

Carpenteria californica

Rosa 'White Pet'

Rehmannia elata

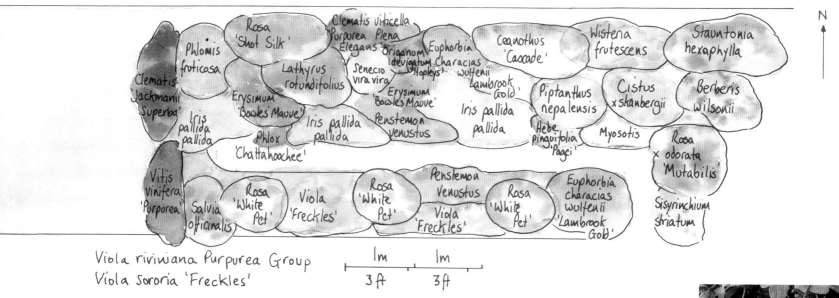

Rosa 'Shot Silk'

Clematis viticella Purpurea Plena Elegans

Phlomis fruticosa

Lathyrus rotundifolius

Senecio vira vira

Origanum laevigatum 'Hopleys'

Euphorbia Characias wulfenii 'Lambrook Gold'

Ceanothus 'Cascade'

Wisteria frutescens

Stauntonia hexaphylla

Clematis 'Jackmanii Superba'

Erysimum 'Bowles' Mauve'

Erysimum 'Bowles' Mauve'

Piptanthus nepalensis

Cistus x skanbergii

Berberis wilsonii

Iris pallida pallida

Iris pallida pallida

Penstemon venustus

Iris pallida pallida

Hebe pinguifolia 'Pagei'

Myosotis

Phlox 'Chattahoochee'

Rosa x odorata 'Mutabilis'

Vitis vinifera 'Purpurea'

Salvia officinalis

Rosa 'White Pet'

Viola 'Freckles'

Rosa 'White Pet'

Penstemon Venustus

Viola 'Freckles'

Rosa 'White Pet'

Euphorbia characias wulfenii 'Lambrook Gold'

Sisyrinchium striatum

Viola riviniana Purpurea Group
Viola sororia 'Freckles'

1m   1m
3 ft   3 ft

N

Clematis 'Jackmanii Superba'

Phlomis fruticosa

Erysimum 'Bowles' Mauve'

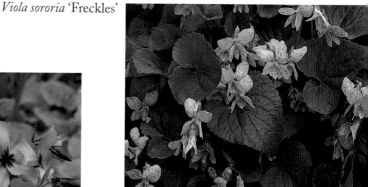

Clematis viticella
'Purpurea Plena Elegans'

Vitis vinifera 'Purpurea'

Viola sororia 'Freckles'

Phlox 'Chattahoochee'

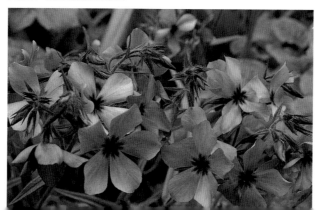

The Summerhouse Beds 145

The Pots

_FOUR LARGE reconstituted stone pots sit on the corners of the
pool. We always plant tulips in them for spring: different types
with varying times of flowering are planted at different depths to
give a longer flowering sequence. We hope they will finish each year
just in time for the planting out of annuals, after the last frosts have
been predicted, usually about 20 May. We generally concentrate on
white and yellow tulips but the lily-flowered 'Burgundy', with deep
mauve-purple flowers, has also been a huge success. When flowering
is over the bulbs are removed and dried. We do not use them again
in the pots but they can be planted elsewhere, for example in the
Kitchen Garden where they are grown as cutting flowers. We
normally replace the compost in the pots only every three or four
years. However, if we have any suspicions of virus we burn the bulbs,
scrub out the pots and introduce new compost.

Our summer schemes vary but are similar each year, with plants
grown from cuttings and seed. For several years we used centrally
placed *Argyranthemum foeniculaceum*, with glaucous leaves and white
daisy flowers, surrounded by a mixture of pink nemesias, the little
mallow-like *Hibiscus trionum*, with cream maroon-centred flowers,
silver helichrysums, and trailing verbenas – both dark blue 'Hidcote
Purple' and 'Silver Anne', a pale pink. In the past we have had red-
flowered flax (*Linum grandiflorum* 'Rubrum'). *Anisodontea* ×
hypomandarum, from South Africa, is another good centrepiece.

Other decorative pots are arranged in the summerhouse. Some
have single specimens such as myrtle or tibouchina, some have a
massing of one salvia (*Salvia uliginosa*, *S. patens* or *S. leptophylla*)
or the salvia-like *Lepechinia salviae*. Others have mixed summer
planting in the same style as the large pots around the pool.
The single specimen containers will be removed and replaced as
the plants' appearance merits. There is *Trachelospermum jasminoides*,
with sweetly scented white flowers, *Melianthus major*, with
wide glaucous pinnate leaves, a white-flowered oleander and
yellow spring-flowering *Corokia cotoneaster* with wiry stems.
But there are many others we have used over the years: daturas

At sunrise in spring, white Tulipa 'Purissima', *planted in the pots at the
corners of the pool, glows beside the golden-variegated leaves of* Iris
pseudacorus. *The early morning light softens the harsh reds and yellows
which predominate in the west border later in the season.*

(now brugmansias), other salvias, and sometimes olearias, another favourite genus, most species being too tender for outside wintering at Tintinhull. All the young plants go in one of the greenhouses during the winter. As they get larger they have to survive being in the summerhouse or are abandoned.

In the niche by the stone seat at the end of the west border we have pots of purple-leaved Australian cordylines and phormiums from New Zealand, and yellow- and red-flowered plants picking up the colour scheme of purple, yellow and red in the border. The bright primrose *Calceolaria integrifolia* is grown from cuttings. There are tender cupheas and *Fuchsia* 'Thalia', *Phygelius capensis* 'Winchester Fanfare' and *Bidens* 'Golden Goddess'. These plants, arranged as a picture, are all viewed from the pavement as you enter the garden by the side door. On the opposite side, by the pale border, there are agapanthus in pots, bulked up with silver helichrysums, evolvulus, or any other blue- or pink-flowered annuals available, all colour coordinated with the border planting.

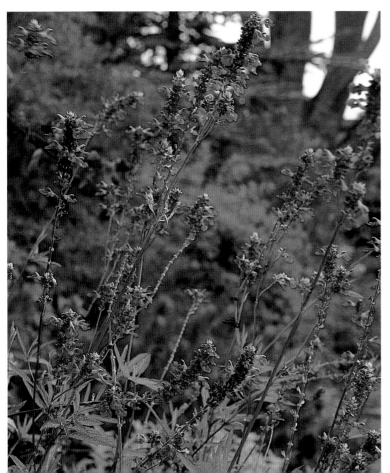

Above left: *In the garden I designed in Michigan, where the summers are very hot, salvias in pots and silver-leaved plants in a majestic urn show planting styles very similar to those used at Tintinhull. In the sunny border behind, eupatoriums and mauve-plumed* Thalictrum rochebrunanum *flourish.*

Left: *The not-altogether-hardy* Salvia uliginosa, *with sky-blue flowers in late summer, seems to perform best when massed in a pot. I have never been so successful with this plant in border schemes and sometimes lose it in a hard winter.*

Opposite: *White daisy-flowered* Argyranthemum foeniculaceum *with glaucous fretted leaves combines with silvery helichrysums and mauve and pink verbenas to sustain summer colour in the main pots around the pool. In the background by the summerhouse, blue* Salvia uliginosa *and silvery* Artemisia arborescens *'Faith Raven', along with plenty of other pot plants, fill this area with flower and foliage interest.*

The Pots 149

Planting the Pale Borders

When planting or replanting a border, it is wise to work to a plan, drawn up on graph paper. However, you should always be ready to make changes to planting shapes and quantities as work proceeds.

In the autumn of 1992 we took all the perennials out of the pale borders in preparation for installing a new watering system. Only the shrubs and grasses were left *in situ*. Some of the perennials were stored in trenches in the Kitchen Garden, while others were potted up, after division, in individual pots. The plants we kept in the Kitchen Garden included *Eupatorium maculatum* 'Atropurpureum', salvias such as *Salvia nemorosa* 'Lubecca', and quantities of pink and mauve phlox. We had discarded the central crowns of all these plants, keeping only the younger outer growth. In pots we had, among others, *Polemonium* 'Lambrook Mauve', *Epilobium angustifolium album*, and both sorts of galega, *Galega officinalis*, the ordinary lavender goat's rue, and the dark blue *G. orientalis*.

With the soil in perfect condition – wonderfully friable through having been worked for so many years – the planting began in early April. The bare-rooted plants had to be put in as quickly as possible, before their root systems dried out, so it was particularly important to work in small, easily manageable sections.

I begin any major planting exercise by placing all the plants in position, arranging them in groups, usually of seven or nine plants (*top*). Then I tackle the groups one at a time. To make quite sure the placing stays as I've planned it, before I move a plant to dig its hole I push my trowel in right next to it, to mark its position. Then I quickly dig

the hole and put the plant in – a salvia is shown here – covering the roots with soil and firming the earth down around it (*above and right*).

All potted plants should be given a good soak before planting. The pool at Tintinhull is handy for this, and I 'dunked' all the pots – a pot of *Galega officinalis* is shown (*opposite, above*). If a plant has filled a pot with roots, you may need to scrape the tightly balled roots and compost carefully away from the sides, with your fingers, as you tip it out.

When a whole group has been planted,

I always cover the area with compost, which identifies the newly planted bit, as well as acting as a mulch (*below*).

The planting schemes in the two sections of the pale border refer one to the other, without being strict mirror images. There are more plants in the longer northern section. When planning the replanting I aimed ideally at having at least two groups of each plant throughout the whole scheme. Vigorous spreaders such as *Galega orientalis* were to occupy sites at either end.

When planting or replanting borders in the spring, remember to leave room for any cuttings which may soon be hardy enough to plant out, as well as for any annuals you will wish to include. I put sticks in the middle of each area I wish to reserve for later planting. In the pale borders I left spaces for plants such as diascias and felicias, from the previous year's cuttings, to be massed in groups in the front of both sections of the border, and for two large groups of the pink dahlia 'Gerrie Hoek'. These and other plants grown as annuals would be put out later in the spring. Silvery artemisias, grown from cuttings, would be planted in a formal rhythm along the front of the beds. Alliums and lilies were to be added in the autumn to perform the following year.

Pruning Roses

WHEN PRUNING a rose in late winter or early spring, the aim should be not only to remove old dead, damaged or diseased wood and stimulate new flowering shoots, but also to produce a shapely bush that will make a decorative contribution to the garden even when the plant is not in flower. Make sure you know what kind of rose you are dealing with, though, for Hybrid Teas, Floribundas and other bush roses are treated differently from species roses and large shrubs which, in general, need little spring attention.

The 'Frensham' roses in the Pool Garden's hot borders (*left*) are Floribundas. Grown in a perennial scheme, they strike quite a formal note; but they must be kept well pruned. Our tight packed-in planting style forces even the roses to grow very tall,

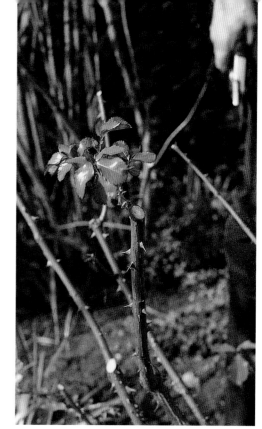

and pruning to a good shape is particularly important. However, we do not cut back as hard as is generally advised for Floribundas, because we want the roses to maintain a good height among the other plants in the border.

Though the 'Frenshams' may be trimmed back in autumn or early winter to prevent wind rock, the real pruning is left until early spring, when I start by cutting back any cumbersome top growth with a pruning saw, using the secateurs to hold the branch steady (*left*). Then I remove any weak, dead or diseased stems (*above left*) and cut away about two-thirds of the wood of each branched stem from the previous season. In the case of an old bush that has become congested you may need to cut out the centre in order to allow in light and air.

Some people treat rose-pruning as a work of art, contemplating each cut very deliberately. I prefer to work swiftly towards a final shape that seems to come almost automatically. Using very sharp secateurs,

I make a slanting cut (from which the rain will run off) above an outward-pointing bud, so that subsequent growth does not cause congestion at the centre of the bush (*above centre and right*). I ensure that at least two viable buds remain lower down the branch, and like to leave the bushes at a height of about 60cm/2ft (*right*).

Some of these 'Frenshams', incidentally, have developed suckers, probably due to their roots being damaged when neighbouring perennials were divided. I slice these out as near to the original root stock as possible.

Like all roses, the 'Frenshams' may need a further trimming of any frost-damaged shoots in late spring, after the final frosts. Once the bushes are in flower there is constant 'summer pruning', or deadheading, to encourage new flowering shoots, as well as for the appearance of each bush. I cut well below the fading flower heads when removing them, and cut tired stems back to a vigorous shooting bud.

Propagating Perennial Lobelia

W E GROW TALL *Lobelia* 'Dark Crusader' in the hot borders, as much for its bronze leaves as for the dark red summer flowers. This half-hardy perennial will survive the winter out of doors in zones where consistently cold weather keeps it dormant, but with us there is the risk that a warm spell will prompt it to put up new shoots which will then be caught by frosts, so we transfer our plants to a cold frame in mid-autumn and divide them in spring.

Having cut down the lobelia stems to about 25cm/10in (*below left*), I dig up the individual plants (*above right*) and put them in a bucket, ready to take behind the scenes to the potting shed. I plant each one up in potting compost, in a 15cm/6in pot, leaving any plantlets that are already coming up attached to the parent (*above, far right*), and firm the soil a little, taking care not to damage the plantlets.

I want my planted-up lobelias to harden

In mid-spring the lobelias begin to send up new shoots, often producing a whole set of new plantlets on the edge of the main crown (*far left*). If you give the pot a sharp knock, compost and plants will slide out on to the potting bench (*left*). Then the little plants can easily be pulled apart (*below left*). Each one is potted up in a separate pot, and the central crown is also repotted. Put a bit of compost in each pot and then, holding the plant with one hand (*bottom left*), press additional compost in around the edge and over the roots until the pot is filled up to about 2.5cm/1in below the rim (it is always a good idea to leave a space between the soil surface and the rim, for ease of watering). Gently firm the compost around the plant (*bottom right*).

The pots should remain in a cold frame, with the lid left off as the weather warms up, for gradual hardening off, until they are put out in their flowering site in late spring.

By this simple process you can easily double the number of your plants – the very nicest part of gardening.

off, so initially I put them in a cold frame with the lid open (*left*). However, the frame must be closed as soon as frost is threatened. The lobelia stems are cut down a bit more before the frame is closed. They will die back during the winter. Remove the stem at the base when it has died, as otherwise it may rot and kill the whole clump.

Small-flowered Clematis

I FIND THE small-flowered species and hybrid clematis infinitely valuable as companion plants. They have a natural appearance better suited to my sort of gardening than the artificial, almost blowzy look of their cousins the large-flowered hybrids. (Although in contradiction to this I have a tender affection for some of the more bizarre doubles, when they are used deliberately to make an exotic statement.)

None of the small-flowered clematis is too flamboyant or attention-seeking, and they associate perfectly with other plants; they clothe high walls or tumble down low ones, mingle with other climbing vines without overrunning them, and scramble through branches of deciduous trees and shrubs. A clematis can be chosen to flower at the same time as the host plant, and intertwine with its blossom – a pink variety of *Clematis montana* weaving through a spring cherry or crab apple. Or it can fit into a scheme of flowery progression – a fruit tree with May blossom, a rambling June rose and a late-flowering clematis can all be grown together.

There are so many different types of clematis that, in a temperate climate, it is possible to have one in flower at almost every season. At Tintinhull we have two winter/early-spring clematis, *C. cirrhosa* var. *balearica* and *C. armandii*, both evergreen. The former, from the Mediterranean, has fern-like leaves and bears its greeny-cream bells during mild spells in the winter, with a final burst in March and April. The later-flowering scented *C. armandii*, from Asia, has handsome almost leathery leaves, translucent when young, and trusses of scented cream flowers. Both these clematis will thrive on a warm wall – in full sun for

Clematis cirrhosa var. *balearica*

C. cirrhosa var. *balearica*, part shade for *C. armandii* – but are also vigorous scramblers if allowed to twine free in the branches of a host tree or large shrub. In Mediterranean climates I have seen these clematis draping tall cypresses with blossom in midwinter.

The real spring season starts with the Alpina clematis, unobtrusive flowerers which seem to blossom indiscriminately in sun or shade. They begin at Tintinhull in

April, but late frosts may damage flower buds. My favourite of the Alpinas is *C.a.* 'Frances Rivis', blue to blueish-purple with long sepals. The *C. macropetala* cultivars are similar but in deeper blue and purple shades.

The montanas come next, thugs compared to other spring clematis, and vigorous enough to clamber into tall trees. The type *C. montana* is white, the named variations are pale to dusky pink and all are fragrant. I prefer the white species or one of the paler pinks such as 'Pink Perfection', although the darker 'Picton's Variety' appeals when draped against grey stone. Another variety, *C.m.* var. *wilsonii*, flowers in June and July with narrow creamy-white flowers, just after its host, *Malus hupehensis*, has carpeted the lawn in fallen blossom outside my bedroom window. Christopher Lloyd describes *C.m.* var. *wilsonii* as giving off 'great wafts of hot chocolate aroma'.

At Hadspen I had beginner's luck with *C. florida* 'Sieboldii', perhaps the most beautiful of all clematis, producing in early summer flowers like a passion flower, white sepals framing clustered petal-like bright purple stamens flecked with pale pink. It is notoriously temperamental: give it star treatment and a sheltered corner.

After this there is a pause before the Texensis and Viticella clematis. The Texans include 'Duchess of Albany', with bell-shaped pink flowers, 'Etoile Rose', with nodding bell-shaped sepals that are silvery pink on the outside and a deep cherry-purple within, and the crimson 'Gravetye Beauty'. All the available Viticella clematis are worth growing. My favourites are 'Alba Luxurians', which has white sepals with green recurved tips, 'Etoile Violette', with purple sepals, double-flowered 'Purpurea Plena Elegans', 'Royal Velours', a dark rich velvety purple, and *C. viticella* itself, with delicate nodding purple flowers. Then there is 'Huldine', a hybrid with some Viticella genes, which starts flowering in midsummer – July here – and continues into autumn. With flowers 10 cm/4 in across, 'Huldine' is the largest-flowered clematis I really like. White sepals are mauve-tinged beneath.

Other late-season flowerers include *C. campaniflora*, with blueish-white bell flowers, *C. flammula*, with deliciously fragrant creamy blossom, the lemon-peel *C. tibetana* ssp. *vernayi* (*C. orientalis* of gardens) and *C. tangutica*. In Britain the last clematis to flower is the cowslip-scented *C. rehderiana*, but in many American gardens, where hotter summers provide more suitable conditions, the glorious white *C. terniflora* (sometimes listed as *C. paniculata* or *C. maximowicziana*) produces a spectacular late-autumn display.

Clematis do require careful siting; they like to search for the sun to flower but need their roots in cool shade. A host shrub will often provide sufficient protection from hot sun, but a position on a wall may get too hot and dry unless the roots are shaded (even a flat stone may be sufficient). All clematis enjoy a mulch in spring and this, as well as encouraging growth, will help keep the soil moist and the roots cool.

Although once established these small-flowered clematis are less trouble than the larger-flowered types and seem more robust, they do benefit from regular attention through the summer. Tendrils, the climbing leaf stalks, need guiding to encourage the flowering shoots to spread out into broad fan-like shapes of colour. (The pruner's task is simplified if they are grown on a wall on a structure of wire or trelliswork.) My husband John used to do this twiddly work meticulously, visiting each clematis in the garden at least once a week. I am too impatient to get perfect results.

When it comes to pruning you can follow specific directions for each type, but the main thing to know – as in all pruning – is whether the clematis flowers on old or new wood. Generally speaking, the harder you cut back in winter the later a clematis will flower – so, at pruning time, you can draw out the length of the flowering period by cutting shoots of any one specimen to different lengths.

On pages 158–9, left to right:
Clematis alpina 'Frances Rivis'
Clematis florida 'Sieboldii'
Clematis 'Etoile Violette'

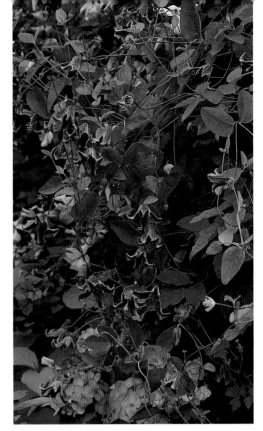

Clematis 'Duchess of Albany'

Clematis flammula

Companionable Salvias

Salvia uliginosa

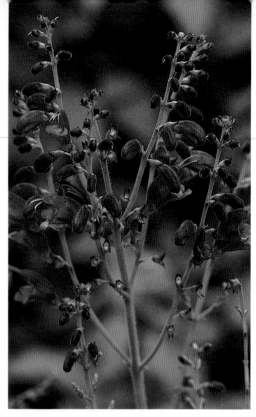

Salvia cacaliifolia

Salvia patens 'Cambridge Blue'

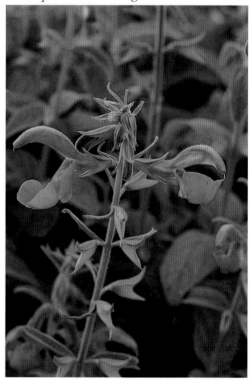

Right: Salvia leucantha

THERE HAS RECENTLY been an explosion in the numbers of different sages available, with flowers covering a huge colour range from scarlet through purple and violet to azure-blue, white and even pale yellow. Many of them make superb garden plants, wonderful for drifts in borders or growing in containers.

Although variable, most salvia flowers have a distinctive upper petal arching forward to resemble the shape of a hood, with calyces and petals often of contrasting hues. Some flowers gape open, others are nearly tubular.

Although all sages need a sunny, well-protected site to give of their best flowering, the common European sage, *Salvia officinalis*, and some of its relatives – such as *S. lavandulifolia* – are hardy to -20°C/-4°F. Most of the more tender sages are easily propagated from seed or cuttings, so can be grown as annuals. The common sage and those from dry areas in California are drought-resistant, but most of the South American sages need plenty of moisture during the summer.

THE BLUE TONES

My favourite salvias are the blues, in all their shades and tints of pure azure, mauve, violet and lavender. At Bettiscombe I plan to have a border of blue salvias, perhaps with some silvery-leaved artemisias and dorycniums added to make the blues seem even brighter.

At Tintinhull I have, at various times, used groups of the sky-blue South American perennial *S. uliginosa* in the pale borders in the Pool Garden, less formally as drifts in the Middle Garden and, most effectively, clumped in pots in the summerhouse. Tall and graceful, it needs a sheltered position with plenty of moisture and does not like competition from neighbouring plants. A tender perennial salvia, the compact dark blue *S. cacaliifolia* from Mexico, is one of the most floriferous of the sages, flowering even in semi-shade and doing especially well in containers. We take cuttings every year. *S. leptophylla* (*S. reptans*), also from Mexico, is smaller in its flowering parts but makes a suckering bushy plant in a pot. I leave it, in its pot, in a greenhouse to die down in winter and reshoot in spring. *S. leucantha*, the tender Mexican sage bush, with chenille-textured violet to lavender flower spikes, thrives without much watering and is especially suitable for pots. It is a late-summer performer in Britain but in its native habitat and in California it flowers all winter. We take cuttings each autumn and overwinter them free of frost.

We grow the bright blue Mexican *S. patens*, the paler 'Cambridge Blue' and

Left: *Salvia sclarea* var. *turkestanica*

Salvia discolor

Salvia elegans

mauve 'Chilcombe' as annuals from both seed and cuttings. They will usually appear again if left in a flower bed but do better if propagated each season. *S. discolor* from Peru has flowers of such a dark violet-blue they appear almost black. We grow it in containers, but I have seen it growing more luxuriously in open ground. It is not at all winter-hardy, so we take cuttings each year.

The common sage, *S. officinalis*, an evergreen shrub from the Mediterranean area, makes a low-growing bush (to 75cm/30in), as useful for foliage as for flowers. *S.o.* 'Icterina' has variegated golden leaves, 'Purpurascens' has reddish-purple foliage and 'Tricolor' has leaves three-toned grey-green, with pink to red marks.

Both the annual clary, *S. viridis*, and biennial *S. sclarea* var. *turkestanica* have flower bracts that are a mixture of white, pink and blue. In *S.s.* var. *turkestanica* the stems are pink-tinted too.

THE REDS
Except in climates where they can be grown outside all through the year (as I find is possible in California and in Texas), I prefer to grow most of the shrubby red-flowered salvias in pots. *S. elegans* and *S. microphylla* varieties are all easy to overwinter if you have a greenhouse. If left outside some of the microphyllas will behave like sub-shrubs and shoot again from the base in spring. At Tintinhull both *S. elegans* and *S. fulgens* make splashes of scarlet in the hot borders.

There are many more salvias to experiment with – it would be a lifetime's work to learn their names and how to use them well in the garden.

The Pea Family

W E ALL DEVELOP preferences for certain plants, finding that, over and over again, and in a variety of situations, they fulfil our expectations. Many years ago I found that goat's rue, *Galega officinalis*, and its cousin *G. orientalis* were important in any border I made. *G. officinalis* and its many modern colour types, with pea flowers varying between pale lavender-blue, lilac, pink and white, produce their massed blooms in midsummer. The vivid darker blue flowers of *G. orientalis* are earlier.

Galegas are Leguminosae, members of the extensive pea family, which includes trees, shrubs, climbers, perennials and annuals. Among the perennials, another essential border plant is the drought-resistant lupin-like false indigo, *Baptisia australis*, a North American native with long racemes of blue flowers carried on erect branching stems clothed with blue-green foliage. It is beautiful all summer, as imposing as a shrub, and by autumn carries decorative black seed pods. The smaller *B. leucantha* has white flowers slightly tinged with purple.

We have no space for the true garden lupins at Tintinhull but have, instead, grown specimens of the tender blue-flowered shrubby *Lupinus albifrons* var. *douglasii* from California. Its silvery-silk leaves and violet flowers make it a superlative pot plant. We also grow the yellow tree lupin, *L. arboreus*.

Indigoferas and lespedezas are also members of the pea family. Both are shrubs to 1m/3ft or so but respond best in the garden to being cut down to the ground

Baptisia australis

Galega officinalis

Lathyrus vernus

Lupinus arboreus

each spring. They need full sun and adequate drainage. *Indigofera heterantha* from the Himalaya has rosy-lilac flowers carried for two months in late summer. Pink *I. kirilowii*, indigo bush, grown successfully in the southern states of America, is also worth attempting in sheltered gardens in cooler climates. The pink and white forms of bush clover, *Lespedeza thunbergii*, are very similar: branching silky sprays are covered in crimson-purple pea flowers in the last months of the season.

Sweet peas are invaluable in the garden. Most often grown as climbers, some will also make sprawling bushes or weave between other plants. Everyone knows and loves *Lathyrus odoratus*, the annual sweet pea, which comes in every colour from white through pink, lavender, crimson and violet-blue to almost black. Grown up tripods in the Kitchen Garden, they make scented columns of colour. The late-flowering perennial pea, *L. latifolius*, will trail down a bank, smother a hedge with blossom, and, in a border scheme, disguise the dying leaves and flowers of earlier-flowering perennials. We have it in one of the borders at Tintinhull but at Bettiscombe I will grow it to rampage over my olive trees. The Persian everlasting pea, *L. rotundifolius*, with salmon-pink flowers, is earlier; at Tintinhull it grows up each year into an early rose, 'Shot Silk'. Lord Anson's blue pea, *L. nervosus*, is tender but worth growing at the base of a warm wall. It has fragrant pale blue flowers and silver leaves. *L. vernus*, with dark purple or pale pink flowers, makes a low bush hardly more than 30cm/1ft high. Very hardy and thriving in well-drained but poor soil, it has ferny, much-divided leaves, which, when interspersed with the small flowers, make an attractive spring mound. It almost vanishes through the summer months but gradually increases its spread as well as seeding in neighbouring corners. I planted it at Tintinhull to give spring effects at the back of the Pool Garden pale borders, and have it at Bettiscombe among golden foliage and lime-green flowerers.

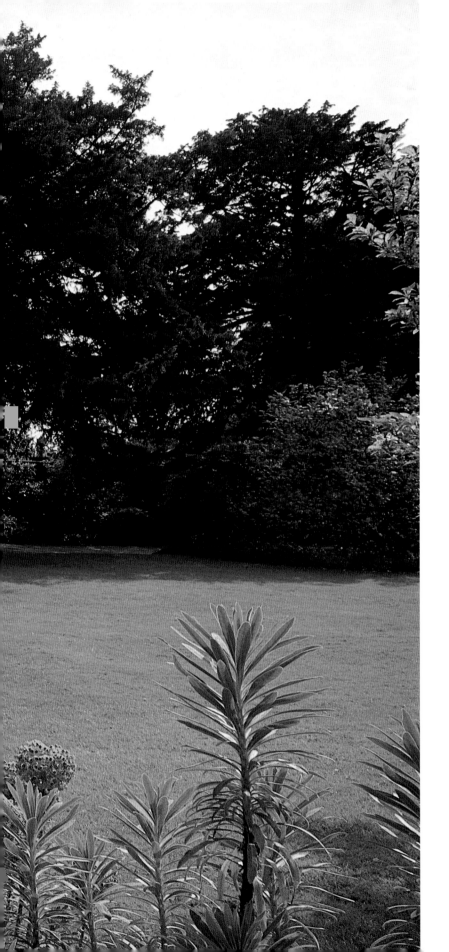

Surrounded by trees – magnolias and old yew trees to the south, the dominant cedar on the northern edge – walls and yew hedging, the Cedar Court, with its central lawn, provides an oasis, a moment of calm after the busy, colourful planting in many other areas of the garden.

THE CEDAR COURT

IN MANY GARDENS, especially in towns, it is the central lawn, a well of green, which provides the setting with a focal point, as pleasing as reflecting water. Most often the lawn is shaped geometrically as a square, rectangle, circle or oval, with some strategically placed trees to silhouette the sky and balance with the mass of the house. Surrounding borders of shrubs and flowers hide perimeter fences or walls to complete the garden design. It is the simplest and often the most satisfying garden arrangement. A green oasis, the lawn also provides a natural recreation area for children and dogs, bridging that awkward gap between the gardener's love of planting and the family's need for an open space.

The lawn in the Cedar Court at Tintinhull fits into this pattern. Its simple greenness, almost uninterrupted by planting, comes as a relief after the more elaborate schemes elsewhere in the garden.

Its layout of a central lawn surrounded by broad borders follows the form of a multitude of other gardens. Although several beds have been carved out for spring-flowering magnolias, the grass, mown in traditional stripes with a cylinder mower, almost forms a square. On the south side it is edged with a broad stone-flagged pavement, in which grow two ancient yew trees; on the north it stretches up to a cedar of Lebanon, probably planted at the beginning of the nineteenth century. Although it has lost many of its spreading lower branches and now has a very sparse outline, this cedar still dominates the garden. Sadly, it has become dangerous, the main

Although much smaller than the lawn of the Cedar Court, the lawn in this Michigan garden is just as much of a haven.

trunk being rotten at its core, and is to be removed. Under the cedar, golden aconites and narcissi and mauve *Crocus tommasinianus* flower early in the year but, as the leaves fade by April, mowing is not interrupted. A wide west-facing border is backed by a high stone wall on which roses, clematis and honeysuckle have a chance to run riot. Sheltered by a yew hedge, Phyllis Reiss's foliage scheme of golden and purple, enhanced by flowers in rich crimson and blue, lies in part shade on the western fringe. The lawn itself is large enough to allow children's games.

The care of grass is certainly not labour-saving; almost any other planting of parterre beds surrounded by hard pathways would be less demanding of time and attention. After being scarified to remove mossy thatch during the winter or early spring, the grass in the Cedar Court is fertilized and treated with a selective herbicide as the growing season begins. It is cut and edged twenty-nine times in an average year, the last mowing often being in a mild spell in December (it is important not to walk on it when it is frost-covered). The areas under the yews and under the cedar need watering in dry periods. In spite of all this work I cannot imagine not having one lawn area in a garden. Usually when I am advising on a garden anywhere in Britain, especially if it is in a small urban space, I will recommend a traditional central lawn (provided always there is enough sun).

Small-flowered narcissi flourish among the leaves of winter aconites and crocus under the old cedar. The grass is cut six weeks after the daffodils have finished flowering.

In my walled garden at Bettiscombe, a lawn, decorated with yew pyramids, is the main garden feature revealed from the house windows. This grass is almost completely surrounded by a yew hedge which, eventually, will effectively screen detailed planting schemes in the rest of this sheltered area from immediate view. I love the idea of secret hidden surprises to be discovered in progression and I find that the smaller the whole garden area the more important it is to erect vertical screens and create separate sections; this increases the feeling of overall space. On the approach side at the front of the house, where the landscape is open, more yew pyramids, this time reinforced by an outer avenue of mulberries, march down the centre of the field to frame an oak tree. The mown grass which sets off the yews merges to make a neat edge with rougher grass, cut monthly during the summer, at the sides – grass which ultimately will become a meadow for naturalized bulbs and flowers, an advantage over Tintinhull where there was no space for this. Hornbeam hedges outline formal French-style alleys of cut grass, as well as hiding future utility and vegetable areas.

The Bettiscombe garden has many of the features of Tintinhull but promises to need much less skilled maintenance. Although grass-cutting and hedge-trimming are labour-intensive, the labour need not be highly trained: both activities require good machines rather than specialized knowledge. In future years the lawns, in both the walled garden and the outer area, and the yew pyramids (by then I hope 4.5m/15ft tall) and yew and hornbeam hedges (probably to 3m/10ft) may well be the only features which are properly maintained, and any flower bed untidiness in surrounding areas will be hidden from immediate view.

At Tintinhull the Cedar Court could be a much simpler scheme than it is. The borders, which do demand attention, could be dispensed with, leaving the trees, including the dominant cedar, the dark colonnade of yews, the grass and the five magnolias – *Magnolia grandiflora* against a south-facing wall, *M. × soulangeana* nearby in a circular bed carpeted with ivy-leaved cyclamen, *M. stellata* and two large specimens of *M. liliiflora* 'Nigra' in square beds on the south side, underplanted with hellebores and Welsh poppies. All this provides sufficient interest without additional frills; and for a weekend gardener it would be quite enough work. In fact, of course, at Tintinhull we make few concessions to reducing maintenance, and managing the existing Cedar Court borders has given me a great deal of pleasure.

In spring, before its leaves unfurl, the wide-spreading Magnolia liliiflora *'Nigra' bears erect goblet-shaped flowers, deep purple on the outside and stained with cream within. Nearby, under the cedar, the hybrid* M. × soulangeana *is also in flower.*

THE PURPLE AND GOLD BORDER

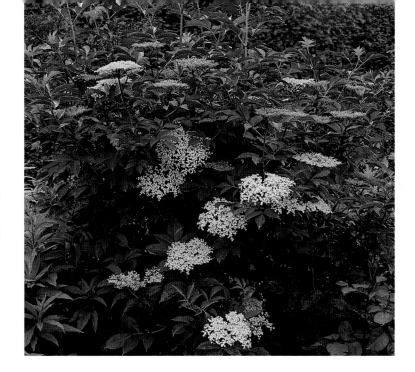

ROBABLY THE GOLD AND purple foliage bed is the best known of all Mrs Reiss's schemes. Gold-variegated dogwoods (*Cornus alba* 'Spaethii'), with startling crimson stems in winter – we cut these back almost to the ground in spring every other year – alternate with purple, copper and bronze foliage plants. Surprisingly, she did not plant the purple-leaved smoke bush she used so frequently throughout the rest of the garden, but she included *Berberis thunbergii* 'Atropurpurea Nana' and *B.* × *ottawensis* 'Superba', the latter one of the best barberries, with yellow and red berries.

Various plants have been added over the years. I have to admit that we were quite pleased when a large *Prunus* × *blireana* keeled over in a storm in 1989. This gave us room to plant two more berberis, *Berberis dictophylla* var. *approximata* (which unfortunately died in 1990) and *B. temolaica*. These are rarer because they are hard to propagate, but they are perhaps the most attractive of all berberis, with distinctive glaucous foliage and young stems covered with a soft bloom. Other additions have been the dark-leaved elder *Sambucus nigra* 'Guincho Purple', and spring-flowering *Viburnum sargentii* 'Onondaga', with bronze young foliage, both toning down the strongest gold/purple contrasts.

All the flowers in this border contain some blue pigment which harmonizes with the dusky foliage. Crimson and pink shrub roses – rose 'Fellenberg', 'Rosemary Rose' with purple-flushed leaves, the Hybrid Musk 'Cornelia', thornless 'Zéphirine Drouhin' and *Rosa glauca*, with its blue-grey leaves and pink flowers – all presenting their best performance in June but also, if deadheaded, providing an almost continual display through the rest of the summer. In spring the bed is carpeted with blue scillas and drifts of *Anemone apennina*, with a corner clump of Solomon's seal, the ordinary *Polygonatum* × *hybridum*. The shrubs are interplanted with vigorous perennials and some annuals, all with dusky purple or bright blue flowers. For blue effects in early summer *Veronica austriaca* ssp. *teucrium* tumbles over the stone edging, while blue salvias – *Salvia patens*, most satisfactory

In the purple and gold border the young shoots of Cornus alba *'Spaethii' contrast with the duller purples of berberis and the bronze foliage of bright-flowered 'Rosemary Rose'. Towards the back of the border is thornless 'Zéphirine Drouhin' with paler pink flowers.* Geranium nodosum *flowers along the edge, with* Veronica austriaca *ssp.* teucrium *and silver-leaved* Salvia argentea.

The flowers of Sambucus nigra *'Guincho Purple', borne in broad heads on purple stalks, are pink in bud and open to pink on the outside and white within. Its bronze leaf tones work beautifully with the other foliage colours in the border, linking the darker purples and the brighter golds.*

if grown each year from seed, and *S. guaranitica*, which is hardy if adequately mulched – flower later and continue into the first frosts. Dark velvet-flowered *Clematis* 'Jackmanii' grows on umbrella-shaped frames. Eupatoriums and bronze-leaved sedums, lythrums and prized *Vernonia* species, brought back as seed from the United States, are late performers and will seed quite prolifically if given the opportunity.

Personally, I so much enjoy the sultry blue-toned colours that if I were redesigning this border today I would probably omit the golden-leaved elements and use green-leaved forms of red-stemmed dogwood for the decorative winter effect. But I remember my inspiring first visit to Tintinhull thirty-five years ago and the impression this foliage border made on my totally untutored eyes. The colour combinations seemed to be just perfect. Over the years I believe Mrs Reiss's scheme has influenced a number of other new gardeners, convincing them that the colour, shape and texture of leaves are at least as important as ephemeral flower colours. In my old garden at Hadspen, in the central border of the kitchen garden, Nori and Sandra Pope now use a mixture of plants with golden, grey and glaucous leaves – euphorbias in quantity, alchemillas and grasses, enlivened by washes of blue-flowered perennials, but with flowers of minimal importance.

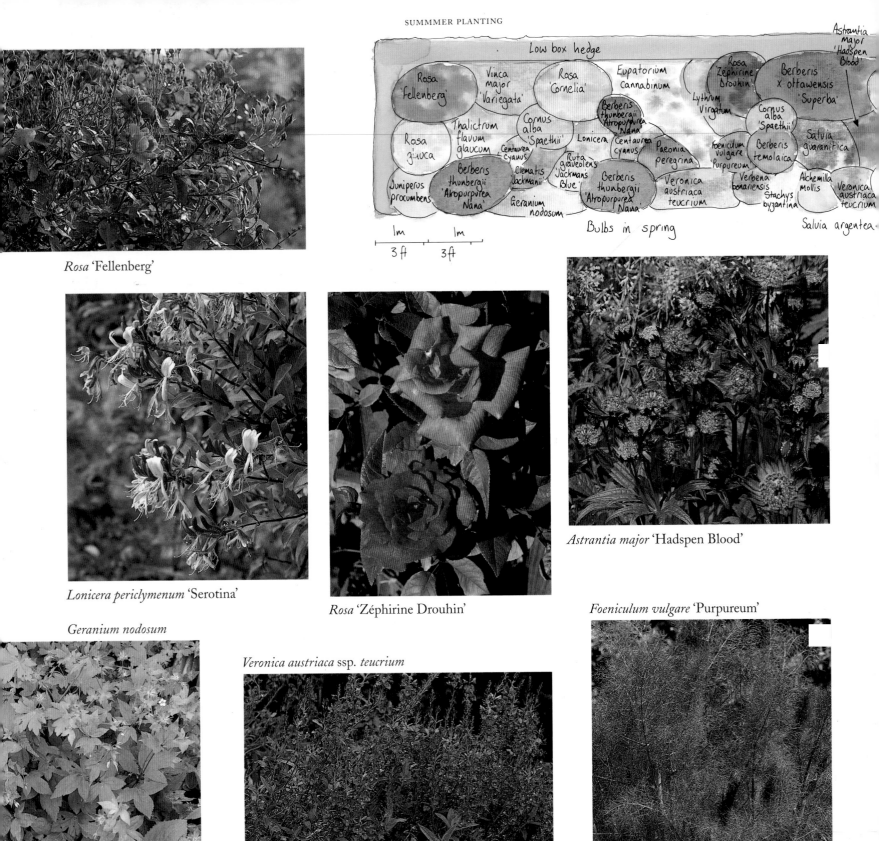

Rosa 'Fellenberg'

Low box hedge

Rosa 'Fellenberg'
Vinca major 'Variegata'
Rosa 'Cornelia'
Eupatorium cannabinum
Rosa 'Zéphirine Drouhin'
Berberis x ottawensis 'Superba'
Astrantia Major 'Hadspen Blood'
Rosa glauca
Thalictrum flavum glaucum
Cornus alba 'Spaethii'
Berberis thunbergii 'Atropurpurea Nana'
Lonicera
Lythrum Virgatum
Cornus alba 'Spaethii'
Salvia guaranitica
Centaurea cyanus
Centaurea cyanus
Paeonia peregrina
foeniculum vulgare 'Purpureum'
Berberis temolaica
Juniperus procumbens
Berberis thunbergii 'Atropurpurea Nana'
Clematis 'Jackmanii'
Ruta graveolens 'Jackmans Blue'
Berberis thunbergii 'Atropurpurea Nana'
Veronica austriaca teucrium
Verbena bonariensis
Stachys byzantina
Alchemilla mollis
Veronica austriaca teucrium
Geranium nodosum

Bulbs in spring

Salvia argentea

1m   1m
3 ft   3 ft

Lonicera periclymenum 'Serotina'

Rosa 'Zéphirine Drouhin'

Astrantia major 'Hadspen Blood'

Foeniculum vulgare 'Purpureum'

Geranium nodosum

Veronica austriaca ssp. *teucrium*

N →

Rosa 'Cornelia'

Eupatorium rugosum

Rosa glauca

Vernonia noveboracensis

Eupatorium cannabinum

Viburnum sargentii 'Onondaga'

Polygonatum x hybridum

Clematis Jackmanii

Cornus alba 'Spaethii'

Lonicera henryi

Cornus alba 'Spaethii'

Sambucus nigra 'Guincho Purple'

Lythrum virgatum 'Rose Queen'

Hosta ventricosa

Salvia guaranitica

Berberis thunbergii 'Atropurpurea Nana'

Sedum maximum 'Atropurpureum'

3 Rosa 'Rosemary Rose'

Berberis thunbergii 'Atropurpurea Nana'

Veronica austriaca teucrium

Salvia argentea

Salvia patens

Veronica austriaca teucrium

Stachys byzantina

Self-seeders

Eupatorium cannabinum. E. perfoliatum,
E. purpureum and E. rugosum

Lythrum salicaria
Sedum maximum 'Atropurpureum'
Vernonia noveboracensis

Lythrum virgatum 'Rose Queen'

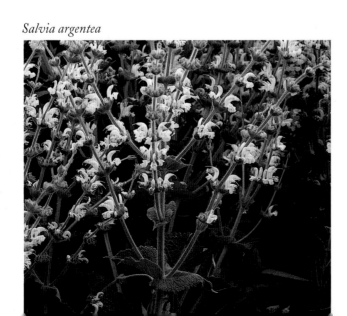

Cornus alba 'Spaethii'

Rosa 'Cornelia'

Salvia guaranitica

Salvia argentea

Rosa 'Rosemary Rose'

Stachys byzantina

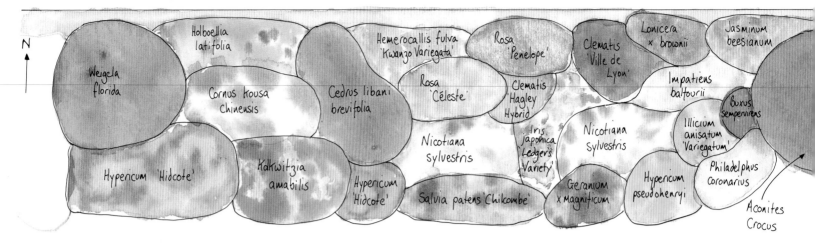

THE CEDAR TREE BORDER

THE CEDAR TREE border is very mixed. Until recently two tree peonies were important here. Sadly, they succumbed to honey fungus, leaving large gaps which we have filled with temporary plantings of *Nicotiana sylvestris*. On the wall behind, the tender Chinese evergreen *Holboellia latifolia* (*H. coriacea* is hardier and very similar), with intensely fragrant white bell-shaped flowers in spring, grows near *Clematis* 'Ville de Lyon', *Lonicera × brownii*, *Jasminum beesianum* and the scarlet-flowered California currant, *Ribes speciosum*, which is trained back as a wall shrub to give it maximum protection and heat. *Hedera helix* 'Sagittifolia', with elegant arrow-shaped leaves, clothes the wall above the door, next to my favourite climbing rose, 'Gloire de Dijon'. The invasive – but annually from seed and easily removed – balsam, *Impatiens balfourii*, is allowed to flower in any empty spaces.

Rosa 'Penelope'

Philadelphus coronarius

Kolkwitzia amabilis

Rosa 'Céleste'

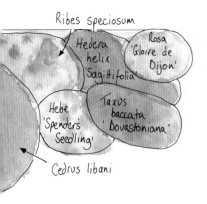

Ribes speciosum

Hedera helix 'Sagittifolia'

Rosa 'Gloire de Dijon'

Hebe 'Spender's Seedling'

Taxus baccata 'Dovastoniana'

Cedrus libani

Wall

Old Blush China rose

Clematis alpina 'Pamela Jackman'

Ceanothus papillosus

Euphorbia characias

Magnolia grandiflora

Clematis macropetala

China rose

Clematis 'The President'

Brachyglottis 'Sunshine'

Rosa pimpinellifolia

Deutzia ningpoensis

Euphorbia characias

Rosa gallica 'Versicolor'

Drimys winteri

Mahonia × media 'Lionel Fortescue'

Euphorbia characias

Rosa gallica officinalis

Rosa 'Stanwell Perpetual'

Actinidia kolomikta

Hebe haastii

Sedum 'Autumn joy'

Sedum 'Autumn joy'

Vinca minor 'Azurea Flore Pleno'

Self-seeder Impatiens balfourii

1m / 3ft · 1m / 3ft

Ribes speciosum

Old Blush China rose

Rosa gallica 'Versicolor'

Mahonia × media 'Lionel Fortescue'

Sedum 'Autumn Joy'

Drimys winteri

Actinidia kolomikta

The Cedar Tree Border 177

THE EAST BORDER

THE OTHER MAIN border in the Cedar Court faces west and is deliberately less colour-orientated, with roses, honeysuckle and clematis draping the high wall behind it. It is given overall coherence by fine shrubs such as the tender semi-evergreen *Hoheria* 'Glory of Amlwch' and the darker-leaved Mediterranean *Phillyrea latifolia*, the latter an ideal formal bush or tree for the border. These are interplanted with Hybrid Musk roses such as 'Penelope' and 'Felicia', shrubs like *Escallonia* 'Iveyi', with erect white flower trusses, *Philadelphus* 'Innocence', with white variegated leaves and scented flowers in midsummer, and *Hydrangea aspera* Villosa Group, a glorious sight towards the end of the summer. The bed is edged with alternating groups of catmint and sedum (*Sedum* 'Autumn Joy'), the latter's fleshy glaucous leaves a strong element of the design from spring onwards and beloved by butterflies when in flower in August and September. White epilobiums (*Epilobium angustifolium album*), tall macleayas, white Japanese anemones (*Anemone × hybrida* 'Honorine Jobert') and *Aster lateriflorus* 'Horizontalis' spread as drifts in their seasons. *Cornus kousa* var. *chinensis*, with creamy bracts and strawberry-like fruits, backed by an old boxwood tree, is a feature close to the south end of the border.

Separated from this border by a path there is a narrow bed planted with yellow, bronze and dark purple irises. Alliums and annual love-in-a-mist (*Nigella damascena* 'Miss Jekyll') also thrive here. A ribbon of mossy saxifrage (*Saxifraga exarata* ssp. *moschata*) makes a cloud of pink in early summer on the outer edge; pink-flowered colchicums (*Colchicum speciosum*) contribute a similar pattern of colour in early autumn on the inner path side. At the southern end of the iris bed, where it is overhung by the *Magnolia liliiflora*, I have planted some shade-tolerant small plants: shooting stars (*Dodecatheon meadia*), *Geranium phaeum* and wake robins, forms of trillium from the Connecticut woods. In late summer *Hosta* 'Royal Standard' has scented lily-like white flowers rising above apple-green foliage.

Under an Asiatic dogwood, Cornus kousa var. chinensis, *the cottagey mixed planting includes* Symphytum × uplandicum *'Variegatum', euphorbias, Welsh poppies and the elegant fern-like* Selinum tenuifolium. *In the iris bed love-in-a-mist and* Allium christophii *extend the flowering season, while groups of catmint along the front of the wall border unify the colour scheme.*

Escallonia 'Iveyi'

Rosa 'New Dawn'

Clematis 'Pagoda'

Hydrangea macrophylla

SUMMMER PLANTING

'Lavatera Barnsley'

Drimys winteri · Actinidia Kolomikta · Actinidia Kolomikta · Clematis terniflora · Rosa 'New Dawn' · Clematis 'Jackmanii' · Lonicera

Rosa 'Stanwell Perpetual' · Hydrangea Macrophylla · Escallonia 'Iveyi' · Anemone 'Honorine Jobert' · Macleaya cordata · Hoheria Glory of Amlwch' · Anemone 'Honorine Jobert'

China rose · Vinca Minor 'Azurea Flore Pleno' · Epilobium angustifolium album · Rosa 'Felicia' · Hydrangea aspeta Villosa · Rosa 'Penelope' · Stachys Macran tha 'Superba'

Aster lateriflorus 'Horizontalis' · Paeonia lactiflora hybrid

Sedum 'Autumn Joy' · Anemone 'Honorine Jobert' · Nepeta 'Six Hills Giant'

Sedum 'Autumn Joy'

1m   1m
3ft   3ft

Self-seeders
Euphorbia stricta
Helleborus foetidus and H. xsternii 'Boughton Beauty'
Lunaria annua
Meconopsis cambrica
Nigella damascena 'Miss Jekyll'
Verbena bonariensis

Iris 'Perry Hill', Iris 'Gay Trip' and Iris 'Bronze Bird' with nigella,

Saxifraga exarata moschata

Nigella damascena 'Miss Jekyll'

Hoheria 'Glory of Amlwch'

Clematis heracleifolia var. *davidiana* 'Wyevale'

Rosa 'Felicia'

Lavatera 'Barnsley'

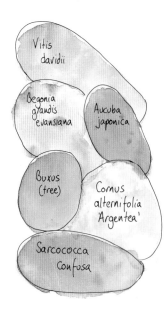

Vitis davidii

Begonia grandis evansiana

Aucuba japonica

Buxus (tree)

Cornus alternifolia 'Argentea'

Sarcococca confusa

Trachelospermum jasminoides

N

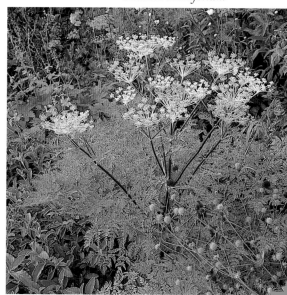

Symphytum × uplandicum 'Variegatum'

Selinum tenuifolium

Philadelphus 'Innocence'

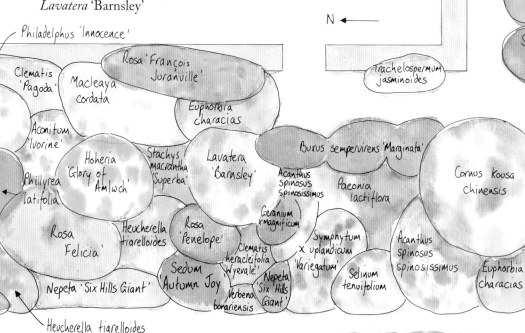

Clematis 'Pagoda'

Macleaya cordata

Rosa 'François Juranville'

Euphorbia characias

Aconitum 'Ivorine'

Hoheria 'Glory of Amlwch'

Stachys macrantha 'Superba'

Lavatera 'Barnsley'

Buxus sempervirens 'Marginata'

Acanthus spinosus spinosissimus

Paeonia lactiflora

Cornus kousa chinensis

Phillyrea latifolia

Geranium × magnificum

Rosa 'Penelope'

Heucherella tiarelloides

Rosa 'Felicia'

Clematis heracleifolia 'Wyevale'

Symphytum × uplandicum 'Variegatum'

Acanthus spinosus spinosissimus

Euphorbia characias

Sedum 'Autumn Joy'

Nepeta 'Six Hills Giant'

Verbena bonariensis

Selinum tenuifolium

Nepeta 'Six Hills Giant'

Heucherella tiarelloides

alliums, Gladiolus communis byzantinus and colchicums

Dodecatheon meadia

Trillium grandiflorum

Euphorbia characias

Geranium maculatum

Hosta 'Royal Standard'

Geranium phaeum

Geranium phaeum 'Album'

Magnolia liliiflora 'Nigra'

Helleborus × sternii 'Boughton Beauty'

Meconopsis cambrica

Hemerocallis fulva 'Kwanzo Variegata'

Dodecatheon meadia

Trillium grandiflorum

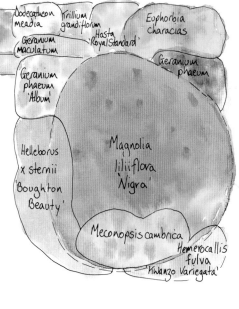

THE MAGNOLIA BEDS

ON THE NORTH SIDE of the Cedar Court, *Magnolia* × *soulangeana* has autumn-flowering ivy-leaved *Cyclamen hederifolium* growing in a large circle around its trunk; during the winter the marbled leaves set off the silver-grey bark and purple-tinged twigs. In the south-west corner the low spreading branches of another *M. liliiflora* 'Nigra', with *M. stellata* at its side, create a woodland situation for spring bulbs and shade-tolerant herbaceous plants such as daylilies, erythroniums, crane's-bill geraniums and hellebores – a mixture of *Helleborus foetidus* and the hybrid *H.* × *sternii* 'Boughton Beauty', both of which seed prolifically. Clumps of Welsh poppies make a yellow wash in season in these shady beds, but their ready seeding habit is less desirable, as they tend to appear throughout the garden and an established seedling is difficult to eradicate in routine weeding. They should be deadheaded as soon as they finish flowering: they can easily become weeds where not wanted and, small though they are, the glimmering yellow flowers catch the eye to spoil a planned colour scheme. This poppy and the Byzantine gladiolus, both desirable plants in their place, had escaped into many beds when we came in 1979; it took several seasons of weeding to contain them. Under one of the magnolias we also have the almost evergreen crane's-bill *Geranium nodosum*, with lilac flowers and glossy leaves, which drifts out under the spreading magnolia and seeds into the adjacent border.

The ivy-leaved Cyclamen hederifolium *from the Mediterranean region which carpets the round bed under* Magnolia × soulangeana *flowers for six weeks in late August and September and most years will survive the occasional sharp frost. Its leaves are attractive all winter, fading only in May, after which the bed is mulched.*

Mushroom compost can be stockpiled and will improve if left to rot down over a few years. We find it useful throughout the garden at Tintinhull but especially under the magnolias, which we mulch heavily, covering the ground *to a depth of 10 cm/4 in. In the neutral soil they might easily develop chlorosis, but the humus-making mulch keeps them healthy. The cyclamen benefit too, and now make a dense mat.*

THE SOUTH SIDE

A WIDE FLOWER BED under the shady north wall of the house grows a collection of hybrids and varieties of *Rosa pimpinellifolia*, all of which flower well before the first June flush of roses in the rest of the garden. Mixed in between the roses are Solomon's seal, white-flowered foxgloves and the hardy twining flame flower, *Tropaeolum speciosum*, with scarlet flowers in late summer. This perennial nasturtium, often seen in northern gardens growing over tall dark yew hedges, is difficult to establish but seems to thrive at Tintinhull. It must have been there for many years. The climbing shade-tolerant rose 'Madame Grégoire Staechelin' has double pink flowers in early June. A spreading *Cotoneaster horizontalis* frames and softens the wide steps to the outer courtyard. In spring tulips grow in the reconstituted stone pots and orange- and red-flowered mimulus, grown each year from cuttings, are used for summer decoration.

To the west, sheltered by the two old yews, another border provides more opportunity for shade-lovers. It has Oregon grape (*Mahonia aquifolium*), viburnums and winter-flowering scented evergreen *Ribes laurifolium*. Scotch burnet roses are interplanted with the maple-leaved perennial *Kirengeshoma palmata*, with primrose shuttlecock flowers in late summer, and a glossy-leaved toad lily, *Tricyrtis formosana*, undercarpeted with groups of *Lamium* 'White Nancy' and Miss Jekyll's favourite fumitory, *Corydalis cheilanthifolia*, with fern-like leaves and pale flowers. Against the wall and almost clothing part of it, the vigorous climber *Sinofranchetia chinensis* thrives but finds it too shady to flower.

Right: *The little ferny corydalis,* Corydalis cheilanthifolia, *one of Miss Jekyll's favourites, grows in dry shade, along with self-seeded cyclamen and chionodoxa, under one of the yew trees in the Cedar Court.*

Left: *The varieties and hybrids of* Rosa pimpinellifolia *will grow, and be spread by suckers, even in deep shade. At Tintinhull* Rosa × harisonii *'Harison's Yellow' and various Scotch burnet roses thrive under the north wall of the house. The climbing Hybrid Tea rose 'Madame Grégoire Staechelin' flowers on the same wall.*

In the Cedar Court reconstituted stone pots are packed with white lamium and orange- and red-flowered mimulus, plants which prefer the light shade on the north side of the house.

Planting out Annuals

Annuals grown from seed sown in early spring, together with tender woody plants rooted from cuttings during the previous autumn, are indispensable at Tintinhull, carrying colour schemes right through the first frosts and infilling so that no bare earth is left visible or allowed to dry out. Many of the annuals go where spring bulbs such as tulips have finished flowering and have been lifted. Others augment a newly planted border scheme for one or two seasons until shrubs and perennials grow together. Perennials can be divided in autumn or spring and replanted to allow space for clumps of annuals. Occasionally a large shrub dies unexpectedly and the gap provides a perfect site for taller, larger-leaved annuals or biennials.

In the Cedar Court two of our treasured tree peonies in the border under the cedar began to fade out at the end of one season. We left them in position until the following spring, hoping for a recovery, but when we finally realized that the ground was probably infected with honey fungus, we resigned ourselves to taking them out. Fortunately we had available some trays of tobacco plants, *Nicotiana sylvestris*, a relatively shade-tolerant annual.

We had sown the nicotiana seed in February, pricked the seedlings out into deep trays in March, and gradually hardened the plants off in closed and then open frames in preparation for planting out, which should ideally have been at the end of May.

Because we were late in planting (it was early June before we took out the tree peonies), it was especially important to water the ground thoroughly (*opposite, below*) before putting in the well-rooted plants. The trays were also soaked in a tank of water until all air-bubbles disappeared. As in all the well-worked Tintinhull borders, the soil is friable and, once it was moistened, it was easy to a dig a hole for each plant (*opposite, above*). I added a handful of dried organic manure before putting the plant in and firming the earth around it (*left, top to bottom*). Positioning the plants 20–30cm/8–12in apart, there was room for a fairly large group in the gap left by one of the tree peonies. Finally, a mulch was applied around the plants to help retain moisture during the months ahead. They flowered in the autumn (*below*).

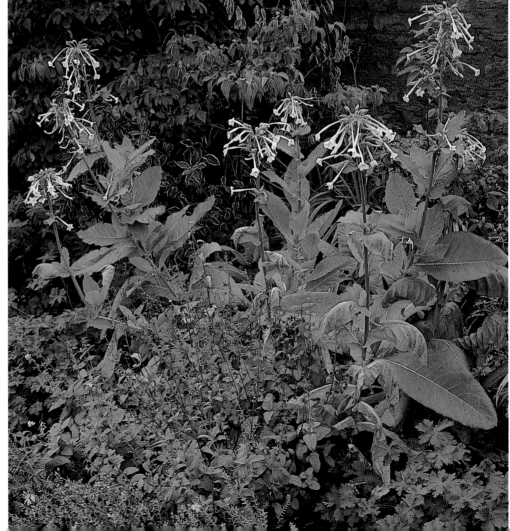

The Stately Magnolias

THE SOUTHERN OR EVERGREEN magnolia, *Magnolia grandiflora*, from the south-eastern states of North America, is pre-eminent. In California and Mediterranean countries, as well as in the southern states, this wonderful magnolia is to be seen growing in the open, making a shapely pyramid and flowering prolifically. In a temperate climate it needs the protection of a warm wall; even there it may not produce its lemon-scented cream globes until it is at least fifteen years old, and then only spasmodically. None the less, *M. grandiflora* is

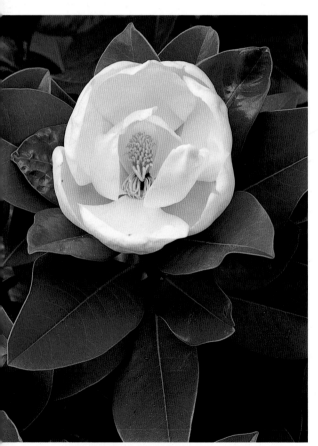

Magnolia grandiflora

handsome enough in year-round leaf and habit to merit a prominent garden place. An old specimen, growing espalier-like to the eaves of a house, is a treasure beyond price.

To get flowers on young plants, choose one of the recommended hybrids or cultivars. *M.* 'Maryland' flowered for Graham Stuart Thomas in its second year. I have used *M.g.* 'Goliath', with polished soft elliptic leaves, reddish-brown felted below. *M.g.* 'Exmouth' is similar, and both flower early in life. At Bettiscombe I grow the American *M.g.* 'Little Gem', which is less vigorous and more suitable for a limited space. Probably the hardiest of all these southern magnolias is the excellent hybrid *M.g.* 'Edith Bogue'.

Another evergreen magnolia is *M. delavayi*, with huge sea-green glaucous leaves and creamy-white scented flowers, but this is definitely tender and, without protection, only for favoured localities.

These are the only genuine evergreens among the cultivated magnolias, but there are many deciduous magnolias which are good for integrating into a shrub scheme, with small plants growing under their branches. Tree-like or bushy, all have fragrant blossoms. Some have upright tulip-shaped flowers (*M.* × *soulangeana* and *M. liliiflora*), others have saucer-shaped open flowers (*M. sieboldii* ssp. *sinensis*), and others, such as *M. kobus* and *M. stellata*, have many-petalled small flowers.

We would all love to succeed with some of the earliest flowerers such as the giant Himalayan pink tulip tree, *M. campbellii*, and *M.c.* ssp. *mollicomata*, which flower gloriously in early spring, their pink blossoms outlined against blue skies, in some Cornish gardens and in California.

However, in less favoured areas the buds are almost inevitably damaged by frosts. The flower buds of *M.c.* 'Charles Raffill' are reputedly more resistant. The goblet-shaped buds open like water lilies to display paler pink inside the petals.

Among the more weather-resistant tulip- or goblet-shaped flowerers you can hardly beat the old favourite *M.* × *soulangeana* and its variants, with flowers in different pinks or white. At Tintinhull the type plant stands as a feature in the Cedar Court, where it flowers, leafless, in April. In the

Magnolia × *soulangeana* 'Lennei'

Magnolia liliiflora 'Nigra'

same lawn are two large spreading *M. liliiflora* 'Nigra' and a Japanese star magnolia, *M. stellata*. Shrubby in habit and seldom exceeding 3m/10ft in height and spread, *M. stellata* has frost-resistant grey hairy buds during winter and also flowers early while leafless. The flowers of the type are snow-white tinged with pink but there are many darker pink cultivars. The hybrids of *M. × loebneri* have much charm. With the habit of *M. stellata* but growing larger, *M. × l.* 'Leonard Messel' has petals with the outer surface of lavender-purple, the inner distinctly paler.

One way around the problem of late frosts is to grow only the summer flowerers, such as my favourite deciduous magnolia, *M. virginiana*, the American sweet bay. The leaves, in warm climates almost evergreen, are long and glossy above, glaucous beneath, and it has small cream globular flowers from mid- to late summer. *M. sieboldii*, *M.s.* ssp. *sinensis* and *M. wilsonii* have pendent saucer-shaped flowers in midsummer. *M. × wiesneri* (*M. watsonii*), needing acid soil, bears its upward-facing saucer-shaped fragrant flowers a bit later.

The list is endless; we would all love to be magnolia collectors but most of us are severely limited by space. Give those you grow the best possible conditions, with shelter from cold winds and plenty of moisture at the roots during the growing period. When planting prepare a wide hole, at least double the width of the container or root system, add a generous supply of organic matter and plant so that the main root system is only just below the soil surface. All ideally prefer acid soil, but except for those few (such as *M. salicifolia* and *M. × wiesneri*) which are definitely calcifuge, most will tolerate some alkalinity, provided they are given plenty of lime-free organic matter to satisfy the shallow, questing roots. Magnolias seldom need pruning. Any shaping necessary should be done after flowering for the deciduous magnolias, in spring for the evergreens.

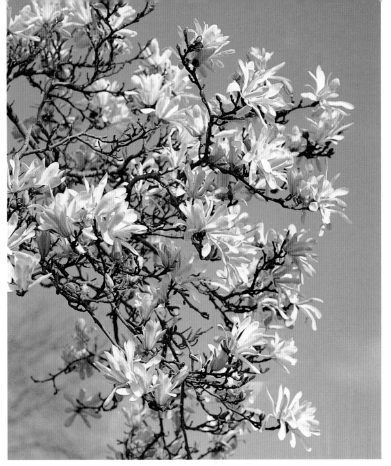

Magnolia × loebneri 'Leonard Messel'

Magnolia stellata

Magnolia wilsonii

Gardening with Cyclamen

THE GARDENING season opens for me each year with the enjoyment of my favourite of all small woodland cyclamens, the spring-flowering *Cyclamen repandum*. The flower smells of violets and is distinctive, with carmine-red – or sometimes pink, or white – upswept, slightly twisted flower petals held above pointed, silver-patterned leaves. This cyclamen needs shade – its leaves will burn in full sun – thriving at Tintinhull under the evergreen oaks as it would in the Mediterranean basin from which it originates. It seeds itself happily and prolifically between ivy and periwinkles, under hellebores and in cracks of paving, and will thrive where water is scarce through most of the year.

In fact *C. repandum* likes exactly the same situation in a garden as the hardier, more vigorous, late-summer-flowering *C. hederifolium*, the most easily grown of all the outdoor cyclamen. *C. hederifolium*, widely distributed all round the Mediterranean, has large scented carmine or white flowers with sharply pointed petals. At Tintinhull the first flowers come in early August and increase in spread and vigour, lasting a good six weeks. The leaves come after the flowers, but start to emerge before the flowering period is over. They are attractive, very variable but basically shaped like ivy, in deep green, marbled in light grey, pewter or even silver, with deep red undersides. In a temperate climate they endure the vagaries of winter weather and remain decorative until dormancy begins in late spring of the following year. They should be top-dressed with leaf mould or any organic mulch to encourage strong new growth. This cyclamen seeds in the most unpromising

Cyclamen repandum

Cyclamen hederifolium

Cyclamen coum

subspecies. In general it has plain green glossy rounded leaves but some have distinctive marblings. The short-stemmed flowers are white, pale pink or deep carmine, with a dark purple blotch at the base of each petal, and open in midwinter. Unlike *C. repandum* and *C. hederifolium*, *C. coum* prefers damp ground – it will thrive next to primroses. Though perhaps less exciting than the other two, it is still a worthwhile plant and it looks splendid massed, as in Lady Anne Rasch's garden at Heale House in Wiltshire. *C. cilicium* is a little trickier and needs more care, with gritty well-drained soil and protective mulches during dormancy. This autumn-flowering Turkish species is a delight, with small, elegantly shaped deep rose-pink flowers accompanied by spoon-shaped leaves.

Between them these cyclamen will provide decorative flowers or leaves to carpet the ground under larger plants at almost every season, only excepting a couple of months at midsummer, when most lose their deciduous leaves and become entirely dormant.

Cyclamen cilicium

places, thriving under deciduous shrubs and trees such as magnolias, but seemingly ready to germinate and flower even in the shade of a yew tree. It makes an ideal subject for growing at the shady base of an evergreen hedge, where almost nothing else except Welsh poppies would survive. At Tintinhull some of the tubers have grown to be almost 30cm/12in across and can occupy an inconvenient amount of space during the dormancy period in summer. I shall miss their maturity when I try to make a new garden. It can take fifty years or so to get cyclamen established and seeding as they do at Tintinhull.

There are two other cyclamen that I find especially useful in the garden. *C. coum*, which has a wide distribution in the wild in the Balkans and the Middle East, may well be an aggregate of many slightly variable

Onions in the Garden: the Alliums

Allium aflatunense 'Purple Sensation'

Most of us grow alliums in the herb or vegetable garden as onions, chives or leeks. But that should be just the beginning. The allium family includes a vast number of species – something like a thousand in all – and the range used regularly in gardens could easily be much increased. Each year I get more enthusiastic about alliums, more aware of their garden possibilities and the pleasure one could have from growing more of the rarer kinds.

Members of the Liliaciae family, all alliums are perennial bulbs. Nearly all have a characteristic smell of garlic or onions and most bear umbels of tiny flowers packed closely together. Beyond that these plants are extremely variable. Coming from very diverse habitats, they have developed different traits. A large bulb, adapted for dormancy in a hot climate, generally signifies that an allium comes from a dry, arid habitat, while alliums from more temperate, cooler climates have smaller, slender bulbs, often clustered on a short rhizome – or indeed may appear to have a fibrous system. The leaves are equally divergent, sometimes short and erect, sometimes long and floppy or thin and thread-like. The leaves of the alliums from hot countries usually begin to fade before the plant comes into flower; those from damp upland meadows retain fresh leaves throughout the summer. Judicious selection can unearth candidates for most garden situations, from baking hot well-drained rockeries, where the dumpy *Allium karataviense* will thrive, displaying its splendid purplish glaucous leaves and pinkish-purple florets, to areas that are moist during the summer growing months, which are suitable for the late flowerers such

as the distinguished greeny-white *A. tuberosum*. No allium, however, will long endure a location that is water-logged during the winter.

At Tintinhull we have never been very adventurous about alliums, partly because of the constraints of the original plant lists; however, we have added various alliums to most of the main borders, and some of these now seed themselves in happy abandon in other parts of the garden. Taking my ideas from what I saw at Sissinghurst, I started by introducing hardy drumstick varieties, with large globular heads of mauve florets, among and around shrub roses. One of the first we planted was *A. christophii* (*A. albopilosum*), with 20cm/8in diameter heads made up of blueish-violet starry florets held on rather stumpy short stalks (up to

40cm/16in). But I really prefer the taller alliums, finding them more graceful, and we soon added the late-flowering blue *A. caeruleum* (up to 80cm/32in), *A. rosenbachianum*, with 1m/3ft stems and violet star-shaped flowers held in a looser spherical umbel, and *A. aflatunense*, with heads of deep violet and stems running to about 1.5m/5ft.

There are many other desirable alliums for which we have never found space at Tintinhull, and I hope that I will have the opportunity to experiment with some of these in my new garden. I certainly plan to try magenta-flowered *A. polyastrum*, with star-shaped florets, *A. macranthum*, with plum-purple bell-shaped flowers, maroon-purple *A. wallichii* and *A. cernuum*, with pinkish flowers and almost evergreen leaves.

Allium christophii

Allium caeruleum

Allium cernuum

BEHIND THE SCENES

IN PRACTICAL TERMS the nitty and gritty side of garden work has no seasonal beginning or end, but there are two definite moments in the year when the rhythms change: in February, and in late June.

Chronologically, mid-February is the most practical moment to start the 'behind the scenes' year at Tintinhull. It is then that the days begin to lengthen perceptibly, and plants in the greenhouse or in cold frames put out new shoots. Adrenaline rises in the excitement of planning and discussing the spring and summer appearance of the garden for the year. And from February on, the 'behind the scenes' work of sowing, pricking out, rooting cuttings and potting on – traditional greenhouse tasks undertaken in preparation for the summer beauty of beds and containers – is almost as important as more obvious routine gardening.

As seeds germinate and plants need pricking out, greenhouses and frames get very full. In our first years at Tintinhull we had two small 3m × 2.5m/10ft × 8ft greenhouses; later we added a third. Two were used for work in progress, while the third, heated to only just above freezing, was for the larger pot plants which benefit from winter protection: cordylines, corokias, correas, *Dodonaea viscosa* 'Purpurea' (before it grew too large and had to stay in the summerhouse where it did not survive), leptospermums and olearias from New Zealand and Australia, myrtles from southern Europe, tender buddlejas and *Jasminum polyanthum* from Asia, *Melianthus major* and bomareas from South Africa, and the dahlia-like *Cosmos atrosanguineus*, both of the latter dormant in winter and needing no water. There were woody salvias and the choosy perennial velvety-flowered *Salvia buchananii* from Mexico, as well as favourites such as *S. clevelandii* from California, and lemon-scented verbena, *Aloysia triphylla* (*Lippia citriodora*), a traditional greenhouse plant in Britain, coming from Chile two centuries ago.

Cold frames are another essential, both for hardening off young plants before they go to their garden sites, and for winter-storing many of the hardiest rooted cuttings, as well as pots of *Francoa sonchifolia*, which sit on the steps in the Eagle Court, and pots of regale lilies for the summerhouse.

The greenhouse and cold frame area at Tintinhull is backed up by a good shed for tools and storage, and a wide potting bench. There are sheltered nursery beds for growing on, but over the years much of the available planting space has been filled with permanent small trees and shrubs, mostly Asiatic and grown from seed: magnolias; a tall *Ehretia dicksonii; Cladrastis sinensis*, which takes twenty years to flower; both *Rhus potaninii* and the varnish tree, *R. verniciflua; Phellodendron amurense; Tetradium daniellii* Hupehense Group (*Euodia hupehensis*); and a spreading *Aesculus parviflora* which flowers in July and August – all of which as they mature provide a 'borrowed' landscape of fine shape and foliage at the back of the garden wall behind the Cedar Court. Smaller woody plants fit into the experimental beds round the Kitchen Garden, and soft-stemmed perennials can be grown there in rows, encroaching on vegetable space.

If we buy in perennial plants – we usually add some new varieties when redoing a bed – we do not expect to be able to use them in a border the first year, but repot them in our own compost or put them out in the Kitchen Garden or our nursery area to grow on for the summer.

WINTER INTO SPRING

As daylight hours lengthen, winter pruning and tidying – even if unfinished – give way to sowing and propagating.

Although we mix our own compost for our big pots (see page 203) we do not find it worthwhile to make up our own mix for seed or for growing on or cuttings; it is too time-consuming. Instead we buy in appropriate proprietary composts. All of those we use contain loam, peat and sand, and a slow-release fertilizer. We have tried using alternatives without peat, such as coir (processed coconut fibre), but we find that they dry out quickly, and young plants need feeding almost immediately. We use plastic trays for seeds, and I prefer square pots for plants that are potted on individually, as round containers take up more space. All must be scrupulously washed after use, and they should be stored in the dark or they will become brittle.

Left: *Some time in winter I examine all my bags of seed, shake their contents on to a saucer and remove any debris. Then I pour the seeds into small polythene or paper envelopes which are stored in silica gel in the refrigerator.*

Right: *The greenhouses in spring are packed with tender plants, potted on from rooted cuttings, and seedlings pricked out from the initial sowing a few weeks earlier.*

All our seeds, whether of annuals, trees, shrubs or perennials, are sown during February and March, and these will include seeds collected in the garden, as well as interesting seeds obtained on my travels (fortunately, seed does not need a phytosanitary certificate), or treasured seeds sent by friends in the States and elsewhere – the new introductions widening the range and interest of plants in the garden. In the autumn we make lists of all the seeds we have gathered, and again work out how many plants we will need for the garden schemes.

Recently, as the garden filled up, most of the trees and shrubs grown from seed at Tintinhull have been given away. But in our earlier years here there was still space for small trees such as the St Lucie cherry (*Prunus mahaleb*), *Aesculus californica* (grown from seed sent by a friend in the International Dendrology Society), and the evergreen *Maytenus boaria* from Chile. Many others grown from seed were planted in my husband John's arboretum in the orchard.

Annuals are a vital element in the garden. They need three months' growing time, to make strong root systems, before being planted out. They will be potted on three or four times during this interval, and will be planted out after the last frost, towards the end of May – or even later, as tulips and forget-me-nots finish and make space in the beds or containers.

We grow mostly species rather than nursery hybrid annuals, but also try new varieties offered by seedsmen. Our own seed includes that of tobacco plants such as *Nicotiana langsdorffii*, *N. sylvestris*, and the grey-leaved South American *N. glauca*, which may reach 2.5m/8ft in a summer. Tobacco plants often self-hybridize to produce interesting variations. We also germinate seed of a few plants which nearly always seed *in situ*, just as an insurance: *Collomia debilis* with apricot flowers; the bright pink *Silene armeria;* the miniature *Polygonum capitatum*, which is allowed to trail over the stones which flank the Pool Garden borders; red and orange Chilean glory-flowers, *Eccremocarpus scaber;* and the square-stemmed mauve *Verbena bonariensis*.

Many of the soft-stemmed tender sages are also grown from seed (the more woody ones are propagated from cuttings). The intense blue *Salvia patens* and the pale 'Cambridge Blue' and mauve 'Chilcombe' germinate easily but dislike being pricked out, so we usually grow them in peat pots to prevent root disturbance. The related *Lepechinia salviae*, with dusky red flowers, and *Lobelia tupa*, with maroon flowers, are treated in the same way.

Seeds of the blue-flowered *Lathyrus sativus* and cream *Hibiscus trionum* are sown for the Pool Garden pots, *Dahlia merckii* for the Kitchen Garden, where it may self-seed in another year, and *Rehmannia elata*, with its strange hooded flowers, for the beds by the summerhouse. The biennial giant thistle, *Onopordum acanthium*, important for its sculptural appearance in the foliage garden at the back of the Fountain Garden, is sown for flowering the following summer, as is the milk thistle, *Silybum marianum*, to go in an odd corner, and Miss Willmott's ghost, *Eryngium giganteum*, for the Pool Garden beds, while white foxgloves can always be fitted in on the north side of the house.

We germinate seeds of hardier perennials and woody plants in case clumps or specimens need renewing after the winter. The sprawling catmint, *Nepeta nervosa*, at the base of the pink 'Mevrouw Nathalie Nypels' roses in the Kitchen Garden needs replacing almost annually; it gets squeezed out by neighbouring plants. More plants of the perennial peas, salmon-coloured *Lathyrus rotundifolius*, and Lord Anson's treasured blue pea, *L. nervosus*, are always welcome.

The seed of *Perilla frutescens* var. *crispa* with dusky purple leaves, which is so perfect for the hot border in the Pool Garden, like that of the blue hyacinth bean, *Lablab purpureus* (*Dolichos lablab*) – of which we need six plants to grow on tripods in the Kitchen Garden – rarely ripens in Britain's cool summers, so I ask for seed each year from friends in the States. Also from the States comes seed for different American eupatoriums and vernonias (from a gardener in Pennsylvania), amsonias – which we have found difficult to establish – and *Baptisia australis*, with blue pea flowers and beautiful black pods; as well as some more Mexican and Californian salvias, most of which are kept in individual pots. We buy in seeds of Swan river daisy (*Brachyscome*), sweet peas for the house, and vegetables for the Kitchen Garden.

Cuttings of tender shrubby plants that will be treated as annuals are taken from overwintered stock plants as they recommence growth. These, when rooted, will replace plants that were rooted the previous August or September and which, in spite of being overwintered in the cold frames, look unhealthy or have not survived. We check how many of each plant we need for all the garden sites, but always grow a few extra. Plants will include anisodonteas, argyranthemums, artemisias, diascias, felicias,

osteospermums and penstemons. Also included will be some of the most important featured plants at Tintinhull, such as *Artemisia* 'Powis Castle' and *Argyranthemum foeniculaceum*, both of which have rapidly expanding root systems and need frequent potting on. And in addition to this, some cuttings of rarer shrubs that have been in the main mist propagator through the winter (with heat and water turned off) will now need potting up.

I enjoy gardening with tender but fast-growing plants. They can either be grouped with hardy perennials and shrubs in the beds, or kept in containers. As the garden at Tintinhull has grown together, there has been less room for tender plants and annuals between the

Above, left and right: *In early spring the dead leaves of the hellebores are tidied away, so that they look at their best when in flower. We also spread a mulch around their crowns and between the clumps to set off the flowers and young leaves.*

permanent planting, and more need for pots. I hope to continue experimenting with them at Bettiscombe.

Potted cuttings that have rooted in the late summer start to grow again in February, and quickly get root-bound unless they are re-potted. They may need further potting by the end of March, which allows them six weeks or so to get well established in their new containers in cold frames before being planted out. We use quite a few anisodonteas, argyranthemums, mimulus, osteospermums, penstemons, and my favourite blue salvias, *Salvia cacaliifolia, S. guaranitica, S. leptophylla* and *S. leucantha*. All these are grown from cuttings, like the more woody sages – the scarlet *S. fulgens* and *S. coccinea*, destined for the hot border in the Pool Garden, the black-flowered *S. discolor* for the summerhouse pots, and forms of *S. microphylla* for the hot borders or for containers.

Ideally, labels for all these plants will have been prepared on wet or freezing winter days, but so many tasks are kept for bad weather that this is seldom achieved. Labelling, however, is essential.

Some outside tasks are also vital February chores, the background to success later in the year. Digging the vegetable garden should be completed as early as possible, and pruning of late-summer buddlejas and small-flowered clematis must be fitted in by the end of the month. If this is done earlier in the winter, unseasonable warm spells may encourage shoots which will be damaged by frosts; if left too late, flowering will be delayed.

Late frosts can damage buds of quite mature plants – early-flowering magnolias, and hydrangeas, such as *Hydrangea aspera* Villosa Group, which do not flower until late summer. The new shoots of young shrubs are also particularly vulnerable, and those still with a small root system may not recover from a hard frost in

April or May. When frosts threaten, it is worth throwing a loose covering of net or fleece over the most vulnerable shrubs – and also over the growing tips of lilies.

In March, all the roses, except for the Scotch burnets, need attention. Bush roses, already trimmed back in November to prevent wind rock, are properly pruned (see pages 152–3). Large shrub roses have their old or dead wood cut out from the base during the winter, but in March any frost-tipped shoots should be removed. Their arching graceful shapes, so valuable in the garden, are easily spoilt if they are wrongly pruned, and branches should only be cut back by a third or so. The most back-breaking rose-pruning at Tintinhull is in the bed of massed apothecary's rose, *Rosa gallica* var. *officinalis*, in the Kitchen Garden. Each shoot needs cutting back to two buds above ground level. It might be worth experimenting, and using hedge clippers or even a strimmer to cut back more ruthlessly.

As soon as rose leaves unfurl, a two-weekly spraying programme against blackspot, mildew and aphids is essential. Use any good rose mixture. Peony tips and lily shoots, both subject to botrytis, can also benefit from being sprayed with a fungicide as they appear.

Spring weeding is followed by mulching with any organic homemade compost or a mushroom compost that we obtain locally. (We hardly ever use farmyard manure, which produces a whole crop of weed seeds.) This will effectively retain moisture in the soil throughout the drier summer months, as well as suppressing weed germination. I try not to mulch where annuals are to go until after they have been planted, then I spread the mulch all around them. It acts as a valuable cosmetic and sets off the young growth of all plants in an attractive workmanlike way.

In March, the hellebores in the north-facing bed in the Eagle Court and under the magnolias in the Cedar Court need their dead leaves cutting away. Then they are mulched. Seedlings which have germinated around their stems are noted, to be dug up later; these, probably mixed offspring of different parents, can be potted up for use in other areas of the garden, or grown on to see if they have any special flower colour or shape.

Sowing Seeds

At TINTINHULL most seeds are sown in February, in half-trays of a suitable seed compost. It is important that the compost should be thoroughly moist. I usually hold the tray in water, almost level with the rim, until all air-bubbles disappear. Then I take it out and press down on it with another tray to level the soil (*below left*). Seed should be scattered quite thinly on the surface of the compost (*below centre*). With very fine seed it may be worth mixing it with sand to ensure a more even distribution. In most cases a thin layer of sieved compost is then shaken over the seeds. However, some seeds, such as those of tobacco plants, prefer to germinate in the light on the surface, and they are left completely uncovered. Others need to be kept in the dark; they can be covered with a layer of glass and newspaper until they have germinated. We place the labelled seed trays on top of the heated soil in the mist propagator, but without the mist in operation.

After germination, as soon as the seedlings are large enough to be handled, they are pricked out into a richer growing compost in larger trays. Generally the seedlings are ready when the second lot of leaves appears. If you can, pot them on with a little soil attached to the wispy roots. Scoop a little clump out of the tray and gently separate them, holding them by the leaves to avoid clasping the fragile stems, then gently firm them into the compost (*right, top to bottom*). We keep our seedlings in the frost-free greenhouse for another few weeks and then harden them off, first in closed frames and later in frames without lids, so that they are well acclimatized before being put out in their flowering sites. During their time in the greenhouse they need little but frequent watering – a gentle spray two or three times a day rather than a good soak – and should be protected from the hot midday sun. The trays will keep damp by capillary action if placed on moist sand or gravel.

Spring into Summer

All through March, April and the first half of May, greenhouses and frames need monitoring. Hot sun can decimate small seedlings, and unexpected frosts, if windows or frame lids are left open, can ruin a whole crop of seeds or cuttings. As the weather warms up the frames can be left open more and more, unless a frost is threatened. It is worth listening to the weather forecast during this anxious period, as one hard frost can do a lot of damage. Plants should never go straight from a greenhouse into the ground but must have a hardening-off period in frames.

In the last half of March and throughout April, perennials that have not been dealt with in the autumn are dug up, split and moved to new sites which have been planned since the end of the previous summer. This gives a chance to fork in compost and prepare the ground more effectively; we only dig when a whole border is renovated. Achilleas, cephalarias, *Clematis recta*, crambes, the white epilobium, eupatoriums, galegas, *Lysimachia ciliata* 'Purpurea', phygelius and veronicastrums are all natural spreaders, and need controlling rather than frequent dividing. Phlox should be lifted at least every three or four years, the central root crown thrown away, and young plants from the outer edge reused. *Aster × frikartii* 'Mönch' should be renewed by cuttings every few seasons.

In April there is still plenty of garden tidying to do: leaves to be swept up, paving to sweep, gravel to rake in the Kitchen Garden, lawns that need feeding and levelling. There are also urgent tasks to prevent trouble a year later. We have very few perennial weeds but,

of course, dandelion and thistle seed is always blowing in from the outlying orchards. Another persistent weed is the attractive perennial arum with smooth green leaves, known as lords and ladies and cousin to *Arum italicum* 'Marmoratum'.

In the main beds and borders weeds are easily spotted, but in the more informal parts of the garden they tend to be overlooked. Annual weeds include the little creeping veronica, *Veronica hederifolia*, pretty with its blue flowers, but extremely persistent, colonizing where it can, and quickly overrunning early-flowering anemones and scillas. It needs weeding out by hand where it germinates all over the garden. This sort of weeding is relatively skilled, as garden plants and seedlings are also appearing, sometimes in unexpected places. We have lost a lot of plants from hasty work done by willing but inexperienced hands.

In April and May, established herbaceous perennials need mulching as they appear, and staking is done in May. We keep this to a minimum, giving support only to the most unruly plants, up to a third of their expected height. We always try to get coppiced hazel, but often have to make do with bamboos and string and some of the circular metal supports. The fast-growing twining clematis all need attention throughout April, May and June: their shoots carefully guided to fan out or clamber into neighbouring shrubs in order to prevent unsightly birds' nest effects.

We prune evergreen trees and shrubs, except for yew and box hedges, in April or May. If they are done any later, there is a danger that new growth made late in the year will be vulnerable to hard

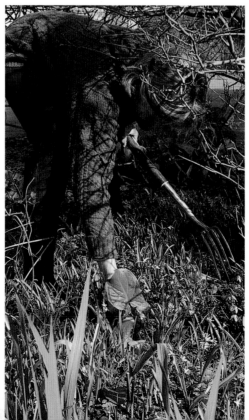

The wild arums are among the most irritating weeds at Tintinhull. We try to dig them out but often break off the stems without getting out the whole root system. In some parts of the garden I occasionally use a contact weedkiller to weaken their growth.

Left: *We have to keep on top of pulling out the annual weeds which germinate as the ground heats up in spring. Most of our weeding is done by hand. I use a hand-cultivator to freshen up the soil but we never use a hoe in the flower beds, as precious seedlings might be lost.*

Below: *In late spring we have the pleasure and excitement of taking plants from the greenhouses and cold frames and putting them out in their permanent positions in the borders. The photographs show new plants of* Coronilla valentina *ssp* glauca *and* Abutilon × suntense *to go in the Eagle Court.*

winter frosts. Winter-flowering laurustinus (forms of *Viburnum tinus*), osmanthus – which needs little formal pruning – itea, rhamnus, and low-growing lavenders and cotton lavenders all need cutting to make good shapes. Spring-flowering viburnums, choisyas, *Osmanthus delavayi* and more tender olearias and other New Zealanders are tidied back after flowering is over. Only the summer-flowering shrubs are left untouched.

During the last ten days of May and the first weeks of June, dead tulip leaves are removed, and some of the bulbs dug up to make space. By now, most of the new plants – annuals and tender shrubs used as annuals – are well hardened off and ready to put out in their permanent sites. Some, such as diascias and lobelias, have already been planted out, earlier in the month. Before planting, all the trays and pots of plants are held in a tank of water until air-bubbles cease to appear. This is always a good idea, but is particularly important for these quick-maturing short-season plants which have to start growing into their sites at once. Where possible, and if there is enough space between neighbouring plants, we prepare the ground by forking it over and incorporating organic compost. I also like to add a handful of dried organic fertilizer to each planting hole. All these plants are heavy feeders, producing a great number of flowers in only a few months.

Some of the plants go in planters of one kind or another, and here soil conditions are more easily controlled. We mix compost for the larger pots, using a mixture of soil taken from the Kitchen Garden, sand and peat. We also add slow-release fertilizer and granules of a water-storing non-toxic gel which swells to make water available to plants' roots throughout periods of drought. The gel is effective for up to five seasons, and much reduces the need to water.

In June, the garden reaches its first flowering peak, with roses and early-flowering perennials. But this is also the beginning of the garden cycle in real terms. During the next months we will be taking seed, making cuttings, and generally undertaking much of the preparation for the garden display of the following year.

Taking Seed

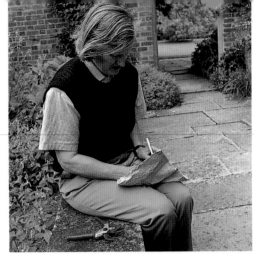

I BEGIN TAKING SEED of perennials, biennials and annuals as soon as any of it is ripe, usually in July. Annuals and biennials are the most important of the seed crops, but we generally take seed of quite a few of the less reliably hardy perennials in case we should have a bad winter.

Seed should be gathered on a dry sunny day, never when it is wet, as it rots very easily. The seed of many flowers, such as the little cream-flowered *Hibiscus trionum*, *Francoa sonchifolia*, greenish-yellow *Nicotiana langsdorffii* and *Salvia patens*, is ripe when it is black and dry, just before the container splits open to distribute it. That of others, such as lathyrus and beans, is contained in pods, and is ready for gathering when the seeds have swollen and the pod itself is completely dry. Yet others have fruit-like outer cases, with the seed protected and hidden inside: seed of these plants, such as *Tropaeolum speciosum*, bomareas and solanums, is gathered when the outer layer begins to dry out. The perennial honesty, *Lunaria rediviva*, has transparent capsules, and seed is ripe

when black (*above left*). I take seed of this only occasionally, as seedlings germinate freely around the established plants.

Seed should be collected in paper bags (it can be stored in plastic after it is fully dry, but not before). I keep fairly large bags from household shopping for this purpose, labelling them carefully with the plant name and the date (*above right*). The bags are then stored somewhere dry, until a winter day when I find the opportunity to clean and sort the seed.

The annual *Hibiscus trionum*, which grows in the Pool Garden, in large pots around the pool, has capsules containing about eight seeds, which I cut off and drop into a bag (*below left*). *Nicotiana langsdorffii*, another annual, has fine seed which can be squeezed out straight into a bag, as can the

similar seed of the perennial *Francoa sonchifolia*. I always collect seed of francoa, in case we lose the parent plants in the cold frame where they overwinter. Most salvia seed is easy to gather: the capsules, each containing one ripe seed, should be pinched to prevent the seed jumping out, then eased off the plant and dropped into a bag (*below centre*). The upward-facing decorative heads of love-in-a-mist, *Nigella damascena*, are gathered in August. If the heads are turned upside down, the seed can be rubbed out into a bag (*below right*). I sometimes save time by cutting off whole flower heads of large thistles, and some of the taller tobacco plants, dropping them straight into the bags for later cleaning and sorting. They can also be hung upside down in their bags, so that the seed falls out as it dries.

Taking Cuttings

C UTTINGS AT TINTINHULL fall into several categories. Every year we take cuttings of plants that may not be reliably hardy, such as abutilon, piptanthus, leptospermums, cistus and the more tender roses. We take a large number of cuttings each year of the tender woody plants that we treat as annuals and of softer-stemmed plants that are used for bedding or containers. These two latter categories include diascias, felicias, woody and soft-stemmed salvias, argyranthemums and anisodonteas. We take woody cuttings from shrubs such as berberis, box, deutzias and spiraeas simply for future replacement of old plants. For most shrubs cuttings are taken when new growth has begun to firm up, probably in midsummer. We take clematis cuttings later in the summer. We also take spring cuttings of perennials, to avoid the bother of division, and of overwintered tender stock plants, to take the pressure off greenhouse space in the winter. Very often heeled cuttings of new growth give appropriate material, but longer branches can be cut up between the nodes to give a number of suitable shoots.

We always take heeled cuttings of tender *Salvia cacaliifolia*, one of the best performers in pots (*left and below left*). Shoots root most easily if taken from a non-flowering branch but this is sometimes difficult to find. Keep the cuttings in an airtight plastic bag and pot them up as soon as possible, following the method described on pages 82–3. In the mist propagator *S. cacaliifolia* cuttings root in a few weeks, but care is needed – this salvia is liable to die off during the winter if over-watered. After the roots are formed the plants are potted individually and overwintered in the greenhouse. They are usually ready to be potted on to larger containers in early spring. The young plants are hardened off in frames before being planted out in full sun.

S. leucantha (*below centre*) flowers later than *S. cacaliifolia* – in warmer climates than ours it will flower all winter. Cuttings can be rooted any time after midsummer.

Some plants, including *Argyranthemum foeniculaceum*, have a very quick-growing root system. With these, as well as taking summer cuttings (*below right*), we generally keep a few stock plants in the greenhouse over the winter and take cuttings of young shoots which grow as the daylight hours lengthen in February.

SUMMER INTO WINTER

From June on, repeat-flowering roses must have their dead heads regularly removed, and others, unless they have attractive fruits, also need unsightly dead blooms taken off. Perennials need deadheading, and in some cases cutting down to the ground in order to encourage new foliage growth. In spite of mulching, we need to keep a look out for weeds, and any purple-flowered foxgloves that appear should be removed before the bees can cross-fertilize with the white ones. (The purple-flowered ones can be identified before they flower by their purple-tinged stems.)

Behind the scenes, seeds of hardy biennials, such as forget-me-nots or winter- and spring-flowering pansies, need sowing in rows in the Kitchen Garden (see page 110). They will be transplanted to their garden sites by the end of September, while the earth is still warm enough for their roots to establish. June is almost the last moment for germinating most biennials outside, from the previous year's seeds, if they are to flower the following year, though some – *Eryngium giganteum*, *Salvia sclarea* var. *turkestanica* and foxgloves among them – may flower the following year if seed is sown *in situ* as soon as it is ripe at the end of July. All can, of course, be raised more easily from seed in the greenhouse in spring, to flower the following year. These seeders are not individually the most important flowers in the garden, but collectively their seeming spontaneity when scattered in drifts through many of the flower beds is part of the Tintinhull look – the 'jungle of beauty' effect.

Around the end of June, the rhythm changes to a more contemplative spiral. As the chores of deadheading, cutting off dead leaves, and watering proceed, thoughts fly to the following year. It is possible to contemplate and consider the garden in a way that cannot be done during the rushed spring and early summer. It is a period for reflection and optimism, with the promise always of doing better next year – every gardener's dream.

With all mixed planting, many of the permanently planted soft-stemmed plants need an annual reshuffle in order to keep both the colour sequence and the proportions of neighbouring plant groups in scale. Taking photographs while performance is at its peak – in June, July, August and September – helps ensure that replanting achieves the desired effects the following year.

The garden must be kept well groomed before the 'dog days' of August, when garden plants can quickly look shabby. Late-flowering plants need to be accompanied by tidy neighbours. It is vital to deadhead not only roses but also irises and early-flowering perennials: columbines (mainly blue forms of *Aquilegia vulgaris*, a flowerer allowed all over the garden), the acid-yellow bracts of *Smyrnium perfoliatum* (leaving some to set seed), and the invasive Welsh poppy, *Meconopsis cambrica*, which will otherwise colonize the garden and be almost impossible to weed out. Summer-flowering shrubs such as lilac, philadelphus, deutzias, sambucus and

Above, left and right: Some alchemilla plants have been allowed to seed in the cracks of stonework. After flowering, alchemilla stems and foliage should be cut right back. The plants will then produce attractive mounds of fresh foliage.

viburnums all have their flowering branches cut out after flowering, to allow new growth on which flowers will be produced next year, and when the dead heads and long stems of the big euphorbias (varieties of *Euphorbia characias* and *E.c.* ssp. *wulfenii*) become unsightly in July, they should be cut back to the hidden base. The large heart-shaped leaves of tall crambes can also look faded, and should be trimmed back, leaving the flower sprays which remain decorative in seed. Long, rooting stems of *Buglossoides purpurocaerulea* can be cut back to the ground in July and August; if it is a dry summer this will be sufficient, but in wet years they will have to be trimmed again if cut too early. During August, crane's-bill geraniums, galegas and alchemillas can be cut back to the ground. Some of the geraniums will flower again, though not the alchemillas or galegas. All will produce new leaves that will last until autumn.

Cuttings of permanent shrubs, which need to be taken from young half-ripened shoots that are not too soft, can be rooted in the mist propagator in late July and in August. Rose shoots taken in July are easily rooted in mist (see page 111), although they can also be grown from hardwood cuttings set in a trench in winter. Cuttings of tender plants to be used as annuals can be taken in July and August from non-flowering shoots. By early September this task should be completed.

August and September bring new bursts of bloom from perennials, and we make a note to increase the range and number of hydrangeas that we know Mrs Reiss loved. Over the years many have disappeared, and this would be a good time to beg cuttings from friends. On the other hand, we have added a lot of other late flowerers to those, such as evening primroses, hollyhocks, ceanothus and hydrangeas, already in the garden: eupatoriums, chelones (copying the Powis Castle borders), cimicifugas, vernonias, veronicastrums – all of which help to disguise the fading stems of the earlier-flowering herbaceous planting. Some cutting back is necessary to set off these late performers. Other efforts go into collecting the seeds we will need for the garden next year.

A beautiful evergreen privet, *Ligustrum quihoui*, with white panicles 20in/50cm long, flowers now in a quiet border where earlier the beauty bush, *Kolkwitzia amabilis*, reigned supreme. The kolkwitzia has had its long flowering fronds cut back to make a shapely bush and to ensure new growth for next year's flowers.

Gardening work becomes more intense again in September. The autumn months are for clearing up and reassessment; for carrying out major tasks of reorganization, for scarifying the lawn, and for pruning shrubs that flower on next year's new shoots, as soon as they are dormant.

Autumn work is vital: moving shrubs as necessary and as they become dormant, and cutting down perennials – but leaving those, such as sedums and grasses, with flowers and leaves which continue to look handsome through the autumn months. Spent annuals must be pulled out, and the last seed gathered and stored. Some of the groups of the hardiest perennials are split and reshuffled now when there is more time than in the spring – though a danger is a wet autumn followed by early hard frosts which freeze water around their newly moved crowns.

Major reconstruction of borders can begin in September. This allows time for digging the beds over. If sterilization is needed, to rid soil of harmful pests and diseases, as well as any build-up of weed seeds, this is the time to do it, while the soil is still warm. Over the years we have had to sterilize the soil in various of the Tintinhull borders, against rose replant diseases. Soil sterilization is not a job for the amateur. The fumigants used are toxic and can only be employed by commercial growers and approved contractors,

who take every precaution in their handling. Borders have to be cleared of perennials, though shrubs can usually be left. Then the professionals apply the fumigant (in volatile liquid or powder form) and seal the surface of the soil with plastic sheeting to retain the vapours. After autumn sterilization woody plants can be replanted in winter and perennials in the following spring.

Throughout October, November and December leaves are swept up and carefully removed from flower beds in which they might 'overlay' emerging shoots of winter or spring flowerers, causing the crowns to rot. For this reason, the large leaves of *Magnolia liliiflora* 'Nigra' are raked up as they fall, on an almost daily basis. Depending on the weather, the lawns need occasional mowing and edging up until Christmas.

Other winter chores include checking and cleaning tools, tidying sheds, checking the watering systems, writing labels for seed trays, and checking lists of plants required for the following season. By February the year's new season begins.

The white epilobium, Epilobium angustifolium album, *is only cut down as the lower leaves begin to look unsightly, at the very end of the season, long after flowering and producing seedheads.*

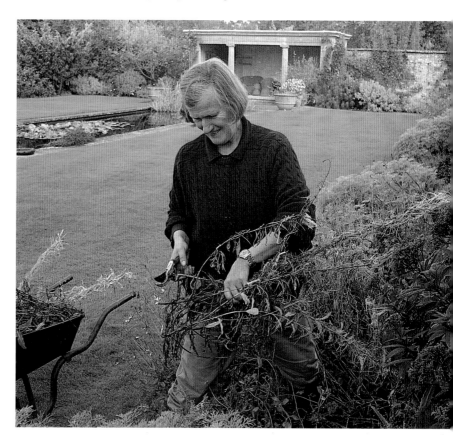

INDEX

Usefulness Zones

The Usefulness Zones quoted after each plant name in the index represent the range of zones, according to the USDA system, in which the plant may be successfully grown in North America. The lower figure gives the coldest zone in which the plant will be hardy without winter protection; the higher shows the limit of its tolerance of hot summer weather. The chart shows the average annual minimum temperature of each zone.

It must be remembered that zoning data can only be a rough guide. Plant hardiness depends on a great many factors, and within any one zone particular regions may be endowed with more or less favorable conditions, just as on a smaller scale in any one garden plants can be positioned in individual situations that will suit their needs to a greater or lesser extent.

°FAHRENHEIT	ZONES	CELSIUS
below -50	1	below -45
-50 to -40	2	-45 to -40
-40 to -30	3	-40 to -34
-30 to -20	4	-34 to -29
-20 to -10	5	-29 to -23
-10 to 0	6	-23 to -18
0 to 10	7	-18 to -12
10 to 20	8	-12 to -7
20 to 30	9	-7 to -1
30 to 40	10	-1 to 4
above 40	11	above 4

ACKNOWLEDGMENTS

AUTHOR'S ACKNOWLEDGMENTS

The idea for this book, originally conceived to be descriptive of Tintinhull and to be written with my late husband, John Malins, came from Frances Lincoln and Erica Hunningher. The present form, more of a personal odyssey, evolved in discussion. We knew from the start that the book would be nothing without Andrew Lawson's pictures: he had been taking the garden over the years and agreed to photograph both there and elsewhere especially for the book. I am most grateful to the garden owners who generously allowed their gardens to be photographed.

Looking after the garden at Tintinhull was a partnership with my husband, John, whose knowledge and gardening wisdom held the garden together. We were wonderfully helped by the skill and dedicated work of Bert Austin and Glynn Jones, the two National Trust gardeners, who, in succession, covered most of our fourteen years. I wish the new gardener, now totally in charge of the garden, great success and happiness in caring for it.

The Frances Lincoln team have as always been inspired and methodical: Jo Christian, my editor, Caroline Hillier, the art director, and Anne Fraser, the picture editor. Tony Lord's encyclopedic knowledge of plant names and their up-to-the-minute changes make the book a reliable guide to current nomenclature. I am very grateful to everyone who has been involved.

PUBLISHERS' ACKNOWLEDGMENTS

Frances Lincoln Limited are grateful to the National Trust for their cooperation. The publishers also wish to offer special thanks to Antonia Johnson, Katherine Lambert and Caroline Taylor for their help in producing this book.

Plan script by Simon Johnson

Design by Studio Gossett

Horticultural consultants Tony Lord, John Elsley
Editor Jo Christian
Picture Editor Anne Fraser
Indexer Penny David
Production Adela Cory
Design assistance Sally Cracknell
Editorial assistance Auriol Miller

Editorial Director Erica Hunningher
Art Director Caroline Hillier
Production Director Nicky Bowden

PHOTOGRAPHIC ACKNOWLEDGMENTS

a = above, b = below, c = centre, l = left, r = right

All photographs copyright © Andrew Lawson, except for the following:
Deni Bown: 138bl, 145br, 174br, 175bc, 180al
Neil Campbell-Sharp: 24, 34ar
John Fielding: 145bc, 174bl, 180b (*Hoheria*), 192b, 193r
Jerry Harpur: 14, 23, 40-41, 149a, 168
Georges Lévêque © FLL: 39, 83a, 94